48: *American Poets, 1880-1945*, Second Series, edited by Peter Quartermain (1986)

49: *American Literary Publishing Houses, 1638-1899*, 2 parts, edited by Peter Dzwonkoski (1986)

50: *Afro-American Writers Before the Harlem Renaissance*, edited by Trudier Harris (1986)

51: *Afro-American Writers from the Harlem Renaissance to 1940*, edited by Trudier Harris (1987)

52: *American Writers for Children Since 1960: Fiction*, edited by Glenn E. Estes (1986)

53: *Canadian Writers Since 1960*, First Series, edited by W. H. New (1986)

54: *American Poets, 1880-1945*, Third Series, 2 parts, edited by Peter Quartermain (1987)

55: *Victorian Prose Writers Before 1867*, edited by William B. Thesing (1987)

56: *German Fiction Writers, 1914-1945*, edited by James Hardin (1987)

57: *Victorian Prose Writers After 1867*, edited by William B. Thesing (1987)

58: *Jacobean and Caroline Dramatists*, edited by Fredson Bowers (1987)

59: *American Literary Critics and Scholars, 1800-1850*, edited by John W. Rathbun and Monica M. Grecu (1987)

60: *Canadian Writers Since 1960*, Second Series, edited by W. H. New (1987)

61: *American Writers for Children Since 1960: Poets, Illustrators, and Nonfiction Authors*, edited by Glenn E. Estes (1987)

62: *Elizabethan Dramatists*, edited by Fredson Bowers (1987)

63: *Modern American Critics, 1920-1955*, edited by Gregory S. Jay (1988)

64: *American Literary Critics and Scholars, 1850-1880*, edited by John W. Rathbun and Monica M. Grecu (1988)

65: *French Novelists, 1900-1930*, edited by Catharine Savage Brosman (1988)

66: *German Fiction Writers, 1885-1913*, 2 parts, edited by James Hardin (1988)

67: *Modern American Critics Since 1955*, edited by Gregory S. Jay (1988)

68: *Canadian Writers, 1920-1959*, First Series, edited by W. H. New (1988)

69: *Contemporary German Fiction Writers*, First Series, edited by Wolfgang D. Elfe and James Hardin (1988)

70: *British Mystery Writers, 1860-1919*, edited by Bernard Benstock and Thomas F. Staley (1988)

71: *American Literary Critics and Scholars, 1880-1900*, edited by John W. Rathbun and Monica M. Grecu (1988)

72: *French Novelists, 1930-1960*, edited by Catharine Savage Brosman (1988)

73: *American Magazine Journalists, 1741-1850*, edited by Sam G. Riley (1988)

74: *American Short-Story Writers Before 1880*, edited by Bobby Ellen Kimbel, with the assistance of William E. Grant (1988)

75: *Contemporary German Fiction Writers*, Second Series, edited by Wolfgang D. Elfe and James Hardin (1988)

Documentary Series

1: *Sherwood Anderson, Willa Cather, John Dos Passos, Theodore Dreiser, F. Scott Fitzgerald, Ernest Hemingway, Sinclair Lewis*, edited by Margaret A. Van Antwerp (1982)

2: *James Gould Cozzens, James T. Farrell, William Faulkner, John O'Hara, John Steinbeck, Thomas Wolfe, Richard Wright*, edited by Margaret A. Van Antwerp (1982)

3: *Saul Bellow, Jack Kerouac, Norman Mailer, Vladimir Nabokov, John Updike, Kurt Vonnegut*, edited by Mary Bruccoli (1983)

4: *Tennessee Williams*, edited by Margaret A. Van Antwerp and Sally Johns (1984)

5: *American Transcendentalists*, edited by Joel Myerson (1988)

Yearbooks

1980, edited by Karen L. Rood, Jean W. Ross, and Richard Ziegfeld (1981)

1981, edited by Karen L. Rood, Jean W. Ross, and Richard Ziegfeld (1982)

1982, edited by Richard Ziegfeld; associate editors: Jean W. Ross and Lynne C. Zeigler (1983)

1983, edited by Mary Bruccoli and Jean W. Ross; associate editor: Richard Ziegfeld (1984)

1984, edited by Jean W. Ross (1985)

1985, edited by Jean W. Ross (1986)

1986, edited by J. M. Brook (1987)

1987, edited by J. M. Brook (1988)

Concise Series

The New Consciousness, 1941-1968 (1987)

Colonization to the American Renaissance, 1640-1865 (1988)

Realism, Naturalism, and Local Color, 1865-1917 (1988)

Contemporary German Fiction Writers

Second Series

Contemporary German Fiction Writers

Second Series

77з8

Edited by
Wolfgang D. Elfe
University of South Carolina

and

James Hardin
University of South Carolina

A Bruccoli Clark Layman Book
Gale Research Inc. • Book Tower • Detroit, Michigan 48226

Manufactured by Edward Brothers, Inc.
Ann Arbor, Michigan
Printed in the United States of America

**Library of Congress Cataloging-in-
Publication Data**

Contemporary German fiction writers. Second series /
edited by Wolfgang D. Elfe and James Hardin.
    p. cm.–(Dictionary of literary biography; v. 75)
"A Bruccoli Clark Layman book."
Includes index.
ISBN 0-8103-4553-6
    1. German fiction–20th century–Bio-bibliography.
2. Novelists, German–Biography–Dictionaries. 3. German
fiction–20th century–History and criticism. I. Elfe,
Wolfgang. II. Hardin, James N. III. Series.
PT772.C593 1988
833'.914'09–dc19
[B]   88-23267
                                                    CIP

Contents

Contents

Plan of the Series

. . . Almost the most prodigious asset of a country, and perhaps its most precious possession, is its native literary product–when that product is fine and noble and enduring.

Mark Twain*

The advisory board, the editors, and the publisher of the *Dictionary of Literary Biography* are joined in endorsing Mark Twain's declaration. The literature of a nation provides an inexhaustible resource of permanent worth. We intend to make literature and its creators better understood and more accessible to students and the reading public, while satisfying the standards of teachers and scholars.

To meet these requirements, *literary biography* has been construed in terms of the author's achievement. The most important thing about a writer is his writing. Accordingly, the entries in *DLB* are career biographies, tracing the development of the author's canon and the evolution of his reputation.

The purpose of *DLB* is not only to provide reliable information in a convenient format but also to place the figures in the larger perspective of literary history and to offer appraisals of their accomplishments by qualified scholars.

The publication plan for *DLB* resulted from two years of preparation. The project was proposed to Bruccoli Clark by Frederick G. Ruffner, president of the Gale Research Company, in November 1975. After specimen entries were prepared and typeset, an advisory board was formed to refine the entry format and develop the series rationale. In meetings held during 1976, the publisher, series editors, and advisory board approved the scheme for a comprehensive biographical dictionary of persons who contributed to North American literature. Editorial work on the first volume began in January 1977, and it was published in 1978. In order to make *DLB* more than a reference tool and to compile volumes that individually have claim to status as literary history, it was decided to organize volumes by topic, period, or genre. Each of these freestanding volumes provides a biographical-bibliographical guide and overview for a particular area of literature. We are convinced that this organization–as opposed to a single alphabet method–constitutes a valuable innovation in the presentation of reference material. The volume plan necessarily requires many decisions for the placement and treatment of authors who might properly be included in two or three volumes. In some instances a major figure will be included in separate volumes, but with different entries emphasizing the aspect of his career appropriate to each volume. Ernest Hemingway, for example, is represented in *American Writers in Paris, 1920-1939* by an entry focusing on his expatriate apprenticeship; he is also in *American Novelists, 1910-1945* with an entry surveying his entire career. Each volume includes a cumulative index of subject authors and articles. Comprehensive indexes to the entire series are planned.

With volume ten in 1982 it was decided to enlarge the scope of *DLB*. By the end of 1986 twenty-one volumes treating British literature had been published, and volumes for Commonwealth and Modern European literature were in progress. The series has been further augmented by the *DLB Yearbooks* (since 1981) which update published entries and add new entries to keep the *DLB* current with contemporary activity. There have also been *DLB Documentary Series* volumes which provide biographical and critical source materials for figures whose work is judged to have particular interest for students. One of these companion volumes is entirely devoted to Tennessee Williams.

We define literature as the *intellectual commerce of a nation:* not merely as belles lettres but as that ample and complex process by which ideas are generated, shaped, and transmitted. *DLB* entries are not limited to "creative writers" but extend to other figures who in their time and in their way influenced the mind of a people. Thus the series encompasses historians, journalists, publishers, and screenwriters. By this means readers of *DLB* may be aided to perceive litera-

*From an unpublished section of Mark Twain's autobiography, copyright © by the Mark Twain Company.

ture not as cult scripture in the keeping of intellectual high priests but firmly positioned at the center of a nation's life.

DLB includes the major writers appropriate to each volume and those standing in the ranks immediately behind them. Scholarly and critical counsel has been sought in deciding which minor figures to include and how full their entries should be. Wherever possible, useful references are made to figures who do not warrant separate entries.

Each *DLB* volume has a volume editor responsible for planning the volume, selecting the figures for inclusion, and assigning the entries. Volume editors are also responsible for preparing, where appropriate, appendices surveying the major periodicals and literary and intellectual movements for their volumes, as well as lists of further readings. Work on the series as a whole is coordinated at the Bruccoli Clark Layman editorial center in Columbia, South Carolina, where the editorial staff is responsible for accuracy of the published volumes.

One feature that distinguishes *DLB* is the illustration policy–its concern with the iconography of literature. Just as an author is influenced by his surroundings, so is the reader's understanding of the author enhanced by a knowledge of his environment. Therefore *DLB* volumes include not only drawings, paintings, and photographs of authors, often depicting them at various stages in their careers, but also illustrations of their families and places where they lived. Title pages are regularly reproduced in facsimile along with dust jackets for modern authors. The dust jackets are a special feature of *DLB* because they often document better than anything else the way in which an author's work was perceived in its own time. Specimens of the writers' manuscripts are included when feasible.

Samuel Johnson rightly decreed that "The chief glory of every people arises from its authors." The purpose of the *Dictionary of Literary Biography* is to compile literary history in the surest way available to us–by accurate and comprehensive treatment of the lives and work of those who contributed to it.

The *DLB* Advisory Board

Foreword

This volume of the *Dictionary of Literary Biography* presents significant West German, East German, and Swiss-German fiction writers who established their literary reputations between the mid 1950s and the mid 1970s. Thus, these writers began their careers at a time when the most obvious effects of World War II had faded and when the integration of the two German states into two opposing political, economic, and military blocs had been completed. All but five of the thirty-nine writers treated in this book were born in the 1920s or 1930s, and most of them experienced Adolf Hitler's Third Reich at a tender age; consequently, National Socialist rule, World War II, and the postwar years figure prominently in their works. It was not sensationalism that led them to treat these topics but conviction: a desire to tell the truth, to come to terms with Germany's guilt, and to prevent the recurrence of a fascist dictatorship. German literature of this period is highly politicized and displays a predominantly leftist orientation. Several of the West German writers in this volume, including Günter Grass, Günter Herburger, Uwe Johnson, Reinhard Lettau, and Martin Walser, were members of the Gruppe 47, a loose organization of German authors that emphasized the political responsibility of the writer. Fourteen of the writers are East German, although four of them moved to the West after establishing their reputations. Their biographies and the discussions of their works reflect the political, social, and cultural developments in East Germany and, in some cases, the clash between the restrictions of socialist realism and the urge for artistic freedom. West German and Swiss-German fiction of the 1960s and 1970s is marked by extensive formal experimentation, particularly in the works of Jürgen Becker, Helmut Heißenbüttel, and Wolf Wondratschek, and—compared to the immediate postwar years—by greater literary sophistication, both of which require a more alert and active reader. Writers such as Max von der Grün, Ludwig Fels, and Brigitte Reimann depict modern industrialized society from the perspective of the worker, while Ingeborg Drewitz, Sarah Kirsch, Irmtraud Morgner, Elisabeth Plessen, Gabriele Wohmann, and Christa Wolf bring a feminist consciousness to bear on contemporary social problems.

The emphasis in this volume is on prose fiction; poetry and drama are treated only to the extent that they are important in the overall evaluation of a writer's life and work. Coverage has not been limited to writers of "serious" literature but includes authors whose works have been termed "Unterhaltungsliteratur" (potboiler literature) by their detractors. This decision was based on the editors' conviction that one of the primary values of literature is its function as a mirror of a given period. It may be that as much can be learned about events and attitudes of the twentieth century from a Willi Heinrich as from the foremost writers of the day.

The entries should be of interest both to experts in German literature and to general readers. Quotations are given in the original language, but English translations are provided in parentheses. German terms and titles not readily understandable to a native speaker of English are also translated. In a departure from German usage, Günter de Bruyn is alphabetized under *D* (rather than *B*) and Max von der Grün under *V* (rather than *G*).

The primary bibliography at the beginning of each entry lists all first editions of the author's books in chronological order. When English translations of a work exist, the first American and British editions are listed. The primary bibliography also lists selected periodical publications and translations into German, forewords, contributions to collections, and books edited by the author. The bibliography at the end of the entry provides a selection of secondary literature on the author.

Contemporary German Fiction Writers, Second Series is a continuation of *DLB 69: Contemporary German Fiction Writers*, First Series, which concentrates on writers who gained recognition in the first decade after World War II. That volume, in turn, is preceded by *DLB 56: German Fiction Writers, 1914-1945* and *DLB 66: German Fiction Writers, 1885-1913*. Future volumes will treat twentieth-century Austrian fiction writers and German writers in the age of Goethe.

—*Wolfgang D. Elfe and James Hardin*

Acknowledgments

This book was produced by Bruccoli Clark Layman, Inc. Karen L. Rood is senior editor for the *Dictionary of Literary Biography* series. Philip B. Dematteis was the in-house editor.

Production coordinator is Kimberly Casey. Art supervisor is Cheryl Crombie. Copyediting supervisor is Joan M. Prince. Typesetting supervisor is Kathleen M. Flanagan. Laura Ingram and Michael D. Senecal are editorial associates. The production staff includes Rowena Betts, Charles D. Brower, Joseph Matthew Bruccoli, Amanda Caulley, Patricia Coate, Mary Colborn, Holly Deal, Mary S. Dye, Sarah A. Estes, Eric Folley, Cynthia Hallman, Judith K. Ingle, Maria Ling, Warren McInnis, Kathy S. Merlette, Sheri Beckett Neal, Joycelyn R. Smith, Virginia Smith, Jack Turner, and Mark Van Gunten. Jean W. Ross is permissions editor. Joseph Caldwell, photography editor, and Penney Haughton did photographic copy work for the volume.

Walter W. Ross and Rhonda Marshall did the library research with the assistance of the reference staff at the Thomas Cooper Library of the University of South Carolina: Daniel Boice, Cathy Eckman, Gary Geer, Cathie Gottlieb, David L. Haggard, Jens Holley, Dennis Isbell, Jackie Kinder, Marcia Martin, Jean Rhyne, Beverly Steele, Ellen Tillett, Carol Tobin, and Virginia Weathers.

Dictionary of Literary Biography • Volume Seventy-five

Contemporary German Fiction Writers

Second Series

Dictionary of Literary Biography

Jurek Becker
(30 September 1937-   )

Jennifer Taylor
Cornell University

BOOKS: *Jakob der Lügner* (Berlin: Aufbau, 1969); translated by Melvin Kornfeld as *Jacob the Liar* (New York: Harcourt Brace Jovanovich, 1975; London: Harcourt Brace Jovanovich, 1976);

Irreführung der Behörden: Roman (Rostock: Hinnstorff/Frankfurt am Main: Suhrkamp, 1973);

Der Boxer: Roman (Rostock: Hinnstorff/Frankfurt am Main: Suhrkamp, 1976);

Schlaflose Tage: Roman (Frankfurt am Main: Suhrkamp, 1978); translated by Leila Vennewitz as *Sleepless Days* (New York: Harcourt Brace Jovanovich, 1979; London: Secker & Warburg, 1979);

Nach der ersten Zukunft: Erzählungen (Frankfurt am Main: Suhrkamp, 1980);

Aller Welt Freund: Roman (Frankfurt am Main: Suhrkamp, 1982);

Bronsteins Kinder: Roman (Frankfurt am Main: Suhrkamp, 1986).

Jurek Becker is one of the best-known authors from the German Democratic Republic (GDR) writing today. While his early works are concerned with the problem of Jewish identity in postwar Germany, his later pieces are highly critical of the societies that have developed on both sides of the Berlin Wall since 1961. Although Becker became disillusioned with the GDR and left in 1977, he also criticizes the Federal Republic of Germany. Like many writers living in exile, Becker is caught in the middle, a victim of his feelings of ambivalence toward both his old and his new country; but, unlike many others, Becker

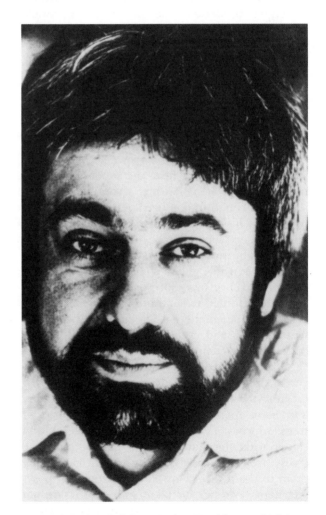

Jurek Becker (Suhrkamp Verlag, Frankfurt am Main)

must also reconcile being German and being a Jew.

Born in 1937, Becker grew up in the Jewish ghetto of Lodz in Poland and in the Ravensbrück and Sachsenhausen concentration camps; his mother died in the camps. In 1945 he and his father settled in East Berlin, where he received his Abitur (high school diploma) in 1955. He joined the Socialist Unity party in 1957 and studied philosophy at the University of Berlin for the next three years. In 1960 he began writing screenplays, television plays, and short stories in German, a language he had begun learning at the age of eleven.

Becker's first novel, *Jakob der Lügner* (1969; translated as *Jacob the Liar*, 1975), was translated into French, Italian, and English and won the Heinrich Mann Prize in the GDR and the Swiss Charles Veillon Prize for literature, both in 1971. A film version, directed by Frank Beyer with a screenplay by Becker, won the Silver Bear award as the GDR entry in the West Berlin Film Festival in 1974.

Jakob der Lügner is the story of Jakob Heym, an unremarkable middle-aged Jew, who, returning home from forced labor in a German-occupied ghetto in Poland, overhears a German radio report that the liberating Soviet army is about four hundred kilometers away. In trying to convince his friends of the news, he changes his story: he did not just hear the report on a German radio but actually owns a contraband radio himself. Jakob's position becomes increasingly untenable as his lies become more complex: every day he must have the Soviets move back and forth, and he must invent small victories and disasters. As the whole ghetto comes to depend on his "radio," Jakob grows more and more to hate his role. He is forced to continue, however, when his best friend commits suicide after learning the truth. In the end everyone is shipped off to the concentration camps, where Jakob dies.

Jakob's story is narrated by a nameless survivor of the camps. The survivor is responsible for creating the past, just as Jakob created the radio. The book opens with the narrator's memories of trees, which were not allowed in the ghetto, and closes with the narrator and Jakob glimpsing trees through the slats of the freight car taking them to the death camps. The narrator proposes alternative endings for Jakob's life, but he cannot change Jakob's story any more than Jakob could make the Soviets appear.

Irreführung der Behörden (Confusing the Authorities, 1973) analyzes the act of writing itself. The book opens with a fairy tale written by Gregor Bienek, a student at Humboldt University in East Berlin in the 1950s: a young couple falls madly in love and imagines that the whole world revolves around them. Later their relationship sours, and they go their separate ways, only to meet again when they have developed more realistic attitudes. Life is no longer perfect for them, but it is more real, and they discover that they prefer it that way. Bienek's situation is similar to that of his characters: his relationship with his wife, Lola, changes from youthful passion to disappointment; in the last scene all of their hidden anger surfaces. Lola asks: "Mich interessiert die Frage, wozu mein Mann schreibt. Ob du es als reinen Broterwerb ansiehst . . . oder ob du noch andere Motive hast" (I'd like to know why my husband writes. Whether you look at it as purely earning a living . . . or whether you have other motives). She feels that literature should have a social purpose and that Bienek has compromised his earlier ideals. Bienek admits that she is right, and, like the hero of his fairy tale, he decides to start confronting reality: "Natürlich hat sie recht, alles in allem und ich weiß das schon lange . . . stets trug ich um die Wunde einen geschickten Verband, der hin und wieder sorgfältig erneuert wurde, jetzt hat sie ihn abgerissen, ich kann mir einen frischen anlegen, oder ich kann darauf verzichten und eine neue Zukunft beschließen" (Of course she's right, all in all, and I've known it for a long time . . . I always cleverly covered my wounds with a bandage which once in a while had to be carefully replaced; now she's ripped it off and I can either put on a new one or I can live without it and try to begin again).

Becker is here presenting the conflict inherent in the role of the writer in the GDR. By the late 1960s and 1970s it was clear that the hopes writers such as Becker, Christa Wolf, and Brigitte Reimann had held in the 1950s for a society in which literature would serve as a vehicle for social change and a forum for public debate had been shattered. It became increasingly difficult for such writers to reconcile their ideals with the realities of the GDR. Just as the love affair in the fairy tale fades, so does the author's relationship with the state as he loses his political idealism; only after the bandages have been removed is he forced to overcome his indifference and to write again. The ambiguity of Becker's presentation underlines the difficulty in which he found himself in the 1970s. Nevertheless, Becker continued to be outwardly successful: he won the Bremen Literature Prize in 1974 and the National Prize for Literature of the GDR in 1975.

Der Boxer (The Boxer, 1976) was Becker's last book to be published in the GDR. Like *Jakob der Lügner*, it is a story within a story. Aron Blank, an old man who survived the concentration camps, and the narrator, a writer, have worked for two years to record Aron's story. It is now finished, but Aron refuses to read it; he claims that the narrator has changed the story in writing it. On the other hand, if it is his story word for word, why would he want to read his own story?

Aron's story is about his son, the boxer. Shortly after the war Aron, who has changed his name to the more German-sounding Arno, finds a boy he thinks is his lost son, Mark, and takes him home to raise him as a German. He tells Mark the story of a boxer–Aron himself–who became strong and self-reliant and gets the boy to learn to box. Determined to make Mark a "normal" member of society–in other words, not Jewish–Aron does just the opposite: he unwittingly turns the boy into an outsider who is painfully aware of his otherness. When Mark leaves the GDR for the West and then goes to Israel, where he is killed in the 1967 Six-Day War, Aron is shocked and bewildered. Why would Mark go to Israel? Where did his sense of Jewishness come from? Aron says, "Sicher könne man ihm viele Fehler im Zusammenhang mit Mark nachweisen, auf keinen Fall aber den, *einen Juden aus ihm gemacht* zu haben. Was das überhaupt sei, fragt er . . . ein Jude, was denn anders als ein Glaubensbekenntnis?" (Certainly you could prove that he's made many mistakes with Mark, but under no circumstances could you say he'd *made a Jew out of him*. What is that anyway, he asked . . . a Jew? What is it other than a religion?).

Aron has tried so hard to become German, to abandon his Jewish identity, that he denies having created a "Jew" out of his son. But Mark's consciousness of his Jewishness was that of Aron, who could not forget the camps, could not forget that he was a Jew. Being Jewish, then, is not a matter of genetics–it is never established whether Mark really *is* his son–or a matter of religion– neither Aron nor Mark is a practicing Jew. Aron and Mark are Jewish because of history, because of what they experienced in the camps, because of what they remember. After those experiences Aron cannot turn himself into "a German," nor could he turn Mark into one. Mark had no place; he could not feel German, but, on the other

hand, he had no Jewish identity to turn to. Aron taught Mark to box to protect him against German anti-Semites. As a result, Mark became aware of his Jewishness and was killed fighting for the Jewish state.

In the fall of 1976 Becker protested the ousting of Reiner Kunze from the Authors' Organization of the GDR. A few months later Becker withdrew from the organization, leaving his position as president of the Berlin chapter. In November he was expelled from the Socialist Unity party after he and other prominent East German authors, including Wolf, Stefan Heym, Sarah Kirsch, and Günter Kunert, signed an open letter to the Honecker government protesting the revocation of the citizenship of the singer-poet Wolf Biermann. In December 1977 Becker was asked to leave the country and was given a two-year visa which allowed him to live abroad without losing his GDR citizenship. He left with the manuscript of the novel *Schlaflose Tage* (1978; translated as *Sleepless Days*, 1979). After six months as a poet in residence at Oberlin College in Ohio and a semester at the University of Essen in the Federal Republic, he settled in West Berlin. At the end of 1979 he received a ten-year visa from the GDR, allowing him to remain an East German citizen until 1989.

In *Schlaflose Tage* Simrock, a thirty-six-year-old schoolteacher in East Berlin, suddenly becomes unhappy with his life. Against school policy, he tells his students that the official May Day demonstration is voluntary, and only nine students attend. He leaves his wife and works for a while in a factory. When his girlfriend Antonia is taken to jail for trying to escape to the West, he is left with only doubt; but he feels that even doubt is a step forward. The tone of the book is critical but moderate. Becker is attacking the everyday process of suppression that exists in all highly bureaucratic societies.

In the West Becker has the freedom to publish but resents his stereotyped role as an exiled critic of the GDR; in the East, where he is still a citizen, he cannot publish. His recent work reveals a preoccupation with the decadence and meaninglessness of Western society. *Nach der ersten Zukunft* (After the First Future, 1980) is a collection of short stories about life in the GDR and in the West, the ghetto, the camps, and being Jewish in Germany. Full of the same black humor that dominates Becker's novels, the stories are reminiscent of the avant-garde narrative tradition of the 1960s and 1970s in the West.

Becker in 1986 (photograph by Anita Schiffer-Fuchs, courtesy of Ullstein Bilderdienst)

In the novel *Aller Welt Freund* (Everybody's Friend, 1982) the thirty-year-old Kilian's suicide attempt is interrupted by his landlady. After the attempt Kilian's life collapses: his girlfriend leaves him, he is thrown out of his apartment, and he loses his job as a newspaper editor. He must resign himself to a society which forbids suicide while it slowly kills all initiative: "Schritt für Schritt bringt sich die Scheißmenschheit um, nach dem schlauesten System, das je ersonnen wurde, doch wenn einer Die Sache für sich selbst erledigen möchte, auf eigene Rechnung sozusagen und vorneweg, dann werden ihm die größten Steine in den Weg gelegt" (Step by step goddamned humanity is killing itself with the most clever system ever invented, but when someone wants to take care of The Thing himself, to foot his own bill so to speak and right away, then they throw the biggest stones in his way).

In the novel *Bronsteins Kinder* (Bronstein's

Children, 1986) Becker returns to the themes of Jewish identity and history. The story is told by nineteen-year-old Hans Bronstein about the life and death of his father, Arno, who had been a concentration camp inmate during World War II. Hans's ironic tone distances him from the narrative: "Vor einem Jahr kam mein Vater auf die denkbar schwerste Art zu schaden, er starb" (A year ago my father was injured in the most serious way thinkable: he died). Hans was born ten years after the war and never knew the horrors of the camps that had become the focus of the lives of both his older sister, who had to be institutionalized, and his father. Hans and Arno live together as if they were strangers. Hans cannot, however, escape from his father's past any more than Mark could in *Der Boxer*. He discovers that his father and two other victims of the Nazis had kidnapped a former concentration camp guard and tortured him. Horrified and confused, Hans is unable to come to terms with his father's obsession, even as it becomes his own.

Becker lives in West Berlin with his second wife, the former Christine Harsch-Niemeyer, whom he married in 1986. His first wife and their children live in the GDR. Like the writings of Isaac Bashevis Singer and Wolfdietrich Schnurre, Becker's works present a surreal world which is so close to reality as to confuse the reader. The elegance and deceptive simplicity of Becker's style enable the reader to identify with the fragmented world of his fiction.

References:

Heinz Ludwig Arnold, "Erzählte Wirklichkeit, Wahrheit unter Zwang," *Deutsches Allgemeines Sonntagsblatt*, 12 October 1980;

Paul Dreykorn, "Drei Bestseller und eine Entdeckung," *Nürnberger Zeitung*, 9 October 1971;

Sander Gilman, "Jüdische Literaten und deutsche Literatur: Antisemitismus und die verborgene Sprache der Juden am Beispiel von Jurek Becker und Edgar Hilsenrath," *Zeitschrift für deutsche Philologie*, 107, no. 2 (1988): 269-294;

Heinrich Goetz, "Vom Schreiben in der DDR," *Hannoversche Allgemeine Zeitung*, 23-24 June 1973;

Peter Graves, "Breaking Out," *Times Literary Supplement*, 20 October 1978, p. 1236;

Max von der Grün, "Die Zeit nach dem Lager," *Deutsche Volkszeitung*, 16 September 1976;

Klaus-Dieter Hähnel, "Jurek Becker: Der Boxer," *Weimarer Beiträge*, 23, no. 7 (1977): 144-150;

Hähnel, "Jurek Becker: Irreführung der Behörden," *Weimarer Beiträge*, 20, no. 1 (1974): 149-153;

Irving Howe, "The Cost of Obedience," *New York Times Book Review*, 16 September 1979, pp. 6, 46;

Eric Korn, "Hope Proffered," *Times Literary Supplement*, 6 February 1976, p. 131;

Fritz J. Raddatz, "Integre Wahrheit–Wahrhafte Literatur," *Die Zeit*, 10 March 1978;

Raddatz, "Wie DDR-Autoren resignieren," *Süddeutsche Zeitung*, 20-21 June 1970;

Marcel Reich-Ranicki, "Das Prinzip Radio," *Die Zeit*, 20 November 1970;

Reich-Ranicki, "Liebe zum Mittelmalz," *Die Zeit*, 25 May 1973;

Reich-Ranicki, "Plädoyer für Jurek Becker," *Frankfurter Allgemeine Zeitung*, 19 February 1977;

Norbert Schachtsiek-Freitag, "Diese fatale Sache mit Kilian," *Kölnische Rundschau*, 24 November 1982;

I. A. White and J. J. White, "Wahrheit und Lüge in Jurek Beckers Roman *Jakob der Lügner*," *Amsterdamer Beiträge zur neueren Germanistik*, 7 (1978): 207-231;

R. A. Zipser, "Interview with Jurek Becker," *Dimension*, 11, no. 3 (1978): 407-416;

Zipser, "Jurek Becker–Writer with a Cause," *Dimension*, 11, no. 3 (1978): 402-406.

Jürgen Becker

(10 July 1932-)

Robert Acker
University of Montana

BOOKS: *Phasen,* by Becker and Wolf Vostell (Cologne: Galerie Der Spiegel, 1960);

Felder (Frankfurt am Main: Suhrkamp, 1964);

Ränder (Frankfurt am Main: Suhrkamp, 1968); partially translated by A. Leslie Willson as "Margins," *Dimension,* 1, no. 2 (1968): 198-217;

Bilder; Häuser; Hausfreunde: Drei Hörspiele (Frankfurt am Main: Suhrkamp, 1969);

Umgebungen (Frankfurt am Main: Suhrkamp, 1970);

Eine Zeit ohne Wörter (Frankfurt am Main: Suhrkamp, 1971);

Schnee: Gedichte (Berlin: Literarisches Colloquium, 1971);

Die Zeit nach Harrimann: 29 Szenen für Nora, Helen, Jenny und den stummen Diener Moltke (Frankfurt am Main: Suhrkamp, 1971);

Das Ende der Landschaftsmalerei: Gedichte (Frankfurt am Main: Suhrkamp, 1974);

Erzähl mir nichts vom Krieg: Gedichte (Frankfurt am Main: Suhrkamp, 1977);

In der verbleibenden Zeit: Gedichte (Frankfurt am Main: Suhrkamp, 1979);

Gedichte 1965-1980 (Frankfurt am Main: Suhrkamp, 1981);

Erzählen bis Ostende (Frankfurt am Main: Suhrkamp, 1981);

Die Türe zum Meer (Frankfurt am Main: Suhrkamp, 1983);

Fenster und Stimmen: Gedichte (Frankfurt am Main: Suhrkamp, 1983).

OTHER: *Happenings; Fluxus; Pop Art; Nouveau Réalisme: Eine Dokumentation,* edited by Becker and Vostell (Reinbek: Rowohlt, 1965);

Elisabeth Borchers, *Gedichte,* selected by Becker (Frankfurt am Main: Suhrkamp, 1976).

Jürgen Becker is one of the leading exponents of experimental, avant-garde literature in Germany. As a member of the so-called Cologne School, a loose grouping of authors with similar theoretical views including Ror Wolf, Gisela Elsner, and Dieter Wellershoff, Becker rejects traditional nineteenth-century aesthetic norms for fiction. He practices instead a highly subjective and fragmentary mode of writing, in which plot and characterization give way to an accumulation of bits of reality permeated by the author's memories and ordered by random associations. Becker was one of several writers who perceived a crisis in literature during the 1960s. These writers—besides Becker, the best known are perhaps Helmut Heißenbüttel, Peter Handke, and Arno Schmidt—attempted to restructure radically the form and content of fiction so that it more accurately corresponds to a rapidly changing empirical reality. Scientific advances have, for Becker, eliminated the illusion of continuity in the world and destroyed the notion that literature can present a cohesive and ordered worldview.

Becker was born in 1932 in Cologne, and the city and its environs play a major role in many of his works. He spent most of his youth in Erfurt but returned to Cologne in 1950. He studied at the university there in 1953 and 1954 and then had a variety of jobs, including a position at the Westdeutscher Rundfunk, the state radio system of North Rhine-Westphalia. He worked as a reader for Rowohlt publishers in Hamburg from 1964 to 1966. In 1973 he directed the theater division of the Suhrkamp publishing house. Since 1974 he has been the director of the radio play division of the Deutschlandfunk, the West German state radio system. In the 1960s Becker concentrated on fiction, but during the 1970s his efforts were directed to radio plays and poetry. In the early 1980s his focus shifted back to fiction. He has won several awards, including the Prize of the Gruppe 47 in 1967, the Literature Prize of the City of Cologne in 1968, the Literature Prize of the Bavarian Academy of Fine Arts in 1980, the Critics' Prize in 1981, and the Bremen Literature Prize in 1986.

Becker feels that he can no longer use the preestablished and worn-out formulas of literature but must search for truth in his own consciousness. He regards himself as a medium, transmitting all that he perceives, remembers, or imagines. Such a transmitting process involves contradictions, ambivalences, and fragmentation, and the multiplicity of experiences necessitates an eclectic style. This position accounts for the varied techniques in Becker's works and the inherent difficulty of most of those works. To counter charges of elitism, Becker maintains–as do many experimental, subjectivist authors–that he acts as an "antenna for mankind"; he believes that his subjective realm has some general characteristics in common with those of others, and that this communality is enhanced by the language he shares with those around him. Even so, Becker's works often leave the reader foundering hopelessly in a sea of private thoughts and experiences devoid of logic and of causal relationships.

Becker's first major prose work was *Felder* (Fields, 1964). Some might dispute the term *prose* for this work because portions of it have lyrical or dramatic qualities. The designation seems appropriate, however, since Becker is consciously reacting against the norm. The book is a montage of 101 sections which cover 146 pages, and Becker attempts to use a different stylistic method for each section. These devices include the manipulation of punctuation and spelling, replacing words with dots, condensed sentences, run-on sentences, blank lines, use of quotations and dialect, topological descriptions, conversations, theoretical statements about his process of composition (it is common for German experimental writers to include such statements in their literary works), and found material. There are no central characters, although several acquaintances of the author are briefly mentioned.

Becker does not try to reproduce reality but to record the effect reality has on him. The fragmentary nature of the work reflects his fragmentary perception of the world. The reader is only given hints as to how the author has been altered or changed by his experiences. There is no clear indication of his progression or regression from one state to another; any relationships among the fragments must be constructed by the reader. Since some critics consider this fragmented style to be more truthful and to correspond more adequately to the way people actually encounter reality, Becker has been called a New Realist.

Becker's next major work, *Ränder* (1968; partially translated as "Margins," 1968), is even more hermetic than *Felder*. The book is divided into eleven sections; the middle section, number

6, consists of a leaf which is blank on both sides, and the other sections correspond symmetrically to each other. The first and last sections, written in normal syntax and everyday language, register the experiences of the author in a variety of situations. The second and tenth sections, which contain no punctuation, represent patterns of associative recollections. The third and ninth sections each contain one five-page-long sentence concerning Becker's experiences as a guest at the Villa Massimo in Rome in 1966. Particularly noteworthy in these sections are his musings on nature, a theme which dominates his later prose and poetry. In the fourth and eighth sections particles of language are arranged on the page like poems to illustrate the fragmented nature of the processes of remembering and forgetting. The fifth and seventh sections continue this disintegration process with linguistic elements scattered at random about the page. This pattern logically leads to the blank pages of the central section.

These chapters represent different levels or stages of experience and the limits of their expression in language. This emphasis on the inadequacy of language brings Becker close to the ideas of Heißenbüttel, who also questions the validity of the communication process. Becker limits himself to what is real for him–his own experiences. He feels that he is unable to penetrate objective reality–only the subjective sphere has validity. Such solipsism led Becker to publish a book in 1971 which contains 281 photographs and no text: *Eine Zeit ohne Wörter* (A Time without Words). The author can observe and record, but he cannot give meaning to reality.

Becker's most recent prose works display a more conventional form, at least linguistically; and while a recognizable plot is still absent, the montage of short pieces in each work gives the impression of diary entries. Becker has called this new direction a "phase of disentanglement" in which the lyric, acoustic, and visual elements of the earlier works have been removed and assigned to separate genres of radio play, photography, and poetry. This separation permits the prose to assume more natural contours. Sometimes the sentences in these works are purposely disjointed and playful, but the syntactic experimentation has been deemphasized. This fact, however, does not make the books any less hermetic. In fact, some passages are more perplexing than those in his earlier works, since Becker has begun to infuse his writing with philosophical speculation and concealed political commentary.

The personal experiences of the author, nevertheless, continue to form the core of these books.

In *Umgebungen* (Surroundings, 1970) Becker for the first time uses explanatory titles to help orient the reader to the many short pieces which constitute the work. The setting is the area in and around Cologne, and as usual the texts form a montage of the memories and reflections of the author, together with descriptive passages and fictitious incidents. Becker tries to preserve fleeting thoughts, feelings, and impressions in a way reminiscent of the "snapshot" poems of Rolf Dieter Brinkmann, another Cologne writer. He comments frequently on the increasing industrialization of Germany, in the course of which the countryside is being overrun by urban centers and industrial complexes. He also displays his dislike for the products of the consumer society, from office buildings to supermarkets.

Erzählen bis Ostende (Narration until Ostende, 1981) inaugurated what some critics believed to be a new direction in Becker's prose. The reader encounters a loose narrative structure—there is a major character, Johann, who works for the news media and is taking a train trip to the Belgian port of Ostende. Here, however, any resemblance to standard fiction stops, and one again finds a series of short titled segments. These fragments depict the memories, perceptions, conversations, dreams, and images that occur to Johann while he is on his journey. The perspective varies between the first and third persons, and the reader is confronted by a collage of "multiple I's" as in the previous works. Many of the texts have philosophical overtones which can make them abstract and confusing. Nevertheless, the reader can discern that the protagonist, a mouthpiece for Becker, prefers the tranquillity of his home and garden to the maddening pace of his high-rise office building, which he portrays in Kafkaesque scenes. Like Becker, who works at a radio station, Johann is in the business of "creating facts," a process about which he has extreme misgivings. There are veiled references to Alexander Kluge, whose cinematic collages are attempts to create an alternative public sphere of information, and to the writer Uwe Johnson, who was concerned with the artist's inability to portray empirical events objectively.

The journey theme—which is growing in popularity among other inward-directed German-language authors, such as Peter Rosei and Franz Böni—also forms the undercurrent to Becker's *Die Türe zum Meer* (The Door to the Sea, 1983). The journey here is one to the furthest realms of the imagination. Divided into four impressionistic chapters—"Auf den Hügeln" (On the Hills), "Geräusche im Tal" (Sounds in the Valley), "Die innere Umgebung" (The Inner Surroundings), and "Besuch im Exil" (Visit in Exile)—this book represents to some degree a return to the hermeticism of the early works. Becker's central concern is still unrelenting self-analysis, but his statements have become so personal that their connection to a larger world and to the reader becomes tenuous. Becker seems to be saying that one can only exist, with the aid of memory and imagination, in a nonlinguistic world and that a more perfect control of language moves one farther away from contact with this world. Relationships with others also seem impossible to achieve, and thus communication between author and reader is illusory. This orientation places heavy demands on the reader. The inklings one can glean of Becker's themes, such as the destruction of nature by technology or the necessity of employing an associative writing style, do not compensate for the irritation of dealing with such a confused work.

Becker has also written radio plays and films; most of these share with his prose an absence of plot and characterization and a conglomeration of voices representing different aspects of consciousness. Becker also wrote a considerable body of poetry, primarily during the 1970s, all of which was republished in a single volume in 1981. Although these poems have a loose structure and do not contain standard stanza, rhyme, or verse patterns, they are not highly experimental in a linguistic sense. What makes them innovative, and a bit difficult, is Becker's use of a concentrated form that makes unexpected jumps and breaks in the thought pattern and thus establishes new semantic relationships. But like his prose works they are diary-like collections of perceptions, observations, memories, and reflections. Thematically, too, there are similar concerns: distrust of an omnipresent technology, a pessimistic outlook regarding progress, a longing for an unadulterated nature whose destruction one faces with resignation, comments on the act of writing, and the importance of memory and the association of ideas for daily existence.

Jürgen Becker has striven to present an alternative literary model of the contemporary world by the use of multiple voices and the refusal to employ a plot or provide connective links. He believes that the resultant fragmentation is a more adequate representation of how people experience reality than the traditional ordering process of prose. For the most part his works have been positively received, albeit among only a small group of readers. Those who criticize him are concerned that Becker's overindulgence in his private world prevents many readers from approaching him and sharing his ideas. Such critics also point out that, as is the case with so many contemporary avant-garde writers, the reader has to be familiar with Becker's theoretical pronouncements and self-interpretations to grasp the intent of his work. This theoretical consideration makes his work elitist to a degree. In spite of these reservations, however, one must admit that Becker and writers of a similar bent have had an influence on mainstream contemporary prose, which has become more introspective in questioning the validity of its methods and assertions.

References:

Peter Bekes, "Jürgen Becker," in *Kritisches Lexikon der deutschsprachigen Gegenwartsliteratur*, edited by Heinz Ludwig Arnold (Munich: Edition text + kritik, 1982), n. pag.;

Bodo Heimann, "Jürgen Becker: *Ränder*," in his *Experimentelle Prosa der Gegenwart* (Munich: Oldenbourg, 1978), pp. 31-38;

Walter Hinck, "Die 'offene Schreibweise' Jürgen Beckers," in *Basis: Jahrbuch für deutsche Gegenwartsliteratur I*, edited by Reinhold Grimm and Jost Hermand (Frankfurt am Main: Athenäum, 1970), pp. 186-203;

Hinck and Hiltrud Gnüg, "Jürgen Becker," in *Deutsche Literatur der Gegenwart in Einzeldarstellungen*, volume 2, edited by Dietrich Weber (Stuttgart: Kröner, 1977), pp. 26-55;

Doris Janshen, *Opfer und Subjekt des Alltäglichen: Denkstruktur und Sprachform in den Prosatexten Jürgen Beckers* (Cologne: Böhlau, 1976);

Leo Kreuzer, ed., *Über Jürgen Becker* (Frankfurt am Main: Suhrkamp, 1972);

Christian Linder, *Schreiben & Leben: Gespräche mit Jürgen Becker* (Cologne: Kiepenheuer & Witsch, 1974);

Hans-Ulrich Müller-Schwefe, *"Schreib' alles": Zu Jürgen Beckers "Rändern," "Feldern," "Umgebungen," anhand einer Theorie simuliert präsentativer Texte* (Munich: Fink, 1977);

Fritz J. Raddatz, "Jürgen Becker," in his *Die Nachgeborenen* (Frankfurt am Main: Fischer, 1983), pp. 202-214.

Peter Bichsel

(24 March 1935-   )

Judith Ricker-Abderhalden
University of Arkansas

BOOKS: *Eigentlich möchte Frau Blum den Milchmann kennenlernen: 21 Geschichten* (Olten & Freiburg im Breisgau: Walter, 1964); translated by Michael Hamburger as *And Really Frau Blum Would Very Much Like to Meet the Milkman: 21 Short Stories* (London: Calder & Boyars, 1968; New York: Delacorte, 1969);

Das Gästehaus: Roman, by Bichsel and others (Berlin: Literarisches Colloquium, 1965);

Die Jahreszeiten (Neuwied & Berlin: Luchterhand, 1967);

Tschechoslowakei 1968, by Bichsel, Friedrich Dürrenmatt, Max Frisch, Günter Grass, Kurt Marti, and Heinrich Böll (Zurich: Arche, 1968);

Des Schweizers Schweiz; Sitzen als Pflicht: Zwei Zeitungsaufsätze (Zurich: Arche, 1969);

Kindergeschichten (Neuwied & Berlin: Luchterhand, 1969); translated by Hamburger as *There Is No Such Place as America: Stories* (New York: Delacorte, 1970); translation republished as *Stories for Children* (London: Calder & Boyars, 1971);

Stockwerke, edited by Heinz F. Schafroth (Stuttgart: Reclam, 1974);

Geschichten zur falschen Zeit (Darmstadt & Neuwied: Luchterhand, 1979);

Museum: Das Museum der Stadt Solothurn 1979, photographs by Max Dörfliger, texts by Bichsel and André Kamber (Solothurn: Kunstverein, 1979);

Der Leser; Das Erzählen: Frankfurter Poetik-Vorlesungen (Darmstadt & Neuwied: Luchterhand, 1982);

Der Busant: Von Trinkern, Polizisten und der schönen Magelone (Darmstadt & Neuwied: Luchterhand, 1985);

Schulmeistereien (Darmstadt: Luchterhand, 1985);

Irgendwo anderswo: Kolumnen 1980-1985 (Darmstadt: Luchterhand, 1986).

OTHER: Niklaus Meienberg, *Reportagen aus der Schweiz*, foreword by Bichsel (Darmstadt & Neuwied: Luchterhand, 1974);

Frank A. Meyer, ed., *Willi Ritschard: Bilder und Reden aus seiner Bundesratzeit*, essay by Bichsel (Zurich: Ringier, 1984).

PERIODICAL PUBLICATION: "Das Ende der Schweizer Unschuld," *Der Spiegel*, no. 1/2 (5 January 1981): 108.

In 1965 the unpretentious and soft-spoken Swiss schoolteacher Peter Bichsel was catapulted to public attention when he received the coveted prize of the Gruppe (Group) 47 at its meeting in Berlin. He was thus honored for a chapter in his then-unpublished novel *Die Jahreszeiten* (The Seasons, 1967) and for his poetic prose miniatures published in 1964 in the slim volume with the curious title *Eigentlich möchte Frau Blum den Milchmann kennenlernen* (translated as *And Really Frau Blum Would Very Much Like to Meet the Milkman*, 1968). At a time when highly intellectualized writings and linguistic experiments were in vogue, Bichsel's charming and seemingly naive vignettes, whose most notable attribute was their utmost economy of expression, delighted the critics. The subsequent success and continuing popularity of this author (sometimes referred to as "the poet of the commonplace") in Switzerland and abroad are astonishing indeed, since for years they were based primarily on three slim volumes of prose, all published in the late 1960s. The miniatures in his first book, in particular, gained worldwide attention. They were translated into many different languages and were anthologized to an almost unprecedented degree.

Bichsel was born on 24 March 1935 in Lucerne, Switzerland, into a middle-class family as the first son of Lina Bieri Bichsel and Willi Bichsel-Schär. Whereas there are few references to his mother, evidence of his love and respect for his father, a house painter, abounds in Bichsel's work. According to his own testimony, there were no books in the family home save for a few painters' manuals, a book about Martin Luther, and the Bible. In 1941 the family moved to Olten, where

Bichsel spent most of his childhood. His school years were overshadowed by a double affliction which seems to have caused him considerable anguish: dyslexia and extreme left-handedness. He attributes his overcoming of these problems to the fact that dyslexia had not been given a label at that time and to a teacher who saw beyond the dreadful spelling and penmanship to recognize Bichsel's potential as a writer. Bichsel admits to still being uncertain in spelling, and he suspects that his much-discussed "Wenig-Schreiben" (modest output), his periodic writer's block, may be linked to these early problems.

A self-proclaimed storyteller, Bichsel likes to reminisce about his first reading experiences. When he was nine an aunt gave him for Christmas what he calls a boring, sentimental children's book, *Christeli* by Elisabeth Müller. It was forced upon him, the reading was torturous, and he did not finish it until 23 December of the following year. But then he was filled with pride and decided to join the ranks of readers. When he discovered the public library at the age of twelve, he eschewed the popular Karl May for the collected works of Goethe and other famous writers and read Adalbert Stifter's *Witiko* (1865-1867) twice, just to prove the incredulous librarian wrong. He became a voracious reader and still considers himself first of all a reader, then a writer.

In 1955 he graduated from teachers' college in Solothurn and taught for two years in an elementary school in nearby Lommiswil. He performed his obligatory service in the Swiss army in 1955 as a medic. His statements about the armed forces are almost always negative; Bichsel abhors strict discipline, unquestioning obedience, and unequivocal decisions, and like his famous compatriot Max Frisch, he tries to destroy the many myths associated with the Swiss military. His marriage in 1956 to Therese Spörri was followed later that year by the birth of a daughter, Christa Maria, and in 1957 by the birth of a son, Matthias. His first attempts at writing occurred during this period. In 1957 the Bichsel family moved to Zuchwil, where *Eigentlich möchte Frau Blum den Milchmann kennenlernen* was written.

Several of these miniatures, which average about two pages in length, first appeared in newspapers in 1962-1963. They immediately gained critical acclaim, and in 1963 Bichsel was invited to participate in the Literary Colloquium in West Berlin, where he met Walter Höllerer, Hans Werner Richter, Peter Weiss, and Günter Grass. The following year Bichsel was invited, upon the

recommendation of the Swiss author and publisher Otto F. Walter, to the meeting of the Gruppe 47 in Siguna, Sweden, where he was allowed to read a few of his pieces before an influential audience of writers and publishers.

The book was enormously popular. Both the expensive limited first edition of twelve hundred and the second edition of six thousand sold out within days. The stories were almost immediately translated into many languages and received critical acclaim throughout the Western world. By 1984 the volume was in its fifteenth printing and had sold over sixty-five thousand copies in German alone.

The book consists of twenty-one short prose pieces, the best known being "Der Milchmann" (The Milkman), "Das kartenspiel" (The Game of Cards), and "Die Tochter" (The Daughter). The plots are notoriously thin. Typically, someone sits and waits, often alone. These individuals rarely have names; the author refers to them as "er" (he), "sie" (she), "jemand" or "man" (someone), "die Tochter," or "die Männer" (the men). In the story "Die Männer" a young woman sits in a café and waits. The men of the title watch her, fantasize about her, toy with the idea of getting to know her, but they do not: "Man hätte sie fragen können," the narrator says. "Man hätte sie ja fragen können" (One could have asked her. One could always have asked her). In "Die Blumen" (Flowers) a man strikes up an imaginary dialogue with a salesgirl in a flower shop. He imagines what he would say to her, but again, he does nothing. The husband in "San Salvador" has purchased a fountain pen with which he writes a good-bye note to his wife, telling her that it is too cold for him there and that he is going to San Salvador. He imagines how she would react. But instead of going, he merely sits and rereads the instructions for the fountain pen.

For the most part, the individuals in Bichsel's stories do not seem to know much about each other, nor does the inconspicuous narrator know much about them; hence the frequent use of the words *vielleicht* (perhaps) and *wahrscheinlich* (probably). As Siegfried Mandel points out, "conjecture becomes compensatory experience" in this solitary type of existence. Like Frau Blum in the title story, Bichsel's men and women carry on imaginary dialogues with persons they would like to get to know, but rarely do they break out of their isolation. Their lives are stifled by stagnation, monotony, and resignation. Bichsel has a propensity for the subjunctive: I could do this or that, his characters tell themselves, or, even more characteristically, in the past subjunctive, I could have done this or that. These are sad stories of lost dreams and missed opportunities, written in a fittingly concise and laconic style.

Bichsel does not psychoanalyze his characters, nor does he parody or comment. Instead of describing speechlessness and isolation, he recreates these conditions through language. His characters speak in clichés if they speak at all, either because they are unable to articulate their thoughts and emotions or because they want to hide them. In Bichsel's paratactical syntax the individual statements stand isolated. Bichsel has an affinity for the conjunction *und* (and) and thus avoids pointing out causal relationships. Instead, he merely registers behaviors and leaves his readers to draw their own conclusions. Similarly, the monotony and repetitiousness of his characters' lives and thoughts are expressed directly in a language made monotonous by regularly recurring words and phrases.

The question remains why Bichsel's miniatures are so extraordinarily popular, since neither the topic—the inadequacy of human relationships in contemporary society—nor the style—more or less objective recording—is all that uncommon. For most critics, the answer is that Bichsel has succeeded like no other writer in capturing the essence of modern existence; with a few suggestive strokes he can sketch a whole life. With his first book, he established himself as a master of reduction and omission. By 1966 he had shared in the Lessing Prize of the City of Hamburg and the Advancement Prize of the City of Olten.

As early as 1971 Bichsel distanced himself from *Eigentlich möchte Frau Blum den Milchmann kennenlernen*. He found the miniatures to be too finished, too complete, and he expressed a strong preference for his second work, the experimental novel *Die Jahreszeiten* (The Seasons). It was published in 1967 by the Luchterhand firm in West Germany, which was to bring out all his subsequent works. He and several other young Swiss authors had followed their friend and supporter Walter when he changed publishing houses.

Die Jahreszeiten was not well received by the critical establishment, although in 1967 it was number two on the best-seller list. In this work Bichsel reflects upon the process of narration: it is a book about a man who writes a book about a fictitious man named Kieninger because he does not want to write a book about himself. In the course of the work a fictional world is created and then is destroyed through anti-illusionary devices. The reader witnesses the frustrations of the narrator, who attempts to tie together disparate pieces of information (details about a house, quotes from the tenants' handbook and insurance policies) and to relate these to the main character. Many alternatives of plot and character are provided, while the narrator bemoans the fact that he is unable to create either a coherent story line or a credible hero. Yet contrary to his expectations, the novel does take shape and the fictitious Kieninger does come alive, although the narrator disavows him in the end: "Der Trottel glaubt, er lebe. Ich täusche ihn" (The fool thinks that he lives. I'm deceiving him). But the narrator and Kieninger turn out to be one and the same person—the narrator did write about himself, after all.

Critics generally agree that the novel, although cleverly devised, is somewhat tiresome. The destruction of the illusionistic basis of fiction is no longer original but has come to be a conventional literary device of the postwar novel. *Die Jahreszeiten* confirms what *Eigentlich möchte Frau Blum den Milchmann kennenlernen* indicated: that Bichsel is more interested in language and the process of writing than in plot or characterization.

In 1968 Bichsel moved to Bellach, where he still resides. Shortly after the move Bichsel gave up his teaching position for journalism. According to his own accounts, he stopped teaching because he did not have enough time for it and because he took it far too seriously to be content with being a bad teacher. Since then he has written many columns about education, and in some ways he has remained a teacher: he considers himself a schoolmasterly author, a moralist, although not the "praeceptor patriae" some critics have called him.

In 1969 Bichsel published a second collection of short stories, *Kindergeschichten* (Children's Stories), which appeared in the United States under the title *There Is No Such Place as America* (1970) and in Great Britain as *Stories for Children* (1971). The original title is misleading: these seven stories are not written for children, nor are they about children. On the contrary, tired old men predominate: the man who wanted to verify that the earth is round, the man who renamed the objects in his apartment, the man who did not want to know any more. Bichsel chose the title *Kindergeschichten* because he was fascinated

Peter Bichsel (photograph by Anita Schiffer-Fuchs, courtesy of Ullstein Bilderdienst)

by the ability of children to ask persistent questions and to imagine hypothetical situations. "What if . . . ?" is one of their favorite questions. They are still capable of envisioning and desiring a different, better world.

In Bichsel's first collection of short stories the individuals do nothing to change their monotonous lives; at best they make plans which they fail to carry out. In the second collection, however, the men (there are no women) rebel, although for the most part unsuccessfully, against the status quo. In "Ein Tisch ist ein Tisch" (A Table Is a Table), one of the most frequently anthologized and analyzed stories in contemporary German literature, an old man, "es lohnt sich fast nicht, ihn zu beschreiben" (hardly worthwhile to describe), is no longer willing to accept his monotonous life; he invents a language that belongs to him alone. The result, however, is that he gives up talking altogether and speaks only to himself. His isolation has become complete.

These stories seem simple, almost simplistic, yet at the heart of several of them is nothing less than epistemological skepticism: the possible fictitiousness of external reality. Previously unquestioned knowledge is suddenly doubted, as in "Die Erde ist rund" (The Earth is Round). An old man who is described by negatives–"Ein Mann, der weiter nichts zu tun hatte, nicht mehr verheiratet war, keine Kinder mehr hatte und keine Arbeit mehr" (A man who had nothing else

to do, was no longer married, no longer had any children or a job)–begins reflecting upon all the things that he once accepted at face value. He "knows" that the earth is round, but he never really believed it; so he sets out to gather proof and is never seen again. Similarly, in "Amerika gibt es nicht" (There is No Such Place as America) the existence of America is questioned: perhaps all those people who claim to have been there have merely gone into hiding somewhere and then come back to tell their yarns about cowboys and skyscrapers! But in Bichsel's work, America and Columbus have also come to stand for the unknown and the courage to seek it out, to question long-accepted "truths," something that precious few of Bichsel's protagonists do.

Like the miniatures in his first volume, the stories in *Kindergeschichten* resemble children's compositions in both style and length. The individuals generally have one trait, as reflected in the titles of the stories–"Der Mann, der nichts mehr wissen wollte" (The Man Who Didn't Want to Know Any More), "Der Mann mit dem Gedächtnis" (The Man with the Memory), "Der Erfinder" (The Inventor)–and that trait is fully developed without any regard to probability. The stories are playful and delightful yet astonishingly complex, so that they appeal both to children and to sophisticated readers. This work, too, was a great success: in the year of its publication alone more than forty-four thousand copies were sold, and it was translated into even more languages than *Eigentlich möchte Frau Blum den Milchmann kennenlernen.* For *Kindergeschichten* Bichsel received the Lessing Prize from the City of Hamburg in 1970.

After *Kindergeschichten* Bichsel did not publish a new book for ten years, to the consternation and frustration of his readers and the critical establishment; the collection *Stockwerke* (Floors, 1974) consists almost entirely of previously published work. But he was by no means idle during these years. He wrote countless essays and columns for newspapers and magazines and a radio play, "Inhaltsangabe der Langeweile" (Summary of Boredom, 1972), for which he received the Swiss Prize for Radio Plays in 1973; he coproduced a film, *Unser Lehrer* (Our Teacher, 1971); he lectured frequently in Switzerland and abroad, most notably in Czechoslovakia, England, Ireland, Australia, and New Zealand; he served as writer in residence at Oberlin College in 1972 and participated in the "German Semester" of the University of Southern California in Los Angeles in 1976. An active member of the Social Democratic party of Switzerland, he served on committees, handed out leaflets, and took part in demonstrations. He was also a friend and political adviser to the federal councilor Willi Ritschard from 1974 until shortly before the popular politician's death in 1983. This unusually close relationship between a high government official and a writer whose columns had become more and more critical of Switzerland attracted national attention. Finally, in 1979, *Geschichten zur falschen Zeit* (Stories at the Wrong Time) appeared. No one seemed too disappointed that it did not contain fiction but forty-seven columns that had been published in the weekly magazine of the Zurich daily *Tages-Anzeiger* from 1975 to 1978. By 1984 the book, for which Bichsel received two prizes, was in its sixth edition.

During the years from 1969 to 1979 Bichsel's approach to writing changed. He no longer drew a sharp distinction between journalistic and literary writing. Although he retained, to a considerable extent, his characteristic style–a preference for plain, unadorned sentences–and his tone–a curious blend of melancholy and playfulness–he no longer simply records human behavior but reflects upon his observations and draws conclusions for his readers. But even as a political columnist, he remains a storyteller. He listens to stories, tells stories, and thinks in stories, but now they serve as points of departure for so-

cial and political commentary; they offer what one critic called "home-spun wisdom." Self-irony is a prominent feature of the columns collected in *Geschichten zur falschen Zeit;* it is self-irony attributed to a fictitious narrator who is a thinly disguised portrait of the author himself.

The columns cover a wide range of issues, large and small. Bichsel is sympathetic toward the poor and powerless, even the heavy drinkers he encounters in the bars, but quite critical of the Swiss establishment: he takes issue with the proverbial Swiss work ethic, with the country's resistance to change, and with its conservative politicians. He deplores Switzerland's excessive political stability, which makes elections rather predictable, and the resulting political apathy. He laments the hardships and frustrations of grassroots political work. He explores such broad topics as democracy in general and the Swiss democracy (where tough questions are not asked frequently enough) in particular, the relationship between justice and the judicial system, the roots of international terrorism, and the roles of the CIA and the Swiss police. His interest in language persists: he shows orthography to be an instrument of repression, writing to be a privilege of the privileged. Even though many of Bichsel's columns deal with politics, he shuns political jargon. His writing is unpretentious, poetic, at times even sentimental.

Seemingly unconcerned about his popularity and unaffected by his fame, he persists in asking probing questions. He knows very well that "wer fragt, ist ein Feind der bestehenden Antworten" (he who asks questions is an enemy of the existing answers). He says, "Vielleicht heißt Erwachsensein, fraglos in Antworten zu leben, Antworten zu haben ohne Fragen" (Perhaps adulthood means to have all the answers without questions); in that case, he does not want to grow up.

Since 1979 Bichsel's popularity and productivity have increased greatly. In the early 1980s he hosted two popular radio programs and made many television appearances. In 1980 he was invited to teach at the University of Essen, and in 1981, the year in which he wrote his controversial essay "Das Ende der Schweizer Unschuld" (The End of Swiss Innocence) for *Der Spiegel,* he was the first foreigner to be elected town clerk of Bergen-Enkheim near Frankfurt am Main, an honorary one-year position that is generally regarded as the most generous stipend for writers in Germany. In 1982, while still residing in Bergen-Enkheim, he was invited to deliver the

"Frankfurter Poetik-Vorlesungen," a famous lecture series; his lectures were published the same year under the title *Der Leser; Das Erzählen* (The Reader; The Narration). The lectures contain important theoretical statements about "Geschichten" (stories) and "Geschichte" (history). Bichsel drew enormous audiences, larger even than those attending the lectures of Günter Kunert, Peter Rühmkorf, Martin Walser, and Adolf Muschg before him, and the lecture anthology sold as if it were a popular novel. The following year Bichsel received a stipend from the Swiss government which permitted him to work on *Der Busant: Von Trinkern, Polizisten und der schönen Magelone* (The Magpie: Of Drinkers, Policemen and the Beautiful Magelone, 1985), a collection of eight short stories about losers, drunkards, eccentrics, and would-be writers toward whom Bichsel is sympathetic in spite of their weaknesses. In these stories the process of writing is once again a prominent theme. As in *Die Jahreszeiten*, Bichsel observes himself writing, reflects upon what he has written, and presents alternative versions; he describes lives which he declares not worth describing. In the same year he published *Schulmeistereien* (Schoolmasteries), a collection of twenty-two essays and speeches that span the years 1969 to 1984. It, too, appeared on the best-seller list shortly after its publication. Many of the essays deal with Bichsel's views on education. He repeatedly attacks the misguided notion among educators that children are unwilling to learn and must be seduced into doing so by all kinds of silly, insulting games.

Irgendwo anderswo: Kolumnen 1980-1985 (Somewhere Elsewhere: Columns 1980-1985) appeared in 1986. A continuation of *Geschichten zur falschen Zeit*, it contains forty newspaper columns written between 1980 and 1985. Familiar topics include Swiss neutrality; politics; unions; the concepts of freedom, justice, and "Heimat" (homeland); and prejudice and discrimination against foreign workers, refugees, the unemployed, and environmentalists. New in this volume are columns devoted to Bichsel's year at Bergen-Enkheim, the so-called Zürcher Unruhen (Zurich unrest) in the early 1980s, and the deaths of Bichsel's father and of Ritschard. In the spring of 1987 Bichsel was guest professor at Dart-

mouth College, where he taught a seminar on the modern German short story.

A master of short prose whose works are frequently compared with those of his compatriot Robert Walser, Peter Bichsel has secured a prominent place among Swiss writers of the generation after Friedrich Dürrenmatt and Max Frisch. He has found a unique, evocative style, to which he has remained faithful in most of his writing. His unassuming nature, his integrity, and his compassion for the less fortunate citizens of his wealthy nation make him one of the most popular writers in Switzerland. His newspaper columns, which one critic called "exemplary public dissent," make him a public figure who must be taken seriously even by those who disagree with his political views.

References:

Hans Bänziger, *Peter Bichsel: Weg und Werk* (Bern: Benteli, 1984);

Hermann Burger, "Des Schweizer Autors Schweiz: Zu Max Frischs und Peter Bichsels Technik der Kritik an der Schweiz," *Schweizer Monatshefte*, 51 (January 1972): 746-754;

Mario Cortesi, *Stimmen zur Schweiz: Mario Cortesi sprach mit Peter Bichsel* (Basel: National-Zeitung, 1968);

Herbert Hoven, ed., *Peter Bichsel: Auskunft für Leser* (Darmstadt & Neuwied: Luchterhand, 1984);

Grete Lübbe-Grothius, "Poetische Meditationen über die provisorische Wirklichkeit: Zu zwei Kindergeschichten von Peter Bichsel," *Schweizer Monatshefte*, 54 (February 1974): 113-119;

Siegfried Mandel, *Group 47: The Reflected Intellect* (Carbondale & Edwardsville: Southern Illinois University Press, 1973);

Rainer Sell, "Stagnation und Aufbruch in Bichsels *Milchmann-* und *Kindergeschichten*," in *Zur Literatur der deutschsprachigen Schweiz*, edited by Marianne Burkhard and Gerd LaBroisse (Amsterdam: Rodopi, 1979), pp. 255-273;

Susanne Steiner-Kuhn, *Schreiben im Dazwischen-Sein: Zu Robert Walser und Peter Bichsel, mit einem Seitenblick auf J. Heinrich Pestalozzi und Otto F. Walter* (Bern & Stuttgart: Haupt, 1982).

Horst Bienek
(7 May 1930-   )

Franz-Joseph Wehage
Appalachian State University

BOOKS: *Traumbuch eines Gefangenen: Prosa und Gedichte* (Munich: Hanser, 1957);
Nachtstücke (Munich: Hanser, 1959);
Werkstattgespräche mit Schriftstellern (Munich: Hanser, 1962; revised and enlarged edition, Munich: Deutscher Taschenbuch Verlag, 1976);
Borges, Bulatovic, Canetti: Drei Gespräche mit Horst Bienek (Munich: Hanser, 1965);
Was war, was ist: Gedichte (Munich: Hanser, 1966);
Die Zelle: Roman (Munich: Hanser, 1968); translated by Ursula Mahlendorf as *The Cell* (Santa Barbara, Cal.: Unicorn, 1972; London: Gollancz, 1974);
Vorgefundene Gedichte: Poèmes trouvés (Munich: Hanser, 1969);
Horst Bienek, translated by Ruth and Matthew Mead (Santa Barbara, Cal.: Unicorn, 1969);
Bakunin, eine Invention (Munich: Hanser, 1970); translated by Ralph R. Read as *Bakunin: An Invention* (London: Gollancz, 1977);
Selected Poems: Johannes Bobrowski, Horst Bienek, translated by Ruth and Matthew Mead (Harmondsworth, U.K.: Penguin, 1971);
Solschenizyn und andere: Essays (Munich: Hanser, 1972);
Die Zeit danach: Gedichte (Düsseldorf: Eremiten-Presse, 1974);
Die erste Polka: Roman (Munich & Vienna: Hanser, 1975); translated by Read as *The First Polka: A Novel* (London: Gollancz, 1978; San Francisco: Fjord Press, 1984);
Gleiwitzer Kindheit: Gedichte aus zwanzig Jahren (Munich: Hanser, 1976);
Septemberlicht: Roman (Munich: Hanser, 1977);
Zeit ohne Glocken: Roman (Munich: Hanser, 1979);
Von Zeit und Erinnerung: Erzählungen, Gedichte, Essays, edited by Margarete and Günter Gorschenek (Gütersloh: Gütersloher Verlagshaus Mohn, 1980);
Der Freitag der kleinen Freuden (Düsseldorf: Eremiten-Presse, 1981);
Erde und Feuer (Munich: Hanser, 1982);
Beschreibung einer Provinz: Aufzeichnungen, Materialien, Dokumente (Munich: Hanser, 1983);

Horst Bienek (photograph by Isolde Ohlbaum, Munich)

Königswald oder Die letzte Geschichte (Munich: Hanser, 1984);
Heimat: Neue Erkundungen eines alten Themas (Munich: Hanser, 1985);
Der Blinde in der Bibliothek: Literarische Porträts (Munich: Hanser, 1986);
Das allmähliche Ersticken von Schreien: Sprache und Exil heute (Munich: Hanser, 1987).

OTHER: Hans Bender, ed., *Junge Lyrik 1956: Eine Auslese,* contributions by Bienek (Munich: Hanser, 1956);
Stig Dagerman, *Spiele der Nacht,* edited by Bienek (Wiesbaden: Limes, 1961);
Hans Henny Jahnn, *Nacht aus Blei,* epilogue by Bienek (Munich: Deutscher Taschenbuch Verlag, 1962);

Alfred Kubin, *Die andere Seite*, epilogue by Bienek (Munich: Deutscher Taschenbuch Verlag, 1962);

Johannes Bobrowski, *Das Land Sarmatien: Gedichte*, epilogue by Bienek (Munich: Deutscher Taschenbuch Verlag, 1966);

Friedrich Ege, comp., *Finnische Lyrik aus hundert Jahren*, edited by Bienek (Hamburg: Merlin, 1973);

Ivan Bunin, *Grammatik der Liebe: Erzählungen*, edited by Bienek (Munich: Piper, 1973);

Bunin, *Das Dorf und frühe Erzählungen*, edited by Bienek (Munich: Deutscher Taschenbuch Verlag, 1976);

Ivan Goll, *Gedichte 1924-1950*, edited by Bienek (Munich: Deutscher Taschenbuch Verlag, 1976);

Edith Södergran, *Feindliche Sterne: Gesammelte Gedichte*, epilogue by Bienek (Munich: Limes, 1977);

Arthur Silbergleit, *Der ewige Tag*, epilogue by Bienek (Berlin: Europäische Ideen, 1978);

Isaak Babel, *So wurde es in Odessa gemacht*, edited by Bienek (Berlin: Ullstein, 1980).

Horst Bienek is known as the author of several novels drawn from his experiences as a political prisoner in the Soviet Union and as the chronicler of events in his native Upper Silesia during World War II. In addition, Bienek has made a name for himself as a literary critic and film producer.

Bienek was born in Gleiwitz, Upper Silesia (now part of Poland), on 7 May 1930. His father, Hermann Bienek, was a railroad employee; his mother, Valeska Piontek Bienek, helped support the family by giving piano lessons. When he was sixteen his family moved to Köthen-Anhalt in the Soviet Zone. Bienek did not complete high school, but he read extensively for the next two years and developed a particular interest in the French symbolists Baudelaire, Rimbaud, and Mallarmé, who influenced his early writings. In 1948 he won a prize in a competition for young authors; at that time he was working without pay for a daily newspaper, *Die Tagespost* of Potsdam. His first short story, "Warum" (Why), was published in Alfred Kantorowicz's journal *Ost und West* (1949) and his poetry in Peter Huchel's journal *Sinn und Form*. In 1950 Bienek took part in a newly established seminar for young writers at Bad Saarchow; there he was discovered by Martin Gregor-Dellin, a literary adviser for the East German government, who offered Bienek a job

as his assistant. In this position Bienek came to know the writers Günter Kunert, Heiner Müller, and Christa Reinig, who, like him, had grown up among the postwar ruins and had become suspicious of dogma and ideologies.

Bienek composed his first set of serious poems in 1950; they became popular at once, especially an apocalyptic cycle including "Jeder Bruder ist Kain" (Every Brother Is Cain) and "Das Mädchen küßt den Sirius in den Wellen" (The Girl Is Kissing Sirius in the Waves). The poems, which deal with the repercussions of World War II and culminate in an appeal for eternal peace, were displayed in manuscript form in an East Berlin bookstore. Their literary merits were recognized by Stephan Hermlin, whose collections *Die Straßen der Furcht* (Streets of Fear, 1947) and *Zweiundzwanzig Balladen* (Twenty-two Ballads, 1947) Bienek admired. Hermlin mentioned Bienek in a speech at a congress for young writers in East Berlin in the spring of 1951.

In the fall of that year the office where Bienek worked was dissolved by the government, and Bienek began studies under Bertolt Brecht at the Berlin Ensemble. He had just finished writing "Elemente des epischen Theaters in dem Stück *Haben* von Julius Hay" (Elements of the Epic Theater in the Play *To Have* by Julius Hay)– the manuscript for which has been lost–when he was arrested on 8 November 1951. His arrest was Kafkaesque: the police confiscated a West Berlin newspaper in his apartment which contained a report about the resistance group "Rote Kapelle" in the Third Reich. Bienek explained that he had been planning to write a poem about one of the persons mentioned in the article, Liane Berkowicz; but no such name appeared in the article. After seven months of interrogation Bienek was sentenced in May 1952 to twenty-five years in a labor camp in Vorkuta, Siberia, on charges of spying for the West.

Bienek survived the Gulag Archipelago partly due to his intellectual stamina but also because of packages of food and supplies from Reinig. Thanks to Gregor-Dellin, who had preserved some of his manuscripts, Bienek's name was not forgotten: Gregor-Dellin introduced his work to Günter Bruno Fuchs, Richard Salis, Dietrich Kirsch, and other writers. In 1955 Bienek was released under an amnesty program and deported to West Germany. He worked as a literary critic for the Hessischer Rundfunk (Hessian State Radio) in Frankfurt and coedited with

Hans Platschek *blätter und bilder,* a journal for poetry, music, and art, from 1957 until 1961, when he found employment in Munich as a reader and then as an editor for the publishing firm Deutscher Taschenbuch Verlag.

Bienek's first publications after his release from prison appeared in Hans Bender's anthology *Junge Lyrik 1956* (1956). In 1957 Bienek published *Traumbuch eines Gefangenen: Prosa und Gedichte* (Dreams of a Prisoner: Prose and Poems), which deals with his prison experiences. The prose and lyric pieces are written in a surrealistic style which demonstrates a highly versatile linguistic sensitivity.

The short stories of *Nachtstücke* (Night Sketches, 1959) continue the theme of the despair and resignation of people whose existence is threatened. "Das Duell" (The Duel) is the story of two revolutionaries who face the consequences of their planned rebellion. "Das Attentat" (The Assassination) depicts a woman's plan to murder a tyrant. In "Die Aufzeichnungen des Clemens C" (Notes of Clemens C) a medical student takes poison and records its effects on himself. "Der Erdnußverkäufer" (The Peanut Vendor) tells of a peanut vendor who has never been able to sell enough of his product to make a living; one day a stranger demands his entire stock, and the vendor, no longer able to comprehend reality, commits suicide. Two other stories rework Greek legends: "Die Schwestern" (The Sisters) describes the fate of Agamemnon's daughters Electra and Chrysothemis; in "Die Tugend der Penelope" (The Virtue of Penelope) Odysseus's wife yields to her sexual desires during her husband's absence.

In the following years Bienek conducted a series of radio interviews with German-speaking authors, including Friedrich Dürrenmatt, Heinrich Böll, Günter Grass, Martin Walser, Alfred Andersch, and Uwe Johnson; the programs were broadcast on all the major German radio stations. The encounters with other writers contributed to a critical self-examination by Bienek. The interviews were published as *Werkstattgespräche mit Schriftstellern* (Workshop Discussions with Writers, 1962).

Bienek's first novel, *Die Zelle* (translated as *The Cell,* 1972), was published in 1968. Initially the title was to have been "Im Bauche des Wals" (In the Belly of the Whale), a metaphor for Bienek's imprisonment. But by the time he had finished the novel about these traumatic years, *Die Zelle* was the only name that seemed appropri-

ate. The protagonist of the novel, like the author himself, is arrested almost on the thirty-fourth anniversary of the October revolution in Russia. Life in the cell–the suffering, the loneliness, the humiliation, and eventually the intellectual triumph over the physical conditions–is depicted in agonizing detail. Time is almost suspended in the novel. The length of the imprisonment is unknown to the reader. The prison floodlights render differentiation between night and day impossible. The prison doctor, the protagonist's only contact with the outside world, is mute and deaf. The inmate invents new patterns of time based on the changing of the guards. He is hoping for any sort of change, such as a hearing or an interrogation, which would provide a measure of time, but nothing happens. The protagonist finally does not know whether his suffering is real, a dream, or a first sign of mental illness. The end of the novel almost repeats the beginning because time itself has become repetitious; the only difference is that at the end both of the protagonist's legs are bandaged. *Die Zelle* was awarded the Literature Prize of the City of Bremen.

With the completion of *Die Zelle* Bienek's obsession with his imprisonment lessened somewhat. His second novel, *Bakunin, eine Invention* (1970; translated as *Bakunin: An Invention,* 1977), is about a young writer, a nameless anarchist who took part in the revolutionary activities of the 1960s. Wishing to write a biography of Mikhail Bakunin, he travels to Neuchâtel, Switzerland, to interview people who knew the great nineteenth-century anarchist; but they fail to remember anything of significance. The protagonist, who wants to experience the *real* life of Bakunin–the one not contained in the history books–despairs as he realizes that there is no tangible evidence about the subject of his study. Bienek's subtitle, *eine Invention,* indicates that the documentary evidence has been enriched with fictitious data: subjective invention becomes historical evidence. The thoughts and activities of the protagonist are combined with factual and imagined episodes from Bakunin's life. The novel contains excerpts from the writings of Bakunin and Ivan Turgenev as well as from biographies of Bakunin by Max Nettlau and Vera Figner.

Bienek's years in the Soviet Union led to a work on Russian intellectuals who were persecuted by their own government: *Solschenizyn und andere* (Solzhenitzyn and Others, 1972) discusses the lives and works of Aleksandr Solzhenitzyn, Mikhail Bulgakov, Isaak Babel, Osip Mandelshtam, and Bakunin. Bienek's book serves as a protest against all governments that try to suppress their intellectuals. Bienek also edited two volumes of works by the Russian writer Ivan Bunin, *Grammatik der Liebe* (Grammar of Love, 1973) and *Das Dorf und frühe Erzählungen* (The Village and Early Stories, 1976).

Between 1975 and 1982 Bienek published a four-part chronicle of his native city, Gleiwitz, during World War II: *Die erste Polka* (1975; translated as *The First Polka*, 1978), *Septemberlicht* (September Light, 1977), *Zeit ohne Glocken* (Time without Bells, 1979), and *Erde und Feuer* (Earth and Fire, 1982).

The entire action of *Die erste Polka* takes place on 31 August/1 September 1939. With the sounds of airplanes and gunfire in the background, the citizens of Gleiwitz witness the wedding of Valeska Piontek's daughter. The bride and groom dance their first polka in a world that is doomed, leaving the memory of momentary happiness in the face of death. Valeska's son Josel also dances his first polka in the ballroom of the Hotel Oberschlesien; the dance becomes a farewell to his childhood in more than one sense. The rhythmic dance is juxtaposed to the rolling thunder of the German tanks at the Polish border; the first polka turns into a dance of death. Bienek describes the events of the next twenty-four hours in Gleiwitz: the funeral ceremony for Valeska's husband, Josel's escape after killing a sergeant who was trying to rape his girlfriend, and the suicide of the half-Jewish court councillor Montag, an early victim of racial discrimination. Bienek received the Hermann Kesten Prize for *Die erste Polka* in 1975. The novel was made into a film, starring Maria Schell and Erland Josephson and directed by Klaus Emmerich, in 1979.

Before the second volume of the tetralogy appeared, Bienek published a collection of his poetry as *Gleiwitzer Kindheit: Gedichte aus zwanzig Jahren* (Childhood in Gleiwitz: Twenty Years of Poems, 1976). The poems contain painful reminiscences of a civilized Germany that was annihilated by National Socialism. They focus on Gleiwitz, which became a border town after World War I and witnessed the outbreak of World War II. Its people are representatives of a border culture, a conglomerate of German, Polish, and Jewish traditions. Bienek pays special attention to the German heritage, notably the nineteenth-century romantic poet Joseph von Eichendorff, who came from Upper Silesia.

Septemberlicht again reports the events of a single day: 4 September 1939. German armies have advanced into Poland, and the Allies have declared war against Germany. The novel concentrates on the attitudes and thoughts of the characters. The war is only a few days old and has already been pushed into the background. Hitler's voice on the radio, headlines in the *Völkischer Beobachter* (the official newspaper of the Nazi party), and machine-gun fire are occasional reminders that a war is going on. The inhabitants of Gleiwitz live as they would in peacetime: it is not their war. They adjust to the new regime without reflecting on it. They do not care about the future of civilization but only about their personal futures. But National Socialist rule has nevertheless brought changes: the symbiosis between the Germans and the Slavic population has dissolved; fear, the resurgence of old ethnic hatreds, and chauvinism have destroyed a community that had existed peacefully for centuries under the guidance of the Catholic church.

Zeit ohne Glocken takes place on Good Friday, 1943, the day the bells of Gleiwitz's St. Peter and Paul Church are confiscated for military purposes by the Nazi government. The confiscation of the bells signals the beginning of "totaler Krieg" (total war), the desperate effort of the Nazis to prevent defeat. The removal of the bells symbolizes the loss of faith. The thundering of the cannons has faded away; life in Gleiwitz seems to be peaceful again, almost to a paralyzing degree. There are no sirens, bombs, or burning houses in Gleiwitz, even though the people are surrounded by the war. The Jewish writer Silbergleit, who fled to his birthplace from Berlin, has been arrested and is on his way to the death camps. Valeska's daughter has been arrested for consorting with a Russian soldier. The eighteen-year-old Josel has been drafted. Franz, the locomotive engineer, lives through daily torture as he transports Jews to the death camps. The novel describes with startling realism the disintegration of hope. The action is again compressed into a twenty-four-hour period, creating a suspenseful simultaneity.

Erde und Feuer, the final volume of the chronicle of Upper Silesia, portrays the initial months of 1945, when the Soviet troops advance into Germany and the mass exodus begins. Bienek focuses on the confusion and disbelief of his characters as they face a drastic change in their lives. The account incorporates Gerhart Hauptmann's famous speech on the bombing of Dresden.

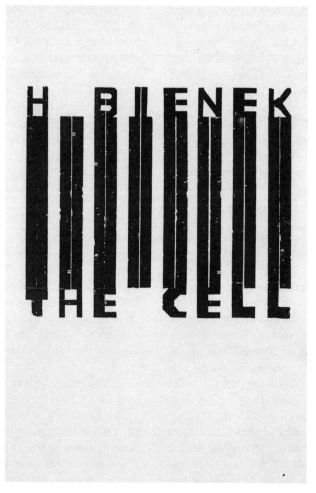

Dust jacket for the English translation of Bienek's autobiographical novel of imprisonment, based on his four years in a Siberian labor camp

In *Beschreibung einer Provinz* (Description of a Province, 1983) Bienek documents his research for the Gleiwitz tetralogy. He contrasts the past and the present and voices concern about political unrest in Silesia, now part of Poland, against the regime of General Jaruzelski. The book is indicative of Bienek's troubled relationship with Germany.

Unlike his previous novels, *Königswald oder Die letzte Geschichte* (Königswald; or, The Last Tale, 1984) has little to do with the author's past. Instead, it depicts a group of German aristocrats who had to escape from their eastern estates when the Soviet army advanced. They are gathered in the Bohemian castle of Königswald, between the Soviets approaching from the east and the Americans from the west. The novel is filled with action: the kidnapping of an SS officer, the retreat of the Germans, the arrival of the Americans, the flight of the aristocrats, and the acquisi-

tion of the territory by the Soviets. The book notes the end of the era of power and influence of the aristocrats.

Bienek's *Der Blinde in der Bibliothek* (The Blind Man in the Library, 1986) contains discussions of authors and their works. Especially noteworthy are his treatments of Else Lasker-Schüler, Nelly Sachs, and Günter Eich, and his introductions of the Swede Stig Dagerman; August Scholtis, a novelist from Bienek's native Silesia; and the poet Arthur Silbergleit, who died in Auschwitz in 1944 and is remembered in *Septemberlicht*. In 1987 Bienek gave lectures at the Universities of Munich and Würzburg that were published as *Das allmähliche Ersticken von Schreien: Sprache und Exil heute* (The Gradual Suffocating of Screams: Language and Exile Today, 1987).

Bienek has also been involved with the film industry. In 1968 he produced a television program about Ezra Pound; the movie version, *Ezra*

Pound, 80, received a prize for best documentary film. Also in 1968 Bienek directed *Beschreibung eines Dorfes* (Description of a Village), based on the 1966 book of the same name by Marie Luise Kaschnitz, who also narrated the film. In 1970 Bienek wrote the script for and directed a motion picture based on *Die Zelle;* the film received international recognition, and Bienek won a gold medal as the best young film director in the Federal Republic of Germany at the 1971 Berlin Film Festival. An English-language version of the film was released in 1974. In 1975 the German television station ARD aired "Beobachtungen in Amerika" (Observations in America), which was directed by Bienek, Jürg Federspiel, Günter Kunert, Gerhard Roh, and Martin Walser; Bienek's contribution was the segment "Gesichter in New York" (Faces in New York). Bienek has also written many essays, articles, and book reviews. He was honored with a residency at the Villa Massimo in Rome in 1960 and received the Hans Jacobi Prize for his poetry collection *Was war, was ist* (What Was, What Is, 1966) in 1967, the Wilhelm Raabe Prize in 1978, the Nelly Sachs Prize in 1981, and the Great Service Cross of the Federal Republic of Germany in 1983.

References:

S. Bauschinger, "Königswald oder Die letzte Geschichte," *World Literature Today,* 59 (Spring 1985): 267;

Ilmars Birznieks, "Horst Bienek: Septemberlicht," *World Literature Today,* 53 (Winter 1979): 104-105;

Günter Blöcker, "Das eigentliche Leben des Michail Bakunin," *Merkur,* 24 (July 1970): 695-698;

W. V. Bloomster, "Beschreibung einer Provinz," *World Literature Today,* 58 (Winter 1984): 100;

Vytas Dukas, "Solschenizyn und andere," *Books Abroad,* 47 (Spring 1973): 379-380;

Manfred Durzak, *Die deutsche Literatur der Gegenwart: Aspekte und Tendenzen* (Stuttgart: Reclam, 1971), pp. 164, 290;

Hans Jürgen Geerdts, "Werkstattgespräche," *Weimarer Beiträge,* 12 (1966): 981;

Christina Grawe, "Gleiwitzer Kindheit," *World Literature Today,* 51 (Spring 1977): 273;

Michael Hamburger, "Dance to the Sound of Gunfire," *Times Literary Supplement,* 25 March 1977, p. 378;

Michael Krüger, *Bienek lesen: Materialien zu seinem Werk* (Munich: Hanser, 1980);

Krüger, "Horst Bienek," in *Schriftsteller der Gegenwart,* edited by Klaus Nonnenmann (Olten: Walter, 1963), pp. 43-46;

Christa Rotzoll, "Feier vor dem Krieg," *Der Spiegel,* no. 39 (22 September 1975): 148-149;

Judith Ryan, "Erde und Feuer," *World Literature Today,* 58 (Winter 1984): 90;

Heinrich Vormweg, "In der Zelle," *Merkur,* 22 (May 1968): 468-470.

Johannes Bobrowski

(9 April 1917-2 September 1965)

Robert Acker
University of Montana

BOOKS: *Sarmatische Zeit: Gedichte* (Stuttgart: Deutsche Verlags-Anstalt, 1961);

Schattenland Ströme: Gedichte (Stuttgart: Deutsche Verlags-Anstalt, 1962);

Levins Mühle: 34 Sätze über meinen Großvater (Berlin: Union, 1964); translated by Janet Cropper as *Levin's Mill* (London: Calder & Boyars, 1970);

Mäusefest und andere Erzählungen (Berlin: Wagenbach, 1965);

Boehlendorff und andere Erzählungen (Stuttgart: Deutsche Verlags-Anstalt, 1965);

Boehlendorff und Mäusefest: Erzählungen (Berlin: Union, 1965)–combines the contents of *Mäusefest und andere Erzählungen* and *Boehlendorff und andere Erzählungen*;

Shadow Lands: Selected Poems, translated by Ruth and Matthew Mead (Denver: Swallow, 1966; London: Carroll, 1966)–includes translations of poems from *Sarmatische Zeit* and *Schattenland Ströme;*

Litauische Claviere (Berlin: Union, 1966);

Das Land Sarmatien: Gedichte (Munich: Deutscher Taschenbuch Verlag, 1966);

Wetterzeichen: Gedichte (Berlin: Union, 1966);

Nachbarschaft: Neun Gedichte; Drei Erzählungen; Zwei Interviews; Zwei Grabreden; Zwei Schallplatten; Lebensdaten (Berlin: Wagenbach, 1967);

Der Mahner: Erzählungen (Berlin: Union, 1967); republished as *Der Mahner: Erzählungen und andere Prosa aus dem Nachlaß* (Berlin: Wagenbach, 1968);

Johannes Bobrowski liest Lyrik und Prosa (Berlin: Union, 1969);

I Taste Bitterness, translated by Marc Linder (Berlin: Seven Seas, 1970)–translations of *Boehlendorff und Mäusefest* and *Der Mahner;*

Im Windgesträuch: Gedichte aus dem Nachlaß, edited by Eberhard Haufe (Berlin: Union, 1970);

Selected Poems: Johannes Bobrowski, Horst Bienek, translated by Ruth and Matthew Mead (Harmondsworth, U.K.: Penguin, 1971)–includes

Johannes Bobrowski (Deutsche Verlags-Anstalt, Stuttgart)

translations of poems from *Sarmatische Zeit* and *Schattenland Ströme;*

Lipmanns Leib: Erzählungen, selected by Wilhelm Dehn (Stuttgart: Reclam, 1973);

Gedichte: 1952-1965 (Leipzig: Insel, 1974);

From the Rivers, translated by Ruth and Matthew Mead (London: Anvil Press Poetry, 1975)–includes translations of poems from *Sarmatische Zeit, Schattenland Ströme*, and *Wetterzeichen;*

*Literarisches Klima: Ganz neue Xenien, doppelte Aus-
　füihrung* (Berlin: Union, 1977).

OTHER: Gustav Schwab, *Die schönsten Sagen des
　　　klassischen Altertums*, edited by Bobrowski
　　　(Berlin: Altberliner Verlag, 1954);
Schwab, *Die Sagen von Troja und von der Irrfahrt
　　　und Heimkehr des Odysseus*, edited by Bo-
　　　browski (Berlin: Altberliner Verlag, 1955);
Hans Clauert, der märkische Eulenspiegel, edited
　　　by Bobrowski (Berlin: Altberliner Verlag,
　　　1956);
Jean Paul, *Leben Fibels*, edited by Bobrowski (Ber-
　　　lin: Union, 1963);
*Wer mich und Ilse sieht im Grase: Deutsche Poeten des
　　　18. Jahrhunderts über die Liebe und das Frauen-
　　　zimmer*, edited by Bobrowski (Berlin: Eulen-
　　　spiegel, 1964);
Samuil Marschak, *Das Tierhäuschen*, translat-
　　　ed by Bobrowski (Berlin: Kinderbuchverlag,
　　　1967); translated by Moya Gillespie as *The
　　　House in the Meadow* (Irvington-on-Hudson,
　　　N.Y.: Harvey House, 1970; London: Chat-
　　　to, Boyd & Oliver, 1970);
Boris Pasternak, *Initialen der Leidenschaft*, trans-
　　　lated by Bobrowski and Günther Deicke (Ber-
　　　lin: Volk und Welt, 1969).

Although Johannes Bobrowski is known primarily for his poetry, he made significant contributions to the development of East German fiction, and his influence was also felt in West
German letters. In the 1960s, when socialist realism and the portrayal of contemporary conflicts
dominated the literary scene in the German Democratic Republic, Bobrowski introduced a fragmented, disjunctive, nonlinear prose in which the
narrator continually intrudes into the story by
questioning the choice of words or the development of the plot. This device serves to remind
the reader of the fictional nature of the work
and the arbitrariness of the creative process. The
disavowal of the omniscient narrator and the skepticism regarding the adequacy of literature to capture reality can also be found in the literary theories of Uwe Johnson and Arno Schmidt. Bobrowski's style, which has its roots in the oral tradition of folk literature and is thus colloquial with
traces of dialect, found many imitators in East Germany, and its influence can be seen particularly
in the works of Christa Wolf. Thematically, too,
Bobrowski broke new ground by attempting, as
in his poems, to come to terms with the roots of
fascism and National Socialism. The historical con-

flicts between German and non-German or between German and Jew lie at the heart of much
of his fiction. The Germans' relationships with
their Eastern neighbors, which had rarely been
treated in German literature, was a topic that
forcefully presented itself to Bobrowski because
of his biographical circumstances. The microcosms he describes are allegories for all of German society, and he uses the past to comment on
the present and the future. He urges the acceptance by the Germans of their guilt for World
War II and its atrocities, hoping that such acceptance will prevent further calamities. The role of
the artist in contemporary society constitutes a
major subtext in much of his oeuvre. The use of
the past to comment on the present became a favorite technique of East German prose in the
mid and late 1960s; in this regard, Bobrowski's influence can especially be discerned in the works
of Rolf Schneider and Manfred Bieler.

Bobrowski was born in 1917 in Tilsit (now So-
vetsk, U.S.S.R.) in East Prussia, not far from Lithu-
ania, to Gustav and Johanna Witzke Bobrowski.
His father, a railroad employee, was of Polish
descent. During his childhood in Tilsit and
Rastenburg (now Ketrzyn, Poland) Bobrowski
was imbued with a deep Lutheran piety. In 1928
the family moved to Königsberg (now Kalinin-
grad, U.S.S.R.), where Bobrowski attended a
college-preparatory high school; one of his teachers was the writer Ernst Wiechert. During these
years he was particularly attracted to music and
painting. During summer visits with his grandparents in the village of Motzischken he learned
much about the culture and history of the Slavic
peoples who lived across the border. His informal study of art history was interrupted in 1937
when he was conscripted into the army. His family moved to Berlin the following year, and
Bobrowski enrolled at the University of Berlin
for one semester in 1941 while on leave from the
army. He married Johanna Buddrus on 27 April
1943; they eventually had four children. During
the war he served in France, Poland, and northern Russia, but he was also a member of the
Bekennende Kirche (Confessing Church), a Protestant resistance group. He was taken prisoner of
war by the Soviets in 1945 and held in the re-
gions of the Don and middle Volga rivers, working as a coal miner and laborer and helping to
organize theater evenings for the POWs. He returned to East Berlin when he was released in
1949. In 1950 he began working as an editor for
a publisher of children's books, and in 1959 he be-

came an editor for the Union Verlag. He died in 1965 from complications after an appendectomy.

Bobrowski wrote his first short story in 1959; most of his approximately three dozen other stories, as well as his novels, were written between 1963 and 1965, shortly after the success of his first two volumes of poetry. Bobrowski claimed that he considered his fiction a natural extension of his poetry: since many of his ideas and themes could not be fully realized in his abbreviated verse forms, he turned to prose to provide more details and greater richness of characterization. Some scholars maintain, however, that Bobrowski only wrote fiction because he was commissioned to do so by publishers eager to capitalize on his instant notoriety as a poet. His first novel, *Levins Mühle* (translated as *Levin's Mill*, 1970), appeared simultaneously in East and West Germany in 1964. Most of his collected stories were published in 1965, again in separate editions in East and West, and the rest were published posthumously in 1967 under the title *Der Mahner* (The Warner). His second novel, *Litauische Claviere* (Lithuanian Pianos, 1966), was written in a few weeks during the summer of 1965. Bobrowski has been honored in East and West Germany as a Christian humanist who spoke out against racial and class distinctions; in the West he is also admired for his innovative and experimental style. He received the Gruppe 47 Prize and the Alma König Prize in 1962, and the Heinrich Mann Prize of the East Berlin Academy of the Arts and the international Charles Veillon Prize from Switzerland for *Levins Mühle* in 1965. He was posthumously awarded the East German F. C. Weiskopf Prize in 1967.

Bobrowski's reflective and introspective style does not always make for easy reading. Events are grouped together only by association, and the connections between them are not always apparent. The novels and stories function on several temporal and thematic levels at once. The narrator gropes for a satisfactory linguistic expression and sometimes must admit his inability to find one. Legends, myths, and fairy tales are combined with historical events to recall unpleasant or suppressed events. Bobrowski's stories are deeply rooted in the landscape of his youth, and this landscape assumes a profoundly symbolic quality. He is not interested in mimetic realism but in studies of human behavior which provide lessons or parallels for the present. The narrator passes no judgments but lets the words and deeds of the characters speak for themselves. All

of these features require the active participation of the reader, who must construct and decipher the narrative along with the author. The works are not, however, extremely esoteric: Bobrowski restricts himself to short pieces—even the novels are not very long—and this brevity permits experimentation without taxing the reader's patience. The predominant use of the present tense and of main clauses helps to draw the reader into the action.

Levins Mühle is set in 1874 in an area of West Prussia inhabited by Germans, Poles, Jews, and Gypsies. (This is the approximate location of the region of Sarmatia, the setting of many of Bobrowski's poems.) The Germans are portrayed as wealthy and powerful property owners and pious Christians; the other groups are shown to be poor and weak, with a great fondness for music. The narrator's grandfather Johannes, a rich miller, floods and destroys a new mill set up by the Jew Levin. Levin loses his lawsuit against Johannes because the Germans in the village—who are, ironically, mostly of Polish descent—conspire to portray Levin to the court as a religious and national enemy. Levin finds comfort and solace with the Gypsies, with whom he composes and sings a street ballad exposing the injustice committed by Johannes. To avenge this insult, Johannes sets fire to the house where Levin has taken refuge. Levin is accused of arson and banished from the village. Nevertheless, the other oppressed villagers, who have acquired from this experience a new sense of solidarity, join forces and defeat the German nationalists in a tavern brawl. Johannes, weary of the constant battles, moves to a larger city to spend his final days spreading German nationalism, hatred, and bigotry.

German intolerance of racial minorities is also a prevalent theme in Bobrowski's poetry; yet there is no false sense of philo-Semitism or denial of complicity on Bobrowski's part—the Germans in the novel fear and hate the Jew because they do not understand him, and Bobrowski does not claim to understand him either. Bobrowski uses Levin's case as a paradigm for all racial prejudice and intolerance, which are linked to nationalism and to power structures in society. The rich invoke religious and nationalistic ideology to justify their domination of the poor. Bobrowski demonstrates the ironies involved in such endeavors: the Christian religion preaches love and tolerance of all people, yet the Germans hated the Jews and based their prejudice partly

Bobrowski in 1964 (photograph by Heinz Köster, courtesy of Ullstein Bilderdienst)

on religion; nationalism in its baser form promulgates the superiority of the state and all its members, yet the Jewish citizens of the state were excluded from this superiority on racial grounds. In so doing he exposes some of the major reasons for the development of fascism and National Socialism. These themes of sin, guilt, nationalism, and the struggle for social equality are not just pertinent to a specific historical locality, but are by analogy important for understanding an even more distant historical past (suggested in the novel by ghosts who appear to Johannes) and for the comprehension of events in contemporary Germany and other countries. The novel has been translated into at least fifteen languages.

Levins Mühle is narrated not in a straightforward linear fashion but in a montage in which the narrator openly expresses his doubts about the truth of the events he recounts and about his ability to render them in an adequate linguistic form. The narrator recalls events in bits and pieces and mixes them with his own reflections, just as the mind does when it remembers something. This imitation of the processes of consciousness is more realistic than the prose of the nineteenth century, which gives a false illusion of

harmony and logic. These particles of language are also, on another level, representative of the fragmentation of contemporary society.

Bobrowski's second novel, *Litauische Claviere*, is similar in theme to the first. It is set in 1936 in the area of the Memel River, where Germans and Lithuanians live side by side and where Bobrowski spent his childhood. Two Germans from Tilsit, Professor Voigt and Concertmaster Gawehn, decide to write an opera about the eighteenth-century Lithuanian pastor and poet Christian Donelaitis. They travel to a small village to visit the local schoolteacher, Potschka, who is an expert on Donelaitis and on Lithuanian folklore. The day of their visit happens to coincide with two rival festivities: the Germans and Lithuanians are celebrating different national holidays in separate parts of town. The German nationalists, who are all portrayed negatively, provoke an incident in which a Lithuanian farmer is killed. No German comes to the aid of the Lithuanians except Voigt. The Lithuanian Potschka is also the center of a controversy because he wants to marry a German woman. Potschka ascends an imaginary "trigonometric tower," where he has a vision of Donelaitis at a marriage celebration. Voigt and Gawehn return home, uncertain whether their project can ever be completed.

The novel demonstrates once again Bobrowski's fondness for constructing simultaneous temporal and spatial levels. Donelaitis, who in his epic poetry supported the oppressed and exploited Lithuanian peasants in their struggle against their cruel German landlords in the eighteenth century, supplies a contrasting image to the fascism developing in the 1930s and offers a positive model for contemporary society and for the future. Potschka, who is the reincarnation of Donelaitis in the 1930s and who can conjure up vivid images of the past, comes back from his trance armed with ideas for the shaping of a new and more equitable society. Voigt, a German who tries to bridge the gap which separates him from his Lithuanian neighbors, is the concrete example of the humanism Donelaitis and Potschka proclaim.

The novel is also a comment on the writer's role in society. J. P. Wieczorek argues convincingly that Bobrowski wanted to demonstrate that the author's function is to provide hope to a cynical world; he was trying to show that his refusal to employ socialist realism and his concentration on the past do not represent formalism or an esoteric retreat from practical affairs but rather provide a method for tackling contemporary problems. Seen in this light, Potschka also serves as an alter ego for Bobrowski: on the one hand, he is the mediator of a Christian-based humanism which he learned from an intensive study of ancient literature and folktales; on the other hand, by descending from his imaginary tower into the real world, he shows that the writer can make practical application of the ideas he has gleaned from his study of history. The artist can contribute to mutual understanding in a troubled world.

Bobrowski again employs his experimental style: the bits and chunks of reality and the intrusions and reflections of the narrator are mixed with quotations from the works of Donelaitis, dreams, and suggested scenes for the opera. At times the reader is hard-pressed to make the necessary connections between these disparate segments, and some passages are purposely vague and open-ended. These features detract from the aesthetic quality of the novel and diminish its impact.

Bobrowski's short stories are miniature versions of his novels. A narrator hesitatingly feels his way along and develops characters and events in the process of writing; events often have little apparent relationship to each other. The language is usually colloquial. The stories contain little plot and no hero; they have no real beginning or end but simply contain a slice of daily life which allows the reader to study human behavior patterns. Simple events in provincial settings are used as parables for large-scale social processes. There are careful descriptions of landscapes, which have precise metaphorical functions within the stories. Bobrowski prefers legends and tales from the past; several stories are set in the seventeenth, eighteenth, and nineteenth centuries, although a few are set in the 1960s. Past and present are often intertwined to demonstrate the need for a change in the tyrannical structures of society.

Like his poems, some of Bobrowski's stories feature great artists and thinkers of the past with whom he feels an affinity: "D. H. B." concerns the Danish composer Dietrich Buxtehude, "Junger Mann am Fenster" (translated as "Young Man at the Window") the philosopher Arthur Schopenhauer, and "Epitaph für Pinnau" (translated as "Epitaph for Pinnau") the writer Johann Georg Hamann. Other stories recall prewar and wartime experiences. "Mäusefest" (translated as "Festival of the Mice") relates the conversations between the moon and an old Jew who is feeding the mice in his house as a German soldier stands guard. In "Der Mahner" (translated as "The Warner") a strange man goes through Königsberg in 1932 calling out "Haltet Gottes Gebote!" (Keep God's commandments!). A German soldier dances wildly about while Jews are being arrested in "Der Tänzer Malige" (translated as "The Dancer Malige"). Still other stories are satires about East German society or allegories about the human condition. "Das Stück" (translated as "The Piece") describes how an author must change his work to conform to the standards of socialist realism before it is accepted for publication. "De homine publico tractatus" is a series of humorous anecdotes about the unorthodox behavior of a postal official whose goal in life is to serve his fellowman. In "Verfolg städtebaulicher Überlegungen" (translated as "In Pursuance of City Planning") the inhabitants of old apartments slated for replacement by new ones are so eager to forget the past that they do not realize that new does not necessarily mean better.

Three stories have as their theme the role of the artist in society. In "Rainfarn" (translated as "Tansy") the narrator becomes invisible one day a year so that he can spy on a group of nudists; he soon grows dissatisfied with his role as a voyeur and longs to take a more active part in society. In "Beschreibung eines Bildes" (translated as "Description of a Picture") a man who has been shipwrecked frantically builds crosses during the day and fires at night to warn other ships away from the perilous waters. In "Boehlendorff" a nineteenth-century poet wanders through the land seeking an answer to the question: "Wie muß eine Welt für ein moralisches Wesen beschaffen sein?" (How must a world be constituted for a moral being?). The only answers he receives are abuse and laughter, and he is driven to suicide. These stories provide the key to understanding all of Bobrowski's fiction: Bobrowski considered himself a moralist and humanist, not just an observer of facts but a passionate participant in life who warns others about the dangers in their path. Drawing from a deep understanding of history and the humanistic tradition, Bobrowski presents the modern reader with a mandate: change society or be doomed to repeat the mistakes of the past.

Bibliography:
Curt Grützmacher, *Das Werk Johannes Bobrowskis* (Munich: Fink, 1974).

References:

Ada G. Beresina, "Johannes Bobrowskis Roman *Litauische Claviere,*" *Weimarer Beiträge,* 5 (1974): 91-106;

Mechthild Dehn and Wilhelm Dehn, *Johannes Bobrowski: Prosa; Interpretationen* (Munich: Oldenbourg, 1972);

Boshidasa Deliiwanowa, "Formen der epischen Kommunikation im Romanwerk von Johannes Bobrowski," *Zeitschrift für Germanistik,* 1 (1980): 277-286;

Bernhard Gajek and Eberhard Haufe, *Johannes Bobrowski: Chronik–Einführung–Bibliographie* (Frankfurt am Main: Lang, 1977);

Johannes Bobrowski: Selbstzeugnisse und Beiträge über sein Werk (Berlin: Union, 1967);

Brian Keith-Smith, *Johannes Bobrowski* (London: Wolff, 1970);

Hans Christian Kosler, "Johannes Bobrowski," in *Kritisches Lexikon zur deutschsprachigen Gegenwartsliteratur,* edited by Heinz-Ludwig Arnold (Munich: Edition text + kritik, 1979), n.pag.;

Christoph Meckel, *Erinnerung an Johannes Bobrowski* (Düsseldorf: Eremiten-Presse, 1978);

Gerhard Rostin, ed., *Johannes Bobrowski: Selbstzeugnisse und neue Beiträge über sein Werk* (Berlin: Union, 1975);

David A. Scrase, "Point Counterpoint: Variations on the 'Fest' Theme in Johannes Bobrowski's *Levins Mühle,*" *German Life and Letters,* 32 (January 1979): 177-185;

Siegfried Streller, "Johannes Bobrowski," in *Literatur der DDR in Einzeldarstellungen,* edited by Hans Jürgen Geerdts (Stuttgart: Kröner, 1972), pp. 292-315;

J. P. Wieczorek, " 'Die Großen taten in verschiedenen Zungen': Johannes Bobrowski's *Litauische Claviere,*" *German Life and Letters,* 35 (July 1982): 355-367;

Gerhard Wolf, *Johannes Bobrowski: Leben und Werk* (Berlin: Volk und Wissen, 1984).

Volker Braun
(7 May 1939-   )

Herbert A. Arnold
Wesleyan University

BOOKS: *Provokation für mich: Gedichte* (Halle: Mitteldeutscher Verlag, 1965; revised, 1965, 1975);

Vorläufiges (Frankfurt am Main: Suhrkamp, 1966);

Kriegserklärung (Halle: Mitteldeutscher Verlag, 1967);

Wir und nicht sie: Gedichte (Halle: Mitteldeutscher Verlag, 1970; enlarged, 1979);

Die Kipper (Berlin & Weimar: Aufbau, 1972);

Das ungezwungene Leben Kasts: Drei Berichte (Berlin & Weimar: Aufbau, 1972; enlarged, 1979);

Gedichte, edited by Christel and Walfried Hartinger (Leipzig: Reclam, 1972; enlarged, 1976, 1979);

Gegen die symmetrische Welt: Gedichte (Halle: Mitteldeutscher Verlag, 1974);

Die Kipper; Hinze und Kunze; Tinka (Berlin & Weimar: Henschel, 1975); published in West Germany as *Stücke* (Frankfurt am Main: Suhrkamp, 1975);

Es genügt nicht die einfache Wahrheit: Notate (Leipzig: Reclam, 1975);

Poesiealbum 115 (Berlin: Neues Leben, 1977); published in West Germany as *Zeit-Gedichte* (Munich: Damnitz, 1977);

Unvollendete Geschichte (Frankfurt am Main: Suhrkamp, 1977);

Der Stoff zum Leben (Pfaffenweiler: Pfaffenweiler Presse, 1977);

Im Querschnitt Volker Braun: Gedichte, Prosa, Stücke, Aufsätze, edited by Holger J. Schubert (Halle: Mitteldeutscher Verlag, 1978);

Training des aufrechten Gangs: Gedichte (Halle: Mitteldeutscher Verlag, 1979);

Gedichte (Frankfurt am Main: Suhrkamp, 1979);

Stücke 2 (Frankfurt am Main: Suhrkamp, 1981)—contains *Schmitten, Guevara oder Der Sonnenstaat, Großer Frieden, Simplex Deutsch;*

Berichte von Hinze und Kunze (Halle: Mitteldeutscher Verlag, 1983);

Hinze-Kunze-Roman (Frankfurt am Main: Suhrkamp, 1985).

Volker Braun (photograph by Bernd Oeburg)

OTHER: Gerhard Wolf, ed., *Sonnenpferde und Astronauten: Gedichte junger Menschen*, contributions by Braun (Halle: Mitteldeutscher Verlag, 1964);

Kipper Paul Bauch, in *Deutsches Theater der Gegenwart*, volume 2, edited by Karlheinz Braun

(Frankfurt am Main: Suhrkamp, 1967), pp. 5-104;

Freunde, in *Neue Stücke: Autoren der Deutschen Demokratischen Republik*, edited by Manfred Hocke (Berlin: Henschelverlag, 1971), pp. 367-387;

Hinze und Kunze, in *Spectaculum 19* (Frankfurt am Main: Suhrkamp, 1973), pp. 83-128.

PERIODICAL PUBLICATION: "Geschichten von Hinze und Kunze," *GDR Monitor*, 3 (1980): 1-4.

Volker Braun's formative years were spent in the German Democratic Republic (GDR); thus he takes for granted many of the postwar German economic, social, and political gains which appeared so laudable to an older generation, and instead of extolling the achievements of socialism he focuses on its problems. This concentration has made him one of the most exciting and controversial writers in German letters, as the many editions of his works in East and West Germany attest. Their history of publication also reflects the complicated relationship Braun has with the authorities of the GDR. Some of his works have been denied permission to be published in the GDR, appearing instead in West Germany; others have not only been published promptly in East Germany but even received prizes there, such as the Heinrich Heine Prize in 1971 and the Heinrich Mann Prize in 1980. As one of the first signatories to the letter by GDR writers protesting the expulsion of the poet Wolf Biermann in 1976, Braun was reprimanded and excluded from the board of the Berlin section of East Germany's writers' organization. Nevertheless, he frequently receives permission to travel and give readings in the West. While Braun thinks of himself primarily as a dramatist, he is better known to many readers as a poet and increasingly as a writer of fiction. An engaged and critical Marxist, his works explore such key issues as the relationship of the individual to a socialist collective, the nature of work and human needs, the interdependence of leaders and led, and the internal contradictions of socialist society and the possibilities for their solution. For Braun, the writer should participate actively in societal change, and the function of writing should be to irritate, to pose questions, and to promote thinking and political action. To express these issues adequately, Braun uses bold strategies, including complex ellipses in his prose and slang in his poetry. One of the

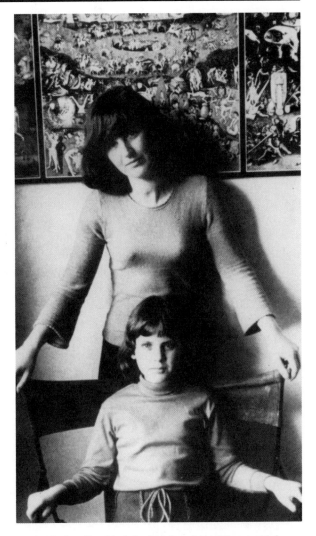

Braun's wife with their daughter Arne (photograph by Roger Melis)

most important contemporary German writers, he is equally fascinating as poet, dramatist, fiction writer, and critic.

Born in Dresden just before the outbreak of World War II, Braun lost his father in the war in 1945. After receiving his Abitur (high school diploma) in 1957, he tried to gain admission to a university but was rejected for political reasons. For the next three years he held a variety of jobs, including machinist and underground construction worker. In 1960 he was admitted to the University of Leipzig, where he studied philosophy until 1964. Braun has worked in various capacities, including reader and assistant director, at several East German theaters: at the invitation of Helene Weigel at the Berliner Ensemble in 1965-1966, at the Municipal Theater in Leipzig in 1971-1972, at the Deutsches Theater Berlin from 1972 to

1977, and again at the Berliner Ensemble since 1977. Braun's literary publications also began in 1965. He traveled to Siberia in 1964; to France in 1971; to Cuba, Peru, and Italy in 1976; and to West Germany on several occasions. In 1980 he toured England, reading from his works.

A few main themes can be found in all of Braun's work, irrespective of genre: the failure of socialism to humanize work and overcome monotony and alienation; the inadequacy of daily life as measured against the utopian promise of socialism; the necessity of fulfilling psychological needs and achieving basic democracy. Braun's aim is always to make poetry an active partner of politics, to have the writer influence social and political affairs as directly as possible, to activate and agitate. To achieve his goals, Braun uses dialectical juxtapositions which not only require the participation of the reader for their understanding but also try to unmask sham and hypocrisy. The constant attempt to break open ossified structures in literature and society, an essential element of his poetry, is also a trademark of his plays and fiction. The plays move from an almost Brechtian didacticism in the early works to a more theatrical, at times surrealistic mode which presupposes considerable sophistication on the part of the audience. His fiction, on the other hand, has begun to shift from the emphasis on individual and psychological needs which followed the earliest collectivist phase of his poetry to an attempted synthesis of the interests of the one and the many, the leaders and the led, the people and the cadres.

Braun's early poems were written in cooperation with the poets Sarah and Rainer Kirsch, Karl Mickel, Biermann, and others with whom he traveled to public readings in imitation of Soviet models. This manner of composition accounts in part for the tone of these poems, in which the public is addressed directly and contemporary issues are discussed. The discrepancy between personal experience and social demands is aggressively stated; and there is a Storm-and-Stress emphasis on the individual, who feels provoked to respond to the inadequacies and injustices of social and political life–as the title of the first collection, *Provokation für mich* (I Am Provoked, 1965), indicates. But the basic idea of Braun's aesthetic, the stress on process as opposed to result, soon led him to adopt a more dialectical depiction of the interdependence between the lyrical "I" and the societal "We," without losing sight of the benefit to so-

Poster for the premiere of the play version of Braun's allegorical tale of an East German Communist functionary and his chauffeur

ciety of the full development of the individual; the second phase of development of his poetry is an investigation into the nature of the collective self. The third phase, beginning in 1969, seems to seek a Hegelian synthesis of the earlier phases. These elements are present in *Wir und nicht sie* (We and Not They, 1970), which includes a comparison of the two German states and asks what might constitute a usable tradition for a German state and literature with revolutionary claims. *Gegen die symmetrische Welt* (Against a World of Symmetry, 1974) poses critical questions about socialism in the GDR and adumbrates possible answers, while establishing links to the tradition of Brecht, Goethe, and Hölderlin. *Training des aufrechten Gangs* (Practicing How to Walk Upright, 1979) plays with the figures of truth seekers and with history; it is interspersed with self-observations and visions of a new life.

A similar thematic unity within a changing theoretical framework characterizes Braun's fiction, as does a consistent, at times brilliant, use of irony. The story *Das ungezwungene Leben Kasts*

(Kast's Free and Easy Life), published in 1972 but written between 1959 and 1968, deals with crucial events in the cultural politics of the GDR. Its first part, "Schlamm" (Mud), can be read as the reductio ad absurdum of the novels favored by the so-called Bitterfeld Program, which called for the realistic depiction of working conditions in an effort to produce a literature commensurate with the political self-image of the new socialist "Arbeiter- und Bauern-Staat" (worker and peasant state). The second part, "Hörsaal" (Lecture Room), discusses how to achieve an adequate artistic treatment of reality, poses the question whether innovations that benefit the common weal also benefit the individual, and shows the disappointment of earlier hopes for the active participation of everyone in the shaping of the future. This demand for participation is also central in the third part, "Bühne" (Stage), where acting in the theater is seen as an anticipation of social and political practice; but Braun makes it clear that alienation and its causes cannot be solved by art. Having toiled in the mud, learned in the lecture room, and experimented on the stage, Kast finally rises to the status of party functionary in part four, "Die Tribüne" (The Rostrum), which was written in 1974 and published in 1979 in an enlarged edition of Das ungezwungene Leben Kasts. Although he is now in a position to make use of all of the experience he has gained, he finds himself cut off from the workers and dies in a car accident. The rise of the worker Hans Kast thus parallels the development of the GDR and parodies the traditional Bildungsroman.

The need to get involved, to act humanely, to mistrust anonymous structures is powerfully underscored in Unvollendete Geschichte (Story without an Ending, 1977). What begins as a conventional love story turns into tragedy when the state security forces begin to investigate young Frank, and his girlfriend Karin is pressured to give him up because she will endanger her own chances for employment by associating with an enemy of the state. Karin's mother is particularly insistent in this regard, while her father gradually comes to see the lovers' side–but not before both have been ostracized, Frank has attempted suicide, and Karin has lost her job. Here two young lives are almost destroyed by innuendo because everyone assumes that the security police would not act without good reason; only when spontaneous human reactions replace the routinized responses, when questions are asked, when involvement displaces indifference does a decent life be-

come a possibility for Karin and Frank and for Karin's father. Braun does not predict the eventual result of their breaking of the mold; the book ends with the sentence: "Hier begannen, während die eine nicht zuende war, andere Geschichten" (Here other stories began while this one had not yet ended).

The dialectical and ironic Braun at his best is found in Berichte von Hinze und Kunze (Reports of Hinze and Kunze, 1983) and Hinze-Kunze-Roman (Hinze-Kunze Novel, 1985). "Hinze und Kunze" is the German equivalent of "Tom, Dick, and Harry"; these are everyman figures representative of the people (Hinze) and the party (Kunze). Because of Braun's complex vision and the intricacies of the situation analyzed–not to mention the exigencies of censorship–the two characters are apt to switch positions and become playfully elusive in their revealing and critical discussions of contemporary East Germany. While Berichte von Hinze und Kunze is clearly modeled on Brecht's "Geschichten vom Herrn Keuner" (Anecdotes of Mr. Keuner, 1930, 1932), Hinze-Kunze-Roman has many similarities to Diderot's Jacques le fataliste (1796). There is no plot to this "novel"; instead, Braun offers a series of conversations between the two protagonists interspersed with reflections on writing, the role of women in society, and a multitude of other topics. Hinze's wife Lisa, who is loved by his boss Kunze, is a third major figure in this witty and at times bawdy collection of tales about life in the GDR.

Kunze and Hinze, the party functionary and his driver, need each other and have settled comfortably into their respective roles: the party leads, the people grumble but follow. But the people do not really want to develop any initiative, nor do they know how to do so because they are not used to exercising such freedom; the party, consequently, is trapped in its dominant role even when it attempts to break out of it by delegating responsibility. Inadequate though the partners in socialism may be and imperfect as their relationship is, they are, nevertheless, engines and recipients of change, moving slowly and uncertainly but moving ahead, even if they are not sure where they are going. Brilliant linguistic tour-de-force passages, a biting wit, and a sustained irony make this one of Braun's most remarkable works, even if it is not easily accessible. A good introduction to Braun's thinking and mode of argumentation is his collection of essays, reflections, poems, and notes Es genügt nicht die einfache

Scene from Braun's play Hinze und Kunze, *as performed at the Städtische Theater in Karl-Marx-Stadt, 1973 (photograph by Sieglinde Gemarius de Kepper)*

Braun in 1985 (photograph by Anita Schiffer-Fuchs, courtesy of Ullstein Bilderdienst)

Wahrheit (The Simple Truth Is Not Enough, 1975).

Braun is, above all, a dramatist. Some of his plays have suffered long delays before being published or performed in the GDR; the reasons for these difficulties appear to be primarily ideological, with Braun running afoul of the political or aesthetic categories of judgment prevalent in the GDR establishment. The early plays were written under the influence of Brecht and deal critically with the relationships between workers and their milieu during the early phase of socialism in the GDR. *Die Kipper* (The Dumpers, 1972), written between 1962 and 1965, and the one-act *Freunde* (Friends, 1971), written in 1965, were not performed until 1972, after the cultural thaw introduced by the Honecker regime. *Hans Faust*, which premiered in Weimar in 1968, is a parodistic modernization of the story of Faust. In Faust and Mephisto, Braun introduces the dialectical pairing of characters which is central to the play version of *Hinze und Kunze*, first performed in Karl-Marx-Stadt in 1973, and to the later book versions.

The second phase of Braun's dramatic writings is characterized by a more experimental, theatrical approach and an emphasis on the conflict between the needs of the individual and those of society. In *Tinka* (1975), written in 1972-1973 and performed in 1976 in Karl-Marx-Stadt, and *Schmitten* (1981), begun in 1968, completed in 1978, and performed in Leipzig in 1982, strong female protagonists challenge basic social and moral assumptions of the GDR. Disturbing questions about male-female relationships, the nature of work under socialism, and the status of women workers in a socialist society may have delayed production of these plays. *Guevara oder Der Sonnenstaat* (Guevara; or, The City of the Sun, 1981), which was written around 1975 and premiered in Mannheim, West Germany, in 1977, and *Großer Frieden* (Great Peace, 1981), which was written in 1976 and staged in Berlin in 1979, locate more abstract discussions of historical issues in distant and exotic settings and use "epic" techniques in their presentation. Both plays fail to come to grips with the key issues they raise, among them the possibility that history may repeat itself and that alienation from work or society may be present in any social or economic

system—notions quite difficult to reconcile with Marxist orthodoxy.

What remains valuable is Braun's ability to show convincingly how initially positive impulses and ideals are transformed in the course of historical application. That is also the key to his fascinating *Simplex Deutsch* (The German Simpleton, 1981), written in 1978-1979 and first staged by the Berliner Ensemble in its experimental theater in 1980. The provocative juxtaposition of historical scenes, ranging from the Russian civil war to present-day West Germany, challenges the audience to either become critically involved or remain the simpletons invoked in the title. Braun's latest play, "Dmitri," written in 1980, exists only as a manuscript. Like Schiller's final fragment, *Demetrius* (1805), it deals with the issue of legitimate versus usurped power. It is to be hoped that unlike Schiller's, this will not be the last play by one of the major theatrical talents writing in German and one of the most challenging critics of accepted or shallow perceptions.

References:

Heinz Ludwig Arnold, ed., *Volker Braun* (Munich: Edition text + kritik, 1977);

David Bathrick, "Geschichtsbewußtsein als Selbstbewußtsein: Die Literatur in der DDR," in *Literatur nach 1945*, edited by Jost Hermand (Wiesbaden: Athenaion, 1979), pp. 273-314;

Manfred Behn, "Volker Braun," in *Kritisches Lexikon zur deutschsprachigen Gegenwartsliteratur*, edited by Arnold (Munich: Edition text + kritik, 1978), pp. 1-13;

Christine Cosentino and Wolfgang Ertl, *Zur Lyrik Volker Brauns* (Königstein: Forum Academicum, 1984);

Wolfgang Emmerich, *Kleine Literaturgeschichte der DDR* (Darmstadt: Luchterhand, 1981), pp. 165-168;

Horst Haase and others, *Geschichte der deutschen Literatur: Literatur der DDR* (Berlin: VEB Volk und Wissen, 1977), pp. 665-668, 748-755;

Christel and Walfried Hartinger, "Volker Braun," in *Literatur der DDR in Einzeldarstellungen*, edited by H. J. Geerdts (Stuttgart: Kröner, 1972), pp. 504-522;

Ulrich Profitlich, *Volker Braun* (Munich: Fink, 1985);

Jay Rosellini, *Volker Braun* (Munich: Beck, 1983).

Günter de Bruyn
(1 November 1926-   )

Valerie D. Greenberg
Tulane University

BOOKS: *Über die Arbeit in Freihandbibliotheken* (Berlin: Zentralinstitut für Bibliothekswesen, 1957);

Hochzeit in Weltzow (Halle: Mitteldeutscher Verlag, 1960);

Wiedersehen an der Spree: Erzählung (Halle: Mitteldeutscher Verlag, 1960);

Der Hohlweg: Roman (Halle: Mitteldeutscher Verlag, 1961);

Einführung in die Systematik für allgemeinbildende Bibliotheken (Berlin: Zentralinstitut für Bibliothekswesen, 1961);

Ein schwarzer, abgrundtiefer See (Halle: Mitteldeutscher Verlag, 1963; revised, 1966);

Maskeraden: Parodien (Halle: Mitteldeutscher Verlag, 1966);

Buridans Esel: Roman (Halle: Mitteldeutscher Verlag, 1968); translated by John Peet as *Buridan's Ass* (Berlin: Seven Seas, 1973);

Hochzeit in Weltzow: Erzählungen (Leipzig: Reclam, 1968);

Preisverleihung: Roman (Halle: Mitteldeutscher Verlag, 1972);

Tristan und Isolde: Nach Gottfried von Straßburg neu erzählt (Munich: Kindler, 1975);

Das Leben des Jean Paul Friedrich Richter: Eine Biographie (Halle: Mitteldeutscher Verlag, 1975);

Märkische Forschungen: Erzählung für Freunde der Literaturgeschichte (Halle & Leipzig: Mitteldeutscher Verlag, 1978);

Im Querschnitt: Prosa, Essays, Biographie, edited by Werner Liersch (Halle & Leipzig: Mitteldeutscher Verlag, 1979);

Neue Herrlichkeit: Roman (Frankfurt am Main: Fischer, 1984);

Frauendienst: Erzählungen und Aufsätze (Halle & Leipzig: Mitteldeutscher Verlag, 1986).

OTHER: "Grischa 44," in *Arnold Zweig: Ein Almanach* (Berlin: Aufbau, 1962), pp. 21-27;

"Berlin, Große Hamburger," in *Städte und Stationen*, edited by Elli Schmidt (Rostock: Hinstorff, 1969), pp. 7-11;

Günter de Bruyn (Günter de Bruyn, Im Querschnitt, *edited by Werner Liersch [Halle & Leipzig: Mitteldeutscher Verlag, 1979])*

Das Lästerkabinett: Deutsche Literatur von Auerbach bis Zweig in der Parodie, edited by de Bruyn (Leipzig: Reclam, 1970);

"Günter de Bruyn über Christa Wolf: Fragment eines Frauenporträts," in *Liebes- und andere Erklärungen: Schriftsteller über Schriftsteller*, edited by Annie Voigtländer (Berlin & Weimar: Aufbau, 1972), pp. 410-416;

"Traumstationen," in *Auskunft,* edited by Stefan Heym (Munich: Autoren-Edition, 1974), pp. 185-195;

Jean Paul, *Leben des Quintus Fixlein,* edited by de Bruyn (Berlin: Der Morgen, 1976);

"Freiheitsberaubung," in *Auskunft 2,* edited by Heym (Munich: Autoren-Edition, 1978), pp. 11-21;

Theodor Gottlieb von Hippel: Über die Ehe, edited by de Bruyn and Gerhard Wolf (Halle & Leipzig: Mitteldeutscher Verlag, 1979);

Friedrich de la Motte Fouqué, *Ritter und Geister: Romantische Erzählungen,* edited by de Bruyn and Wolf (Berlin: Der Morgen, 1980);

Friedrich Wilhelm August Schmidt, *Einfalt und Natur: Gedichte,* edited by de Bruyn and Wolf (Berlin: Der Morgen, 1981);

Christoph Friedrich Nicolai, *Vertraute Briefe von Adelheid B. an ihre Freundin Julie S.,* edited by de Bruyn and Wolf (Berlin: Der Morgen, 1982);

Ludwig Tieck, *Die männliche Mutter,* edited by de Bruyn and Wolf (Berlin: Der Morgen, 1983);

Rahels erste Liebe: Der Briefwechsel zwischen Rahel Levin und Karl Graf von Finckenstein, edited by de Bruyn and Wolf (Berlin: Der Morgen, 1985);

"Fedezeen," in *Spiel ohne Ende: Erzählungen aus 100 Jahren S. Fischer Verlag,* edited by Hans Bender (Frankfurt am Main: Fischer, 1986).

PERIODICAL PUBLICATIONS: "Aussage unter Eid: Hörspiel," *Neue Deutsche Literatur,* 12, no. 4 (1964): 3-39;

"Viktoria," *Neue Deutsche Literatur,* 18, no. 2 (1970): 130-133;

"Wie ich zur Literatur kam," *Sinn und Form,* 24 (1972): 771-775;

"Geschlechtertausch," *Sinn und Form,* 25 (1973): 324-347; republished in *Blitz aus heiterm Himmel,* edited by Edith Anderson (Rostock: Hinstorff, 1975), pp. 1-45; translated by Stephen H. Wedgwood as "Exchange of Sexes," *Dimension,* 6 (1973): 42-73;

"Der Künstler und die Andern," *Sinn und Form,* 27 (1975): 171-178;

"Jean Paul und die neuere DDR-Literatur," *Jahrbuch der Jean-Paul-Gesellschaft München* (1975): 205-211;

"Babylon," *Sinn und Form,* 30 (1978): 765-770;

"Frauendienst," *Neue Rundschau,* 95, no. 4 (1984): 15-22;

"Dämmerungen: Jean Paul und die Politik," *Sinn und Form,* 38 (1986): 1147-1162.

Günter de Bruyn, author of novels, short stories, and essays, is one of the best-known and most respected writers in the German Democratic Republic (GDR). His style owes much to the nineteenth-century realists–Theodor Fontane in particular–and to the irony of the romantic novelist Jean Paul. Nevertheless, de Bruyn's works immerse the reader in the everyday reality of the contemporary GDR. His ironic perspective reveals fundamental conflicts between the socialist ideal and society as it is actually experienced by its less fortunate members. De Bruyn's sympathy is always on the side of the underprivileged. Those characters who have "made it"–whether functionaries, academics, or literati–are subjected to scrutiny which exposes the contradictions and hypocrisy of a rigid class society which subscribes–in theory–to egalitarian ideals. De Bruyn's fiction is, however, neither diatribe nor satire. It is the work of a fine humorist who creates scenes at which a reader can laugh out loud while remaining aware of the poignant, even melancholy context. In de Bruyn readers will find one of the most sensitive and reliable critical interpreters of East German society.

De Bruyn was born in Berlin in 1926 to Carl and Jenny Hilgert de Bruyn. He has lived in Berlin most of his life, although he now spends more time at a country home not far from Frankfurt an der Oder. Berlin and the landscape of the March of Brandenburg are as significant in de Bruyn's work as they are in Fontane's. De Bruyn was conscripted into the army after completing high school in 1943 and was briefly a prisoner of war. In 1946 he returned to Berlin, where he studied to be a schoolteacher. He taught in a village school in Garlitz until 1949. He was trained as a librarian from 1949 to 1953 and worked in libraries until 1961, when he turned to writing full time. His fiction is always closely connected with his experiences, although usually not as directly as in his first novel, *Der Hohlweg* (The Path through the Gorge, 1961), about a young soldier in World War II. Today de Bruyn regards the novel as a failure, feeling that he was too close to the experience to turn it successfully into fiction. Critics agree that it is no more than a creditable first effort.

Berlin provides the setting for the novel *Buridans Esel* (1968; translated as *Buridan's Ass,* 1973), which brought de Bruyn his first interna-

De Bruyn as a ten-year-old schoolboy (Günter de Bruyn, Im Querschnitt, *edited by Werner Liersch [Halle & Leipzig: Mitteldeutscher Verlag, 1979])*

De Bruyn as a librarian in 1955 (Günter de Bruyn, Im Querschnitt, *edited by Werner Liersch [Halle & Leipzig: Mitteldeutscher Verlag, 1979])*

tional success. The "ass" of the title is Karl Erp, a middle-aged head librarian; like the donkey of legend who was unable to decide between two equally tasty bundles of hay, Erp cannot choose between his wife and his young mistress. Erp belongs to the Establishment—he is a member of the ruling Socialist Unity party, a successful professional, the owner of a comfortable home on the Spree River, a husband, and the father of two children. His comfortable life is disrupted when he falls in love with a fellow librarian, the attractive, intelligent, and idealistic Ms. Broder. Eventually Erp moves into her run-down inner-city tenement with communal toilet in the corridor and faulty plumbing. The idealism and sacrifices of comfort which this love requires are too much for Erp; he deserts Ms. Broder and returns home, where he finds that his wife is no longer a mousy subordinate but has begun to emancipate herself. Erp also receives a promotion to a high government post. His career advancement in spite of his personal and ethical failings shows the victory of philistinism in a society that—like any other—rewards its conformists and opportunists.

The novel *Preisverleihung* (Award Ceremony, 1972) is set in another milieu with which de Bruyn is familiar: the world of writers and academic critics. Teo Overbeck, a university instructor of German literature, faces a dilemma: he has been asked to give the laudation for Paul Schuster, a former friend whose novel is to be awarded a prize; Overbeck, however, has discovered that the novel is hackwork, prizeworthy only because it says what officialdom wants to hear. How can the honest and conscientious Overbeck tell the truth without destroying both Schuster and his own career? Added complications are that Overbeck's wife, Irene, was Schuster's lover before her marriage to Overbeck, and that Overbeck's teenaged daughter is actually the product of this liaison. The action takes place on a single day and ends at a party where all the main characters are brought together and the family tensions are resolved. Overbeck, however, does not find a solution to the dilemma of conscience to which he was driven by a self-serving literary and academic establishment.

As is typical for de Bruyn, who regards as his métier the story more than the novel, *Preisverleihung* is short (159 pages). It is also openended: no final answers are provided, fundamental conflicts remain, characters are multifaceted, and human relations are seen in all their complex-

ity. De Bruyn has been called a moralist, yet he provides his readers with no easy or conventional moral guidance. His works convey the sense that because human beings and society—even socialist society—are flawed, idealism is not a realistic option.

It is for his flaws as well as his strengths that de Bruyn is drawn to Jean Paul, of whom he wrote a highly regarded biography published in 1975. De Bruyn calls it his favorite book because he did not feel obliged, as he does in a work of fiction, to disguise himself. He is an admirer of Jean Paul's prose and of his rebellious democratic politics.

The charming tale *Märkische Forschungen* (Researches on the March of Brandenburg, 1978) takes its flavor from eighteenth-century fiction. It is a story of politics and opportunism in the academic establishment. Ernst Pötsch, a country schoolteacher and compulsive amateur researcher, discovers facts about a nearly unknown turn-of-the-nineteenth-century author, Max von Schwedenow, which conflict with the thesis of a major work on Schwedenow about to be published by the influential Professor Menzel. Menzel befriends Pötsch in order to pick his brain; but when Pötsch cannot be deflected from his intention to publish, Menzel crushes him. In the end Pötsch has lost his reputation, his job, and his sanity. Along the way a world of venality, humiliating hierarchy, and rigid class distinctions is exposed. The effect, however, is not harsh but melancholy, ironic, and gently humorous.

In person, de Bruyn has a low-key but entertaining sense of humor. A modest man who guards his privacy, he is at the same time strong-minded and decisive in his views and is known for his integrity. The impression he gives is, above all, one of kindness and gentleness. He won the Heinrich Mann Prize of the Academy of Arts in 1964 and the Lion Feuchtwanger Prize, for which Christa Wolf gave the laudation, in 1981. He has held offices in writers' organizations and has been a member of the GDR's Academy of Arts since 1978. He has two children: Wolfgang, a writer and specialist in American literature, born in 1959; and Nele, born in 1963. He is divorced from their mother and lives with the writer Rosemarie Zeplin. Since 1975 de Bruyn has been allowed to travel to the West; he prefers to visit only the German-speaking countries. Although a social critic, he can by no means be categorized as a "dissident"; he tries to stay out of the public eye, and his political involvement is lim-

Page from the manuscript for de Bruyn's 1968 novel Buridans Esel, *about a middle-aged librarian who cannot choose between his wife and his mistress (Günter de Bruyn,* Im Querschnitt, *edited by Werner Liersch [Halle & Leipzig: Mitteldeutscher Verlag, 1979])* ited to the peace movement. When de Bruyn participated in the 1981 Berlin peace conference of East and West German writers, the critic Dennis Tate reported: "De Bruyn, drawing his inspiration from the Sermon on the Mount, spoke of 'Moral' [morality] as an 'Überlebensstrategie' [strategy for survival], which had been prevented by the 'Machtgebilde der Blöcke und Lager' [power blocs] from developing its true potential."

The reference to the Sermon on the Mount indicates a central theme of de Bruyn's, which appears more frequently in his most recent works: Catholicism. He was raised a Catholic in a Protestant environment and was profoundly influenced by the experience of being an outsider. The autobiographical story "Fedezeen" treats his childhood in the Nazi era with extraordinary artistry. It was selected by the S. Fischer publishing house of Frankfurt am Main to appear in *Spiel ohne Ende* (Game without End, 1986), an anthology celebrating the firm's one hundredth anniversary.

De Bruyn has said that Catholicism is also a prominent theme in the long autobiographical novel he is currently writing. It is to be a chronicle of his generation, beginning in the 1920s and covering several decades. A chapter titled "Frauendienst" (Service to Women), which appeared in the *Neue Rundschau* in 1984, follows the thoughts of a nineteen-year-old man who goes to confession prior to being married. In an epiphany it becomes clear to the young man that his image of the Virgin Mary has always determined which girls he will be attracted to and what his relationships with them will be.

De Bruyn's women characters are presented from a less critical perspective than the men. When asked by Karin Hirdina in 1983, "Warum ironisieren Sie in Ihren Büchern Männer stärker als Frauen?" (Why are men treated with greater irony than women in your books?) de Bruyn responded: "Vor zehn Jahren hätte ich darauf geantwortet, daß ich Frauen positiver beurteile, daß ich ihnen gegenüber eine Verehrungshaltung habe. Aber heute würde ich sagen, es liegt vielleicht daran, daß ich sie einfach nicht so gut kenne" (Ten years ago I would have answered that I judge women more positively, that I revere them. But today I would say that perhaps it is because I just do not know them as well).

In the novel *Neue Herrlichkeit* (New Glory), published in West Germany in 1984 and in the GDR in 1985, the most appealing characters are women: twenty-three-year-old Thilde, a cleaning

*De Bruyn in a village in the March of Brandenburg. This area around Berlin is the setting for much of de Bruyn's fiction (*Günter de Bruyn, Im Querschnitt, *edited by Werner Liersch [Halle & Leipzig: Mitteldeutscher Verlag, 1979]).*

lady; her senile grandmother Tita; and the alcoholic cook Olga. All three are outsiders, members of the most disadvantaged groups, nonparticipants in the ethic and the reality of achievement and success. Each works hard, has suffered greatly, and displays a kind of heroism. All of the characters in the book are physically, mentally, or emotionally handicapped; it is a cast such as one would expect to meet in a painting by Brueghel.

A snowstorm isolates the characters on a farm called Neue Herrlichkeit which serves as a rest home and retreat for the government ministry that employs the main character, twenty-nine-year-old Viktor Kösling. Viktor, privileged by his politician father's prominence and about to begin his own career as a diplomat, has been sent to Neue Herrlichkeit by his domineering mother, who hopes that ten weeks in the country will allow Viktor to write his dissertation. Instead,

Viktor–whose situation is reminiscent of Hans Castorp's in Thomas Mann's *Der Zauberberg* (1924; translated as *The Magic Mountain*, 1927)– falls in love with Thilde and plans to marry her. Thilde, however, is unacceptable to Viktor's parents: she is uneducated, unsophisticated, and, worst of all, her mother lives in West Germany– an insurmountable obstacle to Viktor's career. Viktor, in the tradition of de Bruyn's vacillating protagonists, is a Hamlet-like figure who in the end knuckles under, as he has all his life, to the wishes of others. *Neue Herrlichkeit* is the story of an obsessive love and of failure–failure of character, failure of society. It is a Bildungsroman in reverse–a *Magic Mountain* for the postmodern era–in which every value fails. Literature, philosophy, idealism, and language itself are undermined.

This novel highlights contradictions in the author and his work. Rather than writing such an incisive piece of social criticism, the quiet, gentle Günter de Bruyn can more easily be imagined composing his essays on great writers of the past or editing with Gerhard Wolf the annual series of *Märkischer Dichtergarten* (Writers' Garden of the March of Brandenburg) volumes, which rescue from neglect writers such as Friedrich de la Motte Fouqué, Friedrich Nicolai, and Rahel Varnhagen. But the afficionado of the eighteenth century is also the penetrating observer and recorder of his own time and place. There is a dialectic between his self-effacing modesty and his decisiveness, between his guarded privacy and his active commitment to peace, between socialism and Catholicism. The synthesis of all these facets is achieved in a perspective of profound irony.

Interview:
" . . . die Wahrheit sagen, im Kleinen wie im Großen," in *Auskünfte: Werkstattgespräche mit DDR-Autoren* (Berlin & Weimar: Aufbau, 1974), pp. 41-60.

Bibliographies:
Hans-Michael Bock, "Günter de Bruyn: Werkverzeichnis, Sekundärlituratur," in *Kritisches Lexikon zur deutschsprachigen Gegenwartsliteratur*, edited by Heinz Ludwig Arnold (Munich: Edition text + kritik, 1979), n. pag.;

Margy Gerber and Judith Pouget, "Günter de Bruyn," in *Literature of the German Democratic Republic in English Translation: A Bibliography*, volume 36 (Lanham, Md. & New York: University Press of America, 1984).

References:
Bernd Allenstein, "Günter de Bruyn," in *Kritisches Lexikon zur deutschsprachigen Gegenwartsliteratur*, edited by Heinz Ludwig Arnold (Munich: Edition text + kritik, 1979), n. pag.;

Christel Berger, "Kleinbürger, Spießer, Karrierist–Günter de Bruyns Helden," in her *Der Autor und sein Held* (Berlin: Dietz, 1983), pp. 161-174;

Ted E. Frank, "Günter de Bruyn's 'Preisverleihung': A GDR Novel with a Mission," *University of Dayton Review*, 13 (Winter 1978): 83-91;

Valerie D. Greenberg, "Günter de Bruyn's *Neue Herrlichkeit*: Leveling the *Zauberberg*," *German Quarterly*, 60 (Spring 1987): 205-219;

Karin Hirdina, *Günter de Bruyn: Leben und Werk* (Berlin: Volk und Wissen, 1983);

James Knowlton, "Literature and Its Uses: Günter de Bruyn's 'Preisverleihung' and 'Märkische Forschungen,'" in *Studies in GDR Culture and Society 2*, edited by Margy Gerber and Christine Cosentino (Washington, D.C.: University Press of America, 1982), pp. 177-187;

Werner Liersch, "Der Moralist und die Wirklichheit," in Günter de Bruyn, *Im Querschnitt: Prosa, Essays, Biographie*, edited by Liersch (Halle & Leipzig: Mitteldeutscher Verlag, 1979), pp. 401-420;

Siegfried Mews, "Buridans Esel," in his *Ulrich Plenzdorf* (Munich: Beck, 1984), pp. 90-98;

Gabrielle Elisabeth Schlichting, "Society and the Individual in the Prose of GDR Writer Günter de Bruyn and Its Reception in the German Democratic Republic and West Germany," Ph.D. dissertation, New York University, 1982;

Dennis Tate, "Beyond 'Kulturpolitik': The GDR's Established Authors and the Challenge of the 1980s," in *The GDR in the 1980s*, edited by Ian Wallace (Dundee, Scotland: GDR Monitor, 1984), pp. 15-29.

Tankred Dorst

(19 December 1925-   )

Gerd K. Schneider
Syracuse University

BOOKS: *Geheimnis der Marionette* (Munich: Rinn, 1957);

auf kleiner bühne: versuche mit marionetten (Munich: Juventa, 1959);

La buffonata, libretto by Dorst, music by Wilhelm Killmayer (Mainz & New York: Schott, 1961);

Große Schmährede an der Stadtmauer; Freiheit für Clemens; Die Kurve (Cologne: Kiepenheuer & Witsch, 1962); partially republished as *Two Plays: Große Schmährede an der Stadtmauer; Die Kurve*, edited by Marjorie L. Hoover (New York: Holt, Rinehart & Winston, 1973); translated by Henry Beissel as *Three Plays* (Toronto: Playwrights Co-op, 1976)– contains *Grand Tirade at the Town-Wall; The Curve; A Trumpet for Nap;*

Die Bühne ist der absolute Ort (Cologne: Kiepenheuer & Witsch, 1962);

Die Mohrin (Cologne & Berlin: Kiepenheuer & Witsch, 1964);

Yolimba, libretto by Dorst, music by Killmayer (Mainz & New York: Schott, 1965);

Die mehreren Zauberer: 7 Geschichten für Kinder (Cologne: Kiepenheuer & Witsch, 1966);

Toller: Szenen aus einer deutschen Revolution (Frankfurt am Main: Suhrkamp, 1968); edited by Margaret Jacobs (Manchester, U.K.: Manchester University Press, 1975); adapted for television by Dorst, Peter Zadek, Hartmut Gehrke, and Wilfried Minks as *Rotmord oder I was a German* (Munich: Deutscher Taschenbuch Verlag, 1969);

Sand: Ein Szenarium, by Dorst and Ursula Ehler (Cologne: Kiepenheuer & Witsch, 1971);

Eiszeit: Ein Stück, by Dorst and Ehler (Frankfurt am Main: Suhrkamp, 1973);

Auf dem Chimborazo: Eine Komödie, by Dorst and Ehler (Frankfurt am Main: Suhrkamp, 1975);

Dorothea Merz, by Dorst and Ehler (Frankfurt am Main: Suhrkamp, 1976);

Gesellschaft im Herbst (Frankfurt am Main: Suhrkamp, 1978);

Tankred Dorst (photograph by Regine Will, courtesy of Ullstein Bilderdienst)

Klaras Mutter, by Dorst and Ehler (Frankfurt am Main: Suhrkamp, 1978);

Stücke, edited by Gerhard Mensching, 2 volumes (Frankfurt am Main: Suhrkamp, 1978)– contains *Der Kater oder Wie man das Spiel spielt; Gesellschaft im Herbst; Die Kurve; Große Schmährede an der Stadtmauer; Rameaus Neffe; Die Mohrin; Der Richter von London; Toller; Sand; Kleiner Mann–was nun?; Eiszeit; Goncourt oder die Abschaffung des Todes*, by Dorst and Horst Laube;

43

Die Villa, by Dorst and Ehler (Frankfurt am Main: Suhrkamp, 1979);

Mosch, by Dorst and Ehler (Frankfurt am Main: Suhrkamp, 1980);

Merlin oder Das wüste Land, by Dorst and Ehler (Frankfurt am Main: Suhrkamp, 1981);

Eisenhans: Ein Szenarium, by Dorst and Ehler (Cologne: Prometh, 1983);

Der verbotene Garten: Fragmente über d'Annunzio, by Dorst and Ehler (Munich & Vienna: Hanser, 1983);

Die Reise nach Stettin, by Dorst and Ehler (Frankfurt am Main: Suhrkamp, 1984);

Heinrich oder Die Schmerzen der Phantasie (Frankfurt am Main: Suhrkamp, 1985); revised version, *Theater heute,* 8 (1985): 42-52;

Deutsche Stücke: Werkausgabe, by Dorst and Ehler (Frankfurt am Main: Suhrkamp, 1985)—contains *Dorothea Merz; Klaras Mutter; Heinrich oder Die Schmerzen der Phantasie; Die Villa; Mosch; Auf dem Chimborazo;*

Ich, Feuerbach, by Dorst and Ehler (Frankfurt am Main: Suhrkamp, 1986);

Der nackte Mann (Frankfurt am Main: Suhrkamp, 1986);

Goncourt oder die Abschaffung des Todes (Frankfurt am Main: Schauspiel Frankfurt, n.d.).

OTHER: *Das bunte Fenster: Ein Geschichtenbuch,* edited by Dorst (Munich: Juventa, 1959);

Denis Diderot, *Rameaus Neffe,* translated and adapted by Dorst (Cologne & Berlin: Kiepenheuer & Witsch, 1963);

Ludwig Tieck, *Der gestiefelte Kater oder Wie man das Spiel spielt,* adapted by Dorst (Cologne: Kiepenheuer & Witsch, 1963);

Die Münchner Räterepublik: Zeugnisse und Kommentar, edited by Dorst (Frankfurt am Main: Suhrkamp, 1966);

Sean O'Casey, *Der Preispokal,* translated by Dorst (Berlin: Henschelverlag, 1969);

Hans Fallada, *Kleiner Mann—was nun?,* adapted by Dorst (Frankfurt am Main: Suhrkamp, 1972);

Molière, *George Dandin,* translated and adapted by Dorst (Frankfurt am Main: Suhrkamp, 1977);

Molière, *Drei Stücke,* translated and adapted by Dorst (Frankfurt am Main: Suhrkamp, 1978)—contains *Der Geizige; Der eingebildet [sic] Kranke; George Dandin;*

Thomas Dekker, *Der Richter von London,* adapted by Dorst (Frankfurt am Main: Suhrkamp, 1978);

Dorst in the mid 1970s (photograph by Rosemarie Clausen)

Molière, *Der Bürger als Edelmann,* translated and adapted by Dorst and Ursula Ehler (Reinbek: Rowohlt, 1986).

PERIODICAL PUBLICATION: "Dorothea—eine Frau, die nichts lernt: Zum zweiten Teil der Merz-Erzählung," *Süddeutsche Zeitung,* 25 May 1976, p. 9.

Tankred Dorst is a West German author who presents various aspects of postwar German society in his novels and in his plays, many of which have been shown on German television. He has also adapted works by Denis Diderot, Thomas Dekker, Ludwig Tieck, and Hans Fallada for the modern stage and has translated works by Molière and Sean O'Casey. Manfred Durzak considers him one of the "interessantesten und vielseitigsten Autoren der dt. Gegenwartslit., der die traditionelle Rolle des Dramatikers innovativ erweitert hat, vor allem durch die Einbeziehung des Films bzw. des Fernsehens" (most interesting and most versatile authors of contemporary German literature, one who has extended the traditional role of the dramatist in an innovative manner, above all by working with the medium of film as well as television).

Dorst was born on 19 December 1925 in Oberlind, Thuringia, to Max Dorst, an engineer, and Elisabeth Lettermann Dorst. He was drafted in 1942, taken prisoner by the Americans in 1944, and released in 1947. After completing his Abitur (school-leaving examination) in 1950 he studied German literature, art history, and theater at the University of Munich until 1956. During his student years he became interested in puppet plays. In the 1960s and 1970s he worked for various publishing houses. Since 1970 he has frequently lectured in the United States and other countries, including Australia and New Zealand. He currently lives in Munich as a free-lance writer. He received the Prize of the National Theater of Mannheim in 1960, the Prize of the City of Munich and the Gerhart Hauptmann Prize of the City of Berlin in 1964, the Tukan Prize of Munich in 1969, and the Prize of the City of Florence and the Lisbon Theater Prize in 1970. He is a member of the P.E.N. Club, the Academy of Fine Arts of Munich, and the German Academy for Language and Poetry.

Dorst's early plays reflect his interest in marionettes. In these plays drama is treated as an absolute illusion and the characters as beings with no memory or consciousness. There is hardly anything that distinguishes the characters from each other at the beginning of each play; what they are at the end they have become during the performance, acquiring their individual characteristics in the course of acting out their roles. The figures on the stage are "puppets," and the actions in which they participate are not reflections of reality but parables, symbols, or allegories. Just as the puppets are formed by the events in which they participate, man develops by responding to external circumstances and by interacting with others.

Dorst's view of the theater changed after he began working on *Toller* (1968), a play about the Munich Soviet Republic of 1919. His aim after 1968 was to capture "true reality," which, as Dorst understands it, consists not only of objective facts but also of the effect of external events

Cover for Dorst's 1975 comedy, illustrated with a photograph of the hill climbed by Dorothea Merz and her family and friends

on individuals, whom Dorst considers a mixture of rational and irrational elements. Dorst's main interest is in showing the psychological makeup of individuals.

The impact of political, historical, and social forces on the value system of a bourgeois family is depicted in the plays *Auf dem Chimborazo* (On Mount Chimborazo, 1975), *Die Villa* (1979), *Mosch* (1980), and *Heinrich* (1985), and the novels *Dorothea Merz* (1976), *Klaras Mutter* (Klara's Mother, 1978), and *Die Reise nach Stettin* (The Trip to Stettin, 1984). All of these works are based on the author's family history and portray a middle-class family living in Germany from the 1920s to the 1970s. Asked why he chose to write about his own family, Dorst replied: "Stoffe werden ja nicht glattweg erfunden. Man findet

Cover for Dorst's 1976 novel about life in Germany in the 1920s and 1930s

sie. Man kann gar nicht schreiben ohne Erinnerung. Wenn man nur 'erfindet,' gerät man leicht ins Konstruieren. Ich möchte Realität festhalten, diese hier habe ich erfahren. Oft steckt in dem, was wirklich geschehen ist, mehr Darstellenswertes als in dem, was man erfinden könnte. Die eigene Phantasie ist da ärmer als die wirklichen Begegnungen der Geschichte. Aber ich will Geschichte nicht 'dokumentieren,' obwohl ich auch in diesen Familiengeschichten gleichsam 'historische' Dokumente benutze, wie ich sie in *Toller, Sand, Eiszeit* und *Goncourt* verwendet habe.–Es interessiert mich, Personen in verschiedenen Phasen ihres Lebens zu sehen, wiederzusehen, wiederzuerkennen, und dahinter das Phänomen Zeit: wie Zeit durch Menschen hindurch geht, sie trägt, sie verändert, sie fallen läßt. Und das ist auch ein Zusammenhang, der etwas über unsere

Geschichte sagt" (Material [for a literary work] is not invented. One discovers it. Without memory it is impossible to write. If one only "invents," one slips easily into hypothesizing. I would like to capture reality–this I have experienced. Often there is more that's worthy of being depicted in experience than in what one could invent. One's own imagination is poorer in this regard than the actual historical occurrences. However, I do not wish to "document" history, although I use "historical" documents in these family chronicles as I did in *Toller, Sand, Eiszeit* and *Goncourt.*–I am interested in observing people and recognizing them again in various stages of their lives, and beyond that, the phenomenon of time: how time moves through people, holds them, changes them, and lets go of them. And that is also a context that says something about our history).

The comedy *Auf dem Chimborazo* is chronologically the end of the family saga. In the early 1970s the strong-willed Dorothea Merz, a widow in her late sixties or early seventies, climbs a hill on the border with the German Democratic Republic (GDR); she is accompanied by her sons Heinrich and Tilman, her friend Klara Falk, and Tilman's girlfriend Irene. Their plan to light a fire as a message to Dorothea's friends in the GDR is never carried out because of a family fight. Frequent flashbacks show the fragile nature of the family, which is held together more by social convention and tradition than by true understanding and love.

In the novel *Dorothea Merz* the domineering mother of *Auf dem Chimborazo* is a young girl. In 1925 she marries Rudolf Merz, the owner of a small tool company in Grünitz. Rudolf dies two years later, leaving his wife and their sons, Tilman and Heinrich. The novel consists of eighty-five numbered sections mixing narration, dialogues, diary entries, photographs, and drawings to give a panoramic view of the social, political, and cultural life of Germany in the 1920s and 1930s. Dorst neither condemns nor praises his characters but lets them express their hopes, wishes, and illusions. He says in an interview printed on the cover of *Klaras Mutter* that he wanted to show "daß Menschen eine bestimmte Vorstellung davon haben, wie Leben sein muß, wie man leben soll, daß sie eine Utopie haben und daß diese Utopie sie in Schwierigkeiten mit der Realität, in der sie leben müssen, bringt" (that people have a definite idea of how life ought to be, how one should live, that they have a utopia and that this utopia brings them into conflict with the reality in which they have to live).

Implicit in the novel is Dorst's criticism of the middle class for not appreciating the danger of National Socialism. According to Alan Best, "As Dorst sees matters, both the middle-class and the fascists looked to the past as a justification of the present; by indicating the extent to which his characters have a propensity to debase their cultural tradition and by revealing their unwitting espousal of Kitsch as a way of life Dorst can mount a political attack on the failure of the middle-class to respond to the menace of National Socialism. Given its aesthetic bias, the surrender of the bourgeoisie to the *myths* of National Socialism was inevitable. The failure of the bourgeoisie to discard its traditions when they have outlived their relevance is indicated as a prime cause of the inner moral vacuum which National Socialism so successfully exploited in its drive for political power." As G. P. Butler points out, "Distasteful though [Dorothea] may find [the Nazis], she is unlikely to court the hostility of the political monsters which, by the time this part of her story ends, are just getting into their stride–after all [as Dorothea says], 'Politics is men's business.' "

Klara Falk, who played a peripheral role in *Dorothea Merz*, is the center of *Klaras Mutter*. The excellent relationship between the schoolteacher Klara and her mother suffers when the mother has a love affair with an unemployed Polish laborer. In the end the laborer disappears and the mother commits suicide. Here a vision nurtured by the constant reading of Marxist and nature-tract literature clashes with objective reality, and the question emerges, as it does in most of Dorst's works: what is reality and what is its relationship to truth? Marjorie L. Hoover commented on this novel: "The story thus purified to quintessential events and encounters still projects a subtext of a mother's and daughter's experience, and this quite without the storyteller's presence. For, true dramatist that Dorst is, he remains invisible behind the scenes. Is it thanks to his collaborator Ursula Ehler that this first narrative work of his is in the best sense a woman's story?"

Dorst acknowledged Ehler's help in an interview with Judith Kuckart and Jörg Aufenanger. When he was asked, "Es steht bei ihren Arbeiten dabei: Mitarbeit 'Ursula Ehler.' Ist Ursula Ehler eine . . . " (Your work lists "Ursula Ehler" as coauthor. Is she a . . .), Dorst interrupted and continued: ". . . ist eine ständig gegenseitige Anregung,

Dorst with his collaborator Ursula Ehler (photograph by Lore Bermbach)

und eine Korrektur. Beim Reden werden Personen deutlicher, und beim Reden kann man sich auch korrigieren. . . . Ursula bringt auch Gedanken und Erfindungen ein, die sich mit der Sache verbinden und sie bereichern" (. . . is a permanent mutual inspiration and a correction. Characters become clearer when one talks about them, and by talking one can also correct oneself. . . . Ursula also supplies ideas and inventions which merge with the material and enrich it).

Die Reise nach Stettin takes place in 1944. Heinrich, selected from among his classmates to take part in a training course for marines, violates orders by reading while on watch and is dismissed. But instead of returning to Grünitz he visits his uncle Plinke, Dorothea's brother, in Berlin. Plinke, who owns an orthopedic manufacturing firm, possesses a tremendous vitality which is not broken even when his firm is destroyed in an air raid. He is thinking ahead as he looks at the rubble and calls out to his employee, Miss Zekel: "Baun wir alles wieder auf, Zeck! . . . Baun wir in kürzester Zeit wieder auf. . . . Die Amerikaner haben auch Plattfüße, Zeck" (We will rebuild everything again, Zeck. . . . We will rebuild everything again in the shortest time possible. . . . Americans have flat feet, too, Zeck). But Plinke does not live to carry out his plans; he dies during another air raid. Miss Zekel, who is Jewish, disappears; she has probably been "evacuated," like a group of Jews Heinrich meets on his way home. Heinrich does not fully understand the meaning of his experiences, but he feels that he has changed—that he is now estranged from his countrymen, of whom he says: "Die Welt geht unter, und sie merken es nicht" (The world is disintegrating and they do not notice it). In the assessment of David Scrase, "The tale is told with impressive control and economy in language which conjures up the forties with neat irony, and the attitudes and confusions of a teen-ager in oppressive circumstances are well captured." The question whether Heinrich, or anyone, can live a normal life after these experiences is left unanswered here; it is addressed in the play *Die Villa*, set in the 1945-1948 period, in which Heinrich smuggles people from the East to the West and cigarettes from the West to the East, continually going back and forth, staying nowhere.

To Dorst these private tragedies reflect the tragedies found in society at large. There were many families like the ones described in Dorst's family saga; as Dorst said in an interview, "Die deutsche Geschichte gehört zu ihrer privaten dazu. Ich kann mir diese Personen und ihre Biographien nicht ohne die größere Geschichte der jeweiligen Zeit vorstellen" (German history and personal history are intertwined. I cannot imagine these persons and their biographies outside the larger history of the time).

References:

Peter von Becker, "Eine überraschend schöne Besteigung," *Süddeutsche Zeitung*, 18-19 December 1976, p. 37;

Peter Bekes, "Tankred Dorst," in *Kritisches Lexikon zur deutschsprachigen Gegenwartsliteratur*, edited by Heinz Ludwig Arnold (Munich: Edition text + kritik, 1983), pp. 1-15;

Alan Best, "The Perils of Culture: Tankred Dorst's *Dorothea Merz*," in *Festschrift für Lionel Thomas: A Collection of Essays Presented in His Memory*, edited by Derek Attwood (Hull, U.K.: University of Hull Department of German, 1980), pp. 135-155;

Günter Blöcker, "Der Geist des Familienalbums: Tankred Dorsts fragmentarischer Roman *Dorothea Merz*," *Frankfurter Allgemeine Zeitung*, 24 June 1976, p. 22;

Sieghild Bogumil, "Poesie und Gewalt: Heiner Müller, Jean Genet, Tankred Dorst," *Neue Rundschau*, 96, no. 1 (1985): 52-77;

G. P. Butler, "Sehr bürgerlich," *Times Literary Supplement*, 31 December 1976, p. 1638;

Manfred Durzak, Review of *Deutsche Stücke: Werkausgabe*, *Germanistik*, 27 (1986): 169;

Heinz B. Heller, "Tankred Dorst," in *Deutsche Literatur der Gegenwart in Einzeldarstellungen*, volume 2, edited by Dietrich Weber (Stuttgart: Kröner, 1977), pp. 77-97;

Günther Hennecke, "Parzival im Jahr nach Stalingrad," *Neue Zürcher Zeitung*, 21 June 1985, p. 34;

Georg Hensel, "Tage und Tagträume aus jener Zeit," *Theater heute*, 8 (1985): 34-36;

Walter Hinck, "Reden an die Mauern der Geschichte: Der Schriftsteller Tankred Dorst wird sechzig," *Frankfurter Allgemeine Zeitung*, 19 December 1985, p. 27;

Kurt Honolka, "Gaudi, Ironie und tiefere Bedeutung," *Stuttgarter Nachrichten*, 21 May 1975, p. 10;

Marjorie L. Hoover, "Tankred Dorst: *Klaras Mutter*," *World Literature Today*, 53, no. 4 (1979): 667-668;

Hellmuth Karasek, "Ab ins Tal: *Auf dem Chimborazo*—Berliner Schlossparkaufführung," *Der Spiegel*, 29, no. 5 (1975): 105-106;

Karasek, "Die zweite Eiszeit," *Die Zeit*, 13 April 1973, p. 24;

Hans Christian Kosler, "Zugfahrt in der dritten Klasse: Mit Tankred Dorst auf der *Reise nach Stettin*," *Frankfurter Allgemeine Zeitung*, 18 February 1985, p. 18;

Anton Krättli, "Winter in mieser Zeit: Zu Tankred Dorsts *Die Reise nach Stettin*," *Neue Zürcher Zeitung*, 20 November 1984, p. 20;

Michael Krüger, "Deutsche Auflösung. Nach dem Film das Buch: *Dorothea Merz*," *Süddeutsche Zeitung*, 11 July 1976, p. 88;

Judith Kuckart and Jörg Aufenanger, "Im Gespräch mit Tankred Dorst, anläßlich des Abschlusses der dramatischen Merz-Trilogie," *Theater heute*, 8 (1985): 37, 40-41;

Friederich Luft, "Fallada wird zum Revue-Autor," *Die Welt*, 25 September 1972, p. 15;

W. F. Muthmann, "Der scharlachrote Buchstabe: Wim Wenders' Film nach Nathaniel Hawthornes Roman *The Scarlet Letter*: Veränderungen am Drehbuch von Tankred Dorst," *Süddeutsche Zeitung*, 13 March 1973, p. 22;

Josef Quack, "Stummheit von Mutter und Tochter: Tankred Dorsts Filmerzählung *Klaras*

Mutter," *Frankfurter Allgemeine Zeitung,* 19 February 1979, p. 18;

Stephan Reinhardt, "Oberflächenrealismus: Tankred Dorsts Roman *Dorothea Merz,*" *Frankfurter Rundschau,* 24 January 1977, p. 12;

Kurt Rothmann, "Tankred Dorst," in his *Deutschsprachige Schriftsteller seit 1945 in Einzeldarstellungen* (Stuttgart: Reclam, 1985), pp. 106-110;

Gertrud Runge, "Molière derb," *Die Welt,* 30 December 1968, p. 11;

Wolf Scheller, "Mädchenjahre nach dem Poesiealbum: Multi-Media-Erfolge machen noch keinen Romancier," *Die Presse,* 22-23 January 1977, p. ix;

Scheller, "Von Träumen und Trümmern: Tankred Dorsts fragmentarischer Roman *Dorothea Merz,*" *Rhein-Neckar Zeitung,* 23 August 1977, p. 2;

Lothar Schmidt-Mühlisch, "Vom Menschen voller Fehl und Adel," *Die Welt,* 13 February 1981, p. 19;

Helmut Schödel, "Das Kino schlägt zurück," *Die Zeit,* 22 April 1983, p. 43;

Wolfgang Schreiber, "Mittelalterlicher Bilderbogen," *Neue Zürcher Zeitung,* 10 February 1982, p. 29;

David Scrase, "Tankred Dorst: *Die Reise nach Stettin,*" *World Literature Today,* 59, no. 4 (1985): 584;

C. Bernd Sucher, "Ich weiß nicht, ob das Stück pessimistisch ist," *Süddeutsche Zeitung,* 13-14 September 1980, p. 15;

Sucher, "Tankred Dorsts Heimat," *Süddeutsche Zeitung,* 20 June 1985, p. 37;

Susanne Ulrici, "Ich bin mit dem Stück identisch: Gespräch mit Tankred Dorst über *Die Villa,*" *Stuttgarter Nachrichten,* 19 September 1980, p. 33;

Hans Vetter, "Sehenswertes Ensemble: *Auf dem Chimborazo.* Fernsehspiel von Tankred Dorst," *Frankfurter Rundschau,* 24 May 1977, p. 11;

Jürgen P. Wallmann, "Drei Fremde im Dorf," *Der Tagesspiegel,* 31 December 1978, p. 51.

Ingeborg Drewitz

(10 January 1923-26 November 1986)

Lieselotte Kuntz
University of Georgia

BOOKS: *Und hatte keinen Menschen: Erzählungen* (Berlin: Eckart, 1955);

Der Anstoß: Roman (Bremen: Schünemann, 1958);

Das Karussell: Roman (Göttingen: Sachse & Pohl, 1962);

Im Zeichen der Wölfe: Erzählungen (Göttingen: Sachse & Pohl, 1963);

Die Versuchung [by Benno Meyer-Wehlack]; *Die Kette* [by Drewitz]: *Hörspiele*, edited by Detlef C. Kochan (Paderborn: Schöningh, 1964);

Berliner Salons: Gesellschaft und Literatur zwischen Aufklärung und Industriezeitalter (Berlin: Haude & Spener, 1965);

Leben und Werk von Adam Kuckhoff, deutscher Schriftsteller und Widerstandskämpfer, hingerichtet durch den Strang in Berlin-Plötzensee am 5. August 1943 (Berlin: Friedenauer Presse, 1968);

Eine fremde Braut: Erzählungen (Munich: Claudis, 1968);

Bettine von Arnim: Romantik, Revolution, Utopie (Düsseldorf & Cologne: Diederichs, 1969);

Oktoberlicht: Roman (Munich: Nymphenburger Verlagshandlung, 1969);

Wuppertal: Porträt einer Stadt (Wuppertal: Hammer, 1973);

Wer verteidigt Katrin Lambert?: Roman (Stuttgart: Gebühr, 1974);

Das Hochhaus: Roman (Stuttgart: Gebühr, 1975);

Der eine, der andere (Stuttgart: Gebühr, 1976);

Die Samtvorhänge: Erzählungen, Szenen, Berichte (Gütersloh: Gütersloher Verlagshaus Mohn, 1978);

Gestern war Heute: 100 Jahre Gegenwart (Düsseldorf: Claassen, 1978);

Mit Sätzen Mauern eindrücken: Briefwechsel mit einem Strafgefangenen, by Drewitz and Winand Buchacker (Düsseldorf: Claassen, 1979);

Zeitverdichtung: Essays, Kritiken, Portraits gesammelt aus zwei Jahrzehnten (Vienna, Munich & Zurich: Europa, 1980);

Kurz vor 1984: Literatur und Politik. Essays (Stuttgart: Radius, 1981);

Ingeborg Drewitz (Teutopress—Ullstein Bilderdienst)

Die zerstörte Kontinuität: Exilliteratur und Literatur des Widerstandes (Vienna, Munich & Zurich: Europa, 1981);

Vier Minuten vor Mitternacht (Bornheim: Lamuv, 1981);

Schrittweise Erkundung der Welt (Vienna, Munich & Zurich: Europa, 1982);

Eis auf der Elbe: Tagebuchroman (Düsseldorf: Claassen, 1982);

Unter meiner Zeitlupe (Vienna: Europa, 1984);

Hinterm Fenster die Stadt: Aus einem Familienalbum (Düsseldorf: Claassen, 1985);

Auch so ein Leben: Die fünfziger Jahre in Erzählungen (Göttingen: Herodot, 1985);

Eingeschlossen: Roman (Düsseldorf: Claassen, 1986).

OTHER: *Städte 1945: Berichte und Bekenntnisse*, edited by Drewitz (Düsseldorf & Cologne: Diederichs, 1970);

Die Literatur und ihre Medien: Positionsbestimmungen, edited by Drewitz (Düsseldorf & Cologne: Diederichs, 1972);

Vernünftiger schreiben, Reform der Rechtschreibung, edited by Drewitz (Frankfurt am Main: Fischer, 1974);

Schatten im Kalk: Lyrik und Prosa aus dem Knast, edited by Drewitz (Stuttgart: Radius, 1979);

Hoffnungsgeschichten: Erzählung, Gedicht, Essay, Predigt, Report, edited by Drewitz (Gütersloh: Gütersloher Verlagshaus Mohn, 1979);

Mut zur Meinung: Gegen die zensierte Freiheit. Eine Sammlung von Veröffentlichungen zum Thema Zensur und Selbstzensur, edited by Drewitz and Wolfhart Eilers (Frankfurt am Main: Fischer, 1980);

So wächst die Mauer zwischen Mensch und Mensch: Stimmen aus dem Knast und zum strafvollzug, edited by Drewitz and Johann P. Tammen (Bremerhaven: Wirtschaftsverlag NW, 1980);

Strauss ohne Kreide: Ein Kandidat mit historischer Bedeutung, edited by Drewitz (Reinbek: Rowohlt, 1980);

Land aus dem Meer: Zur Kultur Islands und der Färöer Inseln, edited by Drewitz, Heinz Barüske, and Siguröur Magüsson (Torshavn: Thomsen, 1980);

Ernst Otto, *Ich bin schon lange tot aber trotzdem lebe ich weiter: Gedichte aus dem Zuchthaus,* foreword by Drewitz (Munich: Neuber, 1981);

Wolfgang Erk, ed., *Der verbotene Friede: Reflexionen zur Bergpredigt aus zwei deutschen Staaten,* title essay by Drewitz (Stuttgart: Radius, 1982);

The German Women's Movement: The Social Role of Women in the 19th Century and the Emancipation Movement in Germany, edited by Drewitz, translated by Patricia Crampton (Bonn: Hohwacht, 1983).

Critical opinion in the Federal Republic of Germany regards Ingeborg Drewitz as a political author since she was deeply interested in social and political issues and their treatment in literature. The social relevance of literature is the guiding principle in many of her novels, stories, and plays. Her main concern is to open the reader's eyes to the human aspects of events and to show

him the many sides of an issue. She often treats topics that have received attention in the news media, particularly those concerning the politically persecuted, the socially disadvantaged, and people on the outer fringes of society. Another issue to which Drewitz returns regularly is Germany's Nazi past.

Drewitz uses West Berlin as the setting for her novels, observing the city and its people in times of crisis. Much of her work focuses on "das Kleinbürgertum" (the petty bourgeoisie) during crucial periods in German history: under National Socialism, in the postwar era, and during the period of reconstruction from 1949 to 1952. In addition to her seven novels, Drewitz wrote stories, plays, essays, film scripts, and radio and television plays.

Some of her novels have been coolly received by the critics. Since the conviction that certain categories, such as political literature, are "unliterary" is shared by many critics, the political aspects of Drewitz's writing receive the sharpest disapprobation. But Drewitz was a politically engaged, socially committed writer who exposed grievous shortcomings of life in an industrialized and urbanized society.

Drewitz was born in Berlin on 10 January 1923 to Eugen N. Drewitz, an architect, and Hildegard Vogel Drewitz, a pianist. She studied German literature, history, and philosophy at the University of Berlin. In 1945 she received her doctorate and married Bernhard Drewitz. They had three daughters, born in 1948, 1950, and 1955.

The theme of Drewitz's first novel, *Der Anstoß* (The Impetus, 1958), is the isolation of man in a big urban center. The novel is an unsentimental story about a printer who rescued a prostitute from the streets and now lives with her and their child. He works with diminishing enthusiasm because the welfare of the poor is of greater concern to him than his job. Eventually, he poisons the child and kills himself. A witness to the suicide seeks to find a motive for these acts, but Drewitz offers no solution. The novel is not a detective story; Drewitz's concerns are moral and psychological. She wishes to show how compassion and fellowship develop and lead to the acceptance of such Christian ideals as mercy, guilt, brotherhood, and forgiveness.

Her second novel, *Das Karussell* (The Carousel, 1962), is about the impact of National Socialism and its aftermath on the lives of ordinary German citizens. The Müntzers are a middle-class Berlin family whose fortunes are traced through the rise of National Socialism, World War II, the postwar division of the city, and the materialism of the "economic miracle" of the 1950s. The impression is one of individual destiny giving way to remorseless historical forces.

The nonfiction *Berliner Salons* (1965) is a study of the literary salons which dominated Berlin's social and intellectual life from 1775 to 1806 and during the period of reaction under Prince Metternich from the Vienna Congress of 1815 to the unsuccessful revolution of 1848. Whereas in the novels the male figures were dominant, in *Berliner Salons* and the biography *Bettine von Arnim: Romantik, Revolution, Utopie* (Bettina von Arnim: Romanticism, Revolution, Utopia, 1969) the emphasis shifts to the role of women in society. Although the romantic insistence on the "holy right of subjectivity and individualism" led to an increasing emancipation of women in salons, the subordination of women was still sanctified by custom, religion, and law. These two books show that women in the nineteenth century confronted the same challenges that women face today: emancipation and acceptance as equal partners with men.

In the novel *Oktoberlicht* (October Light, 1969) Drewitz depicts a fifty-year-old journalist who has been released from a Berlin hospital after an operation for cancer; she is not cured, but she is determined to survive. The action takes place on a single day, with the present narrated in the first person and the journalist's memories, which include her activities in the resistance movement against National Socialism, in the third person. Although many of her dreams for the postwar period have not come true, she has gained new vitality and independence from her experiences. Her former husband, on the other hand, and the woman he married after his divorce from the journalist can only sustain themselves with the assistance of alcohol.

The novel *Wer verteidigt Katrin Lambert?* (Who Will Defend Katrin Lambert?, 1974) commences with a report that a woman named Katrin Lambert was found dead in an icy lake in West Berlin. Was it an accident or suicide? A journalist reading the report remembers a girl by the same name who attended school with her. After establishing that the dead woman is her former classmate, she begins an investigation. Through letters and visits with those who had close contact with Katrin Lambert, the journalist reconstructs her past. Katrin lived in West Berlin with her two illegitimate children. It seems that by helping oth-

ers she sought self-realization both in her career as a social worker and in her private life. But in a society in which charity is not considered a virtue, Katrin's concern for others made her vulnerable. Was she finally broken by the demands made upon her by those who needed her help? Another possible motive, which Drewitz leaves vague, is a suggested incestuous relationship between Katrin and her son. The reason for Katrin's suicide–if it was suicide–is never determined. Drewitz said that she began the novel in an attempt to "write myself away from suicide."

The novel *Das Hochhaus* (The High Rise, 1975) is a study of the effect living in a high-rise apartment building has on social relations. The collection *Der eine, der andere* (The One, the Other, 1976) brings together fifteen stories previously published or presented as radio plays.

Drewitz's best-known book, the autobiographical novel *Gestern war Heute* (Yesterday Was Today, 1978), continues the confrontation with National Socialism and the problem of guilt which she began in *Das Karussell*. It depicts four generations of a family whose lives are dramatically affected by political events in Berlin from 1923 to 1979. The focus of the novel is Drewitz's tortuous path of self-discovery as portrayed in that of the character Gabriele, who admits "daß ihr das 'Ich' abhanden gekommen ist" (that she has lost her self) because she cannot defend herself without arrogance and guilt. Critical reaction to *Gestern war Heute* has been mixed; abrupt changes of time and place, a profusion of references, and the inclusion of excerpts from a workbook make the novel difficult to read.

Drewitz's essays on literature and politics are collected in *Mit Sätzen Mauern eindrücken: Briefwechsel mit einem Strafgefangenen* (To Push in Walls with Sentences: Correspondence with a Prisoner, 1979), *Zeitverdichtung* (Time Condensed, 1980), *Kurz vor 1984* (Shortly before 1984, 1981), and *Die zerstörte Kontinuität: Exilliteratur und Literatur des Widerstandes* (The Destroyed Continuity: Exile Literature and Literature of the Resistance, 1981).

The novel *Eis auf der Elbe* (Ice on the Elbe, 1982) uses a diary format to chronicle the experiences of a fifty-five-year-old widowed attorney and her family. The novel is similar to *Gestern war Heute* in its autobiographical motifs and its depiction of a search for identity. As is typical of Drewitz, the setting is Berlin and the characters belong to the middle class. The diary covers five weeks in 1981.

A certain repetitiveness characterizes Drewitz's work: the themes of loneliness and alienation caused by social factors, coming to terms with a questionable past, life in the divided city, and survival under adverse circumstances reappear again and again. But this repetitiveness does not diminish Drewitz's significance as a spokeswoman for the defenseless and the needy. In this capacity she does not fit into the established pigeonholes of literary evaluation.

Drewitz was a cofounder of the Verband deutscher Schriftsteller (League of German Writers) and served as its deputy chairperson from 1970 to 1980. She became a member of the West German P.E.N. Club in 1964 and served many terms as its vice-president. She also founded the Neue Gesellschaft für Literatur (New Society for Literature) and served on its presidium until 1980. In 1977 she convened the Erster Kongreß Europäischer Schriftstellerorganisationen (First Congress of European Writers' Organizations) in Berlin. In 1977-1978 she was director of the Berlin Evangelical Academy. She received the Carl Zuckmayer Prize in 1952, the Jochen Kepper Plaque for her play *Alle Tore bewacht* (All Gates Guarded) in 1955, the Ernst Reuter Award for the radio play "Das Labyrinth" in 1963, the George Mackensen Prize for the best short story of 1970, and the Federal Cross of Merit, First Class, in 1973. Her social commitment and activism were honored with the Ida Dehmel Prize and the Carl von Ossietzky Medal of the International League for Human Rights, both in 1980. She died in Berlin on 26 November 1986.

References:

Titus Häussermann, ed., *Ingeborg Drewitz: Materialien zu Werk und Wirken* (Stuttgart: Radius, 1983);

Bärbel Jäschke, "Ingeborg Drewitz," in *Neue Literatur der Frauen: Deutschsprachige Autorinnen der Gegenwart*, edited by Heinz Puknus (Munich: Beck, 1980), pp. 69-74;

Angelika Mechtel, "Frau und Geschichte," in *Fischer Almanach der Literaturkritik 1978/79*, edited by Andreas Werner (Frankfurt am Main: Fischer, 1980);

Gisela Ullrich, "Ingeborg Drewitz," in *Kritisches Lexikon zur deutschsprachigen Gegenwartsliteratur* (Munich: Edition text + kritik, 1985), pp. 1-8.

Michael Ende
(12 November 1929-)

Donald P. Haase
Wayne State University

BOOKS: *Jim Knopf und Lukas der Lokomotivführer* (Stuttgart: Thienemann, 1960); translated by Renate Symonds as *Jim Button and Luke the Engine-Driver* (London: Harrap, 1963);

Jim Knopf und die Wilde 13 (Stuttgart: Thienemann, 1962);

Der Spielverderber: Eine komische Tragödie in 5 Akten (Frankfurt am Main: Fischer, 1967);

Das Schnurpsenbuch (Stuttgart: Thienemann, 1969; revised, 1979);

Tranquilla Trampeltreu: Die beharrliche Schildkröte. Eine Fabel (Stuttgart: Thienemann, 1972);

Momo oder Die seltsame Geschichte von den Zeit-Dieben und von dem Kind, das den Menschen die gestohlene Zeit zurückbrachte: Ein Märchen-Roman (Stuttgart: Thienemann, 1973); translated by Frances Lobb as *The Grey Gentlemen* (London & Toronto: Burke, 1974); translated by J. Maxwell Brownjohn as *Momo* (Garden City, N.Y.: Doubleday, 1985);

Das kleine Lumpenkasperle (Stuttgart: Urachhaus, 1975);

Lirum larum Willi warum: Eine lustige Unsinngeschichte für kleine Warumfrager (Stuttgart: Urachhaus, 1978);

Das Traumfresserchen (Stuttgart: Thienemann, 1978); translated by Gwen Marsh as *The Dream-Eater* (London: Dent, 1978);

Die unendliche Geschichte: Von A bis Z (Stuttgart: Thienemann, 1979); translated by Ralph Manheim as *The Neverending Story* (Garden City, N.Y.: Doubleday, 1983; London: Lane, 1983);

Der Lindwurm und der Schmetterling, oder Der seltsame Tausch (Stuttgart: Thienemann, 1981);

Das Gauklermärchen: Ein Spiel in sieben Bildern sowie einem Vor- und Nachspiel (Stuttgart: Edition Weitbrecht, 1982);

Die Schattennähmaschine (Stuttgart: Thienemann, 1982);

Phantasie, Kultur, Politik: Protokoll eines Gesprächs, by Ende, Erhard Eppler, and Hanne Tächl (Stuttgart: Edition Weitbrecht, 1982);

Filemon Faltenreich (Stuttgart: Thienemann, 1984);

Michael Ende (dpa–Ullstein Bilderdienst)

Der Goggolori: Eine bairische Mär. Stück in acht Bildern und einem Epilog (Stuttgart: Thienemann, 1984);

Der Spiegel im Spiegel: Ein Labyrinth (Stuttgart: Edition Weitbrecht, 1984);

Norbert Nackendick oder Das nackte Nashorn (Stuttgart: Thienemann, 1984);

Die Archäologie der Dunkelheit: Gespräche über Kunst und das Werk des Malers Edgar Ende, by Ende and Jörg Krichbaum (Stuttgart: Edition Weitbrecht, 1985);

Trödelmarkt der Träume: Mitternachtslieder und leise Balladen (Stuttgart: Edition Weitbrecht, 1986).

OTHER: *Bei uns zu Haus und anderswo*, edited by Ende and Irmela Brender (Stuttgart: Thienemann, 1976);

"Meine Vorstellung," in *Michael Ende zum 50. Geburtstag*, edited by Hansjörg Weitbrecht (Stuttgart: Thienemann, 1979), pp. 65-69;

Mein Lesebuch, edited by Ende (Frankfurt am Main: Fischer, 1983).

PERIODICAL PUBLICATION: "Literatur für Kinder?," *Neue Sammlung*, 21, no. 4 (1981): 310-316.

Michael Ende has achieved international acclaim as an author of fantasy literature. His success came in 1960 with his first novel, *Jim Knopf und Lukas der Lokomotivführer* (translated as *Jim Button and Luke the Engine-Driver*, 1963), and reached its climax with the publication in 1979 of *Die unendliche Geschichte* (translated as *The Neverending Story*, 1983). Although he is considered an author of children's books, Ende insists that his works are intended for readers of all ages; and his major fantasy novels have had a broad reception which has been compared to that of J.R.R. Tolkien's *Lord of the Rings* trilogy (1954-1956). As a writer of utopian fantasy who idealizes the child in all human beings, Ende carries on the tradition of German romanticism. Like the romantics he explores the conflict between utilitarian reason and playful fantasy, celebrates the power of the imagination, and considers art a game that expresses the human being's true freedom. His popular success and his recourse to romantic themes in a technological age make him a cultural and literary phenomenon of considerable interest and critical debate. The question whether his books offer valid solutions to the problems of the twentieth century or merely provide an escapist, juvenile romanticism has led Amity Shlaes to give Ende the ambiguous title "Germany's Pied Piper of Romantic Fantasy."

Born in Garmisch-Partenkirchen in 1929, Ende was the son of Luise Bartholomä Ende and the surrealist painter Edgar Ende. In 1931 the family moved to Munich, settling in 1935 in the artists' quarter of Schwabing, where Ende grew up surrounded by painters, sculptors, and literary figures. He was educated at the Maximilians-Gymnasium. While the creative atmosphere of Schwabing may have fed Ende's literary proclivities, and while his father's surrealism surely influenced the fantastic nature of his fiction, Ende's path to success was not a direct one. In fact, his

search for his artistic identity would barely survive a personal and creative crisis in the early 1950s, when he would nearly give up on writing.

In 1943 the Munich schools were evacuated due to Allied bombing, and Ende was sent back to his birthplace. He started writing at this time and aspired to be a dramatist, although his youthful compositions were mostly poems and stories. After World War II, unable to afford a university education, he accepted a scholarship to study acting at the Otto-Falckenberg-Schauspielschule in Munich. After studies there and at the Waldorf-Schule in Stuttgart, and a brief stint in regional theater, Ende returned to Munich in 1948 with a manuscript for a comedy. His first dramatic work, however, was never published. For the next several years he struggled as a free-lance writer. Through the actress Ingeborg Hoffmann, whom he married in 1964, he had the opportunity to write for cabarets in the early 1950s; he also did some directing for the Munich Volkstheater and wrote film reviews for Bavarian Broadcasting.

During this time Ende experienced the creative crisis that made the crucial difference in his life and literary fortune. For four years he grappled with the theoretical writings of Bertolt Brecht, who prescribed a non-Aristotelian, didactic form of theater based on the breaking of illusion (the alienation effect). Ende, who had been influenced by the surrealists and the anthroposophical ideas of Rudolf Steiner, was not suited for the pragmatic didacticism or alienation of Brechtian dramaturgy, and his study of Brecht's theory left him at a creative impasse. But at the nadir of his career Ende—almost by chance—discovered his true talent. At the urging of an acquaintance who sought a novel to illustrate, he began to write much as a surrealist might, abandoning himself to the "Lust am Fabulieren, ohne Plan, ohne Absicht" (joy of fantasizing, without plan, without intention). More than a year later, in 1958, he finished the story of Jim Knopf. Although almost two more years passed before the manuscript found a publisher, it soon became clear that Ende's role was not as a dramatist but as an author of fantasy literature. Like the hero of his new book, Ende had found himself.

The narrative was so lengthy that it was published as two novels: *Jim Knopf und Lukas der Lokomotivführer* and *Jim Knopf und die Wilde 13* (Jim Button and the Wild 13, 1962). The books recount the adventures of Jim Knopf, a black foundling who leaves the island kingdom of Lummerland (Morrowland in the English translation) on a marvelous journey with Lukas and his personified locomotive Emma. The foundling's search for his identity leads him through fabulous realms and ends with the revelation that he is Prince Myrrhen, the last descendant of Kaspar, one of the Three Kings. This mythic quest for identity reflects Ende's own return to his childhood: "Als ich zu schreiben anfing, wußte ich nicht, wie der zweite Satz aussehen würde. Ich habe es einfach versucht und das geschrieben, was ich in meiner Kindheit geträumt habe, als ich mit der ersten Eisenbahn spielte" (When I began to write, I didn't know how the second sentence would turn out. I simply gave it a try and wrote what I dreamed in my childhood when I played with my first train). The idea of dream transcription recalls the aesthetics of surrealism, which had been part of Ende's youthful experience as the son of Edgar Ende. In writing the novel "ohne Absicht und ohne zu wissen, wie es weitergehen sollte" (without purpose and without knowing how it should proceed), he discovered his view of art as nonfunctional creative activity—that is, as play.

The equation of creativity and play stands at the center of the Jim Knopf adventures, which merge the world of children and play with the realm of adults and work. The novels propose a reconciliation of these apparent opposites through the exercise of the creative faculties: adult and child coexist harmoniously, and work becomes self-fulfilling play. This concept is illustrated by the cooperative engineering of young Jim and his mentor, Lukas. Even after Jim has married and has become the ruler of a kingdom, his greatest joy remains driving his own locomotive, Molly, throughout his realm. This advocacy of play may seem to encourage a regression away from social maturity and responsibility, and some critics labeled Ende an escapist. But this sense of play, which allows both child and adult to free their repressed creativity, explains in part the immediate success of the Jim Knopf books. The first volume won the German Youth Book Prize in 1961 and an honorable mention in the competition for the Hans Christian Andersen Prize in 1962. Both volumes have been widely translated, and the Jim Knopf material has been adapted for television, radio, puppet theater, and parlor games. With these books Ende found not only his literary calling but also financial independence.

Ende tried again to pursue his earlier dramatic inclinations, but his play *Der Spielverderber* (The Spoilsport, 1967) was roundly panned when it was produced in Frankfurt in 1967. After publishing a collection of children's poems in 1969 Ende moved in 1970 to a villa south of Rome. In this idyllic setting, far from his German critics, he returned to the genre that had brought him success and in 1973 completed the fairy-tale novel *Momo oder Die seltsame Geschichte von den Zeit-Dieben und von dem Kind, das den Menschen die gestohlene Zeit zurückbrachte* (Momo; or, The Strange Story of the Time Thieves and of the Child Who Brought Back to the People the Stolen Time; translated as *The Grey Gentlemen*, 1974). Illustrated by Ende himself, *Momo* duplicated the success of the Jim Knopf books and won the German Youth Book Prize in 1974. But despite the illustrated format and the fairy-tale label, *Momo* was clearly not for children only.

The title figure is once again a heroic waif, this time a little girl on a social mission. Momo's task is to save the world from the grey gentlemen, the nefarious thieves of time. The modern world is juxtaposed to an idyllic past when drama (aesthetic play) provided an alternative reality. The decline of this superior civilization led to the modern world, "eine Wüste der Ordnung" (a wasteland of order). In this industrialized, rationalistic, and utilitarian world, parents have no time for their children, play is discouraged, toys are mechanical and leave no room for fantasy, individuality is crushed, and poetry is compromised by being put to commercial use. Behind the crisis are the grey gentlemen, who have plotted to rob the people of their time and, consequently, of their lives. Only the child Momo can see deeply enough into her own heart to grasp the essence of time, foil the villains, and restore the world to its original harmony.

Ende's moral vision in *Momo* not only castigates an industrial-technological society ruled by scientific reason and profit; it also emphasizes the redemptive role he ascribes to imaginative play. Ende has said that "people need a balance against the technical world. Fiction should provide that. Without fantasy the world is just ash." Such views reach back to the eighteenth century and echo the theories of Friedrich Schiller, who viewed aesthetic play as the source of human freedom. Still, the skeptics contend that the social evils symbolized in *Momo* require more concrete action than the fantasy of art and the aesthetic life of the mind.

For these critics the enormous popular success of *Die unendliche Geschichte* only confirms that Ende is merely writing escapist fantasy with mass appeal. *Die unendliche Geschichte* has sold well over 1.5 million copies, has been translated into twenty-three languages, has appeared in pirated editions, and has been adapted as a motion picture (a project from which Ende ultimately withdrew his support because he felt the film trivialized the novel). It won the Buxtehuder Bulle and Wilhelm Hauff prizes in Germany, the Premio Europeo "Provincia di Trento" in Italy, and the International Janusz Korczak Prize in Poland. It was also adopted as a symbol by the West German antinuclear movement.

Ten-year-old Bastian Balthasar Bux is an outsider, a dreamer, a fat little misfit who is teased and taunted by his peers. To escape from his everyday reality Bastian steals a book entitled *Die unendliche Geschichte*, which recounts the plight of Phantásien (Fantastica in the English translation), a realm endangered by a spreading void. As he reads, Bastian realizes that he is the hero who must enter into the fiction in order to save Phantásien.

Using two shades of colored ink, the novel shifts back and forth between the two levels of reality—Bastian's world (red ink) and Phantásien (green ink)—until Bastian accepts the challenge and becomes part of the fictional reality his reading has created. Ende is depicting the act of reading itself and the reader's imaginative role in the creation of the story, thus encouraging the identification of the novel's actual reader with Bastian and forcing the reader to indulge the imagination in aesthetic play, where reality exists only in the interaction of text and mind. Like Bastian, the reader will ultimately return to everyday reality, but he will return with greater respect for the creative powers of fantasy and a defense against the threat of expanding nothingness—the twentieth-century malaise of one-dimensional rationality.

Die unendliche Geschichte is a veritable manifesto of the romantic imagination: its subject is the novel itself; its hero is the reader; its theme is the never ending act of imaginative creation that endows life with meaning. These ideas are based on the esoteric theories of the German romantic writers Novalis and Friedrich Schlegel, a debt Ende proudly acknowledges. The remarkable thing is that Ende has taken the self-reflexive poetics of the German romantics, which is highly abstract and of interest mainly to the scholarly elite, and given it mass appeal.

Whether fantasy adventure or aesthetic reflections, Ende's books remain open to the criticism that they have little to do with correcting social evils and encourage solipsism instead of social action. This charge and the dilemma faced by the writer in modern society have been addressed by Ende in his play, *Das Gauklermärchen* (Circus Clowns' Fairy Tale, 1982), which pits a struggling group of circus players against ruthless industrial powers who would exploit the group for commercial propaganda. Although Ende's players are heroic because they refuse to support the crass concerns of the capitalists, they are helpless to stop the destruction the industrialists beget. With no apologies Ende defines the artist as a humanist, not an activist.

Der Spiegel im Spiegel (The Mirror in the Mirror, 1984) is a collection of surrealistic short stories that emphasizes the dialectical exchange that occurs between text and reader, which act as mirrors reflecting each other. The stories are written in an intentionally ambiguous manner so that they allow no rational interpretation and, as Ende has said, "so daß der Leser verlockt wird, sich miteinzubringen, sozusagen schöpferisch mitzuarbeiten an der Geschichte, während sie entsteht" (so that the reader is tempted to involve himself, so to speak, to collaborate creatively on the story as it is produced). *Der Spiegel im Spiegel* may be Ende's attempt to answer those who view his work only as juvenile fiction. But this highly opaque collection of stories, which is illustrated with his father's art, has not had nearly the success of his earlier books and suggests that Ende has reached the limits of his appeal. It is possible that his readers actually do want escapist fantasy and are not interested in aesthetic reflection.

It is no wonder that Ende's literary crisis was exacerbated by his reading of Brecht's theories of dramatic alienation. Far from discouraging the spectator's involvement in the work, Ende realized that fiction, and especially drama, were based precisely on the spectator's "belief" in the dramatic illusion: "Was soll Desillusion, wo die Illusion das Entscheidene ist?" (Why disillusionment when illusion is the crucial factor?). Recognizing the aesthetic value of illusion and play, Ende turned inward and reached back to the poetics of romanticism. In his view, celebrating the imagination is not turning one's back on society but nurturing the creative faculty that can humanize a dehumanized world.

Interviews:

"Interview mit Michael Ende: 'Es gibt ja sowas wie anthroposophische Klischees, nicht?,'" *Zeitschrift Info,* 3, special number (1983): 7-9;

Zeit-Zauber: Unser Jahrhundert denkt über das Geheimnis der Uhren nach. Franz Kreuzer im Gespräch mit Michael Ende und Bernulf Kanitschneider (Vienna: Deuticke, 1984), pp. 7-23.

References:

Hermann Bausinger, "*Momo:* Ein Versuch über politliterarische Placeboeffekte," in *Literatur in der Demokratie: Für Walter Jens zum 60. Geburtstag,* edited by Wilfried Barner and others (Munich: Kindler, 1983), pp. 137-145;

Alexander von Bormann, "Kulturbücher für Aussteiger? Michael Endes Märchenromane," *Merkur,* 37 (1983): 705-710;

Margarete Dierks, "Michael Ende," *Lexikon der Kinder- und Jugendliteratur,* edited by Klaus Doderer (Weinheim & Basel: Beltz/Pullach: Verlag Dokumentation, 1975), I: 347-349;

Volker Hage, "Der märchenhafte Erfolg," in his *Die Wiederkehr des Erzählers: Neue deutsche Literatur der siebziger Jahre* (Frankfurt am Main, Berlin & Vienna: Ullstein, 1982), pp. 195-200;

Wilfried Kuckartz, *Michael Ende: "Die unendliche Geschichte": Ein Bildungsmärchen* (Essen: Die blaue Eule, 1984);

Pamela Marsh, "Praiseworthy Morals, Unwieldy Fantasy," *Christian Science Monitor,* 9 November 1983, p. 26;

Heidi Mildner, "Graue Rauchmänner und endlose Geschichten," *Literatur konkret,* 7 (1982-1983): 52-55;

Andreas von Prondczynsky, *Die unendliche Sehnsucht nach sich selbst: Auf den Spuren eines neuen Mythos. Versuch über eine "Unendliche Geschichte"* (Frankfurt am Main: Dipa, 1983);

David Quammen, "Fantasy, Epic and Farce," *New York Times Book Review,* 6 November 1983, pp. 14, 39-41;

Amity Shlaes, "Germany's Pied Piper of Romantic Fantasy," *Wall Street Journal,* 28 February 1985, p. 26;

Alexander Stille, "A Movable Feast of Fiction: 'The Neverending Story,'" *Newsweek,* 102 (14 November 1983): 112, 114;

Somtow Sucharitkul, "Falling into Fantasiana," *Washington Post Book World,* 16 October 1983, p. 11;

Reinbert Tabbert, "*Jim Knopf* und die komisch-phantastische Kinderliteratur," *Phantastische Kinder- und Jugendliteratur und Märchen: Tagungsbericht der internationalen Jugendbuchtagung in Gwatt 1982* (Bern: Schweizerischer Bund für Jugendliteratur/Munich: Arbeitskreis für Jugendliteratur, 1982), pp. 55-70;

Hansjörg Weitbrecht, *Michael Ende zum 50. Geburtstag* (Stuttgart: Thienemann, 1979);

Christian von Wernsdorff, *Bilder gegen das Nichts: Zur Wiederkehr der Romantik bei Michael Ende und Peter Handke* (Neuss: Schampel & Kleine, 1983).

Ludwig Fels

(27 November 1946-   )

Bettina Kluth Cothran
Georgia State University

BOOKS: *Anläufe* (Neuwied, Darmstadt & Berlin: Luchterhand, 1973);

Platzangst: Geschichten (Darmstadt & Neuwied: Luchterhand, 1974);

Ernüchterung: Gedichte (Erlangen & Berlin: Renner, 1975);

Die Sünden der Armut: Roman (Darmstadt & Neuwied: Luchterhand, 1975);

Alles geht weiter: Gedichte (Darmstadt & Neuwied: Luchterhand, 1977);

Ich war nicht in Amerika (Erlangen: Renner, 1978);

Mein Land: Geschichten (Darmstadt & Neuwied: Luchterhand, 1978);

Ich bau aus der Schreibmaschine eine Axt: Gedichte und Geschichten, selected by Annie Voigtländer (Berlin & Weimar: Aufbau, 1980);

Vom Gesang der Bäuche: Ausgewählte Gedichte 1973-1980 (Darmstadt & Neuwied: Luchterhand, 1980);

Ein Unding der Liebe: Roman (Darmstadt & Neuwied: Luchterhand, 1981);

Kanakenfauna: Fünfzehn Berichte (Darmstadt & Neuwied: Luchterhand, 1982);

Betonmärchen (Darmstadt & Neuwied: Luchterhand, 1983);

Lämmermann (Frankfurt am Main: Verlag der Autoren, 1983);

Der Anfang der Vergangenheit: Gedichte (Munich & Zurich: Piper, 1984);

Der Affenmörder (Frankfurt am Main: Verlag der Autoren, 1985);

Die Eroberung der Liebe: Heimatbilder (Munich & Zurich: Piper, 1985);

Rosen für Afrika (Munich: Piper, 1987).

PERIODICAL PUBLICATIONS: "Von einem, der sich auszog, das Fürchten zu lernen," *Akzente*, 27, no. 4 (1980): 317;

"Platitudes and Other Poems," translated by Sammy McLean, *Dimension*, 14 (1981): 168-171.

In his poems, short stories, novels, and dramas Ludwig Fels calls attention to an apathetic soci-

Ludwig Fels (photograph by Felicitas Timpe, courtesy of Ullstein Bilderdienst)

ety which ignores those who are at its periphery. In living pictures he expresses provocatively and precisely what he fears, what worries him, and what enrages him. One is touched, even haunted, by the immediacy and urgency of Fels's message, which has reached an increasingly broad audience through books, radio plays, stage productions, and a television adaptation of one of his novels. Fels entered the literary scene in 1973 with a collection of poems, *Anläufe* (Attempts), and a radio play, "Kaputt oder ein Hörstück aus Scherben" (Smashed; or, A Radio Play Made from Broken Pieces). His first novel, *Die Sünden der Armut* (The Sins of Poverty), appeared in

1975. He soon attracted the attention of critics and was awarded several literature prizes: together with Max von der Grün he received the Advancement Prize of the City of Nuremberg in 1974; in 1979 he shared the Leonce and Lena Prize of the City of Darmstadt with Rolf Haufs and Rainer Malkowski; in the same year, his radio plays were recognized by the prize of the *Kulturmagazin des Südwestfunks*; the Literature Prize of the City of Nuremberg followed in 1981 and the Hans Fallada Prize of the City of Neumünster in 1983; and in 1985 he was awarded one of the most prestigious literary prizes of the Federal Republic, the position of "city scribe" of Bergen-Enkheim.

Fels's main topic is day-to-day life at the lower end of the social spectrum in an uncaring society ruled by powerful people concerned with their own physical pleasure, a life from which refuge can be found only in a fantasy world. He speaks out against this existence and holds up a mirror to bourgeois complacency.

Fels was born out of wedlock on 27 November 1946 in Treuchtlingen, a village near Nuremberg. His mother, a cleaning woman, tried to provide a normal family life for him and his two step-siblings, and one of her live-in companions became a father figure to the boy. After finishing the eighth grade Fels entered into an apprenticeship as a painter, which he did not complete. He got into trouble with the law and had a record of misdemeanors. In 1968 he moved to nearby Fürth, where he eked out a living as a construction worker and unskilled factory laborer. He married Rosi Weiß in 1970, and they moved to Nuremberg. Moving to Vienna in 1983, he finally found a home where he did not feel isolated from the people around him. He credits his wife with much of his success. Her income as a technician in the field of mechanical engineering has allowed Fels to work as a free-lance writer since 1973.

As a child, Fels discovered in books a counterbalance to reality: "So hab' ich halt gelesen, um der Misere zu entkommen, um mich einzuigeln in meinen Büchern, in Träume und Phantasien; daheraus ist der Wunsch entstanden, mich zu artikulieren" (I read just to escape a miserable life and to crawl into my books, my dreams and my imagination; out of this situation came the desire to write my thoughts down). Since there was no one with whom he could discuss his new ideas, he resorted to a "Zwiegespräch mit sich selbst" (conversation with himself) in his writings.

Fels's earliest writings were inspired by his first love and the subsequent loss of that love. Later, writing served Fels as a defense against his hostile surroundings. He writes: "... dann kam der Arbeitsprozeß, in den man gesteckt wurde und es begannen Verhältnisse unerträglich zu werden, und ich brauchte einfach ein Ventil, das ich im Schreiben fand" (Then I got caught up in the working process, and life started becoming unbearable. I simply needed an outlet, which I found in writing). The short vignettes of *Platzangst* (Agoraphobia, 1974) reveal Fels's awareness of the society around him and his place in it: "Du weißt, die Macht ist dort, wo oben ist.... Du fühlst dich nicht klein, das ist dein Fehler" (You know the power lies with those on top.... You don't feel small, that is your problem). He depicts life in factories, in bars, on the streets, and in bordellos. Some stories highlight the plight of the worker: in "Schnell, bevor der Tag kommt" (Quickly, before Daybreak) the last man on the late shift turns off the machines, washes up, and sets out to drive home. Fighting the harsh elements in the cold winter's night, he gives in to a moment of reverie about the good meal and the warm bed awaiting him. He pays for this momentary inattentiveness to reality with his life when he hits a tree. The workers' world is one of the main themes in Fels's writing. It is a limited world where exhaustion from hard physical labor does not leave much room for higher endeavors. Most of Fels's stories are set in the winter, when the workers must get up before dawn, go out into an inhospitable environment, and then spend a day of mind- and body-killing work in the factory, the quarry, or the mud of a construction site. Fantasies during the day center on alcohol and sex, which, along with eating, are the mainstays of life outside work. It is a "dog eat dog" world with only an occasional Gastarbeiter (foreign worker)—an outcast of society—displaying feelings of camaraderie and caring.

It is this self-destructive life that the protagonist of *Die Sünden der Armut* is determined to avoid. Ernst Krauter is a sensitive teenager who is apprehensive of the adulthood he is about to enter. Lazy and usually drunk, he feels poverty to be a sin continually committed against him. He expresses his Weltanschauung in a discussion with a clerk at the employment office, where he is looking for a position available to someone who has not learned a trade. The clerk tells him, "Auf Händen werden Sie nirgends getragen" (No one will carry you in his hands). Ernst answers, "Aber mit Füßen getreten immer" (But they always step on me with their feet). The atmosphere is correspondingly oppressive in the shack Ernst shares with his mother and Detlev Richter, her ex-convict lover. His mother is helpless in dealing with a son who does not want to contribute to the family. Only in extreme situations can mother and son show love for each other, as when Ernst attacks Richter for beating his mother or when the mother gets up at night to give her son a slice of bread after he has been beaten by Richter.

The only ray of hope for a better future appears when Ernst begins work at a factory and his mother finds employment as a cleaning woman at a dentist's office. They make plans to buy a motorcycle and to take a vacation in Italy, but these dreams are extinguished when the mother loses her job a few days later. Ernst decides not to go to work any more. A note to his mother reads like a manifesto: "Ich, Ernst Krauter, habe den Vorsatz gefaßt, lieber zu sterben als ewig zu arbeiten" (I, Ernst Krauter, have made a decision to die rather than work day in and day out).

His desire to escape leads him to fantasize about a naive sort of paradise: a valley where he lives naked and alone in a hut, a friend to man and beast alike. Returning from his dream world to reality, however, he finds only sordid bars inhabited by people who have been unable to establish a place in life. There is no indication of a character flaw which may have caused their failure; rather, these people are the victims of an indifferent, uncaring society. Such is the case with Katie, the daughter of a prostitute. She was once an untamed beauty; even now her face shows no trace of evil. Like Ernst, who feels drawn to her, she is the victim of a "Startloch mit Fußangeln" (background that tripped them up before they ever got going). The novel ends without resolving anything and without showing development in any of the characters; it simply paints a picture of the desolateness of these peoples' lives which numbs the reader by its hopelessness. Nevertheless, the book is engrossing. As von der Grün says, its magic lies in a symbiosis of realism and poetry and in a style of uncompromising honesty through which one can learn much about other human beings. Asked about the similarities between his own youth and that of Ernst Krauter, Fels says, "[Es wurde] immer behauptet..., dieser Roman sei stark autobiographisch. Ich habe immer dagegen gesagt, nein, das ist er

nicht. Er ist die Summe von vielen Erfahrungen, worunter auch einige Erfahrungen des Autors gewesen sind" ([It was] always said . . . that this novel was strongly autobiographical. In response I have always maintained that it is not. It is the sum of many experiences, some of which happen to be those of the author).

Autobiographical experiences can also be found in Fels's second novel, *Ein Unding der Liebe* (A Colossus of Love, 1981). Georg Bleistein was conceived and born without the blessing of the church or society; his aunt and grandmother will never let him forget that he is the product of his mother's immoral life-style. Georg does not remember his mother, who lives in another city, and he never knew his father. For his grandmother and aunt he serves primarily as a beneficiary of their "Christian" charity; the love they show him exhausts itself in providing food for him. Having learned to equate food with love early in life, Georg stuffs himself at every opportunity. It is his fate to be employed as a helper in the kitchen of a department store where his appetite can be constantly satisfied.

Realizing that his corpulent appearance will prevent him from establishing a relationship with a girl, he finds solace in eating still more and therefore can never free himself from the vicious circle. Finding all roads to human relationships blocked, he retreats more and more into his own small world, which is limited to food and to masturbation over pornographic literature. His only goal is his dream of doing something good for the one person he feels truly loves him: his mother. In his dream world she needs him and welcomes him with love. But when he finds his mother he turns out to be one more burden in her difficult life. Working by day as a cleaning woman and by night as a prostitute for a pimp who mistreats her, she has been virtually destroyed by work and disease, and her son is helpless to ease her life. Even his final effort to do something worthwhile by destroying the man who ruined her comes to nothing. At the end he sits on a park bench, a derelict in an uncaring world, looking up into a starry sky. The novel concludes with the words: "Die Erde war der fernste Stern" (Earth was the most distant star).

Kanakenfauna (1982) is a collection of fifteen stories depicting people in their daily struggles. Fels explains the title on the first page: *Kanake* is the Polynesian word for human being, a meaning quite the opposite of the derogatory connotation it has when used colloquially to refer to a foreign worker in Germany. Fels, however, does not limit his critical view to human suffering; his compassion extends to all mistreated creatures. In "Ochsentour" (which can be translated literally as "trip of an ox" or figuratively as "something difficult or oppressive to do") an ox who is to be taken to the slaughterhouse refuses to enter the cart in spite of the exertions of three strong men who beat him brutally. "Dann schlang derselbe Mann den Schwanz oben an der dicken Wurzel plötzlich um seine Faust und drehte reißend, bis der Ochs vor Pein und Angst Blut schiß und, mit einem Satz sich ergebend, im Anhänger stand" (Then the same man suddenly wrapped the tail right at its top around his hand and turned it sharply. The ox shit blood in pain and fear. He gave up and with one jump got into the trailer).

The sketches in *Betonmärchen* (Fairy Tales Made of Concrete, 1983) have a nightmarish quality. Fels recalls that as a child he would read fairy tales aloud to himself and react with goose bumps and shivers when cut-off heads of horses began to speak or crowned snakes sucked milk from udders. The story "Morgenmarsch" (Morning March) can send shivers down the reader's spine: dead people in coffins hold axes in their hands, policemen hit corpses with their truncheons, heads are cut open, and decomposition fills the streets. No other work of Fels conjures up images of death and destruction like this one, in which dreams are stillborn like the cement sacks that in one of the stories replace the babies in their mothers' wombs. In "Notwehrversuch" (Attempt at Self-defense), dark, cold death seems to have usurped all life: "Die Zukunft, auf einen Begriff, auf ein Wort reduziert, ist schwarz wie der Tag, und nur Sterben ist schöner" (The future, reduced to one word or one idea, is black like the day, and only dying is nicer). The world has reached an emotional ice age: tears are frozen, and the sun is a snowball. Human relations are impossible in such a world, in which cement is a second skin. Fels has said, "Ich glaube bei keinem anderen Buch war ich verzweifelter als beim Schreiben der *Betonmärchen*" (I think I have never been as despairing as when writing *Betonmärchen*).

Fels confesses that "ich hatte diese Einsamkeit am Schreibtisch satt" (I was sick of this lonely existence at my desk) and enjoyed seeing his writings come to life on the stage. Both of his dramas were judged successes by the critics. *Lämmermann* (1983) was first performed in 1984 in Hamburg. The plot is typical for Fels: the title

character drops out of high school, destroying his parents' hope for a better life for him. Working on construction sites, he is hated by his colleagues for his "learning" and his former aspirations. He lives with his girlfriend, an attractive secretary who dreams of a bourgeois life. Against the stark reality of hard labor in the dirt on weekdays and boring evenings with his parents and their friends on the weekends, Lämmermann builds his own dream world of travels to places with exotic names: Tashkent, Erewan, Baku, Samarkand. His parents and his girlfriend finally come to consider him a "Versager" (loser) and want to have nothing more to do with him. Despairing of his utter loneliness and his inability to communicate with anyone, Lämmermann reverts to the practices of primitive people, who, in his view, have a much better understanding of the meaning of life: in the last scene he undresses and warms himself over a fire made from his clothes.

Life in a dream world and a return to a primitive stage of human existence are also the goals of Hans Walczak, the protagonist of *Der Affenmörder* (The Ape Murderer, 1985), which was first performed in Munich in 1985. In this drama, Fels has explained, a man revolts against a society where communication and understanding are impossible; he prefers insanity to socialized normality. Walczak dreams of making a living by playing the accordion but must endure hard manual labor to support his family. His wife, having refused to get an abortion, is expecting their second child, thus creating more pressure on him. He escapes from his everyday reality by attending a cabaret where a girl named Lucy plays an ape tamed by an animal trainer, her real-life lover. In a "heroic" gesture Hans attempts to save the girl from her degrading life by attacking her "master." At the end he himself is put in the cage by Lucy and her lover. The drama abounds with sexual fantasies expressed in the blunt language typical of Fels's writings.

In *Rosen für Afrika* (Roses for Africa, 1987) Paul Valla longs to travel to Africa, the last wild continent. The situation at the beginning of the novel is more promising for a happy ending than in any of Fels's other stories: Paul comes from the lower class but has had the good fortune to marry Karola, a girl from a well-to-do family. Paul has a job loading baggage at the international airport in Frankfurt am Main which provides him with a window on the world, an open door to all his dream destinations. But his wife becomes pregnant, and Paul fears that the baby will be a rival for Karola's love. When she refuses his demands that she have an abortion, he beats her and kicks her in the stomach. This act is the final blow to a relationship which had been undermined from the beginning by Paul's feelings of inadequacy because of the social gulf between him and Karola. Paul displays an almost pathological urge to destroy himself and the woman he loves. He is obsessed with the world he has created within himself and with the values associated with this world, which are quite unlike more likely partners for Karola. He will not allow himself to be put into the straitjacket of the "normal" life which Karola's parents expect their son-in-law to lead. Unable to bring his dreams to terms with reality, he drifts more and more into drinking and fantasizing. Reality and his daydreams become a blur, in which his robbing of a bank and the subsequent shooting of his friend are no more than incidental happenings. Paul makes no attempt to flee from the police. In his words: "Es hatte keinen Sinn, darüber nachzudenken. Es war schon immer alles vorbei gewesen, von Anfang an.... Das Leben verging, irgendwie, grundlos" (There was no point in thinking about it. Everything was over, from the very beginning.... Life passed by somehow, without rhyme or reason).

A taste for the exotic and a longing for adventure can be noted in many of Fels's works. Although he claims to have no particular literary models, his early preference for adventure stories such as B. Traven's *Das Totenschiff* (1926; translated as *The Death Ship*, 1934), Robert Louis Stevenson's *Treasure Island* (1883), and James Fenimore Cooper's *The Last of the Mohicans* (1826) attest to his fascination with faraway places. An attraction to America, if it ever existed, seems to have been eliminated by a 1977 trip to New York, Washington, Chicago, and Boston. His reactions to the visit are found in the poem *Ich war nicht in Amerika* (I Was Not in America, 1978). Fels highlights the conspicuous comsumption and the sordid, sad subculture of bars, peepshows, and the streets.

Feeling at home anywhere is a problem for Fels. The stories in the collection *Mein Land* (My Country, 1978) are anything but a declaration of love for the land of his birth, and pieces in *Die Eroberung der Liebe: Heimatbilder* (The Conquest of Love: Pictures of My Homeland, 1985) are expressions of his feelings as an outsider. All forms of belonging, whether to other people or to places,

are complicated for Fels. A cynicism bordering on misanthropy which hinders Fels's protagonists in establishing normal human relationships may have its roots in the author's difficult childhood. The story "Besuch einer Mutter" (Visit of a Mother) in *Die Eroberung der Liebe* describes the mother-child relationship as a perfunctory one, in which the two will never get to know each other. One way for Fels to escape this isolation may be the act of writing. He attempts to rewrite the story of his youth, creating a carefree childhood and an enchanting youth that he never really lived. He summarizes his actual life in one of his poems: "Die Hälfte war Rausch; ein Prozent Liebe; Arbeit der Rest" (Half was drunkenness; one percent love; the rest hard work). The reader may be offended by the bluntness and crudity of the language or the vivid depictions of sexual activity in Fels's books, but these are real aspects of the life he observes. *Erlebnisrealismus* (realism of experience) is the term Heinrich Vormweg coined for Fels's writings, which leave an indelible image in the reader's mind. Suffering and a striving for a humane life are at the center of all of Fels's works. His protagonists are at odds with their philistine environment and attempt to retreat into a dream world; thus they are twentieth-century descendants of such romantic figures as E. T. A. Hoffmann's student Anselmus in "Der goldene Topf" (1814; translated as "The Golden Pot," 1827), who lives alternately in the realm of the fantastic and in the bourgeois world around him.

With the exception of some poems in *Dimension*, a publication of the University of Texas at Austin devoted to the translation of shorter pieces of current literature, none of Fels's works have been translated into English. Given his wide range of genres and his reputation in Germany, perhaps more of these remarkable writings will find their way to a broader audience.

References:

Matthias Altenburg, "Sterben vor dem Tod," *konkret*, 3 (1984): 100;

Hanns Joachim Bernhard, "Literatur der BRD am Beginn der achtziger Jahre," *Weimarer Beiträge*, 30, no. 11 (1984): 1808-1829;

Herbert M. Debes and Jürgen Bugler, "Die Schatten an der Wand sind eingebrannte Seelen," *mid-nachrichten*, 8 (Summer 1985): 15-17;

Jörg W. Gronius, "Durch die Wüste–'Lämmermann' von Ludwig Fels," *Sprache im technischen Zeitalter*, 87 (1983): 251-257;

Jörg W. Gronius, "Durch die Wüste–'Lämmermann' von Ludwig Fels," *Sprache im technischen Zeitalter*, 87 (1983): 251-257;

Max von der Grün, "Respekt vor LF," *Nürnberg heute*, 31 (1981): 7;

Marc Günther, "Eine Liebesgeschichte in unmöglichen Verhältnissen," *Theater heute*, 6 (1986): 40-42;

Thomas Hajewski, "Ludwig Fels: Betonmärchen," *World Literature Today*, 58 (Spring 1984): 265;

Hajewski, "Ludwig Fels: 'Die Sünden der Armut,'" *Books Abroad*, 50 (Autumn 1976): 866;

Hajewski, "Ludwig Fels: Ein Unding der Liebe," *World Literature Today*, 56 (Autumn 1982): 675;

Eckhard Henscheid, "Literatur, eine Kolumne," *Merkur*, 38, no. 6 (1984): 687-691;

Michael Hofmann, "Prospering Mutely," *Times Literary Supplement*, 16 October 1981, p. 1212;

Ferdinand van Ingen, "Ludwig Fels: Ein Unding der Liebe," *Deutsche Bücher*, 12 (1982): 25-26;

Ingen, "Ludwig Fels: 'Kanakenfauna,'" *Deutsche Bücher*, 14 (1984): 19-20;

Hans Christian Kosler, "'Die Erde war der fernste Stern,'" *Frankfurter Hefte*, 7 (1982): 68-70;

Karl Krolow, "Vom Abgesang der Bäuche," *Frankfurter Allgemeine Zeitung*, 18 April 1981, p. 73;

Michael Merschmeier, "Baal 1983," *Theater heute*, 24, no. 4 (1983): 4-7;

Gert Niers, "Ludwig Fels: 'Alles geht weiter,'" *World Literature Today*, 52 (Spring 1978): 281;

Stephan Reinhardt, "Ein Unding der Liebe," *Lesezeichen*, 3 (1981): 35-36;

Horst Scharnagl, "Kein humoristischer Schriftsteller," *Plärrer* (10 October 1975): 50-51;

Erasmus Schöfer, "Eine schwarze Messe der Wirklichkeit," *die horen*, 126 (1982): 168-170;

Christian Schultz-Gerstein, "Elendspanorama," *Die Zeit*, 10 October 1975, p. 6;

Schultz-Gerstein, "Mit geballten Fäusten," *Die Zeit*, 12 April 1974, p. 26;

Jürgen Theobaldy, *Veränderung der Lyrik: Über westdeutsche Gedichte seit 1965* (Munich: Edition text + kritik, 1976);

Thomas Thieringer, "Man muß das Tier herauslocken," *Theater heute*, 26, no. 4 (1985): 28-29;

Thieringer, "So zerrissen und schräg klingt die Melodie eines Lebens," *Theater heute*, 26, no. 4 (1985): 26-27;

Michael Töteberg, "Ludwig Fels," *Kritisches Lexikon für deutschsprachige Gegenwartsliteratur*, edited by Heinz Ludwig Arnold (Munich: Edition text + kritik, 1978), pp. 1-9;

Peter Utz, "Die Schwierigkeit, den Kopf zu verlieren," *Schweizer Monatshefte*, 5 (1985): 439-443.

Fritz Rudolf Fries
(19 May 1935-   )

Timothy W. Ryback
Harvard University

BOOKS: *Der Weg nach Oobliadooh: Roman* (Frankfurt am Main: Suhrkamp, 1966); translated by Leila Vennewitz as *The Road to Oobliadooh* (New York: McGraw-Hill, 1968);

Der Fernsehkrieg: Erzählungen (Halle: Mitteldeutscher Verlag, 1969; enlarged edition, Rostock: Hinstorff, 1975);

See-Stücke (Rostock: Hinstorff, 1973);

Das Luft-Schiff: Biografische Nachlässe zu den Fantasien meines Großvaters. Roman (Rostock: Hinstorff, 1974);

Lope de Vega (Leipzig: Reclam, 1977);

Der Seeweg nach Indien: Erzählungen (Leipzig: Reclam, 1978); republished as *Das nackte Mädchen auf der Straße: Erzählungen* (Frankfurt am Main: Suhrkamp, 1980);

Verbannung und Sieg des Ritters Cid aus Bivar (Berlin: Kinderbuchverlag, 1979);

Erlebte Landschaft: Bilder aus Mecklenburg (Rostock: Hinstorff, 1979);

Mein spanisches Brevier: 1976, 1977 (Rostock: Hinstorff, 1979);

Alle meine Hotel-Leben: Reisebilder (Berlin & Weimar: Aufbau, 1980);

Schumann, China, und der Zwickauer See (Frankfurt am Main: Suhrkamp, 1981);

Alexanders neue Welten (Frankfurt am Main: Suhrkamp, 1982);

Das Filmbuch zum Luft-Schiff: Treatment, Drehbuch (Rostock: Hinstorff, 1983);

Leipzig am Herzen und die Welt dazu: Geschichte vom Reisen (Berlin: Aufbau, 1983);

Hörspiele (Rostock: Hinstorff, 1984);

Verlegung eines mittleren Reiches (Frankfurt am Main: Suhrkamp, 1984);

Bemerkungen anhand eines Fundes oder Das Mädchen aus der Flasche: Texte zur Literatur (Berlin: Aufbau, 1985);

Herbsttage in Niederbarnim: Gedichte (Berlin: Aufbau, 1988).

OTHER: *Metamorphose der Nelke: Moderne spanische Lyrik*, edited by Fries, Carlos Rincon, and K. H. Barck (Leipzig: Reclam, 1968);

"Gratulation," in *Der zerstückte Traum*, edited by Gregor Laschen and Manfred Schlösser (Berlin & Darmstadt: Agora, 1984), pp. 86-87;

Bilder eines Jahres: Impressionen, edited by Fries and Heinz Lehmbäcker (Halle: Mitteldeutscher Verlag, 1987).

TRANSLATIONS: Fernando de Rojas, *Celestina: Tragikomödie von Calisto und Melibea* (Leipzig: Dieterich, 1959);

Benito Pérez Galdós, *Misericordia* (Leipzig: Dieterich, 1962);

Miguel de Cervantes, *Die Zwischenspiele* (Leipzig: Insel, 1967);

Estebanillo González, *Sein Leben und seine Taten aufgeschrieben von ihm selbst* (Leipzig: Reclam, 1967);

L. Otero, *Schaler Whisky* (Berlin: Volk und Welt, 1967);

A. Pareja Diezcanseco, *Offiziere und Señoras* (Berlin: Volk und Welt, 1968);

Tirso de Molina, *Don Gil von den grünen Hosen*, translated and adapted for the stage by Fries (Berlin: Henschel, 1968);

Juan Bosch, *Der Pentagonismus oder Die Ablösung des Imperialismus?* (Reinbek: Rowohlt, 1969);

Pedro Calderón de la Barca, *Dame Kobold* (Berlin: Henschel, 1969);

Armand Gatti, *General Francos Leidenswege* (Frankfurt am Main: Fischer, 1969);

Amadis von Gallien (Leipzig: Insel, 1973);

Julio Cortázar, *Das Feuer aller Feuer* (Frankfurt am Main: Suhrkamp, 1975);

Antonio Buero Vallejo, *Die Stiftung*, translated and adapted for the stage by Fries (Berlin: Henschel, 1975);

Miguel Delibes, *Fünf Stunden mit Mario* (Berlin: Aufbau, 1976);

Cortazar, *Rayuela* (Frankfurt am Main: Suhrkamp, 1981).

PERIODICAL PUBLICATIONS: " 'Das Luft-Schiff '–Phantasiereiche Fabulierkunst oder zu geringe Befrachtung: Fritz Rudolf Fries im Disput mit Kritikern," *Neue deutsche Literatur,* 23, no. 7 (1975): 132-149;

"Laudatio für Volker Braun und Paul Gratzik," *Sinn und Form,* 32 (1980): 540-546;

"Für Paul Wiens," *Sinn und Form,* 34 (1982): 707-708;

"Lehrjahre und Entdeckungen," *Neue deutsche Literatur,* 32, no. 9 (1984): 160-164;

"Erich Arendt," *Neue deutsche Literatur,* 33, no. 1 (1985): 93-95;

"Alvarez de Toledo, Alonso: Ehrung," *Neue deutsche Literatur,* 35, no. 8 (1987): 166-167;

"Die Bergwerke zu Falun," *Sinn und Form,* 39 (1987): 188-191;

"Erwiderung," *Neue deutsche Literatur,* 35, no. 8 (1987): 167-168.

In 1979 Fritz Rudolf Fries received the Heinrich Mann Prize for Literature, the highest literary honor of the German Democratic Republic (GDR). The award acknowledged Fries's twenty years of activity as translator, critic, novelist, and author of travelogues, radio plays, and short stories. In conferring the award, the poet Karl Mickel emphasized Fries's role in introducing Spanish and Latin American literature to GDR readers. Mickel lauded Fries as the modern heir to a centuries-old German fascination with the Iberian peninsula, as an artist who fused German and Spanish literary traditions, and as a "Prosadichter, der in zwei Kulturen lebt" (poet of prose who lives in two cultures).

Fries's cultural duality is central to his work. In interviews and speeches he has expressed his indebtedness to both German and Hispanic writers. The German literary figure who had the greatest impact on Fries is the eighteenth-century novelist Jean Paul (Johann Paul Friedrich Richter), whose levity and wit are echoed in many of Fries's novels and short stories. From the Spanish tradition Fries's characters have inherited the lofty idealism of Don Quixote and the prurient desires of Don Juan. Fries has drawn inspiration from Latin America as well; in fact, he maintains that his initial motivation to express himself creatively came from reading the work of the Chilean poet Pablo Neruda: "In meiner Erinnerung beginnt alles mit dem Dichter des *Aufenthalts auf Erden,* mit Pablo Neruda" (I recall that it all began with the poet of *Residence on Earth,* with Pablo Neruda). Fries also credits jazz and the American Beat Generation, especially Jack Kerouac, for influencing his early works. The confluence of these diverse literary traditions has re-

sulted in an artistic voice singular in contemporary German literature; it is at once whimsical and tragic, utopian and engaged, didactic and playful.

Fries, born on 19 May 1935 to a Spanish mother, Amparo Schulze-Manteola Fries, and a German father, Friedrich Fries, spent the first seven years of his life in Bilbao, an industrial city in northern Spain. In the winter of 1942 Friedrich Fries's company transferred him to Leipzig. Fritz Rudolf Fries adapted quickly to life in Germany but maintained his interest in the Hispanic culture. In 1952 he entered Karl Marx University in Leipzig, where he studied English and Spanish and worked closely with the renowned literary scholar and critic Werner Krauss, whom he has identified as his "geistigen Vater" (spiritual father). After completing his studies in 1958 Fries earned a living as a translator of Spanish literature and interpreter at international conferences. In 1960 Krauss, who had become head of the newly created Department for German-French Enlightenment at the Academy of Sciences in East Berlin, employed Fries as a research assistant. Assigned to study the life and writings of the eighteenth-century priest Benito Gerónimo Feijóo y Montenegro, Fries turned his efforts instead to fiction. When asked to present his findings, he handed his mentor the 340-page manuscript of *Der Weg nach Oobliadooh* (1966; translated as *The Road to Oobliadooh,* 1968).

Der Weg nach Oobliadooh chronicles the lives of two graduates of Karl Marx University during the late 1950s. Arlecq finds work with a corporation as a translator and interpreter. Paasch, trained as a dentist, becomes a jazz musician. Inspired by a Dizzy Gillespie tune to seek the land of Oobliadooh, which to him symbolizes an exotic and idyllic existence, Paasch indulges in music, alcohol, and women. When his hedonistic life-style fails to satisfy him, he decides to immigrate to the West and convinces Arlecq to join him. They travel to West Berlin but quickly become disillusioned, return to East Germany, and have themselves committed to a mental institution. For the first time, they find true contentment. But Paasch, a jazz-humming alcoholic, is bound for self-destruction, and Arlecq, in order to survive, must separate himself from him. When Arlecq's pregnant girlfriend eventually locates him, he agrees to marry her and rejoin society as a responsible citizen.

Der Weg nach Oobliadooh belongs to the genre of the Ankunftsroman (arrival novel), an East German literary form created in the early 1960s that portrays an individual's development of a "socialist consciousness." Like other GDR writers of Ankunftsromane, Fries ultimately integrates his main character into society. But Arlecq's path to social integration and Paasch's penchant for Western music were unacceptable models for East German behavior. The Mitteldeutscher Verlag, one of the GDR's leading publishers of contemporary fiction, rejected the novel. Fries then sent the manuscript to the West German publisher Suhrkamp, which immediately accepted it. *Der Weg nach Oobliadooh* appeared in 1966 and was warmly received by critics and public alike. West German literary historian Wolfgang Emmerich has called the novel one of the most important books of the 1960s. Fries's popularity in West Germany cost him his affiliation with the Academy of Sciences. Since 1966 he has continued to live in Petershagen, near Berlin, and has pursued a successful career as a free-lance writer and translator. He married Marianne Wellinghausen on 30 December 1960; they had four children and were divorced in 1981.

In 1969 Fries published *Der Fernsehkrieg* (The Television War), an anthology of short stories that includes vignettes of life in Nazi Germany, Castro's Cuba, and East Germany. The title story condemns American involvement in Vietnam and indicts the sensationalistic media coverage of the conflict. The book was received coolly in West Germany but insured Fries's legitimacy as a writer in East Germany. *See-Stücke* (Sea Vignettes, 1973) is a collection of travel sketches describing East Germany's Baltic Sea coast.

Fries's first major fictional work to appear in East Germany was his 1974 novel, *Das Luft-Schiff* (The Airship). The four-hundred-page work was, in the words of one critic, both "ein Roman und die Poetik eines Romans" (a novel and the poetics of the novel). Fries obscures a relatively simple plot in a dense web of literary experimentation, not only musing on narrative theory but also using diverse narrative perspectives. Despite its complexity, Manfred Hocke of the DEFA studios in Potsdam was so taken with the novel that he asked Fries to adapt it for film. Fries, who had initially considered the work incompatible with the film medium, agreed to do so, and *Das Luft-Schiff* appeared in 1982.

The novel is set between the world wars. Franz Xavier Stannebein, a representative of a German company in Spain, becomes obsessed with the desire to construct "Flugmaschinen groß

wie Walfische" (aircraft the size of whales) and drafts plans that provide for central heating, beds, and other comforts. Stannebein envisions the day when his "airships" will transport great numbers of people from one continent to another. But the technological achievement is secondary for him: he conceives of transportation as a means of transformation. With his "airship" he hopes to free man from his "Leiden, Schwächen und Gemeinheiten" (sufferings, weaknesses and evils) and transport him into a new utopian age. As with Paasch and his search for Oobliadooh, the goal remains vague and unattainable.

In the second half of the 1970s Fries came into greater prominence in both East and West Germany. Along with Christa Wolf, Günter Kunert, Sarah Kirsch, and over seventy other East German artists, he joined the public outcry against the November 1976 expatriation by the GDR of the writer and composer Wolf Biermann. Unlike Kunert, Kirsch, and dozens of others who immigrated to the West, however, Fries decided to remain in East Germany. His major literary undertaking during this period was a biography of the Spanish author Lope de Vega (1977); he also wrote radio plays and published a second anthology of short stories (1978), a children's book on the Cid (1979), and several volumes of impressions of his travels to the Soviet Union, the United States, Cuba, and various European and South American nations. *Mein spanisches Brevier* (My Spanish Breviary, 1979) recounts a visit to Spain which took him back to his hometown of Bilbao after a thirty-six-year absence.

Fries's third major work of fiction, *Alexanders neue Welten* (Alexander's New Worlds, 1982), like *Der Weg nach Oobliadooh*, contrasts two characters: Alexander Retard is a modest, middle-aged academic at a Berlin institute; Ole Knut Berlinguer is a restless man in search of a new life. While Retard has been quietly passing his years between his home in Friedrichshain and the institute, Berlinguer, who in August 1968 was released from his academic position for his support of Alexander Dubcek's reforms in Czechoslovakia, has been traveling the globe as an interpreter and having romantic interludes with women.

Berlinguer, an East German delegation, and a group of fashion models are on their way to Havana to take part in a cultural conference when hijackers force the pilot to fly to a small African nation. On the ground the hijackers negotiate with the local authorities for a guarantee of safe passage. Keeping an East German writer as hostage, they are escorted to a waiting jeep. But as they are driving down the runway, they are ambushed by soldiers, and the hijackers and their hostage are killed. Meanwhile, Berlinguer, the rest of the East German delegation, and the fashion models have disappeared from the plane and are presumed dead.

These dramatic events are described on ten cassettes that Berlinguer has been mailing to Retard from a secret location. Retard, in the meantime, has been asked to look into Berlinguer's final years in Berlin and to submit a report to the academy. Retard's research brings him into contact with Berlinguer's wife, his former lovers, and others associated with him. The investigation into Berlinguer's life becomes a process of self-discovery for Retard; it opens new horizons for him and unleashes his imagination, but, as in the cases of Arlecq and Stannebein, his fantasies lead nowhere.

The search for utopia is a central motif in the works of Fries. While his ideals are usually vague, *Verlegung eines mittleren Reiches* (The Displacement of a Medium-Sized Country, 1984)—much of which was written in 1967—provides a concrete account of life in a Friesian idyll. In the form of a diary the novel chronicles the lives of survivors of a nuclear catastrophe. A preface establishes the location and date: "Sonnenstadt im Jahre des Heils 07" (The City of the Sun in the Year of the Lord 07). The Sonnenstadt, representing the ideal human community, is a concept adopted from Jean Paul; Fries alludes to it in *Der Weg nach Oobliadooh* and in *Das Luft-Schiff*. The survivors have established a society free of contention, hatred, and war; but Fries warns that even this idyllic community represents only an interlude between two catastrophes. A permanent utopia remains elusive.

Fritz Rudolf Fries is a facile and prolific writer who has fused his German and Spanish heritage into a distinctive artistic voice. He brings to German literature a rare combination of playfulness and literary craftsmanship. His novels are humorous without being silly, whimsical without being trivial. He effectively balances Mediterranean vivacity with north European restraint and proves with each new work that he is, indeed, an author who lives in two cultures.

References:

Friedrich Albrecht, "Fritz Rudolf Fries," *Deutsch als Fremdsprache*, 18 (1981): 52-54;

Albrecht, "Zur Schaffensentwicklung von Fritz Rudolf Fries," *Weimarer Beiträge*, 25, no. 3 (1979): 64-92;

Thomas C. Fox, "Oobliadooh or Eikenngettnosettisfekschin: Music, Language and Opposition in GDR Literature," *Germanic Review*, 61 (Summer 1986): 109-116;

Bernhard Greiner, "'Paradies am Ende der Welt': Geschichten zu Fritz Rudolf Fries' Roman *Verlegung eines mittleren Reiches*," in *Apokalypse: Weltuntergangsvisionen in der Literatur des 20. Jahrhunderts*, edited by Günter Grimm and others (Frankfurt am Main: Suhrkamp, 1986), pp. 369-383;

Greiner, "'Sentimentaler Stoff und fantastische Form': Zur Erneuerung frühromantischer Tradition im Roman der DDR," in *Amsterdamer Beiträge zur neueren Germanistik*, volume 11/12, edited by Jos Hoogeveen and Gerd LaBroisse (Amsterdam: Rodopi, 1981), pp. 249-329;

Reinhard Hillich, "Die Brüste der Göttin: Fiktion und Kritik der Fiktion als Gestaltungselemente in Fritz Rudolf Fries' Roman *Das Luftschiff*," *Sinn und Form*, 33 (1981): 141-162;

Werner Liersch, "Spaziergänge in das Reich der Luft," *Neue deutsche Literatur*, 23 (1975): 7, 127-131;

Karl Mickel, "In zwei Kulturen leben: Laudatio zur Verleihung des Heinrich-Mann-Preises 1979," *Neue deutsche Literatur*, 27 (1979): 8, 160-164;

Christoph Rodiek, "Stierkampf und Politik: Motivanalysen zu Feuchtwanger, Sartre und Fries," *Arcadia*, 19 (1984): 153-164;

Cecile Cazort Zorach, "From Grey East to Golden West: Fritz Rudolf Fries and GDR Travel Literature," in *Studies in GDR Culture and Society*, volume 4, edited by Margy Gerber and others (Lanham, Md.: University Press of America, 1984), pp. 137-152.

Günter Grass
(16 October 1927-   )

Alan Frank Keele
Brigham Young University

BOOKS: *Die Vorzüge der Windhühner* (Berlin-Frohnau & Neuwied: Luchterhand, 1956);

Die Blechtrommel: Roman (Darmstadt, Berlin-Spandau & Neuwied: Luchterhand, 1959); translated by Ralph Manheim as *The Tin Drum* (London: Secker & Warburg, 1962; New York: Pantheon, 1963);

Gleisdreieck (Darmstadt, Berlin-Spandau & Neuwied: Luchterhand, 1960);

Katz und Maus: Eine Novelle (Neuwied & Berlin-Spandau: Luchterhand, 1961); translated by Monheim as *Cat and Mouse* (New York: Harcourt, Brace & World, 1963; London: Secker & Warburg, 1963); German version, edited by Edgar Lohner (Waltham, Mass.: Blaisdell, 1969); German version, edited by H. F. Brookes and C. E. Fraenkel (London: Heinemann Educational, 1971);

Die bösen Köche: Stück (Berlin: Kiepenheuer, 1961);

Hundejahre: Roman (Neuwied: Luchterhand, 1963); translated by Manheim as *Dog Years* (New York: Harcourt, Brace & World, 1965; London: Secker & Warburg, 1965);

Hochwasser: Ein Stück in zwei Akten (Frankfurt am Main: Suhrkamp, 1963);

Die Ballerina (Berlin: Wolff, 1963);

Onkel, Onkel! Ein Spiel in vier Akten (Berlin: Wagenbach, 1965);

Rede über das Selbstverständliche (Neuwied & Berlin: Luchterhand, 1965);

Dich singe ich, Demokratie (Neuwied & Berlin: Luchterhand, 1965);

Die Plebejer proben den Aufstand: Ein deutsches Trauerspiel (Neuwied & Berlin: Luchterhand, 1966); translated by Monheim as *The Plebions Rehearse the Uprising: A German Tragedy* (New York: Harcourt, Brace & World, 1966; London: Secker & Warburg, 1967); German version, edited by Brookes and Fraenkel (London: Heinemann Educational, 1971);

Selected Poems, translated by Michael Hamburger and Christopher Middleton (London: Secker & Warburg, 1966; New York: Harcourt, Brace & World, 1966);

*Günter Grass (Fotoagentur Sven Simon–
Ullstein Bilderdienst)*

Ausgefragt: Gedichte und Zeichnungen (Neuwied & Berlin: Luchterhand, 1967);

Four Plays, translated by Manheim and A. Leslie Willson, introduction by Martin Esslin (New York: Harcourt, Brace & World, 1967; London: Secker & Warburg, 1968)–comprises *Flood; Mister, Mister (Onkel, Onkel!* in British edition); *Only Ten Minutes to Buffalo; The Wicked Cooks;*

Der Fall Axel C. Springer am Beispiel Arnold Zweig: Eine Rede, ihr Anlaß und die Folgen (Berlin: Voltaire, 1967);

Über meinen Lehrer Döblin und andere Vorträge (Berlin: Literarisches Colloquium, 1968);

New Poems, translated by Hamburger (New York: Harcourt, Brace & World, 1968);

Über das Selbstverständliche: Reden, Aufsätze, offene Briefe, Kommentare (Neuwied: Luchterhand, 1968);

Briefe über die Grenze: Versuch eines Ost-West-Dialogs, by Grass and Pavel Kohout (Hamburg: Wegner, 1968);

Speak Out! Speeches, Open Letters, Commentaries, translated by Manheim and others (London: Secker & Warburg, 1969);

Davor: Ein Stück in 13 Szenen (Berlin: Kiepenheuer, 1969); edited by Victor Lange and Frances Lange (New York: Harcourt Brace Jovanovich, 1973); translated by Willson and Manheim as *Max: A Play* (New York: Harcourt Brace Jovanovich, 1972);

örtlich betäubt: Roman (Neuwied: Luchterhand, 1969); translated by Manheim as *Local Anaesthetic* (New York: Harcourt, Brace & World, 1970; London: Secker & Warburg, 1970);

Die Schweinekopfsülze (Hamburg: Merlin, 1969);

Freiheit: Ein Wort wie Löffelstiel [by Grass]; *Gegen Gewalt und Unmenschlichkeit* [by Paul Schallück]: *Zwei Reden zur Woche der Brüderlichkeit* (Cologne: Schäuble, 1969);

Poems of Günter Grass, translated by Hamburger and Middleton (Harmondsworth, U.K.: Penguin, 1969);

Theaterspiele (Neuwied: Luchterhand, 1970)—comprises *Hochwasser; Onkel, Onkel!; Noch zehn Minuten bis Buffalo; Die bösen Köche; Die Plebejer proben den Aufstand; Davor;*

Gesammelte Gedichte (Neuwied: Luchterhand, 1971);

Aus dem Tagebuch einer Schnecke (Neuwied: Luchterhand, 1972); translated by Manheim as *From the Diary of a Snail* (New York: Harcourt Brace Jovanovich, 1973; London: Secker & Warburg, 1974);

Der Schriftsteller als Bürger—Eine Siebenjahresbilanz (Vienna: Dr. Karl Renner-Institut, 1973);

Mariazuehren; Hommage à Marie; Inmarypraise (Munich: Bruckmann, 1973); *Inmarypraise* translated by Middleton (New York: Harcourt Brace Jovanovich, 1973);

Liebe geprüft: Sieben Gedichte mit sieben Radierungen (Bremen: Schünemann, 1974); translated by Hamburger as *Love Tested: Seven Poems with Seven Etchings* (New York: Harcourt Brace Jovanovich, 1975);

Der Bürger und seine Stimme: Reden, Aufsätze, Kommentare (Darmstadt & Neuwied: Luchterhand, 1974);

In the Egg and Other Poems, translated by Hamburger and Middleton (New York: Harcourt Brace Jovanovich, 1977; London: Secker & Warburg, 1978);

Der Butt: Roman (Darmstadt & Neuwied: Luchterhand, 1977); translated by Manheim as *The Flounder* (New York: Harcourt Brace Jovanovich, 1978; London: Secker & Warburg, 1978);

50 erfolgreiche Musterreden für betriebliche Veranstaltungen, Jubiläen, Betriebsversammlungen und andere Anlässe (Kissing: WEKA, 1978);

Denkzettel: Politische Reden und Aufsätze (Darmstadt & Neuwied: Luchterhand, 1978);

Das Treffen in Telgte: Eine Erzählung (Darmstadt & Neuwied: Luchterhand, 1979); translated by Manheim as *The Meeting at Telgte* (New York: Harcourt Brace Jovanovich, 1981; London: Secker & Warburg, 1981);

Die Blechtrommel als Film, by Grass and Volker Schlöndorff (Frankfurt am Main: Zweitausendeins, 1979);

Kopfgeburten oder Die Deutschen sterben aus (Darmstadt & Neuwied: Luchterhand, 1980); translated by Manheim as *Headbirths; or, The Germans Are Dying Out* (New York: Harcourt Brace Jovanovich, 1982);

Aufsätze zur Literatur (Darmstadt & Neuwied: Luchterhand, 1980);

Danziger Trilogie (Darmstadt & Neuwied: Luchterhand, 1980)—comprises *Die Blechtrommel, Katz und Maus, Hundejahre;* translated by Manheim as *The Danzig Trilogy* (San Diego: Harcourt Brace Jovanovich/New York: Pantheon, 1987);

Zeichnen und Schreiben, volume 1: *Zeichnungen und Texte 1954-1977* (Darmstadt & Neuwied: Luchterhand, 1982); translated by Hamburger and Walter Arndt as *Drawings & Words Nineteen Fifty-Four to Nineteen Seventy-Seven* (San Diego: Harcourt Brace Jovanovich, 1983);

Bin ich nun Schreiber oder Zeichner? (Regensburg: Schürer, 1982);

Kinderlied (Northridge, Calif.: Lord John Press, 1982);

Ach Butt, dein Märchen geht böse aus: Gedichte und Radierungen (Darmstadt & Neuwied: Luchterhand, 1983);

Widerstand lernen: Politische Gegenreden 1980-1983 (Darmstadt & Neuwied: Luchterhand, 1984);

Zeichnen und Schreiben, volume 2: *Radierungen und Texte 1972-1982* (Darmstadt & Neuwied: Luchterhand, 1984); translated by Hamburger and others as *Etchings & Words Nineteen Seventy-Two to Nineteen Eighty-Two* (San Diego: Harcourt Brace Jovanovich, 1985);

Geschenkte Freiheit: Rede zum 8. Mai 1945 (Berlin: Akademie der Künste, 1985);

On Writing and Politics 1967-1983, translated by Manheim (San Diego: Harcourt Brace Jovanovich, 1985; London: Secker & Warburg, 1985);

Erfolgreiche Musterreden für den Bürgermeister: Rhetorikhandbuch mit Musterreden zu Sitzungen, Versammlungen, öffentlichen Veranstaltungen und behördeninternen Anlässen (Kissing: WEKA, 1986);

Die Rättin (Darmstadt & Neuwied: Luchterhand, 1986); translated by Manheim as *The Rat* (San Diego: Harcourt Brace Jovanovich, 1987);

Mit Sophie in die Pilze gegangen (Göttingen: Steidel, 1987);

Zunge zeigen (Darmstadt & Neuwied: Luchterhand, 1988).

TRANSLATION: *O Susanna: Ein Jazzbilderbuch. Blues, Balladen, Spirituals, Jazz* (Cologne: Kiepenheuer & Witsch, 1959).

PERIODICAL PUBLICATION: "Die Vernichtung der Menschheit hat begonnen," *Die Zeit,* 10 December 1982, p. 11.

Günter Grass is more than a writer; he is a phenomenon. Recognized in Germany by friend and foe alike as a formidable artistic and political force, abroad he is viewed almost as a personification of Germany and of postwar German literature. Yet, Grass has never pandered to his own popularity: what he writes, says, and does is just as likely to strike an open nerve as a responsive chord. His fame and his infamy are both byproducts of his single-minded pursuit of his mission: to make Germany's Nazi experience a moral yardstick—a kind of ethical absolute zero—against which to measure all other movements and ideologies. Beginning his artistic career as a sculptor, he has become a writer of lyric poetry, drama, fiction, ballet libretti, and political tracts; he is also a painter, graphic designer, and etcher. Many of his ideas seem to have been worked out across the various genres in his repertory and reduced to a system of durable symbols which have informed his oeuvre for more than three decades.

For Günter Wilhelm Grass no symbols are more durable than those crafted from his immediate experience. Danzig, now Gdansk, Poland, was at the time of Grass's birth in 1927 a Free City, a German-speaking island in the Polish Corridor to the Baltic created after World War I. After the Nazis came to power in Germany in 1933, they began to organize in Danzig; bringing Danzig home to the Reich became one of their most popular rallying cries. In the early morning of 1 September 1939 the first shots of World War II were fired in the attack on the Polish post office in Danzig. Grass has said that in Danzig the Nazis' rise to power occurred slowly, so that one could take notes.

From his perspective as a child, the impressionable and gifted boy simultaneously noted minute details of life in a petit-bourgeois family in the Danzig suburb of Langfuhr and the making of world war and holocaust. Grass's artistic search for the causes of global evil still concentrates on minutiae: subtleties of language, prejudice, political accommodation, misplaced sexual and religious fervor.

His mother, Helena, was descended from the Kashubians, a Slavic people distinct from the Poles. Members of her family were mostly small farmers who lived near the village of Karthaus, southwest of Danzig. Willy Grass, his father, was German. Grass's paternal grandparents owned a moderately large cabinet-making shop, and his parents kept a small neighborhood grocery store. These environments and those of the schools and churches Grass attended became microcosmic mise-en-scènes for his aesthetic reconstructions of the genesis of evil.

His view of this genesis is that of an insider: he does not exempt himself from guilt. Only his youth prevented Grass from being more responsible for Nazi atrocities. If he had been born earlier, he says, he would have been just as zealous as any other Nazi. As it was, even as a child he was quite involved: at ten he was a member of the Jungvolk, the "cubs" of the Nazi party; at fourteen he became a Hitler Youth; at fifteen a helper at an antiaircraft battery; and at seventeen a tank gunner. Wounded near Cottbus in late April 1945, he was taken to a field hospital in Marienbad, Czechoslovakia, where he was captured by the advancing American forces and placed in a prisoner-of-war camp in Bavaria. As a reeducation measure he was taken to visit the concentration camp at Dachau; the experience led him to question for the first time the validity of the Nazi point of view.

After he was released from the POW camp in the spring of 1946, Grass worked on a farm, then spent a year laboring in a potash mine. In 1947 he moved to Düsseldorf to study art, but the academy was temporarily closed because of a shortage of coal. One of the professors suggested that he become a stonemason instead. When he had completed his apprenticeship, he went to the academy to study sculpting and graphics. In the evenings he was a drummer in a jazz band. Following a trip through Italy in 1951 and a hitchhiking tour of France in 1952, Grass moved to Berlin to study metal sculpture. In 1954 he married a Swiss dancer, Anna Schwarz, through whom he became interested in dance and began to write ballets.

Grass, whose efforts at writing had begun at age thirteen when he entered a "novel" entitled "Die Kaschuben" (The Kashubians) in a contest sponsored by a Nazi school magazine, was awarded the third prize in a poetry contest sponsored by South German Radio in 1955. Subsequently Walter Höllerer published some of Grass's poems, short plays, and essays in his literary magazine *Akzente*. Grass's first book, the poetry volume *Die Vorzüge der Windhühner* (The Advantages of Windchickens), appeared in 1956. His early surrealistic plays *Hochwasser* (1963; translated as *Flood*, 1967) and *Onkel, Onkel!* (1965; translated as *Mister, Mister*, 1967) and his ballet "Stoffreste" (Cloth Remnants) had their premieres in small and experimental theaters around Germany.

In 1955 he read some of his works at the Berlin meeting of the Gruppe (Group) 47, an informal but extremely influential association of politically engaged writers organized in 1947 by Hans Werner Richter. Grass's talent was recognized by the group, and he received encouragement to try his hand at a novel. In 1956 he and Anna moved to Paris, she to study dance and he to work in earnest on the novel. In 1958 Höllerer arranged for Grass to return to Gdansk to research the attack on the Polish post office and other material for the novel. The trip was partially financed by the five-thousand-mark prize of the Gruppe 47, which he won by reading to the group the manuscript for the beginning of the novel, which appeared the next year as *Die Blechtrommel* (translated as *The Tin Drum*, 1962).

Critical reception of *Die Blechtrommel* was polarized: for each of the many literary prizes it was awarded the book elicited protests alleging obscenity and blasphemy. A characteristic case was that of the City of Bremen, whose literary prize was awarded to Grass by the judges but blocked by the Social Democratic municipal senate—by no means a reactionary body—out of concern that the city might be perceived as having given official sanction to a literary anarchist or pornographer.

In a cursory or unsophisticated reading *Die Blechtrommel* might appear to consist merely of the scurrilous, self-indulgent rantings of the misbegotten gnome Oskar Matzerath, an inmate of an institution for the criminally insane. Not only does Grass seem to show the most sympathy toward this character, but it is obvious that the novel is fundamentally autobiographical: Oskar was born in Danzig, where his parents own a neighborhood grocery store, and after the war he moves to Düsseldorf, where he works as a stonemason and a jazz drummer and studies at the Art Academy. But the autobiographical aspects are totally subordinate to the essential intent of the work, which is to investigate the rise of dictatorship, war, and holocaust in the twentieth century. The genius of the novel is that the story of Oskar Matzerath, while based to a certain extent on the biography of Günter Grass, is really a visible, microscopic scratching of an artistic seismograph needle recording not only the violent global upheavals of the twentieth century but also all the subtle foreshocks and aftershocks. Each beat of the sticks on Oskar's mnemonic drum, each jiggle of Oskar's pen recorded on the pages of *Die Blechtrommel* is a reaction to ever larger forces in the ever widening spheres of his family, his neighborhood, Danzig, Germany, and the world.

But Oskar does not simply record these forces; he is a creation and, at the same time, a victim of them. He is a blue-eyed drummer with a messiah complex because Hitler had blue eyes, was known as "the drummer" for his tub-thumping oratory, and believed himself to be the saviour of Germany. His voice breaks glass because he lives in an age that could produce the "Kristallnacht" (Night of Broken Glass), 9-10 November 1938, when Jewish shops and synagogues were destroyed across Germany. He is a liar and murderer because he mirrors the lying and murderous time and place in which he lives. He becomes a Jesus to a gang of vandals because he lives in a society of true believers seeking a Führer. He is a dwarf because he lives in an age

Dust jacket designed by Grass for the controversial 1959 novel that made him famous

of moral dwarves. He grows into a misshapen hunchback in 1945 because it is his fate to reflect the distorted boundaries and values of postwar Germany and the postwar world. *Die Blechtrommel* is not the story of an obscene dwarf based on the autobiography of a vulgar author; it is the story of historical obscenity in the twentieth century, told by an incarnation of the Zeitgeist whose curriculum vitae corresponds to that of the author only to the extent that the author feels that he, too, is typical of his age.

Book One, the first third of the novel, covers the period from the birth of Oskar's mother in 1900 to the burning of the Danzig synagogue and other violent anti-Semitic acts connected with the Kristallnacht, shortly before Christmas 1938. This part ends with a surrealistic evocation of the Advent, not of the Prince of Peace, but of a deadly counterfeit–a kind of Hitlerian Santa Claus: the heavenly gasman, who, as soon as his believers declare faith in him to be the state religion, will unleash the great war and the holocaust. And he will return in the future, hiding

behind a false beard, with more frightening things in his bag: cyanide instead of almonds (Grass has elsewhere noted the similarity of their aromas) and Christmas sausages stuffed with mincemeat made not *for* humanity but *of* humanity.

Book Two begins with the first official act of World War II: the German attack on the Polish post office in Danzig. Within the two chapters which form the exact center of this book the major turning points of the war occur: German armies are halted in Africa and in the Soviet Union, and the Allied invasion of Normandy begins. Book Two ends with the collapse of Germany in 1945, after Soviet armies capture Danzig and proceed to Berlin. Book Three deals with the postwar world from 1945 to 1953. In the latter year narrated time catches up with narrative time, and the Jesus figure Oskar turns thirty–the age at which Christ began to preach.

The links between Oskar's private microcosm and the historical macrocosm are sophisticated and subtle, often appearing to be the accidental result of Oskar's hyperbolic literary style. For example, to the sentence near the beginning of the novel in which he reports his mother's birth Oskar adds an apparently irrelevant interjection to the effect that Germany was deciding at that time to double the size of the building program for its imperial fleet. He then describes his mother's horoscope, which involves confused marital relationships, fish, eels, illness, a celebration of annihilation, and a dwelling in the deadly house. These elements presage his mother's unhappy ménage à trois with her German husband and her Polish cousin Jan Bronski, her death by self-inflicted fish-and-eel poisoning, and, by a system of ever widening symbolic circles, the future of Danzig and of Germany. The beginning of Book Two provides a further example of this linkage. After Oskar's mother's death her two former lovers, the German Nazi cell leader Matzerath and the Polish post-office employee Bronski, embarrassed and concerned that they might be seen together, meet at midnight to play a symbolic game of Skat: "Polen hat einen Grand Hand verloren; die Freie Stadt Danzig gewann soeben für das Großdeutsche Reich bombensicher einen Karo einfach" (Poland has lost a grand slam; the Free City of Danzig has just won a blockbuster diamond full house for the Greater German Reich).

The experiences most clearly linked to historical events are often also the most obscene, grotesque, and shocking. Grass apparently wishes to offend his readers' codes of private sexual morality in the hope of making them offended at global political immorality. Thus, Oskar begins the chapter "Fünfundsiebzig Kilo" (translated as "165 Lbs.") with an account of the problems of the German armies in the east, which he links to a particularly graphic description of his unnatural sexual involvement (he uses his drumsticks as a penis) with Lina Greff, the neglected wife of a homosexual greengrocer and former scoutmaster. As the radio falsely reports that the German Sixth Army is conquering Stalingrad (the radio is often used by Grass as the link between microcosm and macrocosm), Lina's husband works single-mindedly on the construction of a contraption resembling a large balance scale and then hangs himself on it by causing exactly his own weight in potatoes to roll down into baskets suspended from the opposite end. Greff's long history of using dishonest scales and his ensuing trouble with the bureau of weights and measures—hence the macabre manner of his death—as well as a summons by the morals squad on charges of pederasty, compounded by grief at the news of the death on the eastern front of his favorite former boy scout, drive him to suicide. In the microcosm of Oskar's street in a suburb of Danzig, a tangle of dishonest and perverse behavior leading to catastrophe is linked to the larger question of the fortunes of Germany on the eastern front. Weighed in a macabre balance, entangled in a web of dishonest and perverted behavior, Germany, like Greff, commits suicide amid the complexities of the bizarre war machine it has created.

The scene in Greff's cellar when his corpse is discovered is imbued with such a frightening, primal nihilism that Oskar drums out the song he reserves for his encounters with the most absolute evil: "Ist die schwarze Köchin da? Jajaja!" (Is the black cook here? Yesyesyes!). The black cook (called "the black witch" in the English translation), the personification of evil, haunts Oskar throughout the novel. She casts her shadow when the neighborhood children make Oskar drink their concoction of urine and frog's legs and when Greff commits suicide; when the members of the Stäuberbande (Duster Gang) make Oskar their Jesus and perform a vandalistic black mass, they are betrayed by Luzie Rennwand, one of the incarnations of the black cook. Her spirit permeates the Kristallnacht and the Nazi program of euthanasia, from which Oskar is saved only by the Soviet advance; and she stands be-

hind the Zeitgeist Oskar when he causes the death of his mother, when he leads his presumptive father Jan to his death at the Polish post office, when he makes his other presumptive father Matzerath choke to death–significantly–on his Nazi party pin, and when he (probably) murders the nurse Dorothea Köngetter in Düsseldorf.

As his thirtieth birthday approaches, Oskar is about to be released from the insane asylum, where he has blackened the "unschuldiges" (innocent) paper he asked for at the beginning of the novel with the sordid story of his past in the shadow of the black cook. What will the cook, who is getting blacker and blacker, have in store in the future? Will Oskar be pressed into service as a Führer, as a Jesus to the disciples of some future Duster Gang? As in all of his novels, Grass leaves the ending open.

Looking back on the creation of *Die Blechtrommel*, Grass admits to having been obsessed. From the moment he wrote its first sentence, he recounts, the characters of the novel, a wildly expanding family, came to life for him and sat around his typewriter. For his real family, his wife and their twin sons Franz and Raoul, born in 1957, he was present during these years less as a husband and father than as a cloud of tobacco smoke.

Grass moved to Berlin, partly for health reasons, in 1959. On top of his heavy smoking, he had written the book in the damp ground-floor studio which doubled as the furnace room of his flat on the Avenue d'Italie, and he discovered that he had developed tubercles in his lungs. He was also uncomfortable about the nationalist Charles de Gaulle, who had come to power in France. He was made even more uneasy when, for unexplained reasons, he was detained overnight by the French authorities—an experience which, he says, made him downright homesick for the West German police. This event seems to have found its way into *Die Blechtrommel*: on the penultimate page of the novel Oskar recounts that he was arrested on the Avenue d'Italie (at Maison Blanche, the Metro stop closest to Grass's flat at number 111) and that in several faces in the crowd he saw the horrible visage of the black cook.

Before leaving Paris Grass had written a ballet, *Fünf Köche* (Five Cooks), which was produced in 1959 in Aix-les-Bains and in Bonn; a radio play, "Zweiunddreißig Zähne" (Thirty-two Teeth), which was broadcast in 1959 by South German Radio; and two one-act plays, *Noch zehn Minuten bis Buffalo* (translated as *Only Ten Minutes to Buffalo*, 1967), produced in 1959 in Bochum, and *Beritten hin und zurück* (Mounted There and Back Again), produced in 1959 in Frankfurt. He had also written more poems, which appeared in 1960 in the volume *Gleisdreieck* (Three Rail Junction [a dreary railway stop between East and West Berlin]).

And he had begun another large novel, for which he used the working title "Kartoffelschalen" (Potato Peelings) but which was published in 1963 as *Hundejahre* (translated as *Dog Years*, 1965). Grass says that it was the growth of one episode from this novel into a separate novella of almost two hundred pages that helped him to solidify his concept and change "Kartoffelschalen" into *Hundejahre*. In 1961 the novella was published as *Katz und Maus* (translated as *Cat and Mouse*, 1963).

Katz und Maus is set in Danzig during the war. Some of its characters, such as Störtebeker, the leader of the Duster Gang, who returns in *örtlich betäubt* (1969; translated as *Local Anaesthetic*, 1970), also appear in *Die Blechtrommel* and *Hundejahre*, as well. Oskar also puts in several brief appearances in *Katz und Maus*.

Ostensibly, the main character of the novella is the gangling, devout Catholic Joachim Mahlke, who becomes a tank gunner, wins the Knight's Cross, suffers anxiety, and goes AWOL. And yet, interesting as he is, Mahlke may be only the foil to the real subject of the book, the narrator Pilenz. *He* is the character whose mind Grass seems to wish to explore, a mind which sees in Mahlke's life a whole succession of religious symbols. Pilenz draws the reader's attention, sometimes apparently inadvertently, to connections between Mahlke's life, these religious symbols, and historical events.

Pilenz is the archetypal true believer, a disciple in search of his Jesus, whom he finds in Mahlke. That Mahlke's father is dead becomes for Pilenz something akin to a virgin birth. Mahlke's gaunt face and long hair parted in the middle give him, for Pilenz, an "Erlösermiene" (saviour countenance); and when Mahlke plays the *Ave Maria* on a gramophone aboard the partially sunken minesweeper where the boys spend their summers, the sea, Pilenz claims, is stilled. When Mahlke returns from the war, Pilenz sees in his Knight's Cross a symbol of the ineffable Cross, and believes that the Virgin has made Mahlke bulletproof. On the day–which Pilenz goes to some trouble to point out is a Friday–

when Mahlke goes AWOL, Pilenz describes a crucifixion, complete with thorns in the form of unripe "Stachelbeeren" (thornberries [that is, gooseberries]) which cause Mahlke intense stomach pains when he eats them. Mahlke is entombed in the sunken minesweeper, but–unlike Jesus–he does not rise again.

Pilenz is ridden with guilt about the demise of his friend, and with good reason: Mahlke went down into the minesweeper as a result of Pilenz's lies. Mahlke intended to hide in the ship until dark and then have Pilenz row him across the harbor to what he thought was a Swedish vessel and escape from Germany, but Pilenz had a more mythical ending in mind. As Mahlke, with his cans of food, dove into the wreck to swim to his boyhood hideout in the radio shack, which is still above water, Pilenz, the Judas figure, hid the can opener; and he did not return that evening as arranged. It is possible that Mahlke swam away during the night, but it is more likely that, ill and weighted down with cans of food, he drowned before reaching the radio shack. In any case in his own mind Pilenz has contributed to Mahlke's death, and he seeks a resurrected Mahlke whom he can repay for his perfidy and venerate anew.

Pilenz's misguided religious discipleship stands as a symbol for the misguided political discipleship that saw in Hitler the military saviour of Germany. An important clue to this symbolic link between religious and political faith is found in Mahlke's large Adam's apple, the "mouse" of the book's title, which fascinates the "cat," Pilenz, who says that he is forced by the book's author to lead it to each locality "der ihn siegen oder verlieren sah" (which witnessed its victories and defeats). In addition to his odd use of military vocabulary in connection with the Adam's apple, Pilenz connects the growth of this symbol of guilt and of the Fall to the beginning of the war in 1939. Mahlke's Adam's apple, then, is a symbol of Germany's fall. Mahlke's Knight's Cross, normally a symbol of military victory, is here a symbol for Mahlke's and Germany's total defeat. There are two earlier Knight's Crosses in *Katz und Maus*, belonging to an air force pilot and a submariner who visit their old school and give speeches glorifying war. In 1944 Mahlke becomes a tank gunner. With this succession of Knight's Crosses, the stages of Germany's defeat are described: initial superiority in the air and under the sea changes to inferiority, just as

Germany's land arm—its armor—will be the next, and the last, to crumble.

In October 1959 Pilenz travels to a reunion of the order of the Knight's Cross in Regensburg. A military band of the Bundeswehr (West German armed forces) is playing, and during a break Pilenz asks the lieutenant guarding the door to have Mahlke paged. Mahlke does not appear, of course, but the point is clear: Pilenz and the others are true believers seeking a remnant of their Nazi past, celebrating a supposed glory which was in reality a calamity. That the event is supported by the Bundeswehr is a bitter indictment by Grass of postwar militarism, a suggestion that the Bundeswehr is a vehicle for those who seek a resurrection of the messianic glory of the Nazi era.

In 1961, the year his daughter Laura was born, Grass began to involve himself in politics by supporting Willy Brandt and the Social Democratic party (SPD). Over the next dozen years Grass became a major adviser, campaigner, and speechmaker for Brandt and the SPD.

Another of his short plays, *Die bösen Köche* (1961; translated as *The Wicked Cooks*, 1967), like the ballet *Fünf Köche* a spin-off of *Die Blechtrommel* and the idea of the black cook, was produced in 1961 in Berlin. But Grass concentrated most of his literary efforts during this period on *Hundejahre*, which finally grew to nearly seven hundred pages, about the same length as *Die Blechtrommel*. In *Hundejahre* Grass continues to develop the themes, localities, characters, and narrative techniques of *Die Blechtrommel* and *Katz und Maus;* the three books were republished in one volume in 1980 as the *Danziger Trilogie* (translated as *The Danzig Trilogy*, 1987). But *Hundejahre* deals even more specifically than the other two books with the role of the artist in understanding how the past informs the present and thereby determines the future.

In some ways *Hundejahre* demands more of the reader than *Die Blechtrommel*, which, for all its complexity, is unified by the mesmerizing mono- and megalomania of the narrator, Oskar. Here there are three narrators. Herr Brauxel, the owner of a former potash mine—in place of potash he now dredges up the past—who also spells his name Brauksel and Brauchsel, narrates the first of the three books of *Hundejahre*, which is titled "Frühschichten" (Morning Shifts); Book Two, written by Harry Liebenau to his cousin Tulla Prokriefke, is titled "Liebesbriefe" (Love Letters); and Book Three is titled "Materniaden"

(Materniads) after its narrator, the actor Walter Matern.

Brauxel is the leader of this collective of authors, who solicits and pays for Liebenau and Matern's contributions. Brauxel is also the subject of their writings, for he is in reality Eddi Amsel–alias Brauxel, alias Hermann Haseloff, alias Goldmäulchen (Goldmouth)–the childhood friend of Matern and childhood acquaintance of Liebenau. From the multiple narrative points of view a unified story emerges of two "blood brothers" growing up in and around Danzig and experiencing the rise of National Socialism, the war, and the war's aftermath.

Though they are "blood brothers," Eddi and Matern are also opposites: Eddi is sensitive and artistic, a fine singer, portly but skilled at games requiring intelligence and finesse; Matern is more emotional than rational, physically powerful, and prone to brutality. Eddi is half Jewish (his very assimilated, patriotic father dies at Verdun); Matern is Catholic, the descendant of a feared robber.

At first, Matern joins the other children in persecuting Eddi; as often as not, he is the one who calls Eddi "Itzig" (Sheeny). Later, Matern uses his fists to protect his weaker friend, whose artistic creations and Jewishness continue to evoke persecution. But after he joins the Nazi Sturmabteilung (Storm Troopers [SA]), Matern turns on Eddi again and, with eight other brown-shirted members of the SA, beats him up, knocking out all thirty-two of his teeth. Eddi disappears and has his teeth replaced with gold ones—hence the alias Goldmouth and the symbolic thirty-two chapters of his part of the novel. After the war he reappears under the alias Brauxel and engages Matern and Liebenau to help write his story.

It is the story of a gifted mimetic artist. Like Oskar, Eddi is precocious, and like Grass, he begins as a sculptor, making his first significant piece at age five. Eddi's unique gift lies in his ability to see the essences of phenomena and to recreate those essences in sculptures made of the flotsam he fishes out of the river Vistula, which serves as a symbol of the flow of time. His peculiar gift is only intensified by his persecution: even as he is beaten, his tears lend him "eine verschwommene und dennoch übergenaue Optik" (blurred and yet overly precise optical powers). Two or three days after each beating one of Eddi's sculptures, depicting the very essence of the brutality of his tormentors, appears in the landscape. It is because Matern sees a statue of

Grass speaking at an early meeting of the German Writers' Union (photograph by Isolde Ohlbaum, Munich)

himself, multiplied ninefold, striking out in blind rage–a premonition of his attack as an SA man–that he turns from beating Eddi to protecting him. Such is the power of Eddi's vision and of its expression in his art.

For the farmers in his village, who know little and care less about art, Eddi Amsel is a manufacturer of scarecrows. His creations are so startling that they have the power to frighten horses, cows, and even people–not to mention the birds, who fly up in a great cloud at his christening, covering the sun and casting a foreboding shadow upon him. One old crow is so scared that it falls to the ground dead. It is the frightening essence of the things Eddi sees that strikes terror into the hearts of birds, creatures highly sensitive to dangers in the atmosphere (hence their use in mines like Brauxel's).

Young Eddi decides to create something apparently contradictory: a giant bird that has the effect of scaring birds. Made with tar and feathers, it is so terrifying that even the farmers are not interested in purchasing it: hardened fishwives avoid it, and men allow their pipes to go out as they stare at it. Every misfortune which occurs in the village, including the death of Matern's grand-

mother, is blamed on "der große Vogel Piepmatz" (the great cuckoo bird), as one of the villagers calls it. Eventually, Eddi is told that he must destroy the bird and all of his collected raw materials. A great mound is heaped up by eager volunteers, the bird is placed on top, and the whole is ignited. As Eddi watches this ritualistic burning, taunted by cries of "Itzig!," his eyes narrow into "Sehschlitze" (seeing slits) and he has an apocalyptic vision of ritualistic tarrings and featherings, pogroms, autos-da-fé, and holocausts; and he sees that when he is older he will be forced to make an artistic copy of this vision in the form of another giant bird which will burn eternally, "apokalyptisch und dekorativ zugleich" (apocalyptic and decorative at the same time).

Eddi and Matern leave the village and go to high school in Danzig, where they encounter the Matzeraths, Bronski, and Pilenz, as well as Harry Liebenau and his cousin Tulla Prokriefke. Tulla, who also appears in *Katz und Maus*, is a reptilian female temptress, a black cook figure–a double of Luzie Rennwand of *Die Blechtrommel*.

The blood brothers also meet their teachers: the brutal Mallenbrand, a physical-education instructor, and the gentle Brunies, a humanist addicted to sweets who collects stones containing gleaming flakes of mica. While the boys and their teachers are on a trip to the school's retreat in the forest, some gypsies give Brunies a baby girl, whom he names Jenny and who grows up to become a ballerina.

The dramatis personae of *Hundejahre* is completed by the dogs. In the dark beginnings there was a Lithuanian she-wolf, whose grandson, the black dog Perkun, sired the bitch Senta, who belongs to Walter Matern's father. A dog named Pluto is brought from Stutthof, the site of the death camp, to service Senta; and Senta whelps six pups, among them Harras. Harras is purchased by Harry Liebenau's father to be a guard dog in his cabinet-making shop. Later, Harras will sire Prinz, Hitler's favorite black German shepherd.

The visionary Eddi, sensing a historical-mythological symbol, asks Liebenau's permission to sketch Harras, whom he calls Herr Pluto–the hound of hell–and with whom he uses–unheard-of for dogs–the polite form of German address. But Tulla soon chases Eddi away by calling him "Itzig." Thereafter Eddi begins to make brown-shirted sculptures of SA men with pig-bladder heads, pasted-on faces of pro-Nazi celebrities cut from magazines, and a clockwork mechanism which enables them to march and salute. The uniforms for the sculptures are obtained by Matern, who now joins the SA.

Matern is unhappy about Eddi's SA robot-sculptures, especially because of their pig-bladder heads, and accuses Eddi of representing his comrades as "Schweinehunde" (swinish sons-of-bitches). Eddi replies that he merely reproduces with artistic means what life shows him, and he begins to build a replica of Matern. The beating Eddi predicted when he made the scarecrow of Matern striking out ninefold in blind anger now occurs as Matern and eight of his SA friends beat Eddi up and roll him into a snowman in his garden.

Not far away, the sinister Tulla and eight of her followers are making a parallel attack on Jenny Brunies, who is also beaten and rolled into a snowman. Both emerge when a thaw sets in. Eddi leaves for Berlin with a forged passport in the name of Hermann Haseloff. There he becomes the chief of a propaganda company under Josef Goebbels and an important *maître de ballet* who entertains the troops and makes strange, humanoid machines in his basement studio.

After Oswald Brunies is denounced by Tulla and disappears into the death camp at Stutthof, Haseloff comes to Danzig in his black Mercedes and takes Jenny back to Berlin. He sends a truck for Brunies's furniture and collection of micaceous rocks, which are taken to the site of his future potash mine in Lower Saxony. Around the time of the Allied invasion of June 1944 he begins to produce a ballet on which he had been working since childhood, *Die Vogelscheuchen* (The Scarecrows).

The ballet employs the remnants of a troupe of midgets with whom Oskar Matzerath had entertained the troops in occupied France in *Die Blechtrommel*. As described by Jenny in her letters to Harry Liebenau, the ballet is a fantastic allegory of Germany, a microcosmic reproduction of all of Eddi Amsel's apocalyptic visions, with robot scarecrows, a sinister gardener, and a twelve-legged black dog. The ballet ends with the total destruction of the garden in which it is set. The only survivor is the evil old gardener, who is changed into a scarecrow as the curtain falls.

Two officials from the propaganda ministry who attend the dress rehearsal find the plot too sinister and lacking in the life-affirming element for the soldiers at the front. Haseloff is allowed to add a happy ending in which the scarecrows are bound, brought to the surface from their underground lair, and placed in the service of the now wonderfully virtuous gardener. Eddi's art has always truly reflected and predicted reality, however: as the troupe rehearses the new ending a bomb falls on the rehearsal room, smashing Jenny's feet, confirming the correctness of the original finale.

Germany, like the garden of the ballet, is eventually destroyed. At the end of the war Prinz, having deserted Hitler, swam across the river Elbe near Magdeburg "und suchte sich westlich des Flusses einen neuen Herrn" (and sought on the west side of the river a new master). Prinz finds Matern as he is being released from a British antifascist camp and follows him everywhere, despite Matern's attempts to frighten him away. The violent, irrational Matern, former SA thug turned belligerent antifascist, is the new master of the hound of hell, whom he calls Pluto. Matern goes around Germany as the personification of the denazification process, meting out absurd punishments to innocent people–he infects the daughters and wives of his old comrades with gonorrhea–while covering up the guilt in his own soul. But the artist

Eddi Amsel–Grass's alter ego–will not allow Matern or Germany to cover up the guilt. As Brauxel, using a variety of devices, he dredges up all of Matern's evil deeds.

One such device is the toy Erkenntnisbrille (perception eyeglasses) which Brauxel & Co. places on the market in 1955. Made with cheap plastic frames and simple flat lenses–to which are added mica chips from Brunies's Gypsy rocks, making them miniature crystal balls–these eyeglasses impart to the wearer something of the powers of Eddi Amsel: when young people from seven to twenty-one put them on they see what their parents were doing during the war. Unwittingly, Matern buys a pair of these glasses for Walli Sawatzki, the ten-year-old daughter of his SA friend Jochen Sawatzki. When Walli puts them on she sees her father and Matern, along with seven other SA men, beating out Eddi Amsel's teeth.

After completely encircling him with reminders of his past–artistic proofs of his essential identity with Hitler–Brauxel brings Matern to his mine for a final confrontation. Here he is bringing into existence scenes from his sketchbook, *Pandämonium* (the dwelling place of all the demons), which he keeps in his safe. Even the hardened, violent Matern is horrified by the bedlam: by the countless varieties and psychotic activities of the most bizarre scarecrows; by the monstrousness of the fiery gods Perkunos, Pikollos, Potrimpos; by the desensitized birds; by the hellish laughter and the gnashing teeth; by the scarecrow sporting events and religious services; and by the scarecrow emotions of hate, anger, and revenge. "Das ist die Hölle!" (This is hell!) Matern says over and over again. Not so, Brauxel maintains: "Der Orkus ist oben!" (Orcus [Hades] is above ground), and he reminds Matern of Eddi Amsel's motto: "Die Vogelscheuche wird nach dem Bild des Menschen erschaffen" (The scarecrow is created in the image of man).

For all its complexities *Hundejahre* has, at bottom a simple and clear meaning: in Eddi/Brauxel, Grass has created a visionary artist who, like Grass himself, re-creates in his art the hidden and hideous essence of evil. Brauxel's scarecrows are simply copies of the Schweinehunde he sees around him. And like Grass's works–the sales patterns and legal problems connected with Brauxel's magical eyeglasses are identical to those of *Die Blechtrommel* and *Katz und Maus*–Brauxel's works are shocking and horrifying because they reveal real abuses, not imaginary ones. Thus, his

fiery atomic gods are Old Prussian artistic models of atomic weapons, like the ballistic missiles to which men attach the names of gods: Poseidon, Atlas, Nike. Scarecrows populate the globe, from Africa to the atomic testing grounds of Nevada. And yet, as the day of nuclear wrath draws ever nearer, and Brauxel prepares to mirror the event in the great cuckoo bird, the artist focuses his visionary powers primarily on Germany, since it is the primary heir of the hound of hell, and secondarily on the Jews, the blood brothers to the Germans, fated by their common past to write together the history of the future. Near the end of *Hundejahre* the half-Jew Eddi says to the German Matern, "Aber unter allen Völkern, die als Vogelscheuchenarsenale dahinleben, ist es mit Vorzug das deutsche Volk, das, mehr noch als das jüdische, alles Zeug in sich hat, der Welt eines Tages die Urvogelscheuche zu schenken" (But among all peoples which exist as scarecrow arsenals, it is first and foremost the German people, which, even more than the Jewish, has within it all the right stuff to bestow one day the arch scarecrow upon the world).

There were several artistic spinoffs from *Hundejahre*, including a play, *Goldmäulchen*, which was produced in Munich in 1964; the dramatic "öffentliche Diskussion" (public discussion) from Book Three, which was broadcast in 1963 by Hessian Radio; and the ballet *Die Vogelscheuchen*, which was produced at the German Opera in Berlin in 1970. In 1965, the year his son Bruno was born, Grass was awarded an honorary doctorate from Kenyon College in Ohio and the Georg Büchner Prize. That year he made over fifty appearances on a campaign tour for the SPD, during which a firebomb charred his front door. Also that year he wrote his first full-scale drama, *Die Plebejer proben den Aufstand* (1966; translated as *The Plebeians Rehearse the Uprising*, 1966), which was produced in Berlin in 1966.

The play is the story of an East German dramaturge called "der Chef" (the chief)–a figure clearly based on Bertolt Brecht–who is rehearsing a class-conscious, revolutionary version of Shakespeare's *Coriolanus* when the workers' rebellion of 17 June 1953 erupts on the streets outside his theater. The workers appeal to the chief to lend his intellect, his language, and his credibility to their cause, but he refuses, too busy with his art to see the political reality outside. As the uprising fails due to its lack of leadership and is ultimately crushed by Soviet armor, the chief stands alone on the stage, echoes of the workers' words in his ears, and realizes that he has allowed the historic moment to slip away. He resigns and goes into retirement, where voices will haunt him for the rest of his life.

Die Plebejer proben den Aufstand is not an attack on Brecht, as some have supposed; it is a defense of Grass and his political activities, for which he has been widely criticized. Grass's thesis is that the purpose of engaged art is the discovery of truth so that one can then act in reality. To the extent that Brecht slipped into art for art's sake, this play implies, he missed an irretrievable opportunity to change the world.

The number and variety of Grass's activities in the late 1960s show that he was determined not to miss any such chances, artistic or political. In 1966 he traveled to the meeting of the Gruppe 47 in Princeton, to Czechoslovakia, and to Hungary. He campaigned during the state elections in Bavaria. *Katz und Maus* was filmed. With Elisabeth Borchers and Klaus Roehler he edited a poetry series called *Luchterhand Loseblatt Lyrik*. He continued to write and deliver political messages, a small portion of which were published in 1968 as *Über das Selbstverständliche: Reden, Aufsätze, offene Briefe, Kommentare* (On the Self-evident: Speeches, Essays, Open Letters, Commentaries). He began a column for the *Süddeutsche Zeitung* in Munich. A volume of poetry and drawings, *Ausgefragt* (Thoroughly Interrogated), appeared in 1967. That year Grass campaigned in Schleswig-Holstein and Berlin, traveled to Israel, carried on a correspondence with the Czech writer Pavel Kohout that was published in 1968 as *Briefe über die Grenze: Versuch eines Ost-West-Dialogs* (Letters across the Border: An Attempt at an East-West Dialogue), and won the Carl von Ossietzky Medal. The next year he won the Fontane Prize, gave a major speech at the Social Democratic party convention in Nuremberg, and worked on a citizens' committee in Berlin. All during these busy years the indefatigable Grass was preparing a new literary work which appeared in 1969 both as the novel *örtlich betäubt* and as a play, *Davor* (Before That; translated as *Max: A Play*, 1972).

Many critics were perplexed by Grass's new work. Appearing to deal almost entirely with contemporary problems, it did not seem to fit the pattern of the Danzig Trilogy, with its heavy emphasis upon the past. Yet, *örtlich betäubt* is a most logical extension of Grass's earlier work: it has its roots in the juvenile milieu of Oskar and the Duster Gang in prewar and wartime Danzig;

and, like the previous works, it follows its characters and the legacy of that violent period into the present.

The narrator, Eberhard Starusch, is identical with the boy nicknamed "Störtebeker," the leader of the Duster Gang in the Danzig Trilogy. Now a forty-year-old secondary-school teacher of history and German in Berlin, Starusch experiences something like déjà-vu as he and his students, who are the same age he was under Nazism, are confronted with a familiar set of problems: an ex-Nazi, Kurt Georg Kiesinger, is chancellor of West Germany; the country has rearmed; its major ally, the United States, is engaged in what the students consider an unjust, genocidal war of aggression in Southeast Asia. There is something rotten in the state of affairs.

And there is literally something rotten in Starusch: his carious teeth require extensive dental work. Grass had used teeth and tooth decay before as symbols of hidden moral or social putrescence: Pilenz is suffering from a toothache on the first pages of *Katz und Maus;* Matern knocks out all of Eddi Amsel's teeth; Brauxel opens a restaurant called "Die Leichenhalle" (The Morgue), at which tooth pudding is served to a shocked and nauseated Matern. And a poem in *Gleisdreieck* associates the putrescence which is only temporarily masked by toothpaste with the horrible gold teeth of the holocaust: to get rid of the decay lingering from the past, the poem concludes, we must open our mouths.

The question for the characters in *örtlich betäubt* is what to do about present and future decay. Should the treatment of society's ills be "radical" or "moderate"? Should all the teeth be pulled? Should metaphorical bulldozers (which Starusch imagines on the television screen in the dentist's office) be set in motion to clear the world of its corrupt systems? Or should frustration be resisted and more moderate methods of fighting dental and societal decay be used? The dentist argues for moderation and prophylaxis. Ironically, however, he is not above threatening Starusch with pain when Starusch defends violent radicalism. The spineless Starusch immediately recants, for he is really only a verbal anarchist indulging in middle-aged fantasies.

The issue becomes acute, however, when Philipp Scherbaum, Starusch's most gifted student, decides to protest the use of napalm in Vietnam by burning his beloved dachshund Max in front of the Hotel Kempinski on Berlin's Kurfürstendamm. Scherbaum's radical girlfriend Vero

Grass in the mid 1960s (photograph by Fred Stein)

Lewand, a disciple of Mao and Che Guevara–and a reincarnation of Tulla Prokriefke, who helped Matern kill a dog in *Hundejahre*–urges him to go ahead with the immolation.

The teacher is not much help. Like Pilenz, he feels frustrated and impotent; he would like to relive his own exciting past vicariously through Philipp's deed. He is even tempted by his fiancée Irmgard Seifert, another guilt-ridden teacher at the school, to see Philipp as a messiah. On the other hand, he knows better. He is a mature, rational man. He realizes that Philipp is no messiah, that Irmgard is a religious fanatic, and that violence will reap violence. He may even get into trouble himself if his student goes through with the plan. So he lectures Philipp, graphically describing how he will be beaten to death by the matrons eating pastry at Kempinski's when they see him set fire to the dog. Rather than deterring him, however, this lecture convinces Philipp that he is right: people must be shocked into seeing what a violent world they have created.

The solution comes from an unexpected quarter: from history, from the era of the Duster Gang, from the history teacher's own generation. In a trade-union newspaper, seventeen-year-old Philipp Scherbaum discovers an account of seventeen-year-old Helmuth Hübener, the leader of a nonviolent resistance group, who composed and distributed antifascist leaflets and was beheaded by the Nazis in 1942. Hübener's photo soon hangs on Philipp's wall, as that of Che Guevara hangs on Vero's. Now it is Philipp who lectures his history teacher about how Hübener did not waste his time demolishing churches like the Duster Gang, could take stenography, and even knew Morse code. Starusch vaguely recalls once reading something about Hübener, and he is stricken with professional guilt for not teaching his students about Hübener's group instead of regaling them with stories about his own glory days with the Duster Gang.

Later, when the teacher invites him to an antiwar demonstration, Philipp declines because he has a shorthand class. He takes over the editorship of the school paper, which he had previously refused to do, and renames it *Morsezeichen* (Morse Code). His first article will deal with Helmuth Hübener's resistance group and contrast the activities of Kiesinger and Hübener in 1942. He has given up the idea of burning Max and is having his teeth fixed.

Philipp Scherbaum is Grass's new contemporary hero. This hero looks the present clearly in the face. He does not mythologize; he does not seek to be or to follow a messiah; and he rejects easy, violent solutions, patterning his actions after Hübener, who patiently sought to educate and enlighten the German people about Hitler. His heraldic animal could be the snail: representing the slow, patient progress of democracy, freedom, and reason, this animal is Grass's chosen symbol for himself and for his political models.

From the spring to the fall of 1969 Grass participated in a campaign tour for the SPD throughout the Federal Republic, involving almost two hundred appearances and one hundred speeches. An account of this campaign; of Grass's involvement with the archetypal snail Willy Brandt, the heir of the prototypal snail August Bebel, founder of the SPD; of trips to Yugoslavia, France, and Czechoslovakia; of Grass's participation in the Lutheran Church Conference in Stuttgart; and of Brandt's election as chancellor in September 1969 forms the basis for *Aus dem Tagebuch einer Schnecke* (1972; translated as *From the Diary of a Snail*, 1973).

Aus dem Tagebuch einer Schnecke is addressed to Grass's children as an object lesson in history and its application to modern problems. At the beginning of the book Grass tells the twins Franz and Raoul, eleven, Laura, eight, and Bruno, four, that when he observed the election of Gustav Heinemann as federal president in March 1969 he narrowed his eyes into Sehschlitze and saw a giant snail creeping slowly through the hall. She (in German snails are feminine) hesitated, with her feelers out, not wishing to arrive at her goal, not wishing to win. But when Grass promised her a new goal, when he baited her with slices of the future, she crossed the finish line–Heinemann won by a narrow margin–and crept toward the victory of Brandt in September.

The rigors of the campaign include daily confrontations with radical young people, "zugutbehauste Söhne, die vom Proletariat wie von einer Marienerscheinung schwärmen ... neuerdings berufsmäßige Gottesstreiter, die Christi Blut in hegelförmige Flaschen abfüllen" (too-well-housed sons who rave about the proletariat like it was a manifestation of the Virgin Mary ... lately, professional gladiators for God, who pour the blood of Christ into Hegel-shaped bottles). Grass encounters some of these political mystics at the Lutheran Church Conference, where he reads to them about Philipp Scherbaum wanting to burn his dachshund. Their counterpart from an earlier generation is August, a former SS man who takes the microphone at the conference, salutes his old SS comrades, and drinks a flask of potassium cyanide. Eventually Grass visits August's family, hoping to understand his motivation.

As Grass prepares a speech on Albrecht Dürer's engraving "Melencolia I," which he has been invited by the City of Nuremberg to give in 1971 for the celebration of the five-hundredth anniversary of Dürer's birth, he recounts a fictional narrative about Hermann Ott, a teacher in a Jewish school in prewar Danzig and collector of snails, who is nicknamed "Zweifel" (Doubt) because of his disposition to question commonly accepted "facts." After the destruction of the Danzig synagogue Ott flees from Danzig and takes refuge in occupied Poland in the dank cellar of a rural house owned by a sadistic bicycle repairman named Stoma. Stoma's daughter Elisabeth suffers from aphasia brought on by severe melancholy stemming from the death of her child, who was crushed beneath the wheels of a military vehicle during the invasion in September 1939.

Ott's snails, symbols of healing and progress, gradually help erase the psychological damage of the war. A special purple snail which Elisabeth finds in a graveyard magically draws out her melancholy, providing a model for the healing of an entire society, which is the subject of Grass's Dürer speech. Titled "Vom Stillstand im Fortschritt, Variationen zu Albrecht Dürers Kupferstich 'Melencolia I' " (On Standing Still in Progress, Variations on Albrecht Dürer's Etching "Melencolia I"), the speech forms the book's final chapter. It is a brilliant summary of Grass's engagement with political problems and of the writing of his snail diary; an imaginative, often fantastic exploration of the psychosocial roots of depression in suburban housewives and assembly-line workers; and an analysis of the dark side of utopian expectations, whether in the planned societies of the Eastern bloc or in the artificial "say-cheese!" smiles of consumerism and "the American way of life." It is an inventory of the legacies of the black cook, of modern malaises and their historical roots, and it prescribes the snail of patient progress as a cure.

Most of *Aus dem Tagebuch einer Schnecke* was written during 1969; only a few episodes at the end date from 1970 and 1971, an indication that Grass delayed its publication to coincide with the federal elections in 1972. Thus, a literary account of one election campaign became a political tool released just in time to aid in the next.

Grass made about 130 appearances during the 1972 campaign. The elections strengthened the mandate for Brandt and his policies, including improved relations with the Communist bloc. Grass accompanied Brandt on his trips in 1970 to East Germany and to Poland–where Brandt knelt before the Warsaw memorial to the victims of Nazism–as well as to Israel and the United States in 1973.

Yet, Grass was prepared to criticize Brandt and the SPD, as he had earlier when they agreed to form the "Grand Coalition" with Kiesinger as chancellor. When Grass perceives present parallels to past errors, he speaks out–even when his evidence may be too subtle to convince many others, and even when speaking out may offend his friends and closest allies. A case in point occurred in 1972 when Heinar Kipphardt produced in Munich a play by Wolf Biermann on the subject of dragon slaying. The program, which was never released, included pictures of prominent civic leaders. For Grass, the implication was clear: here were dragons that needed to be slain–a veiled call for political assassination. Grass harshly lectured Kipphardt in his column in the *Süddeutsche Zeitung*. The ensuing imbroglio resulted in Kipphardt being replaced as dramaturge, but it also made enemies for Grass on the left–especially among the literati and intelligent-

Dust jacket for Grass's 1969 novel about dentistry and student activism

sia, many of whom had assumed that the stalwart antifascist Grass was their natural ally.

The passage of time has demonstrated that Grass's fears of the revival of something like a Duster Gang of the left may have been well founded. German terrorist groups such as that of Andreas Baader and Ulrike Meinhof began to arise in the early 1970s, in precisely those quarters Grass had predicted: among disenchanted utopian leftists, many of them women, who were impatient with the snail's pace of progress, wanted a new religion of revolution, and felt that humanistic ends justified violent means. While other antifascist authors, such as Nobel laureate Heinrich Böll, were flirting with the allure of violent revolution–Böll's heroes, particularly his female heroes (one of whom, Katharina Blum in *Die verlorene Ehre der Katharina Blum* [1974, translated as *The Lost Honor of Katharina Blum*, 1975], is directly based on Meinhof), are prone to solve their problems with firearms–Grass makes the antifascist Walter Matern the heir of Hitler's dog; an-

alyzes the frustration of middle-aged intellectuals in Eberhard Starusch and the need to find a new messiah and join a crusade in Pilenz, Vero Lewand, and Irmgard Seifert; suggests the alternative nonviolent model of Helmuth Hübener; and reemphasizes in *Aus dem Tagebuch einer Schnecke* his belief in the essential identity and futility of all violent behavior, whether of the left or of the right.

In the middle of his snail diary the campaign-weary Grass inserted four wistful lines saying that someday he would like to rest from his political travails for a while and write about something he really enjoys: "Ich will ein erzählendes Kochbuch schreiben" (I want to write a narrating cookbook). And though he kept up his busy schedule even after the 1972 elections–participating in regional campaigns; making speeches and writing political essays; taking trips to the Soviet Union, Greece, France, Italy, Israel, the United States, Canada, Poland, India, Asia, and Africa; founding with Böll and Carola Stern the journal *L'76 Demokratie und Sozialismus: Politische und Literarische Beiträge* (L'76 Democracy and Socialism: Political and Literary Contributions) as well as, later, the publishing firm L'80 (thereafter the journal was also called *L'80*); supervising the publication of collected editions of his poems, his plays, and a volume of his speeches and essays titled *Der Bürger und seine Stimme* (The Citizen and His Voice, 1974); receiving an honorary doctorate from Harvard in 1976; and working to develop with Luchterhand publishers a model agreement to provide authors with greatly increased rights of participation in important publication decisions–Grass did in fact begin to turn away somewhat from the crush of everyday political affairs to write his cookbook. It was well under way in 1974 when Brandt resigned as chancellor following the revelation that his assistant, Günther Guillaume, was an East German spy. Saddened but more determined than ever, Grass proclaimed that the snail had left the people behind and they must work harder to catch up to her.

The cookbook appeared in 1977 as *Der Butt* (translated as *The Flounder*, 1978). At seven hundred pages, almost the same length as *Die Blechtrommel* and *Hundejahre*, it has an even more complex narrative fabric and an even wider epic scope than the earlier books. Oskar puts in a token appearance, and there are many eyeglasses–reminiscent of Brauxel's Erkenntnisbrille–belonging to the most visionary characters. The narrator is a writer living in Berlin.

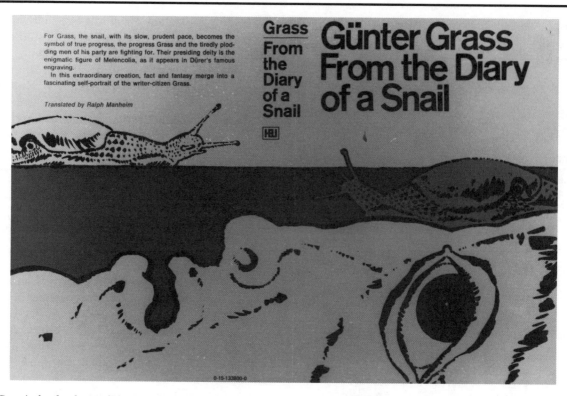

For Grass, the snail, with its slow, prudent pace, becomes the symbol of true progress, the progress Grass and the tiredly plodding men of his party are fighting for. Their presiding deity is the enigmatic figure of Melencolia, as it appears in Dürer's famous engraving.

In this extraordinary creation, fact and fantasy merge into a fascinating self-portrait of the writer-citizen Grass.

Translated by Ralph Manheim

Grass From the Diary of a Snail

Günter Grass From the Diary of a Snail

Dust jacket for the English translation of Grass's account of his participation in the 1969 West German election campaign

A study in yin and yang, *Der Butt* begins with a double impregnation: the narrator physically impregnates his wife Ilsebill, who emotionally impregnates him. Both pregnancies, as well as the parallel development of world history from the stone age to the 1970s, proceed to term in the book's nine sections, which are labeled months. At the end of the ninth month, as history gives birth to the modern world and Ilsebill bears a child–clearly based on Grass's daughter Helena, who was born in 1974 and to whom *Der Butt* is dedicated–the narrator brings forth his emotional "headbirth": the novel itself and its central insight, an extrapolative prediction from the history of male dominance that the future of life on Earth rests with the female.

One strand of the narrative deals with previous embodiments of the narrator and his women, the cooks, from neolithic times to the present. Another strand involves the flounder: he is the fish of the Grimms' fairy tale "Vom Fischer un syner Fru" (The Fisherman and His Wife). A reification of the Weltgeist (world spirit), the flounder advises the male narrator in his various incarnations down through the centuries until, in modern times, it changes sides and begins to advise the women, who place the flounder on trial for his male chauvinist crimes against humanity. A

third important strand of narration, then, involves the empaneling of a feminist tribunal, or "feminal," and the interrogation of the fish.

His dual role as advisor, like the double impregnation, has its analog in what Grass claims were dual versions of the Grimms' fairy tale: the familiar one, in which the insatiably ambitious and acquisitive person is a woman, and another in which it is a man. The latter version was destroyed by the Brothers Grimm, who feared that it might undermine the prevailing pattern of male dominance.

The first cook is Aua, who has three breasts. Actually, all women in the tribe in that age were named Aua and had three breasts. That modern mortals have only two breasts is a symbol of the fact that some third dimension, perhaps a third political possibility, is missing. In fact, the narrator maintains, some feminists, like the mythical Amazons, have only one breast. The Auas amply nurse, nourish, and nurture the tribe, including the adult males, all of whom are named Edek. Thus, their plethora of breasts, which "hügelten landschaftlich" (rose as hills in the landscape), is a symbol of their identity with the earth mother.

Aua has stolen fire from the sky wolf (an adaptation of South American Indian myths), but she uses the fire only for cooking. It is the talking fish–the masculine principle–caught by Edek, the narrator, which suggests that the cooking fires can be used also for smelting metals for weapons. These stone-age hunters already have stone weapons, but whenever they encounter the men of another tribe they hastily confer with Aua, as the other men confer with their Eua or Eia, and hostilities cease as dinner invitations are exchanged.

When the women discover that the men have perverted the cooking fire, they perform a ritual dance around an image of the three-breasted goddess and then throw the new metal weapons into the river. But it is a woman–Mestwina, the tenth-century incarnation of Aua–who commits the first murder: she kills Bishop Adalbert of Prague with a cast-iron cooking spoon. Thus, the metallic, life-taking male principle infringes the organic, life-giving female principle, even in the realm of nourishment. The cooks introduce the potato to Prussia under Friedrich II, thus staving off hunger, and feed poisonous mushrooms to French occupation troops under Napoleon. They smother a lover in bed during the Reformation and feed Jews and other prisoners in the death camp at Stutthof during the Third Reich.

But the bankruptcy of the male principle is at hand: as predicted in the destroyed version of the fairy tale, after man has built bridges over the widest rivers and towers which reach to the clouds, has learned to fly, and wants to journey to the distant stars, all his efforts will collapse as old Mother Earth shakes off his dominion. Even the flounder is disgusted and deserts his sons, who have used their knowledge and power only to create war, misery, and increased hunger.

But who will take over history from the men? It will certainly not be those women who merely imitate men, *Der Butt* maintains. Such a scenario is graphically anticipated in the eighth month, subtitled "Vatertag" (Father's Day). Here the cook is Sibylle Miehlau, the granddaughter of Lena Stubbe, the heroic old Social Democrat who fed the prisoners at Stutthof and was beaten to death while trying to prevent the theft of her supplies. Sibylle is the narrator's former fiancée and the mother of his child; but she has given the child to her mother to raise, has become a lesbian, and has masculinized her name to Billy. On Ascension Day she goes to the lake for a picnic with three other women, Fränki, Siggi, and Mäxchen; all of them are dressed in men's cloth-ing. Fränki, Siggi, and Mäxchen rape Billy with a dildo, an act linked to Ascension Day by being portrayed as a grotesque little crucifixion. A motorcycle gang in black leather observes this atrocity from their metallic cycles. When, newly awakened to her woman- and motherhood, Billy runs away from her "friends" crying "Ich bin eine Frau, eine Frau, eine Frau!" (I am a woman, a woman, a woman!), the seven bikers gang-rape her and then run their heavy machines repeatedly over her body, which is reduced to a pulp.

This episode, the starkest and most shocking thing Grass has ever written, closely parallels the scene in *Hundejahre* where Eddi and Jenny are attacked by the male and female personifications of evil. It demonstrates the bankruptcy of the male principle and the extent to which the male has corrupted the female principle. But it also suggests that in extremis, when the absurdity of male and one-breasted Amazonian violence is most clearly revealed, the fundamental three-breasted female impulse to feed and nurture, inherited by Sibylle from her grandmother Lena Stubbe and from all the cooks back to Aua, may emerge again. If it could take control of history it could provide the third possibility.

It will be opposed by violent women such as the minority on the feminal who vote for the death penalty for the flounder and then throw stones at the others as they return the fish to the sea. For these female terrorists history has simply gone back to the stone age, with masculinized women using stone weapons to take life. For the life-giving women like Maria Kuczorra, the last cook in *Der Butt*, whose husband is shot down by troops in front of the Lenin shipyards in Gdansk during the 1970 strikes over food prices, history moves ahead, not backward; it does not leap to utopia but progresses slowly and surely with the help of a new flounder, a new Zeitgeist.

At the end of the novel the narrator visits Maria in Gdansk. They walk along the beach; have sex, which she initiates; and eat the food she has cooked. Then she runs into the sea and calls out a Kashubian word, loudly, three times, whereupon a new flounder leaps into her arms and speaks with her for a considerable time. The narrator sits on the beach, "fallen out of history," as he describes himself. When she returns she is neither Maria, though she appears to be, nor any of the other earlier cooks, whom she resembles, but Ilsebill. The ending, like that of *Die Blechtrommel,* points to the future. Oskar feared that he would always have the black cook, the personification of the evil principle, coming after him. Here, the male narrator runs after a white cook, the personification of the nourishing principle, who has broken out of the cycle of war and starvation and begun to make the future history of the world a history of peace and plenty.

Reception of *Der Butt* was anything but unanimous or blasé. Many were shocked by such graphic treatment of violence, scatology, and sex. And though it is clearly much more critical of men than of women, many feminists were offended by it. Yet, the novel was so widely acclaimed and sold so many copies that Grass was able in 1978 to endow a rich literary award in the name of his admired "teacher" Alfred Döblin which is administered by the Berlin Academy of Art.

This fictional account of the battle of the sexes was in part suggested by real life: during the writing of *Der Butt* Grass's marriage had been crumbling, and in 1978 it ended in divorce. The next year he married the Berlin organist Ute Ehrhardt, the model for Ulla Witzlaff in the novel. With her he made a trip through Asia which provided the basis for a shorter diary on the model of *Aus dem Tagebuch einer Schnecke* titled *Kopfgeburten oder Die Deutschen sterben aus* (1980; translated as *Headbirths; or, The Germans Are Dying Out*, 1982).

In the meantime he had won several important literary prizes, including the International Mondello Prize in 1977 and the Viareggio Prize in 1978, and had worked on a film version of *Die Blechtrommel;* preparing to film on location necessitated some of the trips to Gdansk fictionalized in *Der Butt.* The director, Volker Schlöndorff, also accompanied the Grasses to the Orient. When the film appeared in 1979 it won the Golden Palm at Cannes.

In 1979 Grass published *Das Treffen in Telgte* (translated as *The Meeting at Telgte*, 1981) as a tribute to Hans Werner Richter and the Gruppe 47. Set in the last full year of the Thirty Years' War, three hundred years before the founding of the Gruppe 47, *Das Treffen in Telgte* is a fictional account of a meeting of war-weary German baroque poets at an inn outside the small Westphalian town of Telgte. Grass had carefully researched this era and these poets for the corresponding section of *Der Butt.* Now he projects onto their time the analogous concerns of the postwar era, including the political factionalism and generational conflicts that racked the Gruppe 47. Simon Dach is the wise, long-suffering analog of

Hans Werner Richter; but who, if anyone, is Günter Grass cannot be answered with certainty: the book is not simply a roman à clef. One poet, however, does stand out from all the rest because of his breaking of taboos, his involvement in practical political matters, and his advising of heads of state: the swashbuckling Grimmelshausen, later to become the author of *Der abenteuerliche Simplicissimus Teutsch* (1669; translated as *The Adventurous Simplicissimus*, 1912), the first great German novel and, in part, a remarkable fictional history of the Thirty Years' War, which is certainly a fitting analogy to Grass's Danzig novels.

Kopfgeburten deals with the problems of world hunger and overpopulation. To accompany him and Ute on their journey to the Orient Grass creates a fictional couple, Harm and Dörte Peters, teachers in Itzehoe, a town north of Hamburg near which Grass's second home at Wewelsfleth is located. In the narrative, which is written in the style of a film script for Schlöndorff, Harm and Dörte try to decide whether to have a child. The overpopulation and the squalor of slums in the Asian countries argue against it. Primitive rituals associated with various mother goddesses, however, awaken deep maternal instincts in Dörte, and she throws her birth control pills into the toilet. The matter is complicated by the xenophobic political speeches of the Bavarian Christian Socialist leader Franz Josef Strauss, who warns that the Germans are dying out, that Turks and other foreigners are taking over the country, and that Germans must increase their birthrate.

In Shanghai Grass tries to imagine what it would be like if the first and third worlds were reversed: what if there were a billion Germans? How does German efficiency compare with Chinese efficiency? Could the developed nations feed people as efficiently as they can kill them? The upshot of Grass's musings is that people in the advanced countries can transcend nationalism and begin to exist on a global scale for the first time. They can turn from war and harness their efficiency as well as their maternal instincts to help fight world hunger. They can stop worrying about dying out and begin to prevent dying. They can stop worrying about having a child and begin to worry about children.

The last paragraph of the book is a symbolic cinematographic summary of the whole argument: back home in Germany, as they drive along in their Volkswagen, Harm and Dörte almost hit a small Turkish boy who runs in front

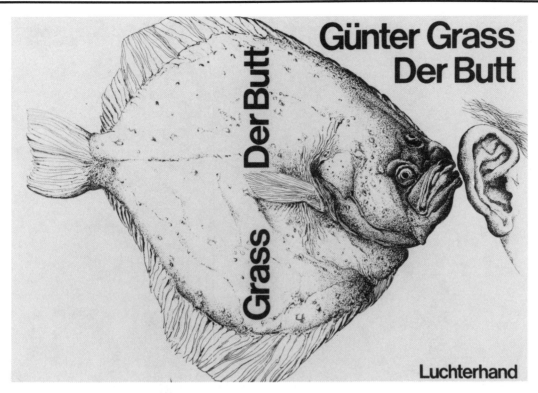

Dust jacket with drawing by Grass for his 1977 "cookbook" which recounts the history of male domination and female heroism

of their car. They stop in time, and the boy and his friends–other Turkish boys–celebrate his survival. Then, in a visionary scene, happy Indian, Chinese, and African children stream out from neighboring streets and yards; they increase and become numberless. They all celebrate with the little Turk whose life has been spared. As the children cheerfully knock on the VW, the childless couple inside "does not know what to say in German"; and the very language Grass uses to describe their speechlessness is pidginized, pulled away from standard German in the direction of that of the children: "und nicht weiß, was sagen auf deutsch."

Grass helped organize meetings of writers from East and West in East Berlin in 1981, The Hague in 1982, and West Berlin in 1983 to promote the cause of peace; made a fact-finding trip to Nicaragua in 1982; participated in 1983 in a conference on the future of democratic socialism; and made a speech at the Social Democratic admonitory commemoration of the fiftieth anniversary of Hitler's rise to power on 30 January 1933. He published the collection *Aufsätze zur Literatur* (Essays on Literature, 1980); two large volumes of graphic art accompanied by selected passages from his writings, *Zeichnen und Schreiben* (1982, 1984; translated as *Drawings & Words Nine-*

teen Fifty-four to Nineteen Seventy-seven, 1983, and *Etchings & Words Nineteen Seventy-two to Nineteen Eighty-two*, 1985); a volume of etchings and poems, *Ach Butt, dein Märchen geht böse aus* (Alas, Flounder, Your Fairy Tale Has An Unhappy Ending, 1983); and a volume of political rebuttals, *Widerstand lernen* (Learn to Resist, 1984). His graphic art was exhibited in well over one hundred galleries worldwide. In Rome in 1982 he was awarded the Antonio Feltrinelli Prize, at the equivalent of approximately eighty-five thousand dollars one of the most richly endowed cultural awards after the Nobel Prize. In 1983 he was elected president of the Berlin Academy of Arts.

In his acceptance speech for the Feltrinelli Prize, "Die Vernichtung der Menschheit hat begonnen" (The Annihilation of Humanity Has Begun), Grass says that literature, even more than the other arts, has always had one reliable ally: the future. Even though Brecht and Döblin were persecuted by Nazism and the Soviet writers Isaac Babel and Ossip Mandelstam by Stalinism, their works outlived these movements; time was on their side. Now, Grass says, the future is not so secure and cannot be taken for granted in the book which he is writing.

The book referred to in this speech appeared in 1986 under the title *Die Rättin* (The She-

Dust Jacket illustrated by Grass for his 1979 novel about a gathering of German poets during the Thirty Years' War

Rat; translated as *The Rat*, 1987). It is informed with an air of eschatology but also with irony and self-parody, in part because it is something of a swan song for Grass as he approaches age sixty. Characters from his previous works are here reunited and come full circle to their beginnings.

Oskar reappears in time for his sixtieth birthday. "Ist abermals die Zeit für ihn reif ?" (Is the time ripe for him once more?), asks the narrator, who is nearly identical with Grass. Oskar Matzerath-Bronski, as he now signs his name, is a film (and erstwhile pornographic video) producer, whom the narrator engages to make a silent movie about acid rain and the death of the forests. For this film Oskar decides on a parody of the Walt Disney style which, with its scarecrows, is reminiscent of Eddi Amsel. He brings together all the figures from the fairy tales to fight to save the forest from the monied interests, in league with corrupt government officials, who are destroying it.

Meanwhile, Oskar's grandmother Anna Koljaiczek, still alive on her farm near Gdansk, is preparing to celebrate her 107th birthday. She invites the far-flung family, all of them characters from earlier novels, to attend. Since it is his gift

to foresee the future (his firm is called Postfuturum), Oskar makes a video of the event before he leaves Düsseldorf. He loads his Mercedes with this prophetic video and other gifts, including some plastic Smurfs, and sets out for Poland.

Interwoven with these strands of narrative is an account of the adventures of five women, including the narrator's wife Damroka–an organist, like Ute Grass–on a boat named *Die Neue Ilsebill* (The New Ilsebill). They set out on a scientific expedition into the Baltic to study the link between pollution and an explosion in the population of jellyfish. Along the way, however, Damroka, their captain, secretly consults with the flounder and is led by him to Vineta, the site of a legendary sunken city off the mouth of the Vistula which was once ruled by women.

The main story concerns the she-rat of the title, which the narrator asks for and receives as a Christmas gift; this incident is a barb aimed at the conservative Bavarian politician Franz Josef Strauss, who had called writers like Grass "Ratten und Schmeißfliegen" (rats and blowflies). The narrator recalls that in Grass's early play *Hochwasser* two speaking rats had commented on human ca-

Grass in 1982 (Werek–Ullstein Bilderdienst)

lamity; and now the she-rat does the same. While the narrator circles the earth in a space capsule, the she-rat stands on a pile of human refuse and gives a nightmarish speech modeled on Jean Paul's "Rede des toten Christus vom Weltgebaüde herab, daß kein Gott sei" (Speech of the Dead Christ from the Top-of-the-World-Building, That There Is No God) in his novel *Siebenkäs* (1796-1797). She says that the human race is gone; only its refuse survives. As the she-rat describes the end of mankind–"Ultimo," as she calls it–the narrator sees the events happening before him on his video screen.

The she-rat begins her account with the Flood, the first global calamity. Noah refused to take rats on board his ark, so the rats saved themselves by digging deep tunnels and air chambers, stocking them with food, plugging them with the living bodies of elderly rats, and waiting for the flood waters to subside. All their survival instincts and heightened powers of perception stem from this time, she says; hence rats unerringly know when to leave a doomed ship. Now, sensing that the entire earth is doomed again, the rats are digging deep underground shelters. Some have begun to make themselves immune to

radioactivity by tunneling under nuclear reactors and into radioactive waste.

The rats, like the dying trees in the forest, have tried to warn the humans that their world is heading for disaster. The rats have ventured forth in large numbers, as have other creatures such as the jellyfish, in mute protest demonstrations, yet humans have failed to realize what they are trying to say. There are cultural warning signs of imminent collapse, such as the phenomenon of punkers who adopt pet rats and dye them zinc green to match their own dyed hair. These children are crying out as well, but no one understands them, either.

The she-rat claims that rats eventually gnawed their way into the giant computers in the East and the West into which doomsday was programmed. Or perhaps it was mice, she concedes. At any rate, it was the humans who had programmed the computers and the missiles, euphemistically called "Peacemakers" and "Friends of the People." Any small, unexpected problem could have set them off.

Ultimo occurs at noon on a Sunday, just as the women on *The New Ilsebill* prepare to descend into the underwater city and just as Oskar's video reaches its end, where it shows the birthday guests watching the video of the birthday party, at which the guests are watching a video of the party. The women and the wooden superstructure of their boat are vaporized; the steel hull drifts aimlessly across the Baltic. Oskar seeks refuge under the skirts of his grandmother, but he and the other birthday guests are desiccated, reduced to shriveled gnomes by the enhanced radiation of the low-blast neutron weapons with which Gdansk is hit. Only the already shriveled 107-year-old Anna Koljaiczek survives, blinded by the flash of the bomb and kept alive on a puree of young rat by the rats, who are now zinc green from the radiation.

When she eventually dies, her mummy and that of Oskar–which is found under her skirts and is taken for that of a newborn–are not eaten as others are but are moved into Gdansk and placed on the altar of St. Mary's church. Here Anna becomes a kind of fertility goddess to the hungry rats, a grotesque new Virgin with Oskar as the Child, the role he played in this very church with the Dusters. The Smurfs are assembled about her in a kind of crèche scene. When one of her fingers breaks off, it seems to point at a group of Smurfs who are tilling the soil. Taking this as a sign, the rats begin to plant and harvest. They subdue mutant pests such as mammalian blowflies and flying snails, and soon they live in abundance.

Shortly before they were vaporized, the five women docked *The New Ilsebill* at Visby, Sweden, and went ashore for the afternoon. There they joined a group protesting the use of animals in medical research. They followed the crowd to a building on the outskirts of town. Rocks were thrown–some of these people are the same violent women who stoned the members of the feminal who acquitted the flounder–and glass was shattered. The women returned to their boat and cast off in haste before the police arrived.

Now, from his vantage point in orbit, the narrator watches the hulk of *The New Ilsebill* moving under its own power into the harbor of Gdansk, again called Danzig. When it docks, human-rats or rat-humans, the products of gene manipulations in the laboratory at Visby who have stowed away on the boat, emerge. They call themselves Manippels, but they are known to the rats as Watsoncricks after the discoverers of DNA. They are blond, blue-eyed dwarves with the heads of rats and three fingers on each hand like the Smurfs, whose language they speak. The rats suspect that they have some swine genes as well, for their tails are those of pigs. Like Eddi Amsel's scarecrows, these monsters retrace the stages of human development: they reinvent fire, drink beer, and march in formation. Naturally, these new evil humanoids exploit the rats, who are finally forced to eliminate them. Thus, the last monstrous creation of the human race is eradicated, the she-rat says.

Like Jean Paul's story, in the end the tale of the she-rat is only a dream. Oskar returns safely from Gdansk, having suffered nothing worse than a minor traffic accident and an attack of prostatism. Damroka writes about an awful American horror film she saw in Visby about half human-half animal monsters, and then returns home, complaining about the women's inability to get along with each other. Everyone, including Volker Schlöndorff, attends Oskar's sixtieth birthday party. Oskar has begun to make the story of the rat-humans into a film titled *Davor und Danach* (Before That and After That), which will end with the total destruction (by monstrous machines out of *Star Wars*) of the forest and the ecological "romantics" who try to save it; but the film is postponed. Humanity has a second chance. It was all just a bad dream. Or was it?

In the end the narrator dreams that there may be a glimmer of hope that humans can act humanely. Though the rats laugh at this hope, he perseveres: just assuming that we humans did still exist, he says, "diesmal wollen wir füreinander und außerdem friedfertig, hörst du, in Liebe und sanft, wie wir geschaffen sind von Natur" (this time we want to be for each other and peace-loving besides, do you hear, loving and gentle, as we are created by nature). "Ein schöner Traum" (a beautiful dream), replies the she-rat before she disappears.

For over three decades Grass has portrayed with remarkable consistency what he sees as the most dangerous insanities of the modern age and has synthesized some reasonable prescriptions for a sane and peaceful world. He knows that these prescriptions are probably futile; he knows that he is a dreamer; he knows that the chances for doomsday are increasing. He has seen his snails stopped in their tracks. Perhaps there will be no future. But he does not give up. He continues to oppose evil by portraying it as evil; his predictions of calamity attempt to avert calamity.

As long as there is a future, and as long as he has breath, a tireless Günter Grass will be working to extend and to humanize that future–writing, drawing, etching, sculpting, lecturing, campaigning, and cooking up ideas in his own controversial and inimitable way.

Bibliographies:

Jean M. Woods, "Günter Grass Bibliography," *West Coast Review*, 5, no. 3 (1971): 52-56; 6, no. 1 (1971): 31-40;

George A. Everett, *A Select Bibliography of Günter Grass (From 1956 to 1973)* (New York: Franklin, 1974);

Patrick O'Neill, *Günter Grass: A Bibliography 1955-1975* (Toronto: University of Toronto Press, 1976);

Susan C. Anderson, *Grass and Grimmelshausen: Günter Grass's "Das Treffen in Telgte" and Rezeptionstheorie* (Columbia, S.C.: Camden House, 1986).

References:

Heinz Ludwig Arnold, ed., *Text + Kritik, Heft 1/1a: Günter Grass* (Munich: Edition text kritik, 1978);

Arnold and Franz Josef Gortz, eds., *Günter Grass: Dokumente zur politischen Wirkung* (Munich: Edition text + kritik, 1971);

Hanspeter Brode, *Günter Grass* (Munich: Beck, 1979);

Nicole Casanova, *Günter Grass: Atelier des métamorphoses* (Paris: Belfond, 1979);

W. Gordon Cunliffe, *Günter Grass* (New York: Twayne, 1969);

Edward Diller, *A Mythic Journey: Günter Grass's "Tin Drum"* (Lexington: University Press of Kentucky, 1974);

Manfred Durzak, ed., *Interpretationen zu Günter Grass: Geschichte auf dem poetischen Prüfstand* (Stuttgart: Klett, 1985);

Rolf Geissler, ed., *Günter Grass: Ein Materialienbuch* (Neuwied: Luchterhand, 1976);

Franz Josef Görtz, ed., *Günter Grass: Auskunft für Leser* (Neuwied: Luchterhand, 1984);

Ronald Hayman, *Günter Grass* (London: Methuen, 1985);

Manfred Jurgensen, *Über Günter Grass* (Bern: Francke, 1974);

Jurgensen, ed., *Grass: Kritik–Thesen–Analysen* (Bern: Francke, 1973);

Alan Frank Keele, *Understanding Günter Grass* (Columbia: University of South Carolina Press, 1988);

Detlef Krumme, *Günter Grass: Die Blechtrommel* (Munich: Hanser, 1986);

Richard H. Lawson, *Günter Grass* (New York: Ungar, 1985);

Irène Leonard, *Günter Grass* (New York: Barnes & Noble, 1974);

Gert Loschütz, ed., *Von Buch zu Buch–Günter Grass in der Kritik: Eine Dokumentation* (Neuwied: Luchterhand, 1968);

Ann L. Mason, *The Skeptical Muse: A Study of Günter Grass' Conception of the Artist* (Bern: Lang, 1974);

Siegfried Mews, ed., *"The Fisherman and His Wife": Günter Grass's "The Flounder" in Critical Perspective* (New York: AMS Press, 1983);

Keith Miles, *Günter Grass* (New York: Barnes & Noble, 1975);

Volker Neuhaus, *Günter Grass* (Stuttgart: Metzler, 1979);

Patrick O'Neill, ed., *Critical Essays on Günter Grass* (Boston: Hall, 1987);

Gertrude Bauer Pickar, ed., *Adventures of a Flounder: Critical Essays on Günter Grass' "Der Butt"* (Munich: Fink, 1982);

John Reddick, *The "Danzig Trilogy" of Günter Grass* (New York: Harcourt Brace Jovanovich, 1975);

Kurt Lothar Tank, *Günter Grass* (New York: Ungar, 1969);

Noel Thomas, *The Narrative Works of Günter Grass: A Critical Interpretation* (Amsterdam: Benjamins, 1982);

Heinrich Vormweg, *Günter Grass, mit Selbstzeugnissen und Bilddokumenten* (Reinbek: Rowohlt, 1986);

Theodor Wieser, ed., *Günter Grass: Porträt und Poesie* (Neuwied: Luchterhand, 1968);

A. Leslie Willson, ed., *A Günter Grass Symposium* (Austin: University of Texas Press, 1971).

Papers:

The Günter Grass Archive is located in the Deutsches Literaturarchiv, Marbach am Neckar, Federal Republic of Germany.

Peter Härtling

(13 November 1933-   )

Egbert Krispyn
University of Georgia

BOOKS: *Poeme und Songs* (Esslingen: Bechtle, 1953);

Yamins Stationen: Gedichte (Esslingen: Bechtle, 1955);

In Zeilen zuhaus: Vom Abenteuer des Gedichts, des Gedichteschreibens und Gedichtelesens (Pfullingen: Neske, 1957);

Unter den Brunnen: Neue Gedichte (Esslingen: Bechtle, 1958);

Im Schein des Kometen: Roman (Stuttgart: Goverts, 1959);

Palmström grüßt Anna Blume: Essay und Anthologie der Geister aus Poetia (Stuttgart: Goverts, 1961);

Spielgeist Spiegelgeist: Gedichte 1959-1961 (Stuttgart: Goverts, 1962);

Niembsch oder Der Stillstand: Eine Suite (Stuttgart: Goverts, 1964);

Janek: Porträt einer Erinnerung (Stuttgart: Goverts, 1966);

Vergessene Bücher: Hinweise und Beispiele (Stuttgart: Goverts, 1966);

Das Ende der Geschichte: Über die Arbeit an einem historischen Roman (Mainz: Verlag der Akademie der Wissenschaften und der Literatur, 1968);

Das Familienfest oder Das Ende der Geschichte: Roman (Stuttgart: Goverts, 1969);

Gilles: Ein Kostümstück aus der Revolution (Stuttgart: Goverts, 1970);

. . . und das ist die ganze Familie: Tagesläufe mit Kindern (Recklinghausen: Bitter, 1970);

Ein Abend, eine Nacht, ein Morgen: Eine Geschichte (Neuwied & Berlin: Luchterhand, 1971);

Neue Gedichte (Darmstadt: Blaschke, 1972);

Zwettl: Nachprüfung einer Erinnerung (Darmstadt & Neuwied: Luchterhand, 1973);

Das war der Hirbel: Wie Hirbel ins Heim kam, warum er anders ist als andere und ob ihm zu helfen ist (Weinheim: Beltz & Gelberg, 1973);

Eine Frau: Roman (Darmstadt: Luchterhand, 1974);

Zum laut und leise lesen: Geschichten und Gedichte für Kinder (Darmstadt: Luchterhand, 1975);

Oma: Die Geschichte von Kalle, der seine Eltern verliert und von seiner Großmutter aufgenommen wird (Weinheim: Beltz & Gelberg, 1975); translated by Anthea Bell as *Oma* (New York: Harper & Row, 1977); translation republished as *Granny: The Story of Karl, Who Loses His Parents and Goes to Live with His Grandmother* (London: Hutchinson, 1977);

Hölderlin: Ein Roman (Darmstadt: Luchterhand, 1976);

Anreden: Gedichte aus den Jahren 1972-1977 (Darmstadt & Neuwied: Luchterhand, 1977);

Theo haut ab: Kinderroman (Weinheim & Basel: Beltz & Grelberg, 1977); translated by Bell as *Theo Runs Away* (London: Andersen Press, 1978);

Hubert oder Die Rückkehr nach Casablanca: Roman (Darmstadt: Luchterhand, 1978);

Ausgewählte Gedichte 1953-1979 (Darmstadt & Neuwied: Luchterhand, 1979);

Ben liebt Anna (Weinheim: Beltz & Gelberg, 1979);

Sophie macht Geschichten (Weinheim: Beltz & Gelberg, 1980);

Nachgetragene Liebe: Erzählung (Darmstadt: Luchterhand, 1980);

Der wiederholte Unfall (Stuttgart: Reclam, 1980);

Meine Lektüre: Literatur als Widerstand, edited by Klaus Siblewski (Darmstadt & Neuwied: Luchterhand, 1981);

Die dreifache Maria (Darmstadt: Luchterhand, 1982);

Vorwarnung: Gedichte (Neuwied: Luchterhand, 1983);

Jakob hinter der blauen Tür (Weinheim: Beltz & Gelberg, 1983);

Das Windrad (Neuwied: Luchterhand, 1983);

Der spanische Soldat oder Finden und Erfinden: Frankfurter Poetik-Vorlesungen (Darmstadt: Luchterhand, 1984);

Ich rufe die Wörter zusammen: Gedichte 1983-84 (Darmstadt: Luchterhand, 1984);

Felix Guttmann: Roman (Darmstadt & Neuwied: Luchterhand, 1985).

Peter Härtling (photograph by Wolfgang M. Weber, courtesy of Ullstein Bilderdienst)

OTHER: "Warum ich nicht wie Theodor Fontane schreibe," in *Fünfzehn Autoren suchen sich selbst*, edited by U. Schultz (Munich: List, 1967), pp. 155-163;

Die Väter: Berichte und Geschichten, compiled by Härtling (Frankfurt am Main: Fischer, 1968);

Christian Friedrich Daniel Schubart, *Gedichte*, edited by Härtling (Frankfurt am Main: Fischer, 1968);

Nikolaus Lenau, *Briefe an Sophie von Löwenthal, 1834-1845*, edited by Härtling (Munich: Kösel, 1968);

Leporello fällt aus der Rolle: Zeitgenössische Autoren erzählen das Leben von Figuren der Weltliteratur weiter, edited by Härtling (Frankfurt am Main: Fischer, 1971);

Die Kopfkissen-Gans und andere Geschichten von großen Dichtern für kleine Leute, introduction by Härtling (Frauenfeld: Hüber, 1978).

PERIODICAL PUBLICATIONS: "Übereinkunft in der Metapher," *Der Monat*, 13 (1960/1961): 56-62;

"Literatur, Politik, Polemik," *Der Monat*, 14 (1962): 45-52;

"Ahnungen von einem neuen Don Juan: Über die Wandlungen von Sexus und Eros in der neueren Literatur," *Stuttgarter Zeitung*, 27 April 1963;

"Literatur und Bildung," *Stuttgarter Zeitung*, 26 March 1966;

"Literatur als Revolution und Tradition," *Akzente*, 14 (1967): 221-223;

"Die wissende Erzählung: Entwürfe für eine Poetik der Gegenwart," *Stuttgarter Zeitung*, 19 December 1970.

The 1960s and 1970s were a period of destabilization in German literature. Notions of sociopolitical relevance eroded the position of the traditional genres in favor of activist, experimental forms. Even established writers were driven off course by the prevailing ideological winds, and artistically motivated prose fiction experienced some lean years. Peter Härtling was one of the few authors who resisted this trend. During those two decades he published a series of novels of the highest aesthetic quality, which through their thematic interrelation constitute a coherent oeuvre.

As is the case with all German writers of his generation, Härtling's biography is dominated by the early experience of Nazism, World War II, and the postwar years of material deprivation. He was born in 1933 in Chemnitz (now Karl-Marx-Stadt in the German Democratic Republic) to Rudolf and Erika Häntzschel Härtling. In 1941 the family moved to Olmütz in Moravia. Härtling's father, a lawyer, died in 1945 in a Soviet prisoner-of-war camp. That year Härtling's mother fled with him and his sister to Zwettl in lower Austria, then to Nürtingen in southwest Germany. After their mother committed suicide in 1946, the children were raised by their grandmother. Härtling attended a humanistically oriented gymnasium in Nürtingen but did not graduate. In 1952, after a brief stint as a factory hand, he became a journalist. Starting out on local papers, from 1955 until 1962 he was literary editor of the national daily *Deutsche Zeitung* in Stuttgart and Cologne; then he became coeditor of the monthly journal *Der Monat* in West Berlin. He held that post until 1970, but in 1967 he had also become editor in chief of the prestigious Frankfurt literary publishing house S. Fischer, rising to general manager the following year. Since the end of 1973 he has been a free-lance writer living in Mörfelden-Walldorf, West Germany. Härtling married Mechthild Maier on 3 July 1959; they have four children.

Härtling is preoccupied with man's ability to know the past. In novel after novel he has explored both individual and collective retrospection–memory and history–and demonstrated the subjective, tentative nature of any reconstruction of the past. Associated with this preoccupation is the notion of a state of timelessness in which people lose their individuality and elude the mnemonic process; Härtling calls this state "Stillstand" (standstill).

Härtling first made his name as a poet. His collections of verse and essays on lyric poetry, which appeared between 1953 and 1962, were major contributions to the upsurge of that genre during those years. In 1959 he published his first novel, *Im Schein des Kometen* (By the Light of the Comet). A technically flawed work, it introduces the memory theme as a middle-aged bar pianist in postwar Germany attempts to evoke his youth. The book also makes extensive use of the music motif which recurs in some of Härtling's later novels.

With the publication of *Niembsch oder Der Stillstand* (Niembsch; or, The Standstill) in 1964 Härtling proved that he had mastered the novel genre. The title figure is the nineteenth-century Hungarian-German poet Nikolaus Franz Niembsch Edler von Strehlenau, who wrote under the pseudonym Nikolaus Lenau. This Byronesque romantic was a tortured soul whose unhappy life included a sojourn in America and eventual insanity. In Härtling's treatment of this material Niembsch's memory after his mental breakdown becomes an endless mirroring of past

and present, and he reaches a "standstill." In dealing with a historical subject Härtling demonstrates the problems involved in reconstructing the past on the basis of documents. The book won the Literature Prize of the German Critics League in 1964 and the Prix du meilleur livre étranger in 1966.

His following novel, *Janek: Porträt einer Erinnerung* (Janek: Portrait of a Memory, 1966), shifts the narrative perspective to a fictitious, though partly autobiographical, figure who attempts through his memories to understand his own past. The subtitle emphasizes the central role played by the mnemonic faculty, which is exercised mainly in Janek's obsessive interest in his father. The process of recalling, rather than its objective, forms the dominant theme of the book.

In his next novel, *Das Familienfest oder Das Ende der Geschichte* (The Family Feast; or, The End of History, 1969), Härtling again uses the subtitle to introduce his main focus. Like *Stillstand*, *the end of history* refers in his terminology to a state in which the object has become timeless, thereby eluding collective and personal memory. The novel concerns a nineteenth-century family whose characteristics, at a reunion of descendants held in 1967, have become unrecognizably blurred.

After an interval which saw the publication of *Gilles* (1970), a play about the French Revolution for which he was awarded the Gerhart Hauptmann Prize; *Ein Abend, eine Nacht, ein Morgen* (An Evening, a Night, a Morning, 1971), a short story revolving around the topic of storytelling; and the collection *Neue Gedichte* (New Poems, 1972), Härtling returned to the novel form with *Zwettl: Nachprüfung einer Erinnerung* (Zwettl: Verification of a Memory, 1973). The novel reverts to the quasi-autobiographical format of *Janek*, with which it has some characters and incidents in common. Against the chaos of the final phase of World War II the theme of the quest for the past is personified in a young boy whose father dies in a POW camp. An obsessive search for the father's grave ultimately yields some bones and a skull, which bear no resemblance to the once-living reality.

Another novel appeared the following year. *Eine Frau* (A Woman) is the biography of a woman from the turn of the century until the present. Like the earlier works, it is a reconstruction of a life; but instead of demonstrating how the contours of a personality become indistinct against the kaleidoscopic backdrop of historical events,

Härtling stresses the woman's essential unity and permanence of character. While the turbulent times affect her outward circumstances, her inner constancy is manifested in her love of music and in the evocation of King David as a guiding force in her life. These motifs suggest a suspension of time, which by implication is identified as the source of chaos and confusion.

With *Hölderlin* (1976) Härtling returned to the format of *Niembsch*. The subject is, again, an earlier German writer who spent the last years of his unhappy life mentally deranged. Since Friedrich Hölderlin is a major literary figure, his life has been documented in great detail. Härtling uses this wealth of information in an attempt to re-create the great romantic poet's personality and the world in which he lived. As he points out, however, the novelist must fall short of the reality of his historical subject: not only are his perceptions conditioned by a greatly changed cultural climate, but he cannot avoid seeing all aspects of Hölderlin's life in the context of his tragic destiny. The novel uses the biographical approach not so much to gain new insights into the subject as to demonstrate the impossibility of really knowing the past.

After the poetry collection *Anreden* (Addresses, 1977) and the children's book *Theo haut ab* (1977; translated as *Theo Runs Away*, 1978) Härtling published his next adult novel, *Hubert oder Die Rückkehr nach Casablanca* (Hubert; or, The Return to Casablanca), in 1978. It is in many respects the reverse of *Eine Frau*: Germany's recent history again provides the setting, but instead of showing a consistent personality against this turbulent background *Hubert* portrays someone who has virtually no ascertainable identity. Like Walter Mitty, the title figure exists only in his own fantasies, which are fueled by movies. Having in several novels dealt with the impossibility of re-creating a past life on the basis of documents or memories, and having described in *Eine Frau* a constant character defined by "timeless" coordinates, Härtling suggests with *Hubert* that a personality may be a chimerical reflection of popular cult heroes. His long-standing preoccupation with the elusiveness of the reality of past individuals here leads to a denial of individuality itself.

The brief narrative with the ambiguous title *Nachgetragene Liebe* (Appended *or* Resented Love, 1980) was followed by the essay collection *Meine Lektüre: Literatur als Widerstand* (My Reading: Literature as Resistance, 1981), in which Härtling postulates a collective memory as the essence of Euro-pean civilization. This notion is developed more optimistically than heretofore in his novel *Die dreifache Maria* (The Threefold Maria, 1982), which once again deals with the life of a nineteenth-century German writer. Eduard Mörike was a maladjusted, retiring person who all his life suffered guilt feelings over an affair he had had as a student. The girl in question had an aura of mystery for Mörike and his circle, although there is evidence that she was little more than a tramp. Härtling develops these facts to present a mirror image of the thesis of his earlier works: collective memory yields an accurate image to the retrospective novelist which eluded the subject's contemporaries. They conceived of themselves and each other in terms of fictitious characters from then-popular operas and novels, not unlike Hubert's identification with Humphrey Bogart. The vagueness of their novelistic depiction is, therefore, attributable not to any inadequacy of man's grasp of the past but to the amorphousness of the original models.

In 1983 there appeared a new collection of poetry, *Vorwarnung* (Forewarning), and another novel, *Das Windrad* (The Windmill). The novel relegates biography to the rank of a minor motif in a clumsily written story about an antiestablishment demonstration. It involves an abortive attempt to build a large wind generator and features a cast of singularly unappetizing flower children of all ages. A laborious rehash of the radicalism of the 1960s, the book is a marked departure from the literary excellence and conceptual cohesion of the rest of Härtling's novelistic work.

Härtling has written several popular children's books. He won the Literature Prize of the Culture Circle of German Industry and the Literary Advancement Prize of Lower Saxony in 1965, the Schubart Prize of the City of Aalen in 1973, the German Youth Book Prize in 1976, the Wilhelmine Lübke Prize in 1978, and the Hermann Sinsheimer Prize of the City of Freinsheim and the Hölderlin Prize of the City of Bad Homburg in 1987. In 1977-1978 he held the honorary position of City Scribe of Bergen-Enkheim.

References:

Burckhard Dücker, *Peter Härtling* (Munich: Beck/ edition text + kritik, 1983);

F. Gallard, "Zeit und Geschichte in Peter Härtlings Romantrilogie," Ph.D. dissertation, University of Paris, 1976;

Elisabeth and Rolf Hackenbracht, eds., *Peter Härtling: Materialienbuch* (Darmstadt & Neuwied: Luchterhand, 1979);

M. F. Lacy, "Afflicted by Memory: The Work of Peter Härtling, 1953-69," M.A. thesis, University of Birmingham, 1969;

Tabah Mirelle, "Peter Härtlings Erzählung 'Niembsch oder der Stillstand': Thematik und Form," *Revue Germanique*, 11 (1981): 190-202;

Kurt Rothmann, "Peter Härtling," in his *Deutschsprachige Schriftsteller seit 1945 in Einzeldarstellungen* (Stuttgart: Reclam, 1985), pp. 157-161.

Willi Heinrich
(9 August 1920-   )

Gerd K. Schneider
Syracuse University

BOOKS: *Das geduldige Fleisch: Roman* (Stuttgart: Deutsche Verlagsanstalt, 1955); translated by Richard and Clara Winston as *The Cross of Iron* (Indianapolis: Bobbs-Merrill, 1956); translation republished as *The Willing Flesh* (London: Weidenfeld & Nicolson, 1956);

Der goldene Tisch: Roman (Karlsruhe: Stahlberg, 1956); republished as *Drei kamen zurück: Roman* (Vienna: Buchgemeinschaft Donauland, 1961); translated by Oliver Coburn as *Crack of Doom* (New York: Farrar, Straus, 1958); translated by Coburn and Ursula Lehrburger as *The Savage Mountain* (London: Weidenfeld & Nicolson, 1958); German version revised as *In stolzer Trauer: Roman* (Gütersloh & Munich: Bertelsmann, 1970);

Die Gezeichneten: Roman (Karlsruhe: Stahlberg, 1958); translated by Sigrid Rock as *Mark of Shame* (New York: Farrar, Straus & Cudahy, 1959; London: Weidenfeld & Nicolson, 1959);

Alte Häuser sterben nicht: Roman (Frankfurt am Main: Fischer, 1960); translated by Michael Glenny as *The Crumbling Fortress* (London: Macdonald, 1963; New York: Dial Press, 1964);

Rape of Honor, translated by Rock (New York: Dial Press, 1961); republished as *Rape of Honour: A Novel* (London: Weidenfeld & Nicolson, 1961); German version published as *In* einem Schloß zu wohnen (Gütersloh & Munich: Bertelsmann, 1976);

Vom inneren Leben (Calw: Ullrich, 1961);

Gottes zweite Garnitur: Roman (Hamburg: Rütten & Loening, 1962); translated by Rock as *The Lonely Conqueror* (New York: Dial Press, 1962; London: Macdonald, 1964);

Ferien im Jenseits: Roman (Munich: Rütten & Loening, 1964); translated by Hans Koningsberger as *The Devil's Bed* (New York: Dial Press, 1965; London: Macdonald, 1966);

Maiglöckchen oder ähnlich: Die Aufzeichnungen der Simone S.: Roman (Munich: Rütten & Loening, 1965);

Mittlere Reife: Roman (Munich: Rütten & Loening, 1966);

Geometrie einer Ehe: Roman (Munich: Rütten & Loening, 1967);

Schmetterlinge weinen nicht: Roman (Gütersloh: Bertelsmann, 1969);

Jahre wie Tau: Roman (Munich: Bertelsmann, 1971);

So Long, Archie: Roman (Gütersloh & Munich: Bertelsmann, 1972);

Liebe und was sonst noch zählt: Roman (Munich, Gütersloh & Vienna: Bertelsmann, 1974);

Eine Handvoll Himmel: Roman (Munich: Bertelsmann, 1976);

Ein Mann ist immer unterwegs: Roman (Munich: Bertelsmann, 1978);

Herzbube und Mädchen: Roman (Munich: Bertelsmann, 1980);

Allein gegen Palermo (Bergisch Gladbach: Lübbe, 1981);

Vermögen vorhanden (Bergisch Gladbach: Lübbe, 1982);

Traumvogel (Munich: Goldmann, 1983);

Männer zum Wegwerfen (Munich: Herbig, 1985);

Freundinnen und andere Erzählungen (Munich: Heyne, 1985);

Die Verführung (Munich: Herbig, 1986);

Zeit der Nymphen (Munich: Herbig, 1987).

Willi Heinrich is one of the most successful writers in postwar Germany; in 1985 sales of his novels exceeded fifteen million copies, and translations of his work have appeared in at least nineteen countries.

Heinrich was born on 9 August 1920 in Heidelberg to Wilhelm and Berta Koch Heinrich; he attended public school from 1926 to 1934 in Karlsruhe, then went to a business vocational school for three years. Drafted in 1939, he was stationed in Czechoslovakia for a year and fought on the eastern front from 1941 to 1945. After the war he returned to Karlsruhe, where he sold groceries and then lottery tickets. Following the success of his first novel, *Das geduldige Fleisch* (The Patient Flesh; translated as *The Cross of Iron*, 1956), in 1955, he turned to writing full-time. On 23 June 1955 he married Erika Stocker. In 1957 they moved to Baden-Baden, and since 1962 they have resided in Bühl-Neusatz.

The main character in *Das geduldige Fleisch* is the twenty-five-year-old Corporal Steiner, whose platoon is left behind in 1943 to protect the retreating battalion from enemy action. Steiner leads his exhausted men through the Soviet-occupied marshland to the German lines. The conflict between Steiner and his superior officer, Stransky, nearly results in Steiner killing Stransky. Stransky is subsequently transferred to a less dangerous place, where he will undoubtedly survive the war; Steiner is killed during the Soviet attack on the Black Sea bridgehead.

The war is seen through the eyes of this simple, ordinary man as he witnesses the killing and mutilation of his friends and comrades. Combat is shown as bringing out both the worst and the best in men. The soldiers' motto is summed up in Steiner's words: "Wer zuerst schießt, lebt am längsten" (He who shoots first lives longest). War is depicted as a personal encounter, and the reader is involved in the immediacy of the bloody action. Heinrich's own experiences undoubtedly entered into the work. Its primary

weakness is the absence of any attempt to seek the reasons for the destruction; Hitler and the political and historical background are hardly mentioned, even though the novel was written ten years after the war. This nonreflective attitude distinguishes *Das geduldige Fleisch* from Erich Maria Remarque's *Im Westen nichts Neues* (1929; translated as *All Quiet on the Western Front*, 1929); the contrast between the two war novels was noted by German critics, who also pointed out Heinrich's implied admiration of heroism. Steiner, the "personified Mars," is reminiscent of Ernst Jünger in his autobiographical *In Stahlgewittern* (1920; translated as *The Storm of Steel*, 1929). The glorification of the hero is also evident in the title of the film based on Heinrich's novel, *Steiner*, coproduced 1977 by Wolf Hartwig of Rapid-Film, Munich, and EMT Limited of London at a cost of fifteen million German marks, with James Coburn as Steiner and Maximilian Schell as Stransky. The reception of the novel was more favorable in America than in Germany. According to *Time*, *The Cross of Iron* "is the most savagely powerful portraiture of men at war on the eastern front since Theodor Plievier's *Stalingrad*. . . . Willi Heinrich, 35, has written this first novel with the passionate intensity of a man plucking shell fragments out of his own memory. A corporal himself in a German infantry division, he marched across 8,000 miles of Russian soil, was severely wounded five times, saw his division lose twelve times its original manpower. In *The Cross of Iron*, Heinrich does what a good war novelist should and few can. He makes the private inferno of his war roar all over again, but as if for the very first time and for all men."

In his second novel, *Der goldene Tisch* (1956; translated as *Crack of Doom*, 1958), Heinrich tries to avoid any ambiguity about his personal stance. Der goldene Tisch (the Golden Table) is a mountaintop near Kaschau in Slovakia which bears silent witness to the annihilation of a German division in December 1944. Heinrich's sharp criticism of the commanding officers led to the initial rejection of the manuscript by the publishing house, which wanted substantial changes in the portrayal of the generals; Heinrich refused to comply. Walter Görlitz's review noted: "Alles [ist] großartig wiedergegeben (inkl. die Psychologie der Partisanen und die Kampfszenen). Mag sein, daß der Verfasser aus eigenem Erleben schöpft. Aber angenommen, daß dies der Fall ist, dann hat ihn dies Erleben in einen Nihilisten verwandelt, der alles Geschehen für sinnlos hält"

(Everything [incl. the psychology of the partisans and the battle scenes] is portrayed superbly. It may be that the author has drawn from his own experience. But assuming this to be the case, then this experience has turned him into a nihilist who looks upon all events as senseless).

In *Die Gezeichneten* (1958; translated as *Mark of Shame*, 1959), his third novel, Heinrich argues that the so-called zero hour of 1945, the complete break with the past, did not really take place. He shows that the Nazi ideology was very much alive at the time of the West German "economic miracle" of the 1950s. He describes parvenus and resentment-laden former Nazis in Nuremberg, a city strongly associated with the Nazi movement. Heinrich's moral outrage with regard to postwar Germany was attacked by Heinz Beckmann, who accused the author of one-sidedness and of presenting a false image of West Germany to readers in East Germany and other countries: "Es ist deprimierend, sich vorstellen zu müssen, daß nun auch der Roman *Die Gezeichneten* im Ausland gelesen und als ein zutreffendes Bild von der charakterlichen, geistigen und politischen Verfassung der Deutschen in der Bundesrepublik hingenommen wird. Doch bewahrt uns vielleicht die erschreckend mangelhafte Qualität dieses Romans vor Übersetzungen" (It is depressing to have to imagine that now the novel *Die Gezeichneten* will also be read abroad, where it will be accepted as an accurate description of the moral, intellectual and political condition of Germans in the Federal Republic of Germany. But the frightfully deficient quality of the work may safeguard us from any translations).

The setting of the war novel *Alte Häuser sterben nicht* (Old Houses Don't Die, 1960; translated as *The Crumbling Fortress*, 1963) is an abandoned village in the French Alps, near the Côte d'Azur, in August 1944. The Germans are retreating after the landing of the Americans in Toulon. A few refugees meet in the village, including Boris, an intellectual Russian emigrant and former Communist; Hanna, a German Jewess, and her uncle; Vieale, a French mayor suspected of collaboration with the Germans, and his wife; and two Swiss, George and Marcel, who had joined the German army but deserted after becoming disillusioned with the Nazis. The high points of this action-filled novel are the love affair between Hanna and George and George's impulsive killing of Gaston, a member of the Resistance. Detmar Heinrich Sarnetzki remarked in the 1977 anthology *Willi Heinrich: Der Autor und sein Werk*:

"Der Stil ist von äußerster Sauberkeit und Präzision, aber manchmal geradezu überwältigend ist die Art, wie die gewaltige Landschaft mit der Handlung verschmolzen ist, fast als Mitspielerin im tragischen Geschehen..." (The style shows extreme purity and precision, but almost overpowering is the way the powerful landscape blends into the action, almost as if it were a part of the tragic events...).

Heinrich's moral outrage is also evident in *Gottes zweite Garnitur* (God's Second Uniform, 1962; translated as *The Lonely Conqueror*, 1962), a novel about racial discrimination. John Baako, a sergeant in the American army stationed in the town of Thüringerstadt, falls in love with Claire, a twenty-five-year-old medical student. In her association with John, Claire violates the social taboo against white girls befriending blacks, who are believed to be sexually more powerful than whites. Heinrich criticizes not only the petit-bourgeois mentality of the small German community but also the white Americans in the garrison who discriminate against the blacks, and the American-born blacks who discriminate against John, who is from Rhodesia. At the end of the novel Claire and John are clearly the moral victors: Claire intends to marry John after his release from a one-year prison term for deserting from the army. The dissatisfaction with this novel arises from its emphasis on a private solution to a social problem; the story ends on a note of resignation rather than one of hope for change. Heinrich's pessimism about human nature is evident in an interview with Heinz Puknus in which he called the ending of the novel "gemessen an der deutschen Wirklichkeit, unrealistisch, wie ich heute selbstkritisch einräumen muß–ich habe das Buch gedanklich praktisch nicht zu Ende geführt. Die Realität ist noch längst nicht so weit, Außenseiter zu integrieren. Denken Sie nur an das Gastarbeiterproblem" (unrealistic, compared with our German reality, as I today have to admit myself–I simply did not think this book to its conclusion. The reality is that we are still not ready to integrate outsiders. Just think of the problems of foreign workers). The strength of the book lies in its portrayal of Claire, with her truly outstanding human qualities: keen insight, courage, and the strength of will to live her own life, even in the face of social ostracism.

The central character of *Ferien im Jenseits* (Holiday in the Hereafter, 1964; translated as *The Devil's Bed*, 1965) is also a woman. Helen

Brazzi, an heiress from Toledo, Ohio, comes to Sicily after World War II to search for her Sicilian-born husband, Genno, who was reported missing in action in 1943. She enlists the help of Clyde Bentley, an American officer who was in charge of her husband's unit when he disappeared. Helen intends to kill Bentley because she suspects that her husband was captured because Bentley deserted him during an enemy attack, but before she can carry out her plan she is kidnapped by bandits and held for ransom in a mountain cave. There she falls in love with Pietro, the leader of the bandits, and she continues to love him even after she learns that he killed her husband. The weakness of *Ferien im Jenseits* is the excessive use of dialogue which does not advance the plot. The reception of the work outside Germany was divided. The critic of *Books and Bookmen* noted that "one of Germany's leading novelists, Willi Heinrich, writes slickly and with the ease of a true professional. He tells a gripping story and at the same time analyzes the variety of love which thrives in an atmosphere of danger and violence." To Martin Shuttleworth, on the other hand, "*The Devil's Bed* by Willi Heinrich is a most unpleasant, cynical, low book." The review in the *Times Literary Supplement* was mixed: "The descriptions of Sicily are excellent but the narrative pace is far too slow, and there are whole chunks of dialogue that fail to further the plot or illumine character and could profitably have been cut. The translation from the German is exceptionally fine." The character of Helen, according to *Kirkus Reviews*, "is reasonably convincing," but the story itself is not: "it doesn't develop with any inevitable logic; you never feel that it was written out of any particular conviction or compulsion."

Heinrich generally succeeds in rendering believable female characters. The heroine and narrator of *Maiglöckchen oder ähnlich* (Lilies of the Valley or Something like That, 1965) is Simone S., a journalist who writes occasional editorials for a small community paper. An ideological and sexual nonconformist, she is drawn to two other nonconformists: the lesbian Lis, a sarcastic photographer who works for the newspaper, and Schulberg, who tries to arouse public opinion against the tax policies of the government and ultimately commits suicide. Themes treated in the novel include media criticism, the continuation of the Nazi mentality, the generation gap, and the sexual abuse of girls by their fathers.

Heinrich's critical stance is maintained in the novel *Mittlere Reife* (Junior Matriculation, 1966). Ruth Stein, who has completed her junior matriculation (tenth grade) and has worked for four years as a secretary in an insurance company, is dissatisfied with her life. She starts moving in higher social circles and becomes involved with the senile Baron von Brandenburg and the rich manufacturer Witkowski. After an affair with Witkowski on his yacht she returns home, but her father rejects her and she goes back to her loyal friend Hans. In the end Ruth is again a low-level employee, resigned to her status. This sense of resignation is a trademark of Heinrich, who remarked in the interview with Puknus: "Die Realität unserer Gesellschaft ist die Resignation vor der Gesellschaft. Ich habe deshalb auch prinzipiell etwas gegen Happy Ends in Büchern" (The reality of our society is resignation before society. I am therefore in principle against happy endings in books).

In *Geometrie einer Ehe* (Geometry of a Marriage, 1967) Irene, a strong-willed, wealthy socialite, is married to the weakling Rudolf, who was erroneously awarded a medal in World War II. Rudolf is drawn to his sister-in-law Katharina, who is softer and more "feminine" than Irene. Both Irene and Katharina's husband know about the affair but say nothing in order to avoid a scandal, and Irene and Katharina ward off a liaison between Rudolf and a third woman from his past. The women in this novel are portrayed as being much stronger than the men, but they are seen from the male perspective.

Heinrich's next novel, *Schmetterlinge weinen nicht* (Butterflies Do Not Cry, 1969), deals with the love of an aging man for a young woman. Karl, a fifty-six-year-old manufacturer, apparently happily married and the father of two grown sons, falls in love with the twenty-year-old Cilly. Inge, Karl's wife, informs Cilly's father about his daughter's affair. Beaten up and thrown out of the house by her father, Cilly discovers her love for a younger man and breaks off her relationship with Karl, who, at the request of his sons, returns to his family. This seemingly happy ending does not negate the book's revelation of the fragility of seemingly stable marriages.

Jahre wie Tau (Years like Dew, 1971) takes the reader back to the 1950s, when the lost generation of World War II attempted to adjust to the postwar value system. Three men have difficulty maintaining their friendship because of their love for the same girl, Marina, whom they smuggle from Lemberg in Soviet-occupied territory to the Western zone. The reception of the work was mixed. The writer Hans Hellmut Kirst points to the disillusioning nature of the book: "Willi Heinrich weiß, woran Menschen leiden können: Ihr Liebesverlangen bleibt zumeist ohne jede Erfüllung, und Träume zerplatzen wie Seifenblasen. Was übrigbleibt: Der Mensch ist sich selbst überlassen! Mit einem Buch von Heinrich– wenn er lesen kann und nicht grübeln will" (Willi Heinrich knows what makes people suffer: their desire for love remains in most cases without fulfillment, and dreams burst like soap bubbles. What remains: Man is left to himself! With a book by Heinrich–if one can read and does not want to think). But to Wolfgang Paul *Jahre wie Tau* is "ein Roman, der gut lesbar ist und die Zeitumstände genau referiert" (a novel which is quite readable and accurately reports the conditions of an era).

Heinrich followed *Jahre wie Tau* with *So Long, Archie* (1972), which deals with a similar situation; but this time three women are in love with one man. Annemarie, Gerda, and Sabine become involved with Archie during his summer vacation. While on the surface *So Long, Archie* is merely an entertaining novel, the underlying issue is the conflict between generations and between conservative and counterculture value systems.

Liebe und was sonst noch zählt (Love and Whatever Else Counts, 1974) is set in the Black Forest, where a valuable piece of real estate is desired by a few speculators. The main theme of the novel is the clash between profiteering and environmental protection; as usual with Heinrich, erotic adventures and political opportunism are also featured.

In *Eine Handvoll Himmel* (A Handful of Heaven, 1976) national prejudice is woven into the action, which revolves around the attempt to integrate the German Helga Beneddetti into the Italian family of her husband, Stefano. When the attempt fails, Helga decides to return to her native Rhineland with the adventurer Dieter Christiansen.

Ein Mann ist immer unterwegs (A Man Is Always on the Go, 1978) shows how business executives deal with the recession of 1974-1975 and contrasts authoritarian with democratic management techniques. The treatment of these issues is trivialized by the insertion of gratuitous sex scenes involving, according to reviewer Evi

Simeoni, wealthy "Orgienfeiernden, ausgeflippten Lustmolchen, die immer die Köpfe zusammenstecken haben, um den neuesten Austausch von Ehefrauen oder Geliebten perfekt zu machen" (orgy-throwing, spaced-out sex maniacs who always find new ways to perfect the newest exchange of wives and girlfriends).

The central character in *Herzbube und Mädchen* (Jack of Hearts and Girl, 1980) is Gundi, an editor in an important publishing house who writes books under a pseudonym. Her adversary is Ralph Staninsky, a famous and wealthy writer, whose arrogant and deprecating description of women motivates Gundi to write a book about his secret life, including his love life. To get details she becomes his secretary. Staninsky, however, knows her true identity, and he uses all means to make her participate in his erotic perversities. There is some humor in the novel, but as Esther Knorr-Anders remarks, "Alles in allem ist diese 'Erotikkomödie' wohl eher ein bürgerliches Trauerspiel" (All in all, this "erotic comedy" is probably more a bourgeois tragedy).

Allein gegen Palermo (Alone against Palermo, 1981) deals with the disappearance of German luxury cars between Gardasee and Sicily. Robert Thiele, a James Bond-type private detective who was expelled from the police force for his unconventional methods and because of the jealousy of his unsuccessful colleagues, is offered five hundred thousand marks by the newspaper magnate Larsen to solve this case and also to find Larsen's runaway wife in Sicily. Thiele is joined in this venture by the beautiful Monika, Larsen's secretary, with whom he falls in love. The pair is hunted by secret agents, as well as by the Mafia, but gets away. According to Knorr-Anders, "Im Grunde ist das Ganze ein Kriminalroman und als solcher spannend. Ein 'Zeitroman,' wie angekündigt, ist es nicht" (Basically, the entire work is a detective story and a thriller. A "novel about contemporary problems," as advertised, it is not).

In *Traumvogel* (Dreambird, 1983) sex and murder are combined. Three couples, Rolf and Karin, Kurt and Ursula, and Walter and Ev, engage in group sex and erotic perversities. This situation changes when Karin meets Roland, a middleaged, wealthy divorced man, with whom she falls in love. Tension arises within the sextet, leading to erotic aggression; between the rest of the group and Karin, who wants to get away; and between the group and Roland, who offers Karin a new life. The book, which is filled with clichés and stereotypes, has little social significance. The major part consists of sex scenes, and the ever-recurring problem is to decide who is to sleep with whom and do what.

The hero of *Männer zum Wegwerfen* (Throwaway Men, 1985) is a goalie who is smuggled from East to West Germany by secret agents. The heroine is the beautiful Marianne Neumann, the first woman he meets in the West. She becomes his manager and girlfriend, turning him into a "new man." Because of his sensational successes on the soccer field he is hunted by agents in both Germanies and also by the Mafia, which fears loss of control of the games. Heinrich attempts to show that soccer is big business and criticizes those who turn this international sport into a money-making enterprise for a few. Marianne is engaged in another international sport: she "scores" in bedrooms in which she ends up with almost every man she meets. She disposes of them as quickly as she meets them, except for the one she loves. This work is a good thriller with well-written dialogue, but as Hellmut Jaesrich points out in his review, "Ein zeitkritisches Werk . . . ist dieser überlange Krimi jedoch nicht" (This overlong detective novel is not a social satire).

Heinrich's novels have generally not been favorably received by German critics. Their immense popularity attests, however, to the perennial appeal of escapist literature and of works about World War II.

References:

Heinz Ludwig Arnold, "Bestsellerautor—unbekannt: Zu Willi Heinrich und seinen Romaneu im Spiegel der Kritik," *Die Tat* (Zurich), 32 (27 May 1967): 34;

Arnold, "Liebe, Lust und Grundstückseinkaüfe," *Frankfurter Allgemeine Zeitung*, 10 September 1974, pp. 20-21;

Heinz Beckmann, "Nach dem Kriegsroman," *Zeitwende*, 30 (1959): 59;

Hans C. Blumenberg, "Das große Bang Bang," *Die Zeit*, no. 7, 4 February 1977, p. 36;

Wolfgang Boehme, "Jederzeit ansprechbar: Willi Heinrich *Ein Mann ist immer unterwegs*," *Zeitwende*, 49 (1978): 252-253;

"Corporal's Inferno," *Time*, 67 (23 April 1956): 120;

Guenther Cwojdrak, "Dem Krieg auf der Spur: Willi Heinrich *Der goldene Tisch*," *Neue deutsche Literatur*, 5, no. 12 (1957): 144-146;

Cwojdrak, "Der Mythus des Zweiten Weltkriegs: Willi Heinrich *Das geduldige Fleisch*," *Neue deutsche Literatur*, 4, no. 7 (1956): 141-145;

"The Devil's Bed," *Books and Bookmen*, 11 (May 1966): 43;

"The Devil's Bed," *Kirkus Reviews*, 33 (1965): 479;

Günther Engels, "Geduldige Leinwand: Notizen zu Sam Peckinpahs Film *Steiner*," *Rheinischer Merkur*, no. 6, 11 February 1977, p. 18;

Walter Görlitz, "Wenn einen der Erfolg nicht schlafen läßt," *Die Welt*, 6 July 1957, p. 26;

Martin Gregor-Dellin, "So Long Willi Heinrich," *Die Zeit*, no. 39, 29 September 1972, p. 7;

Wolfgang Groezinger, "Der Roman der Gegenwart: Kriegs- und Friedenswelt," *Hochland*, 47 (1954-1955): 576-584;

Eberhard Horst, "Wider den Krieg: Willi Heinrich *Der goldene Tisch*," *Neue deutsche Hefte*, 36 (1957): 364-365;

Hellmut Jaesrich, "Fräulein Neumanns Coup: Willi Heinrich fabuliert von Männern zum Wegwerfen," *Die Welt*, 30 March 1985, p. 21;

Jaesrich, "Schnell beim Kern der Sache," *Die Welt*, 4 March 1978, p. V;

Peter W. Jansen, "Aufstand der Drohnen: Willi Heinrichs Roman *Geometrie einer Ehe*," *Frankfurter Allgemeine Zeitung*, 31 October 1967, p. 3;

Hans Hellmut Kirst, "Der neue Willi Heinrich," *Münchner Merkur*, 14 October 1971;

Esther Knorr-Anders, "Gundi seziert einen Großschriftsteller. Willi Heinrichs jüngster Roman: Eher bürgerliches Trauerspiel als erotische Komödie," *Die Welt*, 8 March 1980, p. V;

Knorr-Anders, "Superdetektiv Thiele jagtx Autodiebe: Abenteuer zwischen Rheinland und Sizilien," *Die Welt*, 18 July 1981, p. V;

H. J. Koch, "Mit roten Ohren geturtelt und gestöhnt," *Frankfurter Rundschau*, 25 November 1972, p. XI;

Candida Kraus, "Ich wage überhaupt nichts," *Die Presse* (Vienna), 19-20 August 1972, p. 21;

Roland Leonard, "Ein Papagei zur Belohnung," *Welt am Sonntag–Buchmagazin*, 9 September 1967, p. 67;

Wolfgang Limmer, "Wildwest an der Ostfront: Peckinpahs Film *Steiner*," *Der Spiegel*, 31 (31 January 1977): 126-127;

Peter Mosler, "Ein Autor in Eile und außer Atem," *Frankfurter Allgemeine Zeitung*, 12 May 1978, p. 26;

"Out of Battle: Willi Heinrich, *The Devil's Bed*," *Times Literary Supplement*, 24 March 1966, p. 237;

Wolfgang Paul, "Der Nachkrieg wird bewältigt," *Kölnische Rundschau*, 3 September 1971, p. 26;

Thomas Petz, "Akrobaten sterben schön: Die erste deutsche Großproduktion: Sam Peckinpahs (Anti-) Kriegsfilm *Steiner-Das Eiserne Kreuz*," *Süddeutsche Zeitung*, 24 February 1977, p. 11;

Gerhard Portelp, "Willi Heinrich: *Maiglöckchen oder ähnlich*," *Zeitwende*, 37 (1966): 846;

Heinz Puknus, "Man hat immer ein Brett vor dem Kopf: Willi Heinrichs Weg ins Engagement," *Literatur-Revue*, 8 (1962): 25-27;

Puknus, "Willi Heinrich," in *Kritisches Lexikon zur deutschsprachigen Gegenwartsliteratur*, edited by Heinz Ludwig Arnold (Munich: Edition text + kritik, 1982), pp. 1-10;

Puknus, ed., *Willi Heinrich: Der Autor und sein Werk. Information–Zeugnis–Kritik* (Munich: Bertelsmann, 1977);

Marcel Reich-Ranicki, "Willi Heinrich: 'Maiglöckchen oder so ähnlich,' " in his *Literatur der klei-nen Schritte: Deutsche Literatur heute* (Munich: Piper, 1967), pp. 135-141;

Christa Rotzoll, "Die Bißstelle an seiner Schulter: *Eine Handvoll Himmel*," *Frankfurter Allgemeine Zeitung*, 9 February 1976, p. 18;

Rotzoll, "Gut gemeint: Willi Heinrichs Roman *Die Gezeichneten*/Eine Neuauflage," *Frankfurter Allgemeine Zeitung*, 6 September 1977, p. 22;

Rotzoll, "Trost und Hilfe für den kleinen Mann," *Frankfurter Allgemeine Zeitung*, 9 August 1980, p. 21;

Martin Shuttleworth, "New Fiction," *Punch*, 250 (6 April 1966): 516;

Evi Simeoni, "Held mit Solarium. Wie gehabt: Der neue Roman von Willi Heinrich, *Stuttgarter Zeitung*, 29 April 1978, p. 50;

Hans Jürgen Weber, "Der Krieg als Western Abenteuer," *die Tat*, 18 March 1977, p. 9;

Werner Wien, "Die Gezeichneten," *Neue deutsche Hefte*, 63 (1959): 651-652;

Willi Heinrich: Porträt eines Autors (Munich, Gütersloh & Vienna: Bertelsmann, 1972);

Gerhard Zwerenz, "Der geduldige Heinrich," *twen*, 4 (1963): 86-91.

Helmut Heißenbüttel

(21 June 1921-   )

Robert Acker
University of Montana

BOOKS: *Kombinationen: Gedichte 1951-1954* (Esslingen: Bechtle, 1954);

Topographien: Gedichte 1954/55 (Esslingen: Bechtle, 1956);

Ohne weiteres bekannt: Kurzporträt (Stierstadt: Eremiten-Presse, 1958);

Texte ohne Komma (Frauenfeld: Gomringer, 1960);

Textbuch 1 (Olten & Freiburg im Breisgau: Walter, 1960);

Textbuch 2 (Olten & Freiburg im Breisgau: Walter, 1961);

Textbuch 3 (Olten & Freiburg im Breisgau: Walter, 1962);

Textbuch 4 (Olten & Freiburg im Breisgau: Walter, 1964);

Mary McCarthy: Versuch eines Porträts (Munich & Zurich: Drömer, Knaur, 1964);

Textbuch 5: 3 x 13 mehr oder weniger Geschichten (Olten & Freiburg im Breisgau: Walter, 1965);

Über Literatur: Aufsätze und Frankfurter Vorlesungen (Olten & Freiburg im Breisgau: Walter, 1966);

Textbuch 6: Neue Abhandlungen über den menschlichen Verstand (Neuwied: Luchterhand, 1967);

Was ist das Konkrete an einem Gedicht? 2 Ansätze (Itzehoe: Hansen & Hansen, 1969);

Briefwechsel über Literatur, by Heißenbüttel and Heinrich Vormweg (Neuwied & Berlin: Luchterhand, 1969);

Das Textbuch (Neuwied & Berlin: Luchterhand, 1970);

Projekt Nr. 1: D'Alemberts Ende (Neuwied & Berlin: Luchterhand, 1970);

Auseinandersetzungen (oder Was tut der Seemann mit Margareta), serigraphs by Thomas Lenk, texts by Heißenbüttel (Stuttgart-Möhringen: Manus-Presse, 1970);

Die Freuden des Alterns: 13 mehr oder weniger Gedichte (Duisberg: Hildebrandt, 1971);

Geiger (Stuttgart: Hatje, 1972);

Zur Tradition der Moderne: Aufsätze und Anmerkungen 1964-1971 (Neuwied & Berlin: Luchterhand, 1972);

Helmut Heißenbüttel (Elisabeth Heinrichs, Hamburg)

Gelegenheitsgedichte und Klappentexte (Darmstadt & Neuwied: Luchterhand, 1973);

Das Durchhauen des Kohlhaupts: Dreizehn Lehrgedichte: Projekt Nr. 2 (Darmstadt: Luchterhand, 1974);

Der fliegende Frosch und das unverhoffte Krokodil: Wilhelm Busch als Dichter (Mainz: Akademie der Wissenschaften und der Literatur, 1976);

Der Wassermaler: Das Dilemma auf dem Trockenen zu sitzen, edited by Sybil Albers (Zurich: Lenggstraße 14. Verlag 3, 1976);

Texts, selected and translated by Michael Hamburger (London: Boyars, 1977)–comprises selections from *Textbücher 1-6, Gelegenheitsgedichte und Klappentexte*, and *Das Durchhauen des Kohl-haupts*;

Mümmelmann oder Die Hasendämmerung (Mainz: Akademie der Wissenschaften und der Literatur, 1978);

Eichendorffs Untergang und andere Märchen: Projekt 3/1 (Stuttgart: Klett-Cotta, 1978);

Wenn Adolf Hitler den Krieg nicht gewonnen hätte: Historische Novellen und wahre Begebenheiten. Projekt 3/2 (Stuttgart: Klett-Cotta, 1979);

Die goldene Kuppel des Comes Arbogast oder Lichtenberg in Hamburg: Fast eine einfache Geschichte (Stuttgart: Klett-Cotta, 1980);

Das Ende der Alternative: Einfache Geschichten. Projekt 3/3 (Stuttgart: Klett-Cotta, 1980);

Ödipuskomplex made in Germany: Gelegenheitsgedichte, Totentage, Landschaften 1965-1980 (Stuttgart: Klett-Cotta, 1981);

Von der Lehrbarkeit des Poetischen oder Jeder kann Gedichte schreiben (Wiesbaden: Steiner, 1981);

Die Erfindung der Libido: Das deutsche Epos in der zweiten Hälfte des 19. Jahrhunderts (Mainz: Akademie der Wissenschaften und der Literatur, 1981);

Von fliegenden Fröschen, libidinösen Epen, vaterländischen Romanen, Sprechblasen und Ohrwürmern: 13 Essays (Stuttgart: Klett-Cotta, 1982);

Poesie und Geschichte: Poetik-Seminar Mainz, Wintersemester 1981/82 (Mainz: Von Hase & Köhler, 1983);

Bodo Baumgarten, Malerei (Zirndorf: Verlag für moderne Kunst, 1983);

Versuch über die Lautsonate von Kurt Schwitters (Mainz: Akademie der Wissenschaften und der Literatur, 1983);

Mehr ist nicht zu sagen: Neue Herbste (Stuttgart: Klett-Cotta, 1983);

Von Liebeskunst (Hamburg: Christians, 1986).

OTHER: Ludwig Hohl, *Nuancen und Details*, afterword by Heißenbüttel (Olten: Walter, 1964);

Franz Mon, *Lesebuch*, afterword by Heißenbüttel (Darmstadt & Neuwied: Luchterhand, 1967);

Rudolf Borchardt: Auswahl aus dem Werk, edited by Heißenbüttel (Stuttgart: Klett, 1968);

Eugen Gomringer, *Worte sind Schatten; Die Konstellationen 1951-1968*, edited by Heißenbüttel (Reinbek: Rowohlt, 1969);

John Cage, *Silence*, edited by Heißenbüttel (Neuwied: Luchterhand, 1969);

Antianthologie: Gedichte in deutscher Sprache nach der Zahl ihrer Wörter, edited by Heißenbüttel and Franz Mon (Munich: Hanser, 1973);

Heißenbüttel in 1964 (dpa–Ullstein Bilderdienst)

Max Fürst, *Gefilte Fisch: Eine Jugend in Königsberg*, afterword by Heißenbüttel (Munich: Hanser, 1973);

Max Kommerell, *Gedichte, Gespräche, Übertragungen*, introduction by Heißenbüttel (Olten & Freiburg im Breisgau: Walter, 1973);

Aufklärung über Lichtenberg, contributions by Heißenbüttel (Göttingen: Vandenhoeck & Ruprecht, 1974);

Stuttgarter Kunst im 20. Jahrhundert, edited by Heißenbüttel (Stuttgart: Deutsche Verlags-Anstalt, 1979);

Pravoslav Sovák, *Arbeiten auf Papier*, texts by Heißenbüttel (Stuttgart: Cotta, 1981);

Thomas Lenk, *Skulpturen und Zeichnungen*, texts by Heißenbüttel and Dieter Honisch (Berlin: Hentrich, 1983).

Helmut Heißenbüttel is one of the leading experimental or avant-garde writers in West Germany. For over a quarter of a century he has created works which attempt to reorient the reader's world view through innovative linguistic manipulations. He has also produced many theoretical statements to explain the reasons behind his literary experiments and the results he hopes to achieve. As a critic he has written a host of essays, reviews, statements, speeches, forewords, and afterwords on the gamut of twentieth-century literature and art. As a radio producer in Stuttgart he has introduced the listening public to a wide variety of critical issues in literature, theory, and criticism. He has been a dominant force in shaping postwar German literature, particularly the nontraditional variety.

Heißenbüttel was born in 1921 to Hans and Klara Lorenz Heißenbüttel in the small town of Rüstringen in northern Germany. His father, who was in the navy for twelve years before becoming the town bailiff, wrote essays for the local newspaper. Before World War II Heißenbüttel studied at the Technical College in Dresden. He lost his left arm as a result of wounds sustained in the Soviet Union in 1941. After the war he studied German literature, art history, and English at the Universities of Leipzig and Hamburg. In 1954 he married Ida Warnholz; they have four children. His first book was published in 1954. In May 1955 he began attending meetings of the influential writers' association Gruppe (Group) 47. From 1955 to 1957 he was a reader at the Claassen publishing house in Hamburg. He joined the South German Radio Service in Stuttgart in 1957, and between 1959 and his retirement in 1981 he produced that station's "Radio-Essay" program. He won the scholarship of the Lessing Prize of the City of Hamburg in 1956, the Hugo Jacobi Prize in 1960, the Cultural Award of the State of Lower Saxony in 1962, the Georg Büchner Prize and the Prize of the Committee for Culture of the German Manufacturers' Association in 1969, the Prize of the Blind War Veterans for Best Radio Play in 1971, the International Wine Prize in 1978, and the Order of Merit of the Federal Republic of Germany, First Class, in 1979. He is the director of the literary section of the Academy of the Arts in West Berlin and is a member of P.E.N., the Academy for Literature and Science in Mainz, and the German Academy for Language and Literature in Darmstadt.

Heißenbüttel's main theoretical statements are presented in *Über Literatur* (On Literature, 1966); *Briefwechsel über Literatur* (Correspondence on Literature, 1969), with Heinrich Vormweg; and *Zur Tradition der Moderne* (On the Modern Tra-

dition, 1972). His basic idea is a reshaping of the linguistic relativity theory proposed by Wilhelm von Humboldt in the nineteenth century and later put forward by the American linguists Edward Sapir and Benjamin Lee Whorf. This theory, known as the Sapir-Whorf hypothesis, says that each natural language presents its speakers with a different world view due to the internal structure of the language; thus a native speaker of English sees reality differently from a native speaker of German because their respective languages have forced different interpretations upon their minds. Heißenbüttel extends this view one step further: if people are prevented from obtaining an accurate picture of the world because of their language, then the solution is to change the language.

Language can be changed in two ways, according to Heißenbüttel. The primary method is to change the syntax, which is based on a subject-predicate-object scheme that, he argues, is no longer valid. By eliminating a standard syntax, Heißenbüttel is able to operate with the elements of language much as scientists experiment with material objects: he collects units of language, examines them, arranges them, and recombines them to form new utterances. Because they violate the rules of the standard language, these new statements do not run the danger of repeating the clichés and worn-out ideas inherent in that language. In his search for new expression Heißenbüttel frequently abbreviates language to its bare minimum, in a manner similar to the late phase of expressionist lyric poetry. He also uses permutations and recombinations of words to force the readers to restructure their thought patterns.

The second method of changing language, one that Heißenbüttel has been using in his longer works since 1970, involves the inclusion of considerable quoted material. Heißenbüttel reasons that the concept of individuality, particularly the concept of the individual artist who creates his or her own world order on paper, is outmoded in a scientific and technological age of mass consumerism and mass communication. The only activity left for the author is to quote directly or in paraphrase from the linguistic-cultural milieu of the past and the present. So, in addition to words and morphemes, Heißenbüttel uses phrases or sentences from a myriad of sources as the basis for his new combinations. The resultant montage of language has a twofold purpose: to give the reader an overview of the status quo and at the same time to provide, through a series of new images created by the montage, a fresh view of the world. Heißenbüttel calls these new images hallucinations of reality, and these hallucinations are the ultimate goal of his poetics. Important influences on his work include Theodor Adorno, Guillaume Apollinaire, Hans Arp, Gottfried Benn, Bertolt Brecht, Arno Holz, Stéphane Mallarmé, Filippo Tommaso Marinetti, Ezra Pound, Gertrude Stein, and the linguistic philosopher Ludwig Wittgenstein.

Heißenbüttel's most important publications are a series of six "Textbücher" (Textbooks) that appeared between 1960 and 1967 and were published in one volume as *Das Textbuch* in 1970. Heißenbüttel refers to all of his literary creations as "Texte" (texts), since he rejects genre distinctions; and indeed, it would be impossible to categorize any of these works definitively as poetry, fiction, or drama.

The main theme that runs through the first major division–section A–of *Das Textbuch* is the progressive reduction of the amount of language used to communicate any idea or set of ideas. The earliest texts are made up of short, terse sentences. Nouns and verbs become progressively more abstract. Punctuation marks gradually disappear. Finally, key words–for Heißenbüttel, superfluous words–are omitted. If this procedure were carried any further the text would consist only of a blank sheet of paper. While even this development has been reached in the visual arts, and in one of the early works of Heißenbüttel's fellow language experimenter Jürgen Becker, Heißenbüttel has been reluctant to proceed this far. The texts in section B do not reduce a normal syntax but attempt, to a greater or lesser degree, to destroy it. "Topographien" (Topographies) is the name of an important series of five texts, together only two and a half pages long, in section B. It is here that the destruction of syntax begins. Scattered among grammatically correct sentences are ambiguous and difficult ones that present many possible interpretations, depending on how their elements are linked together. The process of determining variant interpretations demonstrates Heißenbüttel's theoretical aims, for increasing the possible connotations of any one sentence can conceivably increase the expressive potential of language itself.

Many of the other texts in the second section experiment with montage, combining linguistic elements not usually associated with each other. This procedure sometimes results in a

Cover for Heißenbüttel's 1979 experiment in rewriting the history of Europe from the perspective of the year 2000

severe limitation of the number of elements needed for a linguistic structure to carry meaning; it can also result in word-association games. Individual words in this section have been freed from the "domination" of syntax and allowed to enter into new combinations. The extreme variety of these newly formed linguistic constructions can provide the reader with the necessary "hallucination of reality" or alternative vision of the world.

The year 1970 marked a watershed for Heißenbüttel, for most of the works he has published since then are longer and are not marked by the severe syntactic experimentation of the textbooks. In fact, many of the texts approach the traditional form which Heißenbüttel had previously rejected so vigorously. Heißenbüttel, however, has not abandoned his theoretical tenets but has only moved on to his second method of changing language: instead of a montage of words and morphemes, he creates a montage of quoted material. The need to restructure language is still at the center of his concern; he has just chosen larger chunks of language with which to experiment.

Since 1970 Heißenbüttel has called his major works "Projekte" (projects). *Projekt Nr. 1: D'Alemberts Ende* (Project No. 1: D'Alembert's End, 1970) is a gigantic collage of quotations from the works of writers such as Freud, Goethe, Hegel, and Marx as well as from the current intellectual scene. According to Heißenbüttel, the work is a satire of all the ideas in vogue in 1968 in Germany (thus the reference in the title to the great French encyclopedist). Various passages indicate that it is also a parody of Goethe's *Die Wahlverwandtschaften* (1809; translated as *Elective Affinities*, 1854), but only to the extent that it demonstrates the impossibility of a contemporary author proposing a unified world view. There is no longer unanimity of opinion about the world, only a plethora of contradictory views represented by the various quotations. The only stance contemporary literature can take is to quote this material; but since the quoted matter has lost any real meaning, the author is actually only quoting language. It remains the task of the reader to derive new perspectives on the world from the "synthetic authenticity" that Heißenbüttel creates with his quotations. In case the reader should fail to grasp the purpose behind this 390-page "text," Heißenbüttel has included several theoretical commentaries and explanations, a practice not uncommon among avant-garde writers.

Heißenbüttel continues his penchant for quotations in his second project, *Das Durchhauen des Kohlhaupts* (The Splitting of the Cabbage, 1974). Written in a dialogue form reminiscent of a radio play, the thirteen "Lehrgedichte" (didactic poems) contain a grand collage of newspaper headlines, advertisements, clichés, and the lyrics of rock songs. Heißenbüttel performs permutations and combinations on this material, and he includes some parallel texts which force one literally to read "between the lines." His purpose is similar to his aim in *D'Alemberts Ende*, as the mini-interpretations included in the texts attest: to convince the reader of the relativity and lack of certainty in all opinions and ideas, to demonstrate the impossibility of creativity or communication in the contemporary world, and to provide fresh insights through the rearrangement of the quoted material. Since Heißenbüttel believes that linguistic patterns govern one's image of the world, he thinks that an exposure to other thought patterns, particularly when several contradictory ones are juxtaposed, should contribute to heightening or changing one's perception of reality.

An underlying theme of this work, also apparent to some degree in *D'Alemberts Ende*, is death. The title of the book comes from a passage in which Hegel compares death to the insignificant act of splitting a head of cabbage. Heißenbüttel acknowledges the inevitability and meaninglessness of death but defies it by collecting and reproducing printed material on the theme of death.

Heißenbüttel has divided his third project into three separate books: *Eichendorffs Untergang und andere Märchen* (Eichendorff's Demise and Other Fairy Tales, 1978), *Wenn Adolf Hitler den Krieg nicht gewonnen hätte: Historische Novellen und wahre Begebenheiten* (If Adolf Hitler Had Not Won the War: Historical Novellas and True Events, 1979), and *Das Ende der Alternative: Einfache Geschichten* (The End of the Alternative: Simple Stories, 1980). The many short texts that make up each of these works appear to be written in a conventional prose style; thus it would seem that Heißenbüttel has abandoned his experimental stance. A closer look reveals, however, that he has turned his attention to yet another linguistic concern: the concept of narrative fiction. Again and again in these books he calls the reader's attention to the linguistic act of creating a fictional text.

In *Eichendorffs Untergang und andere Märchen* Heißenbüttel is interested primarily in playful quotation and imitation of the works and styles of other writers, but it is often difficult to determine whether his inspiration lies in a particular author, in his own experience, or in his imagination, so thoroughly fused are these disparate elements. Frequently the narrative is interrupted by psychological explanations, by shockingly strong sexual content, or by bizarre events; the theme of aging often intrudes. All of these devices, as well as frequent comments by the author on his style, give the reader the opportunity to observe language in action, to see how language is used to create a narrative style. The reader is gradually supposed to become aware that the concept of narrative fiction is only a fairy tale, that the present technological age has made fiction impossible. All works of literature today, according to Heißenbüttel, are hollow reproductions of that which has already been said.

Cover for Heißenbüttel's 1980 exercise in self-reflection

In *Wenn Adolf Hitler den Krieg nicht gewonnen hätte* Heißenbüttel imagines what Germany would be like in the year 2000 if Hitler had won World War II, and then projects backwards. Walter Benjamin's suicide, Brecht's Danish exile, and Nietzsche's relationship to Lou Salomé are among topics on which he muses in brief texts parodying the essay or the novella. All of these historical references, however, are only pretexts for his reflections on the act of narration. He embellishes history with associations of ideas that spring from his memory and his subconscious; these associations then lead to comments on the nature of fiction and language. Thus history has the same significance for Heißenbüttel as literature: it is a way to investigate the phenomenon of language and to provoke his readers into reexamining their relationship to reality through language.

In *Das Ende der Alternative* Heißenbüttel directs his attention to himself. He quotes from his earlier works and continues some of the narrative strands contained therein. This self-reflection leads Heißenbüttel to comment on his literary technique, on the phenomenon of narration, and on the implications of these for his oeuvre. He realizes as he grows older that there are, as the title suggests, no more alternatives for politics, for his life, for his literary activity, or for the language he has scrutinized so arduously throughout his long career.

Heißenbüttel has written several other works which also contain, to varying degrees, the sort of linguistic experimentation displayed in his major books. *Gelegenheitsgedichte und Klappentexte* (Occasional Poems and Blurbs, 1973), a collection of short pieces written for exhibitions and catalogs of artists, subjects various standard literary methods to critical scrutiny. *Die goldene Kuppel des Comes Arbogast oder Lichtenberg in Hamburg: Fast eine einfache Geschichte* (The Golden Dome of Comes Arbogast; or, Lichtenberg in Hamburg: Almost a Simple Story, 1980) contains twenty-three short selections which examine the contemporary individual's lack of identity in a world governed by purely linguistic memory and associations. *Ödipuskomplex made in Germany* (Oedipus Complex Made in Germany, 1981) is a collection of texts written between 1965 and 1980 which are similar to those in the textbooks. *Von fliegenden Fröschen, libidinösen Epen, vaterländischen Romanen, Sprechblasen und Ohrwürmern* (Of Flying Frogs, Libidinous Epics, Novels of the Fatherland, Speech Balloons and Earwigs, 1982) is a collection of lectures and essays on literary theory written between 1975 and 1981.

Helmut Heißenbüttel may be the most important experimenter with language in contemporary German letters. He outlined his goals early and has adhered to them throughout his career. His works can be difficult, but they reward the patient reader with a host of penetrating insights as well as a certain degree of humor and a fascinating playfulness. They do, however, demand the active participation of the reader, who must draw his own conclusions and continue creative experimentation where Heißenbüttel leaves off. This process requires knowledge of Heißenbüttel's theoretical writings as a basis for approaching his work. Those who do not wish to obtain this knowledge or who are unwilling to engage actively in the creative process will tend, as many critics have done, to dismiss Heißenbüttel as a charlatan. If one approaches his work looking for traditional forms of poetry and prose, one is bound to be disappointed. If, however, one tentatively accepts Heißenbüttel's hypotheses, one might find his conclusion that life and reality have become linguistic fictions not altogether unreasonable. In any case, it cannot be denied that Heißenbüttel has contributed immensely to an increased awareness of and sensitivity to language among contemporary German-speaking authors.

References:

Heinz Ludwig Arnold, ed., *Helmut Heißenbüttel* (Munich: Edition text + kritik, 1981);

Jürgen Becker, "Helmut Heißenbüttel," in *Schriftsteller der Gegenwart*, edited by Klaus Nonnenmann (Olten & Freiburg im Breisgau: Walter, 1963), pp. 143-150;

Robert A. Burns, *Commitment, Language and Reality: An Introduction to the Work of Helmut Heissenbüttel* (Coventry, U.K.: University of Warwick, Department of German Studies, 1975);

Reinhard Döhl, "Helmut Heißenbüttel," *Deutsche Literatur der Gegenwart*, volume 1, edited by Dietrich Weber (Stuttgart: Kröner, 1976), pp. 627-656;

Karl Heinz Köhler, *Reduktion als Erzählverfahren in Heißenbüttels Textbüchern* (Frankfurt am Main: Haag & Herchen, 1978);

Otto Lorenz, "Helmut Heißenbüttel," in *Kritisches Lexikon der deutschsprachigen Gegenwartsliteratur*, edited by Arnold (Munich: Edition text + kritik, 1982), n. pag.;

Hartmut Pätzold, *Theorie und Praxis moderner Schreibweisen: Am Beispiel von Siegfried Lenz und Helmut Heißenbüttel* (Bonn: Bouvier, 1976);

Rainer Rumold, *Sprachliches Experiment und literarische Tradition: Zu den Texten Helmut Heißenbüttels* (Bern: Lang, 1975).

Günter Herburger
(6 April 1932-   )

Jochen Richter
Allegheny College

BOOKS: *Eine gleichmäßige Landschaft: Erzählungen* (Cologne & Berlin: Kiepenheuer & Witsch, 1964); translated by Geoffrey Skelton as *A Monotonous Landscape: Seven Stories* (New York: Harcourt, Brace & World, 1968; London: Calder & Boyars, 1969);

Ventile: Gedichte (Cologne & Berlin: Kiepenheuer & Witsch, 1966);

Die Messe: Roman (Neuwied & Berlin: Luchterhand, 1969);

Training: Gedichte (Neuwied & Berlin: Luchterhand, 1970);

Jesus in Osaka: Roman (Neuwied & Berlin: Luchterhand, 1970); adapted as *Jesus in Osaka: Ein Stück für Arenen, Sportplätze, Zirkus, Kathedralen, Werkhallen, Olympiaden, Flugplätze und Bergkuppen* (Frankfurt am Main, 1971);

Birne kann alles: 26 Abenteuergeschichten für Kinder (Neuwied & Berlin: Luchterhand, 1971);

Birne kann noch mehr: 26 Abenteuergeschichten für Kinder (Neuwied & Berlin: Luchterhand, 1971);

Die Eroberung der Zitadelle: Erzählungen (Darmstadt & Neuwied: Luchterhand, 1972);

Helmut in der Stadt: Erzählung für Kinder (Reinbek: Rowohlt, 1972);

Die amerikanische Tochter: Gedichte, Aufsätze, Hörspiel, Erzählung, Film (Darmstadt & Neuwied: Luchterhand, 1973); "Exhibition oder Ein Kampf um Rom" translated by Andre Lefevere as "Exhibition; or, A Battle for Rome," *Dimension*, 3 (1972): 456-507;

Operette: Gedichte (Darmstadt & Neuwied: Luchterhand, 1973);

Hauptlehrer Hofer; Ein Fall von Pfingsten: Zwei Erzählungen mit einem Nachwort des Autors (Darmstadt & Neuwied: Luchterhand, 1975);

Nüssen und andere Erzählungen (Berlin & Weimar: Aufbau, 1975);

Birne brennt durch: 26 Abenteuergeschichten für Kinder und Erwachsene (Darmstadt & Neuwied: Luchterhand, 1975);

Ziele: Gedichte (Reinbek: Rowohlt, 1977);

Günter Herburger (photograph by Klaus Behr, courtesy of Ullstein Bilderdienst)

Flug ins Herz: Roman, 2 volumes (Darmstadt & Neuwied: Luchterhand, 1977);

Orchidee: Gedichte (Darmstadt & Neuwied: Luchterhand, 1979);

Die Augen der Kämpfer: Roman (Darmstadt & Neuwied: Luchterhand, 1980);

Blick aus dem Paradies; Thuja: Zwei Spiele eines Themas (Darmstadt & Neuwied: Luchterhand, 1981);

Makadam: Gedichte (Darmstadt & Neuwied: Luchterhand, 1982);

Das Flackern des Feuers im Land: Beschreibungen (Darmstadt & Neuwied: Luchterhand, 1983);

Capri: Die Geschichte eines Diebs (Darmstadt & Neuwied: Luchterhand, 1984);

Kinderreich Passmoré: Gedichte (Darmstadt & Neuwied: Luchterhand, 1986).

OTHER: "Saison," in *Aus der Welt der Arbeit*, edited by Fritz Hüser and Max von der Grün (Neuwied & Berlin: Luchterhand, 1966), pp. 270-280;

"Die Verzögerung," in *Porträts*, edited by Walter Karsch (Berlin, Munich & Vienna: Herbig, 1967), pp. 13-19;

"Ende der Nazizeit und andere Gedichte," in *Neue Texte deutscher Autoren*, edited by Martin Gregor-Dellin (Tübingen & Basel: Erdmann, 1971), pp. 152-155;

"Das Allgäu," in *Daheim ist daheim*, edited by Alois Brandstetter (Salzburg: Residenz, 1973), pp. 101-108.

PERIODICAL PUBLICATIONS: "Das Haus," *Augenblicke*, 1 (1961): 59-61;

"Anderer Abend eines Chauffeurs," *konkret*, no. 5 (1965): 28-29, 32-33;

"Tag der offenen Tür," *Der Monat*, 209 (1966): 59-69;

"Training," *Neue Rundschau*, 78 (1967): 637-644;

"Tanker," *Akzente*, 14 (1967): 455-475;

"Dogmatisches über Gedichte," *Kursbuch*, 10 (1967): 150-161;

"Wider die Fernsehfabriken," *Film*, 5 (1967): 40;

"Eine dritte Revolution: Über Enzensbergers 'Kursbuch 9,'" *Der Spiegel*, 21 (July 1967): 82-83;

"Landschaft und Vorfahren," *Der Monat*, 222 (1967): 24-30;

"Bankrott der Väter," *Der Monat*, 226 (1967): 5-8;

"Filmklima," *Film*, 10 (1967): 10;

"Die Tätowierung: Filmprotokoll," *Film*, 10 (1967): 45-56;

"Viktor und Bruno: Catch," *konkret*, no. 16 (1969): 40-45;

"Hope," *Kürbiskern*, 1 (1975): 125-138;

"Palimpsest," *Literaturmagazin*, 3 (1976): 191-199;

"Romankapitel: Wieder anfangen," *Literaturmagazin*, 6 (1976): 84-108;

"Gedichte aus Schwaben," *Akzente*, 23 (1976): 135-138.

Günter Herburger's books have earned him several awards, among them the Literature Prize of the City of Bremen in 1973. He is a successful writer of novels, short stories, poems, children's literature, radio plays, and screenplays. Until 1970 his work was discussed mainly in connection with the Cologne School and its contemporary real-

ism. Since then, Herburger has developed a distinct and unmistakable style of his own.

Herburger was born in Isny im Allgäu on 6 April 1932. After his father's death in 1943 he grew up in the home of his grandfather. He portrays himself as a loner in high school who had little interest in schoolwork and struggled to finish his education. In 1951 he began to study literature, drama, sociology, philosophy, and Sanskrit, first in Munich and then at the Sorbonne in Paris. Lack of money forced him to drop out after a few semesters, and he spent the next ten years drifting through southern Europe and northern Africa. He earned his living at all sorts of odd jobs and experienced life at the fringes of society among tramps, alcoholics, and homosexuals. After a serious illness he returned to Germany and worked as a doorman in Munich and a journalist and television editor in Stuttgart. In 1960 he turned to free-lance writing. He moved to West Berlin in 1964; that year he was invited to join Gruppe (Group) 47, the most influential group of authors in postwar Germany. One year later he received the Berlin Art Prize–Prize "Young Generation," an award given to promising young authors. He moved back to Munich in 1969. During the 1972 elections he worked for the German Communist party; he joined the party the following year. Herburger is married for the third time and has two children. He is a member of the P.E.N. Club of the Federal Republic of Germany.

Herburger's first published work, *Eine gleichmäßige Landschaft* (1964; translated as *A Monotonous Landscape*, 1968), is a collection of seven stories with a common theme. With one exception, all the protagonists are males in their thirties. All of them feel empty and full of rage and try to break out of their present condition, but they all fail. At the end they are resigned, disillusioned, and willing to conform. Herburger shows that beneath the peaceful, orderly, and happy surface of German society lies a monotonous, oppressive, and empty reality that can explode into violence and rebellion at any time. In the title story, for example, the narrator, a bank employee, leads the reader into a well-cared-for park which turns out to be the former concentration camp Bergen-Belsen. As he walks through the park an impotent rage against his monotonous and conforming existence discharges itself in brutal and violent fantasies of raping, torturing, and killing the girl who accompanies him. In reality nothing happens, and the narrator returns to his boring, repressed everyday life.

The attempt to break out is also the major theme of Herburger's first novel, *Die Messe* (The Fair, 1969). Hermann Brix, the thirty-year-old protagonist, refuses his uncle's offer of employment and middle-class status. Instead, he steals money and tries to establish a life of his own. He fails and finally agrees to work at his uncle's furniture factory. His protest against social conformity has shrunk to his secret approval of a man called Jesus who is defacing furniture at a fair with acid.

Despite Brix's final refusal to be integrated into society, the novel follows the traditional pattern of an Entwicklungsroman (novel of development). What sets it apart is Herburger's narrative technique. In his effort to describe every detail and in his refusal to distinguish between the important and the trivial, Herburger pays equal attention to the care of canaries, the production of ice cream, and the names of metro stations in Paris. The sheer quantity of information is supposed to yield a cohesive slice of reality. The actual result, however, is that Herburger's world loses its concreteness and assumes grotesque dimensions. He succeeds in showing reality to be complex and impenetrable; but frequently, this reality resembles a mail-order catalogue with an immense supply of unrelated items.

Herburger's second novel, *Jesus in Osaka*, was published in 1970. In eight loosely connected episodes set in the future he describes Jesus's experiences in a highly industrialized, technological mass society. Jesus, an odd mixture of anarchist, pop star, and Everyman, is the only individualized character in the novel, which criticizes the excesses of capitalism and technology. As a construction worker, a participant in a televised debate with a famous theologian, and an ardent critic of the pope, he demonstrates solidarity with the poor and oppressed. By leaving his cross behind he shows that he refuses to be a symbol of suffering; instead, he actively strives for the improvement of mankind. Herburger repeats the detailed style of narration of *Die Messe,* adding some utopian and exotic features. Whereas his protagonists in the earlier books ended in resignation and conformism, he now offers a vague hope for the future: at the conclusion of the novel Jesus leads a group of children toward a better world of love and brotherhood. The frequent use of stereotyped formulas and crudely rhymed two-line verses is supposed to support

the playful and childlike innocence of Herburger's proposed solution.

In the short-story collection *Die Eroberung der Zitadelle* (The Conquest of the Citadel, 1972) Herburger tries to define his position between the bourgeois world in which he lives and the better society he envisions for the future. He questions the capitalist system of ownership in the title story, criticizes the traditional methods of artistic production in "Figaros Tochter" (Figaro's Daughter), and explores his own role as a writer in "Lenau." His model for the future is the world of the children in "Kongs Kinder" (Kong's Children); although this world is destroyed by the adults, the story ends with a vague reconciliation. The story "Hauptlehrer Hofer," in the volume *Hauptlehrer Hofer; Ein Fall von Pfingsten: Zwei Erzählungen mit einem Nachwort des Autors* (Headmaster Hofer; A Case of Pentecost: Two Stories with an Afterword by the Author, 1975), confirms this utopian model in a more realistic setting. Hofer's efforts to educate the poor and underprivileged fail, but he does not give up: "Absicht und Eifer sind zerstoben, Begeisterung hat sich in Wehmut verwandelt, Hoffnung aber ist geblieben. Deshalb erzählte ich davon" (Purpose and eagerness are scattered; enthusiasm has changed to melancholy; hope, however, has remained. That is why I told this story). Compared to the novels, the narrative style in the stories is more controlled, less associative, and less crammed with details. The stories are also lightened by the introduction of elements from popular culture such as King Kong, Tarzan, and Flipper.

In 1977 *Flug ins Herz* (Flight into the Heart) was published in two volumes; a sequel, *Die Augen der Kämpfer* (The Eyes of the Fighters), followed in 1980. The narrator is a worker, Johann Jakob Weberbeck, whose marriage has failed and who has survived a suicide attempt. He joins a revolutionary worker's group which engages in sociological and genetic experimentation. He suffers imprisonment, experiences the plight of foreign workers, witnesses a mass suicide of adolescents, lives in a backward agrarian utopia called Morgenthau Country, and ends up in the German Democratic Republic. As in the earlier novels, the plot quickly dissolves into loosely connected episodes which are held together by the narrator alone. Surrealistic scenes are followed by critical passages about modern civilization and economics; fairy-tale elements alternate with minute realistic descriptions. The mixture of satire and ideology

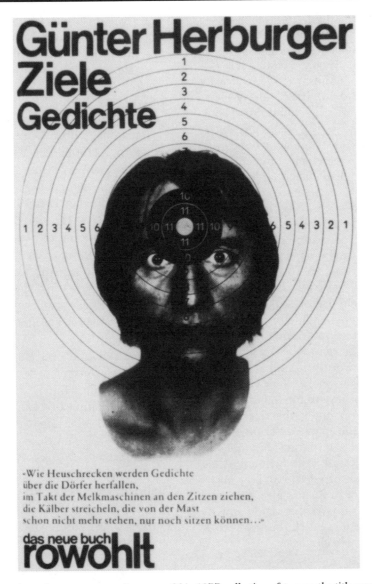

Herburger pictured as a target on the cover of his 1977 collection of poems; the title means "Aims"

and the indulgence in detail lead to a domination of the act of narration over structure and cohesion. There is a noticeable reversion to a more pessimistic outlook in this trilogy.

Children as representatives of a better future are a recurring theme in Herburger's work. In *Birne kann alles* (Birne Can Do Anything, 1971), *Birne kann noch mehr* (Birne Can Do Even More, 1971), *Helmut in der Stadt* (Helmut in the City, 1972), and *Birne brennt durch* (Birne Blows a Fuse, 1975) Herburger addresses children directly. Birne, an electric light bulb with superhuman powers, solves many problems and survives a variety of severe tests. Although Herburger offers detailed, realistic descriptions and introduces modern social conditions and technological phe-

nomena into children's literature, his solutions to the problems he raises are mainly taken from the oversimplified worlds of fairy tales and cartoons. Despite this weakness, the books have found a large readership.

Herburger's radio and television plays have also been successful; in most cases they are based on themes from his fiction and are dominated by the realism of his early phase. Only four of them– "Exhibition oder Ein Kampf um Rom" (broadcast in 1971, published in 1973; translated as "Exhibition; or, A Battle for Rome," 1972), "Die amerikanische Tochter" (The American Daughter, 1973), "Blick aus dem Paradies" (A View from Paradise, 1981), and "Thuja" (1981)–have been published. They reflect the mixture of realism with fantastic, exotic, and parodistic elements that characterizes Herburger's later works.

Herburger has published seven volumes of poetry: *Ventile* (Valves, 1966), *Training* (1970), *Operette* (1973), *Ziele* (Aims, 1977), *Orchidee* (1979), *Makadam* (Macadam, 1982), and *Kinderreich Passmoré* (Realm of the Children, 1986). Themes from the prose works frequently recur in the poems and are expressed in a purposely unpretentious language sometimes tinged with Herburger's native Swabian dialect. The poems mainly depict everyday occurrences and emotions, although they do not exclude utopian and exotic elements. Like the novels, the poems tend to overwhelm by their loquaciousness and suffer at times from lack of formal discipline and linguistic precision.

Herburger's work has received mixed reactions from critics. His children's books and short stories are generally praised, while his novels and some of his poems are seen as daring but unsuccessful experiments. The main objections are directed at an excessive wordiness and concentration on details which make no effort to discriminate between the important and the superfluous. There can be no doubt that Herburger has moved away from the sparse descriptive style of the Cologne School. Herburger himself has named Hermann Broch and Arno Schmidt as his literary models. His use of certain stylistic techniques and his mixing of utopian, satirical, exotic, and realistic elements support this claim; but its strong social commitment gives Herburger's work a unique and unmistakable character.

Bibliography:
Peter Bekes, "Günter Herburger," in *Kritisches Lexikon zur deutschsprachigen Gegenwartsliteratur*, edited by Heinz Ludwig Arnold, volume 2 (Munich: Edition text + kritik, 1978), n. pag.

References:
Yaak Karsunke, "Belanglose Belletristik: Undogmatisches über Günter Herburger," *Kürbiskern*, 2 (1968): 226-232;

Thomas Koebner, "Günter Herburger," in *Deutsche Literatur der Gegenwart in Einzeldarstellungen*, edited by Dietrich Weber (Stuttgart: Kröner, 1977), II: 228-253;

Marcel Reich-Ranicki, *Lauter Verrisse* (Munich: Piper, 1970), pp. 106-112;

Reich-Ranicki, *Literatur der kleinen Schritte* (Munich: Piper, 1967), pp. 103-110;

Ursula Reinhold, "Interview mit Günter Herburger," *Weimarer Beiträge*, 21, no. 12 (1976): 71-80;

Reinhold, "Kritik und Utopie in der Prosa Günter Herburgers," *Weimarer Beiträge*, 21, no. 12 (1976): 81-101;

Kurt Rothmann, *Deutschsprachige Schriftsteller seit 1945 in Einzeldarstellungen* (Stuttgart: Reclam, 1985), pp. 178-183;

Alfons Schiele, "Rollen-Prosa," *Der Monat*, 197 (1965): 87-88;

Heinrich Vormweg, "Ein unvollendeter Roman," *Merkur*, 23 (1969): 490-492;

Vormweg, "Revolutionärer Wille und bürgerliche Existenz: Der Erzähler Günter Herburger," *Akzente*, 20 (1973): 226-236;

Jürgen P. Wallmann, Review of *Die Messe*, *Neue Deutsche Hefte*, 3 (1969): 141-145.

Uwe Johnson

(20 July 1934-23? February 1984)

Robert K. Shirer
University of Nebraska at Lincoln

BOOKS: *Mutmaßungen über Jakob: Roman* (Frankfurt am Main: Suhrkamp, 1959); translated by Ursule Molinaro as *Speculations about Jakob* (London: Cape, 1963; New York: Grove Press, 1963);

Das dritte Buch über Achim: Roman (Frankfurt am Main: Suhrkamp, 1961); translated by Molinaro as *The Third Book about Achim* (New York: Harcourt, Brace & World, 1967);

Karsch und andere Prosa (Frankfurt am Main: Suhrkamp, 1964); "Eine Reise wegwohin, 1960" translated by Richard and Clara Winston as *An Absence* (London: Cape, 1969);

Zwei Ansichten (Frankfurt am Main: Suhrkamp, 1965); translated by Richard and Clara Winston as *Two Views* (New York: Harcourt, Brace & World, 1966; London: Cape, 1967);

Jahrestage: Aus dem Leben von Gesine Cresspahl, 4 volumes (Frankfurt am Main: Suhrkamp, 1970-1973, 1983); translated by Leila Vennewitz as *Anniversaries: From the Life of Gesine Cresspahl*, 2 volumes (New York & London: Harcourt Brace Jovanovich, 1975, 1987);

Eine Reise nach Klagenfurt (Frankfurt am Main: Suhrkamp, 1974);

Berliner Sachen: Aufsätze (Frankfurt am Main: Suhrkamp, 1975);

Begleitumstände: Frankfurter Vorlesungen (Frankfurt am Main: Suhrkamp, 1980);

Skizze eines Verunglückten (Frankfurt am Main: Suhrkamp, 1982);

Ingrid Babendererde: Reifeprüfung 1953 (Frankfurt am Main: Suhrkamp, 1985);

Der 5. Kanal (Frankfurt am Main: Suhrkamp, 1987).

OTHER: Herman Melville, *Israel Potter: Seine fünfzig Jahre im Exil*, translated by Johnson (Leipzig: Dietrich'sche Verlagsbuchhandlung, 1961);

John Knowles, *In diesem Land*, translated by Johnson (Frankfurt am Main: Suhrkamp, 1963);

Bertolt Brecht, *Me-ti: Buch der Wendungen, Fragment*, edited by Johnson (Frankfurt am Main: Suhrkamp, 1965);

Uwe Johnson (Uwe Johnson, Begleitumstände *[Frankfurt am Main: Suhrkamp, 1980])*

"Einer meiner Lehrer," in *Hans Mayer zum 60. Geburtstag*, edited by Walter Jens and Fritz J. Raddatz (Reinbek: Rowohlt, 1967), pp. 118-126;

Das neue Fenster: Selections from Contemporary German Literature, compiled by Johnson (New York: Harcourt, Brace & World, 1967);

"Dead Author's Identity in Doubt: Publishers Defiant," in *Vorletzte Worte: Schriftsteller schrieben ihren eigenen Nachruf*, edited by Karl Heinz Kramberg (Frankfurt am Main: Bärmeier & Nikel, 1970), pp. 116-124;

"Brief an Walser," in *Leporello fällt aus der Rolle: Zeitgenössische Autoren erzählen das Leben von Figuren der Weltliteratur weiter*, edited by Peter Härtling (Frankfurt am Main: Fischer, 1971), pp. 216-217;

"Nachforschungen in New York: Rede bei der Entgegennahme des Georg-Büchner-Preises," in *Büchner-Preis-Reden, 1951-1971*, edited by Ernst Johann (Stuttgart: Reclam, 1972), pp. 217-240;

"Einatmen und hinterlegen," in *Günter Eich zum Gedächtnis*, edited by Siegfried Unseld (Frankfurt am Main: Suhrkamp, 1973), pp. 74-77;

"Erste Lese-Erlebnisse," in *Erste Lese-Erlebnisse*, edited by Unseld (Frankfurt am Main: Suhrkamp, 1975), pp. 101-110;

"Vorschläge zur Prüfung eines Romans," in *Romantheorie: Dokumentation ihrer Geschichte in Deutschland seit 1880*, edited by Eberhard Lämmert and Hartmut Eggert (Cologne: Kiepenheuer & Witsch, 1975), pp. 398-403;

Max Frisch, *Stich-Worte*, edited by Johnson (Frankfurt am Main: Suhrkamp, 1975);

Das Werk von Samuel Beckett: Berliner Colloquium, edited by Johnson and Hans Mayer (Frankfurt am Main: Suhrkamp, 1975);

"Zu *Montauk*," in *Über Max Frisch II*, edited by Walter Schmitz (Frankfurt am Main: Suhrkamp, 1976), pp. 448-450;

Von dem Fischer un syner Fru: Ein Märchen nach Philipp Otto Runge mit sieben Bildern von Marcus Behmer, einer Nacherzählung und einem Nachwort, translated by Johnson (Frankfurt am Main: Insel, 1976);

Margret Boveri, *Verzweigungen: Eine Autobiographie*, edited by Johnson (Munich & Zurich: Piper, 1977).

PERIODICAL PUBLICATIONS: "Mir ist gelegen an Fairness: Erklärung von Uwe Johnson auf der Pressekonferenz des Suhrkamp Verlages am 5. Dezember 1961," *Deutsche Zeitung mit Wirtschaftszeitung* (Cologne), 7 December 1961;

"Ich nenne Hermann Kesten einen Lügner: Uwe Johnsons Erklärung in Frankfurt," *Die Welt*, 9 December 1961;

"Pro Wolf Biermann: Erklärungen von Heinrich Böll, Peter Weiss und Uwe Johnson," *Der Tagesspiegel*, 18 December 1965;

"Beisetzung Giangiacomo Feltrinelli," *Kürbiskern*, 8 (1972): 367-371;

"Besuch im Krankenhaus: Erinnerung an Margret Boveri–Zum 75. Geburtstag der Schriftstellerin," *Die Zeit*, 15 August 1975;

"Ich habe zu danken," *Frankfurter Allgemeine Zeitung*, 8 December 1975;

"Gast war ich gerne: Keine Mafia, sondern Tagung meiner Innung," *Die Zeit*, 15 July 1977;

"Ich über mich," *Die Zeit*, 4 November 1977;

"Ach! Sind Sie ein Deutscher?," *Die Zeit*, 6 February 1978;

"Lübeck habe ich ständig beobachtet," *Vaterstädtische Blätter* (Lübeck), 30 (March / April 1979): 51-57;

"Ein Vorbild," *Literaturmagazin*, 10 (1979): 167-170;

"Ein unergründliches Schiff," *Merkur*, 33 (1979): 537-550;

"Seien Sie vielmals bedankt! Mitteilungen aus der alltäglichen Nachbarschaft eines Schriftstellers," *Die Zeit*, 13 August 1980.

When *Mutmaßungen über Jakob* (translated as *Speculations about Jakob*, 1963), Uwe Johnson's first published novel, appeared in 1959, Johnson immediately became one of the most discussed and most controversial German authors. The novel displayed a virtuosity of language and narrative technique that was remarkable in a first publication, and it incorporated the fact of the division of Germany–and Europe–in a manner that was unprecedented in postwar German literature. Johnson's subsequent work maintained the technical brilliance and linguistic sophistication of *Mutmaßungen über Jakob*, and it continued to examine the juxtaposition of what Johnson called the "beiden Ordnungen, nach denen heute in der Welt gelebt werden kann" (two systems under which one can live in the world today). His persistence in examining the effects of this division on his characters garnered him the titles "poet of both Germanies" and "poet of divided Germany," labels Johnson loathed and rejected. With an insistence on precision of language characteristic of him, he refused to associate himself with the political and ideological connotations these titles carried: "Peinlich ist in solcher Nachrede die Vermutung wahrzunehmen, er befasse sich mit den für ihn vorliegenden 'beiden Deutschland,' weil die Mehrzahl ihn verstimme und er einen Singular vorziehe in einer Wieder-Vereinigung" (It is embarrassing in such slander to perceive the assumption that he concerns himself with the "two Germanies" he confronts, because the plural distresses him and he would prefer a singular in a re-unification). Moreover, Johnson insisted that his thematic concerns were merely a function of his biography and that it was this biography that provided him not only with his themes but also with the skeptical attitude toward language and ideology from which he fashioned his narrative techniques.

Uwe Johnson was born in Cammin in the province of Pomerania on 20 July 1934. His father, Erich Johnson, was a Mecklenburg farmer who became the administrator of a large estate; his mother, Erna Sträde Johnson, was the daughter of a west Pomeranian farmer. He grew up in the small town of Anklam an der Peene. There, by his own account in *Begleitumstände* (Attendant Circumstances, 1980), he learned from his family to be skeptical of the values and the rhetoric of the Nazis. During the last months of the war Johnson, then in his first year of secondary school, was chosen by a state examination commission to attend a National Socialist "Deutsche Heimschule" (German home school) in Koscian, in what is now Poland. When the advance of the Red Army forced a mass exodus to the west, Johnson was young enough to go; the older students had to stay behind to fight, and many of them died.

Johnson's father was interned after the war and died in a camp in Belorussia in 1947 or 1948. Johnson and his mother and sister settled in a village in Mecklenburg; the mother found work as a train conductor. In the difficult year after the war Johnson worked in the village and on the farms around it for food and other necessities. In 1946, following his father's wishes, he began to attend the John Brinkman-Oberschule in Güstrow. At school Johnson wrote and recited a series of connecting texts for a program of folk songs performed by his school choir, and the "junger Güstrower Poet" received his first review in a local newspaper. In *Begleitumstände* he recounts how, as a seventeen-year-old, he felt the need to shape his own unique experience of the conflict between life and art in the form of a story—until he read Thomas Mann's "Tonio Kröger" (1903; translated, 1914): "Dem etwas hinzuzufügen, das erübrigte sich" (Adding anything to

that was unnecessary). For the next few years his literary activity was restricted to reading.

During the years Johnson was in Güstrow the division of Germany grew more sharply defined. The Western occupation zones merged into an economic unit and then, in 1949, became the Federal Republic of Germany (FRG). In the Soviet zone the eastern Social Democrats were merged with the Communists to form the Socialist Unity party, which began to consolidate its power under the watchful eye of the Soviet Military Administration. In 1949, shortly after the birth of the FRG, the German Democratic Republic (GDR) was proclaimed in the East.

Johnson was a leader of his school's chapter of the party youth group, the Freie Deutsche Jugend (Free German Youth [FDJ]), and he supported the policies of the new administration—land reform, opening of the schools to the children of workers and farmers, and exposing schoolchildren to the evils of National Socialism. But his enthusiasm was tempered by the discrepancies he perceived between the version of reality served up by his teachers and representatives of the party and what he could observe himself: "Andere Lehrer wissen, daß der Schüler lügt beim Aufsagen von Lügen, die er von Niemandem weiß als von ihnen selber, und eine Eins schreiben sie ihm an, und der Schüler sieht ihnen zu dabei" (Other teachers know that the student is lying as he recites lies that he knows from no one other than them, and they give him a one—the highest mark—for it, and the student watches them do it).

There was no lack of opportunity to wonder about the meanings of words and descriptions. *Flüchtlinge* (refugees) and *Vertriebene* (those driven out of the former Eastern provinces) became officially *Umsiedler* (resettlers), and the use of any of these terms brought with it a considerable baggage of ideological connotations. Johnson himself benefited from an exercise in redefinition, for he had been classified as the son of middle-class parents and, as such, not eligible for preferential treatment in gaining entrance to a university; but when his mother switched jobs from passenger-train to freight-train conductor he found himself the son of a worker, possessed of new opportunities. Johnson's suspicion of the relationship between observable reality and the words used to describe it never left him, for he found it affirmed in his experiences in both East and West. It forms one of the most significant elements in his development as a writer.

In 1952, after completing the Abitur (school-leaving exam), Johnson became a student at the University of Rostock. In early 1953 he felt the effects of the nationwide effort by the party to discredit the Christian youth organization, the Junge Gemeinde (Young Congregation). This group was accused of being a "Tarnorganisation für Kriegshetze, Sabotage, und Spionage im USA-Auftrag" (front organization in the service of the USA for agitation to war, sabotage, and espionage). All over the GDR members of the Junge Gemeinde were being expelled from the FDJ and from schools and universities. Johnson was called upon to describe to a meeting of the Rostock FDJ a violent attack by two young Christians upon a recruit of the Red Army which allegedly had taken place in Güstrow. He refused, but when ordered to speak he defended the Christians and cited many violations of the GDR constitution by the government. As a result, he was expelled from school and barred from all universities in the GDR. During the upheavals in June 1953, however, the government reached a rapprochement with the church, and those who had been punished and banished during the Junge Gemeinde incident were quietly rehabilitated and reinstated.

Johnson was thus able to continue his university studies. He was no longer comfortable in Rostock, and in 1954 he moved to Leipzig. Over the next two years he worked and reworked his Rostock experiences into his first novel. *Ingrid Babendererde: Reifeprüfung 1953* (Ingrid Babendererde: School-Leaving Examination 1953), which was published posthumously in 1985, is set in a small Mecklenburg town during the week prior to the school-leaving exam in April 1953. The intrusion of the Junge Gemeinde campaign into the lives of Ingrid Babendererde; her boyfriend, Klaus Niebuhr; their good friend Jürgen Peterson, the leader of the school FDJ chapter; and their other friends has devastating effects. The students know that to associate the local Christian youth with the charges against the national organization is patently ridiculous, but the party presses forward with its accusations. Ingrid is called upon to denounce the young Christians, and after first refusing, she makes a speech which results in her being expelled from school and shadowed by state security agents. Klaus, who had stayed away from the proceedings and had implored Ingrid to do the same, withdraws from school the next day, citing violations of the GDR constitution. Jürgen, at odds with his party

and with himself, helps Klaus and Ingrid make their way to West Berlin, where "sie umsteigen in jene Lebensweise, die sie ansehen für die falsche" (they transfer over to the way of life they consider to be the wrong one). Much of what concerned Johnson as a writer for the rest of his life is prefigured in this youthful novel: the gap between reality and the language various ideologies use to reconstruct it; the inability of those who insist upon saying what they mean to find a home in social environments where such directness is rare in public discourse; the celebration of Mecklenburg; and the fear of losing its language and its landscapes.

In July 1956, during the brief period of more tolerant cultural policies between Khrushchev's condemnation of Stalin at the Twentieth Soviet Party Congress and the Hungarian intervention, Johnson submitted the manuscript of *Ingrid Babendererde* to the Aufbau publishing house. The editors showed interest in the book and admiration for the talents of the young writer, but they were unable to resolve their ideological reservations. Over the next year several other prominent East German publishers–Hinstorff, Paul List, and the Mitteldeutscher Verlag–agreed that the novel could not be published. Late in 1956 the cultural-political newspaper *Sonntag* showed interest in the manuscript, but shortly thereafter its editor was arrested for sedition. *Ingrid Babendererde* would, for its time, have been a truly remarkable East German novel, raising issues that were not explored in the GDR until over a decade later by writers such as Christa Wolf and Hermann Kant.

As it became increasingly clear that publication in the GDR was unlikely, Johnson pursued a contact made possible by his Leipzig professor Hans Mayer with the Frankfurt publisher Peter Suhrkamp. Suhrkamp showed initial enthusiasm for *Ingrid Babendererde*, but the novel was ultimately rejected. The contact remained open, however, and, although Suhrkamp did not live to see it, his house became Johnson's sole German publisher.

His studies with Mayer exposed Johnson to some of the great writers of modern world literature, many of whom were rejected by official GDR cultural policies as bourgeois, decadent, and formalist. He read Samuel Beckett, Alfred Döblin, James Joyce, and William Faulkner; he encountered the work of Walter Benjamin; and his respect for Bertolt Brecht deepened.

Johnson at about the time he began writing his massive four-volume novel Jahrestage *(Kindermann)*

Johnson continued to have problems with the authorities. He wrote an examination in which he took the part of the writers who had criticized official cultural policies at the Sixth Writers' Congress of the GDR in 1956. The exam was declared unacceptable, and Johnson only grudgingly agreed to write another. His thesis on Ernst Barlach's novel *Der gestohlene Mond* (The Stolen Moon, 1948) was rejected. And when he finally received his diploma in 1956, no job offers were forthcoming. While a student Johnson had had a practicum with the Leipzig publisher Reclam, and he had hoped for an editorial position when his studies were completed. His political files were so problematic, however, that he remained " 'arbeitslos' in einem Lande, das solchen Zustand abgeschafft haben wollte" ("unemployed" in a country that claimed to have eliminated such a condition). Supporting himself with literary odd jobs on commission from various publishers, he did editorial work for a modern German translation of the medieval epic, the *Nibelungenlied* (1961); translated Melville's *Israel Potter* (1961); and prepared evaluations of manuscripts. During this time he was working on his second novel. In

late 1956 his mother and sister left the GDR and moved to Karlsruhe, and Johnson was able to retain their former room in Güstrow in addition to his room in Leipzig. He traveled frequently by train between the two cities and became intrigued by the world of railway workers his mother had left behind.

The central character of *Mutmaßungen über Jakob* is Jakob Abs, a Dresden train dispatcher who, as can be inferred from the opening sentences of the novel, has been struck and killed by a locomotive while crossing the tracks on his way through the freight yards to work. The reader encounters a puzzling variety of narrative elements as the people who were close to Jakob try to understand his death. There are fragments of three conversations in which it only gradually becomes clear who is speaking, three stream-of-consciousness monologues, and a third-person narrative. These elements are combined, often in mid sentence, into a recounting of various versions and interpretations of the events leading up to Jakob's death. The reader is forced to piece these events together and draw his own conclusions about the death. This process is further challenged by the language used in these narrative strands: fragments of Mecklenburg dialect, English, and Russian are mixed together; highly unusual syntax combines with idiosyncratic punctuation; and the narrator constantly disassembles conventional compound words or assembles unconventional ones. In a 1962 interview with the magazine *konkret* Johnson explained: "Ich habe das Buch so geschrieben, als würden die Leute es so langsam lesen, wie ich es geschrieben habe" (I wrote the book in such a way that people would read it as slowly as I wrote it).

In the fall of 1956 Jakob Abs learns that his mother has left the Mecklenburg town of Jerichow, where she and Jakob had settled with the family of Heinrich Cresspahl after the war, and has gone to the West. Jakob is contacted by Rohlfs, an officer of the East German State Security Service, and learns that Rohlfs had approached Frau Abs in the hope of establishing a working relationship with Cresspahl's daughter Gesine, who has been in the West since 1953 and works as a secretary and interpreter for NATO. Although Frau Abs's response had been to bolt, Jakob agrees to consider Rohlfs's proposal and to meet with him again.

His mother's departure and his encounter with the world of the secret police and espionage intrude into Jakob's well-integrated social role as

119

a responsible worker. When Jakob goes to Jerichow to put his mother's affairs in order he is confronted by another, equally disturbing point of view, for there he meets Gesine's former lover Jonas Blach, a dissident intellectual who has sought refuge with Cresspahl to work on a manuscript critical of the East German political system.

After he returns to work, Jakob's situation is further complicated by the unexpected arrival of Gesine, who makes a clandestine visit to the GDR to check on her father—and perhaps for other reasons. Jakob meets Rohlfs and tells him that he will not approach Gesine. He then makes his way with her to Jerichow, with Rohlfs close on their heels. It is the night of the Soviet intervention in Hungary, and Jakob is worried that Gesine's visit will be seen as part of a plot to stir up trouble in the GDR. He arranges a meeting with Rohlfs, who agrees to guarantee Gesine's safe passage back to the West if she will meet with him later in West Berlin.

After Gesine's visit Jakob returns briefly to work, where he must help dispatch Soviet military trains on their way to Hungary. He obtains leave, ostensibly to visit his mother but in reality to see Gesine, for during her return to the GDR they fell in love. But Jakob does not feel that he belongs in the West, and despite her request that he stay with her, he returns to the GDR. There, as he crosses the tracks in foggy weather on his way back to work, he is struck by a train and killed.

This story leaves the reader with much to ponder. Jakob was clearly a man of exemplary integrity who was disturbed by both personal and political events. His death, whether an accident, suicide, or murder, prevented him from confronting life under the altered circumstances he would have had to face. The perspectives of those who remain—of Gesine, the ex-GDR citizen; of Jonas, the dissident; of Jöche, a worker and friend of Jakob's who participates in one of the conversations; and of Rohlfs, the representative of the state—are all given their due; limited by ideology and interest, none can give a complete or trustworthy account. The narrator can do no more than contribute what he knows and use his skill as editor to weave together the other narrative strands. The reader is invited to join the narrator in his exercise in "Wahrheitsfindung" (discovery of the truth).

Mutmaßungen über Jakob was published by Suhrkamp in July 1959. Johnson chose the same time to move to West Berlin. He had made it a point to have his publishers arrange a residency permit for him in advance, and for the remainder of his life he flatly refused to allow the term *Flüchtling* (refugee) to be applied to him. Over and over he insisted, "Ich bin umgezogen" (I moved).

Mutmaßungen über Jakob attracted enormous critical attention. Although some critics were disturbed by the radical use of language and the modernistic narrative techniques, there was admiration for the virtuosity of this first publication and considerable enthusiasm for a young author who had dared to address the important and neglected theme of the division of Europe. Critics as varied in outlook as Günter Blöcker, Reinhard Baumgart, Gerd Semmer, and Marcel Reich-Ranicki praised the book and saw great promise in Johnson.

Johnson's emergence as an important German literary figure was soon confirmed by various honors. In 1959 he received an invitation to participate in the meetings of the Gruppe (Group) 47, the association of writers organized in 1947 by Hans Werner Richter, at which most of the leading literary personalities of West Germany, Switzerland, and Austria read and discussed their work. In 1960 he was awarded the Fontane Prize of the City of West Berlin for *Mutmaßungen über Jakob*. In 1961 he made his first trip to the United States for an extensive tour of lectures, public readings, and university visits that lasted for four months.

He was already at work on his second published book, *Das dritte Buch über Achim* (1961; translated as *The Third Book about Achim*, 1967). In this novel Johnson continues to examine the effects of divisions, borders, and distance on his protagonist. Because this character is a journalist trying to work outside the limits of his own political and ideological experience, the questions about the relationship of language and reality and about the possibilities of narration that were implicit in the complex form of *Mutmaßungen über Jakob* become explicit—become, in fact, the central theme—in *Das dritte Buch über Achim*.

Karsch, a West German journalist, accepts an invitation from his former lover Karin S., an actress, to visit her in the GDR. There he encounters the cyclist Achim T., Karin's current lover and a national sports hero, and begins to write an article about him. An East German publisher approaches Karsch about expanding the project into a third full-fledged biography of Achim; the other two have been rendered obsolete by

Achim's continual triumphs and the expansion of his social and political role. Karsch is intrigued by the idea, and Achim is initially enthusiastic and cooperative.

Karsch prepares to write a biography of the sort that he understands. Endeavoring to comprehend the development of the individual Achim, he gathers material about the cyclist's childhood and youth, his apprenticeship, an early love affair, and the beginnings of his sports career. At the same time he reads books about cycling, watches Achim's training sessions, and accompanies him to his many public appearances.

As his work progresses, Karsch continually encounters problems in reconciling the personality that emerges from his investigation of Achim's past with the Achim he observes fulfilling the role of national sports hero. What Karsch considers to be important for understanding Achim–his background and development–is often discounted or denied by Achim and the publishers, who are interested only in Achim's current role in East Germany. Anything that calls that role into question has no place in the biography they envision. Karsch finds precisely such contradictory and problematic elements of Achim's development essential for comprehending Achim as an individual, and he is unwilling to ignore them. Ultimately, work on the biography breaks down over apparently incontrovertible evidence that Achim participated in the June 1953 uprising in Leipzig. Karsch returns home and, in an attempt to explain his failure to his friends and to himself, writes an account of his efforts which becomes *Das dritte Buch über Achim*.

This account is carried forward by a series of questions which serve as chapter headings and allow Karsch to reflect upon his experience in the GDR. Karsch's cool, detached descriptions of his literary failure–his research, the rejected drafts of portions of the book, his futile attempts to work out an approach acceptable to Achim, to the publishers, and to himself–repeatedly force him back to the problem of the border: he simply cannot fit his view of an individual identity into a political and social context the presuppositions of which he neither shares nor understands.

Critical response to the novel was largely favorable. Walter Jens felt that Johnson was on the way to greatness, Martin Walser praised his unique prose style, and Blöcker was convinced that Johnson had consolidated his position as the "Dichter der beiden Deutschland" (poet of both Germanies). There were, however, dissenting voices. Karl August Horst called the novel a "trojanisches Pferd" (Trojan horse) and worried about the implications of Johnson's skepticism toward language, while Karlheinz Deschner deprecated Johnson's prose as the ugliest German of its day.

Johnson's efforts to find a voice beyond ideology extended into his public pronouncements and embroiled him in a series of controversies. In late 1961 he went on an extensive reading tour which included a stop in Milan. There he participated in a public round-table discussion at which the keynote speaker was the German writer Hermann Kesten. Kesten's account of the evening, which characterized Johnson as a supporter of the Berlin Wall and an apologist for the GDR, appeared two weeks later in the newspaper *Die Welt*. During the remainder of his tour Johnson found himself besieged by questions and accusations. After obtaining a tape recording of the discussion in Milan, Johnson and the Suhrkamp house held a press conference at which the author took great care to demonstrate how distorted and self-serving Kesten's account had been. In Milan Johnson had discussed the Wall and the reasons it had been built and, characteristically, had tried to keep the discussion free of emotion and polemic. Kesten's denunciation and its appearance in a newspaper well known for its polemical anti-Communism represented precisely the kind of linguistic abuse that Johnson so abhorred and strove to avoid in his own writing. It even led to a discussion in the Bundestag, where the former foreign minister, Heinrich von Brentano, who had previously demonstrated his literary sensitivies by a witless comparison of Bertolt Brecht to the Nazi hero and "poet" Horst Wessel, demanded that Johnson's 1962 fellowship at the Villa Massimo in Rome be revoked. Eighteen years later Johnson still considered this incident so important that he resigned from the German Academy for Language and Literature in Darmstadt after a catalogue it published characterized the incident as a "Streit" (controversy), a term that infuriated Johnson by its neutrality.

Shortly after the Wall was constructed, Johnson began to take an interest in a group of young people who were engaged in helping those who wanted to leave East Berlin. In *Begleitumstände* he discusses an attempt, which he ultimately abandoned, to document the work of this group. In spite of the failure of this project, Johnson's research and association with the group served him well in the novels *Zwei Ansichten* (1965; translated as *Two Views*, 1966) and *Jahrestage: Aus dem Leben von Gesine Cresspahl* (1970-1973, 1983; translated as *Anniversaries: From the Life of Gesine Cresspahl*, 1975, 1987) when he described illegal departures from the GDR. He also drew on this experience for his 1965 essay "Eine Kneipe geht verloren" (A Tavern Is Lost).

In 1962 Johnson married Elisabeth Schmidt, whom he had met in Leipzig and who had just completed a semester studying in Prague. A year later they had a daughter, Katherina.

To use his fellowship at the Villa Massimo Johnson traveled in 1962 to Rome; there he associated with Ingeborg Bachmann and Max Frisch, writers whose work he admired. Also in 1962 he received the International Publishers' Prize for *Das dritte Buch über Achim*. This prize carried the stipulation that he serve on the jury that would determine the following year's award.

Johnson's service on this jury caused more controversy. The jury, which consisted of critics and publishers from all over Europe, met on the island of Corfu in a luxury hotel located in an area where the local people were extremely poor. Although Johnson fulfilled his obligation as a jury member, he publicly criticized the meetings after the prize was awarded, contending that contemporary literature was inappropriately celebrated in such opulent surroundings. His criticism and his refusal to participate in the gala banquet which ended the jury's week of deliberations garnered him considerable unfavorable publicity.

In 1964 Suhrkamp published Johnson's *Karsch und andere Prosa* (Karsch and Other Prose), a collection of three short texts featuring Gesine Cresspahl of *Mutmaßungen über Jakob;* a brief piece about the biblical Jonah written in 1957; and a long text, "Eine Reise wegwohin, 1960" (translated as *An Absence*, 1969), which returns, from quite a different perspective, to Karsch's attempt to write about Achim.

The critics did not respond as positively to the collection as most had to Johnson's first two books. Reich-Ranicki, for example, dismissed the Gesine pieces as sketches from the material for *Mutmaßungen über Jakob* and found the Karsch piece a distressingly conventional retelling of the admired original. In retrospect, however, the collection is important for several reasons. The Gesine pieces demonstrate Johnson's continuing involvement with the Cresspahl family, an involve-

ment that lasted for the rest of his life and produced his masterpiece, *Jahrestage*. The Karsch piece offers a new dimension in Johnson's investigation of the relationship between what one can say and what is perceived: moving beyond the impossibility of writing Achim's biography, it follows Karsch back to the West and portrays the frustrations he experiences trying to write there about the GDR. The ideological barriers Karsch encounters when he tries to describe in print or over the air what he felt and observed in the East are no less onerous than those he had experienced when trying to write about Achim.

Toward the middle of 1964 Johnson began a brief career as a television critic. Believing that the refusal of the West Berlin newspapers to print the schedule of GDR television programs was a foolish denial of reality, he approached the independent *Berliner Tagesspiegel* and proposed that if the paper would print the schedules, he would review the shows. In the next six months Johnson reviewed over a hundred GDR broadcasts. In 1987 Suhrkamp published a collection of these reviews under the title *Der 5. Kanal* (Channel Five).

In 1965 a short novel appeared which returned once again, this time with a narrower focus, to the problems of division, distance, and borders. *Zwei Ansichten* examines the relationship between B., a West German photographer, and D., a nurse from East Germany. B. encounters D. at a party in West Berlin, and the two have what might have remained a brief, casual affair. They have little in common: B. is a rather unremarkable young man from a small town in Schleswig-Holstein who has a passion for automobiles; D. is a quiet woman who regularly travels back and forth between her parents' home in Potsdam and East Berlin, where she lives and works. She has friends in the West and often visits there, but she is content with her life in the East.

The construction of the Berlin Wall, however, adds a new dimension to the relationship of this unlikely pair. After the Wall is erected, B. plans to visit D. in East Berlin and hopes to impress her with his newly acquired foreign sports car. But their meeting does not take place because the car is stolen from in front of his West Berlin hotel and, as he later discovers, is used in a foolhardy attempt to escape from East Berlin. Afraid that he will be suspected of participating in the escape plot, B. decides not to go to the East.

Painting of Johnson by André Ficus (Dr. Siegfried Unseld, Frankfurt am Main)

The Wall gives the relationship an increasingly compelling aura. B. feels an ill-defined, simplistically romantic responsibility to "do something" for D., a feeling which alternately irritates him and puts him in a sentimental frame of mind. D.'s memories of B. are vague, and only when her anger at losing the option of *choosing* to stay in the East combines with a frustrating professional situation at her hospital does she accept B.'s offer of help.

That offer is made in an almost comically offhand manner. The lure of the Wall, the loss of his car, and the personal myth B. has made of D. repeatedly draw B. back to West Berlin from his home in Schleswig-Holstein. He spends much of his time in a bar that happens to be the meeting place for a group of young men and women who help people leave East Berlin. The young female bartender reminds him of his vision of D., and during an evening of too much drinking he writes a letter to D. which he leaves on the bar, a

letter that he probably would not have mailed. The group hand delivers the letter, establishing the contact that leads to D.'s escape.

D. leaves the East by posing as an Austrian tourist on her way to Denmark. Her preparations for flight and the journey itself generate considerable suspense, especially because B. had forgotten the color of D.'s eyes; consequently, the passport provided to D. would not have stood up under close scrutiny.

When B. hears that D. has arrived in Denmark and will be in West Berlin the next day, he makes a hurried trip to Stuttgart to pick up the new sports car with which he wants to greet and to impress her. B. frantically tries to return to Berlin in time, but the car breaks down. When he finally does arrive, he discovers that D. no longer wants to see him. Exhausted and dazed, B. stumbles against a moving bus and suffers a mild concussion. D. visits him in the hospital, but they have little to say to one another. Thereafter they go their separate ways. The shallow reality of their relationship has little to do with the expectations B. or D. had developed in the absence of the other.

The title, *Zwei Ansichten,* identifies the narrative program. The story of B. and D. is told alternately from the perspective of each of the two main figures, with each chapter marking a shift to the other view. The narration, especially when compared with Johnson's earlier works, appears almost traditional; but the two straightforward, chronological, third-person accounts are set against one another. The border is once again a literary category.

Toward the end of the novel the narrator accounts for his acquaintance with the material: he had been on the scene when B. stumbled against the bus, and he had gotten to know D. after her arrival in West Berlin. She recounted her story to the narrator and suggested that he write it down. But, she said, "das müssen Sie alles erfinden, was Sie schreiben. Es ist erfunden" (You have to make up everything that you write. It is made up).

The reduction of the protagonists' names to initials underscores their fundamental anonymity and ordinariness. Many critics were quick to note the correspondence between B. and D. and the German initials for the Federal Republic (Bundesrepublik [BRD]) and the German Democratic Republic (Deutsche Demokratische Republik [DDR]) and to suggest that the characters were somehow representatives of their countries. Johnson denied that he had intended any such association and, in the English translation, rather pointedly provided his characters first names–Dietbert and Beate–which reversed the initials. Johnson wanted to present the different perspectives of ordinary people from both sides of the border.

The critical reception of *Zwei Ansichten* was far less positive than the response to Johnson's earlier work had been. Although critics such as Heinrich Vormweg appreciated the exciting evocation of an illegal exit from East Berlin, they lamented what they perceived as a regression to conventionality; they compared the later with the earlier Johnson and were disappointed. Johnson was unmoved by such criticism: "Es ist eben eine einfachere Geschichte . . ." (It is just a simpler story . . .), he said.

In 1965 the Suhrkamp firm asked Johnson to edit *Me-ti: Buch der Wendungen,* one of the unpublished works in the Brecht archives in East Berlin; the volume was published within the year. Johnson's intense involvement with the manuscript increased his already strong affinity for Brecht's work, and the assignment afforded him the opportunity to meet with writers and other friends in East Berlin. His visits with the singer and writer Wolf Biermann, whose performances and publications had been banned by the East German authorities, resulted in Johnson's being denied access to East Berlin in January 1966.

Johnson had made his second trip to the United States in mid 1965 and, while there, looked for an opportunity to return for at least a year to immerse himself in the American milieu. He did not, however, want an invitation as a writer in residence or guest professor; he was not interested in the isolated, artificial environment of the university but wanted a more conventional job. Helen Wolff, Johnson's American editor, responded with an offer of an editorship in the textbook division of Harcourt, Brace and World, charged with producing an anthology of contemporary German literary texts for high school use. In June 1966 Johnson and his family moved to New York, where they lived on Riverside Drive on the upper West Side of Manhattan. During the first year Johnson completed the anthology *Das neue Fenster* (1967).

Johnson's New York stay provided him with material that would sustain him until his death. By his own account, he "renewed his acquaintance" with Gesine Cresspahl; he began to imagine her as a resident of the upper West Side and to consider how she had come to be there. This re-

newed interest in Gesine and her background led Johnson to the project that would consume most of the rest of his life, the writing of *Jahrestage*. With the help of his American publisher and a grant from the Rockefeller Foundation he was able to remain in New York for a second year and to begin work on the novel.

Jahrestage: Aus dem Leben von Gesine Cresspahl is a massive novel of nearly nineteen hundred pages in four volumes that goes far beyond an examination of the implications of the border between the two Germanies. Gesine seeks to come to terms with her identity in the present–as a German who was born in the Third Reich, was educated under the Nazis and in the formative years of the GDR, left the East in the 1950s and the West in the 1960s, and now lives in Manhattan. She must examine the child that she was, that child's antecedents, and the series of identities she has moved through as the child became the adult.

This extraordinarily ambitious undertaking is presented in the form of a diary with entries for each day from 21 August 1967 to 20 August 1968–a year in the life of Gesine Cresspahl. In these entries Gesine–and often a writer named Uwe Johnson, whom, the reader eventually learns, she has asked to assist her–reflects on her job, on her relationships with her ten-year-old daughter Marie and the other people she encounters, and on the city. The entries reveal Gesine's interest in political and social behavior through her intensive reading of the *New York Times* as she quotes, paraphrases, or simply reacts to the news items that she finds particularly arresting.

This complex evocation of her contemporary life is interwoven with an account of Gesine's background, from her birth in 1933 back to her parents' courtship and marriage and forward through her childhood and education to the present. The narrative, written mostly in the third person but sometimes in the first, is usually straightforward. It also, however, occasionally takes the form of reports of conversations Gesine has with Marie, and imaginary ones with long-dead relatives and acquaintances. Sometimes it represents a transcription of tapes Gesine has made about her life for her daughter "für wenn ich tot bin" (for when I am dead). The interaction of past and present allows Gesine to examine the patterns of behavior that she developed as a child and young adult and to ponder how they operate in her present life. These patterns derive from the continuing influence exerted by the powerful and conflicting figures of her mother and father and their responses to the extreme social and political climate in which they lived.

Gesine was only five years old when her mother, Lisbeth Cresspahl, committed suicide. But the absolute moral standards, the fanatical piety, that drove Lisbeth to take her life had already had a powerful effect on Gesine. When Lisbeth married Heinrich Cresspahl, a cabinetmaker who had immigrated to England and had met her on a visit to his native Mecklenburg, she had agreed to live with him in Richmond, where he had a thriving business. She was unable to feel at home in England, however, and when she became pregnant with Gesine she insisted on returning to Jerichow. There she conspired with her father to force Cresspahl to move back permanently to Mecklenburg, and Cresspahl acquiesced. But the return to Germany and Gesine's birth coincided with the Nazi accession to power, a fact which was an increasingly disturbing source of guilt for Lisbeth. As the Nazis began to implement their policies Lisbeth realized that she could not reconcile what was happening around her with her absolute moral standards. She also realized that she was trapped: her inability to live in England meant that there was no escape from her guilt. To shield herself and her child from this guilt she tried to kill Gesine and twice tried to take her own life. Finally, on 9 November 1938, the Kristallnacht (Night of Broken Glass), in the absence of Cresspahl and the child, she succeeded in killing herself. Gesine sees in herself the legacy of her mother's moral absolutism, and she wishes fervently "daß ich nicht werde wie meine Mutter" (that I not become like my mother).

Heinrich Cresspahl provided a very different example for Gesine. Left responsible for his small daughter, the taciturn craftsman developed a close relationship with her. While conducting his business in apparent harmony with the authorities, he served throughout the war as a British agent. After Germany's surrender he became the mayor of Jerichow and had to struggle with the Soviet military occupation—a struggle which ultimately resulted in a lengthy and debilitating internment. Although Gesine did not always understand the precise nature of his activities, Cresspahl showed her that it was legitimate, even essential, to separate a private sphere of moral and political convictions from the identity one assumes in public.

As an adolescent Gesine had to apply this lesson. Like Johnson, Gesine found the new ideological climate in the Soviet occupation zone both attractive and disturbing. Through the example of her father—and, after his internment, of the young refugee Jakob Abs, who became the head of the Cresspahl household—Gesine developed an abiding belief in progressive socialism. She regarded as essential policies such as redistributing land, providing educational and social opportunities for the children of workers and farmers, and confronting the people with the realities of the Nazi crimes. Her early experience on Johnny Schlegel's prototypical collective farm helped to form her vision of a society of people doing meaningful work and sharing in the benefits of their production.

Gesine could not, however, fail to notice the often appalling disparity between the socialist vision and the reality of the Soviet occupation zone and later of the fledgling GDR. The internment of her father and many other examples of capricious "justice" and heavy-handed rule discredited the ideological claims of the new regime. The 1953 riots in East Germany provided the final blow to Gesine's relationship with the GDR, and she moved to the West.

But neither West Germany nor, later, the United States could provide Gesine with the home she sought. Until 1956 and the ill-fated visit to Jerichow that served as the central event in *Mutmaßungen über Jakob,* she worked as a secretary and interpreter for NATO. After Jakob's visit to West Berlin, when Marie was conceived, and Jakob's subsequent mysterious death, Gesine went to work for a bank. In 1961 she relocated to Manhattan.

Gesine's socialist vision provides her with moral and political principles as rigorous and as uncompromising as those of her mother. But Gesine, who, like her father, must bear responsibility for a small child, cannot afford to allow her moral absolutism free rein. She must be Mrs. Cresspahl, employee of a bank, resident alien in a country of whose political and social policies she does not approve. And she must watch her daughter's steady socialization into a society in which she herself will never feel at home.

She reserves within herself a private sphere in which she can retain her hope, where she can continue to seek the answer to her question, "Wo ist die moralische Schweiz, in die wir emigrieren könnten?" (Where is the moral Switzerland to which we could emigrate?). Initially, there appears to be little prospect of a concrete answer to that question. She is distressed by the careless rhetoric and the radical chic of the American protest movement against the Viet Nam war and is painfully aware of her own modest role in the financial and economic system that supports the war. What she can do is to bear witness: "Es ist was mir übriggeblieben ist: Bescheid zu lernen. Wenigstens mit Kenntnis zu leben" (That is what is left to me: to learn what is going on. At least to live with awareness).

During the year chronicled in *Jahrestage*, however, a focus for Gesine's hope emerges. She is made responsible for her bank's efforts to establish a financial agreement with Czechoslovakia. At first this assignment is merely another aspect of her job. But in the early weeks of 1968 she begins increasingly to note the news from Prague. The rapidly developing promise she sees in the reforms of the Prague Spring captures her imagination, and she begins to believe that her work might also contribute to the establishment of a dynamic socialism under the rule of law. "Für den würde ich arbeiten, aus freien Stücken" (That I would work for freely), she says.

But Gesine is not to have the chance to work for the realization of her socialist vision. The date which, from the beginning of Johnson's work on the novel, had been projected as the last day to be chronicled marked the violent end of the Prague Spring. The ending of the novel is left open; the reader last sees Gesine on a Danish beach shortly before her departure for Prague. It is clear, though, "daß diese Dame und diese Armee notwendig auf einander stoßen würden in dieser Nacht" (that this woman and this army would necessarily collide with one another during this night). Whether this devastating blow to her hopes will cause Gesine to yield to the despair that destroyed her mother, or whether she will continue to bear witness, to maintain her vision as an act of defiance against silence and acquiescence, remains unknown. In any event, the hundreds of pages of *Jahrestage* give voice to that spirit of defiance and stand as a lasting monument to Gesine's–and Johnson's–vision.

Because Johnson's novel appeared in four installments, the last volume nearly ten years after it was originally scheduled to appear, critical response to it also came in stages. After reading the first volume some critics were repelled by the puzzling combination of the daily entries, the shifts between past and present and between first and third person, the large sections of text para-

phrasing or quoting the *New York Times*, and the huge cast of characters. Reich-Ranicki and Helmut Heißenbüttel sought in vain to discern a whole in this first part and failed to see unity between the various levels of narration. Rolf Becker and Hans Mayer, however, showed more awareness of the fragmentary nature of the first volume; they were impressed by the volume in its own right and intrigued by the promise of what was to come. Mayer praised the delicate and complex relationship Johnson was working to establish between past and present, and Becker felt that Johnson's voice had grown stronger, more mature, and more confident.

With the appearance of the second volume in 1971 and the third volume in 1973, critical voices were increasingly respectful. After the second volume was published, Blöcker wrote in the *Frankfurter Allgemeine Zeitung* that Johnson had attained a mastery that left "nahezu alle der mit ihm angetretenen Autoren seiner Generation hinter sich zurück, einen Grass ebenso wie einen Walser, von anderen gar nicht zu reden" (behind nearly all the authors of his generation who had debuted with him, a Grass as well as a Walser, to say nothing of the others).

Although the final volume of the novel had been promised for 1974, what followed was ten years of silence. Rumors of Johnson's personal and physical problems contributed to the growing conviction that *Jahrestage* would remain a monumental and, in the eyes of many, a masterful fragment. When the weekly newspaper *Die Zeit* chose its library of the one hundred best works of world literature in 1978, it included the unfinished novel.

In 1983 the final volume did appear, and the critics were nearly unanimous in their respect for Johnson's accomplishment. To be sure, many critics had individual quibbles–Peter Demetz liked the youthful Gesine far better than the adult; Fritz J. Raddatz felt that Johnson's language had lost its intensity in the final volume; some critics still complained about his alleged overuse of the *New York Times* or about Marie's precocity. These caveats served only to temper the overwhelmingly positive response to the novel as a whole. Seeking adequate comparisons, the critics looked back to Balzac, Fontane, Proust, Joyce, and Thomas Mann. The sense of virtually all the reviews of the final volume is that *Jahrestage* will stand as one of the remarkable literary achievements of the twentieth century.

In 1968, after two years in the United States, Johnson and his family returned to West Berlin, where he continued to work on *Jahrestage*. The following year he joined the P.E.N. Club of the Federal Republic. He also became a member of the Academy of Arts in West Berlin, of which he became vice-president in 1972. In 1971, after publication of the first two volumes of *Jahrestage*, Johnson received the Georg Büchner Prize. Other major literary awards followed: in 1975 the Wilhelm Raabe Prize from the City of Brunswick, in 1978 the Thomas Mann Prize from the City of Lübeck, and in 1983 the Literary Prize of the City of Cologne.

Following the death of Ingeborg Bachmann in late 1973 Johnson spent four days in Klagenfurt, the city of her birth and burial, a city in which she had chosen not to live. The next year he published *Eine Reise nach Klagenfurt* (A Journey to Klagenfurt, 1974), a compilation of statistics, documents, quotations, and observations which form a curious obituary for the poet. By creating an image of Klagenfurt out of the contradictions between its past and present and between the self-image of tourist brochures and the picture that emerges from less flattering statistics, Johnson seeks to identify the city in which Bachmann spent her childhood and to re-create the tensions this place continued to cause for her long after she had left it. Heinrich Böll said in the *Frankfurter Allgemeine Zeitung* for 23 November 1974 that this modest book could be "ein Modell . . . für Biographien–besser noch: auch für Autobiographien" (a model for biographies–better yet: also for autobiographies).

In 1975 Suhrkamp published *Berliner Sachen* (Berlin Affairs), a collection of Johnson's short prose pieces from 1961 to 1970. Most of these had been previously published but were relatively difficult to find. Included were the important theoretical essay "Berliner Stadtbahn" (The Berlin Elevated Railway, 1961); the 1965 account of the "travel agency" that helped people leave East Berlin after the construction of the Wall, "Eine Kneipe geht verloren"; and Johnson's fascinating afterword to a collection of interviews with former citizens of the GDR, "Versuch eine Mentalität zu erklären" (Attempt to Explain a Mentality, 1970).

In 1974 Johnson had moved to the island of Sheerness-on-Sea, Kent, in the mouth of the Thames River. There he intended to find the peace and quiet he needed to finish *Jahrestage*. In 1975, however, he experienced a personal crisis

Johnson in 1983, the year before his death (photograph by Felicitas Timpe, courtesy of Ullstein Bilderdienst)

that had lasting physical and psychological consequences and proved to be a serious obstacle to the completion of his novel. Johnson learned that his wife had had an affair and remained in contact with "einem Vertrauten des S.T.B., des tschechoslowakischen Staatssicherheitsdienstes" (a confidant of the S.T.B., the Czechoslovakian state security agency). The author felt that it was thus possible "seine berufliche Integrität in Frage zu stellen" (to call his professional integrity into question) when he wrote about political developments in Czechoslovakia or the GDR. Johnson experienced serious heart trouble and, after his recovery, a long-lasting writer's block. Johnson and his wife attempted for two years to continue with their marriage; but rumors about their problems became public, and in 1977 they separated.

In the years during and immediately after this crisis Johnson's literary activities were limited to short contributions to German periodicals, a translation into modern German of the Low German fairy tale *Von dem Fischer un syner Fru* (The Fisherman and His Wife, 1976), and the editing of the journalist Margret Boveri's autobiography

Verzweigungen (Ramifications, 1977). In 1977 Johnson became a member of the German Academy of Language and Literature in Darmstadt, from which he resigned in protest two years later over the Kesten affair.

In 1978 Johnson began slowly to work his way back into *Jahrestage*. He also accepted his publisher's invitation to give a series of lectures that would reestablish the poetics chair at the University of Frankfurt. These lectures, which were given in 1979 and published in 1980 as *Begleitumstände*, provide a fascinating account of Johnson's "Erfahrungen im Berufe des Schriftstellers" (experiences in the writer's profession). Throughout the lectures Johnson's almost obsessive concern with concrete, dispassionate language emerges as the unifying theme. His study of German language and literature, he says, awakened in him "eine Vorliebe für das Konkrete. . . für das, was man vorzeigen, nachweisen, erzählen kann" (a preference for the concrete. . . for that which one can exhibit, authenticate, narrate). He reveals important information about his years in the GDR, his beginnings as a writer, and his decision to move to the West. He also examines many of the public controversies that marked his first years in West Berlin and provides detailed documentation supporting and explaining his positions. He concludes the final lecture with a cryptic acknowledgment of the personal crisis that impeded his progress on *Jahrestage* and makes clear his intention to complete the novel.

The short narrative *Skizze eines Verunglückten* (Sketch of a Casualty, 1982) is an account of marital problems similar to those that had proved so destructive for the author. Johnson's narrator, Joe Hinterhand, is a writer living in New York City after serving time in prison for the murder of his wife. Hinterhand had been an exile from the Third Reich, and his wife had betrayed him with a representative of his political enemies. An attempted reconciliation had failed when the private tragedy threatened to become public scandal. The book did not generate a great deal of critical comment, and those who did review it saw it as a thinly veiled account of the unhappy conclusion of the author's own marriage.

After the completion of *Jahrestage* in 1983 Johnson began to make new plans. He wanted to probe more deeply into the family history of the Cresspahls, and he wanted to return to the United States. In September 1983 he made a brief trip to New York, and he planned to go back for a year beginning in June 1984. By the time of his planned departure, Johnson was dead.

The circumstances surrounding Johnson's death underscore the sad, troubled isolation that characterized the last few years of his life. To be sure, he maintained his literary contacts and friendships in West Germany, traveling frequently to the Continent to give readings, attend meetings, or accept prizes. But in Sheerness he spent most of his time alone in his house, striving to finish *Jahrestage* or planning further investigations of the Cresspahl family. His only regular contact with other people on the island was at the local pub, where he usually sat silently at the bar for a few hours every evening. Reports of Johnson's heavy consumption of alcohol are too numerous to discount, and, given the weakened condition of his heart, his drinking must have hastened his end. On or about 23 February 1984 he suffered heart failure and died in his house; his body was not discovered for nearly three weeks.

Uwe Johnson's death deprived contemporary German literature of one of its most original, interesting, and idiosyncratic voices. Johnson, perhaps more than any of his contemporaries, sought a language beyond ideology with which he could present his readers a story that would encourage–or provoke–a reexamination of their preconceived notions. When that quest was most successful, in *Mutmaßungen über Jakob* and in *Jahrestage*, he produced novels that will stand among the finest achievements of postwar German literature.

Interviews:

Horst Bienek, "Uwe Johnson," in his *Werkstattgespräche mit Schriftstellern* (Munich: Hanser, 1962), pp. 86-98;

Arnhelm Neusüss, "Über die Schwierigkeiten beim Schreiben der Wahrheit: Gespräch mit Uwe Johnson," *konkret*, 8 (1962): 18-19;

Michael Roloff, "Interview mit Uwe Johnson," *Metamorphosis*, 4 (1963): 33-42;

Phyllis Meras, "Talk with Uwe Johnson," *New York Times Book Review*, 23 April 1967, pp. 42-43;

Reinhard Baumgart, "Gespräch mit Uwe Johnson (1968)," in *Selbstanzeige: Schriftsteller im Gespräch*, edited by Werner Koch (Frankfurt am Main: Fischer Taschenbuch Verlag, 1971), pp. 47-56;

Gertrud Simmerding and Christof Schmid, "Bichsel, Grass, Johnson, Wohmann: Wie ein

Roman entsteht," in their *Literarische Werkstatt* (Munich: Oldenbourg, 1972), pp. 63-72;

Matthias Prangel, "Gespräch mit Uwe Johnson," *Deutsche Bücher* (1974): 45-49;

Manfred Durzak, "Dieser langsame Weg zu einer größeren Genauigkeit: Gespräch mit Uwe Johnson," in his *Gespräche über den Roman: Formbestimmungen und Analysen* (Frankfurt am Main: Suhrkamp, 1976), pp. 428-460;

Ree Post-Adams, "Antworten von Uwe Johnson," *German Quarterly*, 50 (March 1977): 241-247;

A. Leslie Willson, " 'An Unacknowledged Humorist': An Interview with Uwe Johnson," *Dimension*, 15 (1982): 401-413;

Martin Meyer and Wolfgang Strehlow, "Das sagt mir auch mein Friseur: Film- und Fernsehäußerungen von Uwe Johnson," *Sprache im technischen Zeitalter*, no. 95 (1985): 170-183;

Heinz D. Osterle, "Todesgedanken?: Gespräch über die *Jahrestage*," *German Quarterly*, 58 (Fall 1985): 576-584.

Bibliographies:

Nicolai Riedel, *Uwe Johnson: Bibliographie 1959-1975. Zeitungskritik und wissenschaftliche Literatur* (Bonn: Bouvier, 1976); revised as *Uwe Johnson: Bibliographie 1959-1980. Das schriftstellerische Werk und seine Rezeption in literaturwissenschaftlicher Forschung und feuilletonistischer Kritik in der Bundesrepublik Deutschland. Mit Annotationen und Exkursen zur multimedialen Wirkungsgeschichte* (Bonn: Bouvier, 1981);

Riedel, *Uwe Johnson: Bibliographie 1959-1977. Das schriftstellerische Werk in fremdsprachigen Textausgaben und seine internationale Rezeption in literaturwissenschaftlicher Forschung und Zeitungskritik* (Bonn: Bouvier, 1978).

References:

Derek van Abbe, "From Proust to Johnson: Some Notes after *Das dritte Buch über Achim*," *Modern Languages*, 55 (1974): 73-79;

Heinz Ludwig Arnold, ed., *Uwe Johnson* (Munich: Edition text + kritik, 1980);

Reinhard Baumgart, "Eigensinn: Ein vorläufiger Rückblick auf Uwe Johnsons *Jahrestage*," *Merkur*, 37 (1983): 921-927;

Baumgart, "Ein Riese im Nebel," *Neue deutsche Hefte*, 7 (1960): 967-969;

Baumgart, "Kleinbürgertum und Realismus: Überlegungen zu Romanen von Böll, Grass und Johnson," *Neue Rundschau*, 70 (1964): 650-664;

Baumgart, "Uwe Johnson: *Das dritte Buch über Achim*," *Neue deutsche Hefte*, 9 (1962): 146-148;

Baumgart, ed., *Über Uwe Johnson* (Frankfurt am Main: Suhrkamp, 1970);

Sigrid Bauschinger, "Mythos Manhattan: Die Faszination einer Stadt," in *Amerika in der deutschen Literatur*, edited by Bauschinger, Horst Denkler, and Wilfried Malsch (Stuttgart: Reclam, 1975), pp. 382-397;

Rolf Becker, "Jerichow in New York," *Der Spiegel*, 24 (5 October 1970): 228-230;

Michael Bengel, ed., *Johnsons "Jahrestage"* (Frankfurt am Main: Suhrkamp, 1985);

Günter Blöcker, "Du hast Auftrag von uns, Gesine: Der zweite Band von Uwe Johnsons *Jahrestage*," *Frankfurter Allgemeine Zeitung*, 23 October 1971;

Blöcker, "Roman der beiden Deutschland," *Frankfurter Allgemeine Zeitung*, 31 October 1959;

Blöcker, "Roman der deutschen Entfremdung," *Frankfurter Allgemeine Zeitung*, 16 September 1961;

Hamida Bosmajian, *Metaphors of Evil: Contemporary German Literature and the Shadow of Nazism* (Iowa City: University of Iowa Press, 1979);

Mark Boulby, "Surmises on Love and Family Life in the Work of Uwe Johnson," *Seminar*, 10 (1974): 131-140;

Boulby, *Uwe Johnson* (New York: Ungar, 1974);

Peter Demetz, "Uwe Johnsons Blick in die Epoche: 'Aus dem Leben von Gesine Cresspahl'—der vierte Band der *Jahrestage*," *Frankfurter Allgemeine Zeitung*, 12 November 1983;

Karlheinz Deschner, "Uwe Johnson: *Das dritte Buch über Achim*," in his *Talente, Dichter, Dilettanten* (Wiesbaden: Limes, 1964), pp. 187-202;

Robert Detweiler, "*Speculations about Jacob:* The Truth of Ambiguity," *Monatshefte*, 58 (1966): 24-32;

Edward Diller, "Uwe Johnson's Karsch: Language as a Reflection of the Two Germanies," *Monatshefte*, 60 (1968): 35-39;

Darko Dolinar, "Die Erzähltechnik in drei Werken Uwe Johnsons," *Acta Neophilologica*, 3 (1970): 27-47;

Manfred Durzak, "Mimesis und Wahrheitsfindung: Probleme des realistischen Romans: Uwe Johnsons *Jahrestage*," in his *Gespräche über den Roman: Formbestimmungen und Analysen* (Frankfurt am Main: Suhrkamp, 1976), pp. 461-481;

Durzak, "Wirklichkeitserkundung und Utopie: Die Romane Uwe Johnsons," in his *Der deutsche Roman der Gegenwart,* third edition (Stuttgart: Kohlhammer, 1979), pp. 328-403;

Eberhard Fahlke, "Gute Nacht, New York–Gute Nacht, Berlin. . . : Anmerkungen zu einer Figur des Protestierens anhand der *Jahrestage* von Uwe Johnson," in *Literatur und Studentenbewegung: Eine Zwischenbilanz,* edited by W. Martin Lüdke (Opladen: Westdeutscher Verlag, 1977), pp. 186-218;

Fahlke, *Die "Wirklichkeit" der Mutmaßungen: Eine politische Lesart der "Mutmaßungen über Jakob" von Uwe Johnson* (Bern: Lang, 1981);

Kurt J. Fickert, "Biblical Symbolism in *Mutmaßungen über Jakob,*" *German Quarterly,* 54 (January 1981): 59-62;

Fickert, *Neither Left nor Right: The Politics of Individualism in Uwe Johnson's Work* (New York: Lang, 1987);

Fickert, "Symbol Complexes in *Mutmaßungen über Jakob,*" *Germanic Review,* 61 (Summer 1986): 105-108;

John Fletcher, "The Themes of Alienation and Mutual Incomprehension in the Novels of Uwe Johnson," *International Fiction Review,* 1 (1974): 81-87;

Erhard Friedrichsmeyer, "Quest by Supposition: Johnson's *Mutmaßungen über Jakob,*" *Germanic Review,* 42 (1968): 215-226;

Hans-Jürgen Geisthardt, "Das Thema der Nation und zwei Literaturen: Nachweis an Christa Wolf–Uwe Johnson," *Neue Deutsche Literatur,* 13 (June 1966): 48-69;

Ingeborg Gerlach, *Auf der Suche nach der verlorenen Identität: Zu Uwe Johnsons "Jahrestagen"* (Kronberg: Athenäum, 1980);

Rainer Gerlach and Matthias Richter, eds., *Uwe Johnson* (Frankfurt am Main: Suhrkamp, 1984);

Colin Good, "Uwe Johnson's Treatment of the Narrative in *Mutmaßungen über Jakob,*" *German Life and Letters,* 24 (1971): 358-370;

Werner Gotzmann, "Detektiv, Inquisitor und Don Quichotte: Bemerkungen zu Uwe Johnsons *Jahrestage,*" *Sprache im technischen Zeitalter,* no. 95 (1985): 184-195;

Jürgen Grambow, "Heimat im Vergangenen," *Sinn und Form,* 38 (1986): 134-157;

Christian Grawe, "Literarisch aktualisierte Bibel: Uwe Johnsons Kurzgeschichte 'Jonas zum Beispiel,' " *Der Deutschunterricht,* 25 (February 1973): 34-39;

Michael Hamburger, "Uwe Johnson–eine Freundschaft," *Sprache im technischen Zeitalter,* no. 93 (1985): 2-12;

Ingeborg Hoesterey, "Die Erzählsituation als Roman: Uwe Johnsons *Jahrestage,*" *Colloquia Germanica,* 16 (1983): 13-26;

Karl August Horst, "Im Bauch des trojanischen Pferdes," *Neue Züricher Zeitung,* 7 October 1961;

Sharon Edwards Jackiw, "The Manifold Difficulties of Uwe Johnson's *Mutmaßungen über Jakob,*" *Monatshefte,* 65 (1973): 126-143;

Walter Jens, "Johnson auf der Schwelle der Meisterschaft," *Die Zeit,* 6 October 1961;

Jens, "Privatroman statt Lagebericht," *Die Zeit,* 8 October 1965;

Herbert Kolb, "Rückfall in die Parataxe: Anläßlich einiger Satzbauformen in Uwe Johnsons erstveröffentlichtem Roman," *Neue Deutsche Hefte,* 10 (1963): 42-74;

Anita Krätzer, *Studien zum Amerikabild in der neueren deutschen Literatur: Max Frisch–Uwe Johnson–Hans Magnus Enzensberger und das "Kursbuch"* (Bern: Lang, 1982);

Vera Zuzana Langerova, "Women Characters in the Works of Uwe Johnson," Ph.D. dissertation, Vanderbilt University, 1976;

Sara Lennox, "Die *New York Times* in Uwe Johnsons *Jahrestagen,*" in *Die USA und Deutschland: Wechselseitige Spiegelungen in der Literatur der Gegenwart,* edited by Wolfgang Paulsen (Bern & Munich: Francke, 1976), pp. 103-109;

Lennox, "Yoknapatawpha to Jerichow: Uwe Johnson's Appropriation of William Faulkner," *Arkadia,* 14 (1979): 166-176;

K. H. Lepper, "Dichter im geteilten Deutschland: Bemerkungen zu Uwe Johnsons Erzählung 'Eine Kneipe geht verloren,' " *Monatshefte,* 60 (1968): 23-34;

Eberhard Mannack, *Zwei deutsche Literaturen? Zu Günter Grass, Uwe Johnson, Hermann Kant, Ulrich Plenzdorff und Christa Wolf* (Kronberg: Athenäum, 1977);

Hans Mayer, "Das erste Buch über Gesine," *Die Weltwoche,* 4 December 1970;

Mayer, "Versuch, eine Grenze zu beschreiben: Zu Uwe Johnsons Roman *Mutmaßungen über Jakob,*" in his *Vereinzelt Niederschläge: Kritik und Polemik* (Pfullingen: Neske, 1973), pp. 137-146;

Norbert Mecklenburg, "Großstadtmontage und Provinzchronik: Die epische 'Aufhebung' des regionalen Romans in Uwe Johnsons *Jahrestage*," in his *Erzählte Provinz: Regionalismus und Moderne im Roman* (Königstein: Athenäum, 1982), pp. 180-224;

Mecklenburg, "Zeitroman oder Heimatroman? Uwe Johnsons *Ingrid Babendererde*," *Wirkendes Wort*, 36 (1986): 172-189;

Rolf Michaelis, *Kleines Adreßbuch für Jerichow und New York: Ein Register zu Uwe Johnsons Roman "Jahrestage"* (Frankfurt am Main: Suhrkamp, 1983);

Karl Migner, "Uwe Johnson," in *Deutsche Literatur seit 1945 in Einzeldarstellungen*, edited by Dietrich Weber (Stuttgart: Kröner, 1968), pp. 484-504;

Migner, *Uwe Johnson: "Das dritte Buch über Achim." Interpretation* (Munich: Oldenbourg, 1974);

Migner, "Uwe Johnson *Das dritte Buch über Achim:* Methodische Hinweise zu seiner Erarbeitung," *Der Deutschunterricht*, 16 (1964): 17-25;

Leslie L. Miller, "Uwe Johnson's *Jahrestage:* The Choice of Alternatives," *Seminar*, 10 (February 1974): 50-70;

Richard Allen Murphy, "The Dilemma of the Artist-Writer in the Novels of Uwe Johnson," Ph.D. dissertation, Cornell University, 1967;

Bernd Neumann, *Utopie und Mimesis: Zum Verhältnis von Ästhetik, Geschichtsphilosophie und Politik in den Romanen Uwe Johnsons* (Kronberg: Athenäum, 1978);

Heinz D. Osterle, "Uwe Johnsons *Jahrestage:* Das Bild der U.S.A.," *German Quarterly*, 48 (November 1975): 505-518;

Karl Pestalozzi, "Achim alias Täve Schur: Uwe Johnsons zweiter Roman und seine Vorlage," *Sprache im technischen Zeitalter*, no. 6 (1962-1963): 479-486;

Hansjürgen Popp, "Einführung in Uwe Johnsons Roman *Mutmaßungen über Jakob*," supplementary issue of *Der Deutschunterricht* (1967);

Ree Post-Adams, *Uwe Johnson: Darstellungsproblematik als Romanthema in* Mutmaßungen über Jakob *und* Das dritte Buch über Achim (Bonn: Bouvier, 1977);

Fritz J. Raddatz, "Ein Märchen aus Geschichte und Geschichten: Uwe Johnson: *Jahrestage* 4: Zum Abschluß eines großen Romanwerks," *Die Zeit*, 14 October 1983;

Werner Joachim Radke, "Untersuchungen zu Uwe Johnsons *Mutmaßungen über Jakob*,"

Ph.D. dissertation, Stanford University, 1966;

Marcel Reich-Ranicki, "Dichter der beiden Deutschland?" *Die Zeit*, 24 September 1965;

Reich-Ranicki, "Ein Mann fährt ins andere Deutschland," *Die Zeit*, 16 September 1961;

Reich-Ranicki, "Mutmaßungen wurden Gewißheit: Uwe Johnson macht es sich zu leicht," *Die Zeit*, 13 March 1964;

Reich-Ranicki, "Registrator Johnson," in his *Deutsche Literatur in Ost und West* (Munich: Piper, 1963), pp. 231-246;

Reich-Ranicki, "Uwe Johnsons neuer Roman: Der erste Band des Prosawerks *Jahrestage*," *Die Zeit*, 2 October 1970;

Nicolai Riedel, *Determinanten der Rezeptionssteuerung: Dargestellt am Beispiel der multimedialen Rezeption des schriftstellerischen Werks Uwe Johnsons: Materialien und Grundlagenstudien zu einer kritischen Einführung in die Forschung* (Mannheim: Selbstverlag N. Riedel, 1978);

Riedel, *Untersuchungen zur Geschichte der internationalen Rezeption Uwe Johnsons: Ein Beitrag zur empirischen Forschung* (Hildesheim: Olms, 1985);

Riedel, ed., *Uwe Johnsons Frühwerk: Im Spiegel der deutschsprachigen Literaturkritik* (Bonn: Bouvier, 1987);

Eva Schiffer, "Politsches Engagement oder Resignation: Weiteres zu Uwe Johnsons *Jahrestagen*," in *Der deutsche Roman und seine historischen und politischen Bedingungen*, edited by Wolfgang Paulsen (Bern & Munich: Francke, 1977), pp. 236-246;

Walter Schmitz, *Uwe Johnson* (Munich: Beck / edition text + kritik, 1984);

Franz Schonauer, "Uwe Johnson," in *Schriftsteller der Gegenwart: 53 literarische Porträts*, edited by Klaus Nonnemann (Olten: Walter, 1963);

Peter Schreiner, "Uwe Johnson und seine Welt: Weltsicht, epische Grundform und Sprachstruktur," *Die Zeit im Buch* (1967): 1-8;

Wilhelm Johannes Schwarz, *Der Erzähler Uwe Johnson*, third edition (Bern & Munich: Francke, 1973);

Robert K. Shirer, *Difficulties in Saying "I": The Narrator as Protagonist in Uwe Johnson's "Jahrestage" and Christa Wolf's "Kindheitsmuster"* (Bern: Lang, 1988);

Hugo Steger, "Rebellion und Tradition in der Sprache von Uwe Johnsons *Mutmaßungen über Jakob*," in his *Zwischen Sprache und Literatur: Drei Reden* (Göttingen: Sachse & Pohl, 1967), pp. 43-69;

Gisela Ullrich, *Identität und Rolle: Probleme des Erzählens bei Johnson, Walser, Frisch und Fichte* (Stuttgart: Klett, 1977);

Siegfried Unseld, "Nachwort: Die Prüfung der Reife im Jahre 1953," in *Ingrid Babendererde: Reifeprüfung 1953,* by Uwe Johnson (Frankfurt am Main: Suhrkamp, 1985), pp. 249-264;

Heinrich Vormweg, "Uwe Johnsons Bestandaufnahmen vom Lauf der Welt," in *Zeitkritische Romane des 20. Jahrhunderts: Die Gesellschaft in der Kritik der deutschen Literatur,* edited by Hans Wagener (Stuttgart: Reclam, 1975), pp. 362-380;

Martin Walser, "Was Schriftsteller tun können," *Süddeutsche Zeitung,* 26 and 27 August 1961;

Roland H. Wiegenstein, "Die Grenze des Uwe Johnson," *Frankfurter Hefte,* 16 (1961): 633-634;

Wiegenstein, "Johnson lesen: Vorschläge zu den *Jahrestagen* 1-4," *Neue Rundschau,* 95 (1984): 128-144;

Gotthard Wunberg, "Struktur und Symbolik in Uwe Johnsons Roman *Mutmaßungen über Jakob,*" *Neue Sammlung,* 2 (1962): 440-449;

Erich Wunderlich, *Uwe Johnson* (Berlin: Colloquium, 1973);

Richard E. Ziegfeld, "Exilautor / Exilverleger: Uwe Johnson und Helen Wolff," in *Das Exilerlebnis: Verhandlungen des vierten Symposiums über deutsche und österreichische Exilliteratur,* edited by Donald G. Daviau and Ludwig M. Fischer (Columbia, S.C.: Camden House, 1982), pp. 505-516.

Papers:

The Uwe Johnson Archive is at the University of Frankfurt am Main.

Hermann Kant
(14 June 1926-   )

Manfred Bansleben
University of Alabama in Birmingham

BOOKS: *Ein bißchen Südsee: Erzählungen* (Berlin: Rütten & Loening, 1962);

Die Aula: Roman (Berlin: Rütten & Loening, 1965);

In Stockholm (Berlin: Volk und Welt, 1971);

Das Impressum: Roman (Berlin: Rütten & Loening, 1972);

Eine Übertretung: Erzählungen (Berlin: Rütten & Loening, 1975); selections republished as *Anrede der Ärztin O. an den Staatsanwalt F. gelegentlich einer Untersuchung* (Neuwied & Darmstadt: Luchterhand, 1978);

Der Aufenthalt: Roman (Berlin: Rütten & Loening, 1977);

Zu den Unterlagen: Publizistik 1957-1980 (Berlin & Weimar: Aufbau, 1981);

My Alphabet of GDR Literature (Morgantown: Department of Foreign Languages, West Virginia University, 1981);

Der dritte Nagel: Geschichten (Berlin: Rütten & Loening, 1981);

Unterlagen zu Literatur und Politik (Neuwied & Darmstadt: Luchterhand, 1982);

Bronzezeit: Geschichten aus dem Leben des Buchhalters Farßmann (Berlin: Rütten & Loening, 1986).

Hermann Kant (Poly-Press–Ullstein Bilderdienst)

East German writers fall into three groups: those who have emigrated to the West, those who live in the East but publish in the West, and those who live and publish in the East and represent East German society to the rest of the world. Hermann Kant belongs to the third group. At least since he became president of the German Democratic Republic (GDR) Writers' Association in 1978, Kant has been regarded as the writer who comes closest to representing an official East German view of literature. But Kant is not merely a "literary politician." In the West as well as in the East he is a popular writer who has done much to bring East German literature out of its dogmatism and provincialism and raise it to an international level. Kant's literary reputation rests mainly on three novels which reflect stages in the sociopolitical development of the German

Democratic Republic. These novels have established him as the leading chronicler of GDR history, and he has been awarded the highest literary and political prizes the state has to offer.

Kant was born in Hamburg in 1926 and grew up in a lower-middle-class milieu. He was trained as an electrician, served as a soldier for a few months near the end of World War II, and spent four years as a prisoner of war in Poland. Those four years were a turning point in his life, he says, for it was then that he became an avowed antifascist and Marxist. After his release in 1949 he studied and taught until 1952 at the Arbeiter- und Bauernfakultät (Workers' and Farmers' College) at the University of Greifswald, then studied German literature at Humboldt University in Berlin until 1956. He then worked for a short time as a research assistant and later as a journalist and newspaper editor. Since 1962 he has been a free-lance writer in East Berlin. He is a member of the Academy of the Arts of the GDR. He has served on the board of directors of the Writers' Association since 1963 and was elected vice-president in 1969; in 1978 he rose to the presidency of the association, and in that capacity he has made many lecture tours of eastern and western Europe and the United States.

Throughout his career Kant has been a controversial author of literary and cultural-political newspaper essays. A collection of his journalism from 1957 to 1980 appeared under the title *Zu den Unterlagen* (For the Record) in 1981. The fifty-three selections, which include articles, book reviews, speeches, and literary discussions, deal with the polemics of the time at which they were written and seem dated today.

Kant's aesthetic stems from his dual role as creative writer and journalist. His writing is characterized by virtuosity with language, an occasional tendency toward mannerism, and a general avoidance of metaphor. Kant sees his profession as a political one, as is to be expected of a socialist author. He has warned against both underestimating and overestimating the ability of literature to effect social and political change: literature, he declares, "ist nicht für den Zustand der Welt verantwortlich, aber schon für das, was wir über diesen Zustand denken" (is not responsible for the condition of the world, but it is responsible for what we think about that condition). His works contain extensive reflections on writing and the social responsibility of the writer. Such commentaries can be found above all in his short stories and novels.

Kant's literary career began in the wake of the 1959 Bitterfeld Conference, and the political and literary guidelines drawn up there were binding on him: realism, partisanship, optimism, and comprehensibility. But Kant argues against an overly rigid adherence to that program. In contrast to the black-and-white one-dimensionality of the Bitterfeld literature, "gegen die polierten Charaktere" (against the stylized characters), he presents a many-sided reality. Literature, he maintains, must be as wide and multifarious as life itself, must have "Buckel und Risse" (humps and fissures) just as reality does. Kant's writing is affirmative and at the same time critical: affirma-

tive in that the socialist system is never questioned, critical in that the contradictions, problems, and conflicts in that system are revealed.

Kant made his literary debut in 1962 with *Ein bißchen Südsee* (A Bit of the South Seas), a collection of short stories about daily life during the Nazi period and the postwar years; *Südsee* (South Seas) is a metaphor for the hopes and dreams of the lower classes. The weakest stories in the collection are overburdened with didacticism; the strongest are well-told, humorous tales. Kant emerges in this collection as a naive, pre-literary narrator who spontaneously tells stories about what happened to him. These narratives contain the stylistic features that characterize his novels: a mixture of autobiographical reminiscence and poetic invention, a predilection for anecdote, and theoretical discourses on the craft of writing.

His first novel, *Die Aula* (The Auditorium), appeared in 1963 as a serial in the magazine *Forum* and in 1965 as a book. It made Kant, who had been virtually unknown, one of the most widely read and discussed writers in the GDR. Hailed by critics as one of the most important books of the decade, *Die Aula* underwent many reprintings and was translated into several languages; a stage adaptation ran in East Berlin for nine years; and, partly because of its documentary value, it became a standard textbook in the schools of the Federal Republic of Germany (FRG).

Die Aula is about the early years of the GDR, a period characterized by the polarization of conservative and socialist ideologies. In 1949 the Arbeiter- und Bauernfakultäten were founded to enable working-class citizens to get a college education and become the new socialist cadres. The colleges were closed in 1962 after they had presumably fulfilled their mission. Their success is demonstrated in the novel through the experiences of the members of a workers' and farmers' collective: an electrician becomes a journalist, a carpenter and a farmhand become sinologists, a seamstress becomes an optometrist, and a lumberjack becomes a high government official. Robert Iswall, the electrician who becomes a journalist, was a member of the first graduating class of the Workers' and Farmers' College. He is invited to give the keynote address on the occasion of the closing of the college. Like the unwritten book in Uwe Johnson's novel *Das dritte Buch über Achim* (1961; translated as *The Third Book about Achim*, 1967), Iswall's speech never takes place, for the invitation is withdrawn; but the reader is led to understand that the novel itself is the speech that is never given. Iswall's preparations for the speech–his research, collecting of materials, and attempts to recall the past–form the narrative structure of the novel.

The "modern mode" of narration used in *Die Aula* was praised by East German critics; Western critics, too, admired the virtuosity with which Kant deployed stylistic techniques that until then had been rejected by the tenets of socialist realism as decadent and formalistic. Inner monologue, flashback, and a shifting of time levels are some of the narrative devices that Kant rehabilitated for East German literature. The introduction of a second time level allows analysis and criticism of the past. The present-day level is that of Iswall's journalistic activity, yet any event is taken as an occasion for reminiscence and reevaluation. Present problems such as the destabilization of socialist consciousness, flight from the country, the building of the Berlin Wall, and de-Stalinization are regarded as soluble only through an awareness of history. The importance of historical awareness is suggested in the quotation from Heinrich Heine that serves as an epigram for the book: "Der heutige Tag ist ein Resultat des gestrigen. Was dieser gewollt hat, müssen wir erforschen, wenn wir zu wissen wünschen, was jener will" (The present day is a result of the previous day. To understand what the present holds we must inquire into what yesterday held). Iswall becomes conscious of the past in the GDR through his research for his speech; but on a trip to the Federal Republic, which he experiences as "absurde Fremde" (absurdly foreign), he has the feeling of traveling in a defective time machine. In the FRG Iswall is everywhere confronted with the persistence of the past; he experiences the simultaneity of the old and the new as the division of a nation.

Die Aula combines a reappraisal of the protagonist's individual past with a reappraisal of the society's collective history. Both are filled with contradictions, but these are attributed to human nature and regarded in principle as resolvable. The superiority of the socialist system is taken for granted, and from this standpoint much criticism is leveled at morally questionable or improper behavior, the stupidity and arrogance of government functionaries, and the desire for social status. Kant's critical perspective expresses itself in an all-pervasive irony; as a result of the discussions of this work irony, which had been denounced by East German critics as Western and

Die Gegenwart ist in diesem Augenblicke das Wichtigere, und das Thema ... ist von der Art, daß überhaupt jedes Weiterschreiben davon abhängt.

DAS IMPRESSUM

von Hermann Kant

Dust jacket for Kant's 1972 novel about the rise of an East German editor to a position of political power

decadent, came to be accepted as an expression of newly won political self-assurance. In accordance with Marxist concepts Kant employs irony in two forms: as humor in the presentation of the merely subjective conflicts in the GDR, and as satire in the presentation of fundamental political and economic conflicts in the FRG.

The critical intentions of *Die Aula* were insufficiently acknowledged in both East and West. Whereas the critical aspect was hardly even recognized in the East, in the West it was rejected as oversimplified and superficial. Kant had allegedly defused ideological and philosophical arguments, harmonized the conflicts in the GDR, and avoided taboo subjects. It is true that such topics as the uprisings in the GDR and in Hungary and the building of the Berlin Wall are scarcely mentioned, and these omissions clearly demonstrate the limits of criticism permitted a writer in the GDR. Yet one must not underestimate the critical intent of *Die Aula*, which, particularly for the socialist reader, is quite obvious. The central message of the novel is highly critical: Iswall's invitation to speak is revoked with the justification that the party wants to take its orientation not from the past but from the future. Whereas Iswall is prepared to reassess his past and accept whatever guilt it entails, the state and the party block a reappraisal of their past. Although in *Die Aula* Kant does not violate any taboos, he does significantly enlarge the room for debate. This critical aspect accounts in large part for the continued popularity of the novel in the GDR.

Kant's second novel marks a retreat from the aesthetic and critical advances he made in the first. To overcome the separation of art and life, the first Bitterfeld Conference had decreed that writers should describe the daily production processes in the factories and that workers should turn to writing. That program proved to be unsuccessful. Thus the next Bitterfeld Conference, held in 1964, urged that societal problems be presented from the viewpoint of top management. Kant's second novel, *Das Impressum* (The Imprint, 1972), accorded with this requirement.

David Groth, the editor in chief of a leading magazine in the GDR, receives an offer from the Central Committee of the Socialist Unity party to become a minister of state. The offer sets in motion a process of reflection and self-scrutiny for Groth. The structural parallel to *Die Aula* is obvious, and the critics labeled *Das Impressum* a duplication of the earlier novel and a thin and unsuccessful one at that. That reproach is for the most part justified, for the subtle distinctions, spontaneity, and critical intent that distinguish *Die Aula* are absent from the second novel. Groth's rise from messenger boy to editor in chief is presented as a model of mobility possible only in a socialist society; his ascent also stands for the social and political development of the East German state as a whole.

The novel takes place on a single day, the day on which Groth resists the promotion to minister in the morning and decides to accept it in the evening. The interval between, the recalled biography of the protagonist, takes the form of a multiplicity of anecdotes, episodes, stories, and satirical scenes, connected more associatively than chronologically. The flashback material includes David's youth during the Nazi era, when he witnessed the murder of Jewish fellow citizens and his father's suicide in protest to the regime; his rise in the socialist society of the GDR; the problems of the leaders and planners; and the intellectuals' lack of contact with the workers.

The complexity of *Die Aula* is missing from *Das Impressum*. The characters are mostly types, and the didactic element, although humorously treated, is all too visible. The tension between the social and individual spheres that characterized *Die Aula* is lacking in *Das Impressum*, where Groth's advancement and that of the society are taken as identical. Groth's initial resistance to the promotion as well as his self-doubts disappear with his insight into the strength and the wisdom of the party. Such a standpoint leaves little room for criticism. Whereas the revolt of 17 June 1953 was excluded from *Die Aula*, in this novel it is misused as a mere backdrop for the love story of Groth and Franziska Grewe.

Das Impressum met with a mixed reception in both East and West. Kant's extraordinary skill with language and his literary techniques were again found praiseworthy. Western critics, however, accused him of "ideological purification of history" and of serving as a mouthpiece for the powers that be. Although the reaction in the East was for the most part positive, some critics, comparing the book to novels by Christa Wolf and Günter de Bruyn, found Kant's protagonist lacking in qualities worth emulating, such as depth, honesty, and sensitivity.

A volume of seven short stories, *Eine Übertretung* (An Infringement), appeared in 1975. It consists of more or less successful satires on everyday life in the GDR, including bureaucratic red tape, departmental rivalry, and the timidity of state functionaries with regard to taking responsibility and making decisions. Most of the stories involve comic, at times grotesque situations that Kant takes as starting points for his highly entertaining reflections. The best story, however, does not fit this pattern because of its more serious theme: in "Lebenslauf, Zweiter Absatz" (Curriculum Vitae, Part Two) a young soldier, in flight from the Soviet army near the end of the war, hides in the house of a Polish farmer and is taken prisoner. That story was expanded two years later into Kant's third novel, *Der Aufenthalt* (The Stay, 1977).

Der Aufenthalt is perhaps Kant's most impressive and certainly his most honest novel. Mark Niebuhr, an eighteen-year-old apprentice printer from a small North German town, has been a soldier for only a few months when he is taken prisoner in Poland in January 1945. Accused by a Polish woman of having murdered her daughter in Lublin, Niebuhr is sent to a regular prison, where he is first placed in solitary confinement and later moved to a communal cell with nearly ninety Nazi war criminals. A thirteen-month investigation, however, leads to the conclusion that Niebuhr is the victim of an error, and he is transferred to a work camp for prisoners of war.

Kant called *Der Aufenthalt* a Bildungsroman, and it does loosely fit that designation since it is a story of maturation and self-discovery. Since the traditional journey of the classical form of the genre is, of course, closed to Niebuhr, he has no option other than to turn inward. In doing so, he discovers that he is less a prisoner of his Polish guards than of his own intellectual and moral egocentricity. Before he can open himself to others he must break out of the prison of the self, a condition that seems to be achieved when he wakes up one morning and does not even remember his name. With this event begins the long and arduous journey of coming to a new consciousness: as Niebuhr is forced to dismantle, stone by stone, the wall of a destroyed apartment building in Warsaw, he finds a pencil box bearing the name of a Jewish girl; as he rebuilds the structure in his mind, he imagines the lives of the girl and others in the apartment complex. For the first time he becomes aware of the collective suffering of the Polish people and the collective guilt of the Germans. On a walk through the destroyed city with a Polish lieutenant Niebuhr learns to think critically and to gain perspective on his acquired patterns of thought and prejudice, as well as on himself.

There are two lines of development in the novel: one narrates chronologically the period of captivity and finally establishes Niebuhr's innocence of the crime of which he is accused; the other, moving in the opposite direction, describes a process of reflection which ends in his recognition of his guilt in a larger sense. Niebuhr arrives at the insight that he must understand himself "als ein Glied der **Eimerkette**, als einen Menschen neben Menschen, als einen von den Menschen, ohne die die Unmenschlichkeit nicht gegangen wäre" (as a link in the chain, as a person among persons, as one of those people without whom the atrocity would not have occurred). His family is also retrospectively implicated in the chain of guilt; Niebuhr had always thought of his parents as decent people, but now he realizes that even though they did not side with the Nazis, neither did they aid those few who openly opposed the regime.

When the Polish lieutenant finally leaves him with his newfound self-insight, Niebuhr

Drawing of Kant by Doris Kahane (Wolfgang Beutin and others, Deutsche Literaturgeschichte *[Stuttgart: Metzler, 1984])*

must admit that the causes of the catastrophe remain incomprehensible. Nor is he any wiser thirty years later, for although the novel is told from the perspective of the 1970s as Niebuhr recalls his imprisonment, the insights of the older Niebuhr scarcely enter the picture. That Kant did not allow his hero to mature beyond the experience of his captivity brought reproach from critics in both East and West. Compared with the extraordinary complexity and diversity of Christa Wolf's *Kindheitsmuster* (translated as *A Model Childhood*, 1980), a work with a similar theme that appeared a year before Kant's novel, the latter clearly reveals a lack of depth. On the other hand, by omitting his protagonist's experiences under socialism Kant avoided the compromises he had had to make in his earlier novels. What *Der Aufenthalt* loses in complexity it gains in honesty.

Since then Kant has published two more volumes of short stories. The narrator of the title story in *Der dritte Nagel* (The Third Nail, 1981), the bookkeeper Farßmann, serves as the narrator of all five stories in *Bronzezeit* (Bronze Age, 1986). With the exception of one story, the targets of

Kant's satire are again the problems of daily life in a socialist society. The best story is perhaps "Schöne Elise" (Beautiful Elise), in which a detective searches for a young woman who, it turns out, has been sent out by the "Top Board for Transitional Solutions" as a scapegoat to take responsibility for official mistakes. All of the stories are superbly narrated and entertaining.

Kant's sociopolitical standpoint is abundantly evident in his short stories as well as in his novels: the socialist society is indeed a better one, but it is still not the best conceivable. His works are both partisan and critical. The critical tendency is much less pronounced after *Die Aula;* it is revoked in *Das Impressum* and avoided in *Der Aufenthalt.* At the 1973 Writers' Conference Kant spoke out for a partnership between literature and politics, only to retract the suggestion at the next Writers' Conference in 1978. Since then he has never questioned the primacy of politics over literature. Whether Kant the writer will again emerge from the bureaucrat and whether he will be able to distance himself from politics remains to be seen.

References:

Manfred Durzak, *Der deutsche Roman der Gegenwart* (Stuttgart: Kohlhammer, 1971);

Barbara Einhorn, *Der Roman in der DDR* (Kronberg: Scriptor, 1978);

Ingeborg Gerlach, *Der schwierige Fortschritt* (Kronberg: Scriptor, 1979);

Jost Hermand, *Unbequeme Literatur* (Heidelberg: Stiehm, 1971);

Manfred Jäger, "Hermann Kant," in *Kritisches Lexikon zur deutschsprachigen Gegenwartsliteratur,* edited by Heinz Ludwig Arnold (Munich: Edition text + kritik, 1984), n. pag.;

Leonore Krenzlin, *Hermann Kant: Leben und Werk* (Berlin: Volk und Wissen, 1980);

Theodor Langenbruch, *Dialectical Humor in Hermann Kant's Novel "Die Aula,"* (Bonn: Bouvier, 1975);

Heinrich Mohr, "Gerechtes Erinnern: Untersuchungen zu Thema und Struktur von Kants Roman 'Die Aula' und einige Anmerkungen zu bundesrepublikanischen Rezensionen," *Germanisch-Romanische Monatsschrift,* 2 (1971): 225-245;

Gottfried Pareigis, *Kritische Analyse der Realitätsdarstellung in ausgewählten Werken des "Bitterfelder Weges"* (Kronberg: Scriptor, 1974);

Silvia and Dieter Schlenstedt, "Modern erzählt: Zu Strukturen in Hermann Kants 'Die Aula,'" *Neue Deutsche Literatur,* 12 (1965): 5-34;

Marc Silberman, "Der Erzähler als Erzieher," in *Zum Roman in der DDR,* edited by Silberman (Stuttgart: Klett, 1980), pp. 152-167;

Wolfgang Spiewok, "Hermann Kant," in *Literatur der DDR in Einzeldarstellungen,* edited by Hans Jürgen Geerdts (Stuttgart: Kröner, 1972), pp. 416-434.

Walter Kempowski

(29 April 1929-   )

Patricia H. Stanley
Florida State University

BOOKS: *Im Block: Ein Haftbericht* (Reinbek: Rowohlt, 1969);

Tadellöser & Wolff: Ein bürgerlicher Roman (Munich: Hanser, 1971);

Uns geht's ja noch gold: Roman einer Familie (Munich: Hanser, 1972);

Der Hahn im Nacken: Mini-Geschichten (Reinbek: Rowohlt, 1973);

Walter Kempowskis Harzreise erläutert (Munich: Hanser, 1974);

Ein Kapitel für sich: Roman (Munich: Hanser, 1975);

Alle unter einem Hut: Über 179 witzige und amüsante Alltags-Minimini-Geschichten in Großdruckschrift (Bayreuth: Loewe, 1976);

Wer will unter die Soldaten? (Munich & Vienna: Hanser, 1976);

Schnoor: Bremen zwischen Stavendamm und Balge (Bremen: Schmalfeldt, 1978);

Aus großer Zeit: Roman (Hamburg: Knaus, 1978); translated by Leila Vennewitz as *Days of Greatness* (New York: Knopf, 1981; London: Secker & Warburg, 1982);

Unser Herr Böckelmann (Hamburg: Knaus, 1979);

Kempowskis einfache Fibel (Brunswick: Westermann, 1980);

Schöne Aussicht (Hamburg: Knaus, 1981);

Herrn Böckelmanns schönste Tafelgeschichten nach dem ABC geordnet (Hamburg: Knaus, 1983);

Herzlich Willkommen (Munich: Knaus, 1984);

Haumiblau: Kindergeschichten (Munich: Bertelsmann, 1986).

OTHER: *Haben Sie Hitler gesehen?: Deutsche Antworten*, compiled by Kempowski (Munich: Hanser, 1973); translated by Michael Roloff as *Did You Ever See Hitler?: German Answers* (New York: Avon, 1975);

Immer so durchgemogelt: Erinnerungen an unsere Schulzeit, compiled by Kempowski (Munich: Hanser, 1974);

Haben Sie davon gewußt?: Deutsche Antworten, compiled by Kempowski (Hamburg: Knaus, 1979);

Walter Kempowski (Teutopress–Ullstein Bilderdienst)

Mein Lesebuch, compiled by Kempowski (Frankfurt am Main: Fischer Taschenbuch, 1979);

Beethovens Fünfte und Moin Vaddr läbt, manuscripts and notes for two radio plays, with a cassette of the plays (Hamburg: Knaus, 1982).

Walter Kempowski's success as a West German writer is remarkable, considering that his works focus on family life in a region which is not part of the Federal Republic of Germany and that narratives with nationalistic themes (that is, emphasizing German customs and conduct) are generally viewed with disfavor by West German critics. In spite of these disadvantages Kempowski's novels and radio plays have been so well accepted that he occupies a prominent position among West German writers. He received the Prize for Developing Writers under the Auspices of the Lessing Prize of the City of Hamburg in 1971; the Prize for Developing Writers under the Auspices of the Gryphius Prize in 1972; the Karl Szuka Prize in 1977; the Lower Saxony Prize in 1979; the Bambi Prize in 1980; and in that same year, together with the filmmaker Eberhard Fechner, the Jakob Kaiser Prize. In 1981 he was awarded the Radio Play Prize of the War-Blinded for *Moin Vaddr läbt* (My Father Is Alive [the play utilizes an invented language somewhat similar to Yiddish]). He also received the Federal Service Cross, First Class, a government award, in 1979. In the fall of 1980 he was appointed professor of literature and pedagogy at the University of Oldenburg.

Born in 1929, Kempowski was the youngest of three children of Margarethe Collasius and Karl-Georg Kempowski. The father ran a successful shipping company in Rostock that was founded by his own father and that would have been inherited by Kempowski's older brother Robert if Rostock had not become part of the Soviet zone after World War II. Walter, six years younger than Robert and seven years younger than his sister Ulla, grew up in a prosperous middle-class family. The mother had been trained in the Montessori method of teaching and had taught a kindergarten class before her marriage; family life was enriched by her ability to supplement the children's school education and by both parents' love of music and books. The two older children belonged to a sports club, but Walter was not an athletic child even before a bout with scarlet fever in 1940. Of the three children, he was the one who inherited the parents' artistic interests: he played the piano and the organ, went to concerts with his mother, and read voraciously.

Kempowski's physical education was taken in hand by the Hitler Youth organization after 1939. With the other children at school he wore a uniform on required occasions, learned to march, went on camping trips, and spent some vacation time working on a farm. Because of his musical ability he was made part of the entertainment program at organized events. When World War II broke out, Robert Kempowski and his father were called to active duty. Ulla worked in a munitions factory until 1943, when she married a young Danish employee of her father's firm and moved to Copenhagen with him. In February 1945 Walter, then almost sixteen years old,

was drafted into the army as a courier. His father was killed near the end of the war.

After the Soviet army entered Rostock in May 1945, the Kempowskis began sending packages of family belongings to relatives in Hamburg as part of a plan to relocate in the American zone. Both brothers joined the LDP, the liberal political party. Robert discovered through his job at the family firm that the Soviets were shipping to the Soviet Union baby clothing, sewing machines, and other relief goods sent to Rostock by the Allies, and he had bills of lading to support such a charge. The idealistic Walter decided to bring the information to the attention of the Allies. He was employed by a printing firm and traveled frequently within East Germany to purchase supplies. With his knowledge of road conditions he was able to escape across the border in November 1947. He made his way to Hamburg and then to Wiesbaden, where he obtained a job as a commissary clerk with the American army. In an interview with intelligence officers, he passed on the bills of lading and descriptions of life in Rostock.

In March 1948 the homesick young man went back to Rostock against the advice of friends in Wiesbaden. Within a week he was arrested by Soviet police and charged with espionage. Robert was also arrested. The brothers were tried together and sentenced to twenty-five years imprisonment. Some weeks after their arrest, their mother was also arrested. In spite of her protests that she knew nothing of her sons' activities, she was sentenced to ten years in a women's work camp. She was unexpectedly released in January 1954 and allowed to resettle in Hamburg. Walter was released in March 1956 and Robert a few months later. They joined their mother in Hamburg, where she was living in a converted barracks on a pension provided by the West German government.

Kempowski had decided in prison that he wanted to become an elementary school teacher. Early in 1957 he began his studies at a teachers' college in Göttingen, completing them in 1960. Appointed to a school in Breddorf, Lower Saxony, he took with him his bride, the former Hildegard Janssen, a teacher he had met when both were students in Göttingen. Their son, Karl-Friedrich, was born in 1961 and their daughter, Renate, in 1962. In 1965 the couple was transferred to the village school at Nartum in Lower Saxony, and they continue to live there, although the school has been closed. In 1977 Kempowski reduced his teaching at a nearby school to half time, and in 1980 he also assumed the position at the University of Oldenburg. He visited the United States in 1981 and still travels extensively to read from his works.

Kempowski's interest in writing began immediately after his release from prison; as he said in an interview in the *Freisinger Tagblatt* for 7 January 1980: "Ich wollte nicht Schriftsteller werden. Nur aufzeichnen, was da passiert war" (I did not want to become a writer. Just to record what had happened there). He experimented with writing techniques, including surrealistic settings and poetry, and in 1963 submitted to the Rowohlt publishing firm a novel in letters that was not published but attracted the attention of Fritz J. Raddatz, a reader for the firm. Within a few months, after several discussions with Raddatz, Kempowski settled on the style he still employs: an objective, impersonal technique in which the narrator functions only as a reporter of events. Short, pithy paragraphs with little dialogue and few adjectives distinguish Kempowski's writing. Emotional tone and warmth are added by the frequent inclusion of scraps of doggerel and slang expressions. Perhaps influenced by his reading of Kafka, Kempowski uses the comma more than the period; as a result, the reader is propelled along a series of paratactic clauses until he finds himself at the end of the paragraph. The reader begins to take part in and relive the reported events as he fills in descriptions and makes connections. Much of the commercial success of Kempowski's early novels is based on this participatory response.

In 1969 Rowohlt published *Im Block* (In the Block), Kempowski's account of the huge factory workroom that served as a prison cell for him and hundreds of other men. That was not, however, a good time to bring out revelations of East German prison life; the public was more interested in the political consequences of the student movement of the past year. *Im Block* sold only twelve hundred copies and has long been out of print. Kempowski reworked the entire content of the book into *Ein Kapitel für sich* (A Chapter in Itself, 1975).

In 1960 and 1961 Kempowski had composed a chronicle of Kempowski family vicissitudes for family members only, using material gathered from his relatives. Adapting this material to his new reportorial style, he wrote between 1968 and 1970 the novel *Tadellöser & Wolff* (1971). This book established him as a writer, but

he remained committed to his teaching career. In the 1980 newspaper interview he said, "Ich liebe diesen Beruf. Ihn habe ich mir in den Jahren der Haft erträumt. Ich habe es nie bereut" (I love this profession. I dreamed about it in the years of prison. I have never regretted it).

Tadellöser & Wolff opens in 1939 on the day the three Kempowski children, their parents, and their maid move into a larger apartment, and it closes in 1945 on the day the Soviets enter Rostock. The narrator is Walter, who is ten years old at the beginning of the novel, and through his naively objective eyes the reader sees a mixture of trivial and significant moments so representative of life in that traumatic wartime period that Germans who read the book recaptured part of their own past. The novel immediately became popular, and in the same year several passages were dramatized for radio as "Träumereien am elektrischen Kamin" (Dreams beside the Electric Hearth). In 1974 an episode describing a family vacation was published separately, with photographs, as *Walter Kempowskis Harzreise erläutert* (Walter Kempowski's Trip to the Harz Mountains), and in 1975 the entire novel was made into a film for television.

"Tadellöser und Wolff!" proclaims the father when something pleases him. The adjective *tadellos* means excellent, flawless. The firm of Loeser and Wolff provided Karl-Georg Kempowski with his favorite cigars; by combining the adjective with the firm name, he had a unique exclamation, a Schnack (a bit of chitchat or joke) for appropriate occasions. This is by no means the father's only Schnack; there are at least two dozen more, and the narrator records them without translation or explanation. From the context a reader can usually understand at least the attitude behind the outcry. So many details of the family's life emerge that Kempowski and his relatives have become a sort of representative public family, and personal questions are often posed to them without the least hesitation or sense of impertinence by journalists and private citizens alike. Although the book is labeled "Roman" (novel) and the inside cover bears the inscription "Alles frei erfunden!" (Everything has been freely invented!), it is common knowledge in Germany that the work is autobiographical in almost every detail. A family friend named Cornelli is invented, the mother's maiden name is changed to de Bonsac, and the name of Ulla's husband is fictional; events, however, are reported as the author remembers them or as they were told to him by relatives, and all dates are accurate. Descriptions include exact architectural details of many buildings that no longer exist.

The success of the book led Kempowski to conceive of a multivolume fictional chronicle of his family that would be at the same time an account of middle-class German life and a picture of a crucial period of German history. The intention behind the series is thus both literary and sociological: the wealth of historical, architectural, and personal details not only brings a particular family to life but also brings back into view, for study and evaluation, a way of life that no longer exists. Kempowski decided to begin the chronicle in 1900, a generation before his own birth, and end it in 1963, a date of significance to him as the true beginning of his writing career. Each volume is called a novel, but invented material is rare.

Uns geht's ja noch gold (We're Still Doing Well [a family colloquialism], 1972) begins on 1 May 1945, the day the previous novel ended, and continues the family saga to 8 March 1948, when Walter is arrested. He is again the narrator, but here he becomes the main character for the first time. His older brother returns home and takes a job in the shipping firm; their mother is employed for a time as a cleaning woman. The rigors of daily life in postwar Rostock are reported in an impersonal, objective tone, but even so, the reader realizes the courage and unexpected strength the mother brings to her new role of family provider after receiving the news of her husband's death. At the beginning of the novel Walter is sixteen years old and must return to high school. He rebels, becomes a truant, is expelled, finds a job, joins the Liberal party, escapes to the West (of special interest to Americans is his wide-eyed report of wastefulness in the army commissary job he obtains in Wiesbaden), returns to Rostock, and is arrested. The final paragraph of the book illustrates the tension and ambiguity that Kempowski's reportorial style creates: "Im Morgengrauen holten sie mich aus dem Bett. Zwei trugen Lederjacken. Da hast du was zu melden, wenn du wieder rüberkommst, dachte ich" (At dawn they fetched me out of bed. Two wore leather jackets. You've got something to report when you get back, I thought).

The first two novels, with their extraordinary amount of detail, were hailed as even more descriptive of life in the Third Reich than the work of Günter Grass or Siegfried Lenz. One reviewer praised Kempowski's ability to characterize without caricature, to appraise without prejudice.

In 1973 and 1974 Kempowski brought out two unusual collections of reminiscences–not his own but those of strangers asked at random to give their memories to the author. *Haben Sie Hitler gesehen?* (1973; translated as *Did You Ever See Hitler?*, 1975) is a transcription from tapes of 230 answers of people questioned in public places in the course of Kempowski's travels. Kempowski originally collected this material for use as background in *Tadellöser & Wolff*, but the responses were so fascinating that he decided to publish them separately. The respondents are identified only by occupation and year of birth. *Immer so durchgemogelt* (Always Tricked My Way Through, 1974) records recollections of early school experiences of unidentified people. Although these responses are amusing and surprisingly frank, the collection is of interest mainly in West Germany. The title comes from the admission of a book dealer that he learned very little in elementary school.

Ein Kapitel für sich is Kempowski's account of his eight years in prison. It reveals his admiration for the work of William Faulkner, for in addition to Walter's first-person account (the *Im Block* material) the novel also contains chapters attributed to Robert and their mother, as well as several letters from Ulla in Copenhagen to her Uncle Richard de Bonsac in Wiesbaden and his replies. Faulkner used this multiple-perspective technique in *The Sound and the Fury* (1929) and *As I Lay Dying* (1930). Robert's chapters give the reader a general view of prison conditions and of the other prisoners; he was more gregarious than his brother. The mother's account shows even more clearly than *Uns geht's ja noch gold* her courage and resourcefulness. Kempowski obtained this material by taping conversations with his mother before her death in 1969. Her chapters are more lively than the others, rich in descriptive details and dialogue.

Walter's chapters occupy most of the novel and show his development to manhood in the unusual environment of prison. The book is thus a bildungsroman of sorts; even the negative impact of the delicately described homosexual episodes and the periods of solitary confinement contribute to Walter's education. He learns to take responsibility for himself and to rely on his own judgment in the matters of friendship, intellectual interests, and goals. The youth who had copied his brother's hairstyle and mannerisms discovers

Kempowski

Der Chronist
des deutschen Bürgertums

Albrecht Knaus Verlag

Publisher's advertisement for Kempowski's series of novels about the history of his family

preferences of his own in the stultifying confines of prison and pursues them with a vigor that disgruntles his brother, who complains about Walter's independence when they are imprisoned together. This book, along with *Uns geht's ja noch gold,* was made into a television movie for a Kempowski film festival that also included *Tadellöser & Wolff* and aired in December 1979 and January 1980.

Aus großer Zeit (1978; translated as *Days of Greatness,* 1981) includes chapters ostensibly written by former friends and neighbors of the Kempowski and de Bonsac families as well as by various family members. Each person is responding to a request from the anonymous narrator to contribute to the family history, which begins in the year 1900 in the home of Walter Kempowski's grandparents in Rostock. The book

ends in 1918 with the marriage of his parents. This is a massive novel with leisurely, technically accurate descriptions of landscape, life, and customs in Rostock and in Wandsbek, the district of Hamburg where the de Bonsacs reside. The reader who has already met the family will find here the origin of many sayings and incidents alluded to in the other novels; he knows already that the grandparents' coldness, rigidity, and even cruelty did not repeat themselves in Karl-Georg and Margarethe's parental roles but produced the opposite effect. In *Aus großer Zeit* the reader learns so much about Margarethe's childhood that her courage during and after World War II becomes even more striking.

In 1979 another book of anonymous responses, *Haben Sie davon gewußt?* (Did You Know about It?), appeared. The question refers to the concentration camps, and the answers come, again, from strangers Kempowski encountered on reading tours.

Schöne Aussicht (Beautiful View, 1981) begins just after the marriage of Karl-Georg and Margarethe. Births, illnesses, and family traumas, including Karl-Georg's infidelity, are reported, as well as such historical events as the flight of the *Graf Zeppelin* over Rostock in 1936. The anonymous narrator introduces Walter to the chronicle at the age of three. The second half of the novel is highlighted by the description of a summer family reunion in 1936 when Wilhelm de Bonsac, Margarethe's father, rents a castle on the North Sea coast and gathers his four children and their families for a vacation. Whether or not this episode actually happened, it is charmingly portrayed, especially the surprise of the three Kempowski children when they see their father in a bathing suit for the first time. This book ends as Karl-Georg Kempowski decides to rent a new apartment of six rooms with central heating, a balcony, and a splendid view. The title of the book thus refers to the future of the family rather than its present. It also ironically reflects the general mood in Germany at the time, for economic conditions had improved after the collapse of the Weimar Republic and the appointment of Adolf Hitler as chancellor in January 1933.

According to publicity releases, the chronicle is complete with the appearance in 1984 of *Herzlich Willkommen* (Hearty Welcome). Walter is once again the narrator. The novel begins in March 1956 when he arrives at his mother's home in Hamburg after his release from prison. Following a short visit with his sister in Copenhagen, he enters the Pädagogische Hochschule at Göttingen to prepare for a teaching career. He is now twenty-seven years old and is accepted as a student even though he was expelled from the gymnasium in the mid 1940s and never completed the examinations that lead to the Abitur (certificate of competency). Kempowski gives a wonderfully precise picture of his student quarters in the home of a retired couple. He describes his professors and his daily round of domestic and study activities in great detail and reports his friendship with and growing love for Christa, a music student, with far more color and dialogue than he used in previous novels. In fact, Christa and her sisters are more fully depicted than any of the Kempowski family are in the earlier books of the chronicle. By the end of 1957 Christa and Walter are betrothed. She visits his

family in Hamburg at Christmas and meets the Danish relatives who have arrived for another de Bonsac reunion. The book and presumably the chronicle end at this reunion; but since Kempowski originally planned to conclude the history in 1963, there may yet be another volume.

Kempowski's continuing interest in elementary education is indicated by his collections of stories and recordings of his boyhood experiences for children. In the field of higher education he has contributed to knowledge of Germany's social structure in the twentieth century not only through the chronicle and response books and several radio plays based on them but also through his collection of photographs and memorabilia, as well as paper models of Rostock buildings and churches that he has made and has agreed to donate to the University of Oldenburg.

Asked in a 1980 interview by Ulla Plog-Handke for his definition of a good teacher, Kempowski said, "Einer, den sie vergessen" (One whom they will forget). Perhaps Kempowski will be forgotten as a classroom teacher and as the mentor of aspiring writers who attend the workshops he periodically offers at his home, but his publications have earned him a place in German literary history. Incorporating techniques he admired in the writings of Kafka and Faulkner, he has created a style that enables him to do what he originally set out to do–"nur aufzeichnen, was da passiert war"–with both commercial and critical success.

Interviews:
Volker Hage, "Eine Art Gedächtnistraining," *Akzente*, 19, no. 4 (1972): 340-349;

Irmela Schneider, "Schreiben als Erfahrung von Geschichte: Ein Gespräch mit Walter Kempowski," in her *Die Rolle des Autors: Analysen und Gespräche* (Stuttgart: Klett, 1981), pp. 108-112.

References:
Günter Alfs and Manfred Rabes, *"Genauso war es .... ": Kempowskis Familiengeschichte "Tadellöser & Wolff" im Urteil des Publikums* (Oldenburg: Holzberg, 1982);

Manfred Dierks, *Autor, Leser, Text: Walter Kempowskis künstlerische Produktivität und Leserreaktionen am Beispiel "Tadellöser & Wolff"* (Munich: Francke, 1981);

Dierks, *Walter Kempowski* (Munich: Beck, 1984);

Franz Josef Görtz, "Walter Kempowski als Historiker," *Akzente*, 20, no. 3 (1973): 243-254;

Ute Greber-Dierkes, "Ein Nachmittag bei Walter Kempowski," *Der Literat*, 27 (1985): 233-234;

Volker Hage, "Ein Kapitel für sich: Walter Kempowskis deutsche Familienchronik," in his *Die Wiederkehr des Erzählers* (Frankfurt am Main: Ullstein), pp. 166-194;

Manfred Jurgensen, *Erzählformen des fiktionalen Ich: Beiträge zum deutschen Gegenwartsroman. Handke, Bernhard, Wolf, Kant, Grass, Lenz, Kempowski* (Bern: Francke, 1980), pp. 176-207;

B. M. Kane, "Scenes from Family Life: The Novels of Walter Kempowski," *German Life and Letters*, 28, no. 4 (1975): 418-426;

Siegfried Lenz, "Gespräch mit Walter Kempowski," in his *Über Phantasie* (Hamburg: Hoffmann & Campe, 1982), pp. 105-157;

Günther Mahal, "Literarische Erfolgsbildung–am Beispiel Walter Kempowski," in *Festschrift für E. W. Herd*, edited by August Obermeyer (Dunedin, New Zealand: University of Otago Press, 1980), pp. 151-166;

Norbert Mecklenburg, "Faschismus und Alltag in deutscher Gegenwartsprosa: Kempowski und andere," in *Gegenwartsliteratur und Drittes Reich*, edited by Hans Wagener (Stuttgart: Reclam, 1977), pp. 11-32;

Ulla Plog-Handke, "Dorfschulmeister Walter Kempowski," *Brigitte* (January 1980): 110-113;

Kurt Rothmann, "Walter Kempowski," in his *Deutschsprachige Schriftsteller seit 1945 in Einzeldarstellungen* (Stuttgart: Reclam, 1985), pp. 209-212;

Sylvia Schwab, *Autobiographik und Lebenserfahrung: Versuch einer Typologie deutschsprachiger autobiographischer Schriften zwischen 1965 und 1975* (Würzburg: Königshausen & Neumann, 1981);

Patricia Haas Stanley, "An Examination of Walter Kempowski's *Ein Kapitel für sich*," *South Atlantic Review*, 47, no. 1 (1982): 38-50;

Klaus Wagner, "Die Suche nach dem Vater," in *Deutsche Literatur 1981: Ein Jahresüberblick*, edited by Hage (Stuttgart: Reclam, 1982), pp. 36-41;

Dietrich Weber, "Walter Kempowski," in *Deutsche Literatur der Gegenwart in Einzeldarstellungen*, volume 2, edited by Weber (Stuttgart: Kröner, 1977), pp. 278-296.

Sarah Kirsch

(16 April 1935-   )

Ann Clark Fehn
University of Rochester

BOOKS: *Die betrunkene Sonne/Der Stärkste*, by
  Kirsch and Rainer Kirsch (Berlin-Ober-
  schöneweide: Staatliches Rundfunkkomitee,
  1963); "Die betrunkene Sonne" adapted as
  Die betrunkene Sonne (Leipzig: Schulze,
  1966), and as *Die betrunkene Sonne: Ein Melo-
  dram für Kinder*, music by Thilo Medek
  (Frankfurt am Main: Hansen, 1978);
*Berlin-Sonnenseite: Deutschlandtreffen der Jugend in
  der Hauptstadt der DDR Berlin 1964*, by
  Kirsch and Rainer Kirsch (Berlin: Neues Le-
  ben, 1964);
Gespräch mit dem Saurier: Gedichte, by Kirsch and
  Rainer Kirsch (Berlin: Neues Leben, 1965);
Gedichte (Leipzig: Reclam, 1967);
Landaufenthalt: Gedichte (Berlin & Weimar: Auf-
  bau, 1967);
Gedichte (Ebenhausen: Langewiesche-Brandt,
  1969);
*Hänsel und Gretel: Eine illustrierte Geschichte für
  kleine und große Leute nach der gleichnamigen
  Märchenoper von Adelheid Wette und Engelbert
  Humperdinck*, text by Kirsch, pictures by Wer-
  ner Klemke (Leipzig, Frankfurt am Main,
  London & New York: Peters, 1972);
*Die Pantherfrau: Fünf unfrisierte Erzählungen aus
  dem Kassetten-Recorder* (Berlin & Weimar: Auf-
  bau, 1973);
*Die ungeheuren bergehohen Wellen auf See: Erzählun-
  gen* (Berlin: Eulenspiegel, 1973);
Zaubersprüche (Berlin & Weimar: Aufbau, 1973);
Es war dieser merkwürdige Sommer: Gedichte (Berlin:
  Berliner Handpresse, 1974);
Caroline im Wassertropfen (Berlin: Junge Welt,
  1975);
Zwischen Herbst und Winter (Berlin: Kinderbuch-
  verlag, 1975);
Rückenwind: Gedichte (Berlin & Weimar: Aufbau,
  1976);
Musik auf dem Wasser: Gedichte (Leipzig: Reclam,
  1977);
Wiepersdorf (Ebenhausen: Langewiesche-Brandt,
  1977);

*Sarah Kirsch (photograph by Peter Probst, courtesy of
Ullstein Bilderdienst)*

Katzenkopfpflaster: Gedichte (Munich: Deutscher Ta-
  schenbuch Verlag, 1978);
Wintergedichte: Poetische Wandzeitung (Ebenhausen:
  Langewiesche-Brandt, 1978);
Sommergedichte: Poetische Wandzeitung (Ebenhau-
  sen: Langewiesche-Brandt, 1978);
Wind, text by Kirsch, pictures by Kota Taniuchi
  (Hamburg: Wittig, 1978);
Ein Sommerregen, text by Kirsch, pictures by Taniu-
  chi (Hamburg: Wittig, 1978);
Schatten, text by Kirsch, pictures by Taniuchi
  (Hamburg: Wittig, 1979);
Sieben Häute (Berlin: Anabis, 1979);

Drachensteigen: Vierzig neue Gedichte (Ebenhausen: Langewiesche-Brandt, 1979);

La Pagerie (Stuttgart: Deutsche Verlags-Anstalt, 1980);

Papiersterne: 15 Lieder für Mezzosopran und Klavier, text by Kirsch, music by Wolfgang von Schweinitz (Stuttgart: Deutsche Verlags-Anstalt, 1981);

Erdreich: Gedichte (Stuttgart: Deutsche Verlags-Anstalt, 1982);

Der Winter: Gedichte (Hauzenberg: Pongratz, 1983);

Sarah Kirsch: Poems, translated by Jack Hirschman (Santa Cruz, Cal.: Alcatraz Editions, 1983);

Katzenleben: Gedichte (Stuttgart: Deutsche Verlags-Anstalt, 1984);

Landwege: Eine Auswahl 1980-1985 (Stuttgart: Deutsche Verlags-Anstalt, 1985);

Hundert Gedichte (Ebenhausen: Langewiesche-Brandt, 1985);

Conjurations: The Poems of Sarah Kirsch, translated by Wayne Kvam (Athens: Ohio University Press, 1985);

Irrstern: Prosa (Stuttgart: Deutsche Verlags-Anstalt, 1986);

Allerlei-Rauh: Eine Chronik (Stuttgart: Deutsche Verlags-Anstalt, 1988).

RECORDING: *Sarah Kirsch liest Gedichte aus "Rükkenwind" und aus dem Manuskript; Sarah Kirsch liest Gedichte zeitgenössischer Autoren,* Verlag Langewiesche-Brandt, #0647014, 1978.

Ingrid Bernstein—the future Sarah Kirsch—with her father, mother, uncle, and grandfather in Limlingerode, circa 1937 (courtesy of Sarah Kirsch)

OTHER: Anna Achmatova, *Ein niedagewesener Herbst,* translated by Kirsch and Rainer Kirsch (Berlin: Volk und Welt, 1967);

Novella Matveeva, *Poesiealbum 6,* translated by Kirsch (Berlin: Junge Welt, 1967);

Vietnam in dieser Stunde: Künstlerische Dokumentation, contributions by Kirsch (Halle: Mitteldeutscher Verlag, 1968);

"January," "Dandelions for Chains," "Before the Sun Rises," translated by Gordon and Gisela Brotherston, in *East German Poetry,* edited by Michael Hamburger (New York: Dutton, 1973), pp. 152-155;

Margarete Neumann, *Am Abend vor der Heimreise,* afterword by Kirsch (Berlin: Aufbau, 1974);

Helga Schubert, *Lauter Leben: Geschichten,* afterword by Kirsch (Berlin: Aufbau, 1975);

"Weites Haus/Large House," in *German Poetry 1910-1975,* translated and edited by Hamburger (New York: Urizen, 1976), pp. 490-493;

Christoph Meckel, ed., *Nürnberger Blätter für Literatur IV: Sonderband Poesie,* contributions by Kirsch (Fürth: Klaussner, 1978);

Gisela Kraft and Oskar von Torne, eds., *Lu Xun Zeitgenosse,* contributions by Kirsch (Berlin: Leibniz-Gesellschaft für kulturellen Austausch, 1979);

Bettina Wegner-Schlesinger, *Wenn meine Lieder nicht mehr stimmen,* foreword by Kirsch (Reinbek: Rowohlt, 1979);

"Jeder Hof hat seine Amsel," in *Literatur und Kritik: Aus Anlaß des 60. Geburtstages von Marcel Reich-Ranicki,* edited by Walter Jens (Stuttgart: Deutsche Verlags-Anstalt, 1980), pp. 151-152;

Hans mein Igel, text adapted from the Brothers Grimm by Kirsch, pictures by Paula Schmidt (Cologne: Middlehauve, 1980);

"Vier deutsche Schriftsteller, die in Berlin leben, rufen zum Frieden auf," by Kirsch, Thomas Brasch, Günter Grass, and Peter Schneider, in *Mut zur Angst: Schriftsteller für den Frieden*, edited by Ingrid Krueger (Darmstadt & Neuwied: Luchterhand, 1982), pp. 18-19;

Elke Erb, *Trost*, foreword by Kirsch (Stuttgart: Deutsche Verlags-Anstalt, 1982);

Michael Müller, ed., *Der Sprayer von Zürich: Solidarität mit Harald Naegeli*, contributions by Kirsch (Reinbek: Rowohlt, 1984);

Annette von Droste-Hülshoff, edited by Kirsch (Cologne: Kiepenheuer & Witsch, 1986).

PERIODICAL PUBLICATIONS: "Gedichte," *Sinn und Form*, 28 (May/June 1976): 583-588;

"Zwei Gedichte," *Akzente*, 23 (August 1976): 291-292;

"Seit er fort ist und andere Gedichte/Since He Is Gone and Other Poems," translated by Stewart Florsheim, *Dimension*, 12 (1979): 344-345;

"Über Nicolas Born," *Deutsche Akademie für Sprache und Dichtung: Jahrbuch* (1979): 112-113;

"Poems from *Rückenwind* and *Zaubersprüche* by Sarah Kirsch," translated by Helmbrecht Breinig and Kevin Power, *Boundary 2*, 8 (Spring 1980): 190-197;

"Zwei Gedichte/Two Poems," translated by Breinig and Power, *Dimension*, 14 (1981): 280-281;

"Then We Shall Have No Need of Fire," translated by E. Castendyk Briefs, "Red," "The Rest of the String," translated by Ewald Osers, *Journal of Translation*, 10 (Spring 1983): 47-48;

"Der Winter: Gedichte," *Akzente*, 30 (February 1983): 3-15;

Review of Heinz Czechowski, *An Freund und Feind: Gedichte*, *L'80*, nos. 29-32 (1984): 165-166;

"Wetterzeichen," *Frankfurter Anthologie*, 8 (1984): 223-225;

"Wermutengel," *Frankfurter Anthologie*, 9 (1985): 195-197;

"Four poems," translated by Charles Fishman and Marina Roscher, *New Letters*, 51, no. 4 (1985): 70-72;

" 'Earthly Kingdom' and Other Poems," translated by Agnes Stein, *Comparative Criticism*, 7 (1985): 183-192.

Sarah Kirsch is one of the best-known and most respected poets writing in the German language today. Her rhythms are so distinctive that reviewers, adopting a phrase of Peter Hacks's,

have come to speak of the "Sarah-Sound," and she is frequently cited both for the intensity of her images and for the contradictions they present to everyday perception and to conforming habit. As influences on her language, themes, and ideas she and others name Bettina von Arnim; Annette von Droste-Hülshoff; Adalbert Stifter; the Russian poet Anna Achmatova, whose work she has translated; the European and American modernists she and other writers in the German Democratic Republic (GDR) came to know in the 1960s; older contemporaries such as Johannes Bobrowski and Günter Eich; and the circle of colleagues with whom she has shared public readings since the beginning of her career. Her achievements have been recognized in both East and West by a series of major literary prizes, including the Heinrich Heine Prize of the GDR in 1973, the Petrarch Prize in 1976, the Austrian Prize for European Literature in 1981, and the Friedrich Hölderlin Prize in 1984. Perhaps more indicative of the rise of her reputation is that since the 1970s her works have appeared without any descriptive copy on the dust jackets.

Kirsch was born Ingrid Bernstein in 1935 in Limlingerode, a village on the southern edge of the Harz Mountains, and grew up in the city of Halberstadt. She adopted the name Sarah before she began publishing to show her solidarity with the Jewish victims of the Holocaust. As the daughter of a worker (a telecommunications mechanic) in the GDR, founded in 1949, she participated enthusiastically in socialist youth activities. After earning her secondary school diploma she studied biology at the University of Halle, where she received her diploma in 1959. Her colleague Elke Erb sees in this training the beginning of the attention to detail for which her lyric poetry is known.

In Halle she met the writer Rainer Kirsch, whom she married in 1958. Together with him she joined a circle of aspiring writers coached by Gerhard Wolf. After being admitted to the GDR Writers' Association she attended the Johannes R. Becher Institute for Literature from 1963 to 1965. There she had the opportunity not just to practice her own writing but also to read works of world literature not easily obtainable in the GDR outside the institute. Along the way, in accordance with the ideal of solidarity between workers and writers declared at the 1959 conference in Bitterfeld, she worked in factories and on a collective farm.

Bernstein and her mother at Halberstadt in 1941 (courtesy of Sarah Kirsch)

In 1968 Kirsch and her husband were divorced, and she moved to East Berlin. Her son Moritz was born the following year. During the early 1970s she gained wide recognition in both German states for her work. In 1976 she was among the East German writers who protested the revocation of the GDR citizenship of the singer/poet Wolf Biermann; as a result she was expelled from the Socialist Unity party and from the Writers' Association. On 28 August 1977 she moved with her son to West Berlin. She went to Rome in 1978, where she spent seven months at the Villa Massimo as the guest of the government of the Federal Republic, and subsequently traveled in southern France and the United States. In 1981 she moved to a village near Bremen and in 1983 to Tielenhemme in Schleswig-Holstein.

Unlike most GDR authors living in the Federal Republic, Kirsch enjoys travel privileges between East and West. She does not consider herself an exile poet. Although she often expresses pleasure in the isolation of her rural home, she belongs to the P.E.N. writers' organization and occasionally engages in political action. In 1980, for example, she joined Günter Grass, Thomas Brasch,

and Peter Schneider in an open letter to Chancellor Helmut Schmidt regarding peace efforts.

She began her career writing children's literature, an activity which she continued to pursue after her move to the West. Her first published work, coauthored with Rainer Kirsch, was a radio play for children, *Die betrunkene Sonne* (The Drunken Sun, 1963). Like her poetry, her children's stories tend to stay close to nature, and they often move with matter-of-fact swiftness between the realistic and the fantastic. In *Caroline im Wassertropfen* (Caroline in the Drop of Water, 1975), for example, a girl and her friends shrink to a size that lets them voyage through microscopic realms.

As her talent for poetry emerged, Kirsch became part of a group of young poets that included Rainer Kirsch, Biermann, Volker Braun, Bernd Jentzsch, Günter Kunert, Karl Mickel, and Heinz Czechowski. They came to public attention through readings organized by Stephan Hermlin and because of a heated debate on the role of lyric poetry in the collective state conducted in 1966 in the official newspaper *Neues Deutschland* and in *Forum*, the organ of the GDR youth organi-

Bernstein at about eighteen years (courtesy of Sarah Kirsch)

in the Country," and many of the poems describe the experiences of a city dweller set free in nature. Nevertheless, allusions to GDR life are frequent enough to give the title a secondary sense: "Residence in a (or This) Country." Here, as in her later poetry, Kirsch combines poignant evocations of idyllic harmony with reminders that the idyll is far from being a reality. Although in this volume the GDR is "mein kleines wärmendes Land" (my small country that warms me), she does not shy away from critical turns of thought. For example, recurrent images of flying appear as political commentary on a country that does not allow its citizens to travel outside the Eastern bloc; they also are used to express criticism of American atrocities in Vietnam and to describe the general longings of humans pinned down by physical and psychological constraints.

Landaufenthalt and two later collections published while Kirsch was still living in the GDR, *Zaubersprüche* (Incantations, 1973) and *Rückenwind* (Tail Wind, 1976), were recognized as significant achievements by readers in both German states. The poems in these volumes move primarily within the sphere of the personal and private but do not exhaust themselves there. Instead, through imagery that is at once concrete, evocative, and subtly political, they describe a wide range of experiences. Particularly prominent, especially in *Zaubersprüche*, is the pain of a difficult love relationship; the persona's appeals to a recalcitrant lover, her "Herzkönig" (King of Hearts), can be taken on a personal level and simultaneously as political commentary because of Kirsch's characteristically multilayered language, which is full of ambiguous, potentially double meanings. " 'Privat' würde ich als ein Schimpfwort empfinden" (The word 'private' is a derogatory term for me), Kirsch noted in a 1975 interview for Western readers.

Even though Kirsch maintained that her move from the GDR to the Federal Republic was simply a change of residence, her poetry took some time to adjust to the change. Between 1977 and 1981 she published one thin volume of poems, *Drachensteigen* (Kite-Flying, 1979), and an even thinner collection of prose pieces, *La Pagerie* (1980), named after a small palace in the Provence. Except for the first fifteen poems of *Drachensteigen*, nine of which were written in the GDR, these two volumes consist of travel poems from Italy and the Provence, respectively. Although many of the poems contain the observant detail that marked Kirsch's earlier lyrics, the

zation. These poets maintained, against strong criticism, that lyric poetry could fulfill its socialist function without conforming to traditional constraints on socialist art. Kirsch drew reproof for her frank admissions that she did not attempt economic analysis in her poetry and that she was not convinced that the human condition had been so much changed through the technological and socialist revolution as to affect poetry. Despite these attacks, the vigor and imagination of Kirsch and the others produced a "lyric-boom" that began in the 1960s and lasted into the 1970s.

Gespräch mit dem Saurier (Conversation with the Dinosaur, 1965), Kirsch's first published volume of poetry–or rather half-volume, because she shared it equally with Rainer Kirsch–features childlike verses and rhymes but does not hide its political edge: in "Hierzulande" (In This Country), for example, snails opine that progress can be achieved only by using slime. Her mature style emerged in 1967, the date of *Landaufenthalt*. This title translates in a primary sense as "A Stay

Kirsch with her husband, the writer Rainer Kirsch (left), and the poet Bernd Jentzch in Jena, circa 1960 (courtesy of Sarah Kirsch)

Kirsch with her son Moritz in East Berlin, circa 1973 (courtesy of Sarah Kirsch)

Kirsch (left) with the East German writer Christa Wolf in Mecklenburg, circa 1974 (photograph by Helga Paris)

Kirsch in West Berlin in 1978 (photograph by Stefan Moses)

travel scenes lack the rich, disquieting ambiguity and political undercurrent of her previous work. Mention of the GDR is casual and reminiscent of diary entries: "Ach wie danke ich meinem vorletzten Staat, daß er mich hierher katapultierte" (How I thank my next-to-last state for catapulting me here [to Italy]); references to her new home, the Federal Republic, are prominently absent, as if to avoid coming to terms with a country she had dismissed in *Rückenwind* as "Wolfsland" (land of the wolves).

In her more recent volumes of poetry, *Erdreich* (Earthly Kingdom, 1982) and *Katzenleben* (Cat's Life, 1984), Kirsch once again seems to be at home. Directing her attention to the United States and West Berlin in *Erdreich* and to rural Schleswig-Holstein in *Katzenleben*, she explores dimensions of memory, foreboding, and pleasure with imagery drawn from nature and from literary tradition. As the title of the later book reflects, cats appear frequently; they accumulate into a complex self-image–detached, restless, vain, and hedonistically able to settle down wherever they please.

In addition to the poetry for which she is best known, Kirsch has written several volumes of prose–but only under the broadest definition can they be said to belong to a single genre. Near the beginning of her career in the GDR she took on some journalistic assignments, which, like her translations, were procured for her by the Writers' Association as part of its support and encouragement of aspiring writers. More significant was *Die Pantherfrau* (The Panther Tamer, 1973), which attracted wide attention in part because of the name she had made for herself as a poet but also because of the project itself. Invited by the Aufbau publishing house to do a documentary for the "Year of the Woman," she taped and transcribed interviews with five women: an old-time Communist revolutionary, a mid-career party official, a successful young manager and former competitive swimmer, a worker, and the animal trainer of the title. By East German standards the women talk with considerable frankness about their personal and professional lives. Kirsch's *Fünf unfrisierte Erzählungen aus dem Kassetten-Recorder* (Five Undoctored Stories from the Cassette Recorder, 1973), as the book is subtitled, indicates her desire to avoid the idealizing practices of GDR journalism, and she limits herself to the words of her subjects to guarantee authenticity. Nevertheless, she brings something close to authorial voice to the narratives by editing them, by

selecting phrases as titles for each interview, and by repeating some of the speaker's sentences as a kind of summary or distillation at the end of each piece. This last technique, in particular, allows her to underscore character traits and to emphasize common themes, such as the difficulty of reconciling career demands with love and family.

Also in 1973 Kirsch published *Die ungeheuren bergehohen Wellen auf See* (The Enormous, Mountain-high Waves on the Sea). These seven stories, written between 1968 and 1972, vary in length from two to twenty-five pages and describe the daily lives of women in the GDR from perspectives that range from the unusual to the fantastic. Although problems such as rape, broken engagements, and desperate childlessness form their cores, the ironic and matter-of-fact narrative style pointedly avoids pathos; and the startling events, including a wedding financed by a father for someone else's daughter after his own daughter has been jilted by the groom ("Der Schmied von Kosewalk" [The Blacksmith of Kosewalk]), shake the conventions of socialist realism.

One of the stories in this collection, "Blitz aus heiterm Himmel" (A Bolt from the Blue), was originally solicited by Kirsch's colleague Edith Anderson. Inspired by Hacks's 1970 drama *Omphale*, Anderson asked prominent East German authors, male and female, to write stories in which a sex change occurs. After a large number had accepted the challenge, Anderson began a difficult struggle to get the volume published. She finally succeeded in 1975, albeit in a form somewhat different from what she had originally planned. Kirsch's contribution exemplifies the challenge this extraordinary volume presented to social tradition and sexual taboos. Beneath the surface gaiety of her story lie sharp social analysis and deep-seated skepticism, for her lovers find themselves able to cooperate and share only after the woman suddenly becomes a man. " 'Jetz, wo ich selbern Kerl bin, jetz kriekich die Ehmannzipatzjon' " (Now that I'm a guy, I'm getting e-man-cipated), observes the former woman. Both partners enjoy the freedom, easy camaraderie, and mutual consideration of their suddenly equal lives–but the change ends the sexual relationship that previously brought them great pleasure.

Kirsch's next prose pieces, *La Pagerie* and *Irrstern* (Comet, 1986), are quite different from the two earlier volumes; indeed, they are closer to poetry than to prose. With the exception of

Page from manuscript for an unpublished work by Kirsch (courtesy of Sarah Kirsch) her earliest work, her poetry has often included elements of prose. Her images are evocative but not obviously metaphorical; and they tend to stress the concrete and the everyday, though with elements of the fantastic and fairy tales intermixed. Both in *Zaubersprüche* and in *Rückenwind* the poems and the order in which they are placed yield a quasi narrative. Although iambic, trochaic, or dactylic rhythms are often used, the poems' surfaces are characteristically roughened by prose cadences and colloquialisms; enjambments are the rule rather than the exception. In most of the poetry collections occasional prose texts appear, distinguished only by a justified right margin and by a slightly greater concentration of other prose elements. While *La Pagerie* continues this practice, yielding texts that defy easy categorization, *Irrstern* can comfortably be called prose, even though it is prose with the unmistakable stamp of Kirsch's lyric poetry. Most of the pieces are only half a page or so in length; the longest, "Galoschen" (Galoshes), is almost four pages long. Many are narratives describing events and objects from the daily life of the North Sea country–a visit to a neighbor, the opening of a new village tavern, the birth of a lamb–and use punctuation and hypotaxis, both of which are rare in Kirsch's poems; but they often dissolve into the rhythmic, evocative phrases and ambiguous syntactic constructions for which her poetry is known. Similarly, the prosaic frames yield regularly to imaginative transformations of the real and familiar: the elderly neighbor suddenly appears as a fairy-tale-like figure of Time, with twelve rowdy geese named for the months of the year; the new tavern keeper brings donkeys, a peacock, a machine gun, and a knife-wielding wife to the village for a while and then disappears. Other pieces remain grounded in empirical reality but move unexpectedly into reflections on the Falkland war, a dying friend in East Berlin, or the possibility that the comfortingly concrete may be only an illusion.

With *Allerlei-Rauh* (Many-Furs, 1988) Kirsch has extended her reach yet further into the realm of prose. This volume satisfies her long-standing ambition to write a sustained narrative of significant length; it is about one hundred pages long. The title, which also appears as a heading for a section of *Drachensteigen*, is borrowed from a Grimm tale about a golden-tressed princess who—wearing a coat made of the pelts of many kinds of animals—flees home and privilege

to escape the incestuous demands of her widowed father. Despite ironic changes, Kirsch preserves much of the original story, splitting it in two and inserting it into a chronicle of life in Schleswig-Holstein and reminiscences about a happy summer from her days in the GDR. Many strands of this chronicle converge in the experience of pleasure: "Eine Taube fliegt über uns hin mit einer Kornblume im Schnabel und sagt: Merkt euch, das ist das Glück!" (A dove flies over us with a cornflower and says: Pay attention, this is happiness!). In a literary tradition highly conscious of the temptations of self-satisfaction and escapism, this is dangerous ground for Kirsch to tread. As in much of her poetry, the construction of self is strongly autobiographical. A sentence at the beginning parodies convention by telling the reader both that the work is entirely fictional and that all the names have been "verwechselt" (mixed up). Halfway through the book the convention dissolves in an extended description of a couple named Christa and Gerhard and a paragraph of self-reflection on this venture into the narrative prose that is Christa Wolf's territory. The work is unabashedly experimental: like her poetry, it is characterized by syntactic ambiguities, associative leaps, and the accumulative recurrence of ironically distanced images, but these features are here stretched onto the expanded frame of prose. With this book the author who wrote against the grain of socialist tradition with her stubbornly autobiographical poetry seeks a new direction but continues to assert the necessity of autobiography. Where this experimentation will lead remains an open question.

Interviews:

Karl Corino, " 'Privat' würde ich als ein Schimpfwort empfinden: Gespräch mit Sarah Kirsch," *Deutschland-Archiv*, 8 (October 1975): 1085-1087;

Bernd Kolf, "Gespräch mit Sarah Kirsch," *Europäische Ideen*, 17 (1976): 15-18;

"Ein Gespräch mit Schülern: 4 frühe Gedichte," in *Erklärung einiger Dinge: Dokumente und Bilder* (Ebenhausen: Langewiesche-Brandt, 1978), pp. 5-51;

Klaus Wagenbach, "Von der volkseigenen Idylle ins freie Land der Wölfe: Ein Gespräch mit Sarah Kirsch," *Freibeuter*, 2 (1979): 85-93;

Hans Ester and Dick von Stekelenburg, "Gespräch mit Sarah Kirsch," *Deutsche Bücher*, 9, no. 2 (1979): 100-113.

Bibliography:

Walter Helmut Fritz, "Sarah Kirsch," in *Kritisches Lexikon zur deutschsprachigen Gegenwartsliteratur*, edited by Heinz Ludwig Arnold (Munich: Edition text + kritik, 1985).

References:

Edith Anderson, "Genesis and Adventures of the Anthology *Blitz aus heiterm Himmel*," in *Studies in GDR Culture and Society 4*, edited by Margy Gerber and others (Washington, D.C.: University Press of America, 1984), pp. 1-14;

Charlotte E. Armster, " 'Merkwürdiges Beispiel weiblicher Entschlossenheit'–A Woman's Story–by Sarah Kirsch," in *Studies in GDR Culture and Society 2*, edited by Gerber and others (Washington, D.C.: University Press of America, 1982): 243-250;

Manfred Behn-Liebherz, "Sarah Kirsch," in *Neue Literatur der Frauen: Deutschsprachige Autorinnen der Gegenwart*, edited by Heinz Puknus (Munich: Beck, 1980), pp. 158-165;

Christine Cosentino, "Die Lyrikerin Sarah Kirsch im Spiegel ihrer Bilder," *Neophilologus*, 63 (July 1979): 418-429;

Adolf Endler, "Sarah Kirsch und ihre Kritiker," *Sinn und Form*, 27 (January/February 1975): 142-170;

Ann Clark Fehn, "Authorial Voice in Sarah Kirsch's *Die Pantherfrau*," in *Erkennen und Deuten: Essays zur Literatur und Literaturtheorie, Edgar Lohner in memoriam*, edited by Martha Woodmansee and Walter Lohnes (Berlin: Schmidt, 1983), pp. 335-346;

Franz Fühmann, "Vademecum für Leser von Zaubersprüchen," *Sinn und Form*, 27 (March/April 1975): 385-420;

Almut Giesecke, "Zum Leistungsvermögen einer Prosaform: Analysen zu 'Der Schmied von Kosewalk' von Sarah Kirsch und 'Juninachmittag' von Christa Wolf," *Weimarer Beiträge*, 23, no. 8 (1977): 110-139;

Peter J. Graves, ed., *Three Contemporary German Poets: Wolf Biermann, Sarah Kirsch, Reiner Kunze* (Leicester, U.K.: Leicester University Press, 1985);

Peter Hacks, "Der Sarah-Sound," *Neue Deutsche Literatur*, 24, no. 9 (1976): 104-118;

Ursula Heukenkamp, "Sarah Kirsch: 'Die Pantherfrau,' " *Weimarer Beiträge*, 21, no. 8 (1975): 120-133;

Eva Kaufmann, "Für und wider das Dokumentarische in der DDR-Literatur," *Weimarer Beiträge*, 32, no. 4 (1986): 684-689;

Heidrun Loeper, " 'Ehmannzipatzjon' und Kassetten-Recorder," *Neue Deutsche Literatur*, 22, no. 8 (1974): 144-147;

Heinrich Mohr, "Die Lust 'Ich' zu sagen:· Versuch über die Lyrik der Sarah Kirsch," *Lyrik–von allen Seiten: Gedichte und Aufsätze des 1. Lyrikertreffens in Münster*, edited by Lothar Jordan and others (Frankfurt am Main: Fischer, 1981), pp. 439-460;

Mary Elizabeth O'Brien, "The Divided Woman: Female Protagonists in Contemporary GDR Literature," *New German Review*, 1, no. 1 (1985): 41-54;

Fritz J. Raddatz, "Eine neue Subjektivität formt neue Realität," in his *Traditionen und Tendenzen: Materialien zur Literatur der DDR* (Frankfurt am Main: Suhrkamp, 1972), pp. 167-211;

Marcel Reich-Ranicki, "Sarah Kirsch: Der Droste jüngere Schwester," in his *Entgegnungen: Zur deutschen Literatur der 70er Jahre* (Stuttgart: Deutsche Verlags-Anstalt, 1981), pp. 319-332;

Kurt Rothmann, "Sarah Kirsch," in his *Deutschsprachige Schriftsteller seit 1945 in Einzeldarstellungen* (Stuttgart: Reclam, 1985), pp. 223-226;

Jürgen Serke, "Sarah Kirsch: 'Wie wir zerrissen sind und ganz nur in des Vogels Kopf," in his *Frauen schreiben: Ein neues Kapitel deutschsprachiger Literatur* (Hamburg: Gruner & Jahr, 1979), pp. 184-199;

Margaret Stoljar, "Das Ende der Utopie: Kunert und Kirsch als Modelle einer neuen Exilliteratur," in *Tendenzwenden: Aspekte des Kulturwandels der 70er Jahre*, edited by David Roberts (Frankfurt am Main, Bern & New York: Lang, 1984), pp. 163-182;

Florian Tielebier-Langenscheidt, "Werbung für deutsche Gegenwartsliteratur: Ein Beitrag zur Theorie und Praxis der Literaturvermittlung," *Archiv für Geschichte des Buchwesens*, 23 (1982): cols. 1-386;

Silvia Volckmann, *Zeit der Kirschen: Das Naturbild in der deutschen Gegenwartslyrik. Jürgen Becker, Sarah Kirsch, Wolf Biermann, Hans Magnus Enzensberger* (Königstein: Forum Academicum, 1982);

Jürgen P. Wallmann, "Sarah Kirsch: *Irrstern*," *Literatur und Kritik*, 209/210 (November/December 1986): 469-471.

Alexander Kluge
(14 February 1932-   )

Gretel A. Koskella
George Washington University

BOOKS: *Die Universitäts-Selbstverwaltung: Ihre Geschichte und gegenwärtige Rechtsform* (Frankfurt am Main: Klostermann, 1958; New York: Arno Press, 1977);

Kulturpolitik und Ausgabenkontrolle: Zur Theorie und Praxis der Rechnungsprüfung, by Kluge and Hellmuth Becker (Frankfurt am Main: Klostermann, 1961);

Lebensläufe (Stuttgart: Goverts, 1962); translated by Leila Vennewitz as *Attendance List for a Funeral* (New York: McGraw-Hill, 1966); German version revised as *Lebensläufe: Anwesenheitsliste für eine Beerdigung* (Frankfurt am Main: Suhrkamp, 1974);

Schlachtbeschreibung (Olten & Freiburg im Breisgau: Walter, 1964); translated by Vennewitz as *The Battle* (New York: McGraw-Hill, 1967); German version republished as *Der Untergang der Sechsten Armee* (Munich: Piper, 1969); revised as *Schlachtbeschreibung: Der organisatorische Aufbau eines Unglücks* (Munich: Goldmann, 1978); revised as *Schlachtbeschreibung* (Frankfurt am Main: Suhrkamp, 1983);

Abschied von gestern: Protokoll (Frankfurt am Main: Verlag Filmkritik, 1967);

Die Artisten in der Zirkuskuppel: Ratlos; Die Ungläubige; Projekt Z.; Sprüche der Leni Peickert (Munich: Piper, 1968);

Öffentlichkeit und Erfahrung: Zur Organisationsanalyse von bürgerlicher und proletarischer Öffentlichkeit, by Kluge and Oskar Negt (Frankfurt am Main: Suhrkamp, 1972);

Filmwirtschaft in der BRD und in Europa, by Kluge, Michael Dost, and Florian Hopf (Munich: Hanser, 1973);

Lernprozesse mit tödlichem Ausgang (Frankfurt am Main: Suhrkamp, 1973);

Gelegenheitsarbeit einer Sklavin: Zur realistischen Methode (Frankfurt am Main: Suhrkamp, 1975);

Neue Geschichten: Hefte 1-18. "Unheimlichkeit der Zeit" (Frankfurt am Main: Suhrkamp, 1977);

Alexander Kluge (photograph by Bernd Kammerer, courtesy of Ullstein Bilderdienst)

Die Patriotin: Texte, Bilder 1-6 (Frankfurt am Main: Zweitausendeins, 1979);

Geschichte und Eigensinn, by Kluge and Negt (Frankfurt am Main: Zweitausendeins, 1981);

Neue Geschichten: Hefte 19-28. "Der Angriff der Gegenwart auf die übrige Zeit" (Frankfurt am Main: Suhrkamp, 1984);

Die Macht der Gefühle (Frankfurt am Main: Zweitausendeins, 1984);

Theodor Fontane, Heinrich von Kleist und Anna Wilde: Zur Grammatik der Zeit (Berlin: Wagenbach, 1987).

OTHER: *Bestandsaufnahme: Utopie Film,* edited by Kluge (Frankfurt am Main: Zweitausendeins, 1983).

Alexander Kluge's unique position in modern German literature results from his diversified background as a film producer, social commentator, lawyer, and writer of fiction. All of these elements combine in his work to produce a rich collage of varying styles and techniques, often highly experimental in tone and quality. For several years during the 1960s Kluge was a leading figure among young West German writers who rejected traditional narrative forms in favor of a more cold-blooded, objective portrayal of modern reality using highly innovative techniques. His best-selling *Schlachtbeschreibung* (1964; translated as *The Battle,* 1967) was heralded as a model for the new "documentary" novel; in any case it was one of a few such novels ever written. Even after interest in literary experimentation faded with the end of the student and cultural unrest of the late 1960s, Kluge continued to publish difficult, often enigmatic short stories and "Hefte" (workbooks) attacking the ills he saw in modern society. Above all, Kluge is a leader among contemporary authors in exploring the links between modern-day Germany and its wartime heritage.

Kluge was born in 1932 to Ernst and Alice Hausdorf Kluge in Halberstadt (now in the German Democratic Republic), where his father practiced medicine. In April 1945, during the final phase of World War II, his parental home was destroyed in an air raid. Within a year his parents had divorced, and his mother had remarried and moved to Berlin, where Kluge joined her. This dramatic juncture in Kluge's early life was to haunt him in later years. It came to symbolize a turning point at which the secure world he had known as a child suddenly collapsed, to be replaced by a world of chaos and upheaval that continued well into the postwar years.

After finishing high school in Berlin, Kluge continued his education in Marburg, Freiburg, and Frankfurt, obtaining his doctorate in law in 1956 with a dissertation on university self-regulation. During the final years of his studies he worked as a legal intern in the Frankfurt law practice of Hellmuth Becker, where he was exposed to practical politics and policy-making. In late 1958 he began his career in film production as an observer in the studios of Fritz Lang. His first short film appeared in 1960. Frustrated by the restrictions imposed on young filmmakers by the German film industry, he helped found the so-called Oberhausen Group, which issued a manifesto in 1962 proclaiming the need for artistic freedom and announcing the birth of the new German film. The following year Kluge set up his own production company, Kairos-Film, and became codirector of a new film department at the University of Ulm. His first full-length motion picture, *Abschied von gestern* (English title: *Yesterday Girl*), met with great success in 1966; it is based on the short story "Anita G" from his first collection, *Lebensläufe* (1962; translated as *Attendance List for a Funeral,* 1966). The leading role in the film was played by his younger sister, Alexandra Kluge.

Following the success of *Schlachtbeschreibung* and his early films, Kluge's popularity suffered a decline that was due in part to the changing political climate in Germany. His experimental style had fit in with the modernist movement of the 1960s; the end of the student protests and the return to more traditional models in the early 1970s left him in a position of artistic isolation, a position he examines in his less well-received 1967 film *Die Artisten in der Zirkuskuppel: Ratlos* (The Artists in the Big Top: Perplexed). The main character, Leni Peickert, is an artist whose efforts to create a new form of circus are thwarted because her ideals prove to be too abstract for her audience; she decides to resort to a more pragmatic approach. In an analogous manner Kluge turned from literary experimentation to nonfiction as a means of promoting social and cultural change.

The German war experience and its aftermath are principal themes in Kluge's films, fiction, and nonfiction. At the center of the modern German experience he sees a basic "loss of meaning" which is symbolized for him by the destruction of his childhood home. He describes this loss of meaning in the preface to the short-story collection *Lernprozesse mit tödlichem Ausgang* (Learning Processes with Fatal Outcomes, 1973): "Sinnentzug. Eine gesellschaftliche Situation, in der das kollektive Lebensprogramm von Menschen schneller zerfällt, als die Menschen neue Lebensprogramme produzieren können" (Deprivation of meaning. A social situation in which people's collective program for life is disintegrating faster than people can produce new life programs).

In his films and writing Kluge tries to capture collective social issues and experiences. His

Kluge in 1966 (photograph by Heinz Köster, courtesy of Ullstein Bilderdienst)

fiction is concerned with public rather than private matters, laying out in literary form the ideas elaborated in his theoretical writings. Recurring themes in his books and films are World War II, the capitalist work ethic, and the powerlessness of the individual vis-à-vis the powers that control him–the legal establishment, the military, and the forces of political and historical change. He writes large-scale works in which a wide range of historical material as well as contemporary and science-fiction elements are compiled into collages. These collages convey a sense of the copresence and complexity of the past, present, and future in modern consciousness and in the forces of historical change.

Kluge adapts the montage techniques of

filmmaking to his writing, combining apparently arbitrary sequences of disparate and often dissonant elements (documentary and pseudodocumentary reports, ironic illustrative material, anecdotes, and interviews, as well as pure fictional narrative) to form a complex collage of associated themes. He is intentionally allusive, asking the reader to form his own impressions from the barrage of materials rather than allowing them to be dictated by an imposed aesthetic order. Like many avant-garde German writers of the 1960s, Kluge dismisses as mere "Begriffsimperialismus" (conceptual imperialism) the neat formulas with which literature seeks to encapsulate reality. Instead, he chooses an almost Brechtian technique of critical distancing, adopting a cold-blooded, totally dispassionate style to deal with extremely emotional issues. Kluge admits that his works may appear confusing and incomplete to the reader; indeed, this effect is the one at which he aims in his portrayals of the ambiguity he sees at the center of modern reality. His unusual style constitutes his version of literary realism. He challenges the reader to remain critically active, to create his own associations, and to come to his own conclusions.

Lebensläufe foreshadows the major themes and styles of Kluge's later work. The stories are case histories of people imprisoned in their milieus. Characteristically, the narrator refuses to dwell on the potentially tragic personal dimensions of what he is describing; adopting a laconic, understated style, he passes over details perfunctorily, as though totally removed from the human issues involved. The brief, clipped sentences are more reminiscent of journalistic reporting than of literary narrative. The story "Anwesenheitsliste für eine Beerdigung" (Attendance List for a Funeral) begins with a list of family members and friends attending a funeral; one or two adjectives depict the state of mind of each person. As the story unfolds, it becomes clear that these emotions have nothing to do with the loss of a loved one but result from petty jealousies and small-mindedness. Even though the deceased's life is described in some detail, neither the reader nor the funeral guests are prompted to feel any sorrow. The same dispassionately abrupt style is used in "Anita G.," which follows in accelerated narrative tempo the flight of an East German girl from the West German police and ends with her nervous breakdown in prison after the birth of her child.

Schlachtbeschreibung deals with the defeat of Hitler's Sixth Army at Stalingrad. Third Reich field manuals, troop reports, drawings, photographs, interviews, and sermons delivered to the troops by army chaplains are interlaced with clearly invented material. Each section offers a limited perspective on what is happening, adding up to a picture of the huge web of inefficiency that drives the war machine. Kluge attempts to depict what he describes in the subtitle of the 1978 revision of the novel as *Der organisatorische Aufbau eines Unglücks* (The Organizational Making of a Disaster).

The book was initially attacked by critics on the grounds that it fails as an objective documentary work. Kluge's interplay of fact and fiction, however, as he makes clear in later editions of the work, is intentional. Our very definitions of experience and reality are fictions, Kluge claims. In *Schlachtbeschreibung* he attempts to show that the motives which lead to and sustain war are layers of falsification, "böse Fiktionen" (evil fictions) driving history in the direction of calamity.

Die Artisten in der Zirkuskuppel: Ratlos; Die Ungläubige; Projekt Z.; Sprüche der Leni Peickert (The Artists in the Big Top: Perplexed; The Unbeliever; Project Z.; Sayings of Leni Peickert, 1968), *Gelegenheitsarbeit einer Sklavin* (Occasional Work of a Domestic Slave, 1975) and *Die Patriotin* (The Female Patriot, 1979) contain sketches and outlines for Kluge's film projects. All exemplify his theory of social realism, which is outlined in *Gelegenheitsarbeit einer Sklavin:* they are conglomerations of brief scenes strung loosely together to create commentaries on modern reality that are left totally open for the reader or viewer to interpret.

The short stories in *Lernprozesse mit tödlichem Ausgang* were written at about the same time as the theoretical study *Öffentlichkeit und Erfahrung* (Public Life and Experience, 1972), which Kluge wrote in collaboration with Oskar Negt, a professor of sociology. Both books criticize the passive attitude of the modern worker toward the hierarchies which control him. In *Lernprozesse mit tödlichem Ausgang* Kluge resorts to literary irony to create cameos of individuals without self-knowledge being victimized by the tediousness of their jobs. A cheated gigolo, the residents of a retirement home in Venice, and a university professor all realize too late that they have not really lived at all. Both books attempt to revitalize the ideals of sociopolitical change inspired by the student movement.

Kluge's lengthiest collection of short stories and sketches, *Neue Geschichten: Hefte 1-18, (1977)* (New Stories: Workbooks 1-18) brings together apparently arbitrary sequences of anecdotes and occasional jottings as well as longer prose pieces in eighteen so-called workbooks. More than in any previous work, it is Kluge's own personality and personal memories which provide the unifying force behind this loose assemblage of roughhewn texts. He reiterates his favorite historical themes: the German war experience, the Adenauer era, and the student protest movement of the 1960s. He describes the disconnected texts as snapshots behind which the reader begins to discern a tragic causality haunting the present as well as the past, a causality he defines in his subtitle as the *Unheimlichkeit der Zeit* (Uncanniness of Time).

Kluge with his sister Alexandra (Alexander Kluge, Die Macht der Gefühle *[Frankfurt am Main: Zweitausendeins, 1984])*

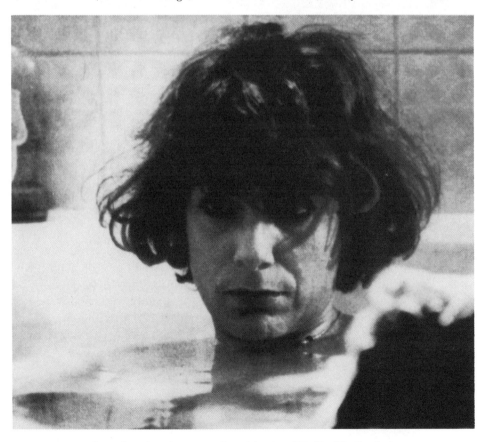

Alexandra Kluge in a scene from Kluge's 1979 film Die Patriotin

The postwar turning point in modern German history–the so-called Nullpunkt (zero point)–is symbolized in the second workbook, which describes from multiple perspectives the 1945 air raid on Kluge's hometown of Halberstadt. By recreating the air raid, Kluge attempts again to fathom, as he did in his Stalingrad novel, a devastating historical event. He is at pains, however, to avoid any personal perspective, defining his characters as purely functional figures–soldiers, generals, volunteers, members of a wedding party: "Zwölf Minuten später sind alle verschüttet" (Twelve minutes later they are all buried alive). He uses interviews and pseudodocumentary protocols parody the cliché-ridden jargon of law and bureaucracy.

A further sequence of workbooks, *Neue Geschichten: Hefte 19-28*, was published in 1984. In the interim Kluge produced another theoretical work, *Geschichte und Eigensinn* (History and Obstinacy, 1981), compiled from three years of discussion and research with Negt. This daunting, over one-thousand-page compilation of essays and illustrations deals polemically with the effect on modern consciousness of capitalist methods of production. In all his books and films Kluge attempts to capture the extent to which modern socioeconomic and political influences combine to mold human experience and public values. His use of illustrations, newspaper quotations, and excerpted passages from historical, legal, and administrative sources create a pseudo-objective, documentary approach in which the author's intentions are implied rather than stated. Underlying Kluge's works is the attempt to make the reader more critical of the forces which threaten to mold his consciousness.

References:

Heinz Ludwig Arnold, ed., *Alexander Kluge* (Munich: Edition text + kritik, 1985);

Thomas Böhm-Christl, ed., *Alexander Kluge* (Frankfurt am Main: Suhrkamp, 1983);

Andrew Bowie, "New Histories: Aspects of the Prose of Alexander Kluge," *Journal of European Studies*, 12 (September 1982): 180-208;

Gloria Behrens and others, "Gespräche mit Alexander Kluge," *Filmkritik*, 12 (December 1976): 562-600;

Jan Dawson, "Alexander Kluge," *Film Comment*, 10 (November/December 1974): 51-57;

Manfred Durzak, "Alexander Kluge: Zwischen Dokument und Fiktion," in *Die deutsche Kurzgeschichte der Gegenwart*, edited by Durzak (Stuttgart: Reclam, 1980), pp. 292-300;

Christoph Eykmann, "Erfunden oder vorgefunden? Zur Integration des Außerfiktionalen in die epische Fiktion," *Neophilologus*, 62 (1978): 319-334;

Bodo Heimann, "Film und deutsche Gegenwartsliteratur," in *Deutsche Gegenwartsliteratur: Ausgangspositionen und aktuelle Entwicklungen*, edited by Durzak (Stuttgart: Reclam, 1981), pp. 424-443;

Peter W. Jansen and Wolfram Schütte, eds., *Herzog, Kluge, Straub* (Munich: Hanser, 1976);

Gottfried Just, "Von der Literatur zum Film: Alexander Kluge," in *Reflexionen: Zur deutschen Literatur der sechziger Jahre*, edited by Klaus Günther Just (Pfullingen: Neske, 1972), pp. 56-60;

Rainer Lewandowski, *Alexander Kluge* (Munich: Beck, 1980);

Lewandowski, *Die Filme von Alexander Kluge* (Hildesheim & New York: Olms, 1980);

David Roberts, "Die Formenwelt des Zusammenhangs: Zur Theorie und Funktion der Montage bei Alexander Kluge," *Zeitschrift für Literaturwissenschaft und Linguistik*, 46 (1982): 104-119;

Dietmar Voss, "Emanzipation der Sinne und Unsinnlichkeit der Emanzipation: Zur ästhetischen Theorie Alexander Kluges," *Das Argument*, 22 (January/February 1980): 20-32;

Wilhelm Vosskamp, "Alexander Kluge," in *Deutsche Literatur der Gegenwart in Einzeldarstellungen*, edited by Dietrich Weber (Stuttgart: Kröner, 1977), II: 297-317.

Günter Kunert
(6 March 1929-   )

Valerie D. Greenberg
Tulane University

BOOKS: *Wegschilder und Mauerinschriften: Gedichte* (Berlin: Aufbau, 1950);

Der ewige Detektiv und andere Geschichten (Berlin: Eulenspiegel, 1954);

Unter diesem Himmel: Gedichte (Berlin: Neues Leben, 1955);

Jäger ohne Beute (Berlin: Neues Leben, 1955);

Der Kaiser von Hondu: Ein Fernsehspiel (Berlin: Aufbau, 1959);

Tagwerke: Gedichte, Lieder, Balladen (Halle: Mitteldeutscher Verlag, 1961);

Das kreuzbrave Liederbuch (Berlin: Aufbau, 1961);

Erinnerung an einen Planeten: Gedichte aus fünfzehn Jahren (Munich: Hanser, 1963);

Tagträume (Munich: Hanser, 1964);

Kunerts lästerliche Leinwand (Berlin: Eulenspiegel, 1965);

Der ungebetene Gast: Gedichte (Berlin & Weimar: Aufbau, 1965);

Verkündigung des Wetters: Gedichte (Munich: Hanser, 1966);

Unschuld der Natur: 52 Figurationen leibhafter Liebe (Berlin & Weimar: Aufbau, 1966);

Im Namen der Hüte: Roman (Munich: Hanser, 1967);

Die Beerdigung findet in aller Stille statt: Erzählungen (Munich: Hanser, 1968); includes "Fahrt mit der S-Bahn," translated by Marjorie Meyer as "Ride on the S-Bahn," in *Thinking It Over: 30 Stories from the German Democratic Republic*, edited by Hubert Witt (Berlin: Seven Seas, 1976), pp. 166-170;

Günter Kunert (Berlin: Neues Leben, 1968);

Kramen in Fächern: Geschichten, Parabeln, Merkmale (Berlin & Weimar: Aufbau, 1968);

Betonformen; Ortsangaben (Berlin: Literarisches Colloquium, 1969);

Warnung vor Spiegeln: Gedichte (Munich: Hanser, 1970);

Notizen in Kreide: Gedichte, edited by Witt (Leipzig: Reclam, 1970; revised, 1975);

Ortsangaben (Berlin & Weimar: Aufbau, 1971);

Offener Ausgang: Gedichte (Berlin & Weimar: Aufbau, 1972);

Günter Kunert (Archiv)

Tagträume in Berlin und andernorts: Kleine Prosa, Erzählungen, Aufsätze (Munich: Hanser, 1972); "Zentralbahnhof," translated by Duncan Smith as "Central Station," in *The Prose Poem: An International Anthology*, edited by Michael Benedikt (New York: Dell, 1976), pp. 215-217;

Die geheime Bibliothek (Berlin & Weimar: Aufbau, 1973);

Gast aus England: Erzählung (Munich: Hanser, 1973);

Im weiteren Fortgang: Gedichte (Munich: Hanser, 1974);

Der Hai: Erzählungen und kleine Prosa, edited by Dietrich Bode (Stuttgart: Reclam, 1974);

Der andere Planet: Ansichten von Amerika (Berlin & Weimar: Aufbau, 1974);

Der Mittelpunkt der Erde: Prosa (Berlin: Eulenspiegel, 1975);

Das kleine Aber: Gedichte (Berlin & Weimar: Aufbau, 1975);

Warum schreiben: Notizen zur Literatur (Berlin & Weimar: Aufbau, 1976);

Jeder Wunsch ein Treffer (Hannover: Middelhauve, 1976);

Berliner Wände: Bilder aus einer verschwundenen Stadt (Munich: Hanser, 1976);

Keine Affäre: Geschichten (Berlin: Berliner Handpresse, 1976);

Kinobesuch: Geschichten (Leipzig: Insel, 1976);

Unterwegs nach Utopia: Gedichte (Munich: Hanser, 1977);

Ein anderer K: Hörspiele (Berlin & Weimar: Aufbau, 1977); "Ein anderer K," translated by A. Leslie Willson as "A Different K," *Dimension*, 10 (1977): 462-503;

Ein englisches Tagebuch (Berlin & Weimar: Aufbau, 1978);

Camera obscura (Munich & Vienna: Hanser, 1978);

Heinrich von Kleist: Ein Modell (Berlin: Akademie der Künste, 1978);

Bücher Nachträge (Berlin: Berliner Handpresse, 1978);

Verlangen nach Bomarzo: Reisegedichte (Leipzig: Reclam, 1978);

Drei Berliner Geschichten (Berlin & Weimar: Aufbau, 1979);

Ziellose Umtriebe: Nachrichten von Reisen und vom Daheimsein (Berlin & Weimar: Aufbau, 1979);

Die Schreie der Fledermäuse: Geschichten, Gedichte, Aufsätze, edited by Dieter E. Zimmer (Gütersloh: Bertelsmann, 1979);

Unruhiger Schlaf: Gedichte (Munich: Deutscher Taschenbuch Verlag, 1979);

Abtötungsverfahren: Gedichte (Munich: Hanser, 1980);

Kurze Beschreibung eines Moments der Ewigkeit: Kleine Prosa (Leipzig: Reclam, 1980);

Verspätete Monologe: Prosa (Munich: Hanser, 1981);

Diesseits des Erinnerns: Aufsätze (Munich: Hanser, 1982);

Stilleben: Gedichte (Munich: Hanser, 1983);

Die letzten Indianer Europas: Ein Essay (Hauzenberg: Pongratz, 1983);

Abendstimmung: Gedichte–Holzschnitte, by Kunert and Heinz Stein (Hauzenberg: Pongratz, 1983);

Leben und Schreiben (Pfaffenweiler: Pfaffenweiler Presse, 1983);

Kain und Abels Brüderlichkeit (Hauzenberg: Pongratz, 1984);

Zurück ins Paradies: Geschichten (Munich: Hanser, 1984);

Windy Times: Poetry & Prose by Günter Kunert, translated by Agnes Stein (New York: Red Dust, 1984);

Vor der Sintflut; Das Gedicht als Arche Noah: Frankfurter Vorlesungen (Munich: Hanser, 1985);

Der Wald (Hamburg: Ellert & Richter, 1985);

Berliner Nächte: Laternenbilder, by Kunert and Michael Engler (Hamburg: Ellert & Richter, 1986);

Berlin beizeiten: Gedichte (Munich: Hanser, 1987);

Lesarten: Gedichte der Zeit (Munich: Piper, 1987);

Zeichnungen und Beispiele, edited by Joseph A. Kruse (Düsseldorf: Droste, 1987).

OTHER: Bertolt Brecht, *Kriegsfibel,* appendix and translations of English picture captions by Kunert (Berlin: Eulenspiegel, 1955);

Nikolaus Lenau, *Gedichte,* edited by Kunert (Frankfurt am Main: Fischer, 1969);

Christopher Middleton, *Wie wir Großmutter zum Markt bringen: Gedichte und Prosa,* translated by Kunert and Ernst Jandl (Stierstadt im Taunus: Eremiten-Presse, 1970);

Brecht, *Über die irdische Liebe und andere gewisse Welträtsel in Liedern und Balladen,* edited by Kunert (Berlin: Eulenspiegel, 1971);

Michael Hamburger, ed., *East German Poetry: An Anthology,* translated by Hamburger, Middleton, and Christopher Levenson, selections by Kunert (New York: Dutton, 1973), pp. 87-108;

Dimension: Sonderheft DDR-Literatur, edited by Kunert (Austin: University of Texas Press, 1973);

Edgar Allan Poe, *E. A. Poes Erzählungen,* afterword by Kunert (Berlin & Weimar: Aufbau, 1974);

Ivan Turgenev, *Vorabend,* foreword by Kunert (Berlin: Neues Leben, 1976);

Agnes Stein, ed., *Four German Poets: Günter Eich, Hilde Domin, Erich Fried, Günter Kunert,* translated by Stein, selections by Kunert (New York: Red Dust, 1979), pp. 12-156;

Marlies Menge and Rudi Meisel, eds., *Städte, die keiner mehr kennt: Reportagen aus der DDR,* foreword by Kunert (Munich: Hanser, 1979);

Ulenspiegel: Zeitschrift für Literatur, Kunst und Satire. Ein Querschnitt von 1945 bis 1950, edited by Kunert and H. Sandberg (Munich: Hanser, 1979);

Jahrbuch für Lyrik, volume 3, edited by Kunert (Königstein: Athenäum, 1981);

Eike Geisel, Im Scheunenviertel: Bilder, Texte und Dokumente, foreword by Kunert (Berlin: Severin & Siedler, 1981);

Mein Lesebuch, selected by Kunert (Frankfurt am Main: Fischer, 1983);

Heinz Teufel, *Auf Noldes Spuren: Fotografien,* foreword by Kunert (Hamburg: Grube & Richter, 1983);

Norbert Hinterberger, *Die klaren Sachen: Gedichte,* foreword by Kunert (Hamburg: Knaus, 1983);

Sarah Kirsch, *Landwege: Eine Auswahl 1980-1985,* afterword by Kunert (Stuttgart: Deutsche Verlags-Anstalt, 1985).

PERIODICAL PUBLICATIONS: "Aus der Sicht des Autors: Notizen zur Praxis des Schreibens," *Monatshefte,* 72 (1980): 117-120;

"Phasen der Verdinglichung: Überlegungen nach der Lektüre von Jamina Davids Buch 'Ein Stück Himmel,'" *Deutsche Akademie für Sprache und Dichtung, Darmstadt: Jahrbuch,* 1 (1983): 72-78.

In 1979, when he received a long-term visa to leave the German Democratic Republic (GDR) and settled near Itzehoe in the Federal Republic of Germany, Günter Kunert was one of the most widely read authors in the GDR, despite having been the target of increasing official criticism in the years prior to his departure. Even while living in the East he had been published, widely read, and quoted in West Germany; a 1984 West German bibliography of critical literature on Kunert lists over two hundred items. With some justification, therefore, Kunert considers himself not an "East German author" but a "German author."

Born in Berlin in 1929, four years prior to the Nazi takeover of Germany, Kunert was subjected to discrimination and persecution as a child because his mother was Jewish. His educational opportunities were limited to grade school and an apprenticeship in a retail store until 1946, when he spent five semesters at an institute for applied art in Berlin. Soon, however, he switched from graphic art to literature, publishing poetry and satirical prose in the magazine *Ulenspiegel* in 1948. When the German Democratic Republic was founded in 1949 Kunert

Cover for Kunert's 1978 collection of prose pieces

joined the ruling Socialist Unity party (SED). His generation, which also included the novelist Christa Wolf, believed that the evils of fascism would be replaced in the socialist state by humanitarianism, justice, and progress.

Kunert's poetry and prose of the 1950s reflect this optimism. During this period he met Bertolt Brecht and was influenced by Brecht's use of dialectic in his Lehrgedichte (didactic poems) and epigrams. Kunert's early poems are simple, epigrammatic, close to prose, and often have a surprising reversal at the end. Their goals are to warn readers to avoid the evils of the past and to raise their social consciousness. In the 1960s his poems grew more complex, becoming characterized by paradox and antithesis. Several early volumes show the influence of Brecht in their use of song and ballad forms. In 1962 he received the Heinrich Mann Prize of the GDR.

The poems in *Der ungebetene Gast* (The Uninvited Guest, 1965) signal a drastic shift toward criticism of socialist society and a dark view of the future. This change brought upon Kunert the opprobrium of the cultural authorities, although he still won the Johannes R. Becher Prize in 1973. At this time the works of other authors of Kunert's generation, such as Wolf's *Nachdenken über Christa T.* (1968; translated as *The Quest for Christa T.*, 1972), also reveal a process of disillusionment. Kunert has been called a pessimist, even a nihilist–appellations he rejects. He argues, however, that hope is a dangerous illusion which permits people to escape from the necessity of trying to do something about the evils of the world. His poem "Aufgabe" (the title is a play on words; it can mean giving up, abandoning, or renouncing something; mailing a letter; or a task, duty, or mission) expresses this stance in the first and last stanzas:

> Die Hoffnung aufgeben
> wie einen Brief ohne Adresse
> Nicht zustellbar und
> an niemand gerichtet
> ....
> Die schwerste Aufgabe ist:
> aufgeben können
> Wer mit der Hoffnung anfängt
> hat seine Lektion schon
> gelernt.
>
> (To relinquish hope
> like a letter without an address
> Not deliverable and
> directed to no one
> ....
> The most difficult task is:
> to be able to give up
> Whoever begins with hope
> has already learned his
> lesson.)

"Aufgabe" appears in the volume *Unterwegs nach Utopia* (En Route to Utopia, 1977). In another poem in the book, "Unterwegs nach Utopia II," Kunert expresses his view of utopia as a bitter illusion:

> Auf der Flucht
> vor dem Beton
> geht es zu
> wie im Märchen: Wo du

> auch ankommst
> er erwartet dich
> grau und gründlich
>
> Auf der Flucht findest du
> vielleicht einen grünen Fleck
> am Ende
> und stürzest selig
> in die Halme
> aus gefärbtem Glas.
>
> (On the flight
> from concrete
> things happen
> as in a fairy tale: wherever you
> arrive
> it is waiting for you
> gray and solid
>
> On the flight you find
> perhaps a green spot
> at the end
> and plunge joyously
> into the blades
> of colored glass.)

What worries Kunert most are the threats brought about by technology in combination with human moral incapacity and inability to learn from–or even remember–the past. He notes in poems and essays the rampant destruction of nature in the name of "progress" and greed; alienation and bureaucratization; and the possibility of nuclear war. For Kunert writing is a way to survive; as he says in *Warum schreiben* (Why Write, 1976): "Solange man schreibt, ist der Untergang gebannt, findet Vergänglichkeit nicht statt, und darum schreibe ich: um die Welt, die pausenlos in Nichts zerfällt, zu ertragen" (As long as one is writing, destruction is held off, mortality does not happen, and that is the reason I write: in order to endure the world, which is continually disintegrating into nothingness).

Kunert was able to travel rather freely for an East German citizen, including a semester as a visiting associate professor at the University of Texas in Austin in 1972. A product of this sojourn is *Der andere Planet* (The Other Planet, 1974), a book of essays on America. Kunert's portrait of New Orleans, for example, reflects in its mood and tone the almost mythical quality that city possesses in the eyes of Europeans, but at the same time his sharp observer's eye takes in the seamy side of life there, the poverty and social injustice. Kunert's impressions of jazz at Preservation Hall, the lazy flow of the Mississippi,

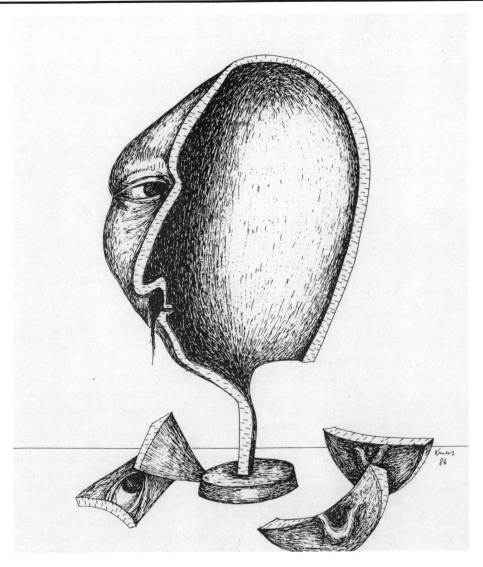

Self-portrait by Kunert: "Portrait of the Artist as a Coconut" (Günter Kunert, Zeichnungen und Beispiele [Düsseldorf: Droste, 1987])

Mardi Gras, and the tropical heat and foliage recreate the atmosphere of a city that clearly captured his imagination and emotions, while his attention to voodoo and cemeteries, the history of slavery, and the War of 1812 show a sense of social and historical context that Americans often lack about their own country. The volume *Ein englisches Tagebuch* (An English Diary, 1978) resulted from his year as writer in residence at the University of Warwick in 1975. Kunert also published collected travel impressions in prose in *Ortsangaben* (Indications of Places, 1971) and in poetry in *Verlangen nach Bomarzo* (Longing for Bomarzo, 1978). His critical interpretations of places he has visited bear no resemblance to conventional travel writing: precise observations of de-

tails serve as springboards for social criticism or philosophical reflections on the lessons of the past for the present. In addition to travel, Kunert is fascinated by ancient civilizations, such as the Etruscan; he considers the study of the distant past a source of strength. He calls himself a frustrated archaeologist.

Irony, satire, and black humor are common in Kunert's short stories, as are elements of the grotesque and surreal. His stories have been included in science fiction anthologies, although technology does not play a major role in them. They often have a dreamlike quality and a sense of horror and impending doom which the potential victim can neither understand nor control. In "Fahrt mit der S-Bahn" (1968; translated as

"Ride on the S-Bahn," 1976) a Berlin commuter looking out of the window of his train notices in the wall of a nearby building a window which has never been there before. As the train passes the window he sees a group of people engaged in animated conversation. One of them is the commuter himself; the rest are old friends of his, some of them long dead and forgotten. From then on he searches desperately and fruitlessly for the building with the window, for he knows somehow that if he finds it and enters to join himself, the city's terrible past–with its wars, suffering, and guilt, which includes the commuter's own private guilt–will be undone. A particularly Kafkaesque example is "Zentralbahnhof" (1972; translated as "Central Station," 1976), the tale of a man who receives a summons to appear at an appointed time for his execution, which will take place in booth 18 of the men's room at the Central Station. He spends a tortured day and night trying to find support from other people, who advise him to obey the summons and assure him that the word *execution* must be a printing error. He arrives at the specified time and enters the booth, confident that the whole thing must be a mistake. Fifteen minutes later workers remove his corpse and take it to the cellar of the station. Smoke, supposedly from locomotives, often hangs over the station, although trains never enter or leave it. Kunert has illustrated these and other stories and volumes of poetry with his own line drawings. Since he is a graphic artist, visual impressions play a dominant role in his work; Kunert says that he has a visual memory.

A master of the epigram, parable, satire, and other short forms, Kunert is considered by critics to have been unsuccessful with his two long works of fiction, the novel *Im Namen der Hüte* (In the Name of Hats, 1967) and the long story *Gast aus England* (Guest from England, 1973). Kunert says in the foreword to *Im Namen der Hüte* that his intent in the novel "ist eine absolute Unmöglichkeit erklärtes Ziel" (is an absolutely impossible goal) of "das Vergessen vergessen zu machen, und das Erinnerungsvermögen als persönliche und gesellschaftliche Potenz zu konstituieren" (causing forgetting to be forgotten and making memory a personal and social force). The setting is Berlin "in jenen merkwürdigen, fantastischen, grotesken Jahren nach 1945" (in the strange, fantastic, grotesque years after 1945). The young war veteran Henry discovers that he can read others' thoughts when he dons their hats. In the course of Henry's pica-

resque adventures postwar German society is shown as *not* having begun afresh with a clean slate ("the zero hour"), but rather as repeating thoughtlessly the errors of the past. With the improving economy, Henry loses his ESP and status as an outsider, becoming an anonymous member of the establishment and a mindless participant in the conventions of work and family. Critics have considered the passivity of the protagonist, who is incapable of analyzing his experiences, a weakness of the novel and have criticized the concentrated multiplicity of styles, ranging from lyrical to documentary, which place heavy demands on the reader.

Gast aus England is a mystery with Kafkaesque qualities; in his foreword, Kunert calls it a fairy tale. The story relates a series of absurd misunderstandings, missed rendezvous, and mistaken identities, including taking a living person for a corpse. One critic, Michael Hamburger, describes the narrative as less suspenseful than Kunert's shorter fiction; the episodes that take place in England are based on fragmentary and incorrect information, since they were written before Kunert had a chance to get to know that country well.

By the late 1970s official harassment had reached a level where Kunert felt unable to write, although he was never prohibited from publishing. Increased pressure resulted from his signing a letter with other leading writers of the GDR, including Christa Wolf, protesting the revocation of the singer/poet Wolf Biermann's citizenship while he was on a concert tour of West Germany in 1976. A consequence of Kunert's signing was his expulsion from the SED in 1977.

Kunert's production since moving to the West has been prodigious. In addition to the volumes of poetry, several of which are illustrated by Kunert, of particular interest are *Leben und Schreiben* (Life and Writing, 1983) and *Vor der Sintflut; Das Gedicht als Arche Noah* (Before the Flood: The Poem as Noah's Ark, 1985). The former, a beautifully printed book with lithographs by Horst Sobotta, consists of a series of brief pieces that explore the writing process, writer's block, history, time, and language–all in Kunert's characteristically lucid prose. *Vor der Sintflut*, a series of lectures Kunert gave in Frankfurt, begins with the proposal in the title–that poetry serves as an "ark" in troubled times. But the first lecture dispenses with that hopeful option and concludes that the most a poem can be is a "Taschenausgabe" (pocket edition) of an ark, more

Kunert in 1987 (photograph by Detlev Moos, courtesy of Ullstein Bilderdienst)

like a mere "Flaschenpost" (letter in a bottle)–
"eine Botschaft über unsere innere und äußere
Befindlichkeit, eine kompetente Selbstdiagnose,
ohne die Konsequenz einer Therapie" (a message
about our inner and outer condition, a compe-
tent self-diagnosis without therapeutic consequences). The second lecture treats Kunert's own
development and growth as a poet; the third discusses Bertolt Brecht and Johannes R. Becher; in
the fourth, which deals with the work of other
poets, Kunert maintains that no poet writing in
German today can escape the heritage of Kleist,
Hölderlin, and Heine. The last lecture, "Absolut
unernst gemeinter Rat für geneigte Hörer und
Leser" (Absolutely Unserious Advice for Willing
Listeners and Readers), is a self-ironic, satirical address that undercuts the serious tone of the earlier lectures and establishes direct contact with
his audience. Kunert has also won literary awards
in the West, including the honorary position of
writer in residence of the town of Bergen-
Enkheim in 1983 and the Heinrich Heine Prize

of the City of Düsseldorf in 1985; become an edi-
tor of *Literaturmagazin;* and been elected to the
German Academy for Language and Poetry in
Darmstadt.

Perhaps Kunert's most important source of
support is his wife, the former Marianne Todten,
whom he married in 1952. All of his books are
dedicated to Marianne, who is his indispensable
critic and helper. When one meets the Kunerts,
it is obvious that they are a team. They live surrounded by their cats–as many as eight at one
point–which they took with them when they
moved to the West. Animals are important to
Kunert; he has called them "bessere Menschen"
(better people), like human beings in a state of innocence before they abandoned nature.

Kunert is a quiet, mild-mannered, friendly,
yet somewhat reserved man; his wry sense of
humor is incongruous with his melancholy countenance, which he has compared to the face of a wal-
rus. Kunert is known for his forthrightness and
the integrity of his character and his work.

Kunert in his garden

In a 1984 article in the Hamburg weekly *Die Zeit* on an emerging tendency in literature toward the mythical and irrational, the critic Fritz J. Raddatz calls Kunert "the most radical herald of the end of the enlightenment." Raddatz quotes from a May 1984 lecture, "Literatur als Mythos" (Literature as Myth), in which Kunert asserts that there can be no literature without mythical content; he equates myth with "ein Weltbewußtsein . . . das grundiert ist von Staunen und Erschrecken" (a consciousness of the world . . . founded upon awe and dread). In the short essay "Zu Bildern von Bomarzo" (On Images at Bomarzo) in *Verspätete Monologe* (Belated Monologues, 1981) Kunert remembers wandering through the park at Bomarzo, Italy, whose inscrutable statues cause him to speculate on the mysterious and the irrational. This secret realm is necessary to human beings and closer to truth because it reflects the subconscious, yet it is missing from modern plastic, technological civilization.

Many critics agree that Kunert's themes and concerns have made his a representative contemporary sensibility. Kunert, however, refuses to be pigeonholed or associated with any "ism" or ideology; in particular, he will not accept the common association of his writings with pessimism, nihil-

ism, or defeatism. He describes himself as "einen eher nüchtern und klar sehenden Autor, der das, was er sieht, entsprechend reflektiert" (an author who is matter-of-fact and sees things clearly, and who accurately reflects what he sees). His work, an evolving corpus with a consistent style and worldview, defies limiting classifications.

Interviews:

Hans Richter, "Selbstausdruck und Gesellschaftsbezug," in *Auskünfte: Werkstattgespräche mit DDR-Autoren,* edited by Anneliese Löffler (Berlin & Weimar: Aufbau, 1974), pp. 463-484;

Fritz J. Raddatz, "I'd Rather Be Dead than Think the Way Kunert Does: Interview with Wolf Biermann and Günter Kunert," translated by David Caldwell, *New German Critique: An Interdisciplinary Journal of German Studies,* 23 (Spring-Summer 1981): 45-55;

Linda DeMeritt and Jochen Richter, "Documentation: Günter Kunert," *German Quarterly,* 61 (Winter 1988): 97-108.

Bibliography:

Margy Gerber and Judith Pouget, "Günter Kunert," in *Literature of the German Democratic Re-*

public in English Translation: A Bibliography (Lanham, Md. & New York: University Press of America, 1984), pp. 79-89.

References:

Peter Bekes, "Günter Kunert," in *Kritisches Lexikon zur deutschsprachigen Gegenwartsliteratur*, edited by Heinz Ludwig Arnold (Munich: Edition text + kritik, 1984), n. pag.;

Anthony Bushell, "Günter Kunert and His Possibilities of Poetry," *Forum for Modern Language Studies*, 18 (January 1982): 39-46;

Theodore Fiedler, "The Reception of a Socialist Classic: Kunert and Biermann Read Brecht," in *Bertolt Brecht: Political Theory and Literary Practice*, edited by Betty Nance Weber and Hubert Heinen (Athens: University of Georgia Press, 1980), pp. 147-158;

Valerie D. Greenberg, " 'Those uneven mirrors . . . ': Literature, Art, Science and the Example of Günter Kunert and M. C. Escher," forthcoming in *Mosaic* (1989);

Erich P. Hofacker, "Faltering Steps: Günter Kunert's 'Unterwegs nach Utopia,' " *Germanic Review*, 57 (Winter 1982): 1-8;

Dieter Jonsson, *Günter Kunert: Literatur im Widerspruch. Mit Materialien* (Stuttgart: Klett-Cotta, 1980);

Jonsson, *Widersprüche–Hoffnungen: Literatur und Kulturpolitik der DDR. Die Prosa Günter Kunerts* (Stuttgart: Klett, 1978);

Lisa Kahn, "Orpheus in the East: Günter Kunert's Orpheus Cycle," *Modern Language Quarterly*, 38 (March 1977): 78-96;

W. Clark Kenyon, "Günter Kunert's 'Schatten entziffern,' " *University of Dayton Review*, 13 (Winter 1978): 77-82;

Michael Krüger, ed., *Kunert lesen* (Munich: Hanser, 1979);

Allan D. Latta, "G. Kunert's 'Der Hai': Socialist Realism and Beyond," *Seminar: A Journal of Germanic Studies*, 16 (1980): 242-258;

Nancy A. Lauckner, "Günter Kunert's Image of the USA: Another Look at 'Der andere Planet,' " in *Studies in GDR Culture and Society Three*, edited by Margy Gerber and Christine Cosentino, translated by Lauckner and Duncan Smith (Lanham, Md.: University Press of America, 1983), pp. 125-135;

I. Rosalie Motz, "Poetic Consciousness in Günter Kunert's Prose," Ph.D. dissertation, University of Washington, 1978;

Fritz J. Raddatz, "Die Aufklärung entläßt ihre Kinder," *Die Zeit*, Overseas Edition, 6 July 1984, pp. 13-14;

James R. Reece, "Cultural Politics and the Literary Avant-Garde in East Germany: The Case of Günter Kunert," *Journal of the Pacific Northwest Council on Foreign Languages*, 2 (1981): 142-146;

A. Leslie Willson, " 'Grenzverschiebung': Günter Kunert's Humanistic Stance," in *From Kafka and Dada to Brecht and Beyond*, edited by Reinhold Grimm, Peter Spycher, and Richard A. Zipser (Madison: University of Wisconsin Press, 1982), pp. 49-61.

Reiner Kunze
(16 August 1933-)

Wulf Koepke
Texas A&M University

BOOKS: *Die Zukunft sitzt am Tische: 26 Gedichte*, by Kunze and Egon Günther (Halle: Mitteldeutscher Verlag, 1955);

Vögel über dem Tau: Liebesgedichte und Lieder (Halle: Mitteldeutscher Verlag, 1959);

Wesen und Bedeutung der Reportage (Berlin: Deutscher Schriftstellerverband, 1960);

Aber die Nachtigall jubelt: Heitere Texte (Halle: Mitteldeutscher Verlag, 1962);

Widmungen: Gedichte (Bad Godesberg: Hohwacht, 1963);

Reiner Kunze (Berlin: Neues Leben, 1968);

Sensible Wege: Achtundvierzig Gedichte und ein Zyklus (Reinbek: Rowohlt, 1969);

Der Löwe Leopold: Fast Märchen, fast Geschichten (Frankfurt am Main: Fischer, 1970);

Der Dichter und die Löwenzahnwiese (Berlin: Berliner Handpresse, 1971);

Zimmerlautstärke: Gedichte (Frankfurt am Main: Fischer, 1972); translated by Ewald Osers as *With the Volume Turned Down, and Other Poems* (London: London Magazine Editions, 1973); translated by Lori Fischer as *Zimmerlautstärke: With the Volume Down Low* (Amherst, Mass.: Swamp Press, 1981);

Brief mit blauem Siegel: Gedichte (Leipzig: Reclam, 1973);

Die wunderbaren Jahre: Prosa (Frankfurt am Main: Fischer, 1976); translated by Joachim Neugroschel as *The Wonderful Years* (New York: Braziller, 1977); translated by Osers as *The Lovely Years* (London: Sidgwick & Jackson, 1978);

Wintereisenbahnerhochzeit (Windeck: Windecker Winkelpresse, 1978);

Der Film Die wunderbaren Jahre: Lesefassung des Drehbuchs (Frankfurt am Main: Fischer, 1979);

Auf eigene Hoffnung: Gedichte (Frankfurt am Main: Fischer, 1981);

Ergriffen von den Messen Mozarts (Hauzenberg: Edition Toni Pongratz, 1981);

Reiner Kunze (Reiner Kunze, Der Film Die wunderbaren Jahre *[Frankfurt am Main: Fischer, 1979])*

Eine stadtbekannte Geschichte (Olten & Freiburg im Breisgau: Walter, 1982);

Gespräch mit der Amsel: Frühe Gedichte; Sensible Wege; Zimmerlautstärke (Frankfurt am Main: Fischer, 1984);

Eines jeden einziges Leben: Gedichte (Frankfurt am Main: Fischer, 1986).

OTHER: "Über die Lyrik als dichterisches Heldendasein des Lyrikers und des Volkes" and "Gedanken über das Lied," in *Fragen des lyrischen Schaffens,* edited by the Deutscher Schriftstellerverband (Halle: VEB

172

Verlag Sprache und Literatur, 1960), pp. 5-37;

Mir gegenüber, edited by Kunze and Heinz Knobloch (Halle: Mitteldeutscher Verlag, 1960);

Kurt Heinze, *Das Brot auf dieser Erden*, edited by Kunze (Weimar: Volksverlag Weimar, 1962).

TRANSLATIONS: Jan Skácel, *Der Wind mit Namen Jaromir* (Berlin: Volk und Welt, 1961);

Milan Kundera, *Die Schlüsselbesitzer* (Berlin: Bloch, 1962);

Die Tür: Nachdichtungen aus dem Tschechischen (Bad Godesberg: Hohwacht, 1964);

Ladislaw Dvorsky, *Der Schatz der Hexe Funkelauge* (Prague: Dilia, 1964);

Ludvik Kundera, *Neugier* (Kassel: Bärenreiter Verlag, 1966);

Josef Topol, *Fastnacht* (Berlin: Henschelverlag, 1966);

Skácel, *Fährgeld für Charon* (Hamburg: Merlin, 1967);

Ludvik Kundera, *Der Abend aller Tage* (Prague: Dilia, 1967);

Vladimir Holan, *Nacht mit Hamlet* (Hamburg: Merlin, 1969);

Antonín Brousek, *Wunderschöne Sträflingskugel* (Darmstadt: Bläschke, 1970);

Holan, *Vor eurer Schwelle* (Darmstadt: Bläschke, 1970);

Milos Macourek, *Eine Tafel, blau wie der Himmel* (Hauzenberg: Edition Toni Pongratz, 1982);

Vit Obrtel, *Sommertraum: Gedichte in Prosa* (Hauzenberg: Edition Toni Pongratz, 1982);

Skácel, *Wundklee* (Frankfurt am Main: Fischer, 1982).

Reiner Kunze came of age in the German Democratic Republic (GDR) and began his writing career as a hopeful socialist. As conflicts with the authorities increased, his poems lost much of their romantic musicality and acquired a terseness and sarcastic wit modeled on the style of Bertolt Brecht. Kunze's epigrammatic creations contain less rationality than Brecht's, but they have more open emotions and even some lighthearted humor. Kunze is a master of the short form in both poetry and prose, an enemy of superfluous words and of dogmatism. His 1981 collection of poems *Auf eigene Hoffnung* (For My Own Hope) bears the motto: "Des Fahnenhissens bin ich müde" (I am tired of hoisting a flag).

Kunze was born in 1933 to Ernst and Martha Kunze in Oelsnitz, Germany, in the Erzgebirge region on the Czech border. There had been miners–including his father–and craftsmen in his family, and he was expected to follow in their footsteps. But the new socialist authorities after 1945 were looking for gifted youngsters from the working class. Against the wishes of his parents Kunze stayed in school, and after his Abitur (school-leaving examination) in 1951 he began the study of German literature and journalism at the University of Leipzig. While there he married a fellow student named Inge; they had a son, Ludwig. Kunze received his diploma in 1955; the same year his first published poems appeared, along with some by Egon Günther, in a volume titled *Die Zukunft sitzt am Tische* (The Future Sits at the Table).

Kunze lectured at the university while working on his doctorate. He began to develop doubts about Communism as a result of the persecution of East German intellectuals and the 1956 Soviet invasion of Hungary. Soon he found himself being denounced by colleagues as a counterrevolutionary. The pressures led to a heart attack in 1959, when Kunze was only twenty-six. After he recovered, he left the university without receiving his degree; his first marriage ended in divorce at about the same time. He worked for a year in a factory but eventually suffered a nervous breakdown. A new lease on life came with the chance to live and write in Czechoslovakia from 1960 to 1962.

On 8 July 1961 he married Elisabeth Mifka, a Czech doctor who had started a correspondence with him after hearing his poems read on the radio in 1959. Kunze adopted her daughter, Marcela, from an earlier marriage. In 1962 Kunze brought his family to the GDR; they settled in Greiz in Thüringia.

When troops of the GDR joined the Soviets in quelling the Prague Spring in 1968, Kunze resigned from the Socialist Unity party. Thereafter, although the Reclam Verlag in Leipzig published a collection of Kunze's poems, *Brief mit blauem Siegel* (Letter with a Blue Seal) in 1973, most of his works appeared in the West. The volume of short prose *Die wunderbaren Jahre* (translated as *The Wonderful Years*, 1977), published in 1976, made clear how far his alienation had gone. The same year he joined other East German writers in signing a letter protesting the GDR's revocation of the citizenship of the singer-poet Wolf Biermann. Kunze's opposition was reinforced by

Kunze and Elisabeth Mifka at their wedding in 1961 (courtesy of Reiner Kunze)

the difficulties his daughter encountered because of him. He finally left the GDR on 13 April 1977 and now lives in Obernzell, near Passau in Bavaria. Welcomed in the West as an anti-Communist, Kunze has refrained from political involvement in the matter of East-West confrontation.

Kunze began as a lyrical poet in the romantic manner of Heinrich Heine, but his verses soon became terser, more epigrammatic, and more like prose; one can observe a consistent trend toward the style of *Die wunderbaren Jahre*. His writing during his last years in the GDR is on the border between poetry and prose, whereas his poetry written in the West has regained lyric qualities.

Kunze discounts his earliest poems and dates his real beginnings from his stay in Czecho-

slovakia; he calls the volume *Widmungen* (Dedications, 1963) his "opus 1." He has included some of the poems from *Widmungen* in his 1984 collection *Gespräch mit der Amsel* (Dialogue with the Blackbird). They are poems of love and nature, with fairy-tale motifs and surprising metaphors; many of them come close to the form of a lied. But they also show how politics, such as the division of Germany, intrude into this lyrical world and tear it apart.

The volumes *Sensible Wege* (Sensitive Paths, 1969) and *Zimmerlautstärke* (1972; translated as *With the Volume Turned Down*, 1973) show the progressive intrusion of hostile forces into nature and human relations. Obvious symbols document his fight for personal freedom. In the poem "Der Hochwald erzieht seine Bäume" (The High Forest Educates Its Trees) in *Sensible Wege* the

Kunze (left) with the Czechoslovakian writer Milan Kundera, circa 1960 (courtesy of Reiner Kunze)

trees are planted at regular intervals so that they become taller, but they lose their lower branches and stop breathing. They have only one thing to say: "Holz" (wood). They are nothing but useful tools and providers of material; their individuality and joy in life are gone.

Harsh epigrams, on the border between poetry and prose, criticize Communist tactics. An example is "Kurzer Lehrgang" (Short Course):

Dialektik
Unwissende damit ihr
unwissend bleibt

werden wir euch
schulen

Aesthetik
Bis zur entmachtung des
imperialismus ist
als verbündet zu betrachten

Picasso

Ethik
Im mittelpunkt steht
der mensch

Nicht
der einzelne

(*Dialectics*
Ignorant people so that you
remain ignorant

we shall
train you

Aesthetics
Until the overthrow of
imperialism, to be
considered as an ally is

Picasso

Ethics
Our first preoccupation is
the human being
Not
the individual)

The dialectics of party education keep the ignorant people ignorant but well indoctrinated; tactical considerations dictate considering Picasso an ally, although his art would be banned; party ethics talks about the "human being" and "humanity" but ignores the individual.

The poems become shorter and shorter. One of the shortest is "Selbstmord" (Suicide) in the "Monologe mit der Tochter" (Monologues with the Daughter) section of *Zimmerlautstärke*:

Die letzte aller türen

Doch nie hat man
an alle schon geklopft

(The last of all doors

Michael being arrested by East German police in a scene from the West German film of Kunze's Die wunderbaren Jahre
(Reiner Kunze, Der Film Die wunderbaren Jahre *[Frankfurt am Main: Fischer, 1979])*

Yet one has never
knocked on all of them)

This poem is a father's desperate attempt at encouragement for his daughter, who cannot see
any future for herself. The poems in the book
are born out of the perception of irreconcilable
contradictions in the socialist system. The title
poem makes the point clearly:

Dann die
zwölf jahre
durfte ich nicht publizieren sagt
der mann im radio

Ich denke an X
und beginne zu zählen

(Then those
twelve years
I was not allowed to publish says
the man on the radio

I am thinking of X
and begin to count)

While the antifascist writer boasts of his persecution during the Nazi years, the listener thinks of
a friend whose works could not be published in
the GDR and begins to count the years of his enforced silence.

Die wunderbaren Jahre (the title is the German translation of a phrase from Truman Capote's *The Grass Harp*, [1951]) consists of short anecdotes, often with harsh punch lines. In one of
them, Michael, an unconventional youngster who
plays the guitar, is being watched by the police
after having been caught reading the Bible. He
wants to hike in the Polish mountains but cannot
get permission to leave the country. He tries to
reach the Baltic Sea but is not allowed to enter Berlin, through which all trains to the north must
pass, during the World Youth Festival. Again and
again, he is shipped back to his hometown and released. "Sie können gehen" (You can go now), he
is told. "Wohin?" (Where to?), he asks. The "wonderful years" are the teenage years, but in the
GDR they are marred by the heavy hand of po-

Kunze in 1976 (Binder/Thiele–Ullstein Bilderdienst)

life in West Germany; but he soon felt at home, as he says in the poem "Ich bin angekommen" (I Have Arrived) in *Auf eigene Hoffnung:*

Ich bin angekommen

Lange ließ ich auf nachricht
euch warten

Ich habe getastet

Doch ich bin angekommen

Auch dies ist mein land

Ich finde den lichtschalter schon
im dunkeln

(I have arrived

I made you wait a long time
for news
I felt my way

But I arrived

This, too, is my country

I find the light switch
in the dark)

lice, school principals, and party officials. From an early age children are educated to fight the enemy–whoever that may be. With their normal need for rebellion or only for a distinctive behavior and appearance, the teenagers become the enemy. Sometimes Kunze describes "normal" generational conflicts, but he deals mostly with the suppression of independent thinking and behavior by the authorities. Some of the incidents are funny, but most are deadly serious.

Part of the book is concerned with the Soviet invasion of Czechoslovakia in 1968, the suffering of Czech artists and writers, and the underground solidarity of the people against the aggression, even in the GDR. These pointed anecdotes are a merciless indictment of the police state, German authoritarianism, and Soviet superpower politics, but not of socialism as such. They reveal Kunze's sympathy with opposition forces in both East and West.

Kunze was received in the West with much fanfare. The 1980 West German movie of *Die wunderbaren Jahre*, which Kunze wrote and directed, was misinterpreted by some in the West as an attack on the possibility of East-West détente. Kunze had some problems adjusting to

In *Auf eigene Hoffnung* the poet experiences not only his new home but also the wide world, since he now has the freedom to travel to other countries. His observations are still terse and often critical, but more genuine humor creeps in. He is still not free from politics, however; he has to resist ideologues of all sorts who claim him for their causes. As he puts it ironically in "Ideologenwunschbild hier wie dort" (Desired Image of Ideologues Here and There):

Melde, schriftsteller K.
angetreten

Kopf bei fuß

(I report, writer K.
has fallen in

Head at foot)

"Kopf bei Fuß" is a play on the military command "Gewehr bei Fuß" (rifle at foot), meaning "at ease, wait for orders."

Kunze's children's books, especially *Der Löwe Leopold* (Leopold the Lion, 1970), are quite

Kunze reading from his work at the University of Stockholm in 1980 (photograph by Wilfried Bauer)

successful. He has something of a child's view of the world and can make the reader see familiar things as if for the first time. His production is slow; he is a severe judge of the quality of his works. Secondary literature on Kunze has increased much faster than his oeuvre itself, and he is besieged by critics and scholars who interpret his works. He answers them in the playful but frank poem "Grob" (Rude) in *Auf eigene Hoffnung*:

Von hundert germanisten liebt die dichtung einer
Berufen ist zum germanisten außer diesem keiner

Interpretationshilfe
Außer diesem einen
mag der autor keinen

(Of a hundred Germanists only one has a love for
    poetry
no one, except this person, has a true calling to be
    a Germanist

Aid to Interpretation
Besides this one
the author likes none)

Kunze, who started out as a romantic poet in the manner of Heine–writing about nature, love, friendship, and the innocent world of children–was forced by political pressure to become a terse and satirical social critic in the style of Brecht. Rejected by the socialist country in which he initially believed, he had to make a fresh start in the West, but not without leaving some of the most poignant prose and verse documents of state tyranny in the East. In the West he has remained a social critic, but his romantic vein and his humor have returned. *Die wunderbaren Jahre*, his essays, and his children's books are meticulously crafted pieces, as are his poems.

Kunze won the Translation Prize of the Czech Writer's Society in 1968; the German Children's Book Prize in 1971; the Literature Prize of the Bavarian Academy of Arts and the Mölle Literature Prize of Sweden in 1973; the Georg Trakl Prize of Austria, the Andreas Gryphius Prize, and the Georg Büchner Prize, all for *Die wunderbaren Jahre*, in 1977; and the Bavarian Film Prize in 1978. He is the antithesis of the trends of the modern age: he is anti-ideological; he is against commercialism and shuns opportunism; he publishes little, and then only short pieces. And yet, of the writers from the GDR who moved to the Federal Republic, Kunze has been one of the most successful. This may be because his opposition to East German society transcends politics: he defends the rights of the individual. There is a need for such a defense in any society.

References:

Heinrich Böll, "Die Faust die weinen kann," in his *Einmischung erwünscht: Schriften zur Zeit* (Cologne: Kiepenheuer & Witsch, 1977), pp. 366-369;

Werner Brettschneider, *Zwischen literarischer Autonomie und Staatsdienst: Die Literatur der DDR*, second edition (Berlin: Schmidt, 1974), pp. 238-245;

Karl Corino and Jürgen P. Wallmann, "Interviews mit *Reiner Kunze*," *Deutschland-Archiv*, 10 (1977): 660-666;

Corino, ed., *Reiner Kunze: Die wunderbaren Jahre—Lyrik, Prosa, Dokumente* (Frankfurt am Main: Fischer, 1978);

Peter Gardner, Review of *The Wonderful Years*, *Saturday Review*, 4 (28 May 1977): 28;

Peter Graves, Review of *Die wunderbaren Jahre*, *Times Literary Supplement*, 12 June 1977, p. 724;

Graves, ed., *Three Contemporary German Poets: Wolf Biermann, Sarah Kirsch, Reiner Kunze* (Leicester, U.K.: Leicester University Press, 1985);

Martin Greenberg, Review of *The Wonderful Years*, *New York Times Book Review*, 24 April 1977, pp. 15, 35;

Michael Hamburger, "Brecht und seine Nachfolger," in his *Literarische Erfahrungen* (Neuwied & Darmstadt: Luchterhand, 1981);

Manfred Jäger, *Sozialliteraten: Funktion und Selbstverständnis der Schriftsteller in der DDR* (Düsseldorf: Bertelsmann Universitätsverlag, 1973), pp. 102-115;

Otto Knörrich, "Reiner Kunze," in his *Die deutsche Lyrik seit 1945*, second edition (Stuttgart: Kröner, 1978), pp. 351-355;

Wulf Koepke, "Reiner Kunze," in *Die deutsche Lyrik 1945-1975*, edited by Klaus Weissenberger (Düsseldorf: Bagel, 1981), pp. 373-382;

Andreas W. Mytze, ed., *Über Reiner Kunze* (Berlin: Europäische Ideen, 1976);

John Updike, "Discontent in Deutsch," *New Yorker*, 53 (26 September 1977): 136-144;

Jürgen P. Wallmann, "Sensible Wege: Ein Porträt des Schriftstellers Reiner Kunze," in *Lyrik von allen Seiten*, edited by Lothar Jordan, Axel Marquardt, and Winfried Woesler (Frankfurt am Main: Fischer, 1981), pp. 461-484;

Wallmann, ed., *Reiner Kunze: Materialien und Dokumente* (Frankfurt am Main: Fischer, 1977);

Rudolf Wolff, ed., *Reiner Kunze: Werk und Wirkung* (Bonn: Bouvier, 1983).

Siegfried Lenz

(17 March 1926-   )

Hans Wagener
University of California, Los Angeles

BOOKS: *Es waren Habichte in der Luft: Roman* (Hamburg: Hoffmann & Campe, 1951);

Duell mit dem Schatten: Roman (Hamburg: Hoffmann & Campe, 1953);

So leicht fängt man keine Katze (Hamburg: Agentur des Rauhen Hauses, 1954);

Der einsame Jäger (Gütersloh: Rufer, 1955);

So zärtlich war Suleyken: Masurische Geschichten (Hamburg: Hoffmann & Campe, 1955);

Das schönste Fest der Welt: Hörspiel (Hamburg: Hans Bredow-Institut, 1956);

Das Kabinett der Konterbande (Hamburg: Hoffmann & Campe, 1956);

Der Mann im Strom: Roman (Hamburg: Hoffmann & Campe, 1957);

Jäger des Spotts: Geschichten aus dieser Zeit (Hamburg: Hoffmann & Campe, 1958); republished as *Jäger des Spotts, und andere Erzählungen*, edited by Robert H. Spaethling (New York: Norton, 1965);

Brot und Spiele: Roman (Hamburg: Hoffmann & Campe, 1959);

Das Feuerschiff: Erzählungen (Hamburg: Hoffmann & Campe, 1960); title story translated by Michael Bullock as *The Lightship* (New York: Hill & Wang, 1962; London: Heinemann, 1962);

Zeit der Schuldlosen; Zeit der Schuldigen (Hamburg: Hans Bredow Institut, 1961); edited by Albert R. Schmidt (New York: Appleton-Century-Crofts, 1967);

Das Wunder von Striegeldorf: Geschichten (Frankfurt am Main: Hirschgraben, 1961);

Zeit der Schuldlosen: Drama (Cologne: Kiepenheuer & Witsch, 1962); edited by P. Prager (London: Harrap, 1966);

Stimmungen der See: Erzählungen (Stuttgart: Reclam, 1962);

Stadtgespräch: Roman (Hamburg: Hoffmann & Campe, 1963); translated by Bullock as *The Survivor* (New York: Hill & Wang, 1965);

Der Hafen ist voller Geheimnisse: Ein Feature in Erzählungen und zwei masurische Geschichten (Lübeck: Matthiesen, 1963);

Lehmanns Erzählungen oder So schön war mein Markt: Aus den Bekenntnissen eines Schwarzhändlers (Hamburg: Hoffmann & Campe, 1964);

Das Gesicht: Komödie (Hamburg: Hoffmann & Campe, 1964);

Der Spielverderber: Erzählungen (Hamburg: Hoffmann & Campe, 1965);

Haussuchung: Hörspiele (Hamburg: Hoffmann & Campe, 1967);

Flug über Land und Meer: Nordsee–Holstein–Nordsee, by Lenz and Dieter Seelmann (Brunswick: Westermann, 1967); republished as *Wo die Möwen schreien: Flug über Norddeutschlands Küsten und Länder* (Hamburg: Christians, 1976);

Das Wrack, and Other Stories, edited by C. A. H. Russ (London: Heinemann, 1967);

Deutschstunde: Roman (Hamburg: Hoffmann & Campe, 1968); translated by Ernst Kaiser and Eithne Wilkins as *The German Lesson* (London: Macdonald, 1971; New York: Hill & Wang, 1972);

Leute von Hamburg: Satirische Porträts (Hamburg: Hoffmann & Campe, 1968);

Die Augenbinde: Schauspiel; Nicht alle Förster sind froh: Ein Dialog (Reinbek: Rowohlt, 1970);

Versäum nicht den Termin der Freude (Memmingen: Visel, 1970);

Lotte soll nicht sterben (Copenhagen: Grafisk/St. Paul: EMC, 1970); republished as *Lotte macht alles mit* (Munich: Lenz, 1978);

Gesammelte Erzählungen (Hamburg: Hoffmann & Campe, 1970);

Beziehungen: Ansichten und Bekenntnisse zur Literatur (Hamburg: Hoffmann & Campe, 1970);

Verlorenes Land–Gewonnene Nachbarschaft: Die Ostpolitik der Bundesregierung (Kiel: Wählerinitiative Nord, 1971);

Die Herrschaftssprache der CDU (Kiel: Wählerinitiative Nord, 1971);

Das Vorbild: Roman (Hamburg: Hoffmann & Campe, 1973); translated by Douglas Parmée as *An Exemplary Life* (New York: Hill &

Siegfried Lenz (Sven Simon, Bonn)

Wang, 1976; London: Secker & Warburg, 1976);

Der Geist der Mirabelle: Geschichten aus Bollerup (Hamburg: Hoffmann & Campe, 1975);

Einstein überquert die Elbe bei Hamburg: Erzählungen (Hamburg: Hoffmann & Campe, 1975);

Elfenbeinturm und Barrikade: Schriftsteller zwischen Literatur und Politik (Hamburg: Hoffmann & Campe, 1976);

Die frühen Romane (Hamburg: Hoffmann & Campe, 1976);

Die Wracks von Hamburg: Hörfunk-Features (Oldenburg & Hamburg: Stalling, 1978);

Heimatmuseum: Roman (Hamburg: Hoffmann & Campe, 1978); translated by Krishna Winston as *The Heritage* (New York: Hill & Wang, 1981; London: Secker & Warburg, 1981);

Himmel, Wolken, weites Land: Flug über Meer, Marsch, Geest und Heide, by Lenz and Seelmann (Hamburg: Christians, 1979);

Gespräche mit Manès Sperber und Leszek Kolakowski, edited by Alfred Mensak (Hamburg: Hoffmann & Campe, 1980);

Drei Stücke (Hamburg: Hoffmann & Campe, 1980);

Der Verlust: Roman (Hamburg: Hoffmann & Campe, 1981); translated by Ralph R. Read as *The Breakdown* (Seattle: Fjord, 1986);

Über Phantasie: Gespräche mit Heinrich Böll, Günter Grass, Walter Kempowski, Pavel Kohout, edited by Alfred Mensak (Hamburg: Hoffmann & Campe, 1982);

Elfenbeinturm und Barrikade: Erfahrungen am Schreibtisch (Hamburg: Hoffmann & Campe, 1983);

Ein Kriegsende (Hamburg: Hoffmann & Campe, 1984);

Der Verzicht (Neu-Isenburg: Edition Tiessen, 1985);

Exerzierplatz: Roman (Hamburg: Hoffmann & Campe, 1985);

Das serbische Mädchen: Erzählungen (Hamburg: Hoffmann & Campe, 1987).

OTHER: Julius Stettenheim, *Wippchens charmante Scharmützel, erträumt von Julius Stettenheim, in Erinnerung gebracht von Siegfried Lenz und Egon Schramm: Satiren*, edited by Lenz (Hamburg: Hoffmann & Campe, 1960);

Uwe Schultz, ed., *Fünfzehn Autoren suchen sich selbst: Modell und Provokation*, contributions by Lenz (Munich: List, 1967);

Liselotte Lenz, *Waldboden: Sechsunddreißig Farbstiftzeichnungen*, text by Lenz (Hamburg: Knaus, 1979);

Elsbeth Weichmann, *Zuflucht: Jahre des Exils*, foreword by Lenz (Hamburg: Knaus, 1983);

Hans Jordan, ed., *Auf Verlegers Rappen: Von Büchermachern und Buchverkäufern*, contributions by Lenz (Munich: Ehrenwirth, 1986).

Next to Günter Grass and Martin Walser, Siegfried Lenz is the most highly acclaimed and popular living German novelist and author of short stories; along with Grass, Walser, and Heinrich Böll, he has helped to shape the path of German literature since 1951. His breakthrough as a writer came in 1968 with the publication of *Deutschstunde* (translated as *The German Lesson*, 1971). By 1975 this novel had sold over a million copies and had been translated into nineteen foreign languages. Since 1968 most of Lenz's books have been on the German bestseller lists. His oeuvre mostly consists of novels and short stories but also includes dramas, radio plays, travel books, and essays.

Lenz was born on 17 March 1926 in Lyck, a small town in Masuria, East Prussia (now Elk, Poland); his father was a civil servant. Like his classmates, he became a member of the Hitler Youth organization. Upon being drafted into the navy in 1943 he was released from taking the final exam at the gymnasium. He served on one of the last German cruisers in the Baltic Sea, the *Admiral Scheer*. During the final months of the war he was a soldier in Denmark, where he deserted and allowed himself to be taken prisoner by the British. After his release in 1945 he studied philosophy and German and English literature at the University of Hamburg with the intention of becoming a teacher. While a student he began contributing to the newspaper *Die Welt*; in 1948 he left the university to join the newspaper's staff. In 1950 he became an editor for *Die Welt*, in which his first short stories and the novel *Es waren Habichte in der Luft* (Hawks Were in the Air, 1951) were published. Since 1951 he has lived in Hamburg as a free-lance writer, spending the summers at his vacation home on the Danish island of Ahlsen. He became a member of the influential writers' organization Gruppe 47 in the early 1950s. He has traveled extensively, going to Africa in 1951, making a lecture tour of Australia in 1968, and serving as a visiting lecturer at the University of Houston in 1969. Since 1965 he has been active as a campaign speaker

for the Social Democratic party. In 1970 he and Grass accompanied Federal Chancellor Willy Brandt to Warsaw for the signing of the German-Polish treaty, which marked the beginning of a more conciliatory era in relations between the two countries. Lenz has received many literary awards, including the René Schickele Prize in 1952, the Gerhart Hauptmann Prize in 1961, the Literature Prize of the City of Bremen in 1962, the Prize of the German Free Masons for Literature in 1970, and the Thomas Mann Prize of the City of Lübeck in 1985. In 1976 he was given an honorary doctorate by the University of Hamburg. He and his wife Lieselotte, whom he married in 1949, have no children.

Lenz's fictional works are written in a realistic style. He rarely experiments with form; he generally tells a straightforward story and creates a vivid atmosphere through the use of precisely observed details; he is particularly noted for his descriptions of the sea. Although he is not an avant-garde writer, his stories and novels are never just superficial entertainment: they always make a statement about the way the world is and the way it should be and present the reader with situations that require moral decisions. In the 1950s and 1960s Lenz's uncompromising moral standpoint manifested itself in parables of guilt and atonement; in the 1970s and 1980s his work became less obviously didactic and more psychological in character. Lenz neither insults his readers nor forces his ideas upon them; instead, he tries to persuade them gently with rational arguments.

The plot of *Es waren Habichte in der Luft* resembles that of a detective story; its atmosphere is similar to that of a Russian epic. The setting, though not explicitly identified, is obviously Finnish Karelia shortly after World War I. The main characters are the teacher Stenka, who is persecuted by the Communist government for a murder he has not committed; the young Erkki, whose fiancé Manja has been killed; and the ideologist Aati, Stenka's persecutor. At the end Stenka and Erkki flee together, but Stenka is shot to death at the border while Erkki escapes to freedom. The novel is typical of German postwar literature in that it combines existentialist ideas with an exciting plot. Time and place are only hinted at; Marxism/Leninism is not named as the ideology. The novel presents a model situation which characterizes a general human condition. Stenka's persecution is portrayed as typical of human experience: everyone is tortured by love, hate, and all kinds of needs, and no one can escape.

Lenz, circa 1973, about the time his novel Das Vorbild *was
published (Kindermann)*

Stenka resists in spite of the fact that he will probably not succeed. The story is full of graphic symbols, such as the ever-present hawks that find
their human counterpart in the cold, inhuman ideologist Aati. Ideology is the negative force which
the teacher, the representative of humanism and
freedom of thought, resists. The novel, written
during the late 1940s, reflects the influence of
French existentialism on German literature. The
cold war, the existence of the two newly founded
German states, and the flight of many Germans
from East to West are present in allegorical form.

Lenz's next novel, *Duell mit dem Schatten*
(Duel with the Shadow, 1953), continues in the existential vein of *Es waren Habichte in der Luft*. An elderly German colonel returns to the African des-
ert to try to come to terms with an old guilt:
during World War II he had taken the uniform
of his severely wounded driver in order to hide
his own identity from his captors and had left
the driver to die. The colonel cannot justify his actions to himself; the past cannot be undone; only
the present exists. But the present cannot be mastered, either: the colonel dies after losing control
over his daughter Biggi, who has gained the sym-

pathy and support of two young Englishmen.
The style of the novel is artificially exotic and pa-
thetic. The characters appear wooden, and the
theme of existential guilt does not fit the story. Unlike most of Lenz's novels, this one has never
been reprinted.

So zärtlich war Suleyken (So Tender Was
Suleyken, 1955) is a collection of delightfully humorous stories about the idiosyncrasies and follies of the inhabitants of the imaginary village of
Suleyken in Masuria; Lenz is said to have written
the stories to give his wife an impression of his
homeland. All the flawed characters are made lik-
able by the pervasive humor. The stories lack
any reference to the politics of the 1950s; in the village of Suleyken, Lenz created a utopian small-
town society that is a stark contrast to his own troubled time. In 1971-1972 thirteen of the twenty
stories were filmed and broadcast on German television.

The novel *Der Mann im Strom* (The Man in
the River, 1957) replaces existential themes with
concrete social criticism. The fifty-year-old Hamburg diver Hinrichs changes the birth date on his
papers in order to secure work. With his many
years of experience he is able to save his company a great deal of money in raising a sunken
ship. In the end, however, his forgery is discovered, and he loses his job. The problems of an
aging worker in a modern industrial economy constitute the main theme of the book, which becomes overly didactic. In contrast to the conscientious Hinrichs, the young people, such as his
daughter Lena's boyfriend Manfred, try to make
money quickly in dishonest ways; the inexperi-
enced Manfred drowns while trying to steal batter-
ies from an old submarine. Lenz's ideal of the
hardworking man who realizes happiness in the
confines of his modest home is something of a
throwback to the neorealistic novels of the 1920s
and 1930s. But in spite of its flaws, *Der Mann im
Strom* is a gripping social-critical novel. It was
filmed in 1958.

Some of the stories in Lenz's collection *Jäger
des Spotts* (Hunter of Ridicule, 1958) show the influence of Ernest Hemingway. Like his American
model, Lenz is interested in people who fail in
spite of great efforts but prove themselves in the
face of failure. The title story is reminiscent of
The Old Man and the Sea (1952): an Eskimo kills a
vicious musk-ox, but bears eat the meat. "Das
Wrack" (The Wreck) is clearly influenced by
"After the Storm" (1932): a diver finally succeeds
in reaching a sunken ship thought to contain valu-

ables, only to discover that its cargo consisted of horses. But for Lenz it is not the achievement of a goal but the struggle itself that is important. The collection also contains several stories of a socially critical, satirical nature which link Lenz to other German authors of short satires of the time, such as Heinrich Böll. Like Böll, Lenz uses social outsiders to criticize contemporary German society. The collection as a whole demonstrates his talent as a writer of short stories; some critics have argued that Lenz's abilities may be more suited to short stories than to novels.

The novel *Brot und Spiele* (Bread and Games, 1959) is an account of the last race of an aging long-distance runner, Bert Buchner, interrupted by flashbacks that tell the story of his life; the race results in Buchner's defeat. Buchner has misused sports by making a career out of them and by wanting to win at any price; he has betrayed the ancient Greek ideal of sports as free play. In Lenz's opinion sports have been corrupted by the constant desire to achieve new records. His ideal is the person who has a normal profession and participates in sports during his spare time. He criticizes the fickleness of the sports clubs, the sponsors, and the public who make an athlete into a hero and then drop him as soon as he no longer fulfills their wishes and dreams.

In the story collection *Das Feuerschiff* (The Lightship, 1960) Lenz is no longer trying to imitate Hemingway. In fact, the story "Der Anfang von etwas" (The Beginning of Something) is a reply to Hemingway's "The End of Something" (1925). In Lenz's story Hoppe, a sailor who has missed his ship, goes to a pub, where he reads in the newspaper that the ship has been rammed by a tanker and has sunk with no survivors. His name is included in the list of victims. Seeing a chance for a new life, he throws his luggage into the river in a symbolic act. Lenz wanted to demonstrate that, in contrast to Hemingway's views, nothing ends with the end of a story, while every beginning has a story that precedes it.

Other anti-Hemingway elements are to be found in the title story (translated as *The Lightship*, 1962), which is a classic novella. Freytag, the captain of a lightship that is soon to be withdrawn from service, takes his son Fred on his last watch. Three men who apparently have been shipwrecked are brought on board; they turn out to be criminals who soon take over the vessel. Because his crew is unarmed, Freytag refuses to try to resist the bandits. He had lost his son's respect

because of an incident in Greece several years earlier; his inaction now only confirms Fred's contempt for him. Only when they try to sail with the lightship, thus endangering all other boats in the area by leaving the channel unmarked, does he resist. He is shot and wounded, but the crew overpowers the criminals. By supporting Freytag's attitude, Lenz is condemning senseless heroism. The story may also be read as a political parable: Freytag's highest value is order; when order, as symbolized by the lightship's fixed position in the channel, is disturbed, it is time to resist.

The theme of political responsibility is also dealt with in Lenz's novel *Stadtgespräch* (Talk of the Town, 1963; translated as *The Survivor*, 1965). Daniel, the leader of the resistance against an occupying power in a Nordic country, is seriously wounded in an unsuccessful attempt to capture a general who is visiting a small town. The foreign commander of the town takes forty-four of its leading citizens hostage and demands that Daniel surrender. Daniel's comrades persuade him not to do so, arguing that his importance as a symbol of resistance is more important than the hostages' lives, and the hostages are executed. After the occupiers are ousted, a discussion ensues in the town about what Daniel should have done. The novel has two themes. The first is the moral question of whether the deaths of the hostages were justified for the purpose of keeping alive the spirit of resistance against an unjust occupation. Lenz answers with a theory of the relativity of truth: what seems to be true at one time will not necessarily appear to be true later. The second theme of the novel, indicated by the original German title, is the discussion among the citizens in which Daniel becomes a scapegoat for the townspeoples' own failure to act or to speak out against the invaders; the citizens were happy to have a resistance movement as long as they did not have to participate in it. This lack of commitment is their guilt: innocence in a guilty world is not possible. Thus, the book is part of the contemporary discussion about collective guilt which Lenz has addressed in several of his works. The novel has several weaknesses, among them the vagueness of time and place, the theoretical nature of many of the discussions, and the construction of an extreme situation. In his next novel, *Deutschstunde,* Lenz was able to correct these flaws.

Before the appearance of *Deutschstunde* Lenz published two more collections of stories. *Lehmanns Erzählungen oder So schön war mein*

Markt (Lehmann's Tales; or, My Market Was So Beautiful, 1964) is a series of nostalgic accounts by a black-marketeer who experienced the greatest time of his life from 1945 until his career came to an abrupt end as a result of the currency reform of 1948. (While a student at the University of Hamburg between 1945 and 1948, Lenz had supported himself by engaging in black-market activities.) In contrast to the Suleyken stories, these tales do not depict a wholesome environment but a world that was great only in the eyes of the social outsider; to most people, it was a time of deprivation. The narrator derives his humorous effects from this implied contrast and from his attempts to raise the intellectual and artistic level of his narration by quoting from or alluding to famous works of literature, usually at inappropriate moments. *Der Spielverderber* (The Spoilsport, 1965) contains primarily social-critical stories which show the influence of the past on the present. The past of the Third Reich plays the main role, as in the title story: the social outcast Joseph Wollina has the uncanny ability to "remember" things he has never been told–for example, that his teacher's clock belonged to a former colleague who had been forced by the Nazis to emigrate; in a psychiatric demonstration, he writes on the blackboard Slavic names of people who were the head physician's patients during the war. When he uncovers insurance fraud by a shipping company, he is arrested for attempted blackmail. Lenz's message is that the society of the Federal Republic exists only because it is able to forget the past. If one does not play along, one becomes a social outcast and may be considered a criminal. "Schwierige Trauer" (Difficult Mourning) is the diatribe of a son who has just learned of his father's death. At the end of World War II the father, the mayor of an East German town, had followed Nazi orders to save the town's historical documents rather than the lives of its citizens. For Lenz, one human life is more important than the whole history of a city.

The impact of the Third Reich on the present is also one of the themes of *Deutschstunde*, one of the biggest German best-sellers after 1945 and considered by some critics to be Lenz's masterpiece. In 1954 the narrator, Siggi Jepsen, has been placed in a juvenile detention center in Hamburg for stealing paintings. He has been assigned to write an essay on "Die Freuden der Pflicht" (The Joys of Duty), which he works on for several months and which becomes a review of his life. During the Third Reich his father, a police-

man in the fictional north German town of Rugbüll, was supposed to enforce an order issued to his friend Max Nansen (modeled on the expressionist painter Emil Nolde) not to paint anymore. The policeman considers it his duty to carry out the order; the painter considers it *his* duty to continue painting. Thus two concepts of duty clash with one another: "Mein Vater hob die Hand, sichelte langsam in Höhe des Koppels und sagte warnend: Du weißt, Max, wozu ich verpflichtet bin.–Ja, sagte der Maler, ja, ich weiß, und damit du es genau weißt: es kotzt mich an, wenn ihr von Pflicht redet. Wenn ihr von Pflicht redet, müssen sich andere auf etwas gefaßt machen" (Slowly my father raised one hand and fumbled at his belt. Slowly he said: "I'm warning you, Max. You know what my duty is." "Yes, I know," the painter said. "And I want you to know: it makes me puke to hear you people talk about duty. When your lot talks about duty, others can look out for trouble"). Jepsen follows orders to the point of surrendering his other son to the Gestapo. Watching over the painter becomes such an obsession with him that even after the war he does not stop hunting for and destroying Nansen's pictures. To protect the paintings, Siggi steals them from galleries and hides them–the crime that led to his incarceration. Nansen, speaking for the author, demands that Jepsen use his own critical faculties and moral judgment to assess the validity of his orders before carrying them out; individual responsibility and a critical attitude are held up by Lenz as the true qualities of a good citizen. He points out, however, that the old concept of duty is still present in the Federal Republic, as evidenced by the topic assigned to Siggi and by the fact that the father is still a policeman in Rugbüll. Lenz's book is a "German lesson" for his readers, whom he wants to educate to evaluate critically Germany's past and present. *Deutschstunde* was broadcast on German television as a two-part motion picture in January 1971.

In the novel *Das Vorbild* (The Model, 1973; translated as *An Exemplary Life*, 1976) a committee of three pedagogues of widely different temperaments and backgrounds meets in Hamburg to select, for inclusion in a school reader, a biography that can serve as a role model for German youth. They propose, discuss, and reject a series of stories and finally agree on the life of Lucy Beerbaum, a world-famous biologist who, after the colonels took power in Greece, voluntarily imposed upon herself the same conditions under which her imprisoned Greek friends were living

Lenz in 1983 (Teutopress–Ullstein Bilderdienst)

until she died from pneumonia. The committee's proposals are rejected by the pompous publisher, for whom they do not meet the standards of fashionable educational theories. By introducing many exemplary figures, including some from the narrative frame, and then discarding most of them, Lenz wishes to demonstrate that there are no longer any universally acceptable role models for today's youth. He wants to teach his readers to look critically at their environment and develop criteria for evaluating other people in the same manner as his three experts. The problem with Lenz's novel–which was coolly received by the critics–is that all the stories and all the characters seem contrived and theoretical; even Lucy Beerbaum's life lacks realism and excitement. The novel does, however, continue the direction of *Deutschstunde* in turning away from the Third Reich toward criticism of contemporary West German society.

Der Geist der Mirabelle: Geschichten aus

Bollerup (The Spirit of the Yellow Plum: Stories from Bollerup, 1975) is a collection of humorous tales and anecdotes about the inhabitants of an imaginary village in Denmark. Most of them read as if they belong in a farmer's almanac of fifty years ago. The same cannot be said of the collection of more serious stories which appeared during the same year, *Einstein überquert die Elbe bei Hamburg* (Einstein Crosses the Elbe River near Hamburg). Some of the stories experiment with style. In "Die Phantasie" three authors of different artistic persuasions discuss the relation of reality to literature by constructing stories about a seemingly poorly matched couple in the pub where they are meeting. "Die Mannschaft" (The Team) describes a game of German handball from the various viewpoints of the eleven players. This theme of perspectivism, of the relativity of experience, comes out most clearly in the title story, which in three long sentences describes Einstein's crossing of the Elbe River in the light of spatial and temporal relativity.

The novel *Heimatmuseum* (Homeland Museum, 1978; translated as *The Heritage*, 1981) traces the fate of a local history museum in Masuria from its founding. The Nazis attempt to change its contents so as to turn it into a German frontier museum; after it has been reestablished in Schleswig after the war, German refugee organizations again try to eliminate all objects that would reveal the Polish heritage of Masuria. At this point the rug weaver Zygmunt Rogalla, the museum's caretaker and the nephew of its founder, sets it on fire to protect it from further misuse. The novel is narrated by Zygmunt from his hospital bed, where he is recovering from burns suffered in the fire. Lenz stresses the right of the Poles to live in Masuria and pleads for the exercise of reason against the continuing hatred of Germany's Polish neighbors. He also traces the ideological misuse of the term *Heimat* (homeland) over the past fifty years.

With *Der Verlust* (1981; translated as *The Breakdown*, 1986) Lenz gives up all social-critical and political themes in favor of psychology. Ulrich Martens, a city tour guide, suffers a stroke and loses his power of speech; he can only make meaningless sounds. His girlfriend, Nora Fechner, a spinsterish librarian, cannot face his handicap and refuses to visit him in the hospital. Lenz shows that the inability to speak leads to exile into oneself; he also deals with the more important handicap of his two characters, their inability to communicate their feelings for each other. What is lacking in the novel is motivation for the characters' actions; only Martens comes across as fully believable and realistically drawn, especially in the depiction of his illness and his fight to restore his speech.

In the novella-length narrative *Ein Kriegsende* (An End of the War, 1984) Lenz returns to the moral questions and model characters of his earlier stories and novels. Near the end of World War II a German minesweeper leaves its safe harbor in Denmark to pick up wounded soldiers on the coast of Kurland. Since the Baltic Sea is dominated by Soviet submarines and airplanes, the crew takes over the ship and returns to Denmark. The crew members are tried for insubordination and mutiny, and two of them are executed. As in *Deutschstunde* the theme is again that of conflicting duties. The order to proceed to Kurland, given by the captain, is countered by the mate, who represents the voice of reason. The mate argues that getting home safely is also a duty. The question is: up to what point must a sol-

dier obey orders, and under what conditions does he have the right to disobey? The situation is complicated by the fact that Germany had already capitulated to the British, so that it was not even clear whether the boat was still under German jurisdiction. The situation may seem too contrived to be credible, but it would have been quite possible in May 1945. Lenz does not take sides between the captain and the mate, leaving the reader to draw his own conclusions. The story was of immediate interest because of the public discussion of soldierly obedience in the wake of the stationing of American Pershing rockets in Germany.

In the novel *Exerzierplatz* (Drill Ground, 1985) the Zeller family flees from East Prussia after World War II and builds a new life in Schleswig-Holstein. After many years of work the head of the family creates a large tree nursery on a devastated drill ground in which the remnants of the past are physically present. The story is told by a social outsider, the naive Bruno, who is Zeller's helper and to whom Zeller wants to leave one third of the land after his death. He realizes that Bruno, who has an intimate love for the trees, is more deserving than his own sons. When the family has Zeller declared incompetent and placed under guardianship, Bruno decides to leave to help his boss. Bruno is good-natured, hardworking, loyal, and unsuspecting; consequently, he easily falls victim to the strong and scheming members of society. He represents the natural way of behaving, like Zeller, only on a less sophisticated level. By having him tell the story, Lenz allows the reader to draw conclusions about the behavior of the other characters rather than having a more intelligent narrator interpret it for them. At times, however, Bruno's style of narration appears to be more sophisticated than his background would warrant. The theme of the book is the rebuilding of life in Germany on the basis of a militaristic past, symbolized by the old drill ground. The story is paradigmatic of the pulling together of all forces after the war to build a new society and of the later quarrel between the old and the new generations, the younger of which knows nothing about the hardships of the past but takes wealth and success for granted.

The fifteen stories of the 1987 collection *Das serbische Mädchen* (The Serbian Girl) were written during the preceding twelve years; consequently, several of them are thematically linked to Lenz's earlier novels. For example, "Der Redenschreiber" (The Ghostwriter), with its critical attitude toward national prejudice, is related to *Deutschstunde* and *Heimatmuseum*: a ghostwriter retreats with his family to a lakeside cabin to write a speech for a state secretary on the German national character while, in a subtle way, he experiences those supposedly German character traits and modes of behavior he is trying to write about. "Motivsuche" (Searching for a Motif) is the story of a judge in a Mediterranean country (probably Greece) who, after an earlier error of justice, passes judgment on the new government. A parallel story involves two men in search of an appropriate locale for a film scene who allow love to influence their judgment of a boy who, because of poverty, had stolen from them; in this case the stories of *Das Vorbild* come to mind. "Fast ein Triumph" (Almost a Triumph) is another rejection of the Hemingway ethos, showing that a daredevil attitude is not heroic if it endangers others: a man with little experience of the sea buys a boat and, instead of having it towed around a peninsula as he is advised to do by the locals, rows it home himself through a great storm. He arrives safely, but a member of the search team that is looking for him is washed overboard. Thus the protagonist's victory over the elements is regarded by the others not as a triumph but as folly. Other stories deal with a variety of topics. The title story is about a girl who naively believes in the love of a German boy she met while he was vacationing in Serbia, follows him to Germany, is disappointed, and is unknowingly used on her way home by Yugoslav smugglers to divert the attention of the border guards. In "Der Mann unseres Vertrauens" (The Man of Our Confidence) a newspaper correspondent of an eastern European country is sent to Sweden, where he has a car accident. Since he is not immediately heard from, he is suspected of defecting and will never be able to rid himself of his colleagues' suspicion of him. In "Die Prüfung" (The Examination) a student passes a test in an interview with a professor with whose wife he was romantically involved before her marriage to the professor. With his ability to make his point by means of subtle hints, to play with perspectives, and to concoct surprise endings, Lenz again proves himself a master of storytelling.

Siegfried Lenz remains a moderate traditionalist who is able to tell a story and create a true-to-life atmosphere like few other contemporary writers. In addition to telling interesting stories, his goal is always a moral one. In confronting his readers with extreme situations or questionable decisions, he engages them to think for themselves; he makes them realize that right and wrong cannot always be distinguished in a clear-cut manner. Lenz does not antagonize the reader; rather he takes him along on his narrative explorations, makes a pact with him, and stimulates his thinking in a truly democratic manner, questioning prejudice and political dogmatism.

References:

Heinz Ludwig Arnold, ed., *Siegfried Lenz*, second edition (Munich: Edition text + kritik, 1982);

Winfried Baßmann, *Siegfried Lenz: Sein Werk als Beispiel für Weg und Standort der Literatur in der Bundesrepublik Deutschland*, second edition (Bonn: Bouvier, 1978);

Geoffrey P. Butler, "Zygmunt's Follies? On Siegfried Lenz's *Heimatmuseum*," *German Life and Letters*, new series 33 (January 1980): 172-178;

Manfred Durzak, "Zeitromane mit moralischen Kunstfiguren: Das Romanwerk von Siegfried Lenz," in his *Gespräche über den Roman: Formbestimmungen und Analysen* (Frankfurt am Main: Suhrkamp, 1976), pp. 204-224;

Theo Elm, *Siegfried Lenz—"Deutschstunde": Engagement und Realismus im Gegenwartsroman* (Munich: Fink, 1974);

Esther N. Elstun, "How It Seems and How It Is: Marriage in Three Stories by Siegfried Lenz," *Orbis litterarum*, 29, no. 2 (1974): 170-179;

Kenneth J. Eltis, "A Study of the Novels of Siegfried Lenz," Ph.D. dissertation, Macquarie University, Sydney, 1972;

Sumner Kirshner, "From the Gulf Stream into the Main Stream: Siegfried Lenz and Hemingway," *Research Studies*, 35 (June 1967): 14-147;

Hans Lachinger, "Siegfried Lenz," in *Deutsche Literatur seit 1945 in Einzeldarstellungen*, edited by Dietrich Weber, third edition (Stuttgart: Kröner, 1976), pp. 479-511;

Hagen Meyerhoff, *Die Figur des Alten im Werk von Siegfried Lenz* (Frankfurt am Main: Lang, 1979);

Edward Mornin, "Taking Games Seriously: Observations on the German Sports-novel," *Germanic Review*, 51 (November 1976): 278-295;

Brian Murdoch, "Ironic Reversal in the Short Stories of Siegfried Lenz," *Neophilologus*, 58, no. 4 (1974): 406-410;

Murdoch, *Siegfried Lenz* (London: Wolff, 1978);

Robert H. Paslick, "Narrowing the Distance: Siegfried Lenz's *Deutschstunde*," *German Quarterly*, 46 (March 1973): 210-218;

Hartmut Pätzold, *Theorie und Praxis moderner Schreibweisen: Am Beispiel von Siegfried Lenz und Helmut Heißenbüttel* (Bonn: Bouvier, 1976);

Trudis Reber, *Siegfried Lenz*, second edition (Berlin: Colloquium, 1976);

Nikolaus Reiter, *Wertstrukturen im erzählerischen Werk von Siegfried Lenz* (Frankfurt am Main: Lang, 1982);

Colin Russ, "The Macabre Festival: A Consideration of Six Stories by Siegfried Lenz," in *Deutung und Bedeutung: Studies in German and Comparative Literature. Presented to Karl-Werner Maurer*, edited by Brigitte Schludermann, Viktor G. Doerksen, Robert J. Glendinning, and Evelyn Scherabon-Firchow (The Hague & Paris: Mouton, 1973), pp. 275-293;

Russ, "Siegfried Lenz," in *Deutsche Dichter der Gegenwart: Ihr Leben und Werk*, edited by Benno von Wiese (Berlin: Schmidt, 1973), pp. 545-559;

Russ, ed., *Der Schriftsteller Siegfried Lenz: Urteile und Standpunkte* (Hamburg: Hoffmann & Campe, 1973);

Peter Russell, "The 'Lesson' in Siegfried Lenz's *Deutschstunde*," *Seminar*, 13 (February 1977): 42-54;

Russell, "Siegfried Lenz's 'Deutschstunde': A Northern German Novel," in *German Life and Letters*, new series 28 (July 1975): 405-418;

Albert R. Schmitt, "Schuld im Werke von Siegfried Lenz. Betrachtungen zu einem zeitgemäßen Thema," in *Festschrift für Detlev W. Schumann zum 70. Geburtstag*, edited by Schmitt (Munich: Delp, 1970), pp. 369-382;

Wilhelm Johannes Schwarz, *Der Erzähler Siegfried Lenz* (Bern & Munich: Francke, 1974);

Gudrun Uhlig, *Autor, Werk und Kritik: Inhaltsangaben, Kritiken und Textproben für den Literaturunterricht*, volume 3: *Koeppen und Lenz* (Munich: Hueber, 1972), pp. 85-167;

Hans Wagener, *Siegfried Lenz*, fourth edition (Munich: Beck/edition text   kritik, 1985);

Albrecht Weber, *Siegfried Lenz: Deutschstunde* (Munich: Oldenbourg, 1973);

Rudolf Wolff, ed., *Siegfried Lenz: Werk und Wirkung* (Bonn: Bouvier Verlag Herbert Grundmann, 1985).

Reinhard Lettau
(10 September 1929-   )

Otto F. Best
University of Maryland at College Park
and
David S. Roth
University of Maryland at College Park

BOOKS: *Schwierigkeiten beim Häuserbauen: Geschichten* (Munich: Hanser, 1962); translated by Ursule Molinaro as *Obstacles* (New York: Pantheon, 1965); translation included in *Obstacles*, translated by Molinaro and Ellen Sutton (London: Calder & Boyars, 1966);

Auftritt Manigs (Munich: Hanser, 1963); translation included in *Obstacles*, translated by Molinaro and Sutton (London: Calder & Boyars, 1966);

Feinde (Munich: Hanser, 1968); translated by Agnes Rook as *Enemies* (London: Calder & Boyars, 1973);

Gedichte (Berlin: Literarisches Colloquium, 1968);

Immer kürzer werdende Geschichten & Gedichte & Porträts (Munich: Hanser, 1973);

Frühstücksgespräche in Miami (Munich: Hanser, 1977); translated by Lettau and Julie Pradi as *Breakfast in Miami* (London: Calder/New York: Riverrun Press, 1982);

Zerstreutes Hinausschaun: Vom Schreiben über Vorgänge in direkter Nähe oder in der Entfernung von Schreibtischen (Munich & Vienna: Hanser, 1980);

Herr Strich schreitet zum Äußersten (Stuttgart: Reclam, 1982).

OTHER: James Thurber, *Lachen mit Thurber*, edited by Lettau (Hamburg: Rowohlt, 1963);

Die Gruppe 47: Bericht, Kritik, Polemik. Ein Handbuch, edited by Lettau (Neuwied & Berlin: Luchterhand, 1967);

Täglicher Faschismus: Amerikanische Evidenz aus 6 Monaten, translated by Lettau and Hanns Zischler, edited by Lettau (Munich: Hanser, 1971);

Franz Kafka, *Die Aeroplane in Brescia und andere Texte*, edited by Lettau (Frankfurt am Main: Fischer, 1977);

Reinhard Lettau (Binder/Thiele–Ullstein Bilderdienst)

Karl Marx, *Love Poems of Karl Marx*, edited by Lettau and Lawrence Ferlinghetti (San Francisco: City Lights, 1977).

Reinhard Lettau was born on 10 September 1929 in Erfurt, Thuringia, to Reinhard F. and Gertrude Felsberg Lettau. He studied German literature, comparative literature, and philosophy at the University of Heidelberg and at Harvard University. He married Mary Gene Carter on 4 September 1954; they have three children. Lettau received his doctoral degree from Harvard in 1960 with a dissertation titled "Utopie und Roman" (Utopia and Novel). He taught at Smith College in Northampton, Massachusetts, from 1957 until 1965. From 1965 to 1967 he lived in West Berlin as a free-lance writer. Since 1967 he has taught German literature and creative writing at the University of California in San Diego. In 1979 Lettau was awarded the Radio Play Prize of the Blind War Veterans for his adaptation of his *Frühstücksgespräche in Miami* (Discussions at the Breakfast Table in Miami, 1977; translated as *Breakfast in Miami*, 1982).

Lettau's stories and poems often verge on the grotesque and frequently illustrate the absurdity of human behavior; he is influenced by both Franz Kafka and James Thurber. As a storyteller he writes wittily about the incongruity which results when objective reality conflicts with subjective perception. His wit is also evident in his use of language: he separates words from the objects to which they refer, causing any analysis on the part of his characters to fall short of the reality for which it is intended. His language is ready to escape into a new reality that displaces the reality originally referred to.

In the collection of stories *Schwierigkeiten beim Häuserbauen* (Difficulties in Housebuilding, 1962; translated as *Obstacles*, 1965), for example, perceived reality eventually becomes the accepted reality. In "Ärger mit der älteren Generation" (translated as "Annoyance with the Older Generation") the farewell party of a traveler bound for America transforms itself into a farewell party for the guests. Similarly, in "Herr Stumpf erliegt einem Trugschluß" (translated as "Mr. Stumpf Succumbs to a Misapprehension") a fireman, after visiting a castle, is seemingly transformed into the owner of the castle and is recognized as such by the other characters in the story. "Wettlauf" (Race; translated as "The Obstacle Course") begins in the realm of the ordinary but rapidly degenerates into uncertainty. Faber, the main character, is chased by a doppelgänger who imitates his every action. After his attempts to elude his double fail, Faber decides to take out after him. The result is a chase "in hot pursuit of his own heels," representing Faber's attempt to regain his own identity and reestablish a definite frame of reference in order to escape the morass of possibilities into which he has fallen.

Manig, the hero of the story collection *Auftritt Manigs* (Enter Manig, 1963; translation included in *Obstacles*, 1966), is treated like a tracing powder that is thrown into turbulent water to expose hidden currents: Lettau uses Manig to iso-

late and depict behavioral patterns, only to cleverly undo them. Manig is portrayed predominantly through pantomime, and some of his gesticulations are clownlike. Manig's problem is that he mistakes the notion of an object for the thing itself; this confusion leads him to weigh notion and thing against each other until the objects lose their meaning entirely. Lettau disrupts reality by equating the thing with the word and the absolute with the relative, and by separating image from reality through leaps in logic and optical illusions. Manig's world, as compared to that of *Schwierigkeiten beim Häuserbauen*, is reduced to the smallest possible number of elements, and the broad descriptions used in *Schwierigkeiten beim Häuserbauen* shrink in *Auftritt Manigs* to bare suggestion.

Feinde (1968; translated as *Enemies*, 1973) draws from a larger realm of existence than *Auftritt Manigs* and picks up where *Schwierigkeiten beim Häuserbauen* leaves off. The witticisms in *Feinde* center around the question "Who is the 'enemy?'" This question was asked in the last story of *Schwierigkeiten beim Häuserbauen*, "Kampfpause" (translated as "Pause in the War"). War is ridiculed in *Feinde* as an extreme of human behavior and a general defect in human character.

Having proved himself a master of what O. F. Best calls the "arabeske Witz" (arabesque witticism) in *Auftritt Manigs* and *Feinde*, Lettau attempts to move into new territory as a social critic in *Täglicher Faschismus* (Daily Fascism, 1971). In this work freedom of expression, normally considered a characteristic of a free, democratic society, is depicted as having fascist qualities. Lettau presents a series of banalities drawn from newspapers to expose fascism in American society. His evidence fails to convince; the arbitrary selection and juxtaposition of items results in distortion.

In Lettau's earlier collections of stories a trend toward greater conciseness and brevity is evident. The title of *Immer kürzer werdende Geschichten & Gedichte & Porträts* (Shorter and Shorter Stories & Poems & Portraits, 1973), which combines *Schwierigkeiten beim Häuserbauen*, *Auftritt Manigs*, and *Feinde* with some additional stories, poems, and "portraits," indicates Lettau's use of a concentrated style to depict everyday events with such precision that hidden elements suddenly become obvious. The stories further attest to the author's refusal to accept unquestioningly the commonplace and the established.

Frühstücksgespräche in Miami is a series of forty-three scenes in which characters enter, speak their piece, and exit. The characters, deposed Latin American dictators living in an old hotel in Miami, are reminiscent of comic strip figures. *Frühstücksgespräche in Miami* ridicules dictators and the people who support them. The topical nature of the subject matter, however, proves to be a disadvantage to Lettau: his use of current political events places his witticisms on a ball and chain, and the capricious games played in earlier works are reduced to mere slogans.

Zerstreutes Hinausschaun (Scattered Observations, 1980) is a collection of essays, sketches, letters, and reviews originally published between 1965 and 1979 in newspapers and magazines. The unifying element in these heterogeneous literary and political pieces is the author's determination to take language literally. Lettau's method of getting closer to the truth is an objective, unemotional use of language, following Karl Kraus's dictum that language is not the handmaiden but the mother of ideas.

Lettau's *Gedichte* (Poems, 1968) contains pointed, witty occasional verse that cannot be fully understood unless the reader has some knowledge of the events referred to. Puns and thought-provoking games based on names, events, and situations lead to surprising combinations but end in platitudes. Here again, Lettau is most engaging when he takes thoughts and deeds literally and leads them to their absurd conclusions in wittily contrived games.

References:

Thomas I. Bacon, "Two from Germany," *Furman Studies*, 21, no. 4 (1974): 7-12;

Otto F. Best, "Reinhard Lettau oder über den 'arabesken Witz,' " *Basis*, 1 (1970): 89-98;

Christopher Harris, *Reinhard Lettau and His Use of the Grotesque* (Warwick, U.K.: University of Warwick, 1972).

E. Y. Meyer

(11 October 1946-)

Malcolm J. Pender
University of Strathclyde

BOOKS: *Ein Reisender in Sachen Umsturz: Erzählungen* (Frankfurt am Main: Suhrkamp, 1972; revised, 1983);

In Trubschachen: Roman (Frankfurt am Main: Suhrkamp, 1973);

Eine entfernte Ähnlichkeit: Erzählungen (Frankfurt am Main: Suhrkamp, 1975);

Die Rückfahrt: Roman (Frankfurt am Main: Suhrkamp, 1977);

Die Hälfte der Erfahrung: Essays und Reden (Frankfurt am Main: Suhrkamp, 1980);

Sundaymorning: Theaterstück, translated from Bern dialect into Swabian dialect by Wolfgang Kunz (Frankfurt am Main: Suhrkamp, 1981); republished in Bern dialect (Bern & Munich: Edition Erpf, 1984);

Plädoyer: Für die Erhaltung der Vielfalt der Natur beziehungsweise für deren Verteidigung gegen die ihr drohende Vernichtung durch die Einfalt des Menschen (Frankfurt am Main: Suhrkamp, 1982);

Das System: Theaterstück (Frankfurt am Main: Suhrkamp, 1983).

OTHER: "Bieler Tagebuch 1976," in *Literatur aus der Schweiz,* edited by Egon Amman and Eugen Faes (Zurich & Frankfurt am Main: Suhrkamp, 1978), pp. 73-104;

"Ein Buch für Winterabende," introduction to Robert Louis Stevenson, *Entführt, oder Die Erinnerungen des David Balfour an seine Abenteuer im Jahre 1752,* translated by Michael Walter (Frankfurt am Main: Insel, 1979);

"Max Frisch zum 70. Geburtstag," in *Begegnungen: Eine Festschrift für Max Frisch zum siebzigsten Geburtstag* (Frankfurt am Main: Suhrkamp, 1981), pp. 146-153;

"Das sprechende Tier oder Der nichtrationalisierbare Rest: Zu Edgar Allan Poe, seinem Gedicht *Der Rabe* und dem sich darauf beziehenden Essay 'Die Methode der Komposition,' " afterword to Edgar Allan Poe, *Der Rabe,* translated by Hans Wollschläger and Ursula Wernicke (Frankfurt am Main: Insel, 1981);

Geräusche: Eine Schweizer Anthologie, edited by Meyer and Beatrice Steiner (Karlsruhe: Literarische Gesellschaft [Scheffelbund] Karlsruhe, 1982).

PERIODICAL PUBLICATIONS: "Eine Art 100-Mark-Mißverständnis um zwei Hälften," *Schweizer Monatshefte,* 62 (January 1982): 53-57;

"Reise nach Sibirien," *Schweizer Monatshefte,* 66 (June 1986): 511-514.

Having started publishing in the 1970s, E. Y. Meyer belongs to the so-called third generation of German-Swiss writers since World War II–Max Frisch and Friedrich Dürrenmatt constituting the first generation, the writers who began publishing in the 1960s the second. Almost all of Meyer's fiction is set in precisely defined Swiss locations, but the problems he addresses transcend this local framework. Meyer's novels, stories, essays, and plays take issue with the development of the modern world. On the one hand, he believes that Western society in the second half of the twentieth century is the prisoner of an ethical outlook, derived from the philosophy of Immanuel Kant, which places exclusive emphasis on the duty of the individual to compete and to achieve; the idea that self-fulfillment may be attained through enjoyment of life and pleasure in what it offers is at best tolerated peripherally. The individual thus leads a life devoid of balance. On the other hand, the technological age has fostered an arrogance toward the nontechnological past, from which it thinks it has nothing to learn; the present has cut itself adrift from the continuity of human history. The material prosperity of the technological society creates a sense of security which is shown to be false by the individual's response to the stimuli which purport to cater to his needs but in fact create new desires. The solution is not, in Meyer's view, a matter of causing the pendulum to swing totally the other way–that is neither feasible nor desirable–but of creating an equilibrium between disorder and order, risk and security. Thus the Switzerland depicted in Meyer's writings, with its strong work ethic and its achievement of a level of prosperity which is the envy of its neighbors, far from being an example for emulation, represents a warning to the rest of the world. Meyer's work, especially his two novels, has attracted wide critical acclaim, and he is one of the most important and respected younger writers in Switzerland today.

Born on 11 October 1946 in Liestal, near Basel, to Jakob and Maria Fleig-Meyer, Peter Meyer calls himself E. Y. Meyer partly to distinguish himself from others with this common surname and partly to separate his role as a writer from his other roles. He spent the later part of his childhood and received his secondary education in Biel. He studied German history and philosophy at the University of Bern from 1967 to 1969 but broke off his studies to train as a primary-school teacher. In the 1960s his many-sided interest in the arts found expression not only in writing but in painting, filmmaking, and acting. He still produces impressive collages. On 29 May 1971 he married Gaby Martin; they were divorced on 5 July 1979. From 1971 to 1974 Meyer taught in a primary school near Bern. His first book, a collection of short stories, was published in 1972. After his first novel appeared in 1973, he resigned his teaching post to live by his writing. He has traveled widely, mainly in Europe and Scandinavia; in 1979 he lived in Israel, and in 1983 he spent three months in New York on a travel scholarship. Meyer lives in Bern with his second wife, the former Florica Malureanu, whom he married on 24 December 1985. He has won several literary prizes for his novels and plays, including the prestigious prize of the Swiss Schiller Foundation, awarded in 1984 in recognition of the quality of his entire oeuvre.

Meyer's life exemplifies the problems he portrays: his decision to relinquish his teaching job and accept the insecurity of a career as a writer reflects his belief in the existential necessity of risk in human life. The high seriousness of his resolve and his belief in the efficacy of writing as a means of combating the depredations of the world on the individual are reflected in his statement in 1982 that, having once lived and worked as a full-time writer, anything else would be for him "Ablenkung" (a distraction).

Ein Reisender in Sachen Umsturz (A Traveler in Matters of Subversion) attracted favorable critical attention in 1972 for its author's ability to show the dark depths which lie beneath the surface of everyday life: a man walking home one evening becomes involved in a bus journey which culminates in the collapse of a mountain; a worker on an outing discovers unexpected dimensions to a well-known tourist spot; a former patient of a psychiatric hospital learns of the forces of evil abroad in the countryside on Twelfth Night; a woman recounts a dream which has left her with "ein Gefühl des Nichtmehrzurückkönnens und des Alleinseins" (a feeling of being unable to get back and of being alone), a reaction common to all the protagonists of the stories after an irreversible dislocation of perceived reality experienced by each. The sense of disorientation is heightened for the reader by the pedantically precise descriptions of locality.

Full recognition of Meyer's talent came with the publication in 1973 of his first novel, *In Trubschachen*, the day-by-day account of a stay from 26 December to 3 January in the small town of Trubschachen in the Emmental. The central figure has come here partly for a change of scene, partly to advance a piece of academic work on Kant. The initial impact of the town and the orderly functioning and copious meals of the hotel induce feelings of well-being and confidence. Gradually, however, the protagonist's sense of control over his destiny is undermined. Subsequent observations lend ambiguity to the pristine images he encountered on his arrival; he learns of the economic forces that ruthlessly determine life in the surrounding valleys, of the alcoholism and incest there, and of the rigid social gradations and familial tensions in the town itself. Simultaneously, he becomes aware that he is making no progress with his work. As he leaves, he contemplates the miscarriage of his confident resolve against the constant reminders of the ephemerality and thralldom of human life he has experienced in the past week. The visual symbol of this new outlook is the town's little graveyard, visible from all the vantage points of his various walks, which has gradually come to make manifest the baselessness of the order and stability represented by the hotel.

The novel contains two discourses. "Emmentaler Rede" (Discourse on the Emmental), given by a local teacher, indicates how the geographical features of the area influence the lives of the inhabitants by shaping their traditions. "Rede von der Pflicht" (Discourse on Duty), given by the protagonist, examines the relationship between the unintegrated drives in the individual in modern society and the separation of duty and inclination in the philosophy of Kant; the discourse advocates the replacement of duty as the guiding principle in life by happiness. Both discourses, each of equal length, act by their positions in the novel as anchors in its formal structure and by their content as pointers to the determining influence on human life of environment and ethos.

The main feature of the novel's narrative technique is that the central figure is referred to at all times by the indefinite pronoun *man* (one). The device destroys the reader's expectation of a fictional reality by eliminating a sense of firm personal identity. At the same time, the doubt and ambiguity arising from this device convey to the reader the experience of the central figure and subvert the solid values usually associated with an idyll in the Swiss countryside. Trubschachen becomes the symbol of a larger world.

The three long short stories published in 1975 under the title *Eine entfernte Ähnlichkeit* (A Distant Resemblance) continue Meyer's investigation of the individual's tenuous relationship to experience. In the title story the writer, struck by the resemblance of an occupant of an old people's home to the Swiss author Robert Walser, makes the acquaintance of the old man, whose personality has little similarity to that of his supposed model; "Die Erhebung der Romanfiguren" (The Revolt of the Characters in the Novel) describes the mixed reaction of the people of a village to their portrayal in a writer's first novel (there is a clear parallel to the situation created by *In Trubschachen*); and in "Groß-Papa ist wieder da" (Grandad Is Back) the narrator reflects on the ambiguity of his knowledge about his grandparents and on what his personality owes to them. In all three stories the uncomplicated assumptions and easy certainties of everyday life contrast with the complexity of reality; yet the more precisely the individual seeks to picture reality to himself, the more he realizes that he is capable of creating only "a distant resemblance" to it.

Critics were virtually unanimous in welcoming Meyer's second novel, *Die Rückfahrt* (The Journey Back, 1977), as his major achievement; his previous works, one critic claimed, were the bricks from which this new great edifice was built. The dramatic opening dream of the hero, Albin Berger, symbolizes the dislocation of the individual in modern society: the cathedral of Bern, at the top of which Berger and his friend and mentor Effinger are standing, splits asunder between them; as both plunge earthward, Effinger roars

out an indistinct challenge to Berger to make something of himself. Berger awakes from the dream in the clinic in Lucerne where he has been receiving therapy: he was driving a car involved in an accident which killed Effinger and is suffering from amnesia and paralysis of his right hand. The first section of the novel takes place in the clinic, where a major part of Berger's therapy consists of lengthy philosophical discussions with the doctor in charge of his case. The second section is set in Italian Switzerland, where Berger goes to convalesce with his new girlfriend and to visit her mother, Ebet Thormann, an artist. Ebet embodies the harmonious relationship between the individual and his experience that had been discussed in the previous section. In this synthesis art has a central function: first, it provides a channel to the unconscious, whose integration into daily life is necessary for personal salvation; second, art is form, and it is the individual's ability to give shape to the inchoate nature of life which sustains and fulfills him. In this double sense, reality must be approached as the greatest work of art. The third section of the novel is Berger's written reconstruction of his life from the point at which, influenced by Effinger, who had been curator of monuments for the Canton of Bern, he decided to become a writer. It was shortly after making that decision that he had the fatal accident.

There are three main difficulties in Berger's relationship with society up to the point of the accident. First, there is a clash between his awareness that everything in life except death is relative and his observation of a society so persuaded of the absoluteness of its values that it can brook nothing but conformity. Second, the consumer society disorients its members by relentlessly creating desires for material things. Berger's gradual accumulation of technological gadgets–culminating in his acquisition of the fateful car–runs parallel to his mounting personal dilemma as he fails to find a role for himself in society: he abandons his teaching post because he feels unable to counter the propagation of false values to the children in his charge. Third, technological society, dissociated from its past, does not encourage the individual to live at one with his own past.

Die Rückfahrt has been seen by critics as a modern Bildungsroman; but whereas this genre traditionally had to do with the integration of the hero into a given society, *Die Rückfahrt* posits the idea that personal integration in Western society at the end of the twentieth century–of which Switzerland is here a microcosm–must take place *against* the prevailing social trends. Berger, like the protagonist of *In Trubschachen*, becomes a symbolic figure. He gradually recovers from the amnesia by confronting his past; his right hand slowly regains its functions so that he is able to commit his past to paper, thus re-creating his relationship to the world and actively forming a perception of life. Berger's journey through his past and origins and his shaping in words of this experience represent a way of neutralizing the alienation of modern life. The journey back is a necessary first step in what Effinger calls the task "das Leben . . . irgendwie sinnvoll hinter sich zu bringen" (of getting through life in some meaningful fashion). The circular structure of the novel, opening with the consequences of the accident and closing with the accident itself, reflects Berger's attempt to heal the rupture with the past symbolized by the splitting in two of the cathedral tower and points to the limitations of human achievement in a way which repudiates contemporary notions of progress.

A selection of Meyer's essays appeared in 1980 as *Die Hälfte der Erfahrung* (The Half of Experience). The title, taken from Goethe, suggests that empirical experience constitutes only half of experience because it becomes comprehensible only if it is related to an intellectual framework. But as Meyer points out, the whole experience which thus emerges is itself subject to the original limitation, so that a continuous process of synthesis takes place. It is the disregard for this subtle and vital process against which Meyer inveighs in a second collection of essays, *Plädoyer* (Plea, 1982). The major piece in this volume has to do with a large, modern concrete school situated in a featureless expanse of land near Bremen in West Germany. The place of education, with its menacing exterior and inhospitable interior, becomes, as it creates standardized patterns of behavior in those inside, a symbol of the simplifying deformations imposed on the complexity of life by modern society. The title of this collection refers to Meyer's plea for a restoration of the sophistication necessary to life, without which humans are robbed of their individuality and reduced to the level of witless monsters.

Meyer's lifelong interest in the theater is manifested in his two plays, *Sundaymorning* (1981) and *Das System* (The System, 1983), both of which have been awarded prizes. *Sundaymorning* addresses the question of how the artist, himself subject to the problems of life and the inescapable in-

fluences of the modern world, can present to his fellowmen, either in painting or in words, pictures deriving from a vision of the wholeness of life. The two heroes, a painter and a writer, are shown in three situations which highlight the pressures militating against their ability to produce such pictures. At the end, it is not clear whether one of them at least will be able to overcome these difficulties and rise to the act of synthesis. In contrast to the Swiss setting of *Sundaymorning*, against which, as in the novels, wider problems are discussed, *Das System* is set in a psychiatric clinic in the south of France and examines the concept of mental normality. It shows how the framework of any conceptual system designed to differentiate between normal and abnormal is not only bound to lack sufficient flexibility to cope with the flux of reality but also tends to set itself up as absolute. As in the novels, an innocent outsider becomes the medium through which the implications and effects of this conflict between reality and system are examined. In the play reality avenges itself by disrupting the artificial constraints a system seeks to impose and by restoring the balance lacking in such a system.

In the essay "Reisen nach Deutschland" (Journeys to Germany) in *Plädoyer* Meyer discusses his own background. His father was a Swiss from the border area where Switzerland adjoins Germany; his mother was a German from the other side of the border. Meyer, growing up on the Swiss side of the border, frequently went to Germany to visit his mother's relatives. He was thus able to observe both border areas, which were in some ways more similar to one another than to the centers of their respective countries yet at the same time bore unmistakable resemblances to those centers. Meyer suggests that borderlands are stimulating in a way that the secure center of a country can never be. The essay is a brilliant depiction of how his upbringing imparted to him the feelings for nuance and complexity of relationship that are reflected in his writing. Indeed, he calls writing a "Grenzland-Beruf" (profession of the borderland) and himself, although now living in Bern, still a "Grenzlandbewohner" (inhabitant of the borderland). In 1981 the critic Dieter Bachmann described Meyer as the "great outsider" in contemporary German-Swiss writing because he avoids ephemeral trends and modish views. But it might be more appropriate to hold to Meyer's concept of the borderland and to reflect on his characteristically circumscribed claim that those who live there "sehen von Natur aus sozusagen etwas mehr" (by nature see a little more, as it were).

References:
Dieter Bachmann, "Neue Schweizer (Heimat-) Literatur: Eine dritte Generation etabliert sich," *Die Weltwoche* (Zurich), 23 March 1972;
Bachmann, "Die Zertrümmerung des Gesichtsfeldes: Notizen zu E. Y. Meyer. Eine Vermißtenanzeige," *Tages-Anzeiger-Magazin* (Zurich), 81 (31 December 1981): 22-25;
Anton Krättli, "E. Y. Meyer," in *Kritisches Lexikon zur deutschsprachigen Gegenwartsliteratur,* edited by Heinz Ludwig Arnold (Munich: Edition text + kritik, 1983);
Betrice von Matt, ed., *E. Y. Meyer* (Frankfurt am Main: Suhrkamp, 1983).

Irmtraud Morgner

(22 August 1933-   )

Helga Slessarev
University of Cincinnati

BOOKS: *Das Signal steht auf Fahrt: Erzählung* (Berlin: Aufbau, 1959);
Ein Haus am Rand der Stadt: Roman (Berlin: Aufbau, 1962);
Hochzeit in Konstantinopel: Roman (Berlin & Weimar: Aufbau, 1968);
Gauklerlegende: Eine Spielfraungeschichte (Berlin: Eulenspiegel, 1970);
Die wundersamen Reisen Gustav des Weltfahrers: Lügenhafter Roman mit Kommentaren (Berlin & Weimar: Aufbau, 1972);
Leben und Abenteuer der Trobadora Beatriz nach Zeugnissen ihrer Spielfrau Laura: Roman in dreizehn Büchern und sieben Intermezzos (Berlin & Weimar: Aufbau, 1974);
Amanda: Ein Hexenroman (Berlin & Weimar: Aufbau, 1983);
Die Hexe im Landhaus (Zurich: Rauhreif, 1984).

OTHER: "Notturno: Erzählung," in *Neue Texte: Almanach für deutsche Literatur* (Berlin & Weimar: Aufbau, 1964), pp. 7-36;
"Sündhafte Behauptungen (Annemarie Auer)," "Vexierbild (Günter Kunert)," "Bootskauf (Ludwig Turek)," in *Liebes- und andere Erklärungen: Schriftsteller über Schriftsteller,* edited by Annie Voigtländer (Berlin & Weimar: Aufbau, 1972), pp. 13-16, 201-208, 371-376;
"Das Seil: Erzählung," in *Die Anti-Geisterbahn,* edited by Joachim Walther (Berlin: Der Morgen, 1973), pp. 147-157;
"Spielzeit: Erzählung," in *Der Weltkutscher und andere Geschichten für Kinder und große Leute,* edited by Frank Beer (Rostock: Hinstorff, 1973), pp. 70-73;
"Diskussionsbeitrag zur Arbeitsgruppe II 'Literatur und Geschichtsbewußtsein,'" in *VII. Schriftstellerkongreß der Deutschen Demokratischen Republik: Protokoll (Arbeitsgruppen)* (Berlin & Weimar: Aufbau, 1974), pp. 112-113;
"Bis man zu dem Kerne zu gelangen das Glück hat: Zufallsbegünstigte Aufzeichnungen über den Oberbauleiter vom Palast der Republik nebst Adjutanten und Ehefrau," in *Bekanntschaften,* edited by Alice Uscoreit (Berlin & Weimar: Aufbau, 1976), pp. 36-60.

PERIODICAL PUBLICATION: "Rede auf dem VIII. Schriftstellerkongreß der DDR," *Neue Deutsche Literatur,* 8 (1978): 27-32.

On the basis of her novels *Leben und Abenteuer der Troubadour Beatriz nach Zeugnissen ihrer Spielfrau Laura* (Life and Adventures of the Trobadour Beatriz as Chronicled by Her Minstrel Laura, 1974) and *Amanda* (1983), Irmtraud Morgner must be considered one of the outstand-

Irmtraud Morgner (photograph by Isolde Ohlbaum, Munich)

engineer inspired the creation of characters in several of her novels. Literature did not play a role in her childhood until the age of twelve, when she discovered a suitcase filled with paperback editions of classical German literature in the attic. She studied literature at the University of Leipzig from 1952 to 1956, then became an editor of *Neue Deutsche Literatur*. She left the magazine in 1958 to pursue a career as a free-lance writer. She was married to the lyricist Paul Wien, who died in 1982; they had one child. Morgner now lives in East Berlin.

According to her most sympathetic critic in the GDR, Annemarie Auer, Morgner's early production, such as the story *Das Signal steht auf Fahrt* (The Signal Is Down for the Train, 1959), indicated that she was "stark im Glauben" (strong in faith); that is, she tried to live up to the dictates of socialist realism. For example, in her second published work, the novel *Ein Haus am Rand der Stadt* (A House on the Edge of the City, 1962), she depicted a bricklayers' brigade and the influence of work on changing consciousness. Her real strength, however, became apparent only after the Twentieth Party Congress of the Soviet Communist party in 1956 and the subsequent reinterpretation of the Stalin era. The initial disenchantment of Morgner's generation is depicted in her novel "Rumba auf einen Herbst" (Rumba Dedicated to an Autumn), which was written in 1964 but never published independently because its point of view was not tolerated by the East German Socialist Unity party (SED) at the time. Parts of the work are, however, inserted in *Leben und Abenteuer der Trobadora Beatriz nach Zeugnissen ihrer Spielfrau Laura*, which may be the most comprehensive introduction to life in the GDR ever written. Before the publication of this novel, a few shorter novels and narratives appeared in which Morgner seemed to be testing her new approach by imitating storytellers like Scheherazade, Laurence Sterne, and E. T. A. Hoffmann.

Bele H., the heroine of *Hochzeit in Konstantinopel* (Wedding in Constantinople, 1968), entertains her lover with a different story each day for twenty-one days. In these stories she mixes everyday reality–for example, the life of her grandmother–with whimsical elements such as her dream of flying in a hospital bed. Paul's mathematical mind has no appreciation for such fantasies; he clings to his philosophy of achievement through science and self-discipline: "Er glaubte, daß sie ihn liebte, weil er ein begabter

ing narrative talents in German literature today. She combines the tradition of romantic imagination and poetic theory with that of the picaresque novel in works that are often fantastic or whimsical but at other times strongly realistic. Portrayals of life and personalities in the German Democratic Republic (GDR) are interwoven with imaginary figures and scenes drawn from various literary traditions to highlight the shortcomings of present conditions, particularly regarding relationships between the sexes, or to present utopian models yet to be achieved. The seriousness of her concern with questions of war and peace, society, and technological development is offset by the humor and playfulness of her presentation. The preciseness of her language gives the reader the feeling of seeing things just as they are in spite of Morgner's distortions of reality.

Irmtraud Morgner was born in 1933 in Chemnitz, which was renamed Karl-Marx-Stadt in 1953. Her father's occupation as a locomotive

Wissenschaftler war. Sie liebte ihn, weil er ein begabter Liebhaber war, Gedanken hatte sie notfalls selbst" (He believed that she loved him because he was a gifted scientist. She loved him because he was a gifted lover; if ideas were needed, she had them herself). In the end she leaves him to pursue "das absolute Experiment" (the absolute experiment).

While *Hochzeit in Konstantinopel* is preceded by a verse from the Goliardic song collection *Carmina Burana* (1937), Morgner's next novel, *Gauklerlegende* (Juggler Legend, 1970), is introduced by a minstrel's prayer for a full experience of love. The story of Wanda and Hubert, written in very simple language, tells about Wanda's love affair with a juggler who steps out of the dollhouse display in a museum and reappears first among the booths of the Christmas fair, then at a conference Hubert is attending. At one point he glances out of Hubert's own body–making the reader wonder whether he is less the antagonist of Hubert, whose work deals with the theory of play, than his alter ego. The story ends with the marriage of Hubert and Wanda and the fairytale cliché, "und wenn sie nicht gestorben sind, leben sie heute noch glücklich und zufrieden" (and if they have not died, they are still living happily and contentedly today).

While *Gauklerlegende* expresses the youthful dream of not being bound by the realism of a society lacking in playful imagination and adventure, *Die wundersamen Reisen Gustav des Weltfahrers* (The Marvelous Journeys of Gustav the World Traveler, 1972) represents the longing of the older generation to expand its horizons. Bele H., the heroine of *Hochzeit in Konstantinopel,* is the narrator. According to her, "Großvater Gustav war von Kultur ein Lügner, nicht von Natur. In ihm arbeitete die Schöpferkraft der Machtlosen. Zu ungeduldig, um warten zu können, eignete er sich die Welt an, bevor sie ihm errungen war" (Grandfather Gustav was a liar not by nature but as a result of his culture. The creative force of the powerless was working in him. Too impatient to wait, he appropriated the world before it had been conquered for him). The novel's motto, taken from Jean Paul's *Leben des vergnügten Schulmeisterleins Maria Wuz* (Life of the Cheerful Schoolmaster Maria Wuz, 1793; translated as "Maria Wuz," 1881), points to the literary forerunner of the hero. Gustav, a retired railroad engineer, takes an old locomotive on trips to the lands of the Siamese Cats, the Amazons (at the Amazon River), and a tyrannical order in Asia,

and to the sexless society of the planet Feribdol. The equipment for this last trip into space is awarded to Gustav by the Soviet Union in recognition of his service to imagination. At the time Morgner wrote the novel, a general reconsideration of imaginative writing and a rehabilitation of romanticism was taking place in the GDR.

Morgner's narrative genius, which first emerged in individual segments of *Hochzeit in Konstantinopel,* became fully evident in 1974 with the publication of *Leben und Abenteuer der Trobadora Beatriz nach Zeugnissen ihrer Spielfrau Laura.* This formidable novel won great acclaim from critics and scholars, who discovered references to a large part of the German cultural tradition and compared the work to Grimmelshausen's *Der abenteuerliche Simplicissimus Teutsch* (1669; translated as *The Adventurous Simplizissimus,* 1912), Goethe's *Wilhelm Meisters Wanderjahre* (1829; translated as "Wilhelm Meister's Travels," 1840), or Thomas Mann's Joseph novels or *Doktor Faustus* (1947; translated as *Doctor Faustus,* 1948). They saw it, in conjunction with Christa Wolf's stress on the imagination in *Lesen und Schreiben* (1968; translated as *The Reader and the Writer,* 1977) and Anna Seghers's *Sonderbare Begegnungen* (Strange Encounters, 1973), as the beginning of a new literary development in the GDR. In the last story in *Sonderbare Begegnungen* Seghers imagines a meeting of Gogol, E. T. A. Hoffmann, and Kafka in Prague–a meeting possible only if historical time is suspended in favor of poetic invention, as Hoffmann had demanded. Such departures from strict socialist realism characterize several East German writings of recent years, but none more than Morgner's *Leben und Abenteuer der Trobadora Beatriz nach Zeugnissen ihrer Spielfrau Laura* and *Amanda.*

Beatriz, the Comtessa de Dia, one of the few woman troubadours, has been kept alive in the fashion of Sleeping Beauty for 810 years. Her own time had deeply disappointed her longing for equality as a woman artist. Persephone had allowed her 810 years of sleep in exchange for her promise to work for a matriarchal society afterward. In the meantime, however, Beatriz's sister-in-law Melusine had kept her informed about the goings-on in the world by means of hypnosis and enlisted her in the opposition within Persephone's organization. Beatriz will, therefore, strive not for a matriarchy but for a sexually equal society. After a cruel awakening in 1968 at the hands of a highway construction crew, Beatriz travels through the south of France to Paris and discovers that the emancipation of women is still in the future. A German journalist, Uwe Parnitzke, tells her about "the promised land," the GDR, and she moves there in the hope of pursuing her profession as a woman troubadour. But even the GDR turns out to be a male-dominated society, and her impatience makes her appear fanatical compared to Parnitzke's ex-wife Laura Salman, a former student of literature and now a subway-train engineer and single mother. (Critics have said that in her treatment of Laura and her son Wesselin, Morgner gives the most touching and realistic description of a mother-child relationship and the best portrait of a child in German literature). Beatriz engages Laura as her minstrel, to seek contracts for the literary works the two women will produce. Laura's stories are interspersed throughout the novel; a montage is thereby created, as indicated by the subtitle *Roman in dreizehn Büchern und sieben Intermezzos* (Novel in Thirteen Books and Seven Intermezzi).

The intermezzi are the segments of the earlier novel "Rumba auf einen Herbst" and tell the story of Laura's former husband, Uwe Parnitzke, a journalist struggling with the political changes after Stalin's death and with the meaning of some scientific research on which he is supposed to report. His own insecurities had made him jealous of Laura's accomplishments and had led to their divorce. The intermezzi also offer background information about the androgynous Benno Pakulat, who is introduced to Laura by Melusine and becomes Laura's second husband. Laura sends Beatriz on a tour of southern Europe to search for the unicorn, the powder of whose horn mixed in the drinking water would induce people to love each other. This would be a more beneficial approach than the bombs and other revolutionary tools favored by Beatriz. Beatriz fails in her quest, returning not with a unicorn but with a little dog.

The juxtaposition of different historical times and of societies with different ideologies, as well as fairy-tale elements, enable Morgner to show the developments still needed before humanity will fulfill its potential. This literary strategy is similar to that of romantics such as Jean Paul and Hoffmann. But there are also many realistically drawn passages, such as the stories of Laura's and Benno's fathers, whose dedication to work is now almost outdated because of technological advances and changes in the attitudes of the young: Johann Salman's last trip on his locomotive *Pauline* is described with great sensitivity. An-

Morgner in 1976 (photograph by Peter Probst, courtesy of Ullstein Bilderdienst)

other story tells of a woman scientist who can only combine her career with her housework by flying through the air in order to save time; reprimanded by her colleagues, she loses her self-confidence and plunges to her death. This story adumbrates Beatriz's death from a fall while washing windows. She has assumed more and more of Laura's household duties; since Laura has taken on more and more of Beatriz's original tasks, the latter seems no longer to be needed. On the day of Beatriz's funeral Laura reads aloud the story of Valeska Kantus, a nutrition expert who changed her sex. She was able to retain her female consciousness and to return to her female form during lovemaking but otherwise enjoyed full recognition of her work and her husband's participation in household duties.

The underlying theme of the novel is the attempt to write history from the point of view of women without excluding a strong sensitivity for male experiences. The contrast between the two types of experience is expressed when Melusine interviews the Russian chess champion Solowjew, who explains his extraordinary accomplishments as the consequence of the exclusion of all other interests; this fanaticism can also be found in outstanding scientists and artists and projects, so the argument goes, a peculiarly male attitude. To women Solowjew ascribes an intellectual realism which might bring equally outstanding results of a different kind. A few pages later, in a conversation with the chief editor of the Aufbau publishing house, Laura links the structure of women's writing to their life-style: women must find time for their writing between such activities as housework and child care, and so their prose is pressed forth like the air from a pneumatic hammer. The montage of short pieces that make up the novel thus expresses the truth of the writer's life. The novel received the Heinrich Mann Prize of the East German Academy of Arts.

In 1983 Morgner published a 139-chapter sequel to *Leben und Abenteuer der Trobadora Beatriz nach Zeugnissen ihrer Spielfrau Laura* with the title *Amanda: Ein Hexenroman* (Amanda: A Witches' Novel). Here Beatriz has come back to life as a siren in the shape of an owl with a woman's head. She has lost her voice and lives hidden in the Berlin Zoo rewriting Irmtraud Morgner's one-sided story of Laura Salman. Additional material for the story comes from the Brocken archives furnished to Beatriz by Isebel, the leader of a faction of witches in Hörselberg. The novel's motto is taken from E. T. A. Hoffmann, and its structure is equally indebted to him. But the description of the Brocken region is inspired by the tradition of Tannhäuser as well as Goethe's *Faust* (1808, 1832; translated, 1838) and other legendary and historical sources. Morgner pays tribute to Goethe's verse play *Pandora* (1810), which, in the relationship between Prometheus and Pandora, foreshadows a better mankind. In her own novel, however, this goal is not reached; the struggle of the human forces against the old hierarchies of angels and devils ends in disaster.

Both realms, the angelic and the satanic, represent the tradition of patriarchism. The women's organizations struggling against these realms in the GDR and in the imaginary Brocken region do not agree on strategy: Isebel's faction strives for the destruction of men and the establishment of a matriarchy, while another witches' group, led by Amanda, hopes to free men and women and to reunite each person with the part of herself or himself that had to be suppressed. This notion that people are split into one half which conforms to society and a more creative and imaginative suppressed half underlies the

structure of the novel because Amanda is the other half of which Laura had been deprived during her student years. At that time Laura had lived with Konrad Tenner but had not been ready to marry and have children. After Chief-Devil Kolbruk cut off her rebellious half–Amanda–Laura became the willing worker and homemaker depicted by Morgner; but Tenner lost interest in her. Amanda has since resided in Hörselberg; she intends to be reunited with Laura and has actually written Laura's segments of *Leben und Abenteuer der Trobadora Beatriz nach Zeugnissen ihrer Spielfrau Laura*.

Laura herself has been interested in alchemical experiments since her youth. Recognizing the role supportive women have played for men, she has been trying to conjure up Orplid, the fantastic island of Eduard Mörike's novel *Maler Nolten* (Painter Nolten, 1832) as a support system. Because of limitations on her time, she advertises for an assistant and hires Konrad Tenner's present wife, Vilma, who has postponed her rebelliousness until age forty. With her help Laura tries to create an elixir that could serve as a substitute for sleep–she still does not know how to cope with her work, her personal interests, and Wesselin's needs–but she invents instead a "phoenix elixir" which brings her back to life after she commits suicide.

Between the two novels Benno Pakulat had become jealous of Laura's relationship to Amanda and had turned to drink. After his death in a car accident, Laura develops relationships with several other men. Konrad Tenner turns out to be something like the "eternal male," a ghostwriter for the patriarchy represented by the Chief-Angel Zacharias and the Chief-Devil Kolbruk, who both try to win Laura's favor. Tenner is set against Heinrich Fakal, who is conscious of his two halves and willing to help Laura steal the potion that can bring about the reunification of the split selves of all humans. But he is betrayed by Tenner, and the ending is a parody of *Faust:* Laura laments Heinrich, and a voice from the background states "Er ist gerichtet" (He has been sentenced). There is no final "ist gerettet" (has been saved), and in the last chapter the witches are driven out of Berlin.

Morgner has announced plans to expand the two volumes into a trilogy, but it would appear to be difficult to sustain the themes of the second volume, particularly since Morgner, like Christa Wolf in *Kassandra* (1983; translated as *Cassandra: A Novel and Four Essays*, 1984), has begun to link the issue of patriarchal power within modern societies with those of war and peace among the superpowers and the threat of atomic war.

Interviews:

Joachim Walther, "Irmtraud Morgner," *Meinetwegen Schmetterlinge* (Berlin: Der Morgen, 1973), pp. 42-54;

Ursual Krechel, "Das eine tun und das andere nicht lassen," *konkret*, no. 8 (1976): 43-45;

Gabi Swiderski, "Der Planet braucht Hexen: Interview mit Irmtraud Morgner," *Rote Blätter*, no. 4 (1983): 65-67;

Eva Kaufmann, "Interview," *Weimarer Beiträge*, 30 (1984): 1494-1514.

References:

Matthias Altenburg, "Stimme auf Buchseiten," *konkret*, no. 5 (1983): 97-99;

Annemarie Auer, "Trobadora unterwegs oder Schulung in Realismus," in her *Erleben—erfahren—schreiben* (Halle: Mitteldeutscher Verlag, 1977), pp. 286-342;

Christel Berger, "Fragen der Moral und die neueste Prosaliteratur der DDR," *Deutsche Zeitschrift für Philosophie*, 25, no. 8 (1977): 984-993;

Sigrid Damm, "Irmtraud Morgner: *Leben und Abenteuer...*," *Weimarer Beiträge*, 21, no. 9 (1975): 138-148;

F. C. Delius, "Ich habe gelesen," *konkret*, no. 5 (1975): 43;

Jürgen Engler, "Die wahre Lüge der Kunst. Irmtraud Morgner: 'Amanda,'" *Neue Deutsche Literatur*, 31, no. 7 (1983): 135-144;

Hans Jürgen Geerdts, "Die Arbeiterklasse in unserer neuesten epischen Literatur," *Neue Deutsche Literatur*, 8, no. 7 (1960): 117-141;

Patricia Herminghouse, "Die Frau und das Phantastische in der neueren DDR-Literatur: Der Fall Irmtraud Morgner," in *Die Frau als Heldin und Autorin: Neue kritische Ansätze zur deutschen Literatur*, edited by Wolfgang Paulsen (Bern & Munich: Francke, 1979), pp. 248-266;

Sonja Hilzinger, *"Als ganzer Mensch zu leben...," Emanzipatorische Tendenzen in der neueren Frauen-Literatur der DDR* (Frankfurt am Main, Bern & New York: Lang, 1985), pp. 126-151;

Helmut Hirsch, "Scherz, Ironie und tiefere Bedeutung," *Neue Deutsche Literatur*, 21, no. 8 (1973): 140-143;

Peter Hölzle, "Der abenteuerliche Umgang der Irmtraud Morgner mit der Trobairitz de Dia," in *Mittelalter-Rezeption,* edited by Jürgen Kühnel and others (Göppingen: Kümmerle, 1979), pp. 430-445;

Sheila K. Johnson, "A New Irmtraud Morgner: Humor, Fantasy, Structures, and Ideas in *Amanda: Ein Hexenroman*," in *Studies in GDR Culture and Society, 4: Selected Papers from the Ninth New Hampshire Symposium on the German Democratic Republic*, edited by Margy Gerber (Lanham, Md.: University Press of America, 1984), pp. 45-64;

Eva Kaufmann, "Der Hölle die Zunge rausstekken ... Der Weg der Erzählerin Irmtraud Morgner," *Weimarer Beiträge*, 30 (1984): 1515-1532;

Werner Liersch, "Erzählen im Ensemble," *Neue Deutsche Literatur*, 17, no. 8 (1969): 158-160;

Biddy Martin, "Irmtraud Morgners 'Leben und Abenteuer der Trobadora Beatriz,'" in *Beyond the Eternal Feminine: Critical Essays on Women and German Literature*, edited by Susan Cocalis and Kay Goodman (Stuttgart: Heinz, 1982), pp. 421-439;

Martin, "Socialist Partriarchy and the Limits of Reform: A Reading of Irmtraud Morgner's Life and Adventures of Troubadora Beatriz as Chronicled by Her Minstrel Laura," *Studies in Twentieth Century Literature*, 5 (Fall 1980): 59-74;

Werner Neubert, "Aus einem Gutachten," *Neue Deutsche Literatur*, 22, no. 8 (1974): 103-105;

Neubert, "Satire im sozialistischen Roman," *Sinn und Form*, 17, no. 1 (1965): 66-80;

Ingeborg Nordmann, "Die halbierte Geschichtsfähigkeit der Frau: Zu Irmtraud Morgners Roman 'Leben und Abenteuer der Trobadora Beatriz nach Zeugnissen ihrer Spielfrau Laura,'" in *DDR-Roman und Literaturgesellschaft*, edited by Jos Hoogevenn and Gerd Labroisse (Amsterdam: Rodopi, 1981), pp. 419-462;

Klara Obermüller, "Irmtraud Morgner," in *Neue Literatur der Frauen: Deutschsprachige Autorinnen der Gegenwart*, edited by Heinz Puknus (Munich: Beck, 1980), pp. 178-185;

"Pariser Gespräch über die Prosa der DDR," *Sinn und Form*, 28, no. 6 (1976): 1164-1192;

Klaus Schuhmann, "Auf der Suche nach dem 'wirklichen Blau,'" in *Selbsterfahrung als Welterfahrung*, edited by Schuhmann and Horst Nalewski (Berlin & Weimar: Aufbau, 1981), pp. 136-148;

Alice Schwarzer, "Auch Genossen sind nicht automatisch Brüder," *konkret*, no. 9 (1976): 57-58;

Jürgen Serke, "Eine Feministin, die Männer nicht aufgibt," in his *Frauen schreiben: Ein neues Kapitel deutschsprachiger Literatur* (Hamburg: Gruner & Jahr, 1979), pp. 292-294;

Sigrid Töpelmann, "Hausbesitzerseele contra Arbeiterseele," *Neue Deutsche Literatur*, 11, no. 6 (1963): 159-162;

Paul Wiens, "Märchenreise ins Morgnerland samt vier legendenwiderlegenden Männerreden," in his *Liebes- und andere Erklärungen* (Berlin & Weimar: Aufbau, 1972), pp. 242-251;

Gerhard Wolf, "Abschied von der Harmonie," *Sinn und Form*, 27, no. 4 (1975): 840-846;

Manfred Wolter, "Trobadora startbereit," *Sinn und Form*, 29, no. 1 (1977): 207-209.

Adolf Muschg

(13 May 1934-   )

Judith Ricker-Abderhalden
University of Arkansas

BOOKS: *Im Sommer des Hasen: Roman* (Zurich: Arche, 1965);

Gegenzauber: Roman (Zurich: Arche, 1967);

Rumpelstilz: Ein kleinbürgerliches Trauerspiel (Zurich: Arche, 1968);

Fremdkörper: Erzählungen (Zurich: Arche, 1968);

Das Kerbelgericht: Hörspiel (Zurich: Arche, 1969);

Mitgespielt: Roman (Zurich: Arche, 1969);

Papierwände: Aufsätze über Japan (Bern: Kandelaber, 1970);

Die Aufgeregten von Goethe: Politisches Drama in 40 Auftritten (Zurich: Arche, 1971);

Liebesgeschichten (Frankfurt am Main: Suhrkamp, 1972);

High Fidelity oder Ein Silberblick: Szenario (Basel: Lenos, 1973);

Albissers Grund: Roman (Frankfurt am Main: Suhrkamp, 1974);

Der blaue Mann: Erzählungen (Berlin: Volk und Welt, 1974);

Von Herwegh bis Kaiseraugst: Wie halten wir es als Demokraten mit unserer Freiheit? (Zurich: Limmat, 1975);

Entfernte Bekannte: Erzählungen (Frankfurt am Main: Suhrkamp, 1976);

Gottfried Keller: Ein literarisches Porträt (Munich: Kindler, 1977);

Besuch in der Schweiz: Erzählungen, edited by Heinz F. Schafroth (Stuttgart: Reclam, 1978);

Noch ein Wunsch: Erzählung (Frankfurt am Main: Suhrkamp, 1979);

Besprechungen 1961-1979, edited by Jean François Bergier (Basel, Boston & Stuttgart: Birkhäuser, 1980);

Baiyun oder die Freundschaftsgesellschaft: Roman (Frankfurt am Main: Suhrkamp, 1980);

Literatur als Therapie? Ein Exkurs über das Heilsame und das Unheilbare (Frankfurt am Main: Suhrkamp, 1981);

Die Tücke des verbesserten Objekts (Bern: Im Waldgut, 1981);

Leib und Leben (Frankfurt am Main: Suhrkamp, 1982);

Übersee: Drei Hörspiele (Stuttgart: Reclam, 1982);

Ausgewählte Erzählungen 1962-1982 (Frankfurt am Main: Suhrkamp, 1983);

Blue Man & Other Stories, translated by Marlis Zeller Cambon and Michael Hamburger (Manchester, U.K.: Carcanet New Press, 1983; New York: Braziller, 1985)—comprises "The Scythe Man *or* The Homestead," "Blue Man," "Reparations *or* Making Good," "Brämi's View," "Grandfather's Little Pleasure," "What Else?";

Das Licht und der Schlüssel: Erziehungsroman eines Vampirs (Frankfurt am Main: Suhrkamp, 1984); translated by Patricia Crampton as *The Light and the Key* (New York: Braziller, 1988);

Adolf Muschg (photograph by Isolde Ohlbaum, Munich)

Unterlassene Anwesenheit: Erzählungen (Leipzig: Reclam, 1984);

Empörung durch Landschaften: Vernünftige Drohreden (Zurich: Rauhreif, 1985);

Goethe als Emigrant: Auf der Suche nach dem Grünen bei einem alten Dichter (Frankfurt am Main: Suhrkamp, 1986);

Der Turmhahn und andere Liebesgeschichten (Frankfurt am Main: Suhrkamp, 1987);

Deshima: Filmbuch (Frankfurt am Main: Suhrkamp, 1987).

OTHER: Donald Barthelme, *Unsägliche Praktiken, unnatürliche Akte*, translated by Muschg and Hanna Muschg (Frankfurt am Main: Suhrkamp, 1969);

Erwin Fieger, *Japan: Sunrise-Islands*, texts by Muschg (Düsseldorf: Accidentia, 1971);

"Kellers Abend: Ein Stück aus dem 19. Jahrhundert," in *Spectaculum 23* (Frankfurt am Main: Suhrkamp, 1975), pp. 40-53;

Fritz Zorn, *Mars*, foreword by Muschg (Munich: Kindler, 1977); translated as afterword in Zorn, *Mars*, translated by Robert and Rita Kimber (New York: Knopf, 1982);

Johann Wolfgang von Goethe, *Wilhelm Meisters Wanderjahre*, afterword by Muschg (Frankfurt am Main: Insel, 1982).

Adolf Muschg, one of the few Swiss authors to have had a major impact on German literature since Max Frisch and Friedrich Dürrenmatt, is considered one of the best storytellers now writing in German. He made his literary debut at the age of thirty-one with his novel *Im Sommer des Hasen* (The Summer of the Hare, 1965), which received the kind of critical attention generally reserved for works of major, well-established writers. The novel was reviewed in all leading newspapers in Germany and Switzerland and became an instant best-seller, and its author, who was awarded several literary prizes for it, was hailed as an important new talent. Thus Muschg established himself in Germany, where the reputations of Swiss authors are generally made or lost, with his first work.

Muschg was born on 13 May 1934 to Friedrich Adolf and Frieda Anna Ernst Muschg in the wealthy community of Zollikon, the "Gold Coast" of Lake Zurich. He grew up in rather modest, lower-middle-class circumstances in a somewhat puritanical and repressive home atmosphere. In his revealing Frankfurt lectures, published as *Literatur als Therapie? Ein Exkurs über das Heilsame und das Unheilbare* (Literature as Therapy? An Excursus on the Wholesome and the Incurable, 1981), he introduces himself as the only child of a teacher and a nurse twenty-six years her husband's junior. His father, who was almost at retirement age when his son was born and apparently was often mistaken for the boy's grandfather, was not particularly close to his son. Walter Muschg, the renowned Germanist, and Elsa Muschg, author of youth books, were Adolf Muschg's considerably older half brother and half sister. One of Muschg's lasting memories of his early childhood is that of perpetual silence in the house, a silence imposed by the father and interrupted only by the clatter of his typewriter. Muschg was twelve years old when his father died.

According to his own testimony, Muschg grew up under the strong influence of his mother. For this pious, self-effacing woman with great expectations for her only offspring, he had to be the perfect son. Apparently she had a strong desire to nurture, and Muschg learned early to view illness as a means of gaining love. Not surprisingly, hypochondria came to play a dominant role in his life and works.

Muschg began his high school education in 1946 at a boarding school in Schiers and completed it in 1953 at the gymnasium in Zurich. From 1953 until 1959 he studied German literature, English, and psychology at the University of Zurich and at Cambridge University. He wrote his doctoral thesis on Ernst Barlach under the direction of Emil Staiger and received his Ph.D. from the University of Zurich in 1959. He taught at a high school in Zurich from 1959 until 1962, at the International Christian University in Tokyo from 1962 until 1964, at the University of Göttingen from 1964 until 1967, at Cornell University from 1967 to 1969, and at the University of Geneva in 1969-1970. Since 1970 he has been professor of German literature at the Federal Institute in Zurich. He lives in Kilchberg with his wife, the writer Hanna Johansen, whom he married in 1967, and their two sons, Philipp Jonathan and Benjamin Niklas. Muschg also has a son, Conrad Michael, from a previous marriage.

Since the mid 1960s Muschg has been keenly interested in politics and has become a prominent public figure in Switzerland and, to a lesser extent, in Germany. He is a frequent commentator on a wide range of social and political issues. In the late 1960s and early 1970s he took a particular interest in the student protest movement, an interest reflected in several of his works. He is an active member of the Social Democratic party and ran unsuccessfully for election to the Ständerat (the body that represents the cantons in the Swiss federal government) in 1975. From 1974 until 1977 he served on the federal commission that revised the Swiss constitution. Most recently, he has been a vocal critic of the Swiss government's policies concerning refugees from third world nations who seek political asylum in Switzerland.

Im Sommer des Hasen is based on Muschg's experiences in Japan from 1962 until 1964, although the events in the novel are largely fictitious. According to the oriental calendar, 1962 was the Year of the Hare, which is said to favor love. One of the longer subplots in the novel involves a tender love story between a married Swiss man and a Japanese girl; in 1987 Muschg developed this story into a screenplay titled *Deshima*. But the book is not so much about Japan as about various individuals' reactions to a foreign culture. The same holds true for Muschg's novel *Baiyun oder die Freundschaftsgesellschaft* (Baiyun; or, The Friendship Society, 1980), which he wrote after a brief journey to China.

In *Im Sommer des Hasen* a Swiss company celebrating the one hundredth anniversary of its representation in Japan invites six young men to spend half a year in that country if they agree to write up their experiences as contributions to a commemorative volume. The men, joined by Bischof, the company's public relations officer, spend the last week of their trip at a Japanese resort, where they read and discuss each other's contributions. All of this is related by Bischof, three weeks after his return from Japan, in the form of a lengthy report which doubles as a letter of resignation. The narrator introduces the six individuals, describes his relationship to them and their relationships to each other, reproduces their contributions, and relates the group's reactions to the contributions. He also reveals a great deal about his lower-middle-class background and career aspirations, the business world, academia, the consumer society, hypochondria, homosexuality, time, death, and the process of writing. The reasons for Bischof's resigning are never made clear; in fact, he apologizes for having gone to such length in explaining himself in the letter (that is, the novel) without providing an answer. It seems that he wants to start a new life and to live more fully.

Although the novel won critical praise not only for Muschg's eloquence and superb style but also for his powers of observation and analytical intellect, some reservations were voiced concerning the book's form. The structure was perceived to be a somewhat artificial one designed to tie together a multiplicity of loosely connected short prose pieces. Some critics suspected that Muschg's real strength lay in short prose. A few years later, when Muschg began to publish volume upon volume of superb short stories, these critics were vindicated.

Muschg realized how fortunate he had been with his first novel when his subsequent two novels, *Gegenzauber* (Counterforce, 1967) and *Mitgespielt* (1969), did not produce very favorable responses. In fact, Muschg was unable to dupli-

Miyoko Akaza as Tae, Leon Askin as Frank Nievergelt, and Marius Müller-Westernhagen as Patrick Goßler in a scene from
Deshima, *a 1987 film based on an episode from* Im Sommer des Hasen, *Muschg's autobiographical first novel. Muschg wrote
the screenplay for the film, which was directed by Beat Kuert.*

cate his earlier success until *Liebesgeschichten* (Love
Stories) appeared in 1972.

Gegenzauber is a rather lengthy satirical
novel that chronicles the fates of an old house in
suburban Zurich called the "Soldanella" and of a
group of young people who attempt, by an imaginative hoax, to save it from destruction. The
house is to be torn down to make room for a
new highway. The countercultural "Soldanella"
community loses in its confrontation with the establishment and is ultimately expelled from its
"Garden of Eden," but not until it has its fun at
the expense of its formidable opponent.

Muschg indicates in the preface to his third
novel that *Mitgespielt* was an outgrowth of a 1959
writing project in which his students were to describe the murder of a high school teacher. More
than ten years later Muschg completed the project. The title is a play on words: *Mitspielen* means
both "to take part in a game" and "to play a dirty
trick on someone." The novel is a mystery involving a middle-aged homosexual teacher of German history and his class. When one of the students disappears under suspicious circumstances,

the teacher becomes a prime suspect for murder.
As it turns out, he is a victim of sorts himself and
dies a "natural" death while sunbathing.

These two novels met with considerable skepticism. Terms used affirmatively in connection
with Muschg's first novel–eloquence, linguistic
virtuosity–became grounds for criticism. To
many critics Muschg's facility with language all
too often became an end in itself, to the detri-
ment of the subject matter. It is true that these
early works suffer from occasional effusiveness,
verbosity, and lack of substance, whereas his later
ones, particularly his short stories, are exemplary
for their great restraint and depth.

Muschg, looking for unobtrusive language
that neither detracted from his subject nor covered it up, first found an adequate style in the volume of short stories *Fremdkörper* (Foreign Objects,
1968). It marked a new beginning in his writing:
a clear-cut move from prolixity to economy, from
pathos to greater detachment. The five stories
were almost universally praised. Showing his psychological insight, Muschg provides superbly written variations on the theme of human estrange-

ment. With great sensitivity, at times with humor bordering on the macabre, he depicts individuals who for various reasons have become alienated from one another. During the next ten years Muschg published three more volumes of equally acclaimed short stories: *Liebesgeschichten, Entfernte Bekannte* (Distant Acquaintances, 1976), and *Leib und Leben* (Life and Limb, 1982), all of which deal, in one way or another, with estrangement.

Muschg is probably best known for *Liebesgeschichten*, his first work published in Germany. One story in particular, "Der Zusenn oder das Heimat" (translated as "The Scythe Man *or* The Homestead," 1983), is brilliant, perhaps one of the great pieces of short fiction of the twentieth century. A widower accused of incestuous relationships with his two grown daughters, fearing that his spoken words are inadequate, attempts to explain in writing what led to the unlawful acts. In the curious, at times humorous, speech patterns characteristic of simple people trying to write in what they consider to be sophisticated language, this father tries to convince the Court of Enquiry that he "den Verkehr niemals als solchen betrieb, sondern damit die Mädchen etwas Freundliches hatten im Leben" (never committed those relations for their own sake, but only so that the girls should have some kindness in their lives), that he did it "nicht wegen dem Fleisch, sondern weil das Fleisch mit einer Seele geplagt ist, und nichts mehr zu hoffen hat, wenn es keine Wärme findet" (not because of the flesh, but because the flesh is tormented by a soul and has nothing left to hope for if it finds no warmth). The story is a strong indictment of a small mountain community where prejudice and slander prevail, where charity and compassion are in short supply.

This poignant story reveals Muschg's rare ability to enter the hearts and minds of the men, women, and children who populate his fictional world, regardless of their age or social class, and to articulate their sense of the world. In his short stories he refrains from commenting or interpreting and permits his protagonists and their stories to speak for themselves. Thus each story has its own unmistakable timbre, each character his own idiom. Although Muschg's narratives are vivid testimonies to the absence of love and the omnipresence of estrangement, indifference, misunderstanding, insecurity, and failings of all sorts, they are not pessimistic in tone. Muschg neither judges nor condemns. Instead, he pleads convinc-

ingly, with great compassion but without sentimentality, for a more humane world.

But the reader is left with the impression that in Muschg's fictional world lives are wasted, opportunities are missed. "Das versäumte Leben" (the wasted life) is a prevalent theme both in Muschg's short stories and in some of his novels. Governed by questionable norms and mores, his characters tend to conceal their true feelings and needs and ultimately lose their ability to act spontaneously. Sensuality and sexuality are suppressed or perverted, hidden frustrations manifest themselves either outwardly in the form of aggression and auto-aggression or inwardly in the form of real and imagined illnesses. Ultimately the body asserts itself and claims its due. Sometimes, for instance when the protagonists suddenly become aware of their deceit and self-deceit and their situation becomes intolerable, crimes are committed. In analytical fashion narrators, psychologists, or investigators then try to uncover the causes of these seemingly inexplicable suicides, homicides, or collapses. In *Leib und Leben*, for instance, a professor of criminal justice recounts from his prison cell what prompted him to shoot the speaker at a ceremony honoring his achievements. The belated recognition that much of his fame was based on publicly sanctioned self-deception led to his first honest action, a first misguided step toward true self-realization.

Many of Muschg's tales are peopled with individuals who fancy themselves in control but suddenly lose their footing, as if the ground were cut from under them. Such is the case in the best-known narrative of *Entfernte Bekannte*, "Brämis Aussicht" (translated as "Brämi's View," 1983). Brämi, a middle-aged farmer, is watching the innocent departure of his family for the fields when suddenly there is a silent catastrophe: "Es war nichts geschehen, aber als er die Treppe hinaufging wusste er, es war alles vorbei, und erkannte, es war nie etwas gewesen. Es war ein umfangreicher, dabei völlig lautloser und immer weiterdauernder Zusammenbruch" (Nothing had happened, but as he was climbing the stairs, he knew that it was all over and realized there had never been anything. It was a total, yet utterly soundless continuous collapse). This moment of absolute honesty is followed by Brämi's suicide. After having spent a lifetime making themselves invulnerable, protecting themselves against the unfamiliar and the unexpected, against death, indigence, hurt, or loss, Muschg's characters must confront their vulnerability.

Muschg in 1988 (Pressefoto Kindermann–
Ullstein Bilderdienst)

Muschg's fourth and probably still his best-known novel, *Albissers Grund* (Albisser's Motive, 1974), was acclaimed by the critical establishment, especially in Germany, and won him the coveted Hermann Hesse Prize. It is one of several works that reflect the era of the student protest movement which influenced him profoundly. As Muschg pointed out on several occasions, the protest movement made it impossible for him to live his life as he had before and forced him seriously to explore his own position and that of his fellowman. In the 1980s, however, reflecting upon those turbulent times, he has become more critical of his own generation's involvement in the protest movement.

Albissers Grund chronicles the psychological, professional, and sociopolitical development of a lower-middle-class Swiss male born in the late 1930s who gets caught up in the political unrest of the late 1960s and early 1970s. It is a detective novel that revolves around the question suggested in the title: what were the motives of the teacher of English, Dr. Peter Albisser, for shooting his therapist, Constantin Zerutt? From a variety of more or less reliable sources the reader is

able to piece together Albisser's background and curious relationship to Zerutt, although the author refuses to provide a definitive answer to the central question. Among the themes treated in the novel are the mother-son relationship, the search for brother figures, the fear of father figures, an excessive need for security, hypochondria, and narcissism. Albisser's suffering is caused by the society of which he is a product; thus many Swiss institutions and attitudes come under fire in the novel.

Like Günter Grass's *Kopfgeburten oder Die Deutschen sterben aus* (1980; translated as *Headbirths; or, The Germans Are Dying Out*, 1982), Muschg's *Baiyun oder die Freundschaftsgesellschaft* chronicles the experiences of a group of privileged central Europeans in the People's Republic of China. An official Swiss delegation consisting of Bernhard Bosshard, a psychologist who narrates the novel; six experts in various other fields; and the neurotic wife of an industrialist who was unable to make the trip himself are guided through postrevolutionary China by representatives of the Chinese Friendship Society. The reader witnesses the participants' curiosity and fascination, their embarrassment and frustrations. Superbly rendered impressions of the strange land alternate with in-depth analyses of the complex relationships of the participants with one another and with their hosts. When the tyrannical leader of the delegation, Prof. Hugo Stappung, is accidentally poisoned by the industrialist's wife, the "travelogue" turns into a detective novel.

Set in Amsterdam, *Das Licht und der Schlüssel: Erziehungsroman eines Vampirs* (1984; translated as *The Light and the Key*, 1988) is Muschg's most ambitious novel to date. It deals with the relationships of art and life, truth and deception, literature and therapy, body and soul, life and death, and contains sophisticated discourses on traditional medicine, the therapeutic potential of art, the process of artistic creation in general and writing in particular, the nature and function of art, and the contemporary art scene. It concludes with an eighty-page epistolary treatise on the still life that includes masterful descriptions of paintings. The narrator is Constantin Samstag, vampire, art connoisseur, and therapist of sorts, who maintains symbiotic relationships with three physicians' beautiful wives on whose blood he feeds. He is a storyteller as well: when he writes, he is neither dead nor alive but "un-tot" (un-dead). In the case of a stewardess suffering from a rare incurable disease–

characteristically, a form of auto-aggression–Samstag does not imbibe her blood but brings her back to life through a nightly storytelling ritual. In the process, the vampire-artist himself gains in vitality and becomes more human. Samstag is commissioned by a blind tobacco tycoon to find a unique still life from the golden age of Dutch painting that will restore his sight; in the end, however, there is doubt as to whether this character really exists. As Michael Butler put it in the *Times Literary Supplement*, "Samstag and his employer turn out to be two halves of one consciousness (character is too strong a word), and the multiple stories spun from it to have no firm root in any fictive reality."

Illness, both literal and figurative, has long been a dominant theme in Muschg's oeuvre. Besides his first play, *Rumpelstilz* (1968), a tragedy about a supreme hypochondriac and his cancer-stricken wife, two works about illness have attracted considerable attention. Muschg's sympathetic foreword to the diatribe *Mars* (1977; translated, 1982) by Fritz Zorn was written as a favor to the publisher, who assumed–wrongly as it turned out–that the vitriolic yet moving account by an obscure thirty-year-old high school teacher of his struggle with terminal cancer needed the endorsement of a well-known author. The work became an instant best-seller both in Switzerland and abroad. For Muschg and Zorn, cancer diagnoses the great failures of the society as a whole, its lack of vitality, its hostility to living; the fear of cancer is a specific form of the fear that one may not have a chance to develop, that one may stand in one's own way. In his popular 1980 Frankfurt lectures, which appeared the following year as *Literatur als Therapie?*, Muschg concludes that literature is not therapy for the writer and probably not for the reader. He does, however, say that for him art and therapy have essentially the same goal of enabling individuals to live more fully.

The greatest success of Muschg's career is his brilliant four-hundred-page literary biography of the nineteenth-century writer Gottfried Keller (1977). There was unprecedented agreement among the critics that Muschg had made a major contribution to scholarship on Keller. According to his own testimony, he tried to destroy the traditional image of Keller so as to show the man in all his ambiguities. In similar fashion, he fought a stereotypical image of Goethe in his most successful play, *Die Aufgeregten von Goethe* (1971), an adaptation and completion of Goethe's

unfinished play about the French Revolution, which shows Goethe to have been a political reactionary.

It appears that the prose fiction of Adolf Muschg will continue to overshadow his contributions to the stage, television, and radio, some of which contain clever and witty if not brilliant dialogue. Whether he is an aesthetic realist, an enlightened humanist, or a poetic realist, as he has been called by various critics, whether he follows in the footsteps of Robert Walser, Martin Walser, or Max Frisch, he has firmly established himself as a master of the short story. An erudite scholar, a superb stylist, and an astute observer of contemporary middle-class Swiss society, he provides valuable commentaries on many contemporary issues that go well beyond Switzerland.

Interviews:

Georges Ammann, *Gespräch mit Adolf Muschg* (Basel: Reinhardt, 1969);

Rolf Kieser, "Interview mit Adolf Muschg," in *Basis: Jahrbuch für deutsche Gegenwartsliteratur*, volume 8 (Frankfurt am Main: Suhrkamp, 1979), pp. 61-70;

Judith Ricker-Abderhalden, "An Interview with Adolf Muschg," *Studies in Twentieth Century Literature*, 8 (Spring 1984): 233-248.

References:

G. P. Butler, "The Tortuous Road from A to Z," *Times Literary Supplement*, 3 January 1975, p. 4;

Michael Butler, "The Cure as Symptom," *Times Literary Supplement*, 4 January 1985, p. 17;

Jochen Hieber, "Porträt des Künstlers als Vampir," *Frankfurter Allgemeine Zeitung*, 2 October 1984;

Anton Krättli, "Kunst- und Vampirgeschichten," *Schweizer Monatshefte* (January 1985): 81-86;

Krättli, " 'Leib und Leben' oder Ernst und Unernst," *Schweizer Monatshefte* (June 1982): 523-527;

Ernst Pawel, "Ice Age of the Spirit: 'The Blue Man' and Other Stories by Adolf Muschg," *New York Times Book Review*, 19 May 1985, p. 12;

Judith Ricker-Abderhalden, ed., *Über Adolf Muschg* (Frankfurt am Main: Suhrkamp, 1979);

Heinz F. Schafroth, "Adolf Muschg," in *Kritisches Lexikon zur deutschsprachigen Gegenwartsliteratur*, edited by Heinz Ludwig Arnold (Munich: Edition text + kritik, 1982), n. pag.;

George Steiner, "Springs of Sadness," *New Yorker*, 61 (8 July 1985): 71-73;

Renate Voris, *Adolf Muschg* (Munich: Beck/edition text + kritik, 1984);

Voris,"Biographie–Roman–Autobiographie:Adolf Muschgs 'Gottfried Keller,' " *Jahrbuch der deutschen Schillergesellschaft*, 27 (1983): 283;

H. M. Waidson, "The Near and the Far: The Writings of Adolf Muschg," *German Life and Letters*, 28 (July 1975): 426-437.

Heinz Piontek
(15 November 1925-   )

H. M. Waidson
University College of Swansea (University of Wales)

BOOKS: *Die Furt: Gedichte* (Eßlingen: Bechtle, 1952);

Die Rauchfahne: Gedichte (Eßlingen: Bechtle, 1953; enlarged, 1956);

Vor Augen: Proben und Versuche (Eßlingen: Bechtle, 1955);

Wassermarken: Gedichte (Eßlingen: Bechtle, 1957);

Buchstab–Zauberstab: Über Dichter und Dichtung (Eßlingen: Bechtle, 1959);

Mit einer Kranichfeder: Gedichte (Stuttgart: Deutsche Verlags-Anstalt, 1962);

Weißer Panther: Hörspiel (Stuttgart: Deutsche Verlags-Anstalt, 1962);

Kastanien aus dem Feuer: Erzählungen, Kurzgeschichten, Prosastücke (Stuttgart: Deutsche Verlags-Anstalt, 1963);

Die Zwischenlandung: Hörspiel (Hamburg: Hans Bredow-Institut, 1963);

Windrichtungen: Reisebilder. Mit einer autobiographischen Skizze (Stuttgart: Reclam, 1963);

Randerscheinungen: Gedichte (Darmstadt: Bläschke, 1965);

Klartext: Gedichte (Hamburg: Hoffmann & Campe, 1966);

Die mittleren Jahre: Roman (Hamburg: Hoffmann & Campe, 1967);

Außenaufnahmen: Erzählungen (Baden-Baden: Signal, 1968);

Liebeserklärungen in Prosa (Hamburg: Hoffmann & Campe, 1969);

Männer, die Gedichte machen: Zur Lyrik heute (Hamburg: Hoffmann & Campe, 1970);

Tot oder lebendig: Gedichte (Hamburg: Hoffmann & Campe, 1971); translated by Richard

Heinz Piontek (photograph by Felicitas Timpe, courtesy of Ullstein Bilderdienst)

Exner as *Alive or Dead* (Greensboro, N. C.: Unicorn, 1975);

Die Erzählungen (1950-1970) (Munich: Langen-Müller, 1971);

Klarheit schaffen, edited by Friedrich Bentmann (Karlsruhe: Volksbund für Dichtung [Scheffelbund], 1972);

German: From Language to Literature, by Piontek and John M. Troyanovich (New York: Van Nostrand, 1972);

Helle Tage anderswo: Reisebilder (Munich: Langen-Müller, 1973);

Leben mit Wörtern: Zum 50. Geburtstag des Autors (Percha: Schulz, 1975);

Gesammelte Gedichte (Hamburg: Hoffmann & Campe, 1975);

Die Zeit der anderen Auslegung: Gedichte (Darmstadt: Bläschke, 1976);

Dichterleben: Roman (Hamburg: Hoffmann & Campe, 1976);

Das Schweigen überbrücken: Meditationen, Gedichte, Szenen, Erzählungen (Gütersloh: Mohn, 1977);

Wintertage, Sommernächte: Gesammelte Erzählungen und Reisebilder (Munich & Vienna: Langen-Müller, 1977);

Gesammelte Erzählungen (Munich: Goldmann, 1977);

Träumen, Wachen, Widerstehen: Aufzeichnungen aus diesen Jahren (Munich: Schneekluth, 1978);

Wie sich Musik durchschlug: Gedichte (Hamburg: Hoffmann & Campe, 1978);

Dunkelkammerspiel: Spiele, Szenen und ein Stück (Percha: Schulz, 1978);

Das Handwerk des Lesens: Erfahrungen mit Büchern und Autoren (Munich: Schneekluth, 1979);

Juttas Neffe: Roman (Munich: Schneekluth, 1979);

Vorkriegszeit: Ein Gedicht (Munich: Schneekluth, 1980);

Was mich nicht losläßt: Gedichte (Munich: Schneekluth, 1981);

Werke in 6 Bänden, 6 volumes (Munich: Schneekluth, 1981-1985)—includes as volume 2 *Die Münchner Romane (Die mittleren Jahre, Dichterleben, Juttas Neffe)* and as volume 6 *Zeit meines Lebens: Autobiographischer Roman;*

Erscheinungen, edited by teachers of German at the Weilheim Gymnasium (Weilheim, 1983);

Die Zeit einer Frau: Sechs Erzählungen, edited by Rainer Malkowski (Stuttgart: Reclam, 1984);

Damals, damals und jetzt: Heinz Piontek zum 15. November 1985, edited by Exner and Michael Schmidt (Munich: Schneekluth, 1985);

Helldunkel: Gedichte (Freiburg im Breisgau: Herder, 1987).

OTHER: *Aus meines Herzens Grunde: Evangelische Lyrik aus vier Jahrhunderten,* edited by Piontek (Stuttgart: Steinkopf, 1959);

John Keats, Gedichte. Auswahl, translated by Piontek (Wiesbaden: Insel, 1960);

Beispiele: Zwölf Erzählungen von zehn Autoren, contributions by Piontek (Stuttgart: Deutsche Verlags-Anstalt, 1962);

Neue deutsche Erzählgedichte, edited by Piontek (Stuttgart: Deutsche Verlags-Anstalt, 1964);

Augenblicke unterwegs: Deutsche Reiseprosa unserer Zeit, edited by Piontek (Hamburg: Hoffmann & Campe, 1968);

Ensemble: Lyrik, Prosa, Essay, edited by Piontek and Clemens Graf Podewils (Munich: Oldenbourg, 1969);

Deutsche Gedichte seit 1960: Eine Anthologie, edited by Piontek (Stuttgart: Reclam, 1972);

Apropos Wien: Essays und Feuilletons, contributions by Piontek (Vienna & Munich: Jugend und Volk, 1973);

Lieb, Leid und Zeit und Ewigkeit: Deutsche Gedichte aus tausend Jahren, edited by Piontek (Hamburg: Knaus, 1981);

Ja, mein Engel: Die besten deutschen Kurzgeschichten, selected by Piontek (Munich: Schneekluth, 1981).

Heinz Piontek has confirmed his place as a leading German poet by the collections of verse he has published since the early 1950s. His three novels of contemporary life in Munich and the autobiography of his early years have made a significant contribution to modern narrative prose. He has also been a successful short-story writer since the 1950s. In addition, he has written radio plays, travel literature, and literary criticism and has edited anthologies of poetry.

Piontek was born in Kreuzburg, Upper Silesia (now Poland), on 15 November 1925 to Robert and Marie Piontek. His father, who had contracted a lung disease as a result of exposure to poison gas in World War I, died in 1928. Piontek's high school education was interrupted when he was drafted in 1943. After he was released from a prisoner-of-war camp in 1945, he passed his Abitur (school-leaving examination) as a mature student. He held a series of jobs, including construction work and sign painting, before entering the University of Munich in 1946 to study literature, philosophy, and art history. He became a free-lance writer in 1948. He lives in Munich with his wife, the former Gisela Dallmann, whom he married on 14 July 1951.

Piontek in 1966 (photograph by Karoly Forgacs, courtesy of Ullstein Bilderdienst)

Each of Piontek's Munich novels concentrates on the relationships and problems of a male figure and those close to him against a carefully delineated background of urban and suburban life. Robert Hanke, the protagonist of *Die mittleren Jahre* (The Middle Years, 1967), marries shortly after the end of the war and becomes a teacher of English and German literature. His daughter Tania is born in 1953. Robert's life loses its normality when he falls obsessively in love with Harriet, a married woman. His wife, Katharina, begins to overeat and to neglect her appearance, and Robert's drinking affects his work at school. There is desperation in the lovers' holiday in Holland, where their expectations of a more carefree life in surroundings where they are not known are disappointed. During a later holiday in Italy Robert's behavior is particularly difficult, and Harriet commits suicide by walking into the sea. Back in Munich, Robert returns to Katharina, who forgives him. When she is killed in a traffic accident, Robert is overwhelmed by

the outcome of his unplanned and irresponsible living. At his wife's grave he thinks: "Eine andere Hand, eine stärkere, liebevollere, würde sich unserer Vergangenheit wie ihrer eigenen Sache annehmen, sie zu Ende zu führen" (Another hand, stronger and more loving, would take on our past as if it were its own and bring it to a conclusion). The novel ends with indications that Robert will take up with another woman, Karin. Clearly he is indifferent to his daughter, who has been living with foster parents, and is unwilling to take much responsibility for her. Robert has experienced love as painful and doom-laden: for all his faults, he remains a hero with whom the reader will often identify.

The main concerns of Achim Reichsfelder in *Dichterleben* (Poet's Life, 1976) are his literary vocation and his relations with women. His first wife, Marie-Claire, with whom he went to school during the war years, is ambitious for him, and for a time they are frequent guests at literary parties. In the later 1950s literary fashions change, and Achim's publisher tries to persuade him to write more prose. Achim's health deteriorates; he no longer sleeps with his wife; and their two children are not developing as he would like. He divorces Marie-Claire, goes on a long journey, and meets and marries Ulla Rossbach, who is not as pretentious socially as Marie-Claire. This marriage also does not last, but Reichsfelder is ready to pursue a quieter and less ambitious way of living than he had done previously; he finds translation work congenial and lives alone in an inner-city apartment. The foregoing is told in flashbacks; the novel opens with Reichsfelder recovering from the flu at the age of fifty. He has been living alone for ten or twelve years. He remains unwell and apathetic for some weeks, gradually extending his walks to shops and other public places. During his convalescence a young stranger named Janko Machwitz calls on him; Janko belongs to a younger generation that cannot understand why their elders allowed the traditional "bürgerlich" (bourgeois) order of civilization to be restored after the war. Janko helps Achim when the latter is accosted and harassed by a strange woman in the Hofgarten, and invites Achim to be a guest of his family at their large country house. The younger man admires Achim's poetry and would like him to start writing original work again. Achim's views on the future of poetry are pessimistic: "Von der Poesie ist nichts Entscheidendes mehr zu erwarten. Es ist noch die Frage, ob sie überleben wird" (Nothing decisive is to be expected of poetry any longer. The question is whether it will survive). Janko looks after Achim, as far as Achim will let him. The older man finds more congenial quarters in a northern suburb but is the victim of a street attack; the novel ends with the doctors believing that they can pull him through.

Jutta Hellmiss in *Juttas Neffe* (Jutta's Nephew, 1979) lives alone in Munich. She was born in Landschütz near the former German-Polish border, where her father was stationmaster. At the ages of twelve and thirteen she surprised everybody at her school by her exceptional ability at throwing the javelin. In January 1945 she, her brother Norbert, and their mother resettled in South Germany, in the American zone. She became noted for her skill with the javelin but failed to pass the examination to allow her to train as a sports teacher and is now on the staff of a publishing firm that specializes in books on sports. She learns from her brother that his son Reimund has disappeared after failing his Abitur for a second time and feels that it is up to her to find her nephew and direct him to a life of stability. Meanwhile Reimund drifts about Munich exploring various life-styles; his aunt makes inquiries at places where Reimund is known to have been, such as a commune of theology students whose ideals include these thoughts: "Fortschritt sei Selbstbegrenzung, Selbstversorgung, Gewaltlosigkeit. Bald werde eine vierte Welt existieren" (Progress is self-limitation, provision for oneself, nonviolence. Soon a fourth world will come into being). While he is on his own, Reimund comes across Janko Machwitz, of *Dichterleben,* who offers him his hospitality. Subsequently Reimund stays with another man, whose homosexual advances he fiercely resists. At this point he learns from a newspaper item that his aunt led a horse through the streets displaying a notice inquiring for information about her nephew. Reimund makes his way to the top of a tower and threatens to jump. Police and firefighters arrive, but Reimund asks for his aunt Jutta to be summoned. The novel ends with the anticipation that the aunt's care for the boy will lead to the end of his despair and restlessness and enable him to be happily settled with a clear but probably unassuming goal in life. *Juttas Neffe* is a novel with insight into the instabilities of individuals and groups, but with a message of hope.

Piontek has written several volumes of short stories. His first collection, *Vor Augen* (In Public, 1955), presents terse, concise narratives. The problems caused for the Germans by the westward advance of the Soviets in 1945 are portrayed in "Verlorene Stadt" (Lost Town); the transient nature of happiness is shown in "Wie Rauch im Wind" (Like Smoke in the Wind); a dangerous mistake in identity confronts a man who makes a forced landing in his glider in "Nach der Landung" (After the Landing). These stories are neatly and deftly crafted and impressive in their precision. *Kastanien aus dem Feuer* (Chestnuts out of the Fire, 1963) comprises stories written between 1956 and 1963. The overwhelming impact of events that are beyond the comprehension of a boy in "Verlassene Straßen" (Deserted Streets), a man's sense of failure at a time of stress in "Tag und Nachtgleiche" (Equinox), and an old woman's nervousness at moving home in "Bäume im Wind" (Trees in the Wind) are among the surprising yet wholly believable situations depicted in these stories. "Ein ziemlich schwerer Fall" (A Rather Difficult Case) satirizes a man of letters. The difficulties of an Italian worker in Germany reach tragic proportions in "Goldregenland" (Land of Golden Rain). "Auf dem Lande" (In the Country) focuses on a young construction worker's disturbed relationship with a girl from a middle-class background. A marriage is threatened by the wife's ruthless and aggressive father, and the latter's death in a road accident is welcome news, especially to the son-in-law, in "Dornbüsche" (Thorn Bushes). "Winterlamento" (Winter Lament) centers upon a pastor who has a deeply meaningful experience during the last days of World War II. Scenes of childhood are precisely evoked in "Der Photograph war schon bestellt" (The Photographer Had Already Been Booked), in which a boy is taken by his mother to be a guest at a wedding where the bridegroom fails to appear. A somewhat older protagonist builds a model airplane in "Flieger, grüß mir die Sonne" (Flier, Greet the Sun for Me) but realizes that the other boys' planes are better than his, and he does not exhibit his model. In addition to stories, *Wintertage, Sommernächte* (Winter Days, Summer Nights, 1977) contains a selection of descriptive essays. People and places are evoked in Piontek's stories with imagination and vigor.

Zeit meines Lebens (Time of My Life, 1985) is subtitled *Autobiographischer Roman* (Autobiographical Novel); Piontek explains that everything in the book is drawn from life, and that he has called it a novel to avoid being involved in arguments with those who may doubt his veracity—such skeptics are welcome to regard it as fiction.

The author's youth in Kreuzburg, a small town near the Silesian-Polish border, during the interwar and war years up to 1943 is graphically evoked. When his father died in 1928, Piontek's mother was left to provide for Heinz and his older sister Inge. School friendships allow for a lively series of character portraits of boys and girls. The Nazis came to power during Piontek's first year at school; the author recalls that his grandmother on his mother's side was the only member of the family who expressed hostility to Hitler. There appears to have been little opposition to National Socialism in Kreuzburg in the 1930s; Piontek joined the "Jungvolk" at the suggestion of his sister's boyfriend, Günter Hentschke, who saw to it that he was not subjected to any unpleasant exercises. The advent of war in 1939 was ominously marked by the movement of troops through Kreuzburg to the Polish frontier and beyond, but for the first years of the war Piontek and his friends noticed relatively little change in their environment. Piontek was a good student and a promising athlete. He learned to appreciate the classics of German literature, and in the Hitler Youth movement he became knowledgeable about airplanes. When visiting his sister, who was working in a part of Germany that had recently been annexed from Poland, he became aware of the hostility between Germans and Poles. Mother and son received the first news of Hitler's invasion of the Soviet Union with foreboding. The author describes the tension between his impulse to loyalty and his revulsion from violence; it was difficult for him to conceive of a German state that would not have the familiar features of Nazism, and fatalism dominated his general outlook at that time. This substantial narrative concludes as Piontek is about to leave school for the army; the news from the Russian front, where Günter Hentschke lost his life, is ominous.

As a critic Piontek has been fair minded and effective in his appreciation of German and other authors since the 1950s. He has also shown good judgment and skill as an editor in the anthologies of poetry, both contemporary and from earlier centuries, which he has compiled. His short stories are compelling narratives, and his three novels form a unity in their approach to human relationships and their evocation of the landscape of Munich. The autobiography is also impressive prose writing. His lyrical poetry is generally serious but also reveals a quiet humor; it is closely observed, often concentrated and lapidary. All in all, there can be no doubt of the substantiality of Piontek's contribution to contemporary German literature. He won the Andreas Gryphius Prize in 1957, the Munich Literature Prize in 1967, the Eichendorff Prize in 1971, the Cultural Circle Award of the Federation of German Industry in 1974, the Georg Büchner Prize in 1976, the Werner Eckg Prize in 1981, the Upper Silesian Cultural Prize of the State of North Rhine-Westphalia in 1983, and the Federal Order of Merit in 1985.

References:

Annette Deeken, "Heinz Piontek," in *Kritisches Lexikon zur deutschsprachigen Gegenwartsliteratur*, edited by Heinz Ludwig Arnold (Munich: Edition text + kritik, n.d.), V: 1-7, A-H;

Richard Exner, "Heinz Piontek," in *Die deutsche Lyrik 1945-1975*, edited by Klaus Weißenberger (Düsseldorf: Bagel, 1981), pp. 186-197;

Walter Helmut Fritz, "Heinz Piontek," in *Handbuch der deutschen Gegenwartsliteratur*, edited by Hermann Kunisch, second edition (Munich: Nymphenburger Verlagshandlung, 1970), II: 105-107;

Otto Knörrich, *Die deutsche Lyrik der Gegenwart 1945-1970* (Stuttgart: Kröner, 1971), pp. 234-240;

Franz Lennartz, "Heinz Piontek," in his *Deutsche Schriftsteller des 20. Jahrhunderts im Spiegel der Kritik* (Stuttgart: Kröner, 1984), III: 1331-1335;

J. C. Middleton, "The Poetry of Heinz Piontek," *German Life and Letters*, new series 13 (1959-1960): 55-59.

Papers:

A Piontek archive has been established in the Manuscripts Section of the Bavarian State Library in Munich.

Ulrich Plenzdorf

(26 October 1934-   )

Siegfried Mews
University of North Carolina at Chapel Hill

BOOKS: *Die neuen Leiden des jungen W.* (Frankfurt am Main: Suhrkamp, 1973); edited by J. H. Reid (London: Harrap, 1979); translated by Kenneth P. Wilcox as *The New Sufferings of Young W.: A Novel* (New York: Ungar, 1979);

Die Legende von Paul und Paula; Die neuen Leiden des jungen W.: Ein Kino- und ein Bühnenstück (Berlin: Henschel, 1974);

Die Legende von Paul & Paula: Filmerzählung (Frankfurt am Main: Suhrkamp, 1974); translated by Christiane E. Keck as "The Tale of Paul and Paula: Filmscript," *Dimension*, 16, no. 1 (1987): 49-113;

Karla; Der alte Mann, das Pferd, die Straße: Texte zu Filmen (Berlin: Henschel, 1978);

Legende vom Glück ohne Ende (Frankfurt am Main: Suhrkamp, 1979);

Plenzdorfs "Die neuen Leiden des jungen W.," edited by Peter J. Brenner (Frankfurt am Main: Suhrkamp, 1982);

Gutenachtgeschichte (Frankfurt am Main: Suhrkamp, 1983);

kein runter kein fern (Frankfurt am Main: Suhrkamp, 1984).

Ulrich Plenzdorf suddenly became a household name in the German Democratic Republic (GDR) in 1972-1973, the years during which his *Die neuen Leiden des jungen W.* (1973; translated as *The New Sufferings of Young W.*, 1979) was produced on several stages and published in novel form. The virtually unknown scriptwriter from East Berlin attracted major attention for his treatment of the longings, problems, and doubts of young people in a socialist society that claimed to have eliminated the causes of individual maladjustment and unhappiness. Plenzdorf had not sought the role of spokesman for discontented youth, but his desire to probe the relationship between socialist ideals and actual conditions thrust him into the center of discussions that far exceeded the confines of a literary debate.

Ulrich Plenzdorf (courtesy of Plenzdorf)

The few biographical facts that are known do not provide a satisfactory explanation of Plenzdorf's development as a writer of controversial works. He was born in 1934 in a workers' district in Berlin; both of his parents were politically active Communists who were incarcerated during the Nazi period. After completing secondary school in 1954 Plenzdorf began to study Marxism-Leninism at the Franz Mehring Institute in Leipzig, but he left in 1955 to become a stagehand—a step that precluded his becoming a member of the privileged class of functionaries. After serving in the army from 1958 to 1959, Plenzdorf resumed his studies at a film academy in Potsdam; since 1963 he has been employed by the state-controlled East German film company DEFA.

From the beginning of his career as a scriptwriter, Plenzdorf was exposed to the problem confronted by most writers in the GDR: the risk of incurring the displeasure of the authorities by deviating from the party line. After Plenzdorf wrote the script for the film *Mir nach, Kanaillen* (Follow Me, Scoundrels, 1964) on a comparatively safe historical subject, he ran into difficulties with his second script, *Karla*, whose fate clearly illustrates the dilemma he faced. The film based on Plenzdorf's screenplay was never released, owing to its critical view of the school system in the GDR. Written in 1964-1965, the script could only be published in 1978, after a more liberal cultural stance had been adopted in 1971 at the eighth party congress of the ruling Sozialistische Einheitspartei Deutschlands (Socialist Unity Party of Germany [SED]).

In the screenplay, the novice teacher Karla, an honest and straightforward young woman, obtains her first job at a secondary school in a small town in the provinces. There she encounters a principal who seems to violate every educational concept she was taught at the university in East Berlin. Whereas Karla believes that teaching should foster independent thinking, the principal insists on rote learning and reducing complex issues to simplistic formulas—particularly in the ideological realm. Instead of encouraging open discussion, he expects the students to reiterate his pronouncements mindlessly. But Plenzdorf modifies the initial confrontation, in which Karla represents all the progressive ideas, by endowing the principal with redeeming features; conversely, Karla loses all sense of proportion in erroneously surmising that the principal, a pioneer who helped build socialism from the rubble of World War II, had been a Nazi. Yet, when she is praised as an exemplary teacher by a delegation from Berlin, it seems that the conflict between her and the principal has been resolved in her favor.

But Plenzdorf avoids such an unambiguous and optimistic ending by having Karla engage in a nocturnal swimming excursion with a male student—an action that so damages her profes-

sional reputation that the principal has no choice but to send her off to a school in the country. The conflict between the official representative of the school system and the young innovator thus remains unresolved. Such a compromise, however, still seemed to imply too much criticism of the GDR's educational policies and institutions for the film to be permitted to be shown in public.

As a result of his experiences with *Karla*, Plenzdorf expected that his next film project, *Die neuen Leiden des jungen W.*, would not be made available to the public at all. It was perhaps this expectation that induced Plenzdorf to write a radical first version during 1968-1969 that was not published until 1982. In this version the adolescent Edgar Wibeau runs away from his small-town home to East Berlin, where he hides in a cottage that is destined to be razed. After his plans to become an artist fail, he joins a team of house painters and devises a new kind of spray gun that malfunctions and destroys itself when he puts it to the test. After he makes an abortive suicide attempt, the spray gun is rebuilt and Edgar is credited with inventing a revolutionary new tool that is bound to increase productivity. Thus, the former outsider, who has fled the stifling atmosphere of his hometown, is not only fully accepted but honored by society. He has achieved a degree of individual freedom that is denied others, a freedom that appears to be the result of his defiance of prevalent social norms.

In the later versions of *Die neuen Leiden des jungen W.* Edgar is electrocuted when his spray gun malfunctions. Furthermore, the spray gun cannot be rebuilt; thus it cannot be ascertained whether it was a useful invention or merely an idée fixe. In these versions Edgar retells from the hereafter the events that led to his demise; from his superior perspective he views some of his previous actions and attitudes in a critical light. But his occasionally ironic self-criticism is far removed from the ritualistic mea culpa declarations that are intended to keep errant individuals in the GDR in the socialist fold. Hence *Die neuen Leiden des jungen W.* retained a critical potential that was immediately perceived by young spectators when the dramatic version premiered. Plenzdorf's text articulated the conflict between their own desire for happiness and fulfillment, on the one hand, and the demands of a strictly regimented society whose norms were determined by an older generation, on the other. *Die neuen Leiden des jungen W.* achieved a rare distinction among literary works: the play and novel versions were vigorously debated in schools, shops, and factories.

The touchstone of critical comment in the GDR was the death of the protagonist, a well-adjusted, promising youth. Attempts to minimize the significance of Edgar's death by explaining it as a device that enabled Plenzdorf to establish an interesting narrative perspective, or to contrast the redeemed, dead Edgar with the living, unrepentant youth, were not very persuasive. East German critics attributed Edgar's nonconformism and ultimate demise to his penchant for blue jeans and, by inference, his having been corrupted by Western decadence. Conversely, critics in the West proffered opinions that ranged from declaring Edgar the victim of a society that does not tolerate individualistic deviations from the norm, to the opposite view that he is basically a traditional hero in the mold of socialist realism, with whom the author dispenses in the end precisely on account of his inability to function in a collective. Edgar's death led to persistent questioning that confirms the open-endedness, previously not the rule in East German literature, of *Die neuen Leiden des jungen W.*

Such questioning notwithstanding, Edgar is not opposed to communism per se. Rather than the sociopolitical system and its ideological underpinning, Edgar attacks the pressure to conform in dress and appearance. Edgar's attitude toward work is indicative of his acceptance in principle of the East German emphasis on productivity and achievement: although he initially spends his time in the cottage without a job, he is aware of the temporary nature of such an existence and recognizes the role played by work in the process of socialization. Yet, he refuses to subordinate his entire life to work and insists on the importance of leisure activities. Thus he is able to respond enthusiastically to J. D. Salinger's classic novel of adolescence, *The Catcher in the Rye* (1951), and to identify with its protagonist, Holden Caulfield, who is hardly addicted to work. Plenzdorf's and Salinger's protagonists have certain similarities, such as their youthful protests against societal norms and institutions, their subjective narrative perspectives, their flippant tone, and their frequent use of jargon; yet, there are also substantial differences. Whereas Holden is a deliberate non-achiever who clings to his lost childhood and has few prospects for the future, Edgar accepts responsibility for his actions and seeks to regain access to society–albeit on his own terms.

Plenzdorf in 1977 (photograph by Peter Probst, courtesy of Ullstein Bilderdienst)

As the title of Plenzdorf's work indicates, another literary source inspired *Die neuen Leiden des jungen W.* Despite his initial revulsion, Edgar begins to read and appreciate Goethe's epistolary novel *Die Leiden des jungen Werthers* (1774; translated as *The Sorrows of Werther*, 1779) when he finds himself in a situation similar to that of Goethe's protagonist: he falls in love with a young kindergarten teacher he nicknames Charlie, a colloquial modernization of Werther's Charlotte. Charlie is engaged to a stiffly pedantic young man who shows little sympathy for Edgar's unorthodox life-style and behavior. As his love for Charlie intensifies, Edgar identifies more and more with Werther. Plenzdorf's frequent use of quotations from Goethe's narrative in tapes Edgar sends to his friend Willi–the modern equivalent of Werther's letters–serves as the vehicle for some of Edgar's most vehement criticism of the socialist work ethic, an ethic which extols collectivism and stifles individuality.

Critical objections to Plenzdorf's employment of the Goethean model focused on the allegedly undignified way in which Edgar discovers

Goethe–in an outhouse. Since the cover and title page of the book are missing, Edgar is not able to identify either author or text and reads the novel unhampered by his prejudice against "recommended" literature. In view of the fact that the cultural policies of the SED dictate obeisance to the democratic and humanistic cultural heritage of which the mature Goethe of the classical Weimar epoch is an important part, it is significant that Plenzdorf chose a work from Goethe's Storm and Stress period. Hence his protagonist engages in an unorthodox, fresh, and engaged reading of *Die Leiden des jungen Werthers* that is in marked contrast to the reception of Goethe by those who put the classical author on a pedestal without bothering to familiarize themselves with his works.

At the ninth plenary session of the Central Committee of the SED in May 1973, First Secretary Erich Honecker issued a veiled warning against the detrimental effects for socialist morale of devoting too much attention to individual difficulties in plays and films. Although Honecker did not mention Plenzdorf by name, his pointed use of the term *Leiden* (sufferings) clearly alluded to *Die neuen Leiden des jungen W.* The explicit references to Plenzdorf's much-discussed work in the narratives of such East German writers as Volker Braun and Rolf Schneider demonstrate, however, that the problematic relationship between the individual and society could no longer be declared nonexistent by administrative fiat or by strict adherence to the party line.

Although Plenzdorf was not able to repeat the phenomenal success of *Die neuen Leiden des jungen W.*, he had hit upon a formula that enabled him to continue writing well-received works. The filmscript *Die Legende von Paul & Paula* (The Legend of Paul & Paula, filmed in 1973, published in 1974; translated as "The Tale of Paul and Paula: Filmscript," 1987) offers a variation of Plenzdorf's central concern, the question of how the individual can achieve personal happiness and fulfillment in a rigidly conformist society. In his choice of the unconventional heroine Paula, an unskilled Berlin supermarket cashier with at best a rudimentary political consciousness; in his explicit depiction of sexual encounters; and in his realistic portrayal of the workaday world, Plenzdorf again came close to violating official taboos. Paula achieves happiness when she is united with Paul, who abandons his promising career as a functionary to be with her. Favoring private bliss over duty and hard work

would seem to set a dangerous precedent for viewers of the film; but Plenzdorf defuses this potentially explosive issue by superimposing upon the plot features derived from the realm of legend. For example, when Paul prepares to move in with Paula, the stage direction states that he is supposed to look as beautiful as a prince in a fairy tale; furthermore, the love of Paul and Paula, an omnipotent love that overcomes all obstacles, pertains to legend rather than real life. The legendary elements do not, however, obscure the realistic depiction of everyday life in East Berlin that was particularly appreciated by moviegoers in the GDR.

The novel *Legende vom Glück ohne Ende* (Legend of Unending Happiness, 1979), a continuation of *Die Legende von Paul & Paula*, offers a variation of Paul's progression from overachievement and adjustment to lack of achievement and maladjustment. After Paula's death Paul meets Laura, who bears a striking resemblance to Paula; as it turns out, this resemblance is purely external. Whereas Paula had cherished such qualities as love, trust, and compassion, Laura has a rational, pragmatic attitude. Although she leads Paul to resume his duties and rejoin the establishment, he becomes an outsider again when he suffers an accident that leaves him partially paralyzed. Paul's last concession to conformity is his consent to marry Laura, but in the end he disappears without a trace. He leaves behind his legacy of nonconformism, radical demands for personal fulfillment, a strong desire for new forms of communal living, and a model of emancipatory relations between the sexes–a legacy that, Plenzdorf implies by his choice of the term *legend* in the title of the novel, represents a challenge rather than reality.

Although the excessively long novel has a rather slender plot and relies too heavily on chance, *Legende vom Glück ohne Ende* achieved a formidable popular success in the GDR–in 1981 a serialized version was printed in an edition of one hundred thousand copies–owing to its presentation of an unsentimental love story that does not rely on escapism but takes place in an environment familiar to its readers. Moreover, Paul's critical comments about a host of minor and major annoyances–from the lack of produce in the supermarkets to the high-handed manner of some officials–struck a sympathetic chord in the reading public.

In contrast to *Legende vom Glück ohne Ende*, *Gutenachtgeschichte* (Bedtime Story, 1983) is a slim work that only approximates book length on account of copious illustrations and large type. Addressed to children, *Gutenachtgeschichte* is not, as its title suggests, a wholesome or uplifting story intended to put children to sleep; rather, the narrator seeks to subvert the genre by instilling in his readers/listeners critical awareness in an antiauthoritarian vein.

In 1978 Plenzdorf was permitted to travel to Klagenfurt, Austria, where he and other authors gave readings from their unpublished works. Plenzdorf read his brief narrative *kein runter kein fern* (You Are Permitted Neither to Go Out Nor to Watch TV, 1984) and was awarded the Ingeborg Bachmann Prize for this uncompromising and challenging work that, although widely anthologized in West Germany, has not been published in East Germany. The story is told from the perspective of a ten-year-old boy who suffers from a learning disability and a speech impediment; he is mercilessly punished for his failure in school by his achievement-oriented father and bullied by his policeman brother. In the stream-of-consciousness narration the boy's ungrammatical and sometimes incoherent utterances are contrasted with the empty rhetoric of a radio announcer who reports on the festivities on the occasion of the twentieth anniversary of the GDR. The Rolling Stones' song "I Can't Get No Satisfaction" serves as the leitmotif for the boy's misery, which at the end of the story reaches catastrophic dimensions: rumor has it that the official celebrations in East Berlin will be supplemented by an appearance of the Rolling Stones on the roof of a building near the western side of the Berlin Wall, but the rumor proves to be false; the boy and other lovers of the Stones' music who have congregated on the eastern side of the wall are savagely beaten by the police, one of whom is the boy's brother.

This unrelentingly pessimistic story, which portrays the individual as a helpless victim of societal institutions and familial oppression, is not typical of Plenzdorf. He usually gives his protagonists—practically all of whom are maladjusted young outsiders—a measure of independence and resourcefulness that allows them occasionally to strike back or beat the system. But *kein runter kein fern* is a further literary expression of the unresolved conflicts between the individual and society in the GDR, between the espoused ideal of socialism and its actual application, between official rhetoric and real living conditions—conflicts that Plenzdorf has made it his task to articulate and expose in the hope of heightening awareness and effecting gradual change.

References:

Ute Brandes, "Toward Socialist Modernism: Ulrich Plenzdorf's *kein runter kein fern*," *Studies in GDR Culture and Society*, 4 (1984): 107-123;

Brandes and Ann Clark Fehn, "Werther's Children: The Experience of the Second Generation in Ulrich Plenzdorf's *Die neuen Leiden des jungen W.* and Volker Braun's *Unvollendete Geschichte*," *German Quarterly*, 56 (1983): 608-623;

Aleksandar Flaker, *Modelle der Jeans Prosa: Zur literarischen Opposition bei Plenzdorf im osteuropäischen Romankontext* (Kronberg: Scriptor, 1975);

Juergen K. Hoegel, "Language, Metaphor, and Strategy of Composition in Ulrich Plenzdorf's Novel *Die neuen Leiden des jungen W.*," *University of Dayton Review*, 13, no. 2 (1978): 37-48;

Georg Jäger, *Die Leiden des alten und neuen Werther: Kommentare, Abbildungen, Materialien zu Goethes "Leiden des jungen Werthers" und Plenzdorfs "Neue Leiden des jungen W."* (Munich: Hanser, 1984);

Eberhard Mannack, *Zwei deutsche Literaturen?: Zu G. Grass, U. Johnson, H. Kant, U. Plenzdorf und C. Wolf* (Kronberg: Athenäum, 1977);

Siegfried Mews, *Ulrich Plenzdorf* (Munich: Beck/ edition text + kritik, 1984);

Walter E. Riedel, "Some German Ripples of Holden Caulfield's 'Goddam Autobiography': On Translating and Adapting J. D. Salinger's *Catcher in the Rye*," *Canadian Review of Comparative Literature*, 7 (Spring 1980): 196-205;

Gisela Shaw, "Ideal and Reality in the Works of Ulrich Plenzdorf," *German Life and Letters*, 35, no. 1 (1981): 85-97.

Elisabeth Plessen
(15 March 1944-   )

Helga W. Kraft
University of Florida

BOOKS: *Fakten und Erfindungen: Zeitgenössische Epik im Grenzgebiet von fiction und nonfiction* (Munich: Hanser, 1971);

Mitteilung an den Adel: Roman (Zurich: Benzinger, 1976); translated by Ruth Hein as *Such Sad Tidings* (New York: Viking, 1979);

Kohlhaas: Roman (Zurich: Benzinger, 1979);

Zu machen, daß ein gebraten Huhn aus der Schüssel laufe (Zurich: Benzinger, 1981);

Stella Polare (Frankfurt am Main: Suhrkamp, 1984).

OTHER: Katja Mann, *Meine ungeschriebenen Memoiren*, edited by Plessen and Michael Mann (Frankfurt am Main: Fischer, 1974); translated by Hunter and Hildegarde Hannum as *Unwritten Memories* (New York: Knopf, 1975; London: Deutsch, 1975);

"In Freiheit flüchtig: Über die Frauengestalten in Alfred Anderschs Romanen," in *LGW 64 Literaturwissenschaft–Gesellschaftswissenschaft*, edited by Volker Wehdeking (Stuttgart: Klett, 1984), pp. 118-131;

"Ostholstein: In Poesie besingen," in *Lieben Sie Deutschland? Gefühle zur Lage der Nation*, edited by Marielouise Janssen-Jourreit (Munich: Piper, 1985), pp. 294-298.

PERIODICAL PUBLICATION: "Die Kinderfrau (Ostholstein)," "Konservatismus im Angebot: 'Die Trägheit der Seele. Vier Modelle,'" *Kursbuch*, 73 (1984): 63-72.

TRANSLATIONS: Marguerite Duras, *Savannah Bay* (Frankfurt am Main: Fischer, 1985);

John Webster, *Die Herzogin von Malfi* (Hamburg: Rowohlt, 1985);

William Shakespeare, *Wie es euch gefällt* (Hamburg: Rowohlt, 1986);

Shakespeare, *Julius Caesar* (Hamburg: Rowohlt, 1986).

Elisabeth Plessen is one of many German writers of the 1970s who attempted through auto-biographical works to come to terms with their personal histories and the legacy of Nazism. Accounts of father-son and mother-daughter conflicts flooded the literary market, and historical figures were popular topics in literature. Plessen's novels contributed to the "documentary literature" of the 1970s and 1980s, in which actual public and private records were incorporated into fiction and drama. After the crisis experienced in the 1960s by writers who abandoned literature for political activism, precise documentation seemed to her necessary for historical understanding.

Elisabeth Charlotte Marguerite, Countess of Plessen was born on 15 March 1944 in Neustadt, Holstein, where she was raised on her parents' large estate, Schloß Sierhagen. She spent her college preparatory years in boarding schools, going on to study history, philosophy, and German philology in Paris and Berlin. She distanced herself from her aristocratic background as childhood experiences with refugees and the student activism of her university years alienated her from its value system. She received a doctorate in German from the Free University of Berlin with a dissertation investigating experimental writings based on historical facts. She then traveled to the West Indies, South America, and the Soviet Union before establishing herself as an independent writer of poems, essays, radio plays, stories, and novels. After living for several years in Berlin and Munich she traveled to the United States and Australia and finally settled in Hamburg. In the 1980s she has translated plays from French and English into German; these plays have been produced in Hamburg and other German cities.

Plessen's early works deal with German "Vergangenheitsbewältigung" (coming to terms with the past) from a woman's point of view; they challenge the accepted socialization process and the use of violence for the "common good." Calling into question traditional historical writing that claims to be objective and doubting the truth of many so-called historical facts, she presents a new way of entering into a dialogue with the past by investigating the subtle influence of personal history and the effect of the social environment on private relationships. Plessen's work skirts the borderline between fact and fiction.

Her first book was her dissertation, *Fakten und Erfindungen: Zeitgenössische Epik im Grenzgebiet von fiction und nonfiction* (Facts and Fiction: Contemporary Epic Literature in the Border Area of Fiction and Nonfiction, 1971), which demonstrates that reality is always shaped according to the point of view of the observer. Focusing on works by Ernst Schnabel, Franz Kafka, Truman Capote, and Per Olov Enquist, Plessen notes that nonfiction novelists "rekapitulieren ihre Unterlagen nicht einfach, sondern inszenieren sie. Da sich die Wertigkeit der einzelnen Dokumente in der Koordinierung mit anderen verändert, erbringen sie damit mehr als nur 'Zweifel am Text', nämlich die konstruktive Dekonstruktion von Ideologie" (don't simply recapitulate their documents but stage them. Since the value of individual documents changes in juxtaposition to others, they cause more than "doubt in the text," namely a constructive deconstruction of ideology).

Plessen's collection of stories *Zu machen, daß ein gebraten Huhn aus der Schüssel laufe* (To Make a Fried Chicken Walk Out of the Serving Bowl, 1981) forms a kaleidoscopic pattern of reality from daily occurrences, memories, fantasies, and feelings. Plessen's stream-of-consciousness narration often imperceptibly blends realistic observations with the expression of a deep inner urgency, imbuing the prose with a magical quality. An almost romantic style has been attributed to her work. The publisher's remark on the dust cover that in her writings "das Wirkliche unwirklich erscheint und das Phantastische real" (the real appears unreal and the fantastic appears real) recalls Friedrich Schlegel's description of the nineteenth-century romantic writer's aim. Yet Plessen is no neoromantic; a reading of her major novels will dispel this notion.

Plessen transformed the experiences of her youth into the first portrayal of a father-daughter conflict in German literature in *Mitteilung an den Adel* (Message to the Aristocracy, 1976; translated as *Such Sad Tidings*, 1979), for which she received the Critics' Prize for Literature. The novel shows that the private sphere is intricately interwoven with the political one; but because this interdependence is not normally recognized, unquestioned stereotypes and anachronistic values are perpetuated. In *Mitteilung an den Adel* Plessen experiments with innovative stylistic techniques. No story unfolds; several levels of time are presented simultaneously. In the early 1970s the journalist Augusta is notified of the death of her father, C. A., and leaves Munich to attend the funeral on the large family estate in northern Germany. Time elapses in the ordinary way as Augusta narrates her trip. On a second time level she reproduces memories of her past. As a student in Berlin in the late 1960s she had been a member of a student organization opposing the government and the established parties. After she signed her name to a protest document, her father had disowned her.

As Augusta drives on the Autobahn, she tries to deal with the fact that her father's death has been partly blamed on her shaming the family name. In a series of imagined conversations with her father she tries in retrospect to confront his looming image. She recognizes that her attempts to arrive at a mutual understanding stem from a certain similarity to C. A. and a love-hate feeling for him. She also needs to resolve the fears that bind her too tightly to those structures of the past that she despises. Her imaginary conversations reveal a traumatic childhood lived in the inflexible traditions of the aristocracy. The physical and mental abuse suffered by Augusta and her brother and sister resulted from the social system rather than from her father's personal inhumanity. She now wants to make her father understand that his values must be reexamined, that analytical thinking and facts must supersede his rigid stereotypes and generalizations. She tries to make him see that the agribusiness he rebuilt after the war into a large money-making enterprise was dependent on the poverty of his workers. In the aristocrat's life thinking, feeling, and doing are in disharmony; his personal sphere is split from his public and political consciousness. The father condemns the violence of the student movement, but he is a fanatical big-game hunter; he adores his wife's youthful face in an old photograph, but he has hardly anything in common with her in later life. The unconscious stress such discrepancies cause manifests itself in alcoholism.

On a third time level Plessen quotes from a fragmentary narrative written by Augusta's father after World War II. His attempt to shape his war experiences into a novel are embarrassingly trivial and naive. No ethical "Vergangenheitsbewältigung" can be observed in his writing; instead, there is praise for heroic deeds and the contention that there will always be war. The daughter cannot condone such blindness to what really happened in Nazi Germany. As she nears her father's estate she realizes that the funeral will be a superficial show in which she cannot participate, and she decides to turn back. In this generational struggle, in which a daughter emancipates herself from her past and reaches an equal position opposite a powerful father, the "message to the aristocracy" is to become conscious of its rigidity and inhumanity. Although Augusta admits her own inability to reform society and expresses disappointment with the student movement, she has at least learned to recognize the problems plaguing the country that is symbolized by her father. Plessen's personal history thus serves to criticize the fatherland as well as the father.

Plessen's experiments in combining historical fact and fiction move from the personal to the public sphere in her novel *Kohlhaas* (1979), another indictment of the aristocracy. She invites readers to follow the narrator's difficult and painful attempt to re-create the sixteenth-century rebel Kohlhaas and what he must have experienced during his attempt to obtain justice from a corrupt government. No attempt is made to present objective truth; the narrator first does meticulous research on the period, then rethinks it subjectively and augments her findings with personal experience and creative guessing. To her horror, she sees that nothing has changed much since Kohlhaas's time; she finds that human rights continue to be violated and that material concerns, corrupt governments, terrorism, and failed rebellions are still part of human life.

The story of Kohlhaas has inspired writers for centuries; Heinrich von Kleist's novella "Michael Kohlhaas" (1810) was made into a movie in the 1970s, and the American writer E. L. Doctorow modernized the story in his novel *Ragtime* (1975) at about the same time Plessen wrote her version. She starts with the end to avoid suspense. She wants her readers to follow critically the narrator's attempts to make Kohlhaas believable to herself, to form their own picture of the peasant leader who assembled a group of rebels to burn and loot in order to draw attention to his unsuccessful search for justice after his horses were illegally impounded at the Brandenburg-Saxony border. While Kleist freely fictionalized the story to include an ideological message for his contemporaries, Plessen never twists the facts. In the end Kleist has the horses returned to Kohlhaas, who can go to his execution knowing that justice has triumphed for the next generation. In Plessen's novel the horses die before Kohlhaas can regain them, a fact confirmed by historical accounts. She is interested in studying different types of rebels and the fate of rebellions. In Kohlhaas she recognizes not only a rebel fighting for his human rights but also a man who endangers his family in the name of abstract moral values; in Nickel Minckwitz, a rebel leader who does not appear in Kleist's story, she draws a professional adventurer who eventually sells out for profit; even more emphatically than Kleist, Plessen presents a Martin Luther who has accommodated himself to the forces in power. The narrator concludes that the rebellion, which involved violence and murder, was self-defeating: the authorities received public support for instituting an even more reactionary regime than existed before. No glimmer of hope is held out: Kohlhaas's torture and slow death point to a grim future for human rights. Plessen wrote the novel at a time when grass-roots movements had sprung up in Germany; she demonstrates that the grass-roots methods of Kohlhaas do not work. The question whether nonviolence would be a practical alternative is left open. The novel constitutes her coming to terms with the realities of the 1970s, when the political climate in Germany became more conservative if not reactionary and introspection and a withdrawal into the private sphere became common.

In her novel *Stella Polare* (North Star, 1984) Plessen focuses on personal relationships in the 1980s. Luise von Kai, a writer, spends a few months with Max Fischer, a physician and writer, in a beautiful house in northern Italy; many other guests come and go. The characters gain full dimension mainly through conversations, the dominant narrative technique of the novel, or stream-of-consciousness reflections. Plessen shows how seductive it is for a woman to abandon herself to traditional love. Luise and Max have agreed not to work during their stay in Italy; Max, however, always lives in his work. He needs to be surrounded by people for inspiration; Luise, on the other hand, has always worked in solitude. Her love for Max is in direct conflict with her work and her need for independence. Max's patriarchal tendencies make him yearn for a family; he resents Luise's creative work because it takes her away from him. Although she has considerably emancipated herself, the effects of the female socialization process are deeply ingrained in her. Dreams of having her lover's child invade her troubled psyche. At first she gladly assumes her duties as a hostess, but the exertions become intolerable. As the outer world intrudes and demands her attention, her relationship with Max becomes more problematic. While Max sporadically escapes from the turbulence created by visitors, she dutifully endures it. The title of the novel reflects the German literary tradition in which northerners travel to Italy to learn a less serious attitude toward life. "Stella Polare" is also the name of a tavern in town where Max plays the pinball machines and becomes inspired to write his next novel while Luise watches. Although remnants of patriarchal conditions still prevail, at the end there is no regression to traditional forms in their relationship. Max leaves; Luise begins to work. They expect to be together again soon.

In this, her most recent novel, Plessen's concern for history moves to the background, allowing her to focus on the present. She attempts to shape a workable personal existence from the changing fragments of facts and fantasies that touch the life of each individual in a different manner. Each new novel by Plessen confronts the dominant currents of German thought. Like the philosopher Jürgen Habermas, she believes that we reflect our history both as individuals and as members of society and that historical knowledge can be used to influence the future.

References:

Ingeborg Drewitz, "Elisabeth Plessen," in *Neue Literatur der Frauen: Deutschsprachige Autorinnen der Gegenwart*, edited by Heinz Puknus (Munich: Beck, 1980), pp. 224-230;

Drewitz, *Zeitverdichtung: Essays, Kritiken, Portraits gesammelt aus zwei Jahrzehnten* (Vienna, Munich & Zurich: Europa, 1980), pp. 284-286;

Helga W. Kraft and Harry Marshall, "Elisabeth Plessen's Discourse with the Past: Two Historical Novels from the 1970s," *Monatshefte*, 77 (1985): 156-169;

Jürgen Serke, "Elisabeth Plessen: Eine Autorin, die niemand haben wollte," in his *Frauen schreiben* (Hamburg: Gruner & Jahr, 1979), pp. 309-310.

Brigitte Reimann

(21 July 1933-20 February 1973)

Judith H. Cox

BOOKS: *Der Tod der schönen Helena* (Berlin: Verlag des Ministeriums des Innern, 1955);

Die Frau am Pranger: Erzählung (Berlin: Neues Leben, 1956: revised, 1962);

Kinder von Hellas (Berlin: Verlag des Ministeriums für Nationale Verteidigung, 1956);

Das Geständnis: Erzählung (Berlin: Aufbau, 1960);

Ein Mann steht vor der Tür: Hörspiel, by Reimann and Siegfried Pitschmann (Berlin: Aufbau, 1960);

Ankunft im Alltag: Erzählung (Berlin: Neues Leben, 1961);

Die Geschwister: Erzählung (Berlin: Aufbau, 1963);

Das grüne Licht der Steppen: Tagebuch einer Sibirienreise (Berlin: Neues Leben, 1965);

Franziska Linkerhand: Roman (Berlin: Neues Leben, 1974);

Brigitte Reimann in ihren Briefen und Tagebüchern, edited by Elisabeth Elten-Krause and Walter Lewerenz (Berlin: Neues Leben, 1983); republished as *Die geliebte, die verfluchte Hoffnung* (Darmstadt: Luchterhand, 1983).

OTHER: "Sieben Scheffel Salz," by Reimann and Siegfried Pitschmann, in *Hörspieljahrbuch I* (Berlin: Henschel, 1961), pp. 63-93.

PERIODICAL PUBLICATION: "Im Kombinat," *Neue Deutsche Literatur,"* 11 (January 1963): 19-47.

Brigitte Reimann, Christa Wolf, and Irmtraud Morgner are representative of the first generation of women writers of the German Democratic Republic (GDR). Reimann's career documents the literary history of East Germany during its first quarter century; her works reflect the issues that confronted society as well as literature in the GDR. Critics regard her early works less for their literary quality than for what Fritz J. Raddatz calls their seismographic aspect: they reveal "die politische Moral, die Hoffnungen und

Verzweiflungen, die Vorstellungen und Klischees, die Ehrlichkeit und die Verstellungen" (the political morality, the hopes and doubts, the conceptions and clichés, the honesty and the disguises) of East Germany. From antifascist themes to Bitterfelder Weg (Bitterfeld Way) and from Ankunft (arrival) literature to Republikflucht (flight from the [German Democratic] Republic), Reimann reflected what was happening in the GDR. Her final work, *Franziska Linkerhand* (1974), along with Morgner's *Leben und Abenteuer der Troubadour Beatriz nach Zeugnissen ihrer Spielfrau Laura* (Life and Adventures of the Troubadour Beatriz as Chronicled by her Minstrel Laura) and Gerti Tetzner's *Karin W.,* both published the same year, marked the beginning in the GDR of a women's literature that featured a new subjectivity and self-realization of the female individual. The development in quality of Reimann's work also parallels that of East German literature: while her early works are considered naive and mediocre, her last novel is regarded as a milestone in the literary history of the GDR. She was finally recognized as an author of serious literature at the same time Western critics began to appreciate East German literature.

Born in 1933 in Burg, a small city in what is today the GDR, Reimann was the daughter of a journalist. After completing high school she worked for two years as a teacher and then in various occupations, including bookselling and reporting. Nothing was more important to her than becoming a writer, but she was afraid that she could not live up to the ideals of the vocation. Her first marriage, which began in 1953, was marked by constant fights and reconciliations, often due to her love affairs–a pattern Reimann would continue most of her life. In 1954 she gave birth three months prematurely to a girl who died immediately. Later that year she took poison after an argument with her husband.

In addition to the problems in her marriage Reimann struggled with her writing career. She worked on several stories and novellas concurrently, unable to apply herself to one project long enough to complete and publish it. Reimann spoke of her struggle "mit meinen ständigen Zweifeln, mit meinem Unvermögen, das auszudrücken, was ich sagen will" (with my constant doubt, with my inability to express what I want to say). Her first published work came late in 1955 with the story *Der Tod der schönen Helena* (Death of the Beautiful Helena). The next year two successful stories, *Die Frau am Pranger* (The Woman at the Pillory) and *Kinder von Hellas* (Children of Greece), appeared. The former, for which *Der Tod der schönen Helena* was a preliminary study, is the tragic story of a young married German woman, Kathrin Martin, who has an affair with a Russian prisoner of war, Alexej, toward the end of World War II. When the villagers discover the relationship, Kathrin is placed in the pillory, spat upon, and stoned. Alexej, the Marxist, displays sentiment and a fine character, while Kathrin's husband Heinrich is thoughtless, coarse, and unable to establish a sensitive relationship with his wife. The plot is simple, the characters are not believably drawn, and the language is fraught with clichés. While barely noticed in the West, *Die Frau am Pranger* had by 1957 become one of the most talked-about books in the GDR. Its popularity led to an East German television version in 1962.

Marxism and love are also the themes in *Kinder von Hellas*, but in this work a conflict arises between them. The setting is the Greek civil war in the late 1940s. Helena and her friend Costas are members of the independence movement against the monarchist government. During one of their raids Costas, realizing that it is impossible to escape alive, convinces Helena to go over to the other side with him and buys their freedom with treasonable statements. Costas loves Helena so strongly that he believes that the struggle against the fascists would be in vain if it included Helena's death. Eventually their treason plays on Helena's conscience, and she returns to the resistance.

Criticism of this work centered on its characterizations: Helena, though only fifteen, behaves and thinks like a politically experienced adult. But Reimann succeeds in demonstrating that during trying times the intellectual view is not always enough, especially for young people.

In 1956 Reimann became a member of the GDR writers' union. In 1957 she wrote that her style had become cooler, more distant, and less sentimental and that she no longer got as passionately involved with her characters as she did with *Die Frau am Pranger* (she cried every time she read it). Late in 1958 Reimann and her husband were divorced; three months later she married the writer Siegfried Pitschmann.

In the story *Das Geständnis* (The Confession, 1960) Martin, a model factory worker, confesses that, as a fifteen-year-old at the end of the war, he turned in a deserter who was subsequently shot by the Nazis. The state institutes no proceedings against him and leaves the decision about his studies to be a teacher up to the firm where he works. Through his confession of guilt during fascist times Martin finds or "arrives at" socialism. This is Reimann's first work to use a worker, instead of a member of the petty bourgeoisie or an intellectual, as the central character. Once again the characterization is unrealistic–Martin is too good to be true.

In 1959 the GDR introduced the Bitterfelder Weg program, which encouraged authors to go to the factories and construction sites and labor alongside the workers. In 1960 Reimann and her husband moved to a large construction site, the "Schwarze Pumpe" (Black Pump) in Hoyerswerda, where they remained for eight years. Their contract called for them to lead a circle of worker-writers, read manuscripts, and conduct book discussions. Reimann also worked one day a week as a pipefitter and later as a welder.

In 1960 and 1961 she and Pitschmann wrote two radio plays: *Ein Mann steht vor der Tür* (A Man Stands at the Door, 1960) and "Sieben Scheffel Salz" (Seven Bushels of Salt, 1961). In the latter work, which they also adapted as a stage play, a new manager joins a work brigade and encounters people who, without being qualified, want to be put in a higher wage bracket. A factory discussion eventually solves the problem, and the manager is finally accepted by the workers. This play is typical of the period's "Brigadestücke" (brigade pieces), a subgenre of East German literature that depicts conflicts and problems on the job and criticizes managerial shortcomings but generally solves the problems in the end. These radio plays earned Reimann and Pitschmann the literature prize of the Free German Trade Union Federation in 1961.

Reimann was awarded the same prize the next year for *Ankunft im Alltag* (Arrival in Everyday Life, 1961), about three high school graduates who spend a "practical" year at the

"Schwarze Pumpe," during which they mature and become dedicated to socialism. This story was Reimann's best work to that time. While the characters are still schematically developed and the language, conflicts, and solutions simple, the story was, in Konrad Franke's view, "sehr viel realistischer, lockerer erzählt, in fast natürlichem Ton" (told in a much more realistic and relaxed way, in an almost natural tone).

Recha, Curt, and Nikolaus react to the work place in various ways, according to their individual backgrounds and character. At first glance *Ankunft im Alltag* is about Recha's attempt to decide whether she loves Curt or Nikolaus, but the actual theme is one which had appeared in *Das Geständnis* and would remain the basis of Reimann's subsequent works: the arrival of young people at socialism–their experiences in production, their conceptions of work, their relations to the rest of the work brigade, and their emotional and intellectual reactions to the system. Recha's choice of Nikolaus in the end is motivated by her newly won insight and understanding of work and life.

The novel caused a great deal of critical discussion in the GDR, much of it negative. But it was popular with the public, as the newspaper *Sonntag* demonstrated in February 1962 when it printed an entire page of letters of praise from readers, as well as a letter from the highly respected writer Anna Seghers defending Reimann.

In January 1963 the journal *Neue Deutsche Literatur* published Reimann's short story "Im Kombinat" (In the Factory). This story is also a direct result of her work at the "Schwarze Pumpe," for as Reimann said, "Ich schreibe nur schwer etwas, was mich nicht ganz persönlich angeht. Ich meine nicht Autobiographie im engen Sinn, sondern Selbsterlebtes, Selbstnacherlebtes" (It is difficult for me to write something that does not concern me very personally. I don't mean autobiography in the narrow sense, but self-experienced, self-reexperienced). Elisabeth Arendt, a young artist at a factory who leads a circle of artists, clashes with Ohm Heiners, an "old Communist" artist who is also employed by the factory. A heated argument results when Heiners asks Elisabeth how she likes his new picture, and she finally musters the courage to tell him that it is bad–he does not know the people he is painting, and his style has not changed in twenty or thirty years. The story is a vehicle for an intellectual discussion of art theories in the socialist society. At the end the conflict is resolved through discussion, and a humiliated Heiners leaves the factory.

Later in 1963 Reimann used Elisabeth Arendt, as well as her brother Uli and her fiancé Joachim, who are mentioned in "Im Kombinat," to deal with the problem of "Republikflucht." In 1960 Reimann's brother had left the GDR, leaving her saddened, hurt, and frustrated. She wondered why no one had written about the tragedy of the division of Germany, and in asking herself what she would have done had she known her brother was planning to leave she got the idea for the story *Die Geschwister* (The Brothers and Sisters, 1963). In the story Elisabeth knows that Uli intends to leave the GDR and, during the course of a day and a half, convinces him to stay. Their older brother, Konrad, had already left the GDR, and he and Elisabeth represent the two poles between which Uli must decide. The story has received critical acclaim because it is a realistic rather than idealistic presentation of the conflict facing Uli. As Peter Hutchinson says, "His choice is not between black and white, but between clearly distinguishable shades of grey." The story is not always convincing, but it is important because it depicts the experiences and disappointment of the first generation of intellectuals to grow up and be educated in the GDR. For this story the GDR's Academy of Arts awarded Reimann the 1965 Heinrich Mann Prize.

In the summer of 1964 Reimann traveled for eleven days with a delegation of the Free German Youth through Siberia. Her next published work, *Das grüne Licht der Steppen: Tagebuch einer Sibirienreise* (The Green Light of the Steppes: Diary of a Siberian Trip, 1965), is a result of that experience. Also in 1964 Reimann divorced her second husband, remarried one month later, and finished the first chapter of what was to be her last work. She had been working on it since 1962, when she became interested in the architecture at Hoyerswerda and conceived the idea of writing the story of a young female architect who comes "jung, begabt, voller leidenschaftlicher Pläne, in die Baukastenstadt und träumt von Palästen aus Glas und Stahl–und dann muß sie Bauelemente zählen" (young, talented, full of passionate plans, to the box-of-bricks city and dreams of palaces of glass and steel–and then has to count building units).

Work on her monumental final novel was a constant struggle for Reimann. In 1968 she was operated on for cancer of the lymph glands after nine months going from doctor to doctor trying to discover what was wrong with her. When she recovered from the operation, she left Hoyerswerda and moved to Neubrandenburg, where she spent the rest of her life moving back and forth from her apartment to the hospital. She divorced her third husband in 1969 and married for the fourth time in 1971. By then she was very sick and weak. In September she wrote that she had lived for months "in einem merkwürdigen Dämmerzustand. Kann nicht mehr schreiben, nicht viel lesen" (in a strange twilight state. Cannot write any more, cannot read much). In a furious race with death she worked when she could. She wrote to a friend that it was not ambition or the desire to publish that drove her but the fear that so much time and so many pages, several of which had turned out quite well, would be wasted: "Eine wirklich gute Schriftstellerin, wie ich es früher erträumte—werde ich doch nicht mehr, und alles, was ich der deutschen Literaturgeschichte zu bieten habe, ist der dubiose Begriff der 'Ankunftsliteratur' " (A really good author, as I earlier dreamed–I shall not be, and all that I have to offer German literary history is the dubious concept of "arrival literature").

Franziska Linkerhand was published posthumously in 1974. Franziska is a middle-class girl who becomes an architect and goes to help build the city of Neustadt. She arrives full of ideas and ideals but finds that the socialist plan is limited to economic and materialistic concerns. She wants to make Neustadt a human, livable, and vibrant city instead of what the current plan has made it– what Marget Eifler calls a "Reißbrettstadt ohne Wohnlichkeit, deren ungesundes Lebensmilieu asoziale Probleme fördert, wie es die steigenden Zahlen der Selbstmorde, Vergewaltigungen und Trunksucht beweisen" (drawing-board city without livability, whose unhealthy milieu promotes asocial conduct, as the rising numbers of suicides, rapes and alcoholism prove). Reimann points to the damage done to the socialist idea by an unbending state apparatus; she blames the state for impairing, instead of furthering, the cooperation and contribution of its members. Reimann creates a vivid and realistic picture of the life-styles and relationships Franziska encounters in Neustadt; according to Eifler, "Ihre Darstellung übertrifft dabei an Lebensechtheit alle anderen Romane ihrer Zeit" (Her portrayal surpasses in authenticity all other novels of her time).

The novel employs a double narrative perspective. Much of it is first-person monologue–intimate, reflective, and autobiographical–directed at Ben, the great love of Franziska's life. Interspersed throughout is an omniscient third-person narrative which allows the reader to view Franziska and her development objectively.

Reimann's criticisms were always intended to be positive; she believed in the GDR but was frustrated with certain aspects of life there. She found in Hoyerswerda that many workers were genuine heroes while others did not look beyond their pay envelopes. She wrote because "Bücher helfen verändern–das ist eine der schlichten Wahrheiten, die ich entdeckt oder wiederentdeckt habe" (Books help to change–that is one of the simple truths that I have discovered or rediscovered).

Reimann died of cancer on 20 February 1973; although almost six hundred pages long, her novel was unfinished. She had hoped to go back through the work to check for inconsistencies, since her ideas had changed over the years; she had also intended to explain more fully Franziska's decision to leave the man she loved and go back to the frustrations of Neustadt. That the novel was left in this unfinished state makes its quality and success even more remarkable. *Franziska Linkerhand* is a much discussed and reviewed book and has achieved high praise from critics in both East and West. Bärbel Jaksch and Heiner Maaß dramatized the novel in 1978, and a DEFA film based on it, "*Unser kurzes Leben* (Our Short Life), premiered in January 1981. The novel has sold more than one hundred thousand copies in the GDR. Brigitte Reimann's fear of always being identified with "Ankunft" literature has proved to be unfounded. It is unfortunate that the world was deprived of her talents just as she developed into a writer of distinction.

Interviews:

"Für mich ist Politik etwas sehr Persönliches: Ein Sonntag-Gespräch zwischen Klaus Steinhaußen und Brigitte Reimann," *Sonntag,* 26 May 1963;

Klaus Höpcke, "Brigitte Reimann schreibt ihren ersten Roman," *Neues Deutschland,* 11 July 1964;

"Wenn die Wirklichkeit sich meldet: Annemarie Auer sprach mit Brigitte Reimann," *Sonntag,* 18 February 1968.

Letters:

Was zählt, ist die Wahrheit: Briefe von Schriftstellern

der DDR, edited by W. Liersch (Halle: Mittel-deutscher Verlag, 1975), pp. 290-330.

Bibliographies:

Hans-Peter Anderle "Brigitte Reimann," in *Mittel-deutsche Erzähler: Eine Studie mit Proben und Porträts* (Cologne: Verlag für Wissenschaft und Politik, 1965), pp. 248-255;

Konrad Franke, *Die Literatur der Deutschen Demokratischen Republik* (Zurich & Munich: Kindler, 1974), pp. 445-448;

Manfred Behn-Liebherz, "Brigitte Reimann," in *Neue Literatur der Frauen: Deutschsprachige Autorinnen der Gegenwart,* edited by Heinz Puknus (Munich: Beck, 1980), pp. 165-171;

Behn-Liebherz, "Brigitte Reimann," in *Kindlers Literaturgeschichte der Gegenwart,* edited by Hans Ludwig Arnold (Munich: Edition text + kritik, 1982), n. pag.

References:

Annemarie Auer, "Das Mögliche," *Neue Deutsche Literatur,* 13 (November 1965): 144-146;

Christel Berger, "Über Prosa junger Autoren," *Weimarer Beiträge,* 19, no. 4 (1974): 169-184;

Ewald Birr, "Das grüne Licht der Steppen," *Der Bibliothekar,* no. 7 (1965): 749-750;

Günter und Johanna Braun, "Die Welt in Hoyerswerda," *Neue Deutsche Literatur,* 12 (January 1964): 111-116;

Herbert Dohms, "Bewährungsprobe," *Neue Deutsche Literatur,* 5 (January 1957): 143-147;

Günter Ebert, "Die verratenen Gefühle," *Forum,* no. 9 (1963): 23;

Ulrich Eggestein, "Die Geschwister," *Alternative,* no. 38 / 39 (1964): 146-147;

Marget Eifler, *Dialiktische Dynamik: Kulturpolitik und Ästhetik im Gegenwartsroman der DDR* (Bonn: Bouvier Verlag Herbert Grundmann, 1976), pp. 100-109;

Elisabeth Elten-Krause, *Brigitte Reimann, 1933-1973* (Neubrandenburg: Das Literaturzentrum, 1978);

Manfred Graupner, "Ankunft im Alltag," *Der Bibliothekar,* no. 8 (1961): 831-832;

E. Günter, W. Liersch, and K. Walther, *Kritik 75: Rezensionen zur DDR-Literatur* (Halle: Mitteldeutscher Verlag, 1976), pp. 137-163;

Peter Hutchinson, *Literary Presentations of Divided Germany: The Development of a Central Theme in East German Fiction 1945-1970* (Cambridge: Cambridge University Press, 1977), pp. 84-90;

Werner Illberg, "Wurzeln im Hier und Heute," *Neue Deutsche Literatur,* 10 (September 1962): 123-128;

Manfred Jäger, "Bemerkungen zu Brigitte Reimanns *Franziska Linkerhand,*" *Amsterdamer Beiträge zur neueren Germanistik,* 11 / 12 (1981): 407-417;

Hans Kaufmann, "Ein Vermächtnis, ein Debüt: Brigitte Reimann: *Franziska Linkerhand;* Gerti Tetzner: *Karen W.,*" in Eva and Hans Kaufmann, *Erwartung und Angebot: Studien zum gegenwärtigen Verhältnis von Literatur und Gesellschaft in der DDR* (Berlin: Akademie, 1976), pp. 193-215;

Wolfgang Knipp, *Zum Verhältnis von Individuum und Gesellschaft in ausgewählten Romanen der DDR-Literatur: Anmerkungen zum sozialistischen Menschenbild* (Cologne: Pahl-Rugenstein, 1980), pp. 150-177, 479-517;

Wolfgang Lehmann, "Die Geschwister," *Der Bibliothekar,* no. 8 (1963): 832-835;

Lehmann, "Nicht ausgenutzte Möglichkeiten," *Neue Deutsche Literatur,* 13 (November 1965): 143-144;

Walter Lewerenz, "Ankunft im Alltag," *Junge Kunst,* no. 9 (1961): 25-27;

Karin McPherson, "*Franziska Linkerhand*—Introduction and Analysis of the Last (Unfinished) Work by the Late GDR Novelist Brigitte Reimann," *University of Dayton Review,* 13 (Winter 1978): 13-24;

Fritz J. Raddatz, *Traditionen und Tendenzen: Materialien zur Literatur der DDR* (Frankfurt am Main: Suhrkamp, 1972), pp. 374-379;

W. Röhr, "Ankunft im Alltag," *Forum,* no. 10 (1962): 6;

Hanns-Jürgen Rusch, "Unser Porträt: Brigitte Reimann," *Börsenblatt für den Deutschen Buchhandel,* 29 (October 1963): 761;

Helmut Sakowski, "Brigitte Reimann," *Neue Deutsche Literatur,* 22 (January 1974): 97-105;

Anna Seghers, "Über eine Rezension," *Sonntag,* 11 February 1962;

Sigrid Töpelmann, "Selbsterlebtes, Selbstnacherlebtes . . . ," *Neue Deutsche Literatur,* 11 (August 1963): 193-197;

Frank Trommler, "DDR-Erzählung und Bitterfelder Weg," *Basis,* 3 (1972): 61-97.

Papers:

Brigitte Reimann's papers are in the Literaturzentrum in Neubrandenburg, GDR.

Gerold Späth

(16 October 1939-   )

Todd C. Hanlin
University of Arkansas

BOOKS: *Unschlecht: Roman* (Zurich: Arche, 1970); translated by Rita and Robert Kimber as *A Prelude to the Long Happy Life of Maximilian Goodman* (Boston: Little, Brown, 1975);

Stimmgänge: Roman (Zurich: Arche, 1972);

Zwölf Geschichten (Zurich: Arche, 1973); republished as *Heißer Sonntag: Zwölf Geschichten* (Frankfurt am Main: Fischer, 1982);

Die heile Hölle (Zurich: Arche, 1974);

Balzapf oder Als ich auftauchte (Frankfurt am Main: Fischer, 1977);

Phönix, die Reise in den Tag: Erzählungen (Pfaffenweiler: Pfaffenweiler Presse, 1978);

Ende der Nacht (Pfaffenweiler: Pfaffenweiler Presse, 1979);

Commedia (Frankfurt am Main: Fischer, 1980);

Von Rom bis Kotzebue: 15 Reisebilder (Zurich & Munich: Artemis, 1982);

Sacramento: Neun Geschichten (Frankfurt am Main: Fischer, 1983);

Sindbadland (Frankfurt am Main: Fischer, 1984);

Verschwinden in Venedig: Geschichten (Pfaffenweiler: Pfaffenweiler Presse, 1985);

Heißer Sonntag/Heiße Suntig: Ein Hörspiel, edited by Bruno Weder (Zurich: Sabe-Verlagsinstitut für Lehrmittel, 1987);

Barbarswila: Roman (Frankfurt am Main: Fischer, 1988).

PLAY: *Unser Wilhelm! Unser Tell!*, translated into French by Claude Chenou as *Nôtre Guillaume Tell*, Théâtre de Carouge, Geneva, 30 April 1985.

Gerold Späth burst upon the German-language literary scene in 1970 with his critically acclaimed first novel, *Unschlecht* (translated as *A Prelude to the Long Happy Life of Maximilian Goodman*, 1975). At a time when the overpoliticization of European literature had raised doubts about the very future of fiction, Späth's baroque narrative signaled the emergence of a young Swiss author who could successfully chart his own course;

Gerold Späth (photograph by Isolde Ohlbaum, Munich)

succeeding works corroborate his ability to write independently of contemporary trends or fads. Frequent laudations in the press, numerous literary prizes and awards, and the acquisition of a major West German publisher–S. Fischer of Frankfurt am Main–attest to Späth's critical success. His acceptance as a popular writer has been hampered by the rambling nature of his prose, the Swiss regionalism of his works, and the intimidating size of his novels (which average well over four hundred pages), as well as by his distaste for self-serving public relations. Nevertheless, the nature and scope of his vigorous prose have attracted increasing critical acclaim and an expanding readership.

Späth's ancestors moved from southern Germany to Switzerland at the turn of the twentieth century, settled in the town of Rapperswil in Canton St. Gaul before World War I, and acquired Swiss citizenship by 1917. The centuries-old Späth organ- and piano-building firm, reputedly one of Mozart's early suppliers, was also transported to the shores of Lake Zurich. Späth was born in Rapperswil on 16 October 1939 to Josef and Martha Rügg Späth. Swiss citizenship and the family's extraordinary dedication to craftsmanship left their mark on his later literary efforts: all of his works depict Switzerland, and many of them are set in his hometown of Rapperswil (or such reincarnations of it as Spießbünzen, Barbarswil, Molchgüllen, or Seestadt); moreover, Späth insists that his writings, like the fine musical instruments created by his family, be skilled pieces of craftsmanship that can endure for centuries. In regard to the question of influences on his writing Späth says: "Meine Familie war immer *jemand*, oder sie dachte jedenfalls, sie sei von gewisser Bedeutung–das ist mir vermittelt worden. Natürlich habe ich das relativiert, doch kann so etwas durchaus prägend sein. Auch der Orgelbau prägt; wie eine Orgel nicht nur für 'die Saison,' sondern für die nächsten hundert, zweihundert Jahre gebaut wird, so schreibe ich Bücher in der Meinung, man könne sie auch 'morgen' noch lesen. Ferner die Ethik des Handwerkers, der sich bewußt ist, eine komplizierte Sache zu machen (Orgeln sind bekanntlich im Prinzip einfach, im Detail ungeheuer kompliziert; außerdem werden sie von Grund auf gebaut, d.h. aus Holzbrettern, Zinnbarren, etwas Blei, Leder etc. macht die Kunst des Orgelbauers ein klingendes Wunderding–auch das prägt; nur ich kann meine Sache von Grund auf so gut machen, wie nur ich es kann). Sonst? Natürlich die regionale Umgebung; das soziale Gefüge hier; das geschichtliche Bewußtsein; die Enge und ihr Gegensatz: die jederzeit zur Verfügung stehende Möglichkeit, vom Zentrum Europas aus in kurzer Zeit jede beliebige Ecke zu erreichen; auch Lektüre prägt: Nachdem ich sehr früh, etwa mit acht Jahren, Twains *Tom Sawyer* gelesen hatte, fand ich, so etwas wolle ich auch einmal machen: ein Buch. . . . Eigentlich wär's die ideale Gelegenheit, den guten Leuten etwas ganz Phantastisches zu erzählen: Vater ein Säufer, Mutter landstörzende Prinzessin, oder war das die Tante?–Womit ich meine, daß diese ganzen Prägungen eben immer relativiert werden müssen; es ist immer alles ein wenig anders, Kleinigkeiten sind meistens viel wichtiger als konstante äußere Zustände" (My family was always *someone*, or at least they thought they had some importance–that much has been passed down to me. Naturally I relativize that in my works, but still, such things can undoubtedly make a lasting impression. Also organ building can be an influence; just as organs are built to last for the next hundred or two hundred years, and not just for the "season," I also write my books so that someone could also read them "tomorrow." Further, there is the ethic of the craftsman who is conscious of doing something complicated [as everyone knows, organs are simple in principle, but terribly complicated in detail; in addition, they are built from the ground up, i.e., from wood planks, from bars of tin, some lead, leather, etc., from which the artistry of the organ builder constructs a miraculously resonating instrument–that, too, leaves a lasting impression; only I can construct my books from the ground up as well as I can]. Otherwise? Naturally, the region where I grew up and still live; the social constellation here; the historical consciousness; the proximity and its opposite: the opportunity to reach any corner of Europe in a short time from this central location; literature also influences me: after having read Twain's *Tom Sawyer* at an early age [I was probably eight at the time], I discovered that someday I, too, wanted to do something like that: a book. . . . Actually, this would be the perfect time to tell your dear readers something really fantastic: my father was a drunk, my mother a marauding princess, or was that my aunt? –By this I mean that all of these influences must constantly be seen in their relative importance; life is always a bit different than we expect, insignificant events are usually more important than the ever-present external conditions). This concluding statement clarifies Späth's apparent disinterest in the dates and major events of his life. His succinct self-portrait, "Ich bin ein Orgelbauer, der gerne Geschichten erzählt" (I am an organ builder who likes to tell stories), ignores causal forces and modestly describes the product.

From 1957 to 1963, following his secondary schooling in Rapperswil, Späth embarked on an apprenticeship in the export trade which took him to Zurich, Vevey, London, and Fribourg. Späth has admitted that his dedication to business was minimal; he would have accepted any profession that permitted him time to write. He was called up in 1958 for military service in a

Rapperswil, Switzerland, Späth's birthplace and the setting for much of his fiction

mountain battalion but was excused from duty due to a back ailment (he currently performs alternative service in civilian defense). In 1964 he married Anita Baumann, his childhood sweetheart, who gave birth to their first child, Veit, in 1967.

By 1968 Späth had decided to pursue his writing career in earnest; thereafter he helped only sporadically in his father's organ workshop as a means of supporting his family. To aid the aspiring writer, *Elle* magazine published a family portrait with a plea for support; as a result of the article, Späth was granted the use of a patron's summer home to concentrate on his writing—before he had actually published a single line. In 1970 Späth returned to Rapperswil with the manuscript for *Unschlecht* and a newborn daughter, Salome.

Späth's early novels are frequently described as picaresque adventures, reminiscent of J. J. C. von Grimmelshausen's *Der abenteuerliche Simplicissimus Teutsch* (1669; translated as *The Adventurous Simplicizissimus,* 1912) in their baroque excesses of language, plot, imagination, and wit. While this description may serve to acquaint read-

ers with Späth's general style and format, it should be taken with extreme caution; a reader concentrating on the traits mentioned will notice the vitality and humor in his stories but overlook the inherent social criticism. For example, Späth often bases his works on fantasies, dreams, hopes, or fears—inevitably involving the acquisition of wealth—shared by many in industrialized, consumer-oriented societies like Switzerland. People often dream of what they would do were they suddenly to receive substantial sums of money. Späth investigates such fantasies.

Unschlecht, for which he won the Conrad Ferdinand Meyer Prize, describes a familiar dream turned nightmare. The orphan and fisherman Johann Ferdinand Unschlecht (the titular name alludes to his simplicity and moral innocence) leads a pleasant if uneventful existence on his island in Lake Zurich near Rapperswil. He is known for his boyish pranks and affectionately dubbed "der größte Tropf am Platz" (the biggest dolt in the place). On his twenty-first birthday his guardian presents him with a new passport and a large inheritance. Unschlecht undertakes to assert his individuality by revising the passport, which reads: "Besondere Kennzeichen–Keine" (Distinguishing features–None); with a ballpoint pen he writes down all his important traits–big feet, long legs, healthy teeth, can wiggle his ears, can fish, can dive; and so on. He can, he presumes, now buy everything he has always wanted: love, influence, and a respected place in the community. With this sudden wealth and his gigantic penis (like most mythic or epic figures, he possesses one heroic trait), Unschlecht is prepared to conquer life.

He soon discovers that his friends and neighbors appreciate his wealth alone, that promiscuity does not equal love, that influence and status cannot be bought. Despite his fondest hopes and dreams, he remains "the biggest dolt in the place." As his disillusionment grows, Unschlecht becomes in turn a thief, an arsonist, a dynamiter, and finally a murderer. He has impetuously sacrificed his innocence and simple joy in life for a promising new identity; now he must flee his home as a wanted criminal and assume still other identities for his very survival. Years later, in the guise of a wealthy and influential foreign businessman, ironically called Guttmann (Goodman), he can only circle Rapperswil from a safe distance, desperately longing for the day when he might dare to return home.

The novel not only represents Späth's first successful literary venture but can be seen, in retrospect, as seminal for his entire oeuvre to date: the major themes of community and identity have been repeated and refined over the years; many of the minor figures in it develop lives of their own in later works; anecdotal structures and character profiles, here in embryonic form, dominate the author's style ten years later.

The title of Späth's second novel, *Stimmgänge* (1972), reflects the micro- and macrocosms of the organ tuner: it refers specifically to the travails of climbing about the organ to tune the pipes, and in general to the travels of the tuner as he ventures out into the world to practice his profession. The title also implies that some things in life can never be "tuned" or set right: the protagonist, Jakob Hasslocher, must sacrifice a potentially disruptive inheritance and marriage in favor of the curative craft of organ building. In this work Späth describes his own novel-writing technique, disguised as a prescription for building fine organs:

> Erstens: Im Kopf alles richtig drehen und genau der Reihe nach einfädeln und keine List vergessen.
> Zweitens: Der Sache einen Anfang und ein Ende geben.
> Drittens: Zwischen Anfang und Ende eine gut gezwirnte starke Blasbalgschnur spannen und zusehen, daß Motor, Schwimmer und Drosselklappe für konstanten Druck sorgen und der Wind nicht ausgeht; außerdem läßt sich an einer straff gespannten Blasbalgschnur alles schön aufknüpfen.
> Daher jetzt die Knöpfe. Was ich stückweise eingefädelt habe, will ich jetzt eines nach dem andern verknoten.

> (First: Turn everything over in your mind and thread the pieces together, one after the other, without forgetting your cunning.
> Second: Give the thing a beginning and an end.
> Third: Between beginning and end tighten a strong, well-woven bellowsline and make sure that the motor, float and throttle-valve provide constant pressure and that you don't run out of wind; moreover, you can tie up everything nicely on a tightly strung bellowsline.
> And now to the buttons. Everything that I have strung up piece by piece, I now intend to knot firmly in place, one after the other.)

From his first novel to his most recent, this narrative approach marks both Späth's strength and his alleged weakness. The vitality, inventiveness, and variety of his miniatures–anecdotes, portraits, adventures, sketches (the "buttons")–have

Dust jacket for Späth's monumental portrait of Rapperswil, which, while still in manuscript, won the first annual Alfred Döblin Prize in 1979

impressed reviewers and readers alike. Yet some critics perceive a weakness in the overall structure, claiming that the plot seems only a vehicle for an unrelated "string" of anecdotal adventures.

Variations on this narrative technique are the twelve short stories written before the publication of *Unschlecht*, which appeared under the title of *Zwölf Geschichten* (Twelve Stories) in 1973. The most significant of these stories is "Heißer Sonntag" (Hot Sunday), consisting of dozens of anecdotes about events and personalities in a small resort town on a hot summer day. This brilliant montage of character sketches was developed into a radio play of the same name (1987).

A more searing and depressing picture of modern Swiss life appears in the novel *Die heile*

Späth reading from his just-published 1984 travelogue-fantasy, Sindbadland, *at the library in Herrliberg, Switzerland (photograph by Gerry Egger, Zurich)*

Hölle (1974; the untranslatable title is a play on words which implies that the consumer paradise may ultimately be unlivable). It consists of portraits of four representative family members whose lives are perversions of their material success. The father is a voyeur and, eventually, a murderer; the mother is obsessed with guilt and fear of cancer; the daughter employs a sleazy gigolo to fill her empty life; and the son commits suicide in his new sports car.

Späth returns to an expanded format with the rambunctious generational novel *Balzapf oder Als ich auftauchte* (Balzapf; or, When I Was Born, 1977), which satirizes the seeking of social status. Insisting that his family has an illustrious history, young Balthazar Zapf proceeds to expose his Gypsy ancestors as criminals, rogues, and eccentrics. To protect the city of Barbarswil from the Zapfs, responsible citizens appoint Balthazar city lifeguard and honorary town crier. In retaliation for this insult Balthazar declares that the city should be razed; after a riot ensues he flees, threatening to return someday and devastate the town.

During the 1970s Späth published four sub-

stantial novels and translated four plays by other authors into Swiss dialect for stage and television; almost two dozen of his stories and opinion pieces appeared in newspapers and journals; in addition, seven of his radio plays were produced in Canada, West Germany, and Switzerland. The short stories in the collectors' volumes *Phönix, die Reise in den Tag* (Phoenix, the Journey into the Day, 1978) and *Ende der Nacht* (End of Night, 1979) have been reprinted in other anthologies of Späth's work.

Ten years after his initial success with *Unschlecht*, Späth stunned readers in 1980 with a monumental expansion of his portraiture: *Commedia* depicts the personalities of over two hundred characters in a type of public opinion poll and concludes with an equally thorough description of their environment as displayed in a museum: the curator leads a group of visitors through a series of rooms and exhibits, then locks them in a dungeon. This complicated novel depicts the isolation of individuals from and within their community. While still an uncompleted manuscript, this work was recognized in 1979 with the first annual Alfred Döblin Prize.

As Späth's reputation has grown, so have his royalties, awards, and subventions, permitting more frequent opportunities for travel. His reading tours, subsidized travel, and private excursions to Italy, Berlin, East Germany, and Alaska were the basis for the travel reports first published in newspapers and then collected in the volume *Von Rom bis Kotzebue* (From Rome to Kotzebue, 1982). The 1983 volume of short stories, *Sacramento*, also features foreign settings; the title story re-creates the lawlessness and greed of the American Wild West. This travel literature culminated in 1984 with the appearance of *Sindbadland*: infected with travel fever, the narrator presents several hundred breathless anecdotes about exotic, bizarre, often grotesque events he has experienced throughout the real world and that of his own imagination. To capture the excitement and suspense of these adventures, Späth narrates each of them in one sentence; some of these sentences are several pages long.

With the play *Unser Wilhelm! Unser Tell!* (Our William! Our Tell!), which premiered in Geneva on 30 April 1985 in a French translation, Späth returns to specifically Swiss material; his staging of this patriotic myth juxtaposes traditional Swiss ideals with the hypocrisies of contemporary society. Späth's renewed concentration on Switzerland produced another major novel, *Barbarswila* (1988), which takes place on a summer day in the town of the title—one of Späth's pseudonyms for Rapperswil. The reader is introduced to dozens of citizens of this community, including Späth's aunt and her beau, a retired lion tamer who has himself been tamed by this chaste old woman; the village idiot, Eugen Höfliger, and his female counterpart, "the beautiful Helen"; the profiteers Benito Rössler and Signor Casagrande; the fisherman Beck, who obsessively chases a mermaid; Alfred Mogelberg, breeder of St. Bernards and bees; and Erna Goll, the desperate wife of a crippled sculptor. It is clear that the narrator, like Späth, is alternately attracted to and repelled by this picturesque and seemingly in-

nocent town. Whether one should expect a new avenue for Späth's talent—he is already an accomplished painter, radio-play author, and television scriptwriter—or whether he continues to write fiction, remains to be seen.

References:

Bruno Bolliger, "Gerold Späths dichterische Welt," *Schweizer Monatshefte,* 55 (June 1975): 233-239;

Hermann Burger, "Der wortgewaltige Ausrufer," *Schweizer Monatshefte,* 58 (April 1978): 309-312;

Franz Josef Görtz, "So stark wie der Gesang der Sirenen," *Frankfurter Allgemeine Zeitung,* 2 October 1984, p. L3;

Hansjörg Graf, "Vier im Teufelskreis," *Frankfurter Allgemeine Zeitung,* 5 August 1974, p. 16;

Todd C. Hanlin, "Individuality and Tradition in the Works of Gerold Späth," in *Blick auf die Schweiz: Zur Frage der Eigenständigkeit der Schweizer Literatur seit 1970,* edited by Robert Acker and Marianne Burkhard (Amsterdam: Rodopi, 1987), pp. 81-94;

Jochen Hieber, "Erzählfeste–Fabulierfreude," *Die Zeit,* 25 November 1977, p. 4;

Wolfgang Hildesheimer, "Pandämonisches Welttheater," *Der Spiegel,* 34 (24 March 1980): 232-235;

Walter Hinck, "Sprachliches Bacchanal auf Rabelais' Spuren," *Frankfurter Allgemeine Zeitung,* 10 November 1977, p. 24;

Rainer Hoffmann, "Menschen und Narren," *Schweizer Monatshefte,* 63 (June 1983): 525-528;

Dominik Jost, "Tutet aus vollem Loch: Ein Schweizer Orgelbauer schrieb einen Orgelmacherroman," *Die Zeit,* 14 September 1973, p. 27;

Anton Krättli, "Jetzt ist jetzt," *Schweizer Monatshefte,* 64 (October 1984): 840-845;

Bernd Neumann, "Schwyzerisch und weltoffen," *Schweizer Monatshefte,* 64 (May 1984): 415-429;

Fritz J. Raddatz, "Ein Globus in Scherben," *Die Zeit,* 8 February 1985, p. 16;

Hans-Dieter Zimmermann, "Jeder Absatz eine neue Geschichte," *Die Zeit,* 16 November 1979, p. 55.

Max von der Grün

(25 May 1926-   )

Alfred L. Cobbs
Wayne State University

BOOKS: *Männer in zweifacher Nacht: Roman* (Recklinghausen: Paulus, 1962);

Irrlicht und Feuer: Roman (Recklinghausen: Paulus, 1963; edited by Jennifer Hampton, London: Harrap, 1974);

Fahrtunterbrechung und andere Erzählungen (Frankfurt am Main: Europäische Verlagsanstalt, 1965);

Feierabend: Dreh- und Tagebuch eines Fernsehfilms, by von der Grün and Hans Dieter Schwarze (Recklinghausen: Paulus, 1968);

Zwei Briefe an Pospischiel: Roman (Neuwied & Berlin: Luchterhand, 1968);

Flug über Zechen und Wälder: Nordrhein-Westfalen, Land der Gegensätze (Brunswick: Westermann, 1970);

Urlaub am Plattensee (Stierstadt im Taunus: Eremiten-Presse, 1970);

Stenogramm: Erzählungen (Düsseldorf: Eremiten-Presse, 1972);

Am Tresen gehn die Lichter aus (Stierstadt im Taunus: Eremiten-Presse, 1972);

Menschen in Deutschland (BRD): Sieben Porträts (Darmstadt & Neuwied: Luchterhand, 1973);

Stellenweise Glatteis: Roman (Darmstadt & Neuwied: Luchterhand, 1973);

Ein Tag wie jeder andere: Bericht (Düsseldorf: Eremiten-Presse, 1973);

Leben im gelobten Land: Gastarbeiterporträts (Darmstadt & Neuwied: Luchterhand, 1975);

Wenn der tote Rabe vom Baum fällt (Munich, Gütersloh & Vienna: Bertelsmann, 1975);

Reisen in die Gegenwart: Vier Erzählungen (Düsseldorf: Eremiten-Presse, 1976);

Vorstadtkrokodile: Eine Geschichte vom Aufpassen (Munich, Gütersloh & Vienna: Bertelsmann, 1976);

Flächenbrand: Roman (Darmstadt & Neuwied: Luchterhand, 1979);

Unterwegs in Deutschland (Düsseldorf: Eremiten-Presse, 1979);

Wie war das eigentlich? Kindheit und Jugend im Dritten Reich (Darmstadt & Neuwied: Luchterhand, 1979); translated by Jan Van Heurck as *Howl Like the Wolves: Growing Up in Nazi Germany* (New York: Morrow, 1980);

Etwas außerhalb der Legalität und andere Erzählungen (Darmstadt & Neuwied: Luchterhand, 1980);

Klassengespräche: Aufsätze, Reden, Kommentare (Darmstadt & Neuwied: Luchterhand, 1981);

Mein Lesebuch (Frankfurt am Main: Fischer, 1981);

Die Entscheidung: Erzählungen (Stuttgart: Klett, 1982);

Späte Liebe: Eine Erzählung (Darmstadt & Neuwied: Luchterhand, 1982);

Friedrich und Friederike: Geschichten (Darmstadt & Neuwied: Luchterhand, 1983);

Unser schönes Nordrhein-Westfalen: Von Menschen und Natur, von Kohle und Kultur: Bildband (Frankfurt am Main: Umschau, 1983);

Die Lawine: Roman (Darmstadt & Neuwied: Luchterhand, 1986).

OTHER: *Aus der Welt der Arbeit: Almanach der Gruppe 61 und ihrer Gäste*, edited by von der Grün and Fritz Hüser (Neuwied & Berlin: Luchterhand, 1966);

Oren Schmuckler, *Unsere Fabrik: Bildbuch*, text by von der Grün and Günter Wallraff (Lucerne & Frankfurt am Main: Bucher, 1979);

Knut Beck, ed., *Das Stefan Zweig Buch*, afterword by von der Grün (Frankfurt am Main: Fischer, 1981);

Anthrazit (Fotogruppe), *Maloche: Leben im Revier*, text by von der Grün (Frankfurt am Main: Eichborn, 1982).

Labor literature of the early postwar period was essentially about coal miners, for the coal industry was a dominant force in rebuilding West Germany and paying its war debt. The leading exponent of this type of literature is Max von der Grün. His novels are exposés of the miners' problems. Employee safety, job-related stress, exploitation of the laborer, job reassignment as a result of automation, and unemployment are among the themes he treats. His works, however, lack the timeless moral vision found, for example, in the writings of Heinrich Böll and Günter Grass. Von der Grün seizes the issues of the moment and abandons the universal for the sensational. In this respect, one can compare his works to many of the anti-Vietnam War plays of the late 1960s and early 1970s.

A self-educated miner, von der Grün wanted to express his concern about his own situation and social position. All of his works indicate that he stands on the side of the underprivileged. From earliest childhood he did not enjoy the privileges his peers did. He grew up Lutheran in a predominantly Catholic area of southern Germany. His mother, Margarethe Mark von der Grün, was also Lutheran; his father, Albert von der Grün, a shoemaker, was a Jehovah's Witness. Von der Grün was born in Bayreuth in 1926 and grew up during the Nazi period; in 1939 his father was imprisoned in the Flossenburg concentration camp as a conscientious objector. Von der Grün attended the public schools in Bavaria, completing his formal education in 1941; subsequently he worked as a merchant's apprentice. In 1943 he was drafted into the paratroops; less than a year later he was captured and spent two and a half years in a prisoner-of-war camp in the southern United States. Returning to Germany in 1948, he worked as a brick mason and, starting in 1951, as a coal miner in the Ruhr valley. In 1954 he married Lieselotte Köhler; one year later their daughter Rita was born.

Von der Grün's first novel, *Männer in zweifacher Nacht* (Men in Double Night, 1962), is based on the author's personal experience as a miner trapped by a cave-in. Seven publishers rejected the manuscript because they found the critical depiction of the miner's world too disturbing. Finally, von der Grün took the manuscript to Dr. Fritz Hüser, director of the Dortmund public libraries and founder of an Archive for Workers' and Socialist Literature. Hüser liked the manuscript and found a publisher, the Paulus Verlag in Recklinghausen, for it. Having encountered a kindred spirit in Hüser, von der Grün helped him to found the Gruppe (Group) 61 in Dortmund. The membership consisted of writers and journalists, among them Günter Wallraff, F. C. Delius, Angelika Mechtel, and Erwin Sylvanus, who wanted to treat the contemporary world of labor and industry and its attendant problems, to critically examine the technological age,

and to conform to the taste of the reading public without experimenting artistically. These authors were members of the bourgeoisie and Social Democrats in the tradition of early-twentieth-century writers of labor literature such as Gerrit Engelke, Heinrich Lersch, and Paul Zech. They wrote not to advance proletarian class consciousness but to give their readers a realistic portrayal of the world of labor at the height of the German "Economic Miracle."

Von der Grün's second book, *Irrlicht und Feuer* (Will-o'-the-wisp and Fire, 1963), became a cause célèbre even before it was published. While the novel was still in manuscript form, some of its most controversial passages appeared in the Catholic weekly *Echo der Zeit*. The firm Westfalia Lünen, producer of the cutting machine criticized in the novel, went to court to block publication of the book; other industrialists turned against von der Grün for what they perceived as an unfavorable representation of the mining industry; and even the Federal Mine Workers Union withdrew its support because of the novel's attack on organized labor. Representatives of the mining industry threatened to have von der Grün reassigned to a lower job category or fired unless he toned down his vitriolic rhetoric or withdrew the manuscript altogether. Von der Grün's failure to comply led to his resignation. Since 1963 he has lived in Dortmund as a full-time writer.

The controversy surrounding *Irrlicht und Feuer* catapulted von der Grün into the limelight. The novel attracted considerable attention at the Frankfurt Book Fair; the East German Writer's Union invited von der Grün for a lecture tour. Both West German Chancellor Konrad Adenauer and East German leader Walter Ulbricht granted the author private audiences. The trials were reported in the press in London, Paris, Moscow, and New York, as well as in the Federal Republic. Ultimately, the courts ruled in von der Grün's favor, and *Irrlicht und Feuer* was published. In 1967 von der Grün divorced his first wife; in 1968 he married Elke Hüser—two years after their son Frank was born.

Even after the Gruppe 61 disbanded in the early 1970s, von der Grün continued to write about the alienation of the worker; implicit in all of his novels is a plea for better working conditions. In each novel the protagonist is angry about his work environment but finally becomes resigned to his fate. In *Männer in zweifacher Nacht* Stacho Hubalek is resigned from the outset to his position as a miner and resents anyone who does not earn his living by hard physical labor. When he and two of his coworkers are trapped underground for five days by a cave-in, his fellow victim Johannes Brinkmann, who is working in the mine to support himself while he studies theology, becomes the target of Hubalek's rage. Although Brinkmann's father is also a miner, in Hubalek's mind the future minister is a representative of the religious-industrial complex which oppresses the worker: "Früher hat uns der Staat ausgemistet, heute die Aktionäre, morgen vielleicht wieder der Staat.... Wirtschaftswunder. –Käse. Arbeiter erleben keine Wunder, die wundern sich über die Wunder der anderen, und schließlich wird alles Wunder auf unseren Rücken ausgetragen" (Earlier the state exploited us, today the stockholders, tomorrow perhaps the state again. Economic Miracle. –Bullshit. Workers experience no miracles; they wonder about the miracles of others, and finally all of the miracles will be achieved by the sweat of our brows).

In *Männer in zweifacher Nacht* von der Grün's personal experience becomes paradigmatic for the situation of the miners in the Ruhr valley. The characters articulate the miners' various moods and complaints. The novel is narrated through inner monologues, dramatic sequences, and dialogues; there is seldom omniscient narration, but this technique is employed when simultaneous events on both sides of the cave-in are commented upon.

In *Irrlicht und Feuer* Jürgen Fohrmann loses his job when the mine in which he has been working is closed down. He finds work first as a helper at a construction site and ends up at an electronic components factory. With each succeeding job Fohrmann finds less and less satisfaction in his work. He is also disillusioned with the materialistic, spiritually empty life-style he and his wife lead. He desires a humanized work environment and an improved quality of life. He feels that the unions have given up their political and moral goals so that the workers might share in the economic prosperity produced by industry. Fohrmann desires to bring about a change in the system, but he vacillates between revolt and resignation and finally concludes that economic need outweighs principle: "Wir möchten gern aufbegehren, weil gegen die herrschenden Zustände aufbegehrt werden muß. Aber wir halten die Schnauze, wir müssen nämlich Geld verdienen, wir müssen nämlich leben, wir wollen leben" (We would very much like to revolt, because one must

rise up against prevailing conditions. But we keep our traps shut, for we have to earn money, we have to live, and we want to live well). Fohrmann realizes that the work which once gave the individual a sense of worth and self-fulfillment has become simply a means of survival.

Irrlicht und Feuer, stylistically more sophisticated than *Männer in zweifacher Nacht*, uses first-person narration instead of inner monologues. The social criticism in the second novel is more aggressive, more direct, and more concrete. Events are presented from the perspective of the workers and expressed in their idiom.

In 1966 the novel was made into a highly acclaimed film for East German television. Two years later the film was acquired by West German television. In preparation for broadcast of the film in the Federal Republic a cross section of over two hundred people from the Ruhr area were asked to view it and answer questionnaires as to whether its depiction of West German coal miners was accurate. The results of the survey, an interview with von der Grün, and a commentary by the director of programming for Southwest German Television were added to the film. The West German press was highly critical of this attempt at censorship. Von der Grün expressed a preference for the East German version.

In *Zwei Briefe an Pospischiel* (Two Letters to Pospischiel, 1968) Paul Pospischiel, a coal miner turned factory worker, is refused a three-day leave of absence. He takes leave without management's approval to help his mother locate the old Nazi who had his father arrested more than thirty years earlier. Pospischiel is fired for the unexcused absence but is reinstated with the support of the union. The union and management, however, come to a compromise solution: Pospischiel is rehired at an inferior position and lower pay than the job from which he was fired. He hates his new job; although the work is not physically demanding, he finds it monotonous and uninspiring. The relief from physical drudgery cannot stamp out his feelings of frustration, exhaustion, and emptiness. Yet Pospischiel is not willing to give up his unrewarding job to look for more satisfactory work: he reasons that he is a slave to industry and that he would be a slave outside industry were he to give up his position.

Like *Irrlicht und Feuer*, *Zwei Briefe an Pospischiel* was made into a film for East German television. The main character was depicted as a class-conscious worker, and emphasis was placed

Max von der Grün (photograph by Anita Schiffer-Fuchs, courtesy of Ullstein Bilderdienst)

on the part of the novel dealing with Germany's "uncompleted past." A year later West German television filmed its own version of the story, which von der Grün felt was more faithful to the novel than was its East German counterpart.

In *Stellenweise Glatteis* (Icy in Spots, 1973) Karl Maiwald, a former truck driver and now chief mechanic for a trucking fleet, discovers that an intercom has been used by management to eavesdrop on conversations of the truck drivers and factory laborers. Feeling that the rights of the workers have been violated, Maiwald calls for a strike and is fired for his action. The union concedes that management has acted properly in firing Maiwald because he had incited revolt in the workplace. The workers are incensed and go on strike in his behalf, and he is reinstated. Maiwald continues to lead demonstrations against the firm, secures the documents to prove his allegations against management, and is fired again. When Maiwald discovers that the union has purchased a considerable amount of stock in the com-

pany, he becomes totally disillusioned and abandons his protest.

Stellenweise Glatteis was made into a film for television only in the Federal Republic, since the internationl broadcasting rights were too expensive for the German Democratic Republic. Critics found the film to be particularly close to the novel. There were several reasions for this faithfulness: von der Grün himself wrote the script, the director took few liberties with the story, and the novel was written in a simple and realistic style that lent itself to the film medium.

Flächenbrand (Wildfire, 1979) deals with the themes of unemployment and political corruption. Lothar, an out-of-work brick mason, takes a job transporting contraband for a businessman. When he learns that the contraband is illegal weapons, he immediately gives up the job. Later he finds employment as a cemetery caretaker and gravedigger. Lothar discovers that some weapons intended for a neo-Nazi group have been buried in the cemetery; he and several other witnesses, including the Social Democrat politician Frank, report this information to the authorities. When Frank learns that a businessman plans to tear down an old neighborhood to construct a luxury high-rise apartment building, he tries to block the project; but he fails because his fellow Social Democrats have been bribed by the businessman who turns out to be none other than the weapons dealer–Lothar's old employer. At the end of the novel Frank's career has been destroyed and Lothar has once again found work as a brick mason. Like most of von der Grün's novels, *Flächenbrand* was made into a successful television film.

Die Lawine (The Avalanche, 1986) demonstrates once again von der Grün's loyalty to the working class. In this novel of intrigue and greed a factory owner wills half of the firm's assets to the workers. At first the workers are skeptical and suspicious of the plan, and several representatives of management are strongly opposed to it and attempt to sabotage it. They fail, and the plan is executed. Management and labor are now partners with a common interest. In this novel one detects a modification of von der Grün's earlier view that management always exploits and enslaves the workers and has no interest in their welfare.

In addition to his major novels, von der Grün has written essays, commentaries, and short stories. Topics in these works span a wide spectrum. In *Urlaub am Plattensee* (Vacation at Plattensee, 1970) a youth from the German Democratic Republic, enticed by the prosperity of the West, is fatally wounded in his attempt to escape from his homeland. The nonfiction *Leben im gelobten Land* (Life in the Promised Land, 1975) is a series of six interviews with foreign workers in the Federal Republic. *Vorstadtkrokodile* (Suburban Crocodiles, 1976) is a short story in which a handicapped child fights courageously to be accepted by his peers. In *Wie war das eigentlich? Kindheit und Jugend im Dritten Reich* (How Was It Really? Childhood and Youth During the Third Reich, 1979; translated as *Howl Like the Wolves: Growing Up in Nazi Germany*, 1980) von der Grün employs a mixture of autobiographical elements, pictures, and documents to depict life under National Socialism. *Klassengespräche* (Conversations among Classes, 1981) is a collection of von der Grün's essays and speeches covering a fifteen-year span. The short story *Späte Liebe* (Late Love, 1982) illustrates the hindrances erected by society to the love of two old people for one another; the story

was made into a highly successful television film before it was published in book form.

In all of Max von der Grün's works one finds concern for those vicitimized by society: the laborer in the mines and in the factories, the aged, the handicapped person, the dropout. Von der Grün, who views the world from the perspective of the underprivileged, is an uncompromising agitator for social justice; therefore, his works continue to attract the public's attention and interest.

Von der Grün has also written radio plays, including "Smog" (1966) and "Vorstadtkrokodile" (1977), and a theatrical revue, *Notstand oder Das Straßentheater kommt* (State of Emergency; or, The Street Theater Arrives, 1969). The latter work premiered on 10 January 1969 at the Ruhr Festival Theater in Recklinghausen. Written during the period of student unrest at German universities at the height of the Vietnam War, it depicts a confrontation between students and workers. The students carry red flags and preach class struggle and revolution. The workers do not understand the students ideologically; have no interest in politics; and distrust the student protesters, to whom they know they will have to look up when the students become leaders in society. Von der Grün was trying to show that despite the presumed solidarity between students and workers at that time, it was impossible for the two groups to communicate with each other.

In 1966 von der Grün was awarded the Laurel Leaf of East German Television for the Film version of *Irrlicht und Feuer*. In 1973 he received the Cultural Prize of the City of Nuremberg. At the Prague Television Film Festival in 1978 he won the Prize of the Prague Television Film Viewers for the film version of *Vorstadtkrokodile*, and in 1978 he was awarded the Wilhelmine Lübke Prize of the Committee for Aid to Senior Citizens for the television dramatization of *Späte Liebe*. He received the Annette Droste-Hülshoff Prize in 1981, the Reinoldus Plaque of the City of Dortmund in 1982, and the Gerrit Engelke Prize of the City of Hannover in 1985.

Interviews:

Lothar Oehlert, "Protokoll eines Interviews mit Max von der Grün," *Basis: Jahrbuch für deutsche Gegenwartsliteratur*, 20 (1972): 112-130;

Heinz Ludwig Arnold, "Gespräch mit Max von der Grün," in his *Gespräche mit Schriftstellern* (Munich: Beck, 1975), pp. 142-197;

Leo Schenk, "Gespräch mit Max von der Grün," *Deutsche Bücher,* 12 (1982): 165-183.

References:

Friedhelm Baukloh, "Wirklichkeit einfangen: Ein Versuch über Max von der Grün und andere neue Realisten," *Eckhart Jahrbuch* (1965/1966): 276-286;

Walter Israel, "Zur kritisch-realistischen Arbeiterliteratur Max von der Grüns," in *Literatur einer Region: Dortmunder Autoren in Darstellungen und Deutschunterricht,* edited by Albin Lenhard (Paderborn: Schöningh, 1981), pp. 39-59;

Hartmut Kircher, "Max von der Grün," in *Deutsche Literatur der Gegenwart,* volume 2, edited by Dietrich Weber (Stuttgart: Kröner, 1977), pp. 128-151;

Martin H. Ludwig, "Max von der Grün: *Irrlicht und Feuer.* Untersuchungen zur literarischen Gestaltung der Arbeitswelt," in *Deutsche Romane im 20. Jahrhundert,* volume 2, edited by Manfred Brauneck (Bamberg: Büchner, 1976), pp. 279-300;

Ludwig, "Technik und Industriearbeit in den Romanen Max von der Grüns," *Der Deutschunterricht,* 28 (December 1976): 36-50;

Hanno Möbius, *Arbeiterliteratur in der BRD. Eine Analyse von Industriereportagen und Reportagenromanen: Max von der Grün, Christian Geissler, Günter Wallraff* (Cologne: Pahl-Rugenstein, 1970);

Stephan Reinhardt, ed., *Max von der Grün: Materialienbuch* (Darmstadt & Neuwied: Luchterhand, 1978); revised as *Max von der Grün: Auskunft für Leser* (Darmstadt & Neuwied: Luchterhand, 1986);

Franz Schonauer, *Max von der Grün* (Munich: Beck, 1978);

Gisela Shaw, "Wie war das eigentlich? The Development of a Theme in the Works of Max von der Grün," *New German Studies,* 8 (Spring 1980): 1-18;

Text Kritik, special Max von der Grün issue, 45 (January 1975);

Noel L. Thomas, "Why Choose *Irrlicht und Feuer* as a Set Book?," *Modern Languages,* 64 (September 1983): 178-184.

Martin Walser
(24 March 1927-)

Michael Winkler
Rice University

BOOKS: *Ein Flugzeug über dem Haus und andere Geschichten* (Frankfurt am Main: Suhrkamp, 1955);

Ehen in Philippsburg: Roman (Frankfurt am Main: Suhrkamp, 1957); translated by Eva Figes as *The Gadarene Club* (London: Longmans, 1959); translation adapted by J. Laughlin as *Marriage in Philippsburg* (Norfolk, Conn.: New Directions, 1961);

Halbzeit: Roman (Frankfurt am Main: Suhrkamp, 1960);

Lese-Erfahrungen mit Proust (Frankfurt am Main & Berlin: Suhrkamp, 1960);

Hölderlin auf dem Dachboden (Frankfurt am Main: Suhrkamp, 1960);

Beschreibung einer Form (Munich: Hanser, 1961);

Mitwirkung bei meinem Ende (Biberach an der Riss: Wege und Gestalten, 1962);

Eiche und Angora: Eine deutsche Chronik (Frankfurt am Main: Suhrkamp, 1962; revised, 1963); edited by A. E. Stubbs (London: Harrap, 1973); adapted by Ronald Duncan as *The Rabbit Race*, in *The Rabbit Race; The Detour* (London: Calder, 1963);

Überlebensgroß Herr Krott: Requiem für einen Unsterblichen (Frankfurt am Main: Suhrkamp, 1964);

Der schwarze Schwan: Ein Stück in zwei Akten (Frankfurt am Main: Suhrkamp, 1964);

Lügengeschichten (Frankfurt am Main: Suhrkamp, 1964);

Erfahrungen und Leseerfahrungen (Frankfurt am Main: Suhrkamp, 1965);

Das Einhorn: Roman (Frankfurt am Main: Suhrkamp, 1966); translated by Barrie Ellis-Jones as *The Unicorn* (London: Calder & Boyars, 1971; New York: Boyars, 1981);

Der Abstecher; Die Zimmerschlacht: Übungsstück für ein Ehepaar (Frankfurt am Main: Suhrkamp, 1967); *Der Abstecher* translated by Richard Grunberger as *The Detour*, in *The Rabbit Race; The Detour* (London: Calder, 1963);

Martin Walser (Fotoagentur Sven Simon—Ullstein Bilderdienst)

Theater, Theater: Ein Bilderbuch des Theaters, by Walser and Karl Hargesheimer (Velber: Friedrich, 1967);

Heimatkunde: Aufsätze und Reden (Frankfurt am Main: Suhrkamp, 1968);

Fiction (Frankfurt am Main: Suhrkamp, 1970);

Ein Kinderspiel: Stück in 2 Akten (Frankfurt am Main: Suhrkamp, 1970);

Hölderlin zu entsprechen (Biberach an der Riss: Thomae, 1970);

Aus dem Wortschatz unserer Kämpfe: Szenen (Stierstadt im Taunus: Eremiten-Presse, 1971);

Gesammelte Stücke (Frankfurt am Main: Suhrkamp, 1971);

241

Die Gallistl'sche Krankheit (Frankfurt am Main: Suhrkamp, 1972);

Wie und wovon handelt Literatur: Aufsätze und Reden (Frankfurt am Main: Suhrkamp, 1973);

Der Sturz: Roman (Frankfurt am Main: Suhrkamp, 1973);

Das Sauspiel: Szenen aus dem 16. Jahrhundert (Frankfurt am Main: Suhrkamp, 1975);

Jenseits der Liebe: Roman (Frankfurt am Main: Suhrkamp, 1976); translated by Judith Black as "Beyond All Love," in *New Writing and Writers 19* (New York: Riverrun, 1982);

Was zu bezweifeln war: Aufsätze und Reden 1958-1975, edited by Klaus Schuhmann (Berlin: Aufbau, 1976);

Ein fliehendes Pferd: Novelle (Frankfurt am Main: Suhrkamp, 1978); translated by Leila Vennewitz as *Runaway Horse: A Novel* (New York: Holt, Rinehart & Winston, 1980; London: Secker & Warburg, 1980);

Der Grund zur Freude: 99 Sprüche zur Erbauung des Bewußtseins (Düsseldorf: Eremiten-Presse, 1978);

Heimatlob: Ein Bodensee-Buch, by Walser and André Ficus (Friedrichshafen: Gessler, 1978);

Wer ist ein Schriftsteller?: Aufsätze und Reden (Frankfurt am Main: Suhrkamp, 1978);

Seelenarbeit: Roman (Frankfurt am Main: Suhrkamp, 1979); translated by Vennewitz as *The Inner Man* (New York: Holt, Rinehart & Winston, 1984);

Die Würde am Werktag (Frankfurt am Main: Fischer, 1980);

Das Schwanenhaus: Roman (Frankfurt am Main: Suhrkamp, 1980); translated by Vennewitz as *The Swan Villa: A Novel* (New York: Holt, Rinehart & Winston, 1982; London: Secker & Warburg, 1983);

Selbstbewußtsein und Ironie: Frankfurter Vorlesungen (Frankfurt am Main: Suhrkamp, 1981);

Heines Tränen: Essay (Düsseldorf: Eremiten-Presse, 1981);

Die Anselm-Kristlein-Trilogie (Frankfurt am Main: Suhrkamp, 1981)–comprises *Halbzeit, Das Einhorn, Der Sturz*;

Versuch, ein Gefühl zu Verstehen, und andere Versuche (Stuttgart: Reclam, 1982);

Brief an Lord Liszt: Roman (Frankfurt am Main: Suhrkamp, 1982); translated by Vennewitz as *Letter to Lord Liszt* (New York: Holt, Rinehart & Winston, 1985);

In Goethes Hand: Szenen aus dem 19. Jahrhundert (Frankfurt am Main: Suhrkamp, 1982);

Liebeserklärungen (Frankfurt am Main: Suhrkamp, 1983);

Gesammelte Geschichten (Frankfurt am Main: Suhrkamp, 1983);

Goethes Anziehungskraft (Constance: Universitätsverlag, 1983);

Meßmers Gedanken (Frankfurt am Main: Suhrkamp, 1985);

Variationen eines Würgegriffs (Stuttgart: Radius, 1985);

Brandung (Frankfurt am Main: Suhrkamp, 1985); translated by Vennewitz as *Breakers* (New York: Holt, 1987);

Säntis (Stuttgart: Radius, 1986);

Heilige Brocken (Weingarten: Drumlin, 1986);

Geständnis auf Raten (Frankfurt am Main: Suhrkamp, 1986);

Dorle und Wolf (Frankfurt am Main: Suhrkamp, 1987).

OTHER: "Ein grenzenloser Nachmittag," in *Hörspielbuch 1955* (Frankfurt am Main: Europäische Verlagsanstalt, 1955), pp. 177-207; revised version in *Spectaculum: Texte moderner Hörspiele*, edited by Karl Markus Michel (Frankfurt am Main: Suhrkamp, 1963), pp. 295-313;

Die Alternative oder Brauchen wir eine neue Regierung?, edited by Walser (Reinbek: Rowohlt, 1961);

Vorzeichen II: Neun neue deutsche Autoren, edited by Walser (Frankfurt am Main: Suhrkamp, 1963);

Franz Kafka, *Er: Prosa*, edited by Walser (Frankfurt am Main: Suhrkamp, 1963);

Der Zeichner Carlo Schellemann, foreword by Walser (Munich: Neue Münchner Galerie, 1964);

Jonathan Swift, *Satiren*, translated by Felix Paul Greve and others, essay by Walser (Frankfurt am Main: Insel, 1965);

Ursula Trauberg, *Vorleben*, afterword by Walser (Frankfurt am Main: Suhrkamp, 1968);

Heinrich Lersch, *Hammerschläge: Ein Roman von Menschen und Maschinen*, afterword by Walser (Frankfurt am Main: Suhrkamp, 1980).

Martin Walser is an innovative and consistently challenging writer who has portrayed the social and cultural development of West Germany precisely and with extraordinary versatility. He is a novelist with an analytical mind who confronts the conflicts of his generation with an immediacy of purpose and a sense of artistic responsibility.

Despite some unproductive experimentation and occasional lapses in his ability to find the exactly appropriate tone, he has become a brilliantly skillful master of his language and an inventive teller of stories. His brilliance, in fact, has led some critics to suspect the ultimate sincerity of his commitment to fundamental social change: they have accused him of indulging in an intellectual game of radical politics in which the uncompromising attacker of the status quo can always feel morally superior because he knows that his extreme proposals will never be implemented.

The tensions within Walser are a reflection of the antagonisms within modern society. He harbors a deep-seated hostility to capitalism because he holds its spirit of unremitting competition responsible for most of the psychological deformations of contemporary life; he is no less opposed to socialism because of its stifling humorlessness and intellectual inflexibility. His best writing is a blend of descriptive realism, aggressive satire, ironic reserve, and humorous generosity. He imbues most of his characters, excluding only the incorrigible fascists, with some part of his own personality. Occasionally he does so somewhat heavy-handedly and as if the weight of moral decision rested only on him; but more often he can be recognized behind his personae in the spirit of playful self-revelation that transforms his fiction into the signature of his time.

Walser was born on 24 March 1927 in Wasserburg, a village on Lake Constance near Lindau. His parents, Martin and Augusta Schmid Walser, owned a small inn that catered primarily to local patrons and had only a negligible share of the lucrative tourist trade. It often provided a stage for traveling performers who aroused in the boy an early interest in the theater. The meager income the inn provided had to be supplemented by the hard-earned profits from a coal dealership. Walser's mother, who came from a large and poor farming family, was a devout Catholic; her husband, however, broken by the recurrent failures of his many business schemes, tried to find consolation in Indian philosophy and theosophical speculation. A diabetic, he died in 1938 at the age of forty-nine, leaving his widow to raise their three sons.

There were many occasions when Walser was made aware of the low esteem in which the community and most of his teachers held his family. He grew up with the conviction that the squabbles and the sordid fierceness of business competition as well as the need for success and social

respectability are driving forces in a petit bourgeois world and that higher education often produces little more than an arrogant attitude of class superiority. Walser attended the high school in Lindau from 1938 until 1943, when he was attached to an antiaircraft station on the home front. A year later he was drafted for labor service and then for military duty in a company of alpine scouts. His older brother Joseph had also been drafted and was killed in action in 1944. American forces took Walser prisoner near the town of Garmisch-Partenkirchen and put him to work in the library of Radio Munich, the Third Reich's central broadcasting station for Bavaria. There he discovered the poetry of Heinrich Heine, which inspired him to write a satirical poem of 120 stanzas about his school experiences. When he recited it during graduation ceremonies in 1946 the principal left the auditorium and nearly succeeded in having Walser's diploma revoked.

In September 1946 Walser enrolled at the College of Theology and Philosophy in Regensburg, an institution with little academic prestige, few books, and a limited number of courses, where it was less his studies than his participation in the student theater that engaged his interest. Walser was not a promising actor, but he wrote good texts for the cabaret performances that, along with a serious and a comic play, were a regular part of the weekly amateur presentations. He transferred to Tübingen University in April 1948 to study literature, history, and philosophy and immediately joined the student theater ensemble there as an actor, writer, and production assistant. Up to this time his mother had been able to support him, but after the currency reform of 20 June 1948, which devalued the old German currency, he was forced to earn his own living. Through his connections with the stage he came to the attention of Helmut Jedele, who was looking for free-lance contributions to the programs of the state-operated radio station in Stuttgart; after three semesters at Tübingen Walser moved to Stuttgart to work for the South German Broadcasting System (SDR), while retaining his status as a student. He began by writing material for the entertainment division and later moved into political and economic analysis. He finished his degree in 1951 with a perceptive dissertation on the prose style of Franz Kafka. His extensive reading; his direct contact with local and national politics as a reporter, interviewer, and editorial writer; and his extensive travels in Europe, includ-

Walser at about the time of publication of his 1972 novel Die Gallistl'sche Krankheit *(dpa)*

ing trips to Poland and Czechoslovakia, gave him experience and insights that were valuable preparation for his work as a playwright and novelist.

Seven of Walser's radio plays were broadcast between 1952 and 1956. This was no small feat in view of the fact that the radio play, much more than the stage play, dominated the dramatic literature of those years and that many prominent authors wrote for the medium. Only one of these plays has been published: "Ein grenzenloser Nachmittag" (No Limits to This Afternoon, 1955), a series of exchanges that reveal the frustrations of a childless middle-aged couple.

Walser's status as an independent contributor rather than a salaried employee of SDR made it easier to sever his ties with the powerful, intellectually stimulating institution that had grown into one of the most influential media organizations in Germany. In December 1956, with his wife, the former Katharina Neuner-Jehle, whom he had married on 20 October 1950, and their four-year-old daughter Franziska, he moved to Friedrichshafen, where his other children, Katharina, Alissa, and Theresia, were born. The fam-

ily moved to the town of Nußdorf near Überlingen on Lake Constance in 1968.

Walser's beginnings as a writer of serious literature, though buttressed by a strong sense of vocation and feeling of self-confidence, were neither spectacular nor marked by quick acceptance among his peers. The members of the Gruppe (Group) 47, an influential informal coterie of avant-garde authors and critics who met annually to read and comment on their recent work, withheld their approval of him until 1955, when his story "Templones Ende" (Templone's End) was awarded the group's annual first prize for the best piece of new writing. But even thereafter Walser's contacts with them were not without constant frictions and serious disagreements, largely because he considered them too removed from involvement in urgent cultural and social issues. And his initial dependence on Kafka as his stylistic model was slow in giving way to a mode of narration that was distinctly his own. Indications of a Kafkaesque parabolic solipsism can be detected in the stories, including "Templones Ende," written between 1952 and 1955 and collected under the title *Ein Flugzeug über dem Haus und andere Geschichten* (An Airplane above the House and Other Stories, 1955). It was only with his first novel, *Ehen in Philippsburg* (Marriage in Philippsburg, 1957; translated as *The Gadarene Club*, 1959), that Walser found his own style–a style that is indebted to Marcel Proust.

Philippsburg could be any major German city during the mid 1950s, the years of the reconstruction boom. It is a place where the power of business and politics and the influence of the culture, entertainment, and information media are intertwined in an impenetrable network of inconspicuous manipulation and corrupt self-interest. This alliance of ruthless profiteers, sanctimonious or cynical opinion-makers, and acquiescent public servants chokes off any form of opposition as it maintains its unscrupulous but seemingly honorable members in positions of wealth and political control. These are insights that come quickly to the novel's protagonist, Hans Beumann, who learns with surprising ease how best to maneuver himself into the role that has been arranged for him. He is a poor young man from the hinterlands–the illegitimate son of a waitress–who, with ambition, pluck, and a talent for timing and one-upmanship, makes a great success of his job as the public relations consultant for a lobbying organization that represents the electronics industry. But his climb into the higher reaches of society is accompanied by a loss of his sense of identity and self-respect; under the guise of modesty and joviality he has become a bully and egomaniac who is no longer capable of genuine feelings. Therefore, he vacillates between his attachment to Anne Volkmann, his employer's daughter, whom he will marry after she has an abortion, and his mistress, Marga. He is torn between remembrance of his social origins and a compulsion to deny them, between his spontaneous inclination to identify with the exploited and his acquired obsession with the trappings of success in the bourgeois world. This world is represented through the paradigmatic life stories of the gynecologist Dr. Benrath, the politically ambitious lawyer Alwin, and the unsuccessful writer Klaff. Each is a failure in his personal relationships as much as he is a menace to a sane society.

Walser's debut as a novelist is distinguished by an ability for precise observation that gives his descriptive passages the quality of authenticity; his evocation of the distinctive nuances and temper of the people who determined the course of German public life is accurately realistic. He did not hide behind symbolism or coyly suggestive indirectness, nor did he fall victim to the voyeurism or "naturalistic" crassness that is always a danger in stories of marital infidelity. Walser's realism expresses an attitude of social criticism that is neither limited to occasional satirical attacks on particular abuses nor satisfied with a stance of intellectual superiority.

Walser was able to write one of the first full-scale exposés of postwar German society because he had developed a narrative perspective–interior monologue–that allowed him to get inside the minds of his figures, to explore their consciousness as well as their subliminal desires and fears. This strategy of interior monologue, which gave him access to recesses of the mind that are not normally within the reach of descriptive realism, became a hallmark of Walser's fiction.

It is used in the story of Anselm Kristlein, which took a trilogy of novels to tell. The first, *Halbzeit* (Half Time, 1960), is nearly nine hundred pages long and was completed after sixteen months of uninterrupted work. The struggling protagonist is a traveling salesman and later an advertising expert, an ambitious, smart, adaptive opportunist whose rise into the ranks of established society is described in exhaustive detail. His story is a panoramic investigation of the private and public attitudes, forms of behavior, social pressures, and power structures that constituted life

in West Germany ten years after the founding of the Federal Republic in 1949.

In the summer of 1958 Walser traveled to the United States to participate in a Harvard International Seminar organized by Henry Kissinger. His encounter there with industrial capitalism at its most powerful and with its methods of self-propagation through advertising contributed to the sense of urgency with which he entered into the political arena in Germany. In 1961 he joined twenty other prominent writers and journalists in proclaiming support for the minority Social Democratic party (SPD) during the upcoming elections for the Bundestag. He edited a collection of position papers, *Die Alternative oder Brauchen wir eine neue Regierung?* (The Alternative; or, Do We Need a New Government?, 1961), of which one hundred thousand copies were sold in four weeks. The first expression of political dissent by a group of major writers during Konrad Adenauer's chancellorship, it signaled the beginning of public opposition by leftist intellectuals to the policies of the ruling Christian Democratic coalition. But Walser's disenchantment with the efficacy of a defeated party establishment was not long in coming. During the federal elections of 1965 he refused to join a group of writers who supported the candidacy of Willy Brandt. The SPD's centrist compromises and its unwillingness to come out clearly against the American commitment to the war in Vietnam prompted Walser's withdrawal from electioneering and solidified his independent stance of opposition.

Das Einhorn (1966; translated as *The Unicorn*, 1971) presents Anselm Kristlein in a new role: he has been commissioned to write a nonfiction book on love, and in the process of research and reflection he becomes his own object of scrutiny. Since he spends most of the novel lying in bed ill, he fails in his contractual obligations. But he does meet the great passionate love of his life, Orli. He becomes the hero of his own story, reencountering himself in many situations that uncertain and deceptive memory calls back and examining his manner of reacting to women, until he is forced to admit that there are no words to express what has vanished irrevocably when he loses Orli's love. At the end he returns to his wife and three children.

On 23 August 1965 Walser had a heart attack which necessitated a three-month stay in hospitals and sanatoriums. He recovered physically but did not immediately regain his creative self-

Walser in 1981, the year he received the Georg Büchner Prize (photograph by Herlinde Koelbl)

assurance. He tried to overcome his feeling of resignation by immersing himself in the study of Karl Marx. The products of his lapse into a form of intellectual paralysis are two books which by general consensus are failures: *Fiction* (1970), a parody of conventional techniques of narration that uses a Munich playboy to exemplify the intellectual sterility of Germany; and *Die Gallistl'sche Krankheit* (Gallistl's Disease, 1972), about the mental life of a middle-aged intellectual whose feelings of inferiority to his successful professional friends lead him first to shut himself up in his room and then to become a Communist.

In the 1970s Walser's major political cause became democratic socialism. In November 1970 he cofounded the "Arbeitskreis Kulturindustrie," a group of authors and other employees of the culture industry who tried to form their own union; in 1972, after their efforts at self-representation failed, they joined the printers' union. He traveled to Moscow to participate in the Fifth Writers' Congress and to Budapest and London to take part in public discussions of political issues. These activities, as well as his widely reported speeches, brought him close to the position of the German Communist party (DKP); but Walser never became a member of the DKP despite his many campaign speeches for Communist candidates between 1972 and 1974. His individualistic, unbureaucratic form of socialism received little support from political organizations of the extra-parliamentary opposition, and his pleas for independence from Moscow went unheeded.

In the concluding novel of the Kristlein trilogy, *Der Sturz* (The Crash, 1973), Anselm is frequently ill and subject to bouts of disgusted indifference toward the things that had previously made his life exciting and enjoyable. He is sick of all the emotional and economic obstacles and compromises that stand in the way of his liberated happiness. At last, trying to pull a stolen sailboat across a snowed-in alpine pass, he loses control of his truck and dies—a futile end, but not without its moments of exhilarating independence.

Walser began writing for major theaters after the completion of *Halbzeit* and soon established himself as the leading West German playwright of the 1960s. He was the first to confront an audience used to the thematic interests of Anglo-American and French authors with specifically German issues; and he broke with much of contemporary stage practice, especially with the absurdist theater and the parable play. He had learned as much as his artistic temperament would allow from the Brechtian technique of a "non-Aristotelian" theater of demonstration, accepting its mixture of critical intellectualism and popular didacticism; but he avoided the obtrusive manner of teaching which had misled Brecht's more dogmatic disciples to regard the stage as a secular pulpit. His plays often exemplify situations in which the latent hostilities caused by habitual abuses of power are forced into the open and then get out of control; and he likes to work with strong, even exaggerated contrasts and violent conflicts. His figures, in other words, tend to become stereotypes; but they never turn into mere abstractions, nor do they lose their complexity. Just as Proust had replaced Kafka as the model for Walser's prose style, so Chekhov took Brecht's place as the teacher from whom he learned most about writing dialogue. Walser is not so much interested in the exemplification of social theories as in the psychology of repression and the mental processes that lead to a resentful acceptance of conformity and authority. Consequently, he prefers dramatic constellations in which a dominant individual, acting with the consent or impotent toleration of a social group, asserts his superiority and coerces others to submit to his will. In this manner Walser shows the fascist personality at work both in anonymous institutions and in the interpersonal relationships of a small group. It is most often the dependency of a servant on his master, of a worker on his boss, or of a wife on her husband that reveals those refined forms of social brutality that are the object of Walser's dramatic exploration. He makes it obvious that such deviant behavior is not the result of individual moral decisions alone: while he does not totally deny personal responsibility, he emphasizes the injustices that are inherent in the structure of bourgeois society. This form of society has not changed significantly since its beginnings in the late eighteenth and early nineteenth centuries, when it made the compulsive individualist and egotist Goethe its spokesman and cultural hero. Such is the critical orientation that informs Walser's work as a playwright down to *In Goethes Hand* (1982), his nonconformist contribution to the 150th anniversary of Goethe's death. Using the great poet's devoted secretary, Eckermann, as its passive protagonist, the play is an attack on the questionable individualism of a great personality and a condemnation of hero worship.

A critique of artists and intellectuals has been an integral part of Walser's work from the beginning. He frequently shows them as vacillating and apologetic handymen of the established powers under whose protection they perform their services. This type of intellectual is represented in the play *Das Sauspiel* (1975; the title is both a sarcastic allusion to the German term for drama [*Schauspiel*] and a reference to a game [*Spiel*] within the play that involves catching a pig [*Sau*]) by the cultural elite of Nuremberg after the Reformation. All of them, from Dürer to Paracelsus and Melanchthon, are defenders of the new status quo and of a law-and-order mentality that keeps the commercial privileges of the city senators intact. Their antagonists—exploited workers, revolutionary Anabaptists, and a radical folk poet who must feign blindness to keep his small corner of the entertainment market—are easily suppressed in the end. In other works Walser depicts the artist or intellectual as an ineffective, self-absorbed loner searching for a social role and exhibiting extreme behavior. The prototype here is Josef Georg Gallistl of *Die Gallistl'sche*

Krankheit, who finds a form of therapy in writing down the story of his affliction.

It would have been easy for Walser to become the spokesman for the psychological and cultural malaise that befell leftist intellectuals during the backlash of the 1970s. Instead, he introduced a new set of fictional characters who represent the anxieties of a wider spectrum of the population. Among them is the aging Franz Horn in *Jenseits der Liebe* (1976; translated as "Beyond All Love", 1982), who has become no less alienated from those around him than Anselm. For fifteen years he has worked for a company that manufactures false teeth, and he now fears that a young ambitious lawyer, Dr. Horst Liszt, is about to take over his position as assistant to the chief executive officer; his anxiety produces a psychosomatic case of lockjaw. This competitor is the one against whom his ever-expanding letter of self-justification, protest, and recrimination is directed in the novel *Brief an Lord Liszt* (1982; translated as *Letter to Lord Liszt*, 1985); in the end, like Kafka's famous letter to his father, it is not mailed. A second group of recurrent figures includes the chauffeur Xaver Zürn, his many relatives in southern Swabia, and the clique of businessmen on whom they all depend not only for their livelihood but also for appreciation; their hope for approval or even understanding is, however, always disappointed. These characters appear in the novels *Seelenarbeit* (Soul-Work, 1979; translated as *The Inner Man*, 1984) and *Das Schwanenhaus* (1980; translated as *The Swan Villa*, 1982), in which Walser turns his attention to the psychological deformations that result from prolonged feelings of personal insufficiency and futility. With touches of humane irony and soothing humor, he subtly explores the problems that bedevil a marriage when the husband is constantly preoccupied with the frustrations of his job and the children have lost respect and affection for their father. It is the description of intimate sorrows and of the societal pressures that cause them that makes books like *Seelenarbeit* and *Das Schwanenhaus* read like the collective autobiographies of the 1980s. Whether it is the story of Xaver Zürn's longing for self-respect or the story of Dr. Gottlieb Zürn's unsuccessful attempt to save a graceful mansion from demolition, Walser is in full control of his material and his style. This mastery is perhaps nowhere more evident than in the novella *Ein fliehendes Pferd* (1978; translated as *Runaway Horse*, 1980), an exploration of the elective affinities and personality differences of two married couples; the husbands, who were friends in high school, are attracted to each other's wives, and the wives to each other's husbands. In the end each of the four people is left with his or her own form of loneliness but also with a new capacity for love, defective though it may be.

It is premature to suggest that Walser has reached the height of his career, but his recent books have received great critical acclaim. He has also gained, though not without opposition, the kind of distinction that is indicated by the choice of candidates for the annual Georg Büchner Prize, which he received in 1981. He also won the Hermann Hesse Advancement Prize in 1957, the Gerhart Hauptmann Prize in 1962, the Schiller Memorial Prize in 1965, and the Bodensee Literature Prize of the City of Überlingen in 1967. He served as writer in residence or guest lecturer at Middlebury College in Vermont and at the University of Texas in Austin in 1973, at Warwick University in 1975, at West Virginia University in 1976, and at Dartmouth College in 1979. He made a lecture tour of Japan in 1977 and presented the Lectures on Poetics at Frankfurt University in October and November 1980. The ten lectures, published as *Selbstbewußtsein und Ironie* (Self-consciousness and Irony, 1981), are a systematic and historical justification of his own theory and practice of literature.

Biography:

Anthony Edward Waine, *Martin Walser* (Munich: Beck/edition text + kritik, 1980).

References:

R. C. Andrews, "Comedy and Satire in Martin Walser's *Halbzeit*," *Modern Languages*, 50 (1969): 6-10;

Thomas Beckermann, *Martin Walser oder Die Zerstörung eines Musters: Literatursoziologischer Versuch über Halbzeit* (Bonn: Bouvier, 1972);

Frederic W. Binns, "Walser, Martin: Marriage in Philippsburg," *Library Journal*, 86 (1 September 1961): 2823;

Ruth Bleuler, "An Investigation of the Style in Walser's Novel *Halbzeit*," M.A. thesis, Pennsylvania State University, 1968;

Louise Cowan, "Flat Surfaces," *National Review*, 11 (21 October 1961): 273-274;

Heike Doane, *Gesellschaftspolitische Aspekte in Martin Walsers Kristlein-Trilogie: Halbzeit, Das Einhorn, Der Sturz* (Bonn: Bouvier, 1978);

M. Dorman, "The Question of Anselm's Identity in *Halbzeit* and *Das Einhorn*," M.A. thesis, University of Birmingham, 1967;

Roger Gellert, "Alois and the Angoras," *New Statesman*, 66 (6 September 1963): 296-297;

John Hall, "*The Rabbit Run* and *Detour*," *Books and Bookmen*, 10 (May 1966): 38;

Georges Hartmeier, *Die Wunsch- und Erzählströme in Martin Walsers Kristlein-Trilogie: Nöte und Utopien des Mannes* (Bern & New York: Lang, 1983);

Ulrike Hick, *Martin Walsers Prosa: Möglichkeiten des zeitgenössischen Romans unter Berücksichtigung des Realismusanspruchs* (Stuttgart: Heinz, 1983);

Martin Krumbholz, *Ironie im zeitgenössischen Ich-Roman: Grass, Walser, Böll* (Munich: Fink, 1980);

Donald F. Nelson, "The Depersonalized World of Martin Walser," *German Quarterly*, 42 (March 1969): 204-216;

Kathryn Rooney, *Wife and Mistress: Women in Martin Walser's Anselm Kristlein Trilogy* (Coventry, U.K.: Department of German Studies, University of Warwick, 1975);

Wilhelm Johannes Schwarz, *Der Erzähler Martin Walser* (Bern & Munich: Francke, 1971);

Klaus Siblewski, ed., *Martin Walser* (Frankfurt am Main: Suhrkamp, 1981);

A. E. Stubbs, "Martin Walser's Fiction 1955-1966," Ph.D. dissertation, University of Southampton, 1970;

Gisela Ullrich, *Identität und Rolle: Probleme des Erzählens bei Johnson, Walser, Frisch und Fichte* (Stuttgart: Klett, 1977);

Anthony Edward Waine, *Martin Walser: The Development as Dramatist 1950-1970* (Bonn: Bouvier, 1978).

Gabriele Wohmann
(21 May 1932-   )

Guy Stern
Wayne State University

BOOKS: *Mit einem Messer,* as Gabriele Guyot (Stierstadt: Eremiten-Presse, 1958);

Jetzt und nie: Roman (Darmstadt, Berlin-Spandau
& Neuwied: Luchterhand, 1958);

Sieg über die Dämmerung: Erzählungen (Munich: Piper, 1960);

Trinken ist das Herrlichste (Darmstadt: Roether,
1963);

*Erzählungen: Im Auftrage des Volksbundes für Dich-
tung,* edited by Reinhold Siegrist (Karlsruhe: Volksbund für Dichtung, 1964);

Abschied für länger: Roman (Olten & Freiburg im
Breisgau: Walter, 1965);

Theater von innen: Protokoll einer Inszenierung (Olten & Freiburg im Breisgau: Walter, 1966);

Erzählungen: Eine Auswahl 1965-1966 (Ebenhau-
sen: Langewiesche-Brandt, 1966); "Die
Schwestern" translated by Elizabeth Rütschi-
Gerrmann and Edna Huttenmaier-Spitz as
"The Sisters," *Dimension,* 7, no. 3 (1974):
450-459;

In Darmstadt leben die Künste: Feuilleton (Darmstadt: Schlapp, 1967);

Die Bütows: Mini-Roman (Stierstadt im Taunus:
Eremiten-Presse, 1967; revised, 1971);

Ländliches Fest und andere Erzählungen (Darmstadt
& Neuwied: Luchterhand, 1968);

Sonntag bei den Kreisands: Erzählungen (Stierstadt
im Taunus: Eremiten-Presse, 1970);

Ernste Absicht: Roman (Darmstadt & Neuwied:
Luchterhand, 1970);

Treibjagd: Erzählungen, edited by Heinz Schöffler
(Stuttgart: Reclam, 1970);

Selbstverteidigung: Prosa und anderes (Neuwied &
Berlin: Luchterhand, 1971);

Große Liebe: Fernsehstück (Bad Homburg: Tsamas,
1971);

Die Gäste: Hörspiel (Basel: Lenos-Presse, 1971);

Der Fall Rufus: Ein Elternabend (Stierstadt im Taunus: Eremiten-Presse, 1971);

Übersinnlich (Düsseldorf: Eremiten-Presse, 1972);

Gegenangriff: Prosa (Darmstadt, Neuwied & Berlin: Luchterhand, 1972);

Gabriele Wohmann (Conti-Press–Ullstein Bilderdienst)

Alles für die Galerie: Erzählungen (Berlin & Weimar: Aufbau, 1972); translated by Ingeborg
McCoy as "Everything for the Gallery and
Other Stories," *Dimension,* 4, no. 1 (1971):
118-143;

*Die Witwen oder Eine vollkommene Lösung: Fernseh-
spiel* (Stuttgart: Reclam, 1972);

Habgier: Erzählungen (Düsseldorf: Eremiten-Presse, 1973);

Paulinchen war allein zu Haus: Roman (Darmstadt:
Luchterhand, 1974);

So ist die Lage: Gedichte (Düsseldorf: Eremiten-
Presse, 1974);

Entziehung: Materialien zu einem Fernsehfilm (Darmstadt & Neuwied: Luchterhand, 1974);

Dorothea Wörth: Erzählung (Düsseldorf: Eremiten-Presse, 1975);

Schönes Gehege: Roman (Darmstadt & Neuwied: Luchterhand, 1975);

Ein Fall von Chemie: Erzählung (Düsseldorf: Eremiten-Presse, 1975);

Ein unwiderstehlicher Mann: Erzählungen (Reinbek: Rowohlt, 1976);

Ausflug mit der Mutter: Roman (Darmstadt: Luchterhand, 1976);

Endlich allein—endlich zu zwein (Düsseldorf: Eremiten-Presse, 1976);

Alles zu seiner Zeit: Erzählungen (Munich: Deutscher Taschenbuch Verlag, 1976);

Böse Streiche und andere Erzählungen (Düsseldorf: Eremiten-Presse, 1977);

Das dicke Wilhelmchen: Erzählungen (Düsseldorf: Eremiten-Presse, 1978);

Frühherbst in Badenweiler: Roman (Darmstadt: Luchterhand, 1978);

Nachrichtensperre (Berlin & Weimar: Aufbau, 1978);

Die Nächste, bitte!: Erzählung (Düsseldorf: Eremiten-Presse, 1978);

Streit: Erzählungen (Düsseldorf: Eremiten-Presse, 1978);

Feuer bitte! (Düsseldorf: Eremiten-Presse, 1978);

Grund zur Aufregung (Darmstadt: Luchterhand, 1978);

Heiratskandidaten: Ein Fernsehspiel, und drei Hörspiele (Munich: Piper, 1978);

Der Nachtigall fällt auch nichts Neues ein: Ein Dialog (Düsseldorf: Eremiten-Presse, 1978; republished with two additional plays, Munich: Deutscher Taschenbuch Verlag, 1979);

Ausgewählte Erzählungen aus zwanzig Jahren, selected by Thomas Scheuffelen, 2 volumes (Darmstadt & Neuwied: Luchterhand, 1979);

Knoblauch am Kamin: Erzählung (Düsseldorf: Eremiten-Presse, 1979);

Paarlauf: Erzählungen (Darmstadt & Neuwied: Luchterhand, 1979);

Wanda Lords Gespenster: Hörspiel (Düsseldorf: Eremiten-Presse, 1979); adapted as *Wanda Lords Gespenster: Drama* (Bad Homburg: Stephanie Hunzinger Bühnenverlag, 1980);

Ach wie gut, daß niemand weiß: Roman (Darmstadt: Luchterhand, 1980);

Vor der Hochzeit: Erzählungen (Reinbek: Rowohlt, 1980);

Wir sind eine Familie: Erzählungen (Düsseldorf: Eremiten-Presse, 1980);

Violas Vorbilder: Erzählung (Düsseldorf: Eremiten-Presse, 1980);

Meine Lektüre: Aufsätze über Bücher (Darmstadt: Luchterhand, 1980);

Ich weiß das auch nicht besser: Gedichte (Munich: Deutscher Taschenbuch Verlag, 1980);

Guilty (Düsseldorf: Eremiten-Presse, 1980);

Stolze Zeiten: Erzählungen (Düsseldorf: Claassen, 1981);

Das Glücksspiel: Roman (Darmstadt & Neuwied: Luchterhand, 1981);

Ein günstiger Tag: Erzählungen (Düsseldorf: Eremiten-Presse, 1981); "Ein günstiger Tag, der heute verwendbar Herr Kleiber" translated by Jutta van Selm as "An Opportune Day, Today's Functional Herr Kleiber," *Dimension*, 8, no. 3 (1975): 542-549;

Komm lieber Mai: Gedichte (Darmstadt: Luchterhand, 1981);

Plötzlich in Limburg: Komödie in 4 Bildern (Bad Homburg: Hunzinger Bühnenverlag, 1981);

Nachkommenschaften: Fernsehspiel (Düsseldorf: Eremiten-Prese, 1981);

Komm donnerstags (Munich: Deutscher Taschenbuch Verlag, 1981);

Einsamkeit: Erzählungen (Darmstadt: Luchterhand, 1982);

Das Trugbild: Erzählung (Hauzenberg: Pongratz, 1982);

Hilfe kommt mir von den Bergen: Hörspiel (Düsseldorf: Eremiten-Presse, 1982);

Geschwister, text by Wohmann, photographs by John Harding (Frankfurt am Main: Fricke, 1982);

Der kürzeste Tag des Jahres: Erzählungen (Darmstadt: Luchterhand, 1983);

Verliebt, oder?: Erzählungen (Darmstadt & Neuwied: Luchterhand, 1983);

Goethe hilf! Neue Erzählungen (Düsseldorf: Eremiten-Presse, 1983);

Gesammelte Gedichte: 1964-1982 (Darmstadt & Neuwied: Luchterhand, 1983);

Bucklicht Männlein: Erzählungen (Berlin & Weimar: Aufbau, 1984);

Der Kirschbaum: Erzählung (Düsseldorf: Eremiten-Presse, 1984);

Ich lese, ich schreibe: Autobiographische Essays (Darmstadt: Luchterhand, 1984);

Passau, Gleis 3: Gedichte (Darmstadt & Neuwied: Luchterhand, 1984);

Hebräer 11, 1: Hörspiel (Düsseldorf: Eremiten-Presse, 1985);

Der Irrgast (Darmstadt: Luchterhand, 1985);

Glücklicher Vorgang (Düsseldorf: Eremiten-Presse, 1986);

Darmstadt: Unterwegs gehöre ich nach Haus. Fernsehfilm (Freiburg im Breisgau: Eulenverlag, 1986);

Der Flötenton: Roman (Darmstadt & Neuwied: Luchterhand, 1987);

Ein russischer Sommer: Erzählungen (Darmstadt: Luchterhand, 1988).

OTHER: Heinz Schöffler, *Über Maler, über Dichter*, contribution by Wohmann (Mainz: Von Hase & Koehler, 1975);

Sylvia Plath, *Briefe nach Hause 1950-1963*, edited by Aurelia Schober Plath, translated by Iris Wegner, afterword by Wohmann (Frankfurt am Main, Berlin & Vienna: Ullstein, 1981);

Anton Cechov, edited by Wohmann (Cologne: Kiepenheuer & Witsch, 1985).

PERIODICAL PUBLICATIONS: "Ein unwiderstehlicher Mann," *Akzente*, 4 (January/February 1957): 79-95;

"Drei Gedichte," *Dimension*, 1, no. 2 (1969): 218-255; translated by Margaret Woodruff as "Three Poems," *Dimension*, 1, no. 2 (1969): 218-225;

Norwegian Wood: Hörspiel, Dimension, 4, no. 2 (1973): 382-468; translated by Minetta Altgelt Goyne as *Norwegian Wood: Radio Play, Dimension*, 4, no. 2 (1973): 382-468;

"Ein günstiger Tag, der heute verwendbare Herr Kleiber," *Stuttgarter Zeitung*, October 1975; translated by Jutta van Selm as "An Opportune Day, Today's Functional Herr Kleiber," *Dimension*, 8, no. 3 (1975): 542-549;

"Zwei Gedichte," *Dimension*, 10, no. 3 (1977): 398-407; translated by Allen H. Chappel as "Two Poems," *Dimension*, 10, no. 3 (1977): 398-407;

"Nachmittag in der Tannenhofstrasse," *Dimension*, 11, no. 1 (1978): 60-77; translated by Selm as "Afternoon on Pine Court," *Dimension*, 11, no. 1 (1978): 60-77.

Since she began writing in 1956 Gabriele Wohmann has been one of Germany's most prolific literary figures. Her works include radio plays, television dramas, plays, poetry, and essays; the forms, however, to which she has returned most consistently are the novel and the short story. Critics frequently acknowledge her mastery of short narratives and consider her to be one of the finest storytellers in West Germany.

Her fiction has become widely known in both parts of Germany, appears with great regularity on West Germany's best-seller lists, and has been translated into at least twelve languages.

Born in Darmstadt in 1932 to Paul Daniel and Luise Lettermann Guyot, Wohmann belongs to the generation of writers that emerged after World War II. Her formative years still provide the thematic underpinnings of much of her fiction. Like many German literary figures she was the child of a clergyman. She has characterized her childhood as secure and protected; her parents, revulsed by Nazism because of their religious and humanitarian convictions, shielded her from its propaganda aimed at children. Wohmann has written an uncharacteristically emotional tribute to her father in her short story "Vaterporträt" (Portrait of My Father) in her collection *Selbstverteidigung* (Self-Defense, 1971) and has drawn on her mother's persona in her novel *Ausflug mit der Mutter* (Outing with My Mother, 1976).

After graduating from high school in Norden, Gabriele Guyot attended the University of Frankfurt for six semesters. She majored in German philology but also attended courses on American, British, and French literature and musicology. Her admiration for Proust, discernible in her early stories, and her discovery of Joyce in Georg Goyert's 1927 translation date from her student years. Her university days may also have given rise to her occasional satirical treatment of professors, as in the story "Antrittsrede" (Speech upon Being Initiated) in the collection *Habgier* (Greed, 1973), in which she also takes aim at unrepentant Nazis. She did not complete her studies; instead she married a fellow student, Reiner Wohmann, in 1953. The couple accepted teaching positions at a private school on the island of Langeoog and, after one year, in Darmstadt. Reiner Wohmann subsequently returned to the university, earned his teaching certificate, and was promoted to the position of Oberstudienrat (senior teacher). Her own teaching career supplied Gabriele Wohmann with the material for such short stories as the often anthologized "Sie sind alle reizend" (All of Them Are Charming) in *Selbstverteidigung*.

In 1956 the prestigious journal *Akzente* accepted Wohmann's story "Ein unwiderstehlicher Mann" (An Irresistible Man), the first work she had ever submitted anywhere. She considers the journal's editor, Walter Höllerer, along with a few other critics and literati such as the writer

Hans Bender, her discoverers. She quit teaching in 1957 to write full time. Her royalties during the first decade of her writing career never exceeded six thousand marks annually; today, with some of her novels selling upward of forty thousand copies in hardback and one hundred thousand in softcover, and with frequent appearances on television and on the lecture circuit, she is financially independent. She is also independent of literary groups or cliques: she attended several meetings of the Gruppe (Group) 47, a post–World War II writers' association, in the early 1960s but now avoids congresses and forums. "Das hat, wie ich meine, mit dem Älter–und Reiferwerden zu tun. Man verhandelt dabei über Trends, den Büchermarkt oder das Lesepublikum. All das hindert, wenn man ein Buch zu schreiben hat" (I attribute that to growing older and more mature. There one discusses trends, the market, or the reading public. All of that is a hindrance when one has a book to write).

She and her husband, who retired from teaching in 1980 to become her literary advisor and manager, live in the artists' colony, Rosenhöhe, in Darmstadt. Though she is a world traveler–the United States is a frequent and preferred destination–she says that she always feels "magnetically drawn back to the roots of Darmstadt and the reclusive refuge of my hedged-in home." Except for vacations, lecture tours, or occasional respites, she imposes an ironclad regimen of daily writing upon herself; the routine results in a major work of fiction and one or two shorter volumes annually. For the most part, she commences writing without knowing the denouement and simply allows the narrative to take over.

Her writing centers almost invariably on the vicissitudes of everyday living, the disintegrating family, the wall that exists even between intimates, the blunders of seeming sophisticates, or the helplessness of those who cannot–or who only barely manage to–cope with life. Her narrative technique, based on a rare acuity in the optical or aural perception of minute or almost inaudible details, has been compared to split-second snapshots, mosaics, or seismographic readings of modern man's daily travail; but an analogy to the painterly technique of Magic Realism more aptly describes Wohmann's narratives. In Magic Realism the painter subjects a miniscule slice of reality, unperceived by the casual observer, to probing scrutiny. The artist can unfold a cosmos, in all its beauty and hideousness, from the pebbles,

plants, insects, and detritus between two ties of a railroad track. Wohmann is unsurpassed in describing the tiny reflex motion of a hand and thereby uncovering repressed or subliminal feelings; bodily symptoms signal psychic malaises. She can characterize the intricacies of a relationship through a table setting. In the novel *Schönes Gehege* (Beautiful Enclosure, 1975) she accomplishes the exposition of characters, events, and atmosphere through a film crew's desultory search for an outdoor setting. Splintered fragments of lives congeal into intelligible chronicles intended as microcosms of today's unstable society. "Mich interessieren immer die gewöhnlichen Schrecken, nicht die sogenannten großen Ereignisse" (I am always interested in the run-of-the-mill terrors, not the so-called great events), she says. For the most part these terrors are experienced by men and women who are less than heroic: they are suppressed, victimized, defeated, and deeply disturbed beneath a placid exterior.

While the situations and people in her narratives are drawn from a circumscribed world, her themes are universal. She often writes of contradictory feelings: eagerness and reluctance to break away from the parental home, the need and fear of being alone, love-hatred between friends and lovers or between mothers and daughters, the intellectuals' complexities as cause for both their pride and their suffering. Critics have pointed out her preoccupation with the emptiness of daily living, the search for vaguely perceived aspirations, the self-doubts of artists, and the fear of aging and dying. What unites all these themes is an even more basic concern of Wohmann's: man's wish to make time stand still and thereby overcome the fear of death. The stories in her collection *Der kürzeste Tag des Jahres* (The Shortest Day of the Year, 1983) strike again and again at the theme of Todesverdrängung (repressing death).

Wohmann has said that she seeks truth beneath false fronts, the face behind a mask, reality behind appearances. In her search for honesty she is unsparing of her characters–even of herself, when her fiction is obviously autobiographical. In describing her style, reviewers use the same adjectives over and over: merciless in uncovering concealed frailties, concise, mordant, ironic, brilliantly witty in her play on words, wickedly comic. Certainly she displays all of these characteristics, but they are tempered, often subtly, by flashes of compassion for her flawed or failed characters.

Wohmann at about the time of publication of her novel Frühherbst in Badenweiler *(1978)*

Appreciation of the microscopic world of her literary works or of her mordant style has by no means been universal. She has gained a large readership and has received some of West Germany's most prestigious awards: a stipend toward a year's stay at the Villa Massimo in Rome in 1967-1968, the Literature Prize of the City of Bremen in 1971, election to the Berlin Academy of Art in 1975 and to the Academy for Language and Literature in 1980, and the West German Order of Merit in 1980. On the other hand, she has been scorned by some critics for what they per-

ceive as repetitiveness in her settings and situations and lack of variation in her characters and their development. That objection ignores the many nuances which, in her small fictional world, can be as momentous as broader diversity elsewhere.

She has also been taken to task for her unremitting destruction of her apparently wholesome characters. Both admirers and detractors have labeled her "die Frau mit dem bösen Blick" (the woman with the evil eye *or* the eye for evil). She defended herself against that stereotype: "Ich habe keinen bösen, sondern einen genau hin-schauenden Blick. Ich beschreibe nicht nur unglückliche Familien, sondern auch glückliche Familien, was alle Menschen zusammenhält *und* Entfremdung. . . . Den Unerträglichkeiten liegen ja Erträglichkeiten zugrunde. Ich habe doch auch das Gute mehrfach dargestellt" (I don't have an eye for evil, but for exactitude. I don't show only unhappy families, but also happy ones, true intimacy and alienation. . . . The unbearable is predicated on the existence of the bearable. And I have portrayed the positive repeatedly). As proof of her lack of aversion to happy scenes Wohmann recounts her first recollection of her creative imagination at work: "Ich war noch in der Volksschule; wir hatten eine Putzfrau, die scheinbar schon seit ewigen Zeiten zu uns kam. Eines Tages hörte ich meine Eltern von ihrer unscheinbaren, armseligen Wohnung reden. Meine Phantasie ließ mir keine Ruhe und verwandelte ihre mir unbekannte Wohnung in einen Märchenpalast" (I was still in elementary school; we had a cleaning woman who seemingly always had been with us. One day I heard my parents speak of her sparse, lowly quarters. My imagination went to work and transformed her unseen flat into a fairy-tale palace). The latest phase in her career, beginning around 1975, finds her frequently reverting to the happier mood of her childhood. But that, too, displeases some of her critics: they describe her collection of satires *Goethe hilf!* (Goethe, Help!, 1983) as too tame and conciliatory.

That charge was scarcely laid against her first published story, "Ein unwiderstehlicher Mann," in which a woman in her late thirties finds herself in the "lächerlichen und unwürdigen . . . auch außerordentlich schmerzhaften Zustand" (ridiculous and undignified . . . and immensely painful situation) of having fallen in love. The man, utterly unaware of her attachment to him, asks for her advice when he feels compelled to make a choice between his wife and a much younger woman. The protagonist finally tells him that in her homeland (the story takes place in America) a person with such a dilemma would shoot himself. He follows her advice, and she muses at the end of the story that even having such a fatal impact on someone else's life is better than having none at all. The desperate attempt to break through isolation and to find love often takes on macabre or pathological forms.

Three volumes of short stories–*Mit einem Messer* (With a Knife, 1958), *Sieg über die*

Dämmerung (Victory over the Twilight, 1960), and *Trinken ist das Herrlichste* (Drinking Is the Most Glorious Thing, 1963)–and a novel, *Jetzt und nie* (Now and Never, 1958), followed her debut publication in rapid succession. In *Jetzt und nie*, set against the background of the West German Economic Miracle of the 1950s, a salesman tries to break out of his humdrum life and marriage. The twenty-four hours covered by the novel are marked by his heavy bouts of drinking, falling in love with a girl at a seaside resort, heart attack, and death.

The inability to start a new life also besets the heroine of *Abschied für länger* (Farewell for a Long Time, 1965). A woman in her early thirties leaves her parental home to be closer to her married lover. But they cannot cut loose from their previous bonds. At the end their inability to communicate, symbolized by his cancer of the larynx, leads to their separation and her return to her parents.

Irony permeates in the "mini-novel" *Die Bütows* (1967), which Wohmann has described as a counter-statement to the traditional sentimental German family novel. The Bütows are pragmatic and achievement-oriented, but their apparent normality hides a proto-fascistic attitude to life. They whip their children in front of visitors, for example, to add shame to the pain. The reader is left with the impression that their xenophobia and loathing for weakness will be perpetuated in their children.

In her collection of short stories *Ländliches Fest und andere Erzählungen* (A Village Celebration and Other Stories, 1968) she adds new shades to her usual palette of gray. The title story is a study in contrasts: party chatter and flirtations alternate with a physician's clinically detailed report on the autopsy of a small child who has apparently been abandoned by her mother. "Atelierbesuch" (Visit to a Studio), in which a conversation about an artist's nonrepresentational paintings defines the relationship of the artist, his wife, and their visitors, uses a lyrical style. "Denk immer an heute nachmittag" (Always Remember This Afternoon), in which a disconsolate child is delivered to a boarding school by his widowed father, who tries to cheer him up with a stream of platitudes, brings Wohmann close to the mastery of dialogue of Ernest Hemingway.

On the other hand, the novel *Ernste Absicht* (Serious Intent, 1970), which consists of an unrelieved inner monologue, became her most Joycean work. A woman in a hospital bed, facing an all but hopeless operation, is assaulted and ultimately defeated by an unceasing stream of recollections of important and trivial events from her life. The critic Martin Gregor-Dellin said of this novel: "Mit enormem sprachlichem Ehrgeiz, beunruhigend durch komplizierte Mehrsträhnigkeit der Erinnerungen und Assoziationen, gelingt G. W. hier eine Lebensrevue vom Grabesrande her" (With enormous linguistic ambition, disquieting through complex, multiple strands of recollections and associations, G. W. successfully evokes the flashback of a life from the edge of the grave). Other critics, however, took the appearance of this novel as a pretext to revive a reproach of the 1960s: that her works lack political engagement.

But in her television play *Entziehung* (Withdrawal, 1974), in which she herself played the role of an addict, and in her novel *Paulinchen war allein zu Haus* (Little Paula Was Home Alone, 1974) she launches caustic attacks on social ills. In the novel, modern child psychology dictates that the warm love a child has enjoyed in the home of her grandparents be replaced by detached and cold affection. The novel not only attests to Wohmann's sensitive understanding of children but shows her as a master of the manipulation of narrative perspectives: she switches effortlessly from the thoroughly "modern" adoptive parents' viewpoint to that of the emotionally deprived eight-year-old. At the end Paulinchen attains a chance for happiness by being sent to a boarding school. The novel was made into a major film for television by the West German author Anne Voss.

In *Ausflug mit der Mutter* Wohmann delineates a mother-daughter relationship from the viewpoint of the daughter. When the father dies, it is not the grieving widow but the daughter, projecting herself into her mother's role, who loses her sense of identity. The book has been described as an unsparing and completely convincing self-examination in which the daughter's guilt at having grown out of her parents' environment is laid bare. Wohmann has described the mother-daughter relationship as one of "die Wurzeln" (the roots) of her writing.

The problem of the artist, explored in many of her short stories, becomes Wohmann's central concern in *Schönes Gehege*. The writer Robert Plath, whom she endows with a good many of her own qualities–such as an attachment to parents and an ambivalent reaction to public poetry readings–has to reconcile his past and present during the filming of a documentary about his life. In the course of the novel he regains former friendships, strengthens his relationship with his wife, and attains clarity about himself as a person and writer. At the end, realizing that the documentary will perpetuate the false image of him created by the media, public relations experts, and himself, Plath withdraws from the project; the film is never made. As the author Geno Hartlaub says in a blurb on the title page of the 1978 reprint of the novel: "Der Schriftsteller Plath bemüht sich geduldig und mit großem Ernst, so schrecklich einfache und schwierige Dinge wie Liebe, Glück und Freundlichkeit wieder zu lernen. Johanna, mit der er eine Ehe der wahren Partnerschaft führt, stellt–im platonischen Sinn–seine verlorene Wesenshälfte dar ... " (The author Plath tries, patiently and most earnestly, to relearn such terribly easy and difficult things as love, happiness and friendliness. Johanna, with whom he maintains a marriage of true partnership, represents–in a platonic sense–the lost half of his being ...). Hartlaub also praises Wohmann's depiction of such currently unpopular subjects as happiness and misfortunes in the private realm rather than the political arena.

She returns to the subject of the artist's life in crisis in *Frühherbst in Badenweiler* (Early Fall in Badenweiler, 1978), the story of the composer Hubert Frey's midlife fears of failing artistic powers, aging, and death. But in this novel grim moments are relieved by outright comic scenes. Asked why she told the novel from a man's perspective and attributed his suffering to his wife's exaggerated careerism, she observed that men deserved equal time and that she deplored the excesses of feminism. "Aber ... ich bin nicht reaktionär" (But I am not a reactionary), she added. *Frühherbst in Badenweiler* remained on the best-seller list of the West German newsmagazine *Der Spiegel* for nearly nine months. Wohmann portrayed a highly intellectual, fiercely independent, yet hurt and vulnerable woman in her short story *Die Nächste, bitte* (Next Woman, Please), published the same year. The narrator provides a portrait of her friend Alma, laying bare her self-pity, her death wish, her hypersensitivity. Only in the last sentence does the narrator reveal that this characterization is a self-portrait.

In *Knoblauch am Kamin* (Garlic at the Fireplace, 1979) Wohmann traces the inhibited, anxiety-ridden progress of a romance started by an advertisement in the personal columns of a newspaper. The ending is left open: will the somewhat hysterical protagonist, desolated by his loneliness, continue the tenuous relationship or indulge in an endless search for a compatible companion? What is *not* said by the two main characters is as important in this narrative as the "reported" dialogue. In the story "Nachsicht mit Kitty" (Forebearance with Kitty), from the collection *Paarlauf* (Running in Tandem, 1979), the guests at a posh suburban party play at rapid cocktail conversations that bar, rather than advance, true communication. This theme of avoiding intimacy through blandness pervades Wohmann's fiction.

Always attuned to the problems produced by contemporary life-styles, Wohmann devotes her novel *Ach wie gut, daß niemand weiß* (Oh How Good That No One Knows, 1980) to the "open marriage" agreement of an unmarried couple. The long years of living together have taken their toll; passion has given way to custom. During professional sojourns in Switzerland and the United States Marlene Ziegler, an attractive thirty-six-year-old psychiatrist, has several liaisons, all of which prove to be unsatisfying. She wavers between the freedom of an emancipated woman and the security of a permanent relationship that may lead to marriage. Wohmann endows her heroine with a capacity for psychologically sophisticated self-analysis, in which Freudian symbols and precepts abound.

Almost simultaneously with this novel, Wohmann edited her book reviews for publication as *Meine Lektüre* (My Readings, 1980); wrote the radio drama *Wanda Lords Gespenster* (The Ghosts of Wanda Lord, 1979), an admittedly autobiographical problem play on the middle-aged heroine's atttempt to cope with aging; and composed another radio play, *Hilfe kommt mir von den Bergen* (Help Comes to Me from the Mountains, 1982), in which two couples suppress under a barrage of small talk the very topic that brought them together: how to cure the handicapped child of one of the couples.

The story collection *Stolze Zeiten* (Proud Times, 1981)—the title is meant ironically—contains one of Wohmann's most resignedly mature stories. "Große Liebe" (Great Love) tells of a small-town librarian who falls in love with a renowned poet but, despite the latter's belated readiness to enter into a relationship with her, settles for a pedestrian marriage to an egotistical schoolteacher and poetaster. In Wohmann's most starkly tragic novel to date, *Das Glücksspiel* (Game of Chance, 1981), the gifted, high-strung young

piano teacher Lily Siemer is driven into madness by her philandering husband, who has abandoned her; a friend who is a hyperactive feminist and devourer of people; an anally preoccupied older man who boards in Lily's home; Lily's brutal stepson; and finally by her insensitive and remote psychiatrist-lover. In one of her public appearances Wohmann mentioned the danger of "Wahrnehmungsmißbrauch" (abuse of perceptiveness), which she likens to the abuse of alcohol. Her hyperperceptive heroine in *Das Glücksspiel* is a victim both of her times and of this self-destructive character trait.

Komm lieber Mai (Come Dear May, 1981) is a collection of narrative poems that use everyday language to describe common experiences that might be the content of Wohmann's short stories. Her unrhymed but rhythmic poems intone the same themes as her fiction. With a few lines– "Sehr dringend ist mein Wunsch/Am Unbedeutend-Eintönigen/Teilzunehmen" (Very urgent is my wish/In insignificant-monotonous events/To take part)–she defines once again her literary mission. This wish to make the ordinary rather than the extraordinary her subject also pervades the anthology *Gesammelte Gedichte* (Collected Poems, 1983), which includes selections from her earliest volumes of lyrics to her most up-to-date creations.

Wohmann's favorite form remains the short story. In her collections *Der kürzeste Tag des Jahres* and *Verliebt, oder?* (In Love, Or?, 1983) her traditional subjects–the attempt to cover anxieties and fears with banalities and loneliness by pretended gregariousness–emerge once again; but her stories continue to sound new notes. In "Zwei Rivalen" (Two Rivals) in *Verliebt, oder?* she achieves hilarious effects when Fabian, a young boy competing with his mother's latest male friend for her attention, mixes a child's language with the sophisticated parlance of his intellectual mother. In the title story, on the other hand, the characters raise traditional religious questions of theodicy and transcendence. These themes have been present in previous stories but are pursued here with added intensity. As Wohmann grows older, she may be returning more often to the world of her father's vicarage.

In the poetry collection *Passau, Gleis 3* (Passau, Track 3, 1984) the frequent poems of loss and leave-taking are countered by the "Der Protest" of the aging in the poem of that name and by the upsurge of the narrator's will "Die Notbremse zu ziehen" (to pull the emergency brake) on the train to oblivion in "Zwei Muscheln" (Seashells). In "Unsere Polaroid-Zukunft" (Our Polaroid Future) a family playing ball achieves its own version of permanence in an ephemeral situation by arresting the flight of the ball with a Polaroid camera. A minor conquest, perhaps, for the family–and for Wohmann, who in so many works rails against time's inexorable passage and here makes it stand still. These poems and the short-story collection *Ein russischer Sommer* (A Russian Summer, 1988) reaffirm Wohmann's ability to depict private lives conducted away from the limelight and devoid of conventional heroism.

The novel *Der Flötenton* (The Tone of the Recorder, 1987) is set against the background of the nuclear accident at Chernobyl. Wohmann shows in episodic fashion how the lives of a large and varied cast of characters are affected by the disaster. At the center of the novel are Anton Asyer, a department head in an international construction firm, and Sandra Hinholz, a renowned player and teacher of the recorder. They meet in Lisbon and engage in a brief affair, then return to Germany and drift apart, overtaken by the routine of everyday life–he by business and other love affairs, she by an even more desultory liaison.

Wohmann has said: "Diese krude Welt, sie gefällt mir nicht" (This crude world displeases me). There are signs in her last few works that she has begun not only to record but to reshape that world.

References:

Irene Ferchl, *Die Rolle des Alltäglichen in der Kurzprosa von Gabriele Wohmann* (Bonn: Bouvier, 1980);

Walter Helmut Fritz, "Gabriele Wohmann: So ist die Lage," *Neue deutsche Hefte*, 22, no. 1 (1975): 138-139;

Martin Gregor-Dellin, "Gabriele Wohmann," in *Lexikon der deutschsprachigen Gegenwartsliteratur*, edited by Herbert Wiesner (Munich: Nymphenburger Verlag, 1981), pp. 533-534;

Rainer Hagen, "Gabriele Wohmann," in *Schriftsteller der Gegenwart*, edited by K. Nonnemann (Olten: Walter, 1963), pp. 325-330;

Werner Helwig, "Gabriele Wohmanns Entzauberungen," *Frankfurter Hefte*, 6 (1980): 68-69;

Yvonne Holbeche, "Portrait and Self-Portrait: Gabriele Wohmann's *Ausflug mit der Mutter*," *Seminar*, 20, no. 3 (1984): 205-217;

Kenneth Hughes, "The Short Fiction of Gabriele Wohmann," *Studies in Short Fiction*, 13, no. 1 (1976): 61-70;

Gerhard P. Knapp, *Gabriele Wohmann* (Königstein: Athenäum, 1981);

Mona Knapp and Gerhard P. Knapp, "Frauenunterdrückungsaugenblicke: Gabriele Wohmanns Roman *Das Glücksspiel*," in *Frauenliteratur: Autorinnen-Perspektiven-Konzepte*, edited by Manfred Jurgensen (Bern: Lang, 1983), pp. 139-160;

Gregor Laschen and Ton Naaijkens, "Kunstfiguren gegen das alltägliche Chaos: Gespräch mit Gabriele Wohmann," *Deutsche Bücher*, 4 (1979): 245-257;

Marcel Reich-Ranicki, "Bitterkeit ohne Zorn," in his *Literatur der kleinen Schritte* (Munich: Piper, 1967), pp. 279-285;

Ekkehart Rudolph, *Protokoll zur Person: Autoren über sich und ihr Werk* (Munich: List, 1971), pp. 192-207;

Michael Christian Rutschky, "Der Wille zur Unangreifbarkeit," *Neue Rundschau*, 86, no. 4 (1975): 727-730;

Heinz Schafroth, "Gabriele Wohmann," in *Kritisches Lexikon zur deutschsprachigen Gegenwartsliteratur*, edited by Heinz Ludwig Arnold (Munich: Edition text + kritik, 1980), n. pag.;

Thomas Scheuffelen, ed., *Gabriele Wohmann: Materialienbuch* (Darmstadt: Luchterhand, 1977);

Klaus Siblewski, ed., *Gabriele Wohmann: Auskunft für Leser* (Darmstadt & Neuwied: Luchterhand, 1982);

Walter H. Sokel, "Quotation and Literary Echo as Structural Principles in Gabriele Wohmann's *Frühherbst in Badenweiler*," *Studies in Twentieth Century Literature*, 5 (Fall 1980): 107-121;

Gisela G. Strand, "Gabriele Wohmann: A Thematic Approach to Alienation," *Michigan Academician*, 9 (Spring 1977): 383-395;

H. M. Waidson, "The Short Stories and Novels of Gabriele Wohmann," *German Life and Letters*, 26, no. 3 (1973): 214-227;

Klaus Wellner, *Leiden an der Familie: Zur sozialpathologischen Rollenanalyse im Werk Gabriele Wohmanns* (Stuttgart: Klett, 1976);

Dieter E. Zimmer, "Weg mit der Tarnung: Das Gespräch mit der Autorin Gabriele Wohmann," *Die Zeit*, 12 December 1974, p. 39.

Christa Wolf
(18 March 1929-   )

Dieter Sevin
Vanderbilt University

BOOKS: *Moskauer Novelle* (Halle: Mitteldeutscher Verlag, 1961);

Der geteilte Himmel (Halle: Mitteldeutscher Verlag, 1963); translated by Joan Becker as *The Divided Heaven* (Berlin: Seven Seas, 1965; New York: Adler's Foreign Books, 1976);

Nachdenken über Christa T. (Halle: Mitteldeutscher Verlag, 1968); translated by Christopher Middleton as *The Quest for Christa T.* (New York: Farrar, Straus & Giroux, 1971; London: Hutchinson, 1971);

Lesen und Schreiben: Aufsätze und Betrachtungen (Berlin: Aufbau, 1972; enlarged, 1973); republished as *Lesen und Schreiben: Aufsätze und Prosastücke* (Darmstadt: Luchterhand, 1972); translated by Becker as *The Reader and the Writer: Essays, Sketches, Memories* (Berlin: Seven Seas, 1977; New York: Signet, 1977);

Till Eulenspiegel: Erzählung für den Film, by Wolf and Gerhard Wolf (Berlin & Weimar: Aufbau, 1973);

Unter den Linden: Drei unwahrscheinliche Geschichten (Berlin: Aufbau, 1974);

Kindheitsmuster (Berlin: Aufbau, 1976); translated by Ursule Molinaro and Hedwig Rappolt as *A Model Childhood* (New York: Farrar, Straus & Giroux, 1980; London: Virago, 1982);

J'écris sur ce qui m'inquiète: Débat dans Sinn und Form sur son dernier Roman (Paris: Centre d'études et de recherches marxistes, 1977);

Kein Ort, nirgends (Berlin: Aufbau, 1979); translated by Jan Van Heurck as *No Place on Earth* (New York: Farrar, Straus & Giroux, 1982; London: Virago, 1983);

Fortgesetzter Versuch: Aufsätze, Gespräche, Essays (Leipzig: Reclam, 1979);

Gesammelte Erzählungen (Darmstadt: Luchterhand, 1980);

Neue Lebensansichten eines Katers; Juninachmittag (Stuttgart: Reclam, 1981);

Kassandra: Vier Vorlesungen; Eine Erzählung (Berlin: Aufbau, 1983); translated by Van Heurck as *Cassandra: A Novel and Four Essays* (New York: Farrar, Straus & Giroux, 1984);

Christa Wolf (photograph by Stefan Moses, Munich)

Voraussetzungen einer Erzählung: Kassandra (Darmstadt: Luchterhand, 1983);

Störfall (Darmstadt: Luchterhand, 1987);

Die Dimension des Autors (Darmstadt: Luchterhand, 1987).

OTHER: *In diesen Jahren: Ausgewählte deutsche Prosa,* edited by Wolf (Leipzig: Reclam, 1957);

Proben junger Erzähler: Ausgewählte deutsche Prosa, edited by Wolf (Leipzig: Reclam, 1959);

Wir, unsere Zeit, edited by Wolf and Gerhard Wolf (Berlin: Aufbau, 1959);

Karoline von Günderode, *Der Schatten eines Traumes,* edited by Wolf (Berlin: Der Morgen, 1979);

Anna Seghers, *Ausgewählte Erzählungen,* edited by Wolf (Darmstadt: Luchterhand, 1983);

Historischer Verein für Hessen, 1934-1983: Vorträge, Exkursionen, Publikationen, edited by Wolf (Darmstadt: Verlag des Historischen Vereins für Hessen, 1983).

Christa Wolf is one of the most prominent postwar German writers. Her works are read and discussed widely in both Germanies, and her reputation is spreading rapidly beyond the German-speaking countries. In addition to her fiction, Wolf has done significant work in the essay form, providing a theoretical basis for her oeuvre.

Christa Ihlenfeld was born in 1929 in Landsberg an der Warthe (today Gorzów Wielkopolski, Poland). Her father, Otto Ihlenfeld, was a salesman. In 1945 the invading Red Army forced the German population in the territories east of the Oder-Neiße line to move to the West; the Ihlenfelds settled in Mecklenburg, where Christa worked as secretary to the mayor of Gammelin. After a stay in a tuberculosis sanatorium she finished school in 1949 in Bad Frankenhausen. She joined the Socialist Unity party and, from 1949 to 1953, studied German literature at the Universities of Leipzig and Jena. In 1951 she married the Germanist and essayist Gerhard Wolf; they have two daughters, Annette and Katrin. After receiving her degree with a thesis on problems of realism in the work of Hans Fallada, she worked as a technical assistant for the East German Writers' Union, as a reader for the Neues Leben publishing house in East Berlin, and as an editor of the periodical *Neue Deutsche Literatur.* From 1959 to 1962 she was a reader for the Mitteldeutscher Verlag in Halle, where she also worked in a boxcar factory. In 1962 she moved to Kleinmachnow, near Berlin, and turned to writing full time. She has traveled widely in Europe and has visited the Soviet Union and, in 1974, the United States. In 1976 she and her husband moved to East Berlin; the same year she joined other prominent East German writers in signing a petition protesting the revocation of citizenship of the poet/singer Wolf Biermann.

Wolf's first work of fiction, *Moskauer Novelle* (Moscow Novella, 1961), was received politely but did not enjoy great success. It is the story of an East Berlin doctor, Vera Brauer, who travels to Moscow in 1959 with a delegation from the German Democratic Republic; the interpreter assigned to the delegation turns out to be Pawel Koschkin, whom she had met fifteen years before when, as a lieutenant in the Red Army, he had participated in the occupation of her hometown of Fanselow. Wolf's attempt to use their love affair as an allegory for international relations between Germany and the Soviet Union fails.

Her breakthrough as a writer came with the novel *Der geteilte Himmel* (1963; translated as *The Divided Heaven,* 1965). Published shortly after the building of the Berlin Wall, the book was an instant success and made Wolf, virtually overnight, the best-known author in the German Democratic Republic (GDR).

After an accident education student Rita Seidel wakes up in a hospital bed and tries to analyze what has taken place. During her convalescence Rita examines the preceding two years of her life: her love for the chemist Manfred Herrfurth, her move from a small village to the city of Halle, her work in a railroad-car factory, her studies to become a teacher, Manfred's flight to the West just before the erection of the Berlin Wall on 13 August 1961, and her accident shortly thereafter. The sequence of events is primarily chronological, although there are flashbacks to Rita's and Manfred's early childhood. The third-person narrator seems to be almost omniscient but shares Rita's questioning attitude, thereby stimulating the reader to participate in the narrative process. The ambiguity of the text allows Wolf to deal with topics that otherwise could not have been discussed in published form in the GDR in the early 1960s.

The economic and political situation of the GDR was precarious at the time the novel was written: the prospering West German economy presented an enormous challenge to East German planners, who had to cope with the loss of thousands of skilled workers and professionals who crossed the open border to West Berlin. This problem was solved by the building of the Berlin Wall, but at a high price: the loss of international esteem for the GDR and of personal freedom for its population. The resulting intensification of the cold war and the fear that it might lead to actual war are woven into the background of Wolf's novel. Wolf's treatment of the "German Question"–the division of Germany–contributed to the enormous success of the book in both East and West.

Although the story takes place in the GDR, Wolf addresses general problems and concerns: the anxieties resulting from leaving the idyllic village for the big city–the feeling of being lost, lonely, and scared–are common in any industrialized nation. The same universality holds true for the love between Rita and Manfred and their separation by external forces. Nevertheless, Wolf's primary intended reader is East German, and she hopes to stimulate that reader to reflection. Hence, even though Halle is portrayed as a product of capitalism, which was replaced by socialism only fifteen years previously, Wolf points out that the water and air pollution produced by industry can no longer be blamed on the old regime. In fact, Rita cannot find any positive aspect to the industrialized city, even though Manfred, who has lived there all his life, tries to show her its hidden beauty.

The village remains a place of refuge for Rita in times of crisis. But, when she returns there after some time away, she notices that it, too, is changing rapidly due to the forced collectivization of agriculture. Wolf is here touching on a topic which was, at the time she wrote the novel, taboo in the GDR: that the collectivization of farms precipitated an increase in the number of people leaving the country, which in turn led to the building of the Berlin Wall.

In depicting Rita's work in the railroad-car factory, Wolf was abiding by the call of the ruling Socialist Unity party to incorporate themes from the working world into literature, a doctrine formulated at the Bitterfeld Conferences in 1958 and 1959. The hope that workers would start writing about their own experiences did not materialize; authors like Wolf, on the other hand, did respond by working in the fields and factories and gaining experiences which became part of their literary works.

Rita is portrayed as an emancipated woman: she selects the man she loves and lives with him; she leaves her village to pursue an education as a teacher in the big city, against the will of her mother; and she volunteers to work as the only woman in a large factory. Thus, she continually matures in understanding, self-confidence, and knowledge, eventually becoming intellectually equal to Manfred, who holds a doctorate in chemistry. In contrast to Rita, Manfred is emotionally stagnating. Ten years older than Rita, raised in the city and having experienced the Nazi era as a child, he is a skeptic and cynic who is less and less able to put up with the inadequacies of the socialist system. Finally, feeling that he is being treated unjustly in his job, he crosses the Berlin border. He assumes that Rita will follow him; but for her such a decision is more difficult: her loyalty to her country goes much deeper than his. Although she does follow him to West Berlin, she returns home the same day. Shortly thereafter, the Berlin Wall is built, precluding any further choice on her part. Then follows, at the novel's conclusion, her "accident," which may be an unconscious suicide attempt.

Suicide was not an acceptable topic in the GDR when the novel was written, and the book could not have been published there if Rita's attempt to take her own life had not been ambiguously disguised as an accident. The critical reception of the novel in the GDR tended to be apologetic, avoiding any mention of the suicide attempt and dwelling on Rita's remaining in the East as a demonstration of her commitment to the socialist state. In Western criticism, on the other hand, the building of the wall and the possibility of a suicide attempt were emphasized. Wolf received the prestigious East German Heinrich Mann Prize for the novel.

Wolf's next novel, *Nachdenken über Christa T.* (1968; translated as *The Quest for Christa T.*, 1971), presented the functionaries in the Ministry of Culture with an even greater headache than had *Der geteilte Himmel*. None of the criteria of the prevailing literary doctrine of socialist realism–the demands for a positive hero, for the setting of an example, for an appeal to the masses, and, most of all, for strict adherence to the policies of the party–seemed to have been met in the book.

At the beginning of the novel the narrator, contemplating the untimely death of her friend Christa T., an aspiring writer, decides that Christa's memory should not die and sets out to write about her. Her nonconformist subject fills the narrator with self-doubt and with skepticism about her own literary attempts. After all, who will read what she writes? Will it ever be published, and if it is, what good will it do? Furthermore, will she ever understand Christa T.'s secret vision of herself? Did the vision ever exist, or was the narrator just imagining or hoping for such meaning in the life of her friend? Why did Christa T. not write? The answer must be sought in her skepticism about her own ability; about language as a vehicle for conveying meaning; and, most important, about whether her subjective and personal concerns could be of interest to a society whose primary concern is to catch up economically with the West. Christa T., the narrator insists, had good intentions of contributing to the new society and possessed the kind of imagination needed to grasp and portray the concerns of that society.

The search for truth is a major theme in the novel. The narrator tries to discover the truth about the life of her dead friend. Like Christa T., she cannot write without speaking the truth; but in a collectivist society the truth is sometimes better not expressed. Christa T., in the final analysis, saw only two options for herself: to say everything or nothing. She knew that her half-hearted attempts to write were not in accordance with the prevailing literary principles; she was keenly aware that her subjective material and sensitive style would be frowned upon as lacking social relevance. Thus, she led the average life of a housewife and mother, unable to break the banal cycle of her existence, and that banality eventually destroyed her spiritually and physically. Dying of leukemia, she realized that her potential would be lost forever, and concluded that she had lived too early. The novel ends on an optimistic note: in the future young, inspired writers will not have to suffer Christa T.'s fate.

The response to *Nachdenken über Christa T.* in the GDR has been notable for its absence, except for a few hesitantly critical reviews when the novel appeared. The reason for the neglect is easy to discern: the novel's implied criticisms of the GDR during its early years. The book was published in the GDR only intermittently and in small editions which were quickly sold out. In West Germany, on the other hand, the response in the media as well as in scholarly discussions has been intense.

In the collection of essays *Lesen und Schreiben* (1972; translated as *The Reader and the Writer*, 1977) Wolf formulates her ideas about what she considers important in modern prose, as well as its function in her society and the world at large. Wolf believes that literature should provide the reader with stimuli for growth. In a technological age literature is more important than ever, but it also faces increased competition from the other media; therefore, it needs to find ways to be innovative and vital to its readers.

In the early 1970s Wolf wrote a film script, *Till Eulenspiegel* (1973), with her husband and pub-lished the short-story collection *Unter den Linden: Drei unwahrscheinliche Geschichten* (Under the Linden Trees: Three Improbable Stories, 1974). The title story uses a dream sequence to express social criticism; in "Neue Lebensansichten eines Katers" (New Perspectives of a Cat) a tomcat comments satirically on his scientist master's attempts to engineer human happiness; the protagonist of "Selbstversuch" (Self-Experiment) decides that she does not want to acquire masculine intellectual and emotional traits and calls a halt to an experimental sex-change procedure.

The autobiographical *Kindheitsmuster* (1976; translated as *A Model Childhood*, 1980), her longest novel to date, deals to a much lesser extent than her previous ones with the GDR. The narrator, Nelly Jordan, tells of her 1971 trip to her hometown–the former Landsberg, now part of Poland–with her husband, her brother, and her daughter Lenka; of her childhood during the Nazi period; of the three years she has spent writing the present book; and of her efforts to explain to Lenka how Nelly and her parents could have failed to oppose the Nazis. Daily middle-class life under fascism is described in detail, often by inserting authentic materials such as newspaper clippings. Such events as the limitation of the freedom of the press and the establishment of concentration camps do not really affect the family; they continue to operate their store and remain largely apolitical, as did so many Germans, not realizing that their disinterest is making possible the consolidation of Nazism.

Kindheitsmuster is daring in suggesting–contrary to the official dogma of the GDR–that East Germans as well as West Germans share in the guilt of the Nazi past. On the other hand, while problems of the 1970s, such as Vietnam, Chile, Greece, and the Middle East, are referred to, critical comments are limited to the non-Communist world, and no mention is made of such topics as the unrest in Poland. Restricting her work in this fashion might have been necessary in view of GDR censorship, but in previous and subsequent books Wolf was able to find indirect means of dealing with issues that could not be openly discussed in the GDR.

The reception of *Kindheitsmuster* was generally positive in both German states. While the novel's complicated structure, with its three levels of narration, was criticized, Wolf was praised for dealing openly and convincingly with the GDR's Nazi past. *Kindheitsmuster* is the one book of Wolf's which is easily obtainable in East Germany.

Christa Wolf DLB 75

Wolf at about the time her novel Kassandra *(1983) was published (Poly-Press–Ullstein Bilderdienst)*

In 1979 Wolf published an experimental novel which, unlike her previous works, has little to do with either her own biography or the history of the GDR: *Kein Ort, nirgends* (No Place, Nowhere; translated as *No Place on Earth*, 1982). Wolf imagines a meeting of the German romantic writers Heinrich von Kleist and Karoline von Günderode at a tea party in the small town of Winkel am Rhein in June 1804. Kleist and Günderode feel out of place not only in society but also in an existential sense. Their struggle to discover new forms of human experience is not limited to theory and writing: they feel the need for productive dialogue, interaction with others of similar mind, friendship, and love. Kleist and Günderode seem destined to fulfill these needs for each other, but in the imaginary encounter they hardly have a chance to progress beyond superficialities. Incorporating quotations from documentary material into her novel—a technique first used by the nineteenth-century author Georg Büchner, whom Wolf admires greatly—helps to lend authenticity to her story, even though the historical figures are manipulated freely. The histori-

cal distance makes it possible for Wolf to explore matters which in some instances are still delicate subjects in the GDR, such as the relationship between the individual and the state, limitations on writing, and the danger of social alienation which may lead to despair and even to suicide—the ultimate fate of both main characters in real life. In spite of their affinity for each other, Kleist and Günderode are unable to break through the sexual and social barriers that separate them. The same problems Kleist and Günderode encounter—societal limitations and pressures; unsatisfactory relationships between men and women, both of whom need to be liberated from traditional roles; and possibly most important, the difficulty of writing freely and truthfully—still cry out for solutions which the socialist society has failed to provide.

In 1980 Wolf became the first author living and writing in the GDR to receive the Federal Republic's most prestigious literary award, the Georg Büchner Prize. That Wolf should be selected for the Büchner Prize seemed particularly appropriate, since she had repeatedly mentioned her admiration and special feeling of affinity for the nineteenth-century author. She sees Büchner's writings as an expression of his sense of responsibility for the great issues that confronted his society and, ultimately, all of mankind. In her Büchner Prize address, published in *Die Dimension des Autors* (The Dimension of the Author, 1987), she pays special attention to Büchner's female characters, who show that only mature, liberated, yet loving women are capable of helping mankind to survive. This insight, Wolf proclaims, holds true even more in modern times. Women, she says, must not leave the responsibility for survival to men because of the male propensity for self-destruction, a tendency which is manifest in all of Büchner's male characters.

The concerns expressed in Wolf's Büchner Prize address are a major theme in her novel *Kassandra* (1983; translated as *Cassandra*, 1984). The novel begins with Kassandra, a prisoner of war awaiting execution, pondering the destruction of her city, Troy, and its civilization. How and why did it happen? What actions or inactions led up to this cataclysmic event? What role did she play in it? These are some of the questions Kassandra attempts to answer as she recapitulates what has happened. Wolf's main themes, expressed allegorically, are the threat of war in the nuclear age; the role, or better nonrole, women play in societies that seem to drift at an accelerat-

262

ing pace toward self-destruction; the unwillingness to negotiate to prevent war; the insane reliance on increasing armaments; economic interests; false concepts of honor and the fear of losing face; and industrialism as the Trojan horse which most societies embrace as a panacea but which might well carry the seeds of civilization's destruction. The novel shows that male-dominated power structures deny input not only to women like Kassandra but to anybody with differing ideas. As soon as Kassandra opposes the views and actions of her father, King Priamos, and his ruling clique, she is excluded from the inner circle and even thrown into the dungeon. Kassandra's plight has an autobiographical basis in Wolf's own need to speak and write the truth no matter what the official policy might be.

Although Kassandra's warnings are not heeded by the men in power, who ignore the truth and thereby bring about the destruction of Troy, the book's message should not be viewed as pessimistic. A thoughtful reader will be forced to ask: what would have happened if the male ruling clique had listened to Kassandra? Could she have saved Troy? The possibility of a positive response represents the optimistic component of this work about war, death, and destruction. That Wolf touched a central nerve of contemporary concerns is evident if one considers the appeal of the work in East Germany, where every new printing seems to be immediately sold out, and in West Germany, where *Kassandra* was on the best-seller list for over a year after it appeared.

Simultaneously with the novel Wolf published *Voraussetzungen einer Erzählung: Kassandra* (Genesis of a Story: Kassandra, 1983), a series of lectures she delivered in Frankfurt am Main in 1982. Wolf describes in detail and without inhibition the impressions, concerns, and research–including a trip to Greece–which went into the writing of her novel. *Voraussetzungen einer Erzählung: Kassandra* was probably never intended for publication in the GDR because of its frankness, particularly in regard to the political issues only touched on allegorically in the novel. When the lectures were finally published in Wolf's own country, certain passages were deleted.

The novel *Störfall* (A Case of Disruption, 1987) appeared one year after the nuclear accident at Chernobyl in the Soviet Union. In this work Wolf juxtaposes the technical failure of the nuclear facility with the occurrence of a brain tumor in the narrator's brother. The novel poses searching questions about the future of humanity in view of man's frailty and the dangers of technology.

Bibliography:
Alexander Stephan, *Christa Wolf* (Amsterdam: Rodopi, 1980).

References:
Manfred Behn, ed., *Wirkungsgeschichte von Christa Wolfs "Nachdenken über Christa T."* (Königstein: Athenäum, 1978);

George Buehler, *The Death of Socialist Realism in the Novels of Christa Wolf* (Frankfurt am Main: Lang, 1984);

Inta Ezergailis, *Woman Writers: The Divided Self. Analysis of Novels by Christa Wolf, Ingeborg Bachmann, Doris Lessing and Others* (Bonn: Grundmann, 1982);

Helen Fehervary, "Christa Wolf's Prose: A Landscape of Masks," *New German Critique*, no. 27 (Fall 1982): 57-88;

Marilyn S. Fries, "Christa Wolf's Use of Image and Vision in the Narrative Structuring of Experience," in *Studies in GDR Culture and Society 2*, edited by Margy Gerber and Christine Cosentino (Washington, D.C.: University Press of America, 1982), pp. 59-85;

Winfried Giesen, *Christa Wolf* (Frankfurt am Main: Universitätsbibliothek, 1982);

Sonja Hilzinger, *Kassandra: Über Christa Wolf* (Frankfurt am Main: Haag & Herchen, 1982);

Charlotte W. Koerner, " 'Divided Heaven' by Christa Wolf: A Sacrifice of Message and Meaning in Translation," *German Quarterly*, 57 (Spring 1984): 213-230;

Sara Lennox, "Trends in Literary Theory: The Female Aesthetic and German Women's Writing," *German Quarterly*, 54 (January 1981): 63-75;

Myra Love, "Christa Wolf and Feminism: Breaking the Patriarchal Connection," *New German Critique*, no. 16 (Winter 1979): 31-53;

Eberhard Mannack, *Zwei deutsche Literaturen?: Zu G. Grass, U. Johnson, H. Kant, U. Plenzdorf, und C. Wolf* (Kronberg: Athenäum, 1977);

Karin McPherson, "In Search of the New Prose: Christa Wolf's Reflection on Writing and the Writer in the 1960s and 1970s," *New German Studies*, 9 (Spring 1981): 1-13;

"The Problems of Purity," *Times Literary Supplement*, 13 August 1971, p. 961;

Klemens Renoldner, *Utopie und Geschichtsbewußtsein: Versuche zur Poetik Christa Wolfs* (Stuttgart: Akademischer Verlag, 1981);

Martin Reso, ed., *"Der geteilte Himmel" und seine Kritiker: Dokumentation* (Halle: Mitteldeutscher Verlag, 1965);

Marion von Salisch, *Zwischen Selbstaufgabe und Selbstverwirklichung: zum Problem der Persönlichkeitsstruktur im Werk Christa Wolfs* (Stuttgart: Klett, 1975);

Klaus Sauer, ed., *Christa Wolf: Materialienbuch* (Darmstadt: Luchterhand, 1979);

Dieter Sevin, *Der geteilte Himmel, Nachdenken über Christa T.: Interpretationen* (Munich: Oldenbourg, 1982);

Alexander Stephan, *Christa Wolf* (Munich: Beck & edition text + kritik, 1976);

Christa Thomassen, *Der lange Weg zu uns selbst: Christa Wolfs Roman "Nachdenken über Christa T." als Erfahrungs- und Handlungsmuster* (Kronberg: Scriptor, 1977);

Heinz-Dieter Weber, *Über Christa Wolfs Schreibart* (Constance: Universitätsverlag, 1984);

John Whitley, "Quest for Christa T.," *Sunday Times* (London), 16 May 1971, p. 33.

Wolf Wondratschek
(14 August 1943-   )

Jochen Richter
Allegheny College

BOOKS: *Früher begann der Tag mit einer Schußwunde* (Munich: Hanser, 1969);

Ein Bauer zeugt mit einer Bäuerin einen Bauernjungen, der unbedingt Knecht werden will (Munich: Hanser, 1970);

Paul oder Die Zerstörung eines Hör-Beispiels: Hörspiele (Munich: Hanser, 1971);

Omnibus (Munich: Hanser, 1972);

Chuck's Zimmer: Gedichte, Lieder (Frankfurt am Main: Zweitausendeins, 1974);

Das leise Lachen am Ohr eines andern: Gedichte Lieder 2 (Frankfurt am Main: Zweitausendeins, 1976);

Männer und Frauen: Gedichte, Lieder 3 (Frankfurt am Main: Zweitausendeins, 1978);

Letzte Gedichte (Frankfurt am Main: Zweitausendeins, 1980);

Chuck's Zimmer: Alle Gedichte und Lieder (Munich: Heyne, 1982);

Früher begann der Tag mit einer Schußwunde und andere Prosa (Munich: Deutscher Taschenbuch Verlag, 1982);

Die Einsamkeit der Männer: Mexikanische Sonette (Zurich: Diogenes, 1983);

Carmen oder Ich bin das Arschloch der achtziger Jahre (Zurich: Diogenes, 1986);

Menschen Orte Fäuste: Reportagen und Stories (Zurich: Diogenes, 1987).

Wolf Wondratschek (photograph by Fatima Ingramhan)

OTHER: Jules Verne, *Der Stahlelefant; Katastrophe im Atlantik,* translated by Wondratschek (Frankfurt am Main, 1967);

Vlado Kristl, *Sekundenfilme,* edited by Wondratschek (Frankfurt am Main: Suhrkamp, 1971);

Mein Lesebuch, edited by Wondratschek (Frankfurt am Main: Fischer, 1982).

PERIODICAL PUBLICATIONS: "Bewegliche Spur im Sichtbaren: Zur Lyrik von Walter Helmut Fritz," *Text + Kritik,* 9 (1965): 9-12;

"Maß und Unmaß des Lobes," *Text + Kritik,* 9 (1965): 34-36;

"Weder Schrei noch Lächeln: Robert Walser und Franz Kafka," *Text + Kritik,* 12 (1966): 17-21;

"Ich bin ein Zehn-Prozent-Autor: Wie es zu *Chuck's Zimmer* kam," *Die Zeit,* 4 July 1975, p. 18;

"Malcolm Lowry in Mexiko," *Tintenfaß,* 8 (1983): 80-94.

Wolf Wondratschek's first volume of fiction, *Früher begann der Tag mit einer Schußwunde* (In Earlier Times the Day Began with a Bullet Wound, 1969), introduced a new tone and style into German literature. Critics were quick to discover and celebrate Wondratschek as a genuine new voice. Although he followed his first book with only two more relatively small volumes of fiction in 1970 and 1972, his texts have become part of the German literary canon and have been included in many anthologies and textbooks. His formal experimentation with the radio play met with similar acclaim and earned him one of the most prestigious awards for this genre. Wondratschek's greatest success, however, came with his poetry collections in the 1970s. Although some critics claim that this success is due to packaging and advertising rather than to the quality of the poems, there can be no doubt that Wondratschek is one of the most widely read poets in West Germany. His six poetry volumes, published between 1974 and 1986, have sold more than one hundred thousand copies.

Wondratschek was born in Rudolstadt, Thuringia, on 14 August 1943. He grew up in Karlsruhe in a middle-class home. His father was an officer in the German army. As some of his early fiction, especially "Über die Schwierigkeiten, ein Sohn seiner Eltern zu bleiben" (On the Difficulties of Remaining a Son of One's Parents), suggests, there were severe tensions between Wondratschek and his parents. According to his own account, he once beat up his father and was thrown out of the house. When his parents wanted him to move back home, he went to court and pleaded for the right to choose his own parents; he lost the case. When his father tried to force him to join the army, he threatened to commit suicide and was allowed to attend a university instead. In 1962 he enrolled at the University of Heidelberg to study literature, sociology, and philosophy. He subsequently went to the Universities of Göttingen and Frankfurt am Main, interrupting his studies in 1964-1965 to work as an editor for the literary magazine *Text + Kritik.* In Frankfurt he became involved in the student protest movement; leftist political tendencies connected with that movement have strongly influenced his writing.

In 1967 he left the University of Frankfurt to become a free-lance writer of poetry, short prose pieces, essays, radio plays, and film scripts. His first book, a selection of short prose texts, was published in 1969. The same year he won the first Leonce and Lena Award for his poem "Als Alfred Jarry merkte, daß seine Mutter eine Jungfrau war, bestieg er sein Fahrrad" (When Alfred Jarry Noticed That His Mother Was a Virgin, He Climbed on His Bicycle). In 1969 he was voted to be the recipient of the prestigious award for outstanding radio plays given by the war-blinded. However, he declined to attend the awards ceremony in 1970 because the president of the Federal Republic of Germany was present. In the same year he accepted a one-year fellowship at the University of Warwick in England. In 1977-1978 Wondratschek gave a series of lectures at American universities. He currently resides in Munich.

In *Früher begann der Tag mit einer Schußwunde* traditional narrative progression is reduced to a succession of sentences. Wondratschek declares: "Nur die Sätze zählen. Die Geschichten machen keinen Spaß mehr. Eine Geschichte ist die Erinnerung an einen Satz" (Only the sentences count. The stories are no longer fun. A story is the memory of a sentence). Unlike the endless and frequently monotonous sentence catalogues of the *nouveau roman,* which add together descriptions of objects, Wondratschek strings together sentences containing perceptions, observations, and opinions. "43 Liebesgeschichten" (43 Love Stories), for example, consists of forty-three sentences, each containing the name of a girl: "Didi will immer. Olga ist bekannt dafür. Ursel hat schon dreimal Pech gehabt" (Didi always wants to. Olga is known for it. Ursel has had bad luck three times already). Each sentence is the germ of a story which the reader is called upon to finish. Whereas the *nouveau roman* overwhelms and oppresses with its detailed observation of reality, Wondratschek's fiction appeals to the imagination of the reader to fill in the blanks or to complete the text. In "Hausaufgaben" (Homework) Wondratschek outlines violent or paradoxical events in sixteen numbered paragraphs; the seventeenth paragraph is an invitation to the reader: "17 (bitte vervollständigen)" (17 [please complete]). The purpose of these pieces is to bring about the active participation of the reader.

Wondratschek avoids slipping into vagueness by relying on ordinary language and experience. As another text from the first volume, "Verschönerung eines Prosastückes von Robert Walser" (Adornment of a Prose Piece by Robert Walser), and Wondratschek's 1966 essay on Walser in *Text + Kritik* suggest, Wondratschek has studied Walser carefully and has learned from him the complexity and malignity of inobtrusive everyday occurrences. By contrasting linguistic elements; by using allusion, paradox, and syllogism; and by withholding information, Wondratschek exposes the clichés, prejudices, inconsistencies, and contradictions of language and ordinary life. The linguistic experiments serve to heighten the social and political awareness of the reader without lapsing into propaganda. Manipulation of language, use of associations and pauses, and elimination of traditional plot give Wondratschek's first book its freshness and appeal.

In his second small volume of fiction, *Ein Bauer zeugt mit einer Bäuerin einen Bauernjungen, der unbedingt Knecht werden will* (A Farmer and a Farmer's Wife Beget a Farmer's Lad Who Absolutely Wants to Become a Farmhand, 1970), the sentence is still the major element. In "Nr. 1843" and "Nr. 2141" a detective-story format strings the sentences together. Sentences such as "Mat Walker dreht durch und schießt. Fat Sam steht im Weg und stirbt" (Mat Walker goes crazy and shoots. Fat Sam is in the way and dies) supply the rough outline of a picture which the reader's imagination is to complete by adding detail and coloring.

The method is most effective when the pieces are short and appeal to common experience, but the texts in Wondratschek's second book are longer than in his first and tend to strain the reader's ability to follow. In "&," for ex-

ample, the abrupt changes between small, coherent blocks lead to confusion rather than to the desired cocreative activity. In other pieces, such as "Trauerfeier" (Memorial Service), the effort to define and explain a political position leads to an essayistic form of narration that abandons the original style; the linguistic experimentation which characterized the earlier volume is sacrificed for the sake of a message which cannot be misinterpreted. In the first text of *Ein Bauer zeugt mit einer Bäuerin einen Bauernjungen, der unbedingt Knecht werden will* Wondratschek quotes William S. Burroughs to support his claim that the work of a writer is mainly "vorgegebenes Material zu sortieren, redigieren & arrangieren" (to sort, edit, and arrange) material which already exists and not to invent coherent fictitious stories; despite this claim, there is in this volume a growing tendency toward cohesion and a stronger emphasis on content rather than formal experiment.

The radio plays in *Paul oder Die Zerstörung eines Hör-Beispiels* (Paul; or, The Destruction of a Radio-Play Example, 1971) are mostly based on earlier fiction pieces. By splitting sentences into isolated phrases and by juxtaposing unrelated sentences, Wondratschek creates acoustic collages. The succession of spoken language is abandoned in favor of simultaneity; the stereophonic signals reach the listener from different directions, much as in a railroad station. Wondratschek's refusal to tell a story draws attention to the language itself, which appears as a collection of empty formulas, hollow phrases, and clichés. The listener is led via the criticism of language to a criticism of the society that abuses the language. The goal is to activate the passive receiver to become an involved sender. "Zufälle" (Coincidences), which is based on a piece of the same title in Wondratschek's first book, conveys the message that the word *Zufall* (coincidence) is used to cover up and excuse any situation that does not fit into the concept of the speakers. In "Freiheit oder ça ne fait rien" (Freedom; or, It Doesn't Matter) the word *Freiheit* (freedom) is cut out of political speeches whenever it occurs, and the hollow pathos is ridiculed. The language of the truck driver Paul in the title piece exposes the repressed sexuality, latent violence, and overwhelming boredom of a typical member of the working class. In all these cases Wondratschek effectively utilizes the techniques of radio to draw attention to the communication process and demonstrates the social attitudes that have led to the widespread abuse of language.

The tendency toward cohesion and emphasis on content that was observable in *Ein Bauer zeugt mit einer Bäuerin einen Bauernjungen, der unbedingt Knecht werden will* is even more obvious in *Omnibus* (1972), which includes pieces written from 1967 to 1971. In addition to some fiction texts in the early style, the book contains film scripts, essays, short prose texts labeled "cartoons," and a radio play. In the longest piece, the film script "Rache" (Revenge), Wondratschek strings pictures together in a way similar to that in which he strings sentences together. The plot which is to connect the individual images, however, is so confusing that it is hard to imagine how a spectator would follow the film. The linguistic method does not carry over into the visual realm because film has to rely on a more realistic presentation than does a literary text. It is therefore understandable that Wondratschek abandoned the project before it was finished. The essays "Jagger" and "Zappa," which were written in a traditional style for newspapers, attack excesses of the rock culture. In similar fashion Wondratschek attacks consumerism in "King Size Filter" and "Versuch über den Volkswagen" (Treatise on the Volkswagen) and the exploitation of sex in "Oktober der Schweine" (October of the Pigs). The "cartoons" are concerned with language. In "Glücksfälle" (Strokes of Good Luck) Wondratschek lists metaphors, idioms, and sentences which, in the context of death, assume surprisingly grotesque meanings: "den Kopf verlieren" (to lose one's head), "im Geld ersticken" (to suffocate in money), "die Pistole gegen die eigene Schläfe halten und hoffen, tief beeindruckt zu werden" (to hold a pistol against one's own temple and hope to be impressed deeply). There are a few pieces in which Wondratschek demonstrates how language is thoughtlessly abused and how clichés and "dead metaphors" can corrupt thinking and language; in most cases, however, these plays with words are merely entertaining. "Kopfschmerzen" (Headaches) and "Die Seereise" (The Voyage) are arranged in the form of poems. In some instances, Wondratschek simply quotes unaltered newspaper reports.

In "Berichtigung einer Person" (Correction of a Person) Wondratschek combines his reductionist style of writing with a coherent story: indirect quotes, observations, memories of specific incidents, and withholding of information are used to describe the upbringing of a boy by his parents; the individual case assumes a universal meaning. In "Berichtigung einer Person"

Wondratschek in 1986, the year his poetry collection Carmen *appeared (photograph by Detlev Moos, courtesy of Ullstein Bilderdienst)*

Wondratschek regains the concentrated intensity which his earlier sentences carried. Overall, however, the texts of *Omnibus* have lost the experimental character and aggressiveness of his early prose and are approaching what Wondratschek himself had denounced as "Geschichten" (stories). "Auf eine Geschichte zu verzichten, ist eine gute Gelegenheit.... Nur die Sätze zählen" (To abandon a story is a great opportunity.... Only the sentences count), Wondratschek had proclaimed in his first book.

The final piece in *Omnibus* is the radio play "Kann das Quietschen der Straßenbahn nur eine Frau gewesen sein?" (Can the Screech of the Streetcar Have Been Only a Woman?). It was produced in 1972 and features four voices who try to recover what no longer exists–silence. In comparison to the plays in *Paul oder Die Zerstörung eines Hör-Beispiels*, this piece returns to the traditional form of the radio play.

Except for essays and articles for newspapers and magazines, many of which are collected in *Menschen Orte Fäuste* (Men Places Fists, 1987), Wondratschek has not written any more prose works. These texts have abandoned all efforts at experimentation with form. By his own admission Wondratschek finds it extremely difficult to write longer narratives. His reductionistic, linguistically conscious prose, which aims at reader participation, is not suited for longer works of fiction. Wondratschek has pushed his particular brand of prose to its limits and exhausted its potential; it seems only natural, therefore, that he has concentrated his efforts on other literary forms.

After *Omnibus* was published Wondratschek dropped out of the literary scene for two years, emerging in 1974 with a small volume of poetry titled *Chuck's Zimmer* (Chuck's Room). In the essay "Ich bin ein Zehn-Prozent-Autor" (I Am a Ten-Percent Writer, 1975) and in the first poems of the new book, "Langes Gedicht über eine Sekunde" (Long Poem about a Second) and "König-Ludwig-Lied" (King Ludwig Song), Wondratschek analyzes his changed attitude toward literature. He denounces his language experimentation as vanity and rescinds his social criticism. Instead, he will now write simple, consumer-oriented poetry which he will publish and sell himself.

Most of Wondratschek's poems are close to the lyrics of the rock-and-roll songs of the late 1960s and early 1970s and could well be set to music. The lines are simple and frequently are repeated, and the language is blunt. The influence of the American subculture of the 1960s with its music, drugs, sex, and dropping-out dominate the poems. Americanisms like *super, freak,* and *show* abound, and it is not coincidental that Wondratschek chose the American name "Chuck" for the major character in many of the poems. Chuck is the personification of the disillusioned, melancholic, self-centered dropout. He appealed to an audience which grew up with rock and roll and was under the spell of American pop culture and promptly claimed a place for his creator among the likes of Bob Dylan, Cat Stevens, the Rolling Stones, and Frank Zappa. Wondratschek recognized this appeal and launched a skillful advertising campaign which made him the uncontested rock poet in Germany.

The volumes *Das leise Lachen am Ohr eines andern* (The Soft Laughter in the Ear of Another, 1976), *Männer und Frauen* (Men and Women, 1978), and *Letzte Gedichte* (Last Poems, 1980) continue the themes and tone of *Chuck's Zimmer.* The imitation of American rock actually results in poems which are written in English, but they do not rival the better American rock lyrics. The tone is either sentimental and melancholic or detached and amusing. The images lose the precision and concreteness of those in *Chuck's Zimmer.* In *Letzte Gedichte* and *Männer und Frauen* the poems become more aggressive and less narcissistic, with more ironic distance and less fashionable weltschmerz. Reactions to political events find their way into Wondratschek's poetry in these volumes; personal experiences and reflections are treated in precise language and have gained in bitterness and intensity. There is a feeling of genuineness which was lacking in some of the poems in *Chuck's Zimmer.* Cynicism, black humor, and sauciness allow Wondratschek to display sensitivity and genuine emotion without sounding artificial or sentimental.

Wondratschek's latest two poetry volumes, *Die Einsamkeit der Männer: Mexikanische Sonette* (The Loneliness of Men: Mexican Sonnets, 1983) and *Carmen oder Ich bin das Arschloch der achtziger Jahre* (Carmen; or, I Am the Asshole of the Eighties, 1986), indicate yet another direction in his artistic development. Not only does he break with his successful method of self-marketing but he also turns away from rock poetry. The Mexican sonnets were inspired by Malcolm Lowry's *Under the Volcano* (1947) and are variations on the themes of that novel: alcohol, longing for love and the impossibility to love, jealousy, loneliness, and Mexico. They are composed in a precise, condensed, and purified language, charged with intense emotion, and present images of great beauty and intensity. *Carmen* combines the irony and cynicism of the earlier poetry with the intensity and beauty of the Mexican sonnets to produce fresh and vital love poetry.

In the sonnet "Tänzer" (Dancers), Wondratschek describes the struggle of the artist for perfection. The dancers long to jump into the light and remain there: "und dann oben bleiben, nahe der Sonne,/nicht wieder fallen, nur einmal nicht,/einmal oben bleiben, nur vielleicht/*einmal* länger, als es möglich ist" (and then to stay there, near the sun,/not to fall back again, only once/once to stay up there, perhaps only/*once* longer than is possible). Some of Wondratschek's latest poems have perhaps reached that moment where they may "stay up there a little longer than is possible." They raise high expectations for the future.

Bibliography:

Otto F. Riewoldt, "Wolf Wondratschek," in *Kritisches Lexikon zur deutschsprachigen Gegenwartsliteratur,* edited by Heinz Ludwig Arnold, volume 5 (Munich: Edition text + kritik, 1978), n. pag.;

Kurt Rothmann, *Deutschsprachige Schriftsteller seit 1945 in Einzeldarstellungen* (Stuttgart: Reclam, 1985), pp. 399-404.

References:

Wolf Donner, "Sätze über Sätze," *Die Zeit*, 30 October 1970, p. 28;

Uwe Herms, "Eine neue Art von Literatur?," *Die Zeit*, 27 July 1975, p. 18;

André Müller, "Ich liebe den Zweikampf! Ein Gespräch mit Wolf Wondratschek," *Die Zeit*, 18 March 1988, pp. 15-16;

Marcel Reich-Ranicki, "Nur Sätze und doch Geschichten," *Die Zeit*, 18 April 1969, p. 33;

Norbert Schachtsiek-Freitag, "Wolf Wondratschek: *Omnibus*," *Neue Rundschau*, 3 (1972): 563-566;

Klaus Seehafer, "Wolf Wondratschek/*Omnibus*," *Neue Deutsche Hefte*, 3 (1972): 152-153.

Appendix I

Pattern and Paradigm

Pattern and Paradigm: History as Design

Judith Ryan

Reprinted from The Uncompleted Past: Postwar German Novels and the Third Reich (*Detroit: Wayne State University Press, 1983), pp. 23-41.*

West German Patterns

In the years immediately following the war, there was much talk, at least in the Federal Republic, of the need to come to terms with the recent past. Once the mental framework of the Nazis was officially gone, a total reorientation of thought became necessary. A particularly difficult problem was the concept of collective guilt; resistance to the Nazis was seen as something that had been virtually impossible. Postwar literature in its early phase was most often a transmutation of historical experience into mythic or metaphorical terms. There were, of course, other attempts to deal with the past in a more direct fashion–Carl Zuckmayer's play *The Devil's General* (1946) comes immediately to mind, but even here, despite the predominant realism, there is an undercurrent of myth in the discreet Satanization implied by the title. Mythic perceptions of the past prevailed by and large, forming a foil against which later treatments, especially the major novels of the sixties, can best be understood.

A complicating factor in the development of postwar German literature was the "zero hour," the sensation that writers were beginning again from a *tabula rasa*. Since Nazi literary traditions had been broken off, while at the same time there was little access to the works of German exiles (due to the strict controls imposed by the Allies), writers felt they were working virtually without precedent, writing almost in a vacuum. Although the notion of the zero hour was overstated, it is certain that these writers were at a loss for appropriate literary models and grasped eagerly at whatever modern literature began to filter into Germany. Some older traditions were still alive, and one of these, the lyric tradition of Rainer Maria Rilke, was already being transmitted by the poets of the "inner emigration" (inward distancing from Nazi ideology). These poets, whose strengths lay largely in the field of a very internalized sort of nature poetry, were among the first to be heard.

The themes and motifs to which they turned after the war remained basically similar to those they had used during their withdrawal– what other reserves did they have to draw upon? But, in the interim, their imagery had undergone a change in meaning and function. Those who wrote lyric poetry in defiance of the political catastrophe around them, sometimes even in concentration camps, could well call upon nature as a force of wholeness and healing, and by positing an identity between the poet and nature, they could find a consistency between outer and inner world which was lacking in their relationship to society and the political regime. And Christian concepts, frequently transposed into nature mysticism, had in themselves the quality of resistance. But when this same use of imagery was continued in the postwar period–Ivan Goll's poetry anthology *De Profundis* (1946) and Walter Höllerer's anthology *Transit* (1956) contain representative samples of such verse–it was more a withdrawal from responsibility than an expression of opposition. One may well ask, therefore, why the reading public did not immediately see it as a suspect form. Partly, it gained legitimacy because it continued the underground traditions whose meaning it now, in fact, sucked dry; it could also be seen as one aspect of the general trend of reviving literary traditions with greater moral integrity than those of the Third Reich; in addition it introduced an element that now seemed lacking, that of myth. The myth sought was no longer the vast and primeval structure of the Germanic past upon which the Third Reich had drawn, nor was it the philosophically demanding superstructure of works like Rilke's *Duino Elegies* (1922). But the nature myth had its own special relevance, for what could be more consoling to this unsettled time than a poetic universe in which individual and nature merged and became one?

Yet a return to nature mythology had inherent within it the tendency to smother, "like a rampant vine," everything within its reach. In the end, both the poet and his imagery were reduced to empty posturing. Wilhelm Lehmann, one of the first poets to gain prominence after the war, epitomizes this trend as he grapples vainly to combine into an evocative, if not logically consistent, network ancient mythology, medieval legend, and a welter of botanical names whose very sound suggests the primeval deities of garden and woodland. In this type of mythological system, both the poet and external reality seem to evaporate before the onslaught of poetic images. It is no accident that when poets such as Paul Celan, Johannes Bobrowski, and Nelly Sachs addressed themselves to the question of the holocaust, weaving into their poetry memories of their experiences in the Third Reich, they were not primarily perceived as political poets. The beauty of their language and imagery lulls the mind away from more than a generalized reflection on the horrors recalled in their verses, and the problems presented, whether embedded in private mythology, in traditional legends, or in mystical thought, are seen as in some way universal, as merely a more terrible repetition of something that has occurred throughout the ages. All three use the elegiac mode, thus raising a serious difficulty, since elegy implies an underlying order that can be re-created in literature. In Nelly Sachs' poetry, suffering is merely a rung on a Jacob's ladder to ultimate transfiguration; Celan's negative godhead is the unknown addressee of the poem, which he sees as a kind of message in a bottle; and if the ancient deities have disappeared from Bobrowski's homeland, their traces still remain, in landscape as well as in memory, to provide the sense of wholeness which serves as a foil to man's sorrow.

In this sense, then, the poetry of the post-war era remained for some time indebted to the concepts of inner emigration. The nature references and the obscure myths and legends that had formed a kind of coded language in opposition poetry had simply been transformed into self-supporting systems of metaphor and myth devoid of genuine political content. How could this have come about? A large part of the explanation lies in a perception of Hitler that was not in any way unique to the German people. Rather than viewing nazism as a social and political evil

with a specific historical genesis, they preferred to regard it as a reincarnation of evil itself. But seeing it in this way meant mythologizing history, in effect equating Hitler with the devil. Furthermore, it transposed the individual's struggle against nazism onto another plane, giving it an added dimension of hopelessness: how could mere political action be expected to be effective against the eternal forces of evil? Only gradually, in retrospect, was it seen that this was to a large extent the inverse of the Nazis' own mythology. But by the time other types of political protest poetry were revived in the late sixties and early seventies, the need for reviewing the Nazi past was no longer so pressing.

It may be objected that poetry, even political poetry, is not an adequate vehicle for an evaluation of the historical position in which the Germans found themselves. But it soon became obvious that even the plays and novels of the early period did not provide the specific social and political contexts necessary for dealing with the past. The question asked was often not so much "Why did no one manage to stop Hitler?" as "Why were we the ones to fall prey to this evil situation?" Turning the question this way put the experiences of the recent past into a particular pattern of thought. The German people were seen as the collective victim of a terrible fate, rather than as a group of morally responsible individuals. An entire historical epoch was reduced to merely one manifestation among many of the eternal struggle between good and evil; history came to be seen in terms of primal myth. As writers groped for structures and forms to express their experience of their own time, they adopted in a somewhat uncritical way this idea of history as a recurrent pattern. Equally at a loss to make sense of what had happened, the German reading public accepted the new myths presented in drama and fiction.

The earliest postwar literature was rooted in the writings of exiles, emigrants, and survivors of the concentration camps, often produced during the war and published either immediately in foreign countries or after the war in Germany. As in lyric poetry, the adequacy of traditional forms was again put to the test. And as in poetry, the coded language that had been used by anti-Nazi writers during the Third Reich seemed to supply the answer to a problem which was most acutely felt: that the enormity of what had been experienced could not possibly be encompassed by familiar literary structures. So the search began for equivalents, parallels, and paradigms; gradually the "slave language" was transformed into a new allegoric mode.

The religious pattern of guilt and redemption lent the first viable framework for this intractable material. Ernst Wiechert's *Forest of the Dead* (1946), a moving testimony to his four months' internment in Buchenwald in 1938, and Bernd von Heiseler's *The Reconciliation* (1953), an attempt at a more elaborated version of the Christian standpoint Wiechert had presented, are typical of this phase; Elisabeth Langgässer's novels *The Indelible Seal* (1946) and *The Quest (Märkische Argonautenfahrt, 1950)* are a more sophisticated version of the same schema.

Aside from Wiechert's relatively simplistic application of the Christian model, his use of nineteenth-century realism presents the major difficulty of his novel. The hero's model in the concentration camp, a man known as Father Kilb, is a petit bourgeois grocery store owner whose idyllic life has been brutally disrupted by his deportation. Much of Kilb's virtue lies in no more than this, the false accusations that make him, in the hero's eyes, a successor to Heinrich von Kleist's seeker after justice in the 1810 novella *Michael Kohlhaas;* the quality which radiates from Kilb like a holy aura is in large measure due to his embodiment of nineteenth-century values. Again and again, Weichert harks back to standards long since gone and no longer entirely appropriate. The protagonist is inwardly purged and steeled by his Buchenwald experience, but his transformation hardly takes place on the same plane as the historical events it must confront.

The guilt-redemption scheme is given an added mythic dimension in Langgässers's *The Indelible Seal,* published in the same year as Wiechert's *Forest of the Dead.* Structured around models from the Jewish and Christian traditions, the novel strives to create a modern legend. Two saints in particular become examples for the central character, Belfontaine, and their lives are interwoven with his reflections in the course of travels from Germany to France and back. Through Belfontaine, the traditional figures of the Wandering Jew and the Eternal Pilgrim are ultimately united as the multiple levels of the narrative come together. Like Wiechert's, Langgässer's view of the recurrent struggle between good and evil is often simplistic, but she overlays it with a typological scheme reminiscent of the relationship between the Old and New Testaments. Langgässer's novel is thus a stepping-stone in the movement towards a mythic depiction of the Nazi era, a development that continued into the fifties. Her modern legend presents the Third Reich as the most cataclysmic of a series of historical catastrophes within the eternal struggle for salvation. In effect, the National Socialist regime is equated with the rule of Satan, and the characters become abstractions whose significance lies in their embodiment of eternal verities. But the novel never quite reaches the level of sophistication attained by Thomas Mann's *Doctor Faustus,* the most masterful of the early mythic novels.

Langgässer's later work on a similar theme, *The Quest,* moves further than its predecessor, linking the religious framework with a mythological one and drawing a parallel between biblical theology and classical mythology. On the surface, it concerns the pilgrimage of seven characters to a Benedictine monastery immediately after the war. On the way, their recapitulation of personal experiences during the Third Reich begins to reveal common configurations behind their apparently dissimilar lives. For the pilgrims, the Argo of classical myth becomes a symbol of man's eternal journeying, and they see themselves as latter-day argonauts. Another image they use for their journey is that of descent into the underworld, suggested by repeated references to Eurydice and Persephone. Their quest is a search for the return of their souls from the realm of darkness. It takes them through the labyrinth of memory and the underworld of guilt; their Golden Fleece is the Christian grace they discover at Anastasiendorf. Just as the image of the voyage conflates different religious and mythic traditions, so the goal of their journeying becomes a mystically superimposed version of various real and mythic places. The upper and lower poles are formed by the contrast between the concentration camp, Theresienstadt, in the past, and the monastery, Anastasiendorf, in the present. Metaphorically, the two poles are the underworld and the Heavenly Jerusalem. Layer upon layer of parallel references become fused in the image of the city, especially the lost city of Troy, which is revealed as the archetype of all cities. Towards the end of the novel, the circular pattern of the city draws up into itself other circles upon which it is superimposed to form an immense symbolic spiral: the mystic rose upon which all is centered.

To be sure, the argonauts are not content to remain at the mystic center. Instead, they bear with them on their return to the outside world the insights gained on their trip to the monastery. In this way the novel's abstractions are brought back to the level of down-to-earth reality. Reinforcing the return to the worldly is the appended tale of two "Children of Medea," orphaned in the winter of 1945 and prevented from perishing only by their involvement with a group of black marketeers.

Yet, although no specific resolutions to the problems of the argonauts are offered at the conclusion, the novel is not open-ended. The seven lives ultimately conform to the same concentric pattern as the architecture of past, present, and future, symbolized by the mystic rose design that seems to underlie the plan of Troy. For all its realistic detail and psychological finesse, the novel reduces history, in the last analysis, to the abstract patterning of myth. Even the potential for resistance, embodied in the figure of the young resistance fighter Irene, is ultimately subordinated to the mystic pattern.

Simultaneous with the mythic trend was a move towards parable and fable, largely the result of the Kafka renascence promulgated by Group 47, writers who deliberately set out to create a new tradition for postwar literature. Included in Group 47 were writers like Günter Grass and Uwe Johnson, who were to make a significant mark in the late fifties and sixties, as well as more restricted talents like Wolfdietrich Schnurre and Hans Erich Nossack.

One of the few full-length novels in the parabolic vein, Schnurre's *The Fate of Our Town* (1959), is made up of an elaborate mosaic of tiny metaphorical prose pieces. Here universalization is based not upon ancient myth but upon modern tropes. Hermann Kasack's *The City Beyond the River* (1947), the allegorical tale of a man's visit to the realm of the dead during the latter part of World War II, was doubtless one of Schnurre's models for *The Fate of Our Town*. While in both cases the central character assumes the role of archivist or chronicler, this implied historiographic view of reality is ultimately subsumed into the patterning of metaphor and allegory. Like Langgässer, Kasack believes in eternal recurrence, although it occurs here less as part of the actual structure than as part of the novel's reflective base. His dependence on mysticism, represented by the figure of the Meister Magus and his pronouncements, lends an optimistic undercurrent to the pervading tone of despair, so that the European catastrophe, as he terms it, is viewed as part of a necessary process that will ultimately return Western culture to what he regards as its Asian ori-

gins. In his parallel novel of a modern chronicler, Schnurre seems to take issue with Kasack's (and possibly also Langgässer's) mystic vision.

Like Langgässer, Schnurre constructs a realm where a number of different time periods interpenetrate and mutually illumine each other. Distinguishable, though not clearly separate from each other, are the present technological world and a vague kind of medieval society that presumably stands for the Third Reich. The spirit of ancient history is embodied in the dust-covered mummy Chrysanthema, who comes to life somewhat precariously in the narrator's household. The narrator himself is presented as a medieval scribe engaged in writing the history of his native town; in the act of writing he begins to reflect more seriously on the nature of his role as chronicler. These reflections mark an important step in the development of fiction about nazism. Unlike Kasack or Langgässer, Schnurre perceives no order in the events of recent history, nor does he wish to impose upon them the intrinsically unrelated order of myth. His complaint that he cannot find the right "epic flow" is not a modish exclamation on the absurdity of the world or the breakdown of the modern novel. "Mankind would be innocent if the bookshelves of our minds were as neatly ordered as our novels," the chronicler cries in despair. In other words, he recognizes a discrepancy not apparent to some other novelists of the period: that mythic structures may organize our chaotic impressions of history too schematically, evoking a response of powerlessness in the face of what appears to be a predetermined pattern.

Set in a city divided and besieged by powers from the east and west, *The Fate of Our Town* is a parable of postwar Berlin. One of its weaknesses lies in the mythologizing of the two major powers as the "sabre riders" from the east and the "army of atonement" from the west. The political criticism implied in these two images may be well taken, but when it is extended throughout the novel it obscures subtleties that need to be brought to light.

Paradoxically, the figure of the archivist turns out to be one of the least emancipatory in the whole book. The isolation enforced by his occupation is exacerbated by his involvement with three strange women, Xeres, Ludwiga, and Chrysanthema, who bear the main burden of the novel's metaphorical structure. Absorbed by these symbols, the narrator retreats further and further from reality (as indicated by his various peculiar love affairs: with a fish, or with a wave, for example) until he ends up in a monastery preparing to write the ultimate message to mankind. Resignation seems to be the only possible "solution" to his dilemma. But even this, while taken seriously by the narrator-scribe, is not viewed without irony by the author himself, who takes pains to make the reader aware of the cost it exacts. At the conclusion of the novel, the monk discovers, in an ancient, dusty room, pages from a book of revelations written by his predecessors long ago; all are illegible. But upon his return to his own cell, he realizes that he will never make use of this insight: "I know that I will remain silent, that I will forget, and that I will never record anything other than what the rules of my order demand of me." The monk's solution is a deceptive way out, and the novel's conclusion must be read ironically.

One possible alternative is provided by a friend of the chronicler, Richard, a circus performer whose professional name is "Achmed, the Unsettling," a reference to similar epithets used about politically engaged writers like Brecht and Dürrenmatt. In this role, Richard stands for the artist who attempts to make people more conscious of their part in the fashioning of history. But alas, as the archivist discovers, "revolutions (in which Richard persists in believing) cannot be started in conjuror's tents." It is symptomatic of this novel that Richard is seen almost entirely through the eyes of the narrator, who views him as a central, if problematic, figure. The difficulty, as Richard himself gradually comes to realize, lies in the fact that criticism of the status quo is useless unless there are forces that can be marshaled to change it. Art that tries to point out what is wrong with society sometimes has the opposite effect from that intended. "As the waves of laughter that surge around Richard when he appears as Achmed die down again, they wash away with them all the misgivings of the good citizens; unrelieved, and glad to have in Achmed an escape mechanism that helps them let off the steam from their consciences that has befogged their minds, they all throng relieved and free out of the hall after the performance." Richard despairs of finding a way to stir the conscience of his public. "It is as if," he complains, "the truth were made of cotton, and if one offers it to people, they stuff it gratefully into their pillows so that they can rest more comfortably." Revolutionary art has always had to contend with this central problem: that aesthetic form might prevent the

work's disturbing message from being fully appreciated. There are ways of avoiding this difficulty, but the question remains whether Schnurre has found a solution. Even Richard is said, ironically, to possess an enviable strength of character that lets him remain in hiding from the authorities for long periods of time: "And who, of all those who ended up becoming guilty along with everyone else, would not have been grateful for the strength of character to descend into the sewers, like Richard, for so long a time?" The fact that Richard uses the sewers as his hiding place indicates Schnurre's critical attitude toward inner emigration.

The poet Ignatius represents another possibility. In contrast to Richard, Ignatius believes that in times of political crisis it is virtually impossible to continue with the traditional role of the poet, that it is in a sense criminal merely to sing the praises of nature's beauty. "He saw no justification any more, he told a stunned group of followers, in tracing the spiraling flights of buzzards up into eternity, and the very idea of singing about the murmuring woods was almost a kind of betrayal." Ignatius' view of poetry bears a remarkable similarity to Brecht's in his famous poem "Bad Times for Poetry," where he says that not nature but political and social problems drive him to his desk and the composition of verse. Ignatius' former devotees do not understand this point. Instead, they cast him out, removing his books from the libraries, beheading his statue in the park, and burning his works in nightly bonfires. Ignatius' decision to start anew with language by cleaning typewriter keys is not any more likely to be politically effective than were his earlier poetic effusions. The narrator-scribe sees the weaknesses of both would-be resisters through art, Richard and Ignatius, but he, too, is unable to find a resolution to the artist's dilemma.

The difficulties of reconstructing this literary mosaic clearly limit the effectiveness of *The Fate of Our Town*. More problematic, however, is the novel's elevation of concrete historical problems to a parabolic plane. By equating the problems of postwar Berlin with the problems of the Third Reich and simultaneously clothing them in medieval garb, Schnurre implies that the problems are perennial in nature. The author himself seems unaware of the insight that flickers briefly in his narrator's consciousness: that the kind of truth which emanates from a timeless and hermetic sphere can scarcely be useful for the here and now. The book's parabolic structure has led it to this dead end; whatever inkling the reader may have of its hidden obverse, the scribe himself cannot help but end in resignation. Like myths, parables reduce our views of history to essentially closed models of thought. Within these frames, free individual action is virtually prohibited.

The mythic view was not restricted to West Germany alone, but also predominated in Switzerland, whose German-language theater was highly influential in the fifties. Of course, Switzerland's essentially conservative humanism was an important factor in the way its writers came to see the history of Nazi Germany. Taking up mythic forms was for them a way of connecting their own literature with the main stream of European modernism; they failed to realize that the great works of the twentieth century had used myth for an entirely different purpose. Whereas the earlier part of the century had needed myth to give coherence to the fragmentation of modern experience, the fifties needed forms that could liberate people from rigidly fixed thought patterns. Swiss writers were in a different position from German writers, and their special type of political engagement tended to take up Brechtian models and essentially turn them in upon themselves. An important element of Brecht's program had been the use of open forms, reflecting his view that the world could be altered and that critical detachment could help individuals to escape the prison of social and psychological determinants. But the Swiss writers, attempting to carry Brecht's dramatic models one stage further, in actuality closed the door that Brecht had carefully left open.

Plays like Max Frisch's *The Firebugs* (1958) or *Andorra* (1961), overtly criticizing the complacent bourgeois mentality and its reluctance to resist prevailing mores, reveal upon closer examination how closed dramatic structures rule out the possibility of individual resistance. Paradoxically, *The Firebugs* attacked rigid systems of thought, while at the same time harking back to paradigmatic forms: the medieval *Everyman* and Greek tragedy. Admittedly, the play is intended as a parody of these models. It stresses repeatedly that fate is a concept more appropriate to drama than to life, but by conflating various paradigms that depend on this notion, the play ultimately gives credence to the idea of inevitability and universality. A major difficulty is *The Firebugs'* intentional applicability to both prewar and postwar situations, including its implicit reference to the Communist overthrow of Czechoslovakia. The play's meaning broadens in scope as its relevance to specific historical issues narrows. Such simplifications are not really commensurate with the moral dilemmas of political reality. Its farcical element, far from emancipating us from these models, as it is intended to do, trivializes and distracts from the issues at hand.

In Frisch's novel *Homo Faber* (1957), there is a similar dilemma. Though it seems to refer mainly to postwar problems, the novel deals in a continuous undercurrent with issues raised by the recent past. Here again, life is viewed as a modern variant of a classical model, in this case, the Oedipus story. Much is made of the question to what extent human beings are determined by some outside force—fate—or by their own actions; what the protagonist calls chance manifests itself exactly as if it were fate. Like *The Firebugs*, the novel suffers from a disparity between two modes of thought: the tragic and the ironic. Insofar as Faber is a modern Oedipus, what happens to him takes on the quality of fate, whether or not he regards it as a random chain of circumstances. Once sequences become repeatable, events can no longer seem like chance occurrences. By basing his tale upon myth, Frisch virtually eliminates the possibility that Faber might have been able to act otherwise. If Faber's blindness is less avoidable than Oedipus', he is still not genuinely free, but a prisoner of his own psychological makeup, and so the determinants of psychology become a modern equivalent for fate. The clash between myth and freedom appears unresolvable.

Even where Frisch moves away from preestablished mythic patterns, as in *Andorra*, he sees the individual as hopelessly locked in to social determinants. The boy Andri, whose father conceals his illegitimacy by claiming that he is a Jewish refugee, is a moving example of how an individual can take on the role assigned to him by society. When the Andorrans finally succumb to the Nazis, they allow Andri to be taken away without protest. True to the period in which it was written, the play's main concern is the problem of identity: on this level, Andri's refusal to believe his father's revelation of the truth about his heritage is perfectly credible. The problem lies in the play's attempt to transform the relationship between Germans and Jews into a piece of general psychologizing in terms of the familiar identity crisis of the late fifties and early sixties. Similarly,

Frisch's portrayal of the turncoat Andorrans, once so proud of how they had protected the supposed Jew, is both a criticism of their self-complacency and a tacit acceptance of social determinism. The drama becomes a paradigm of a modern Everyman and a modern Everypeople. By highlighting the psycho-social determinants of the action, Frisch precludes the Brechtian response: "but they should have acted differently." Instead, the viewer is more likely to respond, "Yes, that's just how it was." A related product of much the same time and much the same type of thought is *The Visit* (1956), by Frisch's compatriot Friedrich Dürrenmatt. Once again, a universalized modern parable is constructed around the idea that people can be easily swayed and that society's morals are less than high-minded. When Claire Zachanassian, returning after a long absence, offers her home town a substantial reward if it agrees to participate in her cruel plans for avenging a former lover, the people are quick to see their advantage. The rapidity with which they allow themselves to become murderers is relevant to the discussion of nazism, but it is overlaid by the fable's universal implications.

Indeed, Dürrenmatt's whole theory of drama revolves–in explicit debate with Brecht–around the concept of the anonymous individual who has no genuine freedom of action. By regarding Hitler and Stalin, not as individuals, but as state machines of carnage, Dürrenmatt argues that there can be no individual guilt in the modern world and, hence, no individual tragedy. Like those of Frisch, Dürrenmatt's plays in the early postwar years are based on classical Greek forms which become ingeniously inverted in their application to the modern predicament. In the modern world there may no longer be fate or the gods, but in their place is not so much individual moral responsibility as a chain of accident and coincidence. "Thus there is no threatening God, no justice, no fate as in the Fifth Symphony, but merely traffic accidents, dikes bursting because of faulty construction, explosions in atom bomb factories, caused by absentminded laboratory assistants." The very grotesqueness of these accidents renders the individual helpless, overwhelmed by them in the same way as he was crushed in the classical Greek drama by fate. The laughter that ensues–and Dürrenmatt calls his plays comedies–is merely the laughter of desperation.

Of Dürrenmatt's plays, perhaps the most relevant to the issue of individual responsibility are

Romulus the Great (1948) and *The Physicists* (1962), although only the former has direct bearing on the Third Reich. Curiously, resistance is not depicted in *Romulus the Great* as the action, but as a passivity that blocks the actions of others. By refusing to intervene, the emperor Romulus allows the Roman Empire to come to its inevitable decline. In the last analysis, though, the operative force is the power of the future. Whereas Romulus believes that he has passed judgment on Rome, he merely leaves it to its inevitable decline. His counterpart, the Germanic emperor Odoaker, implores Romulus to join forces with him to prevent his bloodthirsty nephew Theodoric from ushering in a new age of terror, but their belief in the inevitability of the future turns both emperors away from the path of political or military action. The individual is powerless: "You must submit to your fate. There is no other alternative." The upshot of it all is that one cannot intervene in the course of history without in the end being crushed by fate. Cunningly, Dürrenmatt substitutes the word *reality* for *fate* in contexts that are to be taken without irony (Romulus declares, for example, that the emperors' grand designs for the future have been "corrected by reality"), but the ultimate effect is to create the impression that things could not have turned out otherwise.

However much Dürrenmatt insists that reality is a random chain of accidents, events do seem to have some covert form of patterning in this play. The Roman Empire is suspiciously like the Third Reich, but Romulus is not Hitler; the anticipated bloody reign of Theodoric recalls the Third Reich while not being precisely identical with it. Yet despite these distinctions, the effectiveness of the play as a political statement depends on the similarities, not the differences, between the Roman Empire and our own age.

Active resistance is presented twice in *Romulus the Great*, each time in the form of parody: first on the night of the Ides of March, when the patriotic members of the Empire attempt to assassinate Romulus ("Et tu, cook?"), and again when the royal messenger makes a last desperate attempt on the life of an emperor who has, unbeknown to him, already abdicated his office. The association of Caesar and Hitler could be a fruitful one, but Dürrenmatt does not even indirectly raise ethical issues connected with the assassination of dictators. And Theodoric, the dictator of the future, escapes entirely unscathed. Romulus' pessimistic view that the murder of one dictator would not prevent the rise of a thousand others neatly sidesteps the essential moral dilemma. Moderate humaneness and an essentially fatalistic world view win the day.

Unwittingly, Dürrenmatt implies here through his absurdist stance that the individual has lost all power to determine his own fate. Modern civilization, with its generally amorphous structure, persistently thwarts man's attempt to change it. When Dürrenmatt discusses Brecht's contention that the world can be changed, his only rebuttal is a backhanded compliment to Brecht's technical expertise: "It is often simply the case that Brecht the creative writer sweeps Brecht the dramaturge along with him, a perfectly legitimate phenomenon that only becomes dangerous when it ceases to occur." In the work of Brecht, the audience's reflections form, as it were, the invisible obverse of the play on the stage. In Dürrenmatt, the positive model is actually demonstrated—in this case, in the figure of Romulus. Unfortunately, Frisch and Dürrenmatt, rather than Brecht, are the true representatives of this early phase in the rethinking of the Nazi past. They reflect and help to popularize notions of history in which freedom of action is precluded by the inevitable movement of events.

This entire group of Swiss and German writers of the late forties and fifties translates the events of the recent past into cosmic dimensions, stripping history of its roots in time and endowing it with eternal qualities. When Schnurre's narrator claims that he is the "servant of truth, not Chronos," he speaks for an entire generation of writers who saw the mass guilt of a particular nation at a particular time as the universal, ever-recurring guilt of all mankind. To be sure, they are also aware that the chain must somehow be broken. Schnurre tried to do so by setting up a mosaic that had still to be pieced together, evidently hoping to stimulate a productive and critical response. His abstruseness interferes with this, however, and the reader of *The Fate of Our Town* is more likely to give up in despair. Langgässer and the Swiss writers, by contrast, do not lead outward from the patterns they set up but into the realm of myth and archetype.

In reflecting the view that resistance to Hitler had been virtually impossible, the closed forms thus confirmed, rather than questioned, the reader's belief in inevitability or historic recurrence. Thus the schema-response pattern is relatively static, adopting accepted opinions without provoking new ones. As reflections of a basically pessimistic view of the individual's role in history, these works fulfilled psychological needs but failed to refine political awareness.

Socialist Paradigms

Discontinuity from the prewar to the postwar period was an initial problem in the GDR, as in the Federal Republic, but here there was no talk of a zero hour. Instead, an attempt was made almost from the outset to identify the emerging socialist state with the Communist resistance and to see in the underground resistance movement predecessors of those engaged in building up the new regime. This postulation of a fictitious continuity is problematic in the extreme. In the first instance, model patterns of behavior and thought were not directly transferable from the historical resistance to the socialist state. Moreover, this new vision of the past was at variance with the experience of most East Germans, who had not been directly involved with the resistance against Hitler. The popular paradigm of an East German resistance heritage disregarded moral complexities and dilemmas that did not fit the socialist model. Like the myths and metaphors of its Western counterparts, it closed doors instead of opening them. While resistance had been desirable in the Third Reich, it was no longer so in the Democratic Republic, and the problem finally became so acute that the myth of continuity had to be abandoned. In the late fifties, just as West German literary forms were gradually becoming more open and flexible, East German critics called for a clean break with the past, thus all but eliminating the possibility of probing the issues it had raised. Whereas the reliance on resistance models had unwittingly served an escapist mentality, the new approach disregarded even more radically a psychological need to work through past experience.

The first phase of East German literature rested upon perceptions of historical reality gained from exile, rather than from first-hand experience of nazism. Emigrants to Mexico and Russia naturally found that their view of fascism in Germany was influenced by their experiences in their country of exile. When this understanding of history was coupled with adherence to the strict requirements of socialist realism—the presentation of a model situation and a positive hero—the possibility of critical distancing became even more remote. Despite slight thaws in the official line in the mid-fifties and the early seventies, writers were urged to keep to traditional forms of narration, avoiding more innovative structures, which in the socialist view are only accessible to a literary elite. Against this background, opposition could be expressed only within the accepted paradigm; attempts to break out of the closed model, as in certain works of Anna Seghers, Johannes Bobrowski, and Christa Wolf, were greeted with suspicion.

Only occasionally was the unreality of the socialist paradigm brought to the fore. Stephan Hermlin's short story "Lieutenant Yorck von Wartenburg" (1946), an imaginary account of the last moments in the life of a member of the officers' conspiracy against Hitler, is a good example. Cooped up in his prison cell awaiting execution, Yorck von Wartenburg dreams of a "corrected" version of the unsuccessful assassination attempt of 20 July 1944. Told as if it were real, the dream continues until the penultimate moment, when the dreamer awakes to a terrible awareness of failure. Now at last separating dream and reality, he nonetheless clings to his vision as he dies. Hermlin's vignette should have drawn attention to the real nature of East German resistance myths: that their intended function lies precisely in their unreality, in their correction of what really happened, and in their projection of an ideal to be turned to in the future.

Unfortunately, the East German paradigm has been cast in the mold of a simplified realism which ignores this function of literature. In positing consonance between literary presentation and accepted views of reality, it minimizes the reader's awareness that fiction is rooted in ideology. In calling for agreement from its readers, it denies them their potential for political growth.

This increasing rigidity of the paradigm can be seen in the development of the East German tradition. Bodo Uhse, in *We Sons* (written in 1944 but not published until 1948), is still able to exploit the double optics of limited first-person narration. By pointing out the imperfections of his schoolboy protagonist's understanding of reality, he encourages the reader to develop a more complete vision. By setting his story in the year 1918, he calls upon the reader to think beyond the end of the novel by drawing parallels and making distinctions. And by making the positive hero an absent model (the boy's dead mentor Erxner), he creates a dialectic that demands our participation for its completion.

Similarly, Anna Seghers' early novel *Transit* (published during her exile in 1943) sets up a dialectic between her worker-protagonist and the uncompleted manuscript of which he accidentally gains possession. The blank page at the conclusion of the manuscript corresponds to the novel's orientation towards the future, in which the positive model is to be adapted creatively to a new set of circumstances.

But the comparative subtlety of these more dialectical approaches is soon abandoned. Seghers herself, attempting again and again to soften the edges of the requisite socialist hero, often falls prey to the more typically West German extreme of irrationality and myth. As she broadens the scope of her canvas and tries to encompass the sociopolitical mechanisms of an entire era, as in *The Dead Stay Young* (1949), she balances precariously between the socialist paradigm and its mythic counterpart. Even her formal innovations, much as they resemble the multifaceted technique that Heinrich Böll was to handle with relative success in *Billiards at Half-Past Nine* (1959), fail to modify the overall impression that life falls into a single, vast pattern. In depicting people from different generations and from a range of social classes, Seghers was trying to create an effect similar to that of the frescos of Diego Rivera, whose work she had much admired during her Mexican exile. Artfully arranged and politically expressive, such frescos were complex, but still easy to understand. In this respect they appealed to Anna Seghers' desire to address the non-elitist reader without sacrificing subtlety of form. But in supporting the fresco-like parorama of *The Dead Stay Young* with an underlying symbolic pattern (the generational parallels and the frequent use of leitmotifs), she invalidates her own attempt to perceive history as open-ended. Her conclusion consists of the suggestion that the resistance heritage be handed down through the generation as yet unborn; more appropriate would be an exhortation to rethink prevailing views of resistance.

These problems are not unexpected in a writer like Anna Seghers, originally from the middle class and thus bound to feel torn between innovative literary forms and the prescribed one-dimensional paradigms. But even proletarian writers like Willi Bredel, who were more familiar with social complexities, resolve the issue of continuity between the Third Reich and the postwar period by resorting to the socialist paradigm. Bredel's trilogy, *Relatives and Friends* (1941-53), rests almost entirely on the image of the family heritage as the bearer of the resistance tradition. And Bodo Uhse's unfinished late novel, *The Patriots* (1954), ostensibly a spy story, develops the paradigm through the use of symmetrical arrangements: constellations of characters, parallel or contrasting plots, counterpoint and connections within the underground network in which his characters move. All of these substitute for the mythic substratum of the West German novels and create their own version of closed literary structures. If we compare *The Patriots* with even such second-rate works of West German fiction as Hans Hellmut Kirst's trilogy *Zero Eight Fifteen* (1955), we can see what is missing. Both novels carry the appeal of an adventure story, but Kirst's adds an undercurrent of irony, an assumption that the reader knows better than the characters and can view them with a degree of detachment. By its very nature, socialist realism reduces the potential for ironic presentation. The type of novel that must be read against the grain, by constructing the inverse of the actual story told, is something of a rarity in East German fiction. A look at one exception, Eberhard Panitz' *Unsaintly Sophia* (1975), which begins at much the same point in time as *The Patriots* leaves off and deals, like Uhse's novel, with the Russian involvement in the German underground resistance, may cast some light on the status of ironic structures in East German fiction.

What Uhse had abandoned after *We Sons*, Panitz resurrects for a new purpose: the limited-point-of-view narrator. Everyone seems to know more about Sophia than the narrator, but, fascinated with snippets of information he grasps here and there, he feels impelled to carry on the quest for her identity. The surprise ending–that Sophia, a Russian agent parachuted into Germany toward the end of the war and subsequently mayor of the small town where the story takes place, is actually the mother of the narrator's wife–provides an ironic answer to the question of continuity. Like Christa Wolf's *The Quest for Christa T.* (1968), Panitz' novel places the burden of the detective work on the reader, who has to complete the picture of Sophia that constantly eludes the narrator. Whether her unorthodox way of governing the town is to be read as resistance or merely as human complexity remains unresolved in the novel itself. But the book's two-level approach to the past forms an incipient dialectic for the reader to complete.

The spy story resistance novel was not the only model to be used in East Germany. The middle generation preferred to accept its own views of the past and turn them to account through situational irony. This differs from the open irony of Panitz' *Sophia*, since it depends upon an accepted view of things in the present which forms the criterion for evaluating the past. Franz Fühmann's work is perhaps the best example of this method. His experience of nazism from within, as a product of the German school system and as a soldier in Hitler's army, coupled with his postwar conversion to communism while a prisoner of war in Russia, equip him to be a spokesman for an entire generation. His best short stories, such as "Comrades" (1955) or "The Capitulation" (1958), depend almost entirely upon plot reversals in which the other face of the Nazi view of reality is suddenly revealed. Other works employ elements of dream, fairy tale, and myth uncommon in East German writing. One of his most moving small masterpieces, "Bohemia by the Sea" (1962), uses Shakespeare's unintentional displacement of Bohemia to the seaside in *A Winter's Tale* as a metaphor for an old woman's postwar displacement from her inland home to a seaside town. The image from Shakespeare becomes a suggestive, multilevel bond between her psyche and the narrator's consciousness. More grandiose, but ultimately less convincing, is the use of myth in "King Oedipus" (1966), even though it demonstrates the unmasking of Nazi ideology. But the tale depends on an underlying belief in historical inevitability, whereby World War II is understood as part of a transitional period that parallels the transition from one form of society to another in Sophocles' *Oedipus Rex*. When Fühmann lets his imagery sweep him away, he uses a kind of nature myth not unrelated to the popular metaphors of nazism. His "Barlach in Güstrow" (1963), the one piece which presents resistance to nazism from within, suffers markedly from this fault. One cannot help feeling that Barlach's resistance, his decision to stand firm despite the desecration of his sculptures, is rooted in what amounts to a crypto-fascist mode of thought.

During this period, another group of middle generation writers had begun to develop a new socialist paradigm that took into account personal experience of nazism while also pointing beyond it. Their literary models form a more direct counterpart to the resistance heritage novels than do the stories of Fühmann. Harking back to the traditional German novel of development and education (*Bildungsroman*), this group tries to gain perspective on the past by viewing it in terms of personal development. Erwin Strittmatter's *The Miracle Worker* (1957), Dieter Noll's *The Adventures of Werner Holt* (1960-63), and Erik Neutsch's *Peace in the East* (1974-78) are two-part novels with strong autobiographical elements. All three stress the problematic, even paradoxical, nature of the transition from nazism to socialism. But despite their greater complexities, the development novels can hardly be said to break out of the closed structures of programmatic thought. The close identification of author and protagonist divests the novels of the *Bildungsroman*'s original advantage: its ironic structure. Ultimately, the adventure-story pattern of the positive hero novels prevails here too; the novels show how a character abandons nazism and embraces socialism but do not explore the nature of ideology in general. Individual political and social development follows a consistent pattern, and one novel can almost be substituted for another, so unvarying is the underlying model. In Neutsch's series of novels, the pattern even begins to take on the status of myth, as young Achim, in a schoolboy poem written to his girlfriend after her recovery from an abortion, sentimentally invokes the story of Eurydice. The young woman's return to consciousness from a coma and Achim's ultimate enlightenment after political and sexual ignorance, error, and guilt take on the inevitability of the mythic return from the underworld. Despite this gesture toward myth, the development genre maintains its basic form, though relying rather heavily upon a more inward, psychological presentation.

In this regard, the East German novel lags conspicuously behind its counterpart in the West. Perhaps the most convincing testament to this is Uwe Johnson's second novel, *The Third Book about Achim* (1961), conceived against the foil of GDR theory but published two years after his move to the Federal Republic. Here the idea of history as a product of individual perceptions becomes a cen-

tral theme of the novel. Realism and fiction are thematically linked in a story line that involves a journalist's attempt to write the definitive biography of Achim, an East German cycling champion. Achim's present life seems unintelligible from the journalist's Western point of view, and what he learns about the cyclist's past is simply not acceptable to the party officials who have commissioned the book and who prefer schematic views of continuity to the shifting complexities that Karsch discovers. Johnson's peculiar status allows him to create the unusual phenomenon of a West German response to an East German schema. Unlike its East German predecessors, *The Third Book about Achim* remains defiantly open-ended, constantly teasing and prodding the reader to complete the vision that the journalist has abandoned in despair. In pointing up this issue of subjective perception, Johnson, unlike his journalist Karsch, does not simply throw up his hands in horror or succumb to an unresolved plurality of interpretation. In using the subjective lens to distort historical material almost beyond recognition, he draws attention to the fact that a unified vision of reality is itself a fiction. Although his view of the contrast between East and West is somewhat simplistic, the novelist refrains from codifying them into unyielding models. The discrepancy between the relatively direct mirroring of accepted views one tends to expect from fiction and the puzzlingly elusive version of reality Johnson gives in this novel forces the reader to become more critical of common assumptions. *The Third Book about Achim*, one of the earliest attempts at reader activation in the postwar German novel, points the way to a new genre of reflection on nazism.

But Johnson is an unusual case. We shall see later, in Johannes Bobrowski and Christa Wolf, two other exceptions to the dominant socialist realism of GDR theory; but, in the main, East German novels continue to be locked into a set of relatively inflexible, predetermined patterns.

Appendix II

A Call to Letters

A Call to Letters and an Invitation to the Electric Chair

Siegfried Mandel

Reprinted from Group 47: The Reflected Intellect *(Carbondale & Edwardsville: Southern Illinois University Press, 1973), pp. 1-31.*

Group 47 is a paradox. It is one man, Hans Werner Richter, and at the same time an expanding and contracting constellation identifiable by several constant stars. The group has given its members a publicity platform, and reciprocally some of its members have brought the group an international reputation. Group 47 was conceived, nurtured, fathered, and brought to prominence by Richter, a person of single-minded political idealism, a tenacious social vision and dedication to basic German interests, an unparalleled flair for publicity and its exploitation, and with an iron-cool temperature seemingly devoid of sentimentalism. Anyone who might have had more endearing qualities or lesser egocentricity than Richter would surely have failed to keep alive for more than two decades a loosely-knit association of writers who periodically exhibited their wares (which pleased or antagonized fellow participants and the public), engaged in critical debate over socio-literary-aesthetic issues, and assisted in revitalizing all forms of literary expression inside and outside the fluid group. It kept alive because it never hardened into a school of style or inflexible ideology. At times it initiated new trends, but more often it was a barometer of changing literary tastes, social conditions, and political climates.

Drawing upon his own background, Richter lately has written reminiscence stories, *Blinder Alarm* [False Alarm] (1970)–sketches whose style has moved away from his early realistic novels to a lyrical, ironic prose. The Baltic island of Usedom, and the town of Bansin where he was born in 1908, was populated by fishermen, masons, locksmiths, and peasants from interior villages, and from the time of Kaiser Wilhelm II to the postwar Russian occupation it reflected in a microcosm the experience of much of Germany in all its political periods; little has changed physically, except that presently a few miles away is a barbed wire border with Poland. A sense of nationality reigned supreme, yet his father returned from World War I a Social Democrat (a rare phenomenon in his town) and with stories that told not of glory but of his endless task of emptying bedpots. During Nazi times, his family had to suffer indignities and social ostracism because he did not play along with new political trends. When the second war came contrary to his expectations, he advised his five sons to behave unobtrusively in the army, to be neither heroic nor cowardly, and never to volunteer for anything; they survived the war. He was against war but for the honoring of soldiers, a distinction which made an impact on his son, Hans Werner.

In Berlin, the young Richter started to learn the book trade, joined the Communist party in 1930 and left it in 1933, migrated to Paris but after a year of starvation returned to Berlin under the watchful eyes of the Nazis. After the war started he was recruited into the German infantry for duty in France and Italy and eventually gave himself up to the Americans at Monte Cassino. Again, he began to concern himself seriously with political questions while a German prisoner of war at Camp Ellis in the United States. Because the American officers interfered little in the internal affairs of the prisoner camps, some of the German *Wehrmacht* officers and noncoms cooperated with terrorists who wanted to keep alive the dedication to Nazism and who used discipline and sometimes murder to keep dissenters in line and to prohibit debate. Reeducation came slowly and was speeded up when the defeat of Germany became a certainty. To open a truthful picture of the military and political situations, a POW newspaper was distributed during the winter of 1944 and lasted into early 1946. Along the line, one of the editors of this newspaper, called *Der Ruf* [The Call], was a lawyer, Walter Mannzen, and he was joined by Richter and by Alfred Andersch, among others. When Andersch was released soon after the war, he founded another *Der Ruf* in August 1946 in Munich, with the subtitle "Independent newsleaf of the new generation." Richter made contributions from the start, and with the fourth issue they continued jointly to edit the periodical until April 1947 when the American military government in Bavaria banned further publication under Andersch-Richter auspices.

The issues raised in *Der Ruf* and the solutions firmly advocated have importance in their historical context and carry over into the thinking of what later was Group 47. Some of the fellow POWs, who had worked with both men before, renewed their contributions to the newsleaf. *Der Ruf* found considerable resonance among subscribers in all four zones of occupation and its circulation rapidly rose above 100,000. Within a short time, there also was talk of a political *Ruf* party. Mainly, the newsleaf was politically oriented, but it also contained general cultural articles, fiction and poetry, and journalistic reports which intended to gauge the actual condition of German life and peoples' mentalities. The dual purpose of the newsleaf was to become the voice of the silent generation, the young homecoming soldiers, and to influence the political direction of Germany. In some respect the arguments put forward had jelled during the times of the old POW publication and then received renewed polemical force. The core propositions were the following: the freedom and unity of Germany, a social-humanistic foundation for the new political structure of Germany, a unified socialist Europe, no imposition of the idea of collective guilt upon the German people, and no unnecessary humiliation of Germans. Among other points, *Der Ruf* wanted Germans to play a role in all peace deliberations, called for the speedy return of German prisoners of war from camps all over the map, urged the use of German revolutionary courts–instead of the Nuremberg trials–to deal with Germans who had committed crimes against Germany, and proposed a bridging role or middle position for Germany between East and West.

The contents of the articles which appeared in *Der Ruf* merit more than the mere gloss which critics have accorded them since they reveal attitudes free of the disguises that marked other publications during the postwar era in regard to political, economic, social, and cultural problems. Writers for the publication discarded all niceties and taboos, spoke plainly and often aggressively. Although Germany had capitulated unconditionally, these writers bent no knees to the military government and warned that only a just peace

would have durability. Other than the precondition for a united Germany, the revision of eastern boundaries, and retention of the 1937 geographical status quo, many of the proposals fitted into a somewhat fuzzy blueprint. A recurrent theme is the call for a humanistic socialism which would democratize socialism and socialize democracy and the search for a third way which would be indigenously German. Richter felt that the time was ripe for socialism because the capitalistic order had been weakened by two imperialistic wars and periodic crises while the middle-class supporters of capitalism had been demoralized by Fascist experiments; the whole system was in its decline. Theoretically, the proletariat should be the carrier of future developments but he seemed paralyzed by the magnitude of the tasks though the goal was close. Richter saw irony in the fact that when the liberal middle-class elements needed underpinning from the Left in 1933, it was lacking, while during the postwar years it was forthcoming. The tragedy of the German working class, thought Richter, lay in the lack of effective leadership yesterday and today. *Der Ruf*'s socialism envisaged freedom of political and social choice, including acceptance or rejection of religion, instead of Marxist determinism.

From Paris to Moscow, Communists were particularly upset with Richter's sharp letter, published in *Der Ruf* (February 15, 1947), which struck at M. Marcel Cachin, one of the oldest members of the French Communist party. Cachin had said publicly that the Nazi spirit still prevailed in Germany, that Germans had no regret nor showed penance, that Nazis still were in key positions, and that American and British interests were abetted by the rebuilding of industries in their sectors. Richter responded by accusing M. Cachin of being a traitor to international socialism and reminded him of the boundless disillusion suffered by socialists at the 1939 Stalin-Hitler pact, the alliance between a Fascist Germany and Russia. He recalled further Cachin's defeatist role in urging French workers to lay down their arms when the Germans invaded France. More specifically, Richter noted that Cachin's demand for dismantling factories would pauperize the German worker. Richter condemned Cachin for nationalist revenge tactics which attempted to internationalize instead of socializing the rich industrialist Ruhr, for wanting to dismantle factories instead of unionizing them, for encouraging workers to dynamite the Hamburg dock industry rather than turning it over to the workers.

Cachin's allegiance was to Moscow while Richter favored a new socialistic approach; he thought that it would be a mistake to restore the political parties which exhibited their weaknesses during the Weimar regime of the twenties. The various plans to dismember Germany, as well as Churchill's ideas of decentralized provincialities, were rejected by *Der Ruf* writers. Instead of Churchill's balance-of-power orientation, Richter called for a socialized Europe, a United States of Europe in which Germany would play a cooperative and equal role. Reiterated was the idea that Germany's political hopes for the future would rest on the young homecoming generation and their joining hands with socialist forces throughout Europe. The journalist Nicolaus Sombart expressed the hope that the young Frenchmen would put aside any Clemenceau-like hatreds that resulted in the Versailles Treaty and in return Germans would never again tolerate a Hitler among them.

The socialist economy, as broached, regarded the private ownership of the means of production as obsolete and absurd as slavery; a planned economy and technology were essential. A prescription for healing Germany was given by Mannzen, who proposed to free the economy from the chains of the profit motive and the market mechanisms; socialistic planning was to control the economy. While Germany appreciates American economic assistance and wants the good will of the world, Richter wrote, "Young Germany knows that its future state will be proletarian, but it is not ready to live in a state of beggary." Of course, as Andersch pointed out, the economy and society would need to be reconstructed in order to foster changes that would eliminate the physical and psychic effects of aerial bombings of German cities, to help millions of Germans made homeless in the East, to eliminate the blight of black markets, to end the Babylonian captivity of soldiers, to reverse the paralysis of industries and cities in ruins, to still the voices of hunger and despair. Actually, German industry was not destroyed: about eighty percent was relatively undamaged.

Most of the writers for *Der Ruf* neither spoke softly nor entirely hid a big stick; many battled defensively against the resentment that broke in waves over Germany after the war. An example of countering foreign criticism was set by Walter Kolbenhoff (b. 1908), who won a prize from the POW *Der Ruf* in 1946 and continued to contribute to the new one. The occasion was a book written by Nobel Prize winner Sigrid Undset, translated from a Norwegian manuscript as *Return to the Future* (1942; *Wieder in die Zukunft*, 1944, published in German simultaneously in New York and Zürich). Just before the German march into Norway, she fled to the United States and there learned that her son had been shot by the Germans. As a patriot and mother, her distaste for anything German became unrelenting: "German brutality is boundless whenever they are masters; but when luck turns against them, they beg and whine for mercy. . . . Can anyone doubt that we will again hear such lamentations should the Allies succeed in winning the war against the attackers of free states." She thought, too, that there had been no change over the past thousand years in the *Herrenvolk* or master-race mentality of the Germans. Kolbenhoff made emotional concessions to Mrs. Undset's grief and then launched into admonishments: "Your forefathers, also, Mrs. Undset, once were brutal and unpleasant robbers." Hate should not be directed against those who resisted Hitler, wrote Kolbenhoff, not against the millions of innocent German children who are not responsible for the stupidities of their parents. He reminded Mrs. Undset of Germany's cultural contributions (as if the glories of Weimar allow an absolving of the barbarities in nearby Buchenwald) and the contributions to the socialist movement of Europe. "Other Europeans also suffer from political infantilism," but the best part of the German nation, comments Kolbenhoff, is attempting to find a new way, and the good forces will prevail: "The only solution of the problem is that we achieve union with the life of other nations." He concluded with the optimistic assessment that Germans would seize their "third chance." There is no record of any reply or forgiveness by Sigrid Undset, who had cause to remember, among other things, the destruction by German bombers of the town of Lillehammer where she lived in a house which had been built in the year 1000.

Many of the contributors to *Der Ruf* worked hard to absolve the soldiers of the German *Wehrmacht* from any dishonor; through their contributions to the newsleaf they wanted to restore the pride of the homecomers and their hopes. Alfred Andersch was particularly fulsome in extolling the "astounding military deeds of the young Germans in this war" as against the deeds of the somewhat older Germans who were being tried in Nuremberg; their deeds "stand in little relation to one another." "The warriors at Stalingrad, El Alamein, and Cassino, to whom even their opponents paid respect, are innocent of the crimes at Dachau and Buchenwald"; their defeat was honorable, wrote Andersch, and "the real enemies of the young soldiers who braved death on all European and African fronts are the political and military criminals.... the nation will again have its honor when these traitors are defrocked." *Der Ruf* contributors expressed anger and concern for the six million, mostly young, German soldiers who two years after the war were still in POW camps, doing reconstruction work in Russia, especially in Siberia, felling trees in Canada, mining and working in France and North Africa; they complained about medical attention, food, and housing comforts (which were somewhat unlike those they enjoyed when they were occupiers). Perhaps *Der Ruf* was unaware that sixty percent of Russian POWs in German hands never returned home.

As for the home front, Andersch indicted official and public indifference to the POWs: "Sorrow and empathic suffering is confined to circles of close relatives, to the mothers robbed of millions of sons.... women and girls turn their backs to the apparently hopeless lot of those behind barbed wires." A former student and POW, Friedrich Minssen, in looking around, felt that 1946 had not brought a new start, that despite the help of the Allies "our calorie rations are lower than that since the beginning of the war ... and are not significantly higher than what they were in the German concentration camps"; economic stagnation, hunger, and despair are the signs of peace. The writers for *Der Ruf* resented foreign reporting about the mean, petty, grubbing, and degrading postwar life in Germany, but they too were distressed by the facts. In whatever sphere they felt vulnerable to criticism, they built up defensive arguments which solidified down to the idea that Germans were guilty only in degree; others were guilty too, other nations were imperialists too. They pointed to the appeasement policies of the Western powers during the thirties, symbolized by Neville Chamberlain, which allowed Hitler to have his way, to the inhuman treatment of minorities by Poland and particularly the virulent anti-Semitism of the Soviets, and to other sins by Germany's neighbors. Dietrich Warnesius, a freelance writer, sharply noted, "I do not subscribe to the idea that the German nation is the only instigator of all crimes in this epoch." He pointed out also that Germans were no better or worse than

others, which, however it is taken, is a significant revision of the *Herrenvolk* theory of the Third Reich. To the argument that Germany must be ready to cede territories because it lost the war, it was suggested that this might-is-right notion was practiced by Hitler but should not be turned against post-war Germany. In other words, there was a defensive argument for every hostile foreign feeling, real or anticipated.

As proof that *Der Ruf* did not shut the door to friendly disagreement, it published the personal observations of Stephen Spender, the English poet. Possibly also this was an indirect opening to the international discussions which Richter hoped would link the young Germans to figures such as Arthur Koestler, Ignazio Silone, André Malraux, all of them anti-Fascists and anti-Stalinists, yet of the intellectual Left. Spender was well acquainted with the German as well as the French scene and did not minimize the difficulties of developing cooperative working attitudes between Germans and the rest of Europe. Germans still felt that France's fall was deserved morally and factually; they felt that France's part in the occupation of Germany was unearned and unfair since she had been beaten. The French novelist Vercors, who had founded an underground newspaper during the German occupation, had written an essay in 1945, "Are there decent Germans?" Although his answer was not encouraging and was in line with sentiments of many Frenchmen, Spender did manage to see some hopeful signs of a new chapter in Franco-German relations. Spender, unlike the writers for *Der Ruf*, was suspicious of any new German youth movement: "the young Germans of today are the most tired, unknowledgeable, and intellectually poverty-stricken generation group today." Further, he feared that the German universities were becoming asylums for ex-army officers with nationalistic sympathies. He did find on university rolls the names of German university professors of undoubted integrity, and of the older generation, but as for the rest he was cautious. For one thing, he was disturbed by some who, though they claimed to be anti-Nazi nationalists, still clung to racial theories that stressed the incompatibility between Caucasians and Asians, and the inevitability of East-West conflicts. Certain articles in *Der Ruf* admitted that some university elements still paid homage to the National Socialist madness but that one should not have expected university professors to have set a better example than other segments of German society which swayed with the times; among the scores of professors who could not pass the eighteen-month denazification process were some whose dismissal possibly was unjust. Andersch claimed that the information used by the military authorities should have been made public: "Let the people know." He and others strongly urged the return of émigré scholars to German universities, although there would be social and intellectual difficulties. They could not foresee, however, that the gulf was rarely to be bridged in the future; voluntary émigrés, by and large, gained the taint of "deserters." Some writers made the realistic assessment that Germans at that time were interested in material rather than cultural CARE packages.

Spender also put his finger on another problem, namely, the "astonishing lack of sensitivities to realities in the attitude of most German intellectuals" who glossed over everything casually as if nothing had ever happened. If this is too great a generalization, it is offset by the repetitious and woebegone insistence in most of *Der Ruf* articles that the world ought to recognize how much the Germans had suffered. It seems to me that some of the writers who tried to reestablish the moral equilibrium of Germans adduced arguments and made appeals to the very sentiments which had caused arrogant attitudes toward their European neighbors. Anyone acquainted with the colloquial strata of German life and expression even before the Third Reich knows of the currency of contempt in which the Italians, French, Poles, Czechs, Russians, and non-German Europeans were held. In no inconsiderable way did such ingrained outlooks influence war actions and German occupation policies, including the systematic genocide practiced especially in Poland, which along with other Eastern countries was marked as a slave state; the readiness to denigrate was turned against those who were defined as nonpersons or decadent people or inferior nations. There were signs of postwar German shock at the revelations of the enormity of crimes committed as a consequence of the so-called German nationalist awakening during the Third Reich. The possibility of spiritual regeneration and profound soul-searching, despite or because of half-empty bellies or the fear of retribution, was never greater. But the finger-pointing technique of *Der Ruf* writers continued with questions directed to the German public by W.M. Guggenheimer, for instance, as to "why are we not disturbed by such ugly behavior as the Italians hanging Mussolini and his girlfriend on meat-

hooks, but are only ashamed and disturbed at descriptions of what happened in German concentration camps?" Such mischievous logic and juxtapositions were to be carried to extremes later in the neo-Fascist newspaper *Soldatenzeitung*, which specializes in showing other peoples to have been worse than the Nazis. Precisely such defensive illustrations may account for the argument I heard advanced by some German students that the English were responsible for the first concentration camps during the Boer Wars, that in modern times the Turks, Poles, French, and Russians were also guilty of massacres, as if one crime mitigates another.

The glorification of German soldiers in *Der Ruf* was amplified to extremes in many directions afterward, most spectacularly through a book ingenuously called *The Unloved German*, which became a German best-seller in 1963. Its author, Dr. Hermann Eich, an editor-journalist who learned to perfect his trade as an official of the foreign press section of the Nazi government, made a case for the kindly German soldier as a gay, childish, and children-loving tourist who saved national monuments, raised sanitary and dietary levels in occupied areas, sparing the unfortunate population "the worst," and only made stern reprisals when partisans violated German commandments of war and sportsmanlike rules. In other words, the armed burglars treated their chosen hosts with consideration. When these well-treated hosts presented their bill after the war, Eich was moved to remark, "The true picture of the German occupation from 1939 to 1945 has been obscured by the understandable need of the liberated countries to secure themselves a good place in the queue for reparations." Such cynicism and contempt were far from the intent of those writing for *Der Ruf*, yet others were tempted to abuse the basic premises advocated.

Subject also to misunderstanding was the unity of post-war Europe envisaged by *Der Ruf*. It seemed that some Germans were short on memory while other Europeans could not shake the memory, still fresh, of devastation wrought by two wars unleashed by Germany. The word *unification*, though tempered by the idea of socialistic humanism and national integrity, still carried with it unwitting reminders of the German aim of complete European colonization–from Flanders to the Urals–by Nazi tacticians who used the army as their instrument. *Der Ruf* came on too early and too strong with idealistic slogans which appealed to masses of homefarers, who wanted salve for their wounds. Also it created suspicions of unrelenting German nationalism; it created fears of renewed militarism–an unjust charge in view of the idealistic insistence on worldwide disarmament; it antagonized Communists who liked neither the Cachin letter nor the powerful excerpt-reprints of Arthur Koestler's exposé of Stalinist trials in his novel *Darkness at Noon*; and *Der Ruf*, with its recalcitrant attitudes, disturbed the military government. Pressures mounted against the continuation of this publication, so that in April 1947, with the seventeenth issue still in press, the publication's editors were put out of business because of their "untrustworthy criticism." Yet, given the independent temperament of its writers, *Der Ruf* could not have been less controversial than it was.

Much of the reportage and the fiction published in *Der Ruf* carried the same sociopolitical tone evident in the articles. By and large, they described the apathy of much of the public and the difficulties in turning away from a past which seemed better or no worse than the present. It may have been optimistic to expect too soon a profound rejection of the racial and ideological messages steadily propagated by the schools and mass media during the past thirteen years. Obviously literature can assist in the reorientation of readers by tone and example, without being propagandistic, but it was to take some time before such possibilities became realizable. In some instances, the theoretical and actual groundwork was poured for a postwar literature. Gustav René Hocke (b. 1908) combined the best features of academic and journalistic training in his incisive article "Deutsche Kalligraphie oder: Glanz und Elend der modernen Literatur" [German calligraphy or the glory and misery of modern literature] (*Der Ruf*, November 1946). He called for a new sensitivity to style and clarity of expression, a discarding of the aestheticized language and the subterfuges of those who went into an "inner migration" during the Hitler years, a rejection of the endemic bureaucratese, newspaper and platform rhetoric of the old dictatorship; along with others of *Der Ruf* Hocke insisted on a new, honest, and realistic prose suited to the times. The turn to a realistic simplicity was made, but often the style and content of literature bore an uneasy, tentative, and groping relationship. Human miseries were recorded in sharp matter-of-fact style in stories, but in poems subjective feelings gave a tone of special pleading.

Richter had gathered poems by some thirty German POWs in a volume called *Deine Söhne, Europa* [Your sons, Europe] (1947), which exhibited the trend toward the new simplicity of style but also were shot through with unrestrained elegiac self-pity and recountings of the horrors visited upon Germans during the war and the deprivations endured in prison camps. If these poets or would-be poets could see no suffering other than their own and of those closely related to them, how could it be otherwise for a less articulate and equally self-preoccupied public? The old refrain appears:

> We suffer hunger, hate, and scorn,
> We and our nation
> are put before a world court
> and bear silently, with patience, the bills but not
>   the guilt!
> We were only soldiers.

Mourning for fallen comrades, trench digging, homesickness, tearful portraits of families, the daily waltz of death, war as a bloody lottery, survival, and depression are rendered with litanous tones. Only a few of the poems showed potential power. Wolfdietrich Schnurre (b. 1920) was capable of sketching disillusionment with simple strokes: "I know photos in which our fathers winked,/in battle-gray dress and gay, with flowers on their guns . . . /We followed in their steps but trod upon corpses." The only poet of reputation in the volume was Günter Eich (b. 1907), and he took a drastic departure from his earlier nature lyricism in several poems. One of them, "Inventur," "Inventory," became a manifesto poem for the new style:

> This is my cap
> this my coat,
> here my shaving stuff
> in a cloth bag. . . .

The poem goes on not only to inventory his possessions, pitifully small, but also to suggest a slow orientation to the present, a salvaging operation. The inventory technique was to become, with greater and excruciating elaborateness, a part of German prose and poetry.

After his experience with *Der Ruf*, Richter thought of collaborating with a weekly, *Die Epoche*, but this fell through. Then, in July of 1947, he attended a meeting whose topic of discussion was "The Occupation of the Poet in his Time," sponsored by Stahlberg Publishers. The meeting opened in a well-ordered tea-party atmosphere but then turned into a battle royal between those who supported the belletristic function of literature and those who felt that it was a horror to speak of aesthetics when the time demanded revolutionary engagement on the part of writers; the split was deep. Nevertheless, Richter thought that gatherings where writers read and discussed their work had real possibilities if the participants had certain outlooks in common. Consequently, Richter called a meeting of his own early the following September at the home of Ilse Schneider-Lengyel, an essayist and poetess, in the Bavarian town of Allgau, inviting a small group consisting mostly of contributors to *Der Ruf* and to the poetry anthology which he had edited. The bohemian élan of the group was at no time higher than when members recruited a rickety vehicle, reeking of ersatz gasoline, and piled into it with their shabby suitcases, arriving at their Bavarian retreat grimy and bone-weary and stumbling nude into the sea and capering as if on a vacation. The reading and discussion sessions lasted into the morning hours and the discussants' exhilaration was as boundless as the critical exchanges were unsparing. No masterpieces were pulled out of the rucksacks, and discussions tended to stress content over formal qualities–the "what" transcended the "how." As a matter of record, Wolfdietrich Schnurre gave the first reading, and it was a vignette called "Das Begräbnis des lieben Gottes" [The burial of the dear God] in which a conglomerate of onlookers, gravediggers, and a priest bury God, an occurrence which seems not even to have merited publicity nor have caused any concern: "Loved by no one, hated by no one, today, after long and divine endurance of pain, died: God." The content conveys a totality of apathy by and within the world while sardonic realism and low-brow colloquial dialogues mark the narrative method. The reading was symptomatic of the attempts to do away with pathos and sentimentality, yet it fell into a piteous tone.

The group could hardly wait for its next session and this took place a few weeks later, November 8 and 9, in the city of Ulm. By that time, one of the oldest members of the assemblage, Hans Georg Brenner (1903-62), a translator of Sartre, had knighted it the "Group 47." From the start it was clear that the initiator Hans Werner Richter (whose name means "judge" and has received its share of puns) regarded the meetings, in his own words, as a private matter–a circle of friends and newcomers invited or dropped at his pleasure and conforming to the rules of reading and discussion which he laid down. That the meetings rarely ever became private in the strictest sense is accounted for by the growing presence of outside publicists. Of course, as the attendance at meetings became swollen, there could no longer be assurances of all simply being friends, a euphemism at best. One of the purposes of the Ulm meeting was to discuss a satirical periodical appropriately called *Skorpion,* which would serve as the amplifier for opinions and writings of Group 47. Richter had assembled and printed a trial issue, at his own cost, during the previous summer. As it turned out, the issue slated for publication in 1948 never materialized because the American military government of Bavaria (called by many of the group an occupation dictatorship, *Besetzdiktatur*) thought the publication "nihilistic" and, anticipating its sting, put up obstacles to obtaining a publication license. Even with the removal of such obstacles, group members felt that the current economic situation would have made attempts at publication impracticable.

Although Richter's statement, during an interview, about the characteristics of the "new literature" applied to the contents of the projected *Skorpion,* it held equally true of the literary intent of the writings presented at meetings during the first several years:

> All signs attest to a new language which will be realistic. For the most part, the young generation has still not recovered from the enormous shock of the last years and has withdrawn into an imaginary, romantic world. One example of this is the growing number of lyricists. They still live in another era and their models are Rilke, George, Heyse, Alverdes, and others.

Richter never was to have much of an ear for poetry, but as for prose he insisted on a spontaneous and unambiguous style which prunes away tricks and decorativeness and avoids imitation of earlier German authors. He saw the need for creating a "magical realism," starting from the ABCs of prose and ignoring the criticism and ridicule of snobs. He found a perfect designation for this bare prose in Wolfgang Weyrauch's word *Kahlschlag,* a ruthless and pioneerlike clearing of language thickets. For years, a great deal of crudeness in the readings of the group was mere affectation growing out of the new style. Yet this style was hardly new; it resembled some of the work of the realists and naturalists like Max Kretzer,

Arno Holz, and Johannes Schlaf, who explored the depths of misery in which industrial workers were caught in the 1880s and nineties and whose writings nearly have vanished into obscurity; it resembled also the expressionists' pathos revived by Wolfgang Borchert in 1947. More important, however, was the sure transition from the political journalism of *Der Ruf*–without loss of socialistic ideologies–to the diversity of literary genres (short stories, novels, dramas, poetry, essays). Interest centered mainly on the immediate present while, for the most part, any deep probing of the problematic past was avoided. Matter-of-factness and ridicule seemed to be surgical-literary methods. It was some time before writers of the group regained absolute trust in the lyric instinct and sentiment. Some outside critics regarded the literary activities of the group as regressive rather than progressive in matters of style and content, and only infrequently did some experimentation break through to suggest the possibilities of other directions. The charge of literary provincialism was not entirely unfounded.

Quite rapidly the format of the meetings–and their rituals–took shape. Richter originally wished to recruit a democratic élite in the realm of literature and journalism in order to have, in widening circles, some mass effect; these objectives were to be gained without programmed meetings or a dues-paying organization and without encouraging collective thinking. The meetings were to give unpublished and published members of the younger generation an opportunity to demonstrate their talents. It was understood that those who were invited–by postcards–to meetings were anti-Fascists, anti-militarists, politically liberal or leftist-inclined but not toward the extreme of communistic Stalinism. Most of those invited during the early years shared the common experience of war as soldiers of lowly rank; officers were suspected of having worked too hard for the cause. The invitational process was to give the group internal flexibility, to encourage talent, to discourage dilettantism and commercial writing, and to attract new blood which would give the group vitality and currency. Since the group had no publications organ, it offered instead a visible forum for scouts from all media and an opportunity for fledgling authors, with some toughness, to try their fortunes in what was to become a literary stock exchange. One critic of the group estimated that nine out of ten novitiates failed to gain approval for entrance into the holy–or as some have dubbed it, unholy–order. Richter admitted that criticism during the early stages was somewhat uncivilized and too blunt; it was a reaction to the repression of all criticism during the Hitler years. As a result, novelists like Luise Rinser and Rudolf Krämer-Badoni packed their bags in 1950 and left the group. Rinser became a writer of best-sellers bordering on soap operas, and Krämer-Badoni a free-lance writer and a vocal, as well as bitter, anti-Group 47 critic. Publicity, whether good or bad, through all the media proved to be of invaluable assistance in giving group meetings an aura of newsworthy cultural events.

Even some of Richter's readings received harsh treatment: "In the early years listeners who did not wish the reading to continue turned their thumbs down. At that point, the leader of the meeting had to interrupt the reader and send him back to his seat. He fell through. It was completely immaterial if the reader was a friend, an acquaintance, someone of prominence, an unknown person, or the founder of Group 47." However, Richter pointed out that whoever "could take the sharpest and most devastating criticism without showing an emotional reaction, he could be invited again, certainly," and try anew. The ritual, I think, bore resemblances to that of the university student duels, popular though outlawed, which gave evidence of manliness through physical scars; the group-inflicted scars were psychic. How many new writers were discouraged from continuing is not known, but the number of works by known writers who were dissuaded from inflicting some of their work upon the public is a matter of record.

One device for educating and exhibiting authors who read from their work during group sessions was the "electric chair," a jocular or diabolic designation, depending upon whether one was in or out of it. Nearby would sit the group guardian, Richter, who sized up the mood of the audience or followed his own. At any time he might interrupt the reader in a curt, collective voice to say that the group had heard quite enough. If he was lucky, the reader would be allowed to finish his selection, on the average twenty to thirty minutes with exceptions made for the more prominent members of the group, and then discussion would ensue. In any case, the reader was expected to retain *Haltung*, poise or equanimity, and to listen silently to favorable or unfavorable criticism. Whatever indignation or elation he felt would have to be repressed. Stoic martyrdom or silent suffering had to be learned. From 1947 to

1968, more than two hundred authors submitted themselves to this Prussian ritual and more than a hundred critics and guests, mostly from the mass media, had ringside seats; the guests included persons from many European countries. Through 1955 the group met almost regularly twice a year and then once a year. Three meetings were held outside of Germany in Italy, Sweden, the United States, and one had to be cancelled in Czechoslovakia when the Russians arrived there first in 1968; since then full-scale meetings have been in abeyance.

During the first years, criticism was a rough-and-tumble affair as assorted voices rose from the floor. Gradually, however a phalanx of professional and sophisticated critics–journalistic and academic–stepped into the jury box during the fifties: Walter Jens (1950), Joachim Kaiser (1953), Marcel Reich-Ranicki (1958), Walter Höllerer (1959), and Hans Mayer (1959)–there was no higher court of appeals for redress of instant judgment. The sureness of judgment and computer-like critical reaction of the phalanx is astonishing given the difficulty of following the oral reading of a text whether it is poetry or prose, whether the reading is distinct or mumbled, dramatic or nervously pedestrian. Does indeed the quality of the text unfold to the ear? The question had been debated and is debatable. Only a few poets of the first rank have been able to do justice to their own work by reading from it; certainly neither T. S. Eliot nor Robert Lowell could do the same. Recorded readings of Group 47 poets–ranging from the bellowing of Erich Fried to the subdued renderings of Johannes Bobrowski–also leave much to be desired. Prose and narrative are somewhat easier to manage because the exposition is easier and the language rarely ambiguous. It also seems to me that the out-loud reading of fiction generally tends to inhibit the reader, which may have some virtues. It also may account for the fact that for the most part it has the somewhat puritanical effect of not only purging eroticism, sexuality, coyness, and gross vulgarities from the texts but also discouraging psychologically delicate and emotional explorations. Nevertheless, reading, criticism, and discussion remained the ritual for novices and the stars of the group.

A saving grace of the group has been the ability of members, including Richter, to satirize the proceedings. However, the novelist and dramatist Martin Walser, who in 1955 was awarded one of the few group prizes, went beyond satire in 1964 and called for a sweeping democratization of the rituals and opening the doors to all comers by way of a preliminary jury-screening; he felt that Group 47 had become a power-hungry literary monopoly. Of course, his suggestions went unheeded. A year later in his "Brief an einen ganz jungen Autor" [Letter to a very young author] he gave indirect evidence that his own recovery from group criticism was never complete. Walser advised the eager and young author to write to Richter, Jens, or Höllerer and to subtly note that he has read all the writings of the addressee. Further injunctions were listed: expect to be ignored as a newcomer, demur at being among the first to read, affect humility, anticipate the group's inattentiveness and door-banging at your reading, be prepared for any eventuality, count on the trained concentration of the critics who will listen as might an off-duty detective who involuntarily overhears what is said. He had gone even further at a group meeting in 1961, when tolerance ran low at two o'clock in the morning, to characterize all critics as *Lumpenhunde*, scoundrels. Walser's caricatures of the critics, however, do capture some of their salient features. To wit, Höllerer quickly carves up the reading into small specimens as if for microscope analysis and discovers typical sentences which are further dissected until they satisfy his "microscopic view." He grumbles, may burst into sudden laughter which frightens the novitiate, and as a "grower of cultures" he may give the reader the impression that he is viewed as a new form of bacteria or disease. Then Jens, as if he were approaching a spiny lobster, will handle the reading gingerly and weigh and probe it. He is concerned with measuring readings and assessing the reader's possible place in the Valhalla of contemporary literature. When the work is sweepingly labelled, then Kaiser slowly rises to the task and with elegiac cadences, sighs, and empathic suffering will expose the reading for what it is, gently censuring writing which he himself would have been capable of. In contrast, Reich-Ranicki does not let a moment pass in silence and with rapid-fire strokes repeats the executions visited upon the reading by his fellow critics and applies ideas which had already been conceived before the reading even began. Reich-Ranicki, born in 1920 in Poland, resided in Berlin until 1938 and then in Poland where as a Jew he was shunted to the Warsaw Ghetto; he returned to West Germany in 1958. Somewhat ungallantly and exceeding the limits of satire and taste, Walser intimates that Reich-Ranicki has homesickness for the Eastern spiritual environment from which he came. Obviously, Reich-Ranicki did not belong to the exclusive club of the German homefaring soldiers. The same treatment is accorded Hans Mayer who went into exile in France and Switzerland during the Third Reich and later became a professor at the Leipzig University in East Germany until 1963 when he moved West; Mayer made his first guest-critic appearance at the 1959 group meeting. Walser calls Mayer's critical expressions ballistic hyperboles and "assuredly the most beautiful foreign language in the fatherland." If someone in the audience defends the reader, it gives the "provoked but eager-to-answer" critics an opportunity to go at it again. Sarcastically, Walser suggested that the author prepare a musical-text-for-listening: "It may not turn out to be bad literature." Intended is a sly dig at Kaiser who is a music critic as well.

What Jens said about the group also applies to its own corps of critics, namely, that instead of unity it is "the sum of disharmonies which characterizes Group 47." All the critics have an unimpeachable integrity and in their written reviews of books or performed dramas of writers identified with Group 47 it is hardly possible to detect favoritism or nepotism. In some cases their critiques of group members have been harsher than those of outside critics and their judgments differ more than they coincide. Their assumption is that if an author is worth writing about, he should be able to take it. However, I have the feeling that if the author's ideology is congenial, attempts are made to separate content from method and not to run the author's reputation into the ground. Of course, each of the critics has his own vocabulary and approach, despite the similarity of their social ideas and sympathies. A university professor who also has held visiting professorships in the United States and a lyrical poet as well, Höllerer develops the principle of a basic discrepancy between "the world" and "the I," effecting a counterplay, *Widerspiel,* so that the author's work becomes the "bridge" between the two as well as between "consciousness and vital feeling": "the bridge springs under your footsteps." Jens is a professor of classical philology and a novelist, radio playwright, and adapter of Greek plays. His critical method, perhaps because of academic training, is analytical rather than prescriptive; of himself and others he demands meticulousness and elegance of style; he advises the writer to work intensely and well within

a small compass, to use a pocket mirror rather than a giant telescope to reflect his observations, and to learn modernity from the unpoetically sparse diction of Kafka rather than the monumentality of word and lyric associations of Broch or the imitation-compendia of the so-called realists. By temperament he is moralistic and pacifistic. One of his aims is to identify books with international potential.

Kaiser, like Höllerer, Mayer, and Jens, has doctoral credentials and is a regular literary and music critic for the prestigious *Süddeutsche Zeitung;* he wields an academic style of precise analysis without journalistic cleverness or frills. It took Richter a while to become accustomed to Kaiser's cautious style, but I think that most members of the group approved of his high seriousness. He warned in a news report in 1957 that the group was engaging in fun sessions when it allowed too much time to the stars who read from published works which admitted no change rather than fulfilling the group's function of presenting young and unknown authors to the public. In contrast to his colleagues, Reich-Ranicki is a pyrotechnical phenomenon and probably one of the best instant critics I have seen anywhere. Despite his avowed moralistic and educative intent and insistence that literature must foster a cultural democracy and have sociological relevance, he is the most widely read critic in the mass media. Some note facetiously that he has a sparse and thin broomstick style; he does quite brusquely sweep away what he disagrees with. He is the most polemical of the critics and many of his arguments are incisive and colorful within a logical and lawyerlike presentation. Peter Handke, the latest of the no-longer-young angry men, bitterly rejects Reich-Ranicki's measuring the newest literature by the criteria of naturalness or faithfulness to life, and he labels the critiques as no more than formulas and communiques. The most imposing of the group's critics is the literary historian Hans Mayer, a Marxist, much of whose somewhat cerebral criticism reaches only a special audience interested in socioliterary discussion. He is not bound, as are Kaiser and Reich-Ranicki, to act as a middleman between writer and public or to act as a simplifying interpreter. Among the more aggressive writers of the group, some have chosen to double as essayistic critics and like Helmut Heißenbüttel see it necessary to rid criticism of doctrinaire ideology if criticism and literature are to be effective in rehumanizing society.

Many writers have an inbuilt critical apparatus, which even the sharp group critics were only able to tamper with slightly given the limitations of the reading system and the oral critiques. At best these critiques were able to point to faults and merits by way of sweeping generalities or the dissection of "typical" sentences from the readings. Of course, the critics and audience could discourage, encourage, or kill with apathy any of the readers, but this was also true of published works. In an open society any programmatic intent by critics, if there were the unlikely possibility of critical unanimity, results at best in short-term trends. The changes in social, economic, and political climates, audience tastes, contact with other literatures, the individuality of writers, and conflicts among critics, all contribute to a renewing dynamics of literature. For the most part, Group 47 author-readers themselves pointed to new directions. During the initial postwar phase, one could easily discern a dominance of expressionistic modes, the realistic *Kahlschlag* prose, existential stylizations, the idea of art for man's rather than art's sake, the stress on social content, and other features arising out of the so-called *Trümmerliteratur,* the literature reflecting the ruins of war; the influence of Thornton Wilder and Hemingway was especially pronounced. One foreign visitor to the 1951 group session remarked that the younger authors were trying to catch a train which had departed twenty years earlier. During the early fifties, tentatively but surely, horizons broadened. The deep mistrust of words, slogans, and their values–such as love, honor, duty–which had been corrupted during the Third Reich, gave way to a more confident expression of emotions. With the aid of French, English, and American literature–as well as the discovery mainly of Joyce, Kafka, and Faulkner–it was possible to explore the literature of antirealism, the language of lyricism, surrealism, and to adopt aesthetic means without necessarily losing sight of social purpose. In the sixties, trends became even more diffuse, flowing mainly into two channels: politically active literature, more intense than ever since the end of the war, and avant-gardism which created hybrid forms of literature and aimed a massive assault upon every literary tradition.

In 1948 several German writers, some of whom had cast their lot with the Eastern sector in the hopes of a better political and social future, went to Moscow to receive the gospel of social realism. During a conference Alexander A.

Fadejew told Anna Seghers and other delegates that Stalin regarded writers as "the engineers of the human soul." Fadejew saw it the task of the writer to educate the reader for the future and to view today's reality as a revolutionary development toward it. He extolled Balzac as the model of a realist who showed a capitalistic society in such hateful terms that the reader is caught up in the same emotion and understands that the future cannot be in the direction of such a system. Socialist literature has its humanistic or romantic aspects in that it gives preference to ideal relationships of ideal people, extols the virtues of work, and aims to change life through literature. Through the years, Walter Ulbricht, the late party boss of East Germany, continually exhorted the engineers of the human soul to assist the workers, farmers, and other working people in storming the heights of a socialist, nationalist culture and vanquishing capitalist ideologies and bourgeois habits. The problem of writing primarily for the revolutionary proletariat was formidable and the possibilities of creating anything resembling literature rather than propaganda was limited. Soon a number of writers who were unequal to the rigorous assignment left for the West while others unsuccessfully tried to mitigate bureaucratic policies; they nursed their disillusionments privately, rationalizing that the East, ideologically, was still better than the West. Some who objected to censorship were prohibited from publishing. Even distinguished Marxist critics such as Georg Lukács and Hans Mayer were harshly chastised for undialectical and revisionist attitudes toward socialist realism. In every conceivable way Group 47 tried to keep contact alive with East German writers by hosting them at meetings whenever the Ulbricht regime allowed a short leave of absence, holding small and impromptu discussion sessions with selected members from both sides, and encouraging open-letter exchanges on vital political issues. Although their social and political sympathies were similar, the physical gulf between them remained deep and the vocabulary of East German dogma grew more impenetrable and militant.

If the agreement on political matters between writers and government in East Germany was relatively greater than that in West Germany, it emphasized the ambivalent position of many Group 47 writers. *Der Ruf* subscribed to the myth of a revolutionary working class which could be led in a socialist direction, an idea which faded with the rapid economic strides and subsequent affluence of West Germany, yet the desire remained–and emerged with intensity in the sixties–to change the conservative political structure. Politics demands undivided attention and unrelenting activity as well as energies which writers struggling to make ends meet could not divert from their work. Perhaps the most damning analysis of the naïveté of the nonconformist who typified Group 47 during the fifties was made by the poet and critic Hans Egon Holthusen:

> He himself wishes to be effective politically, he wants political influence, and that means he wishes power; yes, to a certain extent he already enjoys it in that he uses the so-called mass media and has at his disposal newspaper columns, air time, lecture halls, and the patience of book readers. At the same time he retreats from power. With a hysteric mixture of fear, hate, and desire he eavesdrops on power and is ever ready to denounce it as an enemy of the spirit and as immoral, not only power specifically but in general. He finds himself in the soulful condition of a *demivierge*, a half-virgin, known in erotic terminology as the most unappetizing thing in existence.

The last sentence is an example of the no-holds-barred polemical attacks and counterattacks between outside critics and Group 47; the acrimony is earnest but it also gives both parties much-desired publicity, a convertible currency. Holthusen points to the nonconformist's understandable fear and remembrance of the Third Reich, yet he proposes that power need not be evil if it is used in defense of civil and national freedoms and as a counterweight to the consolidating imperialism of Bolshevism. Holthusen posed such issues in 1960, and with many ramifications it became a crucial and on-going debate between pacifists who wanted a geographically neutral Germany and advocators of power-balance politics with the formation of political-military alliances. Holthusen pointed to Günter Eich's Büchner-Prize acceptance speech in 1959, in which Eich called for an active nonconformism and exhorted writers to employ criticism, opposition, resistance, and challenge to power, otherwise "we decorate the slaughterhouse with geraniums." Holthusen accuses the intellectuals of not really wanting to play active politics and even of ignoring Marx's injunction that social life is basically practical. Indeed, nonconformism and practicality rarely went hand in hand in the life of German intellectuals. In the twenties Bertolt Brecht exhorted the intellectual comrade to "join the Workers United

Front, for you are a worker too." They dreamed of storming to victory waving huge red banners, inspired by the cinema of Eisenstein and Pudovkin, Gorky's socialist realism, Erwin Piscator's stagings and Brecht's plays, and Hans Eisler's songs; they proclaimed working-class solidarity but split the various movements wide open through tactical and factional differences. The German Communist party attacked the Social Democrats as the main pillars of the bourgeoisie and joined the Nazis in undermining the Weimar Republic in the expectation that out of the resulting chaos Communists would emerge triumphant. The general disillusionment of the Left was evident in the postwar attempt by writers for *Der Ruf* to chart a new socialist way. But except for the slow-developing trade-union movement there seemed to be no formulation of practical goals.

It must be said clearly that Richter kept programmatic politics out of the group's socioliterary discussions. Those group members who felt inhibited could initiate independent publications such as Hans Magnus Enzensberger's *Kursbuch*. Political protest letters and resolutions were signed by individuals and not by group acclamation, by voluntary and not coercive means; the protests were given weight by the reputation of the signers. The examples are numerous: declaration of indignation against the Soviet military rape of Hungary in 1956, the Anglo-French Suez venture, intentions of atomic armaments for the German army, the French war in Algeria, attempts by the government to encroach on the freedom of television presentations and the press, the American intervention in the Vietnam civil war, Arab threats against the existence of Israel in 1967; they charged some of the press with whipping up public hysteria which resulted in the police slaying of a student demonstrator, Benno Ohnesorg. Many Group 47 authors and critics took similar steps to protest the Soviet military intervention in Czechoslovakia. On the other hand, the left radical mass-circulation magazine *konkret* echoed the Soviet line and excoriated Czech attempts to emulate Western liberalism; it is ironic that *konkret* would deny the Czech socialists the very freedom it enjoys in a so-called bourgeois-capitalist reactionary society. Klaus R. Röhl, editor and publisher of *konkret*, had been a guest at Group 47 sessions, and a number of the group authors–including Peter Rühmkorf, Hubert Fichte, Alexander Kluge, Günter Herburger, Günter Grass, Heinrich Böll, Peter Handke, and Richter–were occasional contributors. There was little difference, however, between Röhl's bitter ridicule–in print–of the group's liberal wing and the attitude toward the group by reactionary government officials. Röhl elevates to political sainthood the revolutionary conclave of Mao, Minh, Castro, Che Guevara, and he is a cheerleader for terrorists, guerillas–from South America to the Middle East; but he does not feel comfortable about encouraging such movements in Germany, especially since his ex-wife Ulrike Meinhof tried to annihilate his publication and later became implicated in criminal terrorist activities. Terror may be good for others but not for Röhl's neighborhood and establishment. The phenomenon of a radical publication achieving mass circulation is attributable to its special formula: prolix nudity, low-brow erotica and pornography, sensational and sadomasochistic photo journalism; occasional articles and polemics by name authors supply a pseudocultural veneer. A reading of several issues is likely to give any foreigner the moral impression that West Germany is the sump hole of the world.

The political spectrum within the fluctuating periphery of Group 47 ranges from the liberal to the ultraleftist, and their political commitments vary accordingly. In general the separation between their essayistic-political writings and their literary work does not prevent a mutual coloring, but this is at a minimum when compared with the fiction of Malraux, Koestler, or Silone. These writers of memorable political novels were themselves caught up actively in the maelstrom of their time and had been able to render the tone and dimensions of totalitarianism of the Left and the Right, as well as the politically colorless masses who were pliable, sullen, or acquiescent; the experiences of these novelists sat deep in the marrow of their bones. Unlike them, the early Group 47 writers could not make literature out of the tension between frustrated political hopes and realities; their disenchantments, by comparison, were played out in a sandbox; their concerns seemed self-centered and piteous while their attacks on the early economic miracle and the conservative, political parliamentarianism (undiscriminatingly called "restoration") as a cause for people's failure to regenerate in a moral and political sense seemed peevish. Moral regeneration rather than lip service to democracy seems to be an elusive process in German life, but many writers associated with Group 47 fought hard to set it in motion. The problem, however, is not an exclusively German one.

To come back for a moment to some of Holthusen's criticism of Group 47, it is hard to disprove that some writing, especially the polemical poetry, seems not to joyously praise total anarchy. True, there are streaks of political infantilism in the group. Holthusen in 1960 also threw cold water on facile comparisons between the German literary rebels, particularly the younger ones, and the American beatniks and the English angry young men, although all share tendentiousness. He notes that the German situation is more complicated because "all of us have to drag with us a political inheritance with which, in all honesty, we cannot appear before the eyes of others. The exhaust gas of a national plunge into hell still poisons the air, oppressive taboos clog the flow of open discussion–a form of self-imposed regulation of speech is not infrequent. How much dishonesty, how much concealed resentment and hidden hysteria on all sides." It is a perceptive and admonitory comment on a significant segment of German social, political, and literary thinking. Yet, I think that Holthusen overshoots the mark with his suggestion that unless writers become politicians, politics be left to the politicians who have proven themselves capable of power and the concomitant arrogance of office. The large body of German civil servants proved capable of serving any system–Fascist or democratic–with equal enthusiasm, as exemplified by some of its senior people, like the expounder of Nazi racism Dr. Hans Globke who was allowed to rise to high position in the Chancellor's Office in Bonn. The number of ex-Nazis in governmental service is even larger in East Germany, though nominally they have been retreaded by the Communist mill. All this has not enhanced the image of the politicians in the eyes of the Group 47 writers in particular. All serious literature is "engaged" literature, one way or another, and most Group 47 authors have increasingly concerned themselves with enlarging the opportunities for participating in the determination of who is to exercise political power and where it is to lead. The dangers to democracy are ever present from the extremes of the Right and the Left, overanxious threats of government actions against the press, provincial accents on patriotism, police powers, the dangerous swings of labor and the *petite bourgeoisie*. Group 47 writers cannot help but be sensitive to such societal affairs; they may exacerbate or meliorate, depress or encourage, aggressively or subtly express their values through the images created by literature; whatever their view or tone–

loud or whispered, polemical or lyrical—it is amplified and made public through the mass media. Their literature is varied. Frequently it is rich descriptively and anemic ideologically, and even provocative in the rejection of ideology or in the portraying of a milieu without political thought; it is cantankerous, often evasive, exploratory mainly in a technical sense, illuminative and obfuscatory, oppositional and noncomformist in respect to the establishment, self-lacerating and self-assertive. The relation of ideology and aesthetic form has been much debated within Group 47 sessions, and the ideal relationship has not been persuasively demonstrated by any of its writers. In discussing their literature, one can only talk of approximations. The social and political aims declared through *Der Ruf* and periodically implied through discussions and polemics have not been achieved; neither a program nor an ideological and aesthetic rationale has ever been worked out; the question of mastering the past never was put in focus—it was overshadowed by concern for the present. In short, here are some reasons for a literature that speaks radically about frustrations and very little of hope. It would have taken a Dostoevsky to measure and delineate the amorphousness and normality of evil, the everyday inurement to evil by the mass of German society during the Third Reich, and the discontents and discomforts, morally and intellectually, of the present. The inheritance, of which Holthusen wrote, still disturbs but it has neither been totally confronted nor mastered in German postwar literature.

Economics, and often a consciousness of world image, rather than culture as fostered through the arts, has dominated modern German life. The catastrophic unemployment picture during the early thirties contributed to the rise of the Nazis, while the recession of the mid-sixties coupled with the radicalization of students resulted in a backlash and a strong resurfacing of the neo-Fascist National Democratic Party. Whether this trend ebbed because the world expressed its alarm and the German public redressed its image or because economic measures deflated the situation, the message is somewhat depressing. Politics and economics have power value while culture gives the veneer of prestige despite its essential impotence. While some writers associated with Group 47 have achieved international visibility, and along with the reputation of the musical arts, have given Germany renewed cultural status, these same writers because of their sociopolitical views are barely tolerated by those who tend to gain most from the fostered image. To what extent their oppositional stance is, or will be, fruitful can only be tangentially indicated, but their work and thinking, their motifs and motives, do reveal the dynamics of the literature which they have created.

Books for Further Reading

Arnold, Heinz Ludwig. *Geschichte der deutschen Literatur aus Methoden: Westdeutsche Literatur von 1945-1971*, 3 volumes. Frankfurt am Main: Athenäum/Fischer Taschenbuch Verlag, 1972.

Bachmann, Dieter, ed. *Fortschreiben: 98 Autoren der deutschen Schweiz*. Zurich & Munich: Artemis, 1977.

Berg, Jan, and others. *Sozialgeschichte der deutschen Literatur von 1918 bis zur Gegenwart*. Frankfurt am Main: Fischer Taschenbuch Verlag, 1981.

Berman, Russell A. *The Rise of the Modern German Novel: Crisis and Charisma*. Cambridge, Mass.: Harvard University Press, 1986.

Brettschneider, Werner. *Zwischen literarischer Autonomie und Staatsdienst: Die Literatur in der DDR*. Berlin: Schmidt, 1972.

Bullivant, Keith, ed. *The Modern German Novel*. Leamington Spa, U.K., Hamburg & New York: Berg, 1987.

Durzak, Manfred. *Die deutsche Kurzgeschichte der Gegenwart: Autorenporträts, Werkstattgespräche, Interpretationen*. Stuttgart: Reclam, 1980.

Durzak. *Der deutsche Roman der Gegenwart: Entwicklungsvoraussetzungen und Tendenzen*, third edition. Stuttgart, Berlin, Cologne & Mainz: Kohlhammer, 1979.

Durzak, ed. *Deutsche Gegenwartsliteratur: Ausgangspositionen und aktuelle Entwicklungen*. Stuttgart: Reclam, 1981.

Duwe, Wilhelm. *Ausdrucksformen deutscher Dichtung vom Naturalismus bis zur Gegenwart: Eine Stilgeschichte der Moderne*. Berlin: Schmidt, 1965.

Eisele, Ulf. *Die Struktur des modernen deutschen Romans*. Tübingen: Niemeyer, 1984.

Emmerich, Wolfgang. *Kleine Literaturgeschichte der DDR*, third edition. Darmstadt & Neuwied: Luchterhand, 1985.

Futterknecht, Franz. *Das Dritte Reich im deutschen Roman der Nachkriegszeit. Untersuchungen zur Faschismustheorie und Faschismusbewältigung*. Bonn: Bouvier, 1976.

Garland, H. B. *A Concise Survey of German Literature*. London: Macmillan, 1971; Coral Gables, Fla.: University of Miami Press, 1971.

Hamburger, Michael. *After the Second Flood: Essays on Post-War German Literature*. New York: St. Martin's Press, 1986.

Hoffmeister, Gerhart, and Frederic C. Tubach. *From the Nazi Era to the Present*. New York: Ungar, 1986.

Hohendahl, Peter Uwe, ed. *Literatur der DDR in den siebziger Jahren*. Frankfurt am Main: Suhrkamp, 1983.

Horst, Karl August. *Kritischer Führer durch die deutsche Literatur der Gegenwart: Roman, Lyrik, Essay.* Munich: Nymphenburger Verlagshandlung, 1962.

Jurgensen, Manfred. *Deutsche Frauenautoren der Gegenwart.* Bern: Francke, 1983.

Koebner, Thomas, ed. *Tendenzen der deutschen Gegenwartsliteratur.* Stuttgart: Kröner, 1984.

Kröll, Friedhelm. *Gruppe 47.* Stuttgart: Metzler, 1979.

Kunisch, Hermann. *Die deutsche Gegenwartsdichtung.* Munich: Nymphenburger Verlagshandlung, 1968.

Kunisch. *Handbuch der deutschen Gegenwartsliteratur,* second edition, edited by Herbert Wiesner, Helge Kähler, and others, 2 volumes. Munich: Nymphenburger Verlagshandlung, 1969-1970.

Langer, Lawrence. *The Holocaust and the Literary Imagination.* New Haven: Yale University Press, 1975.

Mandel, Siegfried. *Group 47: The Reflected Intellect.* Carbondale & Edwardsville: Southern Illinois University Press/London & Amsterdam: Feffer & Simons, 1973.

Natan, Alex, ed. *Swiss Men of Letters: Twelve Literary Essays.* London: Wolff, 1970.

Nonnenmann, Klaus. *Schriftsteller der Gegenwart: Deutsche Literatur. Dreiundfünfzig Porträts.* Olten & Freiburg im Breisgau: Walter, 1963.

Pfeifer, Jochen. *Der deutsche Kriegsroman 1945-60: Ein Versuch zur Vermittlung von Literatur und Sozialgeschichte.* Königstein: Scriptor, 1981.

Raddatz, Fritz J. *Traditionen und Tendenzen: Materialien zur Literatur der DDR.* Frankfurt am Main: Suhrkamp, 1972.

Reed, Donna K. *The Novel and the Nazi Past.* New York, Bern & Frankfurt am Main: Lang, 1985.

Reich-Ranicki, Marcel. *Deutsche Literatur in West und Ost: Prosa seit 1945.* Munich: Piper, 1963.

Robertson, J. G. *A History of German Literature,* sixth edition, edited by Dorothy Reich. Edinburgh & London: Blackwood, 1970.

Rothmann, Kurt. *Deutschsprachige Schrifsteller seit 1945 in Einzeldarstellungen.* Stuttgart: Reclam, 1985.

Ryan, Judith. *The Uncompleted Past: Postwar German Novels and the Third Reich.* Detroit: Wayne State University Press, 1983.

Soergel, Albert, and Curt Hohoff. *Dichtung und Dichter der Zeit,* 2 volumes. Düsseldorf: Bagel, 1961-1963.

Wagener, Hans, ed. *Gegenwartsliteratur und Drittes Reich: Deutsche Autoren in der Auseinandersetzung mit der Vergangenheit.* Stuttgart: Reclam, 1977.

Waidson, H. M. *The Modern German Novel: A Mid-Twentieth Century Survey.* London & New York: Oxford University Press, 1959.

Wiesner, Herbert, ed. *Lexikon der deutschsprachigen Gegenwartsliteratur.* Munich: Nymphenburger Verlagshandlung, 1981.

Contributors

Robert Acker ....*University of Montana*
Herbert A. Arnold ....*Wesleyan University*
Manfred Bansleben ....*University of Alabama in Birmingham*
Otto F. Best ....*University of Maryland at College Park*
Alfred L. Cobbs ....*Wayne State University*
Bettina Kluth Cothran ....*Georgia State University*
Judith H. Cox ....*Birmingham, Alabama*
Ann Clark Fehn ....*University of Rochester*
Valerie D. Greenberg ....*Tulane University*
Donald P. Haase ....*Wayne State University*
Todd C. Hanlin ....*University of Arkansas*
Alan Frank Keele ....*Brigham Young University*
Wulf Koepke ....*Texas A&M University*
Gretel A. Koskella ....*George Washington University*
Helga W. Kraft ....*University of Florida*
Egbert Krispyn ....*University of Georgia*
Lieselotte Kuntz ....*University of Georgia*
Siegfried Mews ....*University of North Carolina at Chapel Hill*
Malcolm J. Pender ....*University of Strathclyde*
Jochen Richter ....*Allegheny College*
Judith Ricker-Abderhalden ....*University of Arkansas*
David S. Roth ....*University of Maryland at College Park*
Timothy W. Ryback ....*Harvard University*
Gerd K. Schneider ....*Syracuse University*
Dieter Sevin ....*Vanderbilt University*
Robert K. Shirer ....*University of Nebraska at Lincoln*
Helga Slessarev ....*University of Cincinnati*
Patricia H. Stanley ....*Florida State University*
Guy Stern ....*Wayne State University*
Jennifer Taylor ....*Cornell University*
Hans Wagener ....*University of California, Los Angeles*
H. M. Waidson ....*University College of Swansea (University of Wales)*
Franz-Joseph Wehage ....*Appalachian State University*
Michael Winkler ....*Rice University*

Cumulative Index

Dictionary of Literary Biography, Volumes 1-75
Dictionary of Literary Biography Yearbook, 1980-1987
Dictionary of Literary Biography Documentary Series, Volumes 1-4

Cumulative Index

DLB before number: *Dictionary of Literary Biography,* Volumes 1-75
Y before number: *Dictionary of Literary Biography Yearbook,* 1980-1987
DS before number: *Dictionary of Literary Biography Documentary Series,* Volumes 1-4

A

C

D

E

F

G

I

J

M

N

O

P

S

Dictionary of Literary Biography

1: *The American Renaissance in New England,* edited by Joel Myerson (1978)

2: *American Novelists Since World War II,* edited by Jeffrey Helterman and Richard Layman (1978)

3: *Antebellum Writers in New York and the South,* edited by Joel Myerson (1979)

4: *American Writers in Paris, 1920-1939,* edited by Karen Lane Rood (1980)

5: *American Poets Since World War II,* 2 parts, edited by Donald J. Greiner (1980)

6: *American Novelists Since World War II,* Second Series, edited by James E. Kibler, Jr. (1980)

7: *Twentieth-Century American Dramatists,* 2 parts, edited by John MacNicholas (1981)

8: *Twentieth-Century American Science-Fiction Writers,* 2 parts, edited by David Cowart and Thomas L. Wymer (1981)

9: *American Novelists, 1910-1945,* 3 parts, edited by James J. Martine (1981)

10: *Modern British Dramatists, 1900-1945,* 2 parts, edited by Stanley Weintraub (1982)

11: *American Humorists, 1800-1950,* 2 parts, edited by Stanley Trachtenberg (1982)

12: *American Realists and Naturalists,* edited by Donald Pizer and Earl N. Harbert (1982)

13: *British Dramatists Since World War II,* 2 parts, edited by Stanley Weintraub (1982)

14: *British Novelists Since 1960,* 2 parts, edited by Jay L. Halio (1983)

15: *British Novelists, 1930-1959,* 2 parts, edited by Bernard Oldsey (1983)

16: *The Beats: Literary Bohemians in Postwar America,* 2 parts, edited by Ann Charters (1983)

17: *Twentieth-Century American Historians,* edited by Clyde N. Wilson (1983)

18: *Victorian Novelists After 1885,* edited by Ira B. Nadel and William E. Fredeman (1983)

19: *British Poets, 1880-1914,* edited by Donald E. Stanford (1983)

20: *British Poets, 1914-1945,* edited by Donald E. Stanford (1983)

21: *Victorian Novelists Before 1885,* edited by Ira B. Nadel and William E. Fredeman (1983)

22: *American Writers for Children, 1900-1960,* edited by John Cech (1983)

23: *American Newspaper Journalists, 1873-1900,* edited by Perry J. Ashley (1983)

24: *American Colonial Writers, 1606-1734,* edited by Emory Elliott (1984)

25: *American Newspaper Journalists, 1901-1925,* edited by Perry J. Ashley (1984)

26: *American Screenwriters,* edited by Robert E. Morsberger, Stephen O. Lesser, and Randall Clark (1984)

27: *Poets of Great Britain and Ireland, 1945-1960,* edited by Vincent B. Sherry, Jr. (1984)

28: *Twentieth-Century American-Jewish Fiction Writers,* edited by Daniel Walden (1984)

29: *American Newspaper Journalists, 1926-1950,* edited by Perry J. Ashley (1984)

30: *American Historians, 1607-1865,* edited by Clyde N. Wilson (1984)

31: *American Colonial Writers, 1735-1781,* edited by Emory Elliott (1984)

32: *Victorian Poets Before 1850,* edited by William E. Fredeman and Ira B. Nadel (1984)

33: *Afro-American Fiction Writers After 1955,* edited by Thadious M. Davis and Trudier Harris (1984)

34: *British Novelists, 1890-1929: Traditionalists,* edited by Thomas F. Staley (1985)

35: *Victorian Poets After 1850,* edited by William E. Fredeman and Ira B. Nadel (1985)

36: *British Novelists, 1890-1929: Modernists,* edited by Thomas F. Staley (1985)

37: *American Writers of the Early Republic,* edited by Emory Elliott (1985)

38: *Afro-American Writers After 1955: Dramatists and Prose Writers,* edited by Thadious M. Davis and Trudier Harris (1985)

39: *British Novelists, 1660-1800,* 2 parts, edited by Martin C. Battestin (1985)

40: *Poets of Great Britain and Ireland Since 1960,* 2 parts, edited by Vincent B. Sherry, Jr. (1985)

41: *Afro-American Poets Since 1955,* edited by Trudier Harris and Thadious M. Davis (1985)

42: *American Writers for Children Before 1900,* edited by Glenn E. Estes (1985)

43: *American Newspaper Journalists, 1690-1872,* edited by Perry J. Ashley (1986)

44: *American Screenwriters,* Second Series, edited by Randall Clark, Robert E. Morsberger, and Stephen O. Lesser (1986)

45: *American Poets, 1880-1945,* First Series, edited by Peter Quartermain (1986)

46: *American Literary Publishing Houses, 1900-1980: Trade and Paperback,* edited by Peter Dzwonkoski (1986)

47: *American Historians, 1866-1912,* edited by Clyde N. Wilson (1986)